AF485367

disha
Publication Inc

CBSE Class 11

BiOLOGY
Chapter-wise Question Bank

NCERT + Exemplar + Practice Questions

with Solutions

In the interest of student community

Circulation of softcopy of Book(s) in pdf or other equivalent format(s) through any social media channels, emails, etc. or any other channels through mobiles, laptops or desktops is a criminal offence. Anybody circulating, downloading, storing, softcopy of the Book on his device(s) is in breach of the Copyright Act. Further Photocopying of this book or any of its material is also illegal. Do not download or forward in case you come across any such softcopy material.

Corporate Office

DISHA PUBLICATION

45, 2nd Floor, Maharishi Dayanand Marg,

Corner Market, Malviya Nagar, New Delhi - 110017

Tel : 49842349 / 49842350

No part of this publication may be reproduced in any form without prior permission of the publisher. The author and the publisher do not take any legal responsibility for any errors or misrepresentations that might have crept in. We have tried and made our best efforts to provide accurate up-to-date information in this book.

All Right Reserved

© Copyright Disha

READ, REVIEW, REWARD!!!

Buying books from Disha just got a lot more Rewarding!!!

We, at Disha Publication, value your feedback immensely and to show our appreciation for our reviewers, we have launched a review contest.

To participate in this reward scheme, just follow these quick and simple steps:

Write a review of the product you purchased on Amazon/Flipkart's website.

Take a screenshot/ photo of your review.

Mail it to **disha-rewards@aiets.co.in**, along with all your details.

Each month, selected reviewers will win exciting gifts from Disha Publication. Note that the rewards for each month will be declared in the first week of the next month on our website

https://bit.ly/review-reward-disha.

Edited by: Rashi Chauhan

Typeset by Disha DTP Team

www.dishapublication.com

Books & ebooks for School & Competitive Exams

www.mylearninggraph.com

Etests for Competitive Exams

Write to us at **feedback_disha@aiets.co.in**

Contents

The Living World

1.1 Why are living organisms classified?

Sol. Classification is a method of grouping living organisms into convenient categories based on some observable characters which make their study easier.

For example, mammals are those who possess mammary glands, hair on body, external pinnae etc.

1.2 Why are classification systems changing every now and then?

Sol. Classification system changes when more information becomes available about the organisms. Additional information are updated from time to time about different organisms at this stage there is a need arises to make changes in the classification system.

1.3 What different criteria would you choose to classify people that you meet often?

Sol. In our day to day life we categorize people based on following criteria :

1. Level of education
2. Profession
3. Height and skin colour
4. Native place
5. Sex
6. Hobbies
7. Nature

1.4 What do we learn from identification of individuals and populations?

Sol. Identification of individuals and populations determine their exact place or position in the set plan of classification.

1.5 Given below is the scientific name of mango. Identify the correctly written name.

(a) *Mangifera Indica*

(b) *Mangifera indica*

Sol. (b) *Mangifera indica*

1.6 Define a taxon. Give some examples of taxa at different hierarchial levels.

Sol. Taxon is a group of real organisms contained in any category. A natural taxon refers to a group of similar, genetically related individuals having certain characters distinct from those of other group.

For example, all the insects form a taxon. So do birds, reptile, algae, grasses, dog, lion and man. Some examples of taxa at different hierarchial levels are :

(a) The taxon of bacteria is monera and their category is kingdom.

(b) The sponges form the taxon porifera and their category is phylum.

(c) *Rosa* is a taxon and genus is its category.

1.7 Can you identify the correct sequence of taxonomical category?

(a) Species $\longrightarrow$ Order $\longrightarrow$ Phylum $\longrightarrow$ Kingdom

(b) Genus $\longrightarrow$ Species $\longrightarrow$ Order $\longrightarrow$ Kingdom

(c) Species $\longrightarrow$ Genus $\longrightarrow$ Order $\longrightarrow$ Phylum

Sol. (c)

1.8 Try to collect all the currently accepted meanings for the word 'species'. Discuss with your teacher the meaning of species in case of higher plants and animals on one hand and bacteria on the other hand.

Sol. Species is one of the basic units of biological classification. A species is often defined as a group of organisms capable of interbreeding and producing fertile offspring. Sometimes more precise or differing measures such as similarity of DNA, morphology or ecological niche are used to define the basis of species. In case of animals, the name of species is defined by the specific name or the specific epithet. For example, gray wolves belong to the species *Canis lupus*, golden Jackals to *Canis aureus* etc. Both of them belong to same genus *Canis*, but species name varies. But species name of plant is only called species epithet. The 'specific name' in botany is always the combination of genus name and species epithet such as *saccharum* in *Acer saccharum* (Sugar maple).

But bacteria are grouped under four categories based on their shape – spherical, rod-shaped, comma and spiral shaped and species of bacteria is according to their shapes. Thus the meaning of species in higher organism and bacteria are different.

1.9 Define and understand the following terms:

(i) Phylum (ii) Class (iii) Family (iv) Order (v) Genus

Sol. (i) **Phylum :** A phylum is group of related classes having some common features. *e.g.*, protozoa.

(ii) **Class :** A class is group of related orders, for *e.g.,* order Rodentia, Lagomorpha and Carnivora all having hair and milk glands are placed in class mammalia.

(iii) **Family :** A family is a group of related genera. The genus *Felis* of cats and the genus *Panthera* of lion, tiger and leopard are placed in the family Felidal.

(iv) **Order :** An order is a group of related families. The family Felidae of cats and the family Coridal of dogs are assigned to the order carnivora. Cats and dogs have large canine teeth and are flesh-eaters.

(v) **Genus :** A genus is a group of species alike in the broad features of their organization but different in detail. As per the rules of binomial nomenclatures, a species can not be named without assigning it to a genus.

1.10 How is key helpful in the identification and classification of organism?

Sol. Key refers to a set of alternate characters in such a manner that helped for identification of plants and animals by selecting and eliminating the characters according to their presence or absence in the organism. Every taxonomic category like family, genus and species has separate taxonomic key. There is species key for the identification of species in a genus and genus key is for the identification of genus in a family and so on.

1.11 Illustrate the taxonomical hierarchy with suitable examples of a plant and an animal.

Sol.

Kingdom
↑
Phylum or Division
↑
Class
↑
Order
↑
Family
↑
Genus
↑
Species

Common name Genus Class	Biological name Family Phylum	Species Order
1. Man *Homo* Mammalia	*Homo sapiens* Hominidae Chordata	*Sapiens* Primata
2. Mango *Mangifera* Dicotyledonae	*Mangifera indica* Anacardiaceae Angiospermae	*Indica* Sapindales

SECTION B   # PRACTICE QUESTIONS 

MULTIPLE CHOICE QUESTIONS

1. Which of the following is **not** a characteristic of life?
(a) Reproduction
(b) Complex chemical organization
(c) Adaptation to environmental changes
(d) Differentiation from cells to tissues

2. The total sum of all the chemical reactions occurring in our body is known as:
(a) metabolism   (b) growth
(c) regeneration   (d) reproduction

3. Which of the following are unique features of living organisms?
(a) Growth and reproduction
(b) Reproduction and ability to sense environment
(c) Metabolism and interaction
(d) All of the above

4. Cell division occurs _____ in plants and _____ in animals.
(a) continuously, only upto a certain age
(b) only upto a certain age, continuously
(c) continuously, never
(d) once, twice

5. Which two points are known as the twin characteristics of growth?
(i) Increase in mass
(ii) Differentiation
(iii) Increase in number of individuals
(iv) Response to stimuli
(a) (i) and (ii)   (b) (i) and (iv)
(c) (ii) and (iii)   (d) (i) and (iii)

6. Identify the correct sequence of taxonomic categories.
(a) Species → Genus → Order → Class → Family → Phylum/Division → Kingdom
(b) Species → Genus → Family → Class → Phylum/Division → Order → Kingdom
(c) Species → Genus → Family → Order → Class → Phylum/Division → Kingdom
(d) Species → Genus → Family → Order → Class → Phylum/Division → Kingdom

7. Which of the following shows the correct example of taxonomic category - Genus?
(a) Potato, tomato and brinjal belong to Solanum.
(b) Monkey, gorilla and gibbon are placed in Mammalia.
(c) Solanum, Petunia, and Datura are placed in Solanacea.
(d) Mangifera indica, Solanum tuberosum, and Panthera leo.

8. Indian Botanical Garden Howrah , Kolkata is famous for:
(a) different varieties of roses
(b) largest banyan tree
(c) medicinal plants
(d) none of these

9. Taxonomic hierarchy refers to:
(a) step-wise arrangement of all categories for classification of plants and animals.
(b) a group of senior taxonomists who decide the nomenclature of plants and animals.
(c) a list of botanists or zoologists who have worked on taxonomy of a species or group.
(d) classification of a species based on fossil record.

10. Which of the following organisms is not correctly matched with its particular ?
    (a) Human beings – *Sapiens*, species
    (b) Lion – *Panthera*, genus
    (c) Cats – Felidae, genus
    (d) *Datura* – Solanaceae, family

ASSERTION & REASON QUESTIONS

DIRECTION (Qs. 1-5) : *These questions consists of two statements. Answer these questions selecting the appropriate option given below:*
(a) Both Assertion (A) and Reason (R) are true and Reason (R) is the correct explanation of Assertion (A).
(b) Both Assertion (A) and Reason (R) are true, but Reason (R) is not the correct explanation of Assertion (A).
(c) Assertion (A) is true, but Reason (R) is false.
(d) Assertion (A) is false, but Reason (R) is true.

1. **Assertion:** The growth of multicellular organisms takes place by cell divisions.
   Reason: The unique features of living organisms are growth, reproduction, ability to sense the environment.
2. **Assertion:** Metabolism is a defining feature of the all living organisms.
   Reason: All the living organisms such as animals, plants, fungi and microbes exhibit the metabolic processes and no any non-living thing shows this process.
3. **Assertion:** The growth of the living organisms takes place internally while the growth of the non-living organisms occurs externally.
   Reason: Growth is a defining characteristic of the living organisms.
4. **Assertion:** The hierarchial system of classification represents the various levels of kinship and named as Linnaean system.
   Reason: The hierarchial system of classification was introduced by Linnaeus.
5. **Assertion:** Key is a type of taxonomical aid that is used for the identification of animals and plants on the basis of similarities and dissimilarities.
   Reason: Every taxonomical category like family, genus and species has separate taxonomic key.

CASE/PASSAGE BASED QUESTIONS

DIRECTIONS (Qs. 1-5) : *Read the following passage and answer the questions that follows.*

On the basis of certain characteristics, things are classified as living or non-living. Reproduction, growth, metabolism and consciousness are characteristics of the living organisms. Metabolic process are not present in the non-living things. Non-living things show growth due to deposition of the materials.

1. Living organisms show growth due to
   (a) Cell division   (b) Reproduction
   (c) Deposition of molecules (d) None of them
2. Self-consciousness is a characteristic of living organisms that is shown by
   (a) All organisms   (b) Only plants
   (c) Only human beings   (d) All of them

3. Which of the following reactions occurs during metabolism?
   (a) Synthesis of small molecules
   (b) Decomposition of complex molecule
   (c) Both option (a) & (b)
   (d) None of them
4. Which of the following statement is true for non-living thing?
   (a) Growth of non-living thing is internally.
   (b) Non-living thing grows due to deposition of materials externally.
   (c) Non-living thing grows both externally as well as internally.
   (d) None of them
5. Anabolism and catabolism are the characteristics of-
   (a) Living organisms
   (b) Non-living things
   (c) Both living & Non-living
   (d) Catabolism is characteristic of living while anabolism is shown by non-living.

VERY SHORT ANSWER QUESTIONS

1. Name the three codes of nomenclature.
2. Who introduced the hierarchy in taxonomy ?
3. What is taxonomy ?
4. What is meant by cytotaxonomy ?
5. Who devised the binomial nomenclature ?
6. What is a type specimen?
7. In which language binomial nomenclature is written?
8. What term is used to describe organisms without well developed nucleus ?
9. Is the inter specific breeding possible? Does it yield sterile or fertile progeny?
10. Give the number and names of obligatory taxonomic categories.
11. What is speciation ?
12. What are correlated characters ?
13. Why classification of plants and animals is necessary?
14. What is cohort or order?
15. Who is the father of Taxonomy?
16. Give botanical and zoological names of the following
    (1) Pea   (2) Wheat
    (3) Man   (4) Potato

SHORT ANSWER QUESTIONS

1. What is systematics? Discuss the criteria of artificial classification.
2. What is a taxonomic aid ?
3. Give the classification of man.
4. What is museum ? How many kinds of museum are found?
5. What is the benefit of manuals and records for scientific study of living beings ?
6. What is the role of characteristics of living beings in classification?
7. What is the significance of a herbarium?
8. Name the major categories used in taxonomy and arrange them in an hierarchical manner.

LONG ANSWER QUESTIONS

1. What are the advantages of scientific names ?
2. What is the difference between living and non-living ?
3. Explain binomial system of nomenclature.
4. What is the role of zoological parks in wildlife conservation?

SOLUTIONS

Multiple Choice Questions

1. **(d)** The characteristics of life include: responsiveness to the environment; growth and change; ability to reproduce; have a metabolism and breathe; maintain homeostasis; being made of cells; passing traits onto offspring. Differentiation from cells to tissues is not a characteristic of life. Like bacteria, it is a unicellular organism and does not posses any tissue. It is still considered alive.

2. **(a)** **Catabolism** – breakdown of substances eg., Respiration **Anabolism** – Formation of substances. eg., Photosynthesis. Catabolism + Anabolism = Metabolism.
   These are defining features of all life forms.
   Simultaneous Catabolism and Anabolism called as **Amphibolism**.

3. **(d)** All living organisms share certain unified and basic characteristics (including energy utilization, regulation or homeostasis, growth, development, reproduction, adaptation) metabolism and interaction.

4. **(a)** All cells arise from pre-existing cells by a process of cell division. Cell division is the phenomenon of production of daughter cell from parent cell. It occurs continuously in plants and only up to a certain age in animals.

5. **(d)** Increase in mass and increase in number of individuals are twin characteristics of growth. Growth is defined as increase in size and mass during the development of an organism over a period of time. It is measured as an increase in biomass and is associated with cell division by mitosis, subsequent increases in cell size, and with the differentiation of cells to perform particular functions.

6. **(d)** Species is the lowest category in basic taxonomic hierarchy and has the maximum common characterstics with other species under the same genus. The genus is an aggregate or a group of closely related species. Family is the group of closely related genera, and has less common characterstics than species or genus rank.
   Order is a higher taxon and is the assemblage of families having similar characterstics.
   Class is a group of related orders.
   Phylum: The classes with similar features are grouped into phylum in animals and division in plants.
   The phyla are grouped into still broader categories, called kingdom.

7. **(a)** Potato, tomato and brinjal are three different species but all belong to the genus *Solanum*. Genus is an assembly of related species which evolved from a common ancestor and have certain common characters. *Solanum* is a polytypic genera with more than one species.

8. **(b)** Indian Botanical Garden, Howrah, Kolkata is known as the largest banyan tree. It is also known as Acharya Jagadish Chandra Bose Indian Botanical Garden. The Great Banyan tree is over 250 years old. The present crown of the tree has circumference of 486 m and the highest branch rises to 24.5 m; it has at present 3772 aerial prop roots reaching down to the ground as a prop root.

9. **(a)** Taxonomical hierarchy (introduced by Linneaus) is arrangement of various taxonomic levels in the descending order, starting from kingdom upto species. The hierarchy indicates the various levels of kinship. The number of similar characters of categories decreases from lowest rank to highest rank *i.e.*, from species to kingdom. There are 7 obligate categories which constitute taxonomical hierarchy. In addition to these obligate categories there are some optional categories are as follows. e.g., Tribe, subclass, superclass, etc.

10. **(c)** Cats belong to the family *Felidae*.

Assertion & Reason Questions

1. **(b)** Multicellular animals are those organisms that contain a large number of cells. A single cell zygote divides and forms a large number of different types of the cells that are responsible for the growth of multicellular organisms. Growth, reproduction, ability to sense the environment and metabolism are the characteristics of the living organisms.

2. **(a)** Metabolism is a process in which anabolic and catabolic reactions takes place in the living organisms. All the living organisms are made of chemicals so all the organisms like animals, plant, fungi and microbes exhibit the process of metabolism. Thus it is a defining characteristic of the living organisms.

3. **(c)** Growth is a process in which the mass and weight of the living and non-living things increases. The living organisms grow internally while non-living things grow externally. Since the non-living things grow by the deposition of materials externally so it is not a defining characteristic of the living organisms.

4. **(a)** The hierarchical system of classification was proposed by Carl Linnaeus so named as Linnaean system. In this system, the organisms are grouped in a systemic levels or order that are called as taxon. Each level of the classification represents a specific taxon.

5. **(b)** Key is an important tool of the taxonomy that is used to identify the organisms on the basis of similarities or dissimilarities for the purpose of classification. Every taxonomic category contains a specific taxonomic key.

Case/Passage Based Questions

1. **(a)** Living organisms show growth due to cell division.
2. **(c)** Self-consciousness is a characteristic of living organisms that is shown by only human beings.
3. **(c)**   4. **(b)**
5. **(a)** Anabolism and catabolism are the characteristic of living organisms.

Very Short Answer Questions

1. International codes of botanical, zoological and bacteriological nomenclature.
2. Linnaeus
3. Taxonomy frames the rules for classification. It is the branch of biology which describes the theory and practice of identifying and classifying living organisms.
4. Classification based on chromosome number.
5. Carolus Linnaeus.
6. Establishment of the name of the new species on the basis of the original speciemen is called type specimen.
7. Latin
8. Prokaryote
9. Yes, both.

10. There are 7 obligatory categories that are : Kingdom - Phylum/Division - Class - Order - Family - Genus - Species.
11. Formation of a new species from an existing one by the appearance of mutation.
12. The common features the species have to qualify for inclusion in a genus are called correlated characters.
13. Classification divides millions of plant and animal species into convenient groups that makes their study easier.
14. Cohort is a unit of classification higher than the family.
15. The Father of Taxonomy is *carrolus Linnaeus* : a swedish botanist.
16.
    (1) Pea → *Pisum sativum*
    (2) Wheat → *Triticum aestivum*
    (3) Man → *Homo sapiens*
    (4) Potato → *Solanum tuberosum*

Short Answer Questions

1. Systematics is the branch of science that deals with the kinds and diversity of all organisms. The system is highly useful in the field for quick identification of organisms. Artificial system often utilizes one or two morphological traits.
2. A taxonomic aid is a storage of record of either live or dead specimens of flora or fauna, which helps scientists in taking reference to study classification.
3.
    Common Name – Human
    Scientific Name – *Homo sapiens*
    Genera – Homo
    Families – Hominidae
    Orders – Primata
    Classes – Mammalia
    Phyla/Division – Chordate
4. Museum in an institution where artistic and educational materials are exhibited to the public. The material available for observation and study are called a collection.
    Kinds of Museums :
    • Art Museum
    • History Museum
    • Applied Science Museum
    • Natural Science Museum
5. Manuals and records basically helps in understanding past flora and fauna of a given area. Take an example of a thriving city. There may had been a dense forest, rich in biodiversity, where we get to see densely populated cities today. The manuals and records of that area helps us in knowing about past richness in biodiversity.

We also come to know extinct species, through manuals and records. Some of the extinct species may be close or distinct relatives of some existing species. We can develop some evolutionary relationships between them.

6. A group of common feature of living beings are placed under a common category of classification and when uncommon under different category. It means more systematic a process for further study, research, protection and recording.
7. HERBARIUM :– A book, case or room containing an orderly collection of dried plants is called Herbarium. It develops interest in Nature for the activists in it. It can be used to gain knowledge and be updated about plants and their scientific names and even compare various samples. If is a small scale it can be proactive to do. One can make projects too from it for schools, colleges and research institutions.
8. The hierachy includes seven obligate categories — kingdom, division or phylum, class, order, family, genus and species. The categories are arranged in descending sequence. In order to make taxonomic position of species more precise, certain categories have been added to this list are called intermediate categories *e.g.*, sub-kingdom, super phylum or super division, sub division, super class, sub class, super order, sub order, super family, sub-family, tribe, sub species, variety, etc.

Long Answer Questions

1. The advantages of scientific names are as following:
    (i) Biologists use universally accepted principle to provide scientific names for the known organisms. Each name is made up of two components mainly. First component of the name describes about the genus of the species, while second component describes about the specific epithet of that organisms. Every species has a single and specific name.
    (ii) It is generally in latin and written in italics, when printed. Two separate underline is put in the hand-written scientific name of the organisms.
    (iii) Every organism known to science has been provided with a scientific name irrespective of its importance.
    (iv) They are comprehensive and are easier to recollect.
    (v) A wrong name can easily be corrected.
    (vi) A newly discovered organism can be easily provided with a new scientific name.

2.

Character	Living	Non-living
Metabolism	Living beings show metabolic activities, which are like biochemical processes.	There is no metabolism.
Reproduction	Living beings produce their future generations.	Non-living do not reproduce.
Growth	Growth in living being is a result of internal processes.	Most of the non-living do not grow. Growth in some, like clouds is a result of accumulation of external substances.
Movement	Living beings show movement.	Non-living are static and if they move then it is a result of some external force.
Nutrition	Living beings take food to carry various life processes.	There is no nutrition in non-living.

3. Binomial nomenclature system was developed by Linnaeus. Binomial nomenclature is the system of providing organisms with appropriate and distinct names consisting of two words, first generic and second specific. The first or generic word is also called genus. It is like a noun and its first letter is written in capital form. The second word or specific epithet represents the species. It is like an adjective. Its first letter is written in small form except occassionally when it denotes a person or place. The two word name is appended with the name of taxonomist who discovered the organism and provided with its scientific name, e.g., *Ficus bengalensis L., Mangifera indica Linn,* The name of taxonomist can be written in full or in abbreviated form. There are several technical names which have three words, e.g., *Homo sapien sapiens, Acacia nilotica indica, Gerilla gorilla gorilla.* Here the first word is generic, the second specific while the third word represents variety (mostly in botanical literature) or subspecies (mostly in zoological literature). If the same scientific name is to be written time and again, the name of the genus can be abbreviated, *e.g., F. bengalensis.*

4. In the early stages, the zoological parks were considered as places of relaxation and enjoyment for public, however, there has been a change in the objective of purposefulness of these parks. The establishment of zoological parks help in providing knowledge about different native and exotic wild mammals, birds, reptiles, fish and flora to the public in general and school children in particular. Since the key to wildlife conservation lies in the education of masses and involvement of voluntary organisations, zoological parks are very useful in spreading knowledge on the wildlife wealth of the country. These are also important centres for organising seminars, training and researches on the management of wildlife species and for study of their social behaviour, breeding and ecological species.

SECTION C   NCERT EXEMPLAR QUESTIONS 

Multiple Choice Questions

1. As we go from species to kingdom in a taxonomic hierarchy, the number of common characteristics:
   (a) will decrease   (b) will increase
   (c) remain same   (d) may increase or decrease
2. Which of the following 'suffixes' used for units of classification in plants indicates a taxonomic category of 'family'?
   (a) – Ales   (b) – Onae
   (c) –Aceae   (d) – Ae
3. The term 'systematics' refers to:
   (a) identification and study of organ systems
   (b) identification and preservation of plants and animals
   (c) diversity of kinds of organisms and their relationship
   (d) study of habitats of organisms and their classification
4. Genus represents:
   (a) an individual plant or animal
   (b) a collection of plants or animals
   (c) group of closely related species of plants or animals
   (d) None of the above
5. The taxonomic unit 'Phylum' in the classification of animals is equivalent to which hierarchial level in classfication of plants.
   (a) Class   (b) Order
   (c) Division   (d) Family
6. Botanical gardens and Zoological parks have:
   (a) collection of endemic living species only
   (b) collection of exotic living species only
   (c) collection of endemic and exotic living species
   (d) collection of only local plants and animals
7. Taxonomic key is one of the taxonomic tools in the identification and classification of plants and animals. It is used in the preparation of:
   (a) monographs   (b) flora
   (c) Both (a) and (b)   (d) None of these
8. All living organisms are linked to one another because:
   (a) they have common genetic material of the same type
   (b) they share common genetic material but to varying degrees
   (c) all have common cellular organisation
   (d) All of the above
9. Which of the following is a defining characteristic of living organisms?
   (a) Growth
   (b) Ability to make sound
   (c) Reproduction
   (d) Response to external stimuli

Very Short Answer Questions

1. Couplet in taxonomic key means ....
2. What is a monograph?
3. *Amoeba* multiplies by mitotic cell division. Is this phenomena growth or reproduction? Explain.
4. Define metabolism.
5. Which is the largest botanical garden in world? Name a few well known botanical gardens in India.

Short Answer Questions

1. A ball of snow when rolled over snow increases in mass, volume and size. Is this comparable to growth as seen in living organisms? Why?
2. In a given habitat we have 20 plant species and 20 animal species. Should we call this as 'diversity or biodiversity'? Justify your answer.
3. International Code of Botanical Nomenclature (ICBN) has provided a code for classification of plants. Give hierarchy of units of classification, botanists follow while classifying plants and mention different 'suffixes' used for the units.
4. A plant species shows several morphological variations in response to altitudinal gradient. When grown under similar conditions of growth, the morphological variations disappear and all the variants have common morphology. What are these variants called?

5. What is the difference between flora, fauna and vegetation? *Eichhornia crassipes* is called as an exotic species, while *Rauwolfia serpentina* is an endemic species in India. What do these terms exotic and endemic refer to?
6. Brinjal and potato belong to the same genus *Solanum*, but to two different species. What defines them as seperate species?
7. The number and kinds of organism is not constant. How do you explain this statement? *Change is law of nature.*

Long Answer Questions

1. *Brassica campestris Linn*
   (a) Give the common name of the plant.
   (b) What do the first two parts of the name denote?
   (c) Why are they written in italics?
   (d) What is the meaning of Linn written at the end of the name?
2. What are taxonomical aids? Give the importance of herbaria and museums. How are Botanical gardens and Zoological parks useful in conserving biodiversity?

SOLUTIONS

Multiple Choice Questions

1. **(a)** Lower the taxa, more are the number of shared characteristics within the members of the taxon. So, the lowest taxon shares the maximum number of morphological similarities. As we move towards the higher hierarchy, *i.e.*, class, kingdom, similarities decrease.
2. **(c)** The names of family, taxon in plants always end with suffix aceae, e.g., Solanaceae, Cannaceae and Poaceae. Suffix **ales** is used for taxon **'order'** while suffix **ae** is used for **'class'** and suffixes **onae** are not used in any of the taxons.
3. **(c)** The word systematics has been derived from the Latin word 'Systema' meaning systematic arrangement of organisms. Linnaeus used 'Systema Naturae' as a title of his publication. It describes the diversity of organisms and their relationship at every level of organisation.
4. **(c)** **Genus** comprises of a group of closely related species with more characte rs in common as compared to species of other genera.
5. **(c)** Division is inclusive of classes with few similar characters of a group of organism. It is equivalent to 'Phylum' used in case of animals.
6. **(c)** **Botanical gardens** and **Zoological parks** are used to restore depleted population, reintroduce species and restore degraded habitats of both exotic and endemic living species.
7. **(c)** **Taxonomic keys** are tools that help in identifying of an organism based on the characters. It includes both monograph and flora.
8. **(b)** All living organisms possess a common genetic material, DNA, but with variations, *e.g.*, DNA in bacteria is circular while in highly evolved eukaryotic cells as plants and animals, DNA is a long double stranded helix.
9. **(d)** Besides growth and reproduction response to an external stimuli or to the environment in which an organism dwells is the most important characteristic of any living organism.
   Howevers, virus (which is not included under living organisms) also show growth and reproduction. Thus, these options are not true.

Very Short Answer Questions

1. Couplet in taxonomic key is a pair of a contrasting characters used as tool for identification to aid in identification of a newly discovered organism.

2. Monograph is a specialised work of documenting information on a particular taxon, *i.e.*, family or genus or on aspect of subject, usually by a single author. The main purpose of monograph is to present primary research and original work.
3. *Amoeba* multiplies by simple mitotic cell divisions giving rise to two daughter *Amoebae*. Growth here is synchronous with reproduction, *i.e.*, increases in number.
4. **Metabolism** is the sum total of all biological reactions occurring in any living cell, which are controlled absolutely by enzymes. These reactions are of two types breaking down reactions (catabolism, e.g., cell respiration) and synthesing reactions (anabolism, e.g., photosynthesis).
5. A botanical garden is dedicated to collection, cultivation and display of wide range of plants labelled with their botanical names.
   The largest botanical garden in the world is Royal Botanical Garden (in Kew, London). In India *the famous well known botanical gardens are*
   (i) National Botanical Garden (NBG) Lucknow, UP.
   (ii) Botanical Garden of FRI, Dehradun (UK).
   (iii) Lloyd Botanical Garden, Darjeeling.
   (iv) Indian Botanical Garden, Sibpur, Kolkata.

Short Answer Questions

1. Living organisms, grow, have metabolism and respond to external stimuli and reproduce as well. These characteristics are not shown by non-living objects.
   In biological terms growth is characteristic feature of all living organisms. It relates to increase in size by accumulation of protoplasm in the cell thus resulting in increase in the size of the cell. Increase in number of cell by cell division on other hand results in the size of individual organism.
   Snow is an inanimate (non-living) object, while rolling over, it gathers more snow on its surface thus, it increases in size by physical phenomenon but not by biological phenomenon. This growth cannot be thus compared to that seen in living organisms.
2. There are existing 20 plant species and 20 animal species in the given habitat. They will exhibit the biodiversity in that given habitat because diversity refers to variation in a broad term and can be applied to any area whereas biodiversity is a degree of variation of life forms within a specified area.

3. ICBN has specified certain rules and principles in order to facilitate the study of plants by botanists. It helps in correct positioning of any organism newly discovered through the pressure of proper identification and nomenclature.

The taxonomic hierarchy, which is used while classifying any plant given below

Kingdom-Plantae

Division-phyta

Class-ae

Order-ales

Family-eae/ceae

Genus-First name of organism usually Latin word and written in italics.

Species-Second word of scientific name, also written in italics.

4. These morphological variants are called **biotypes**. It includes group of genetically similar plants showing similarity when grown in same environmental and geographical regions. The same environment provides them the similar abiotic factors like soil, pH, temperature, etc.

When growth in two different geographical regions, they are exposed to different abiotic characters which affects their growth, and development bringing changes in their external morphological features but, their genetic constitution remain same.

5. Following are the difference between flora, fauna and vegetation

Exotic Species	Endemic Species
Exotic species Any species of a plant living in any other place except its native place. e.g., *Eichhornia crassipes* is a exotic species in India as it is native of Amazonian basin but it was introduced in India.	Endemic species are restricted to a particular area, *e.g.*, *Rauwolfia serpentina* It is an endemic species found only in India.

Flora	Fauna	Vegetation
Plant life occurring in a particular region of time, generally the naturally occurring indigeneous native plant life is flora.	The total number of animals found in a particular region at particular time is known as fauna.	Refers to the plant forms of region. It is a general term used for a plant forms, which does not include a particular taxa or any botanical characteristics.

6. Genus is a taxonomic rank used in bionomial nomenclature comprising of a group of related species sharing few common characters.

Solanum is the largest genus of flowering plants which includes few economically important plants, e.g., potato, tomato, tobacco and brinjal. All these plants show some common morphological structures related to vegetative and reproductive similarities. So, they are are included in the same common genus Solanum.

7. The number and kind of organisms is not constant, because of the following reasons new organism are added due to mechanisms of.

(i) sexual reproduction

(ii) mutation

(iii) evolution

The number of organisms get reduced due to

(i) environmental threats

(ii) loss of habitat

(iii) anthropogenic activities

Long Answer Questions

1. Brassica campestris Linn

(a) The common name of *Brassica compestris* Linn is mustard.

(b) The first part of the name denotes the genetic name and the second part is the species name of the plant.

(c) According to ICBN, all scientific names are comprised of one genetic name followed by a species name, which require to be always written in italics. It is a rule of bionomial nomenclature.

(d) Linn means Linnaeus. He was the first to discover the plant. He identified, named and classified the plant, so the plant is named after him by adding suffix 'Linn', after the scientific name *B. campestris*.

2. The aids which help in identification, classification and naming of a newly discovered organisms (plant or animal) the taxonomic aids.

It could be in the form of a preserved document like herbaria or specimen kept at museums or scientific institutions. Other aids include written document like monography, taxonomic keys, couplets, etc.

A new organism found can be studied while comparing it with living plants and animals living in protected areas like Botanical gardens, Zoological parks, etc.

Botanical gardens helps in conservation of plants by

(i) Plant species growing important local and keeping record of them.

(ii) Growing and maintaining species that rare are and endangered.

(iii) Supplying seeds for different aspects of botanical research.

Zoological parks contribute in conserving biodiversity by

(i) Providing natural environment and open space to animals.

(ii) Providing home to different native and exotic wild animals.

(iii) Rescue of endangered species.

(iv) Facilitating breeding animal and releasing them free.

Thus, both botanical gardens and zoological parks play an important role in conservation of biodiversity.

2 Biological Classification

2.1 Discuss how classification systems have undergone several changes over a period of time?

Sol. Different systems of classification proposed from time to time have undergone several changes from artificial system to phylogenetic system earlier the system of classification was based on one or a few superficial resemblances. For example, animals were classified as aquatic (water dwellers), terrestrial (land dwellers) and aerial (air dwellers). Similarly, plants were classified as herbs, shurbs and trees on the basis of their habit. This system is artificial. The artificial system was then followed by natural system which were based on a number of structural and morphological taxonomic characters. Now, the organisms are classified on the basis of their evolutionary interrelationship. Such classification are phylogenetic.

2.2 State two economically important uses of
(a) heterotrophic bacteria
(b) archaebacteria

Sol. (a) **Heterotropic bacteria :** These bacteria are natural scavengers. The souring of milk into lactic acid and alcohol to vinegar is brought about by some saprophytic bacteria, e.g., Lactic acid bacteria and acetic acid bacteria respectively. A number of antibiotic are extracted from actinomycetes especially from the genus *Streptomyces e.g.* Streptomycin, Chloramphenicol, Oilorotetracycline, Erythromycin, Terramycin etc.

(b) **Archaebacteria** live as symbionts in the rumen of herbivorous animals. Methanogens are present in the guts of several ruminant animals such as cows and buffaloes and they are responsible for the production of methane (biogas) from the dung of these animals.

2.3 What is the nature of cell wall in diatoms?

Sol. The cell wall of diatoms is covered by a transparent siliceous shell (silica deposited in cell wall which is composed of cellulose) known as **frustule.**

2.4 Find out what do the terms 'algal bloom' and 'red tides' signify?

Sol. Algal bloom : When colour of water changes due to profuse growth of coloured phytoplankton, it is called algal bloom.

Red tides : Redness of the red sea is due to luxurient growth of *Trichodesrium erythrium*, a member of cynobacteria (blue green alage).

2.5 How are viroids different from viruses?

Sol. Viroids are simpler than viruses, consisting of a single RNA molecule that is not covered by protein capsid. The genetic material of viruses are surrounded by protein coat.

2.6 Describe briefly the four major groups of protozoa.

Sol. The four major group of protozoa are flagellated protozoan, amoeboid protozoan, sporozoan, ciliated protozoan. The main characters of these group are as follows :

	Characters	Flagellated Protozoan	Amoeboid Protozoan	Sporozoan	Ciliated Protozoan
1.	Asexual reproduction	by longitudinal binary fission	Binary or multiple fission	Multiple fission	Transverse binary fission
2.	Nutrition	Heterotrophic and saprozoic	Holozoic	Heterozoic and saprozoic	Heterozoic Holozoic & saproza
3.	Locomotory	Flagella organ	Pseudopodia	Absent	Ciliapresent
4.	Habitat	Endoparasitic Some symbiotic and endoparasitic	Fresh water	Endoparasitic Endoparasitic	Fresh water
5.	Example	*Trypanosoma*	*Amoeba*	*Entamoeba*	*Paramoecium*

2.7   **Plants are autotrophic. Can you think of some plants that are partly hetrotrophic?**

Sol.   Insectivorous plants are partly heterotrophic.

2.8   **What do the terms phycobiont and mycobiont signify?**

Sol.   Lichens shows symbiotic association between algae and fungi. The fungal component of lichen is called mycobiont and the algal component is called as phycobiont.

2.9   **Give a comparative account of the classes of kingdom fungi under the following:**
     (a)   Mode of nutrition   **(b)   Mode of reproduction**

Sol.   Kingdom fungi has four classes, these are phycomycetes, ascomycetes, basidiomycetes and deuteromycetes. The comparison between these classes are as follows :

		Phycomycetes	Ascomycetes	Basidiomycetes	Deuteromycetes
(a)	Mode of nutrition	Obligate parasites	Parasitic or coprophilous	Parasitic	Parasitic or saprophytic
(b)	Mode of reproduction	Asexual reproduction by motile zoospore	a	Vegetative reproduction is common. Sexual process is represented by plasmogamy and karyogamy.	Asexual reproduction by spores, sexual reproduction is absent.

2.10   **What are characterstic features of Euglenoids?**

Sol.   Euglenoids show the following characteristic features :
     (i)   They store carbohydrates in the form of paramylon.
     (ii)   Since euglenoids are green and holophytic like other plants. Few are non-green and saprophic, some are holotrophic.
     (iii)   They bear a red pigmented eye spot and a gullet near the base of flagellum.
     (iv)   All the euglenoids have one or two flagella which help in swimming.
     (v)   Absence of cell-wall but contain flexible pellicle made up of protein.
     (vi)   Fresh water, free-living found in ponds and ditches.

2.11   **Give a brief account of viruses with respect to their structure and nature of genetic material. Also name four common viral diseases.**

Sol.   Viruses have the following characteristics :
     (i)   All plant viruses have single stranded RNA and all animal viruses have either single or double stranded RNA or double stranded DNA.
     (ii)   Protein virus also contain genetic material RNA or DNA. A virus is a nucleoprotein and the genetic material is infectious. These are obligate parasites, self replicating, non-cellular organisms.
     (iii)   Viruses are smaller than bacteria and their genetic material is surrounded by protein coat called capsid. Capsid is made up of small subunits called capsomeres.

Four common viral diseases are :
     (a)   Cough and cold   (b)   Mumps
     (c)   Influenza   (d)   Small pox

2.12   **Organise a discussion is your class on the topic are viruses living or non-livings ?**

Sol.   Viruses are link between living and non-living. They possess some living character and some non-living characters. Crystallization is non-living character but it can reproduce inside living body.

Actually viruses are metabolically inert when outside the host-cell. They reproduce using the metabolic machinery of the host cell.

SECTION B   PRACTICE QUESTIONS

Multiple Choice Questions

1.   Which of the following characteristic(s) is/are used by Whittaker for the classification of organisms?
     (a)   Mode of nutrition
     (b)   Thallus organisation
     (c)   Phylogenetic relationships
     (d)   All of the above

2.   Which of the following was the criterion used for classifying organisms by the earliest human beings?
     (a)   Morphology   (b)   Sacredness
     (c)   Use   (d)   Habitat

3.   Organisms of which of the following kingdom do not have nuclear membrane ?
     (a)   Protista   (b)   Fungi
     (c)   Monera   (d)   Plantae

4.   How many bacteria are produced in four hours if a bacterium divides once in half an hour?
     (a)   8   (b)   64
     (c)   16   (d)   256

5.   Which of the following pairs come under the group chrysophytes?
     (a)   Diatoms and *Euglena*   (b)   *Euglena* and *Trypanosoma*
     (c)   Diatoms and Desmids   (d)   *Gonyaulax* and Desmids

6. Which of the following is a parasitic fungi on the mustard plant ?
   (a) *Albugo*
   (b) *Puccinia*
   (c) Yeast
   (d) *Ustilago*
7. Yeast is not included in protozoans but are placed fungi because
   (a) it has no chlorophyll.
   (b) some fungal hyphae grow in such a way that they give the appearance of pseudomycelium.
   (c) it has eukaryotic organization.
   (d) cell wall is made up of cellulose and reserve food material is starch.
8. The genetic material of virus includes
   (a) only RNA.
   (b) only DNA.
   (c) RNA and DNA both
   (d) RNA or DNA, *i.e.*, one nucleic acid in a virus.
9. Bladderwort and Venus fly trap are examples of
   (a) insectivorous plants
   (b) parasitic plants
   (c) N_2 – rich plants
   (d) aquatic plants
10. Lichens indicate SO_2 pollution because they
    (a) show association between algae and fungi.
    (b) grow faster than others.
    (c) are sensitive to SO_2.
    (d) flourish in SO_2 rich environment.

ASSERTION & REASON QUESTIONS

DIRECTION (Qs. 1-5) : *These questions consists of two statements. Answer these questions selecting the appropriate option given below:*
(a) Both Assertion (A) and Reason (R) are true and Reason (R) is the correct explanation of Assertion (A).
(b) Both Assertion (A) and Reason (R) are true, but Reason (R) is not the correct explanation of Assertion (A).
(c) Assertion (A) is true, but Reason (R) is false.
(d) Assertion (A) is false, but Reason (R) is true.

1. **Assertion :** Aristotle used simple morphological characters to classify plants.
   Reason : Aristotle is called as father of Biology as well as Zoology.
2. **Assertion :** R.H. Whittaker proposed five kingdom classification and he grouped all the prokaryotic organisms into the kingdom Monera while all the unicellular eukaryotic organisms into the kingdom Protista.
   Reason : He used complexity of structure of the cell and nucleus for the classification.
3. **Assertion :** Mycoplasma is a type of eukaryotic organisms that does not contain cell wall.
   Reason : Cell wall is absent in animals.
4. **Assertion :** Deuteromycetes are a type of fungi that are called as imperfect fungi.
   Reason : In these fungi, only vegetative phases or asexual mode of reproduction are known.
5. **Assertion :** Lichens is a type of symbiotic partnership of a fungus and an alga.
   Reason : Lichen is good indicators of pollution.

CASE/PASSAGE BASED QUESTIONS

DIRECTIONS (Qs. 1-5) : *Read the following passage and answer the questions that follows.*

Kingdom Monera includes all the prokaryotic organisms such as bacteria, cyanobacteria and archaebacteria. In the given diagram a bacterial cell and a nostoc are labelled. Carefully observe the diagrams and answers the questions.

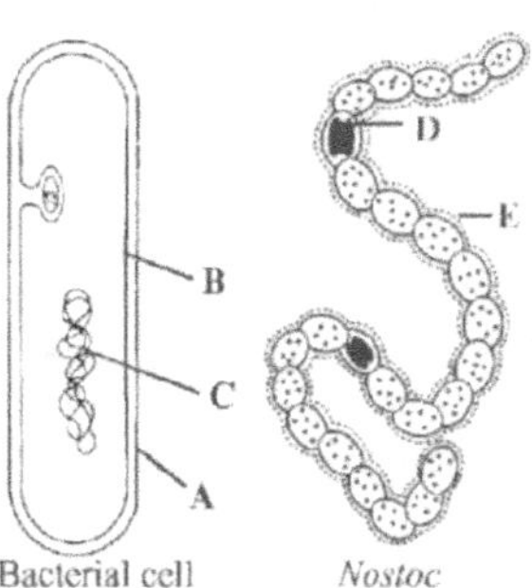

1. What is represented by labelling D?
   (a) Cell membrane
   (b) Cell wall
   (c) Heterocyst
   (d) DNA
2. Which of the following labelling indicates mucilaginous sheath?
   (a) A
   (b) D
   (c) E
   (d) C
3. Nostoc is a type of-
   (a) Algae
   (b) Fungi
   (c) Cyanobacteria
   (d) None of these
4. Which of the following statement is true for Methanogens?
   (a) They produce mainly chlorine gas
   (b) Methane gas is mainly produced by Methanogens
   (c) No any gas is produced by them
   (d) Only CO_2 is produced by them.
5. What is the function of labelling D?
   (a) Nitrogen fixation
   (b) Carbon dioxide fixation
   (c) Photosynthesis
   (d) None of them

VERY SHORT ANSWER QUESTIONS

1. Who wrote the books '*Species Plantarum*' and '*Systema Naturae*'?
2. Name the two kingdoms of the living world proposed by Linnaeus.
3. What are protists?
4. Which organism was earlier placed in plant as well as animals kingdoms and why?
5. Name the 5 kingdoms of organisms in the order of their supposed evolution.
6. Mention 2 traits in which fungi resemble animalia.
7. Define
   (a) Plasmogamy
   (b) Karyogamy
8. What are reterovirus. Give an example
9. Give two salient features of slime moulds.
10. What is called the jokers of microbiology and why?
11. Give the names of two diseases caused by Protozoans

Short Answer Questions

1. Cyanobacteria plays a major role in our ecology. Discuss.
2. What is the role of methanogens?
3. What are lichens? What are the roles of lichen in water pollution ?
4. On what factors is the 5 kingdom classification of Whittaker based?
5. Give the technical terms used for the following:
   (a) Remains of an organism of a former geological age.
   (b) Science of classification of organisms.
   (c) Evolutionary history of a group of organisms.
   (d) Organisms which synthesize their own food, using chemical energy.

6. What are the kinds (shapewise) bacteria found in nature. Name the pathogen with the disease caused
7. Why is
   (i) Basidiomycetes called club fungi?
   (ii) Ascomycetes called sac fungi?

Long Answer Questions

1. Give an account of early work in taxonomy.
2. What are the distinguishing characters of kingdom fungi?
3. Compare the main features of Monera with Protista.

SOLUTIONS

Multiple Choice Questions

1. **(d)** R.H. Whittaker (1969) proposed a five kingdom classification. The main criteria for classification used by him include cell structure, thallus organisation, mode of nutrition, reproduction and phylogenetic relationships.
2. **(c)** Since the dawn of civilisation, there have been many attempts to classify living organisms. It was done instinctively not using criteria that were scientific but borne out of a need to use organisms for our own use – for food, shelter and clothing.
3. **(c)** Monera is the group of prokaryotes. They are basically unicellular, may be mycelial, colonial and filamentous. They do not contain any organized nucleus with distinct membrane.
4. **(d)**

$$1 \xrightarrow{30\ \text{min}} 2 \xrightarrow{30\ \text{min}} 4 \xrightarrow{30\ \text{min}} 8$$
$$\xrightarrow{30\ \text{min}} 16 \xrightarrow{30\ \text{min}} 32 \xrightarrow{30\ \text{min}} 64$$
$$\xrightarrow{30\ \text{min}} 128 \xrightarrow{30\ \text{min}} 256$$

5. **(c)** Chrysophytes are a group of diatoms, golden algae (desmids) and golden brown photosynthetic microscopic protists. Their body is covered by a transparent siliceous shell.
6. **(a)** *Albugo* is the parasitic fungi on mustard and belongs to the class phycomycetes and kingdom fungi.
7. **(b)** The plant body of fungi typically consists of branched and filamentous hyphae, which form a net like structure, known as mycelium. In yeast, the plant body is unicellular but sometimes cells remain attached in short chains, forming a pseudomycelium.
8. **(d)** Viruses are obligate intracellular parasite which can reproduce only by invading and taking over other cells as they lack the cellular machinary for self reproduction. Viruses have either DNA or RNA as the genetic material. Viruses having RNA as the genetic material are known as Retroviruses.
9. **(a)** Bladderwort and venus fly trap are partially antotrophs. They trap insects for obtaining mtrogen and are called insectivorous plants e.g. pitcher plant.
10. **(c)** Lichens are formed by symbiotic relationship between algae or cyanobacteria and fungi. Lichens typically grow in harsh environments most lichens, especially epiphytic fruticose species and those containing cyanobacteria, are sensitive to pollutants. Hence, they have been widely used as SO_2 pollution indicator organisms.

Assertion & Reason Questions

1. **(b)** Aristotle is known as father of Biology and Zoology. He classified plants into trees, shrubs and herbs on the basis of morphological characters. He also classified animals on the basis of colour of blood.
2. **(a)** R.H. Whittaker, classified all the organisms into five kingdom on the basis of cell type, complexcity of structure, mode of nutrition, reproduction and phylogenic relationships. He grouped all the prokaryotic organisms into kingdom Monera and all the eukaryotic unicellular organisms into kingdom protista on the basis of cell type.
3. **(d)** Mycoplasma is a type of prokaryotic organisms that completely lack a cell wall.
   Cell wall is a type of rigid layer that is present outside the plasma membrane. Generally, it is found in plants, fungi and bacteria. Animal cells do not contain cell wall.
4. **(a)** Deuteromycetes are important class of fungi. They reproduce only by the asexual method. They produce spore that are called as conidia. So they are called imperfect fungi.
5. **(b)** An algal and a fungus forms a complex structure that is called as lichen. In lichen algal forms food and supply to the fungi. Fungus absorbs minerals and water from the soil and provides to the algal for the process of photosynthesis. Thus they help each other and show mutualism. Since lichen does not grow in a polluted area so it is a good indicator of pollution.

Case/Passage Based Questions

1. **(c)** 2. **(c)**
3. **(c)** Nostoc is a type of cyanobacteria.
4. **(b)** Methanogens are present in the gut of several ruminant animals and they are responsible for the production of methane gas (biogas) from the dung of these animals.
5. **(a)** Nostoc and Anabaena can fix atmospheric nitrogen in specialised cells called heterocysts.

Very Short Answer Questions

1. Carolus Linnaeus.
2. Plantae and Animalia
3. Protists are unicellular, eukaryotic organisms.
4. *Euglena* because it has locomotary organelle, flexible pellicle, contractile vacuole and reproduce by binary fission like animals and chloroplasts and pyrenoids like plants.
5. Monera, Protista, Fungi, Animalia and Plantae.
6. Heterotrophy and glycogen as reserve food.
7. (a) Plasmogamy – Fusion of protoplasms between two motile or non-motile gametes.
   (b) Karyogamy – Fusion of two nuclei.
8. Reterovirus are organisms that have RNA s as genetic material. For example HIV
9. The two salient features of slime moulds are :
   (1) These do not have cell wall
   (2) These have pseudopodia for movement
10. Jokers of microbiology are mycoplasma as they have no cell wall and no definite shape.
11. Two diseases caused by protozoans are
    (1) Amoebiasis   (2) Malaria

Short Answer Questions

1. Cyanobacteria, also known as 'blue green algae' help in carbon fixation in a major way on the ocean surface. They are helpful in nitrogen fixation in paddy fields leading to a better harvest. About 80% of photosynthesis on ocean surface is done by cynobacteria. So, it can be said that they play a major role in our ecology.
2. Methanogens are type of bacteria which live in the gut of ruminating animals. They assist those animals in digestion and the byproduct of that digestive process is methane. More number of livestock population results in increased methane level in the environment leading to global warming. So, indirectly methanogens can be responsible for global warming.
3. Lichens are symbiotic associations *i.e.* mutually useful associations, between algae and fungi. The algal component is known as **phycobiont** and fungal component as **mycobiont**, which are autotrophic and heterotrophic, respectively. Algae prepare food for fungi and fungi provide shelter and absorb mineral nutrients and water for its partner. Lichens are very good pollution indicators as they do not grow in polluted areas.
4. The five kingdom classification is based upon the following factors :
   (i) Complexity of cell structure — Prokaryotes or Eukaryotes
   (ii) Complexity of organisms body — Unicellular or Multicellular
   (iii) Mode of obtaining nutrition — Autotrophs or Heterotrophs
   (iv) Phylogenetic relationships
5. (a) Fossils   (b) Taxonomy
   (c) Evolution   (d) Autotrophs
6. (1) Coccus (SPHERICAL) Disease : Pneumonia

   pathogen : Streptococus pneumoniae

(2) Bacillus (ROD SHAPED) Disease : Anthrax
   Pathogen : Bacillus *anthrax*
(3) Spirillum (SPIRAL SHAPED) Disease :

   Pathogen :

(4) Vibrio (Comma Shaped) Disease : Cholera

   Pathogen : *Vibro Cholera*

7. (i) After sexual reproduction basidium is formed which form the shape a club and this chin these fungi are called Club Fungi.
   (ii) In sexual reproduction ascospores are formed in a sac like asci and thus this fungi is called sac fungi.

Long Answer Questions

1. Since the dawn of civilisation, there have been many attempts to classify living organisms. It was done instinctively not using criteria that were scientific but borne out of a need to use organisms for our own use – for food, shelter and clothing. Aristotle was the earliest to attempt a more scientific basis for classification. He used simple morphological characters to classify plants into trees, shrubs and herbs. He also divided animals into two groups, those which had red blood and those that did not.
   In Linnaeus' time a **Two Kingdom** system of classification with Plantae and Animalia kingdoms was developed that included all **plants** and **animals** respectively.
   Classification of organisms into plants and animals was easily done and was easy to understand, inspite, a large number of organisms did not fall into either category.
   R.H. Whittaker (1969) proposed a **Five Kingdom Classification**.
   The kingdoms defined by him were named **Monera, Protista, Fungi, Plantae** and **Animalia**. The main criteria for classification used by him include cell structure, thallus organisation, mode of nutrition, reproduction and phylogenetic relationships.
2. The distinguishing characters of kingdom fungi are as follows:
   (i) Fungi are non-vascular, non-seeded, non-flowering, eukaryotic achlorophyllous (nongreen), heterophic (heterophytic) spore bearing, thalloid, multicellular decomposers and mineralisers of organic wastes and help in recycling of matter in the biosphere.
   (ii) In true fungi the plant body is **thallus**. It may be non-mycelial or mycelial.
   (iii) The cell shows eukaryotic organization but lack chloroplast and Golgi bodies. The genetic material is DNA and mitosis is intracellular (karyochorisis).
   (iv) Fungi lack chlorophyll, hence, they do not prepare food by photosynthesis. Thus they can grow everywhere, where organic material is available.
   (v) Fungi are **heterotrophs** that acquire their nutrient by absorption. They store their food in the form of glycogen.
   (vi) The primitive fungi have oogamous type of sexual reproduction where as most advanced ones do not have sexual reproduction.

3. The main features of Monera and Protista are as following :

Monera	*Protista*
I. The kingdom consists of prokaryotic organisms.	I. The kingdom contains eukaryotic organisms.
II. The organisms are unicellular, colonial, mycelial and filamentous.	II. The protists are unicellular or colonial.
III. Cell size is comparatively smaller (0.1-5 mµ).	III. Cell size is comparatively larger (10-100 mµ).
IV. The cell wall if present contains peptidogycans.	IV. The cell wall if present contains cellulose.
V. Flagella, if present are unistranded.	V. Flagella if present are 11-stranded.
VI. There is a single envelop system.	VI. There is a double envelop system.
VII. Ribosomes are 70S in nature.	VII. Cytoplasmic ribosomes are 80S while organelle ribosomes are 70S.
VIII. Membrane bound cell organelles are absent	VIII. Membrane bound cell organelle are present.
IX. An organized nucleus is absent.	IX. An organized nucleus is present.
X. Genetic material is a single double helix molecule of DNA.	X. Genetic material consists of two or more DNA molecules.
XI. Sap vacuoles are absent	XI. Sap vacuoles occur.
XII. Cell division occurs by amitosis as mitotic spindle is absent.	XII. Cell division occurs by mitosis due to presence of spindle.
XIII. Sexual reproduction is absent as meiosis does not occur.	XII. Sexual reproduction is generally present as meiosis can occur.

SECTION C — NCERT EXEMPLAR QUESTIONS

MULTIPLE CHOICE QUESTIONS

1. All eukaryotic unicellular organisms belong to
   (a) Monera
   (b) Protista
   (c) Fungi
   (d) Bacteria

2. The five kingdom classification was proposed by
   (a) R.H. Whittaker
   (b) C. Linnaeus
   (c) Aristotle
   (d) Virchow

3. Organisms living in salty areas are called as
   (a) methanogens
   (b) halophiles
   (c) heliophytes
   (d) thermoacidophiles

4. Naked cytoplasm, multinucleated and saprophytic are the characteristics of
   (a) Monera
   (b) Protista
   (c) Fungi
   (d) Slime molds

5. An association between roots of higher plants and fungi is called
   (a) lichen
   (b) fern
   (c) mycorrhiza
   (d) BGA

6. A dikaryon is formed when
   (a) meiosis is arrested
   (b) the two haploid cells do not fuse immediately
   (c) cytoplasm does not fuse
   (d) None of the above

7. Contagium vivum fluidum was proposed by
   (a) D.J. Ivanowsky
   (b) M.W. Beijernek
   (c) Stanley
   (d) Robert Hook

8. Association between mycobiont and phycobiont are found in
   (a) mycorrhiza
   (b) root
   (c) lichens
   (d) BGA

9. Difference between virus and viroid is
   (a) absence of protein coat in viroid, but present in virus.
   (b) presence of low molecular weight RNA in virus, but absent in viroid
   (c) Both (a) and (b)
   (d) None of the above

10. With respect to fungal sexual cycle, choose the correct sequence of events.
    (a) Karyogamy, Plasmogamy and Meiosis
    (b) Meiosis, Plasmogamy and Karyogamy
    (c) Plasmogamy, Karyogamy and Meiosis
    (d) Meiosis, Karyogamy and Plasmogamy

11. Viruses are non-cellular organisms, but replicate themselves once they infect the host cell. To which of the following kingdom do viruses belong to?
    (a) Monera
    (b) Protista
    (c) Fungi
    (d) None of these

12. Members of phycomycetes are found in
    (i) Aquatic habitats
    (ii) On decaying wood
    (iii) Moist and damp places
    (iv) As obligate parasites on plants
    Choose from the following options.
    (a) (i) and (iv)
    (b) (ii) and (iii)
    (c) None of these
    (d) All of these

VERY SHORT ANSWER QUESTIONS

1. What is the principle underlying the use of cyanobacteria in agricultural fields for crop improvement?

2. How is the five kingdom classification advantageous over the two kingdom classification?

3. Polluted water bodies have usually very high abundance of plants like *Nostoc* and *Oscillitoria*. Give reasons.

4. Are chemosynthetic bacteria autotrophic or heteroterophic?

5. The common name of a pea is simpler than its botanical (scientific) name *Pisum sativum* why then is the simpler common name not used instead of the complex scientific/ botanical name in biology?

SHORT ANSWER QUESTIONS

1. Diatoms are also called as 'pearls of ocean', why? What is diatomaceous earth?

2. There is a myth that immediately after heavy rains in forest, mushrooms appear in large number and make a very large ring or circle, which may be several metres in diameter. These are called as 'fairy rings'. Can you explain this myth of fairy rings in biological terms?

Discuss the mycilial structure in Agaricus and its soil borne nature.

3. *Neurospora* an ascomycetes fungus has been used as a biological tool to understand the mechanism of plant genetics much in the same way as *Drosophila* has been used to study animal genetics. What makes *Neurospora* so important as a genetic tool?

4. At a stage of their cycle, ascomycetes fungi produce the fruiting bodies like apothecium, perithecium or cleistothecium. How are these three types of fruiting bodies different from each other? Discuss the type of fruiting bodies formed by ascomycetes fungus and differentiate accordingly on the basic of there structures.

5. What obsrevable features in *Trypanosoma* would make you classify it under kingdom-Protista?

Discuss cell structure of *Trypanosoma* also discuss its different strain brief.

LONG ANSWER QUESTIONS

1. Algae are known to reproduce asexually by variety of spores under different environmental conditions. Name these spores and the conditions under which they are produced.

2. Apart from chlorophyll, algae have several other pigments in their chloroptast. What pigments are found in blue, green, red and brown algae, that are responsible for their characteristic colours?

3. Make a list of algae and fungi that have commercial value as source of food, chemicals, medicines and fodder.

SOLUTIONS

Multiple Choice Questions

1. **(b)** **Protista** is a group comprising of all unicellular eukaryotic plants and animals. The organisms included in this group are either photoautotrophs, heterotrophs or parasites.

Monera includes prokaryotic organisms like bacteria, unicellular organism.

Fungi are eukaryotic but are mostly multicellular (yeast is unicellular).

2. **(a)** R.H. Whittaker (1969), an American taxonomist divided organism into five kingdoms, in order to develop phylogenetic classification.

(i) Monera   (ii) Protista
(iii) Fungi   (iv) Plantae
(v) Animalia

C Linnaeus developed two kingdom classification.

(i) Kingdom-Plantae
(ii) Kingdom-Animalia.

and Virchow is associated with the discovery of cell theory.

3. **(b)** **Halophiles** are organisms inhabiting areas with high concentration of salts. The name halophiles means 'salt loving'.

Heliophytes are the plants that grow best in sunlight and can not survive in dark conditions.

Methanogens are the bacteria that produce methane as a metabolic byproduct under anaerobic conditions.

Thermoacidophiles are archaebacteria able to survive under strong acidic environments and high temperatures, but cannot tolerate high salt concentrations around them.

4. **(d)** **Slime molds** are saprophytic protists, that move along the dead leaves engulfing organic matter. These are multinucleated with no cell wall and have naked cytoplasm.

5. **(c)** **Mycorrhiza** is a symbiotic association of fungus with the roots of a higher plants like gymnosperms and angiosperms.

6. **(b)** Dikaryon is a cell with two nucleus. This results when two somatic cells fuse but their nucleus do not fuse immediately. Meiosis does not result in such conditions.

7. **(b)** **M.W. Beijerinck** proposed contagium vivum fluidum which means contagious living fluid. This phrase was first used to describe virus, characteristic in escaping from the finest mesh available.

8. **(c)** **Lichens** are organisms comprised of a permanent symbiotic association of a fungus and an alga. The fungal partner is called mycobiont an the algal partner is called phycobiont.

9. **(a)** Viruses contain DNA or RNA as the genetic material and a protein coat, whereas viroids have no protein coat, but only RNA as their nucleic acid. This is the reason why viroids are carried inside viruses. *e.g.*, hepatitis-D is a viroid carried inside the capsid of hepatitis-B virus.

10. **(c)** Plasmogamy means fusion of protoplasm while karyogamy means fusion of nucleus. These two events lead to the formation of zygote ($2n$) which is a diploid structure where meiosis occurs.

11. **(d)** In the five kingdom classification proposed by Whittaker, non-cellular organisms like viruses and viroids are not included. Viruses were not placed in the classification since they are not truly 'living' and hence, they are considered as non-cellular.

12. **(d)** Phycomycetes are fungi that can thrive on dead and decaying wood as saprophytes. These prefer to live in moist and damp places and need water for the movement of zoospore and sexual gametes.

    Few members of phycomycetes are obligate parasites like *Phytophthora infestans* that causes late blight of potato and *Peronospora viticola* causing downy mildew of grapes.

Very Short Answer Questions

1. Cyanobacteria are able to fix atmospheric nitrogen and make it available to the plants and thus are used in agricultural crop improvement. This improves crop yield and also reduces the cost of application of nitrogen fertilisers. *e.g., Anabena* and *Nostoc*.

2. The five kingdom classification, proposed by RH whittaker is based upon cell structure, body structure (unicellular, multicellular), nutrition (autotrophic, heterotrophic) reproduction and habitat either aquatic, terrestrial, or aerial and phylogenetic relationship.

    It is thus more useful as compared to two kingdom system of classification which does not distinguish between prokaryotes and eukaryotes and no other kingdom except plant and animal are identified.

3. Polluted water bodies have high growth of algae due to the presence of nutrient. These nutrients increase the rapid growth of water plants, *i.e.,* algae especially *Nostoc* and *Oscillitoria*, etc., and result in colonies. These colonies are generally surrounded by a gelatinous sheath and leads to the formation of blooms in water bodies.

4. Chemosynthetic bacteria are capable of oxidising various inorganic substances such as nitrates, nitrites and ammonia and use the released energy for production of ATP and thus they are autotrophs and not heterotrophs.

5. The common or vernacular names cause confusion regarding the identification of specific specimen as they change with the change in place whereas the scientific names are in latin and universally accepted and understood. Scientific names are thus preferred over the common vernacular names.

Short Answer Questions

1. Diatoms and desmids are included under chrysophytes, kingdom-Protista. These are the main producers in the ocean. They prepare food for themselves and for the other life forms in the ocean as were a siliceous shell known as frustule cores the body of diatoms, this is the reason they are also called as 'pearls of ocean.

    'Diatomaceous earth' is the accumulation of large deposits of diatoms that forms a siliceous covering extending for several 100 metres formed in billions of years. The material obtained from these deposits is used in polishing and filtration of oils and syrups.

2. The fruiting bodies in *Agaricus* are known as basidiocarps. They form a concentric ring like structure from the mycelium present in the soil. These basidiocarps resemble button in shape and develop to form a ring like structure. This fairy ring structure in *Agaricus* stimulate productivity in plants. This rings are the fruiting bodies of this fungus and the diameter of this fairy ring increases every year due to the spread of mycelium.

3. *Neurospora* fungus can be grown easily under laboratory conditions by providing 'minimal medium' like inorganic salts, carbohydrates source and vitamin (biotin) and thus was selected to be a very good tool in genetics.

    The mutations can be also easily introduced in the fungal cells and meiotic division can be easily seen under X-ray treatment.

4. **Ascomycetes** consist of sporangial sac called ascus. Asci (singular-ascus) may occur freely or in aggregated form with dikaryotic mycelium to form the fruitification bodies called ascocarps.

    The fruitification formed by asci include the following :

    (i) **Apothecium** is cup like structure, *e.g., Peziza.*

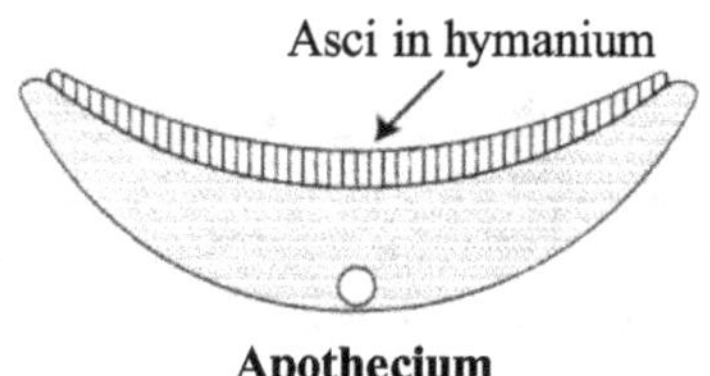

Apothecium

(ii) **Perithecium** is flask shaped, *e.g., Neurospora*

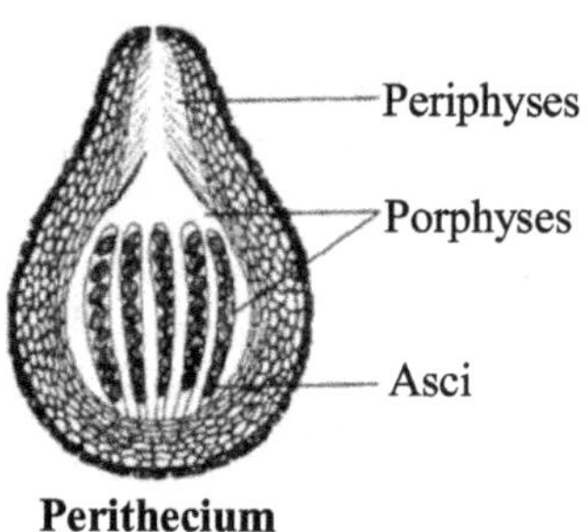

Perithecium

(iii) **Cleistothecium** is closed with a slit, *e.g., Penicilium*

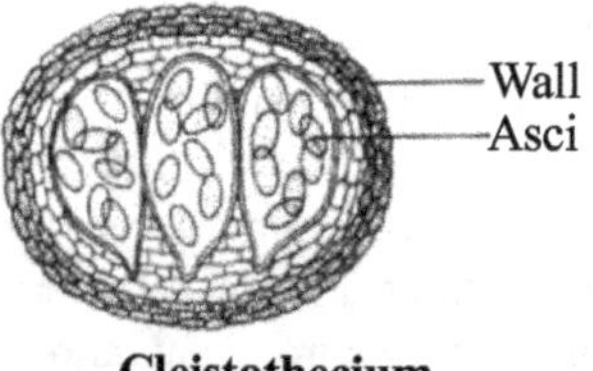

Cleistothecium

5. *Trypanosoma* is included under flagellated protozoans on the basis of locomotary organ. It *resembles Protisia in the following characters.*

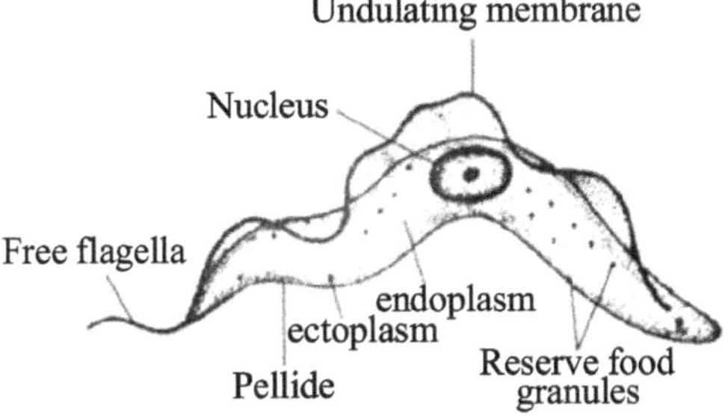

Trypanosoma gambiens

(i) It is unicellular.
(ii) It reproduces asexually *i.e.*, by binary fission.
(iii) Possess centrally located nucieus and also contain an prominent nucleus endosome.
(iv) Reserve food material is in the form of granules.

Long Answer Questions

1. Asexual reproduction in algae is very common mean of reproduction. Algae and their spores exhibit significant diversity and vary greatly in their level of specialisation. *Asexual reproduction by spores and their types include:*

(i) **Zoospores** are mobile flagellated spores. In this protoplasm of each vegetative cell undergoes repeated longitudinal division either into 2 or 4, rarely 8 or 16 daughter protoplasts. Before the onset of division the parent cell loses its fiagella.

Each daughter protoplast after the last series of division secretes a cell wall and a neuromotor apparatus that develops two flagella, eyespots and contractile vacuoles. Each of the daughter cell thus formed resembles the parent cell in all aspects except the small size.

Under favourable conditions formation of zoospores is very common.

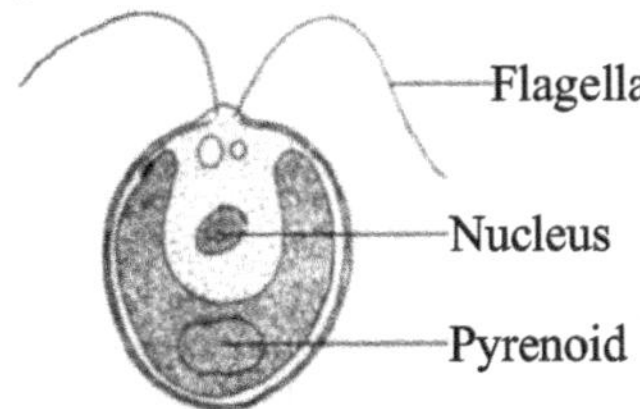

Zoospore of Chlamydomonas

(ii) **Aplanospores** are the non-motile spores. They are formed asexually within a cell, in which protoplast withdraws itself from the parent wall, rounds up and develops into aplanospores which germinate either directly or may divide to produce zoospores.

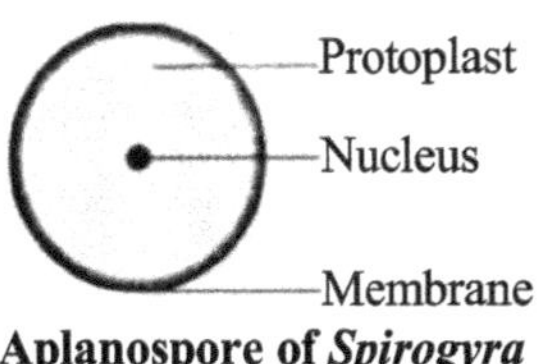

Aplanospore of *Spirogyra*

(iii) **Hypnospores-** In this, the protoplasm withdraws from the cell wall, rounds up and develops a thick wall under unfavourable conditions. These resting spores are called as hypnospores. Due to presence of haematochroma they are red in colour *e.g., Vaucheria, Ulothrix.*

(iv) **Akinetes** are special vegetative thick walled cells present in the filaments which remain under dormant state and resume germination under favourable conditions. They can also withstand unfavourable condition as *Spirogyra*.

(v) **Statospores** are thick walled spores produced in diatoms.

(vi) **Neutral spores** are the protoplast, of vegetative cells directly functioning as spores (*e.g., Ectocarpus*).

2. All photosynthetic organisms comprise of one or more organic pigments that are capable of absorbing visible, radiations, which will initiate the photochemical reaction of photosynthesis. The three major classes of pigments found in plants and algae are the chlorophylls, the carotenoids and the phycobilins.

Carotenoid and phycobilins are called accessory pigments since, the quanta absorbed by theese pigments can be transferred to chlorophyll.

The diversity of light harvesting pigments in alga implies that the common ancestor was primitive and that no close affinity exist between blue, green, red, brown, golden brown and green algae.

Following are the characteristic pigments of different classes.

Class	Common Name	Major Pigments
Chlorophyceae	Green algae	Chlorophyll-*a* and chlorophyll-*b*.
Phaeophyceae	Brown algae	Chlorophyll-*a* chlorophyll-*c*, Fucoxanthin.
Rhodophyceae	Red algae	Chlorophyll-*a*, chlorophyll-*d*, phycoerythrin.

3. **Algae**

Around 70 species of marine algae are used for food, chemical and medicinal purpose.

Food	Medicine	Chemical
Porphyra (?ower), *Rhodymenia* (pulse), *Chondrus* (Trishmoss). *Rhodymenia* (sheep's weed) is also used as fodder *Laminaria, Alariam Macrocystis, Sargassum* are used as food in many countries. The edible brown algae are used as fodder. *Ulva, Caulerpa, Enterom*	**Corollina** - capable in curing worm infection *Polysiphonia-Possess* antibacterial property. **Carrageenan** is an coagulant. Sodium laminarin sulphate acts as anticoagulant.	**Phycolloids :** It includes agar, carrageenin and funori. **Alginic acid** It is a phycocolloid obtained commercially from *Laminaria, Macrocystis* *Nerocystis, Fucus, Sargassum*, etc. It is used as salts in obtaining emulsioins (ice-creams, ointments, toothpastes etc.

Fungi

The role of fungi was established in early history. Since, the beginning of cultivation yeast have been used in making of bread and alcohol. The discovery of penicillin that marked the beginning of a new approach to microbial diseases in human health.

Products of fungi in medicine, chemical and food include.

Around 70 species of marine aigae are used for food, chemical and medicinal purpose.

Medicine	Chemical	Food
Penicillin (*Penicillium notatum* and *P. chyrsogenum*), glyotoxin. Chitrinine (*Trichderma* sp.) (*Pencillium citrinine*). Baccatin-A (*Gibberella baccater*) Ergotine (*Claviceps purpurea*), Clavicin (*Aspergillus clouertus* Flavin (*A, flavours*)	*Aspergilius niger* Mucor in production of citric acid. *Aspergillus niger* and *P. purpurogenum* in production of (gluconic acid). *P. glacum* and A. *gallomyces* forms (gallic acid)	Fermentation-*Aspergillus orzae* yeast-*Saccharomyces roxii* Cheese production-by *Penicillium comemberti* and *penicillium roqueforti* Colour of foods – by *Monoasus purpurreus*.

Plant Kingdom

3.1 **What is the basis of classification of algae?**

Sol. Classification of algae is based upon photosynthetic pigments.

3.2 **When and where does reduction division take place in the life cycle of a liverwort, a moss, a fern, a gymnosperm and an angiosperm?**

Sol.
I. **Liverwort** – The main part of the body of liverwort is thalloid. Haploid gametes are produced from the male and female sex organs gamets fuses to form zygote. Zygote develops in the form of sporophytes. These sporophytes are further differentiated into foot, seta and capsule. As a result of reduction division many haploid spores are produced in capsule.

II. **Moss** – In the first stage in moss primary protonema develops into secondary protonema. Both these stages are haploid . Zygote formed by the fusion of gametes further produce sporophytes.

III. **Fern** – Leaves of sporophyte bear sporangia in which spores are produced by reduction division in meiosis.

IV. **Gymnosperm** – In microsporophylls and megasporophylls that bear microsporangia and megasporangia respectively, reduction division occurs to produce microspores (pollen grains) and megaspore.

V. **Angiosperm** – Main part of the body is sporophytic and bears flowers. Reduction division takes place in anthers of stamen i.e. haploid pollen grains and in the ovary of pistil producing eggs.

3.3 **Name three groups of plants that bear archegonia. Briefly describe the life cycle of any one of them.**

Sol. Three groups of plant that bear archegonia are
1. Bryophyta,   2. Pteridophyta and
3. Gymnosperm.

Life cycle of gymnosperms : The gymnosperms are heterosporous, they produce haploid microspores and megaspores. The two kinds of spores are produced within sporangia that are borne on sporophyll which are arranged spirally along an axis to form strobili or cones. The strobili bearing microsporophylls and microsporongia are called microsporangiate or male strobili. The microspores develop into a male gametophytic generation which is highly reduced, and confined to only limited number of cells. The reduced gametophyte is called pollen grain. The development of pollen grain takes place within microsporangia.The cones bearing megaspo-rophylls with ovules or megasporangia are called macrosporangiate or female strobili. The male or female cones or strobili may be borne on the same tree or different trees. The megaspore mother cell is differentiated from one of the cells of the nucellus. The nucellus is protected by envelopes and the composite structure is called an ovule. The ovules are borne on megasporophylls which may be clustered to form the female cones. The females cones are borne on the main plant body of the sporophyte. The megaspore mother cell divides meiotically to form four megaspore. One of the megaspore enclosed within the megasporangium develops into a multicellular female gametophyte that bears 2 or more archegonia or female sex organs. The multicellular female gametophyte is also remains within megasporangium.

3.4 **Mention the ploidy of the following: protonemal cells of a moss; primary endosperm nucleus in dicot, leaf cell of a moss; prothallus cell of a fern; gemma cell in *Marchantia*; Meristem cells of monocot, ovum of liverwort and zygote of a fern.**

Sol. Protonemal cells of a moss – Haploid (n)
Primary endosperm nucleus in dicot – Triploid (3n)
Leaf cell of a moss – Haploid (n)
Prothallus cell of a fern – Haploid (n)
Gemma cell in *Marchantia* – Haploid (n)
Meristem cells of monocot – Diploid (2n)
Ovum of liverwort – Haploid (n)
Zygote of a fern – Diploid (2n)

3.5 **Write a note on economic importance of algae and gymnosperms.**

Sol. **Economic importance of Algae:**
Algae like *Chlorella*, *Gelidium* (produce agar-agar) are used as food. Many algae like diatoms (used in manufacture of glass, polish, etc), algin (used in vulcanisation, artificial fibres, etc.), are used in industry. *Nostoc*, *Anabaena*, etc., are useful in increasing fertility of soil. Antibiotic chlorellin is extracted from *Chlorella*. Many algae have harmful effect also, for example, *Microcystis*, *Chlrococcus*, *Oscillatoria* cause water blooms and *Cephaleuros* species of algae are parasitic on tea leaves and cause harm to tea industry. Alginic acid are extracted from the members Phaeophycea such as laminaria, Macrocystis and carrageenin is extracted from red algae chondris Crispos.

Economic importance of gymnosperms :
Gymnosperms helps in checking soil erosion. Seeds of *Pinus gerardiana*, *Gnetum gnemon* and *Ginkgo biloba* are eaten. Conifers like *Pinus longifolia*, *Cedrus deodara*, *Picea*, *Tsugo*, etc., produce soft wood. Bark of *Tsugo* yields tannins for making inks, seeds and bark of *Cycas* are used as poultica for wounds and sores. *Ephedra*, *Gnetum*, *Taxus baccata*, *Cycles rumphii* are used for medicinal purposes.

3.6 Both gymnosperms and angiosperms bear seeds, then why are they classified separately?

Sol. Gymnosperms are 'naked seeded' plants because their seeds are not enclosed in fruit wall whereas angiosperm are 'enclosed seeds' as seeds (ovules) are found enclosed in the ovary wall.

3.7 What is heterospory? Briefly comment on its significance. Give two examples.

Sol. Genera like *Selaginella* and *Salvinia* which produce two kinds of spores macro and microspores, are known as heterosporous. The megaspore and microspores germinate and give rise to female and male gametophytes, respectively. The female gametophytes in these plants are retained on the parent sporophyte for variable periods. The development of the zygotes into young embryo takes place within the female gametophytes. This event is considered as an important step in evolution leading to seed habit. Heterospory is considered as the first step towords seed habit. *Selaginella* and *Marsilea*, show seed habit.

3.8 Explain briefly

(i)	**Protonema**	(ii)	**Antheridium**
(iii)	**Archegonium**	(iv)	**Diplontic**
(v)	**Sporophyll**	(vi)	**Isogamy**

Sol.
(i) Protonema : The predominant stage of moss gametophyte which directly develops from spore is known as protonema.

(ii) Antheridium : The male sex organ in bryophytes, pteridophytes and gymnosperms is called antheridium. It bears male gamete.

(iii) Archegonium : It is the female sex organ found in bryophytes, pteridophytes and gymnosperms. It bears female gamete.

(iv) Diplontic : In the life cycle of plants when their diploid stage is dominant for long time then this is called diplontic.

(v) Sporophyll : The sporophyte bears sporangia that are subtended by leaf like appendages called sporophylls.

(vi) Isogamy : When the gametes involved in sexual reproduction are morphologically similar then this is called isogamy. These gametes are physiologically different.

3.9 Differentiate between the following:-
- **Red algae and brown algae**
- **Liverworts and moss**
- **Homosporous and heterosporous pteridophyte**
- **Syngamy and triple fusion**

Sol. Differences between red algae and brown algae are as follows

S.N.	Red algae	Brown algae
1.	Thylakoids in chloroplasts are not stacked.	Thylakoids in chloroplasts are stacked in groups of
2.	Chlorophyll a and Chl.d present.	Chlorophyll a and Chl.c present.
3.	Reserve food is floridean starch.	Reserve food is laminarian.
4.	No flagellated structure are found.	Flagellated structure are present.

Differences between liverworts and moss are as following.

S.N.	Liverworts	Moss
1.	Found in moist shady habitat.	Found in almost all conditions but absent in oceans.
2.	Plant body is dorsoventrally flattened, thalloid.	Plant body is differentiated into 2 stages— protonema stage (no sex organs) and leafy stage (produces sex organs).
3.	Asexual reproduction occurs by formation of gemma.	Asexual reproduction occurs by budding in the secondary protonema.

Differences between homosporous and heterosporous pteridophyte are as following :

S.N.	Homosporus pteridophyte	Heterosporus pteridophyte
1.	Spores are of same type.	Spores are of different type.
2.	It produces monoecious gametophyte.	It produces dioecious gametophyte.
3.	Examples of homosporus pteridophyte *ferns like Adiantum, Pteris*	Examples of heterosporus pteridophytes are *Selaginella, Marsilea, Salvinia, Azolla*

Differences between syngamy and triple fusion are as following.

S.N.	Syngamy	Triple fusion
1.	One of the male gametes fuses with the egg, resulting in the production of diploid zygote or oospore is called **syngamy.**	The second male gamete fuses with the secondary diploid nucleus (formed by fusion of two haploid polar nuclei), producing a **triploid primary endosperm nucleus**. This is called **triple fusion**.
2.	Syngamy results in formation of diploid embryo.	Triploid primary endosperm nucleus forms triploid endosperm.

3.10 How would you distinguish monocots from dicots?
Sol. The dicotyledons are characterised by having two cotyledons in their seeds while monocotyledons have only one cotyledon in their seeds.

3.11 Match the following content of column I with column II

Column I		Column II
(a)	*Chlamydomonas*	**(i)** Moss
(b)	*Cycas*	**(ii)** Pteridophyta
(c)	*Selaginella*	**(iii)** Algae
(d)	*Sphagnum*	**(iv)** Gymnosperm

Sol. (a) (iii) (b) (iv) (c) (ii) (d) (i)

3.12 Describe the important characterstics of gymnosperms.
Sol. The seed forming vascular plants which produce seeds but no fruits are called gymnosperms. General characters of gymnosperm are as follows:
(i)   Fertilization does not require water.
(ii) Leaves may be of two kinds : foliage leaves and scale leaves.
(iii) The ovules are orthotropus.
(iv) Most primitive seed bearing plants.
(v)   Mostly these plants are evergreen.
(vi) Have no ovary wall, seeds are naked.
(vii) Exhibit polyembryony.
Sexual reproduction oogamous type.
(viii) Large, tall and woody trees.

SECTION B — PRACTICE QUESTIONS 

MULTIPLE CHOICE QUESTIONS

1. Mannitol is the stored food in
   (a) *Chara*　　　　(b) *Porphyra*
   (c) *Fucus*　　　　(d) *Gracilaria*
2. Fusion of two gametes which are dissimilar in size is termed as _______ .
   (a) isogamous　　(b) oogamous
   (c) anisogamous　(d) agamous
3. Mosses are of great ecological importance because of
   (a) its contribution to prevent soil erosion.
   (b) its contribution in ecological succession.
   (c) its capability to remove CO from the atmosphere.
   (d) both (a) and (b)
4. The heterosporous pteridophyte belonging to the class lycopsida is
   (a) *Selaginella*　　(b) *Psilotum*
   (c) *Equisetum*　　(d) *Pteris*
5. The spreading of living pteridophytes is limited and restricted to narrow geographical region because
   (a) gametophytic growth needs cool, damp and shady places.
   (b) it requires water for fertilization.
   (c) due to absence of stomata in leaf and absence of vascular tissue.
   (d) both (a) and (b)
6. *Cycas* and *Adiantum* resemble each other in having
   (a) seeds　　　　(b) motile sperms
   (c) cambium　　(d) vessels
7. Angiosperms have dominated the land flora primarily because of their
   (a) power of adaptability in diverse habitat.
   (b) property of producing large number of seeds.
   (c) nature of self pollination.
   (d) domestication of man.

8. If there are 4 cells in an anther, what will be the number of pollen grains?
   (a) 8　　　　　　(b) 4
   (c) 16　　　　　(d) 12
9. Fruits are not formed in gymnosperms because of
   (a) absence of pollination.
   (b) absence of seed.
   (c) absence of fertilization.
   (d) absence of ovary.
10. Double fertilization is exhibited by
   (a) Algae　　　　(b) Fungi
   (c) Angiosperms　(d) Gymnosperms

ASSERTION & REASON QUESTIONS

DIRECTION (Qs. 1-5) : *These questions consists of two statements. Answer these questions selecting the appropriate option given below:*
(a) Both Assertion (A) and Reason (R) are true and Reason (R) is the correct explanation of Assertion (A).
(b) Both Assertion (A) and Reason (R) are true, but Reason (R) is not the correct explanation of Assertion (A).
(c) Assertion (A) is true, but Reason (R) is false.
(d) Assertion (A) is false, but Reason (R) is true.

1. **Assertion :** The fungi are widespread in distribution and they even live on or inside other plants and animals.
   Reason : Fungi are able to grow anywhere on land, water or on other organisms because they have a variety of pigments, including chlorophyll, carotenoids, fucoxanthin and phycoerythrin.
2. **Assertion :** Algin is obtained from algae.
   Reason : Rust of wheat is due to *Puccinia*.

3. **Assertion :** Mosses are evolved from algae.
   Reason : Protonema of mosses is similar to some green algae.
4. **Assertion :** Coconut tree is distributed in coastal areas over a large part of the world.
   Reason : Coconut fruit can float and get dispersed over thousands of kilometers before losing viability.
5. **Assertion :** The endosperm in gymnosperm is formed after fertilisation.
   Reason : The gymnosperm seeds were not formed by triple fusion.

CASE/PASSAGE BASED QUESTIONS

DIRECTIONS (Qs. 1-5) : *Read the following passage and answer the questions that follows.*

Bryophytes are the groups of plants that lack the vascular system. The given figures represents the examples of bryophytes. Observe the diagram and answers the questions.

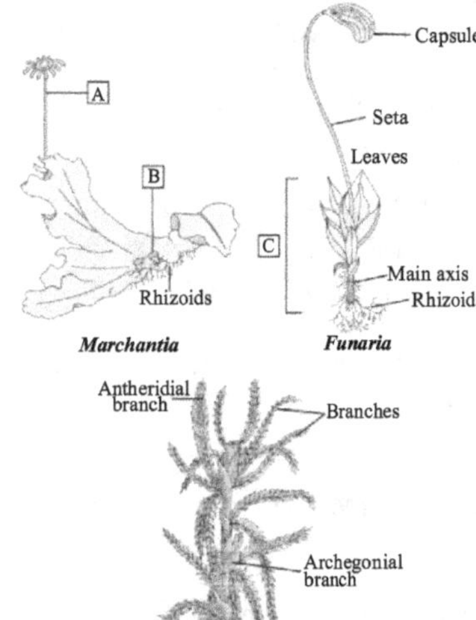

1. Which of the following labelling represents Archegoniophore?
   (a) A   (b) C
   (c) B   (d) D
2. What is indicated by labelling C ?
   (a) Gemma cup   (b) Gametophyte
   (c) Antheridia   (d) Archegonia
3. Which of the following statement is true about Bryophytes?
   (a) They live in soil but require water for reproduction
   (b) They are present in marine water
   (c) Both (a) and (b)
   (d) They do not require water for reproduction
4. Sphagnum is show by labelling :
   (a) C   (b) D
   (c) B   (d) A
5. Gemma cup plays important role in :
   (a) Photosynthesis   (b) Reproduction
   (c) Respiration   (d) All of them

VERY SHORT ANSWER QUESTIONS

1. Which type of food reserve is present in green algae?
2. Which pigment does provide red colour to red algae?
3. Which alga does reproduce sexually by conjugation?
4. Which filamentous structure does appear in mosses due to germination of spores?
5. Which plant group is called vascular cryptograms?
6. Which plant is commonly called as walking fern?
7. Which group of plants produces seed but not fruits?
8. Which part of ovule is haploid in gymnosperm?
9. What is name of megasporophyll bearing ovules of angiosperm?
10. Why gymnosperms fail to produce fruits?
11. Why life cycle of angiosperm is called as diplontic?
12. Which algae is known as Rolling alga?
13. Which are the specialized structures in selaginella which bears adventitious roots?
14. What are the number of cells and nuclei present in embryo sac of angiosperm?
15. Which plant is known as living fossil?

SHORT ANSWER QUESTIONS

1. What are the salient features of pteridophyte.
2. What is numerical taxonomy?
3. What are gemmae? Name two plants that produce gemmae.
4. Differentiate between cytotaxonomy and chemotaxonomy.
5. Differentiate between monocotyledon and dicotyledons.
6. What is the unique feature of bryophyte in compare to other plant groups? Discuss.
7. What are the features of Gemmae found in bryophytes?
8. What is the basis of classification of phylogenetic system?
9. What are the main features of Anthocerotopsida?

LONG ANSWER QUESTIONS

1. Write short notes on the following :
   (a) Peristomial teeth of moss
   (b) Protonema of moss
   (c) Archegonia of moss
2. Give a comparative account of gymnosperms and angiosperms.
3. Describe major features of Plant kingdom.

SOLUTIONS

Multiple Choice Questions

1. **(c)**
2. **(c)** Fusion of two gametes which are of dissimilar size is called anisogamous. Fusion of flagellate gametes of similar size is called isogamous. **Oogamous** is the fusion between **one large, non - motile female gamete** with a **smaller, motile male gamete**. Agamous does not involve the fusion of male and female gametes in reproduction.
3. **(d)** Mosses along with lichens are the first organisms to colonise rocks and hence, are of great ecological importance. They decompose rocks making the substrate suitable for the growth of higher plants. Since mosses form dense mats on the soil, they reduce the impact of falling rain and prevent soil - erosion.
4. **(a)** *Selaginella* is a member of lycopsida, which produce two kinds of spores-macro (large) and micro (small) spores. Thus, known as heterosporous pteridophytes.

5. **(d)** Pteridophytes are the vascular plants (those having xylem and phloem tissues) that reproduce by releasing spores rather than seeds, and they include the highly diverse true ferns and other graceful, primarily forest-dwelling plants. The spreading of living pteridophytes is limited and is restricted to narrow geographical region because its gametophytes require cool, damp, shady places to grow and also it requires water for fertilization.

6. **(b)** *Cycas* (a gymnosperm) and *Adiantum* (known as Maiden hair fern, a pteridophyte) resemble each other in having motile sperms. Seeds, cambium are common in gymnosperms but absent in pteridophytes. True vessels are absent in both pteridophytes and gymnosperms.

7. **(a)** Angiosperms are highly evolved and well adapted land plants. They have both vessels and tracheids in xylem for better conduction of water. Roots are modified into tap roots, adventitious roots, pneumatophores etc. to suit the desired climate.

8. **(c)** 1 microspore mother cell $\xrightarrow{\text{meiotic division}}$ 4 haploid microspores or pollen grains

    4 microspore mother cells = 4 × 4 pollen grains

    = 16 pollen grains.

9. **(d)** The ovules are not enclosed inside the ovary. Instead they are borne naked on the leafy sporophylls, and hence the name gymnosperms (gymnos- naked sperma- seed) is given Double fertilization is absent in gymnosperms.

10. **(c)** Double fertilization is a unique feature exhibited only by angiosperms. It involves both syngamy and triple fusion.

Assertion & Reason Questions

1. **(c)** Fungi lack pigments and are therefore, heterotrophic. The mode of nutrition is either parasitic/saprophytic.

2. **(b)** Certain marine brown algae (algin) produce large amounts of hydrocolloids.

    Puccinia is an unicellular fungi, cause disease in plants like wheat- rust.

3. **(a)** Mosses that belong to the bryophytes have evolved from algae. The fact that protonema has a thallus like body shows that mosses have evolved from algae.

4. **(a)** Coconut tree is distributed in coastal areas since its fruits floats on saline water because salt is more denser than freshwater, so it floats.

5. **(d)** Endosperm is formed when two sperm nuclei inside a pollen grain reach the interior of a female gametophyte (sometimes called the embryo sac). The cell created in this process of double fertilisation develops into the endosperm. Endosperm tissue, produced inside the seeds of most of the flowering plants, following fertilisation. It surrounds the embryo, providing nutrition in the form of starch, may also contain oils and proteins. Endosperm is not found in gymnosperms. It is only found in angiosperms.

Case/Passage Based Questions

1. **(a)**
2. **(b)** Bryophytes possess root-like, leaf-like or stem like structures. Its main body part is haploid. It produces gametes hence is called gametophytes.
3. **(a)**   4.   **(b)**
5. **(b)** Asexual reproduction in liverworts takes places by fragmentation of thalli, called germmacups.

Very Short Answer Questions

1. Starch
2. Phycoerythrin.
3. *Spirogyra*
4. Protonema.
5. Pteridophytes.
6. *Adiantum*
7. Gymnosperm.
8. Endosperm
9. Carpel.
10. Fruits are formed from ovaries. Since the gymnosperm ovules are not enclosed inside the ovaries, they do not produce fruit.
11. Life cycle of angiosperm is called as diplontic because diploid (sporophytic) phase is more prominent and long lived whereas haploid (gametophytic) phase is short lived.
12. Volvox
13. Rhizophores
14. 7 cells and 8 nuclei
15. Cycas

Short Answer Questions

1. Pteridophytes are **vascular cryptogams** *i.e.*, plants of this group possess vascular tissue (*i.e.*, xylem and phloem) for the conduction of water and minerals and for the translocation of foods. They are flowerless and seedless plants.

    General characters of pteridophytes are as following.

    I.   Primary root is short lived. It is replaced by adventitious roots.

    II. All vegetative parts possess vascular tissues. A cambium is altogether absent. In xylem trachea are absent and in phloem companion cells are absent.

    III. Pteridophytes show origin and evolution of stele (*i.e.*, vascular tissue, pericycle and if present the pith).

    IV. Pteridophytes are characterized by having only tracheids in their xylem and only sieve tube in their phloem.

    V.   The main plant body is sporophyte (diploid), usually differentiated into true roots, true stems and true leaves. Stem is usually underground rhizome or an erect trunk as in tree ferns. Leaves are large (megaphyllous) and variously shaped.

2. **Numerical Taxonomy** is based on all observable characteristics. Number and codes are assigned to all the characters and the data are then processed. In this way, each character is given equal importance and at the same time hundreds of characters can be considered.

3. Gemmae are green, multicellular asexual buds, which develop in small receptacles, called gemmae cups, on the thallus.

    The gemmae become detached from the parent thallus and germinate to form new individuals. *e.g.*, *Marchantia, Riccia.*

4. **Cytotaxonomy** that is based on cytological information like chromosome number, structure, behaviour and **chemotaxonomy** that uses the chemical constituents of the plant to resolve confusions, are also used by taxonomists these days.

5. Difference between monocotyledons and dicotyledons are as following:

Monocotyledons	Dicotyledons
Fibrous root system is	Tap root system is present.
Parallel venation is seen on the leaves.	Reticulate venation is seen.
Leaves have a sheathing leaf base.	Leaves have a stalk, the petiole.
Flowers are trimerous.	Flowers are nomally pentamerous.
Seeds have only one cotyledon *e.g.*, Rice, Coconut	Seeds have two cotyledons. *e.g.*, Mustard,

6. In Bryophytes, zygotes do not undergoes reduction devision immediately. They produce a multicellular body called a sporophyte. The sporophyte is not a free-living but attached to the photosynthetic gametophyte and derives nutrition from it.

7. Gemmae are the means of asexual reproduction found in many bryophytes (ex-Liverworts). They are one to many celled, specially produced clonal plant fragments. They are green multicellular, asexual buds which develop in small receptacles called "gemma cups" located on the thalli. Gemmae become detached from the parent body and germinate to form new individual.

8. It indicates evolutionary as well as genetic relationship among organism, it is based on fossil record, biochemical, anatomical, morphological, embryological, physiological, genetics, Karyotype and other studies.

9. These are also known as horn worts because typical horn like appearence are present of their sporophyte. These contains thalloid gametophyte, distinctly dorsiverotral, rhizoids are present, Thalloid do not possess air chambers and scales. Each cell of thallus has a single large chloroplast with a pyrenoid.

Long Answer Questions

1. (a) Peristomal teeth is located just below the operculum. It helps in dispersal of spores by hydroscopic movement of its outer ring while the inner ring do not show the hygroscopic movements.

(b) Each spore produces a filamentous juvenile stage called protonema. Protonema has two types of branches, subterranean non green rhizoidal and green epiterranean branches. Buds develop on green prostrate branches which grow to form new moss plants.

(c) Female reproductive organ of moss is called archegonium.

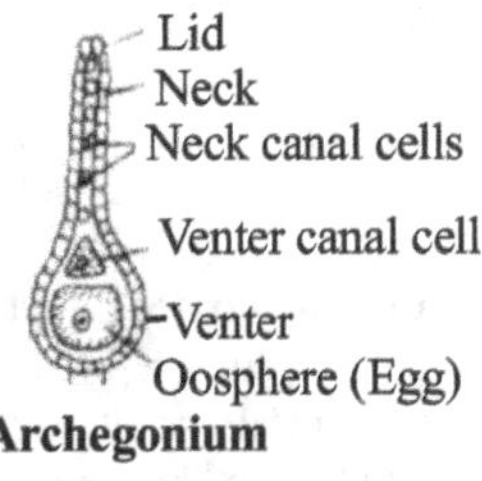

Archegonium

2. Comparison of gymnosperms and angiosperms

	Gymnosperms	Angiosperms
1.	Seeds are naked	Seeds are covered.
2.	Diplontic life cycle.	Diplontic life cycle.
3.	Sporophyte phase is the dominant phase.	Sporophyte is the dominant phase.
4.	Roots are generally tap roots.	Adventitious roots are found in monocots.
5.	Sexual parts are found on strobili.	Sexual parts are on special structures, called, flowers.
6.	Leaves are modified to withstand extreme temperature.	Modification of leaves depends on the given condition and can be of many types.
7.	Economic importance is restricted to ornamentation purposes.	Have wider economic importance.
8.	Don't bear fruits.	Many plants bear fruits.
9.	Pollination is absent	Pollination is present.

3. Features of Plant Kingdom :

- Plants are autotrophic, except some carnivorous plants. They trap photo energy from sunlight and convert it to chemical energy through photosynthesis. Because of this plants are the main channel for supplying energy in the food chain on earth.

- Reproduction in plants can be by any of the following modes: Vegetative or Asexual, and Sexual Reproduction.

- Plant cell is unique because of presence of cell wall and large vacuoles. Green parts of plant contain chlorophyll, which helps them in trapping the photo energy.

- Sizes of plants can vary from microscopic to a very large tree. Plants are mainly divided into Algae, Bryophytes, Pteridophytes, Gymnosperms and Angiosperms.

Diagrammatic Representation of Plant Kingdom.

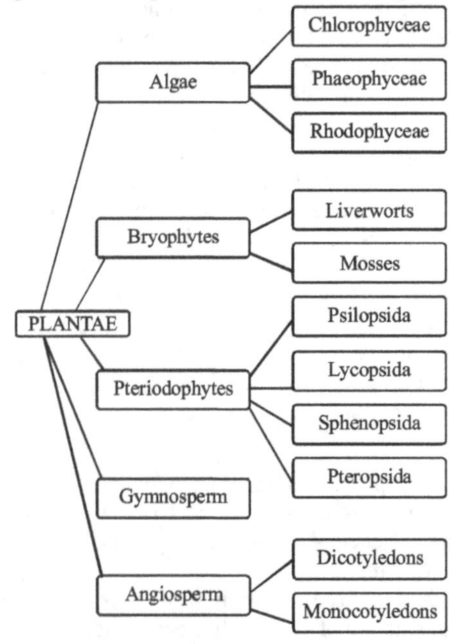

- Lower plants, like algae and bryophytes have thalloid structure, while higher plants, like gymnosperms and angiosperms, have clearly defined roots and stems.
- In higher plants root gives a means to anchor in the soil and helps the plant in taking minerals and water from the soil. Green leaves on the stem help them in photosynthesis.
- Most of the plant growth as a result of photosynthesis. After photosynthesis extra food is utilized to facilitate growth.
- Usually in higher plants growth is unlimited and some taller trees can live a life of more than 1000 years.
- Being the main carbon fixation agents, plants are very important for the whole ecology.

- The whole food basket for humans is being filled by the plant kingdom. Even animal products, like milk and poultry, are indirect results of plant's carbon fixation.
- Plants supply raw materials for a majority of economic activities. Wood for furniture and building materials come from plants. The whole paper industry is dependent on plant kingdom. Think of a life if there was no paper and you may understand the larger impact on human civilization.
- Angiosperms have special organs, called flower, to bear sexual parts. Flowers are helpful tool in facilitating variations and further evolution of the plant kingdom

SECTION C — NCERT EXEMPLAR QUESTIONS 

MULTIPLE CHOICE QUESTIONS

1. Fusion of two motile gametes which are dissimilar in size is termed as
   (a) oogamy
   (b) isogamy
   (c) anisogamy
   (d) zoogamy

2. Holdfast, stipe and frond constitutes the plant body in case of
   (a) Rhodophyceae
   (b) Chlorophyceae
   (c) Phaeophyceae
   (d) All of these

3. A plant shows thallus level of organisation. It shows rhizoids and is haploid. It needs water to complete its life cycle because the male gametes are motile. Identify the group to which it belongs to
   (a) pteridophytes
   (b) gymnosperms
   (c) monocots
   (d) bryophytes

4. A prothallus is
   (a) a structure in pteridophytes formed before the thallus develops
   (b) a sporophytic free living structure formed in pteridophytes
   (c) a gametophyte free living structure formed in pteridophytes
   (d) a primitive structure formed after fertilisation in pteridophytes

5. Plants of this group are diploid and well adapted to extreme conditions. They grow bearing sporophylls in compact structures called cones. The group in reference is
   (a) monocots
   (b) dicots
   (c) pteridophytes
   (d) gymnosperms

6. The embryo sac of an angiosperm is made up of
   (a) 8 cells
   (b) 7 cells and 8 nuclei
   (c) 8 nuclei
   (d) 7 cells and 7 nuclei

7. If the diploid number of a flowering plant is 36. What would be the chromosome number in its endosperm?
   (a) 36
   (b) 18
   (c) 54
   (d) 72

8. Protonema is
   (a) haploid and is found in mosses
   (b) diploid and is found in liverworts
   (c) diploid and is found in pteridophytes
   (d) haploid and is found in pteridophytes

9. The giant redwood tree (*Sequoia sempervirens*) is a/an
   (a) angiosperm
   (b) free fern
   (c) pteridophyte
   (d) gymnosperm

VERY SHORT ANSWER QUESTIONS

1. Food is stored as floridean starch in Rhodophyceae. Mannitol is the reserve food material of which group of algae?

2. The plant body in higher plants is well differentiated and well developed. Roots are the organs used for the purpose of absorption. What is the equivalent of roots in the less developed lower plants?

3. Most algal genera show haplontic life style. Name an alga which is
   (a) Haplo diplontic
   (b) Diplontic

4. In bryophytes male and female sex organs are called .... and ....

SHORT ANSWER QUESTIONS

1. Why are bryophytes called the amphibians of the plant kingdom?
   Amphibians can their in water as well as on terrestrial habitat.

2. Heterospory, *i.e.*, formation of two types of spores—microspores and megaspores is a characteristic feature in the life cycle of a few members of pteridophytes and all spermatophytes. Do you think heterospory has some evolutionary significance in plant kingdom?

3. Each plant group of plants has some phylogenetic significance in relation to evolution *Cycas*, one of the few living members of gymnosperms is called as the 'relic of past'. Can you establish a phylogenetic relationship of *Cycas* with any other group of plants that justifies the above statement?

4. Comment on the life cycle and nature of fern prothallus.

5. How are the male and female gametophytes of pteridophytes and gymnosperms different from each other?

6. In which plant will you look for mycorrhiza and corolloid roots? Also explain what these terms mean.

Long Answer Questions

1. Explain why sexual reproduction in angiosperms is said to take place through double fertilisation and triple fusion. Also draw a labelled diagram of embryo sac to explain the phenomena.

2. Draw labelled diagrams of
   (a) Female and male thallus of a liverwort.
   (b) Gametophyte and sporophyte of Funaria.
   (c) Alternation of generation in angiosperm.

SOLUTIONS

Multiple Choice Questions

1. **(c)** Lower group of plants like algae exhibit great variation in mode of sexual and asexual reproduction. Some algae produce gametes which are not similar in shape, size and structure. Their fusion is called anisogamy. e.g., *Chlamydomonas*. Isogamy is the fusion of similar gametes, zoogamy is sexual reproduction of animals.

2. **(c) Phaeophyceae :** In the members of the class-Phaeophyceae, the plant body is usually attached to the substratum by means of a holdfast and has a stalk called stipe and a leaf like photosynthetic organ called frond.

3. **(d) Bryophyta** is a group of plants which have gametophytic haploid thalloid body. The motile male gametes are produced in special male reproductive structures called antheridia.
   These gametes need thin film of water to swim and reach the female reproductive organ called archegonia. Pteridophytes, gymnosperm and monocots show higher level of organisation.

4. **(c) Prothallus** is usually a gametophytic phase in the life of a pteridophyte. Spore germinates to form a prothalium, it is short lived inconspicuous heart shaped structure with a number of rhizoids developed beneath and bears sex organs, archegonium and antheridium.

5. **(d) Gymnosperms** include medium sized or tall trees and shrubs. Their plants are well adapted to withstand extremes of temperature, humidity and wind. Reproductive organs are usually in the form of cones or strobili. The male cones are made up of microsporophyll and female cones are made up of megasporophyll. The presence of sporophyll (micro and megasporophyll) shows the development of seed habit but seeds develop from naked ovule and are not covered .

6. **(b) Embryo sac** in angiosperm contains 2 synergids, 1 egg cell, 3 antipodal cells and one secondary nucleus.

7. **(c) Endosperm** is a product of triple fusion. One male nuclei ($n = 18$) fuses with diploid secondary nucleus ($2n = 36$), so it becomes triploid ($3n = 54$). Thus, ploidy of endosperm is ($3n$) and chromosomes will be 54.

8. **(a)** The germination of **haploid** spores of mosses produced by sporophyte after reductional division form the protonema. This structure later develops into an independent gametophytic plant.

9. **(d)** *Sequoia sempervirens* is a gymnosperm. It has thick, woody and branched stems. The plant also shows some xeric adaptations which helps it to survive in adverse climatic conditions.

Very Short Answer Questions

1. Mannitol is a reserve food material of the members of Phaeophyceae (brown algae).

2. Root like structure called rhizoids are present instead of roots in less developed lower plants (bryophytes and pteridophytes). The plant tissue system in these is not differentiated into true leaf, stem and roots as it is found in higher plants (gymnosperm and angiosperm).

3. Haplo diplontic type of life cycle is exhibited by *Ectocarpus, Polysiphonia* and *Kelps*. The main plant body is saprophytic in *Fucus* and it shows diplontic type of life cycle.

4. In bryophytes the male sex organ in antheridium and female sex organ is archegonium. **Antheridium** produces flagellate antherozoids which are male gametes.
   Archegonia is the female part which bears a single egg cell.

Short Answer Questions

1. Bryophytes are a group of primitive plants having a dominant gametophytic plant body. These plants can live in soil but depend on water for movement of male gametes called antherozoids to reach the archegonium (female organ bearing egg cell) so that fertilisation can occur, so bryophytes are called the amphibians of the plant kingdom.

2. The production of spores of two different sizes and sexes by the sporophytes of land plants is heterospory. Two types of spores are produced by heterosporic plants. Small spores are microspores which germinate into the male gametophyte and large spores are macrospores which develop into the female gametophyte.

Pteridophytes are intermediate between bryophytes and gymnosperms in the evolution of plants. All bryophytes are homosporous and all gymnosperms are heterosporous. This condition is advanced as sexual dimorphism results in cross fertilisation.

Primitive or earlier pteridophytes are homosporous while later pteriodophytes are heterosporous *e.g.*, *Dryopteris*, *Pteris* homosporous *Selaginella*, *Salvinia*-heterosporous.

3. *Cycas* is an evergreen plant which resembles palm. It has an unbranched stem and large compound leaves. It exhibits phylogenetic relationship with pteridophyte. *Its evolutionary characters include the following*:
   (i) Growth is redundant.
   (ii) Shedding of seed while the embryo is still immature.
   (iii) Minimal secondary growth and manoxylic wood.
   (iv) Megasporophylls are leaf like.
   (v) Sperms are flagellate even when pollen tube is present.
   (vi) Leaf bases are persistent.
   (vii) Ptysix is circinate.
   (viii) Arrangement of microsporangia in well defined archegonia.

4. The life cycle of ferm (*Dryopteris*) clearly depicts the alternation of generation. The gametophytic stage (n) alternates with the sporophytic stage ($2n$) in the life cycle as shown in the figure.

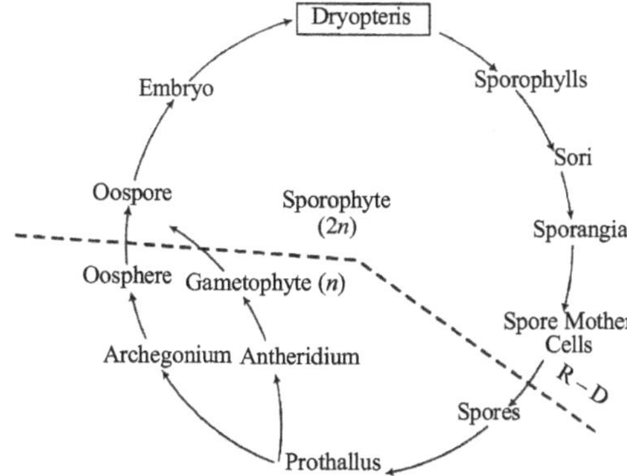

Topographical representation of life cycle of fern

The prothallus of the fern is a multicellular, free living, thalloid, haploid and autotrophic structure. It develops from the spores produced by sporophyte after reduction division.

These spore germinate within a germtube with an apical cell and forms a filament of 3-6 cells and one or two rhizoids at the base which later develops into gametophytic plant.

5. The male and female gametophytes of pteridophytes and gymnosperms different from each other as:

Male Gametophyte of Gymnosperm	Male Gametophyte of Pteridophyte	Female Gametophyte of Gymnosperm	Female Gametophyte of Pteridophyte
A distinct male gametophyte is always present	Male gametophyte is not usually distinct.	A distinct female gametophyte is always present.	Female gametophyte is not usually distinct.
An antheridium is not found.	Antheridium is present	Female gametophyte is retained in the parent plant.	It is independant
Male gametes may or may not be flagellated. Male gametes reach the female gamete through a pollen tube. Water is not required.	Male gametes are flagellated. Male gametes reach the female gamete by swimming in a film of water.	It is enclosed inside an ovule.	It is not enclosed in an ovule.

6. Symbiosis is a type of interaction of two living organisms where both the associated partners derive some benefit from each other both co-exist and flourish well.

Mycorrhiza is a symbiotic association between fungus and the roots of vascular plants. The fungus colonizes the roots of the host either intra or inter cellularly. It helps in the nutrient absorption from soil for the plant. Mycorrhizal associations are present in conifers, *i.e.*, *Pinus, Cedrus, Abies* and *Picea.*

Coralloid roots develop in Cycas. It is produced in clusters at the base of the stem and protrudes out on the ground. It is dichotomously branched and greenish in colour. It contains algal zone in cortex. This algal zone contains blue green algae like *Anabaena* and *Nostoc* which grow in symbiotic association with coralloid roots.

Long Answer Questions

1. An angiospermic plants reproduces sexually by the formation of male and female gametes. The male gamete is a pollen which contains two male nuclei and the female gamete is an egg cell produced in ovule (female gametophyte).

   The pollen grains germinate on the stigma of a flower and the results in growth of pollen through the tissues of stigma and style and reach the egg apparatus. The two male gametes are discharged within the embryo sac. One of the male gamete fuses with the egg cell to form a diploid zygote.

   This fusion is known as **fertilisation** or **syngamy**. The .second male gamete fuses with the diploid secondary nucleus and forms the triploid Primary Endosperm Nucleus (PEN). This fusion is known as triple fusion.

   Because of the involvement of two fusion, this event in angiosperms is termed as **double fertilisation**. The zygote then develops into embryo and PEN develops into endosperm which provides nourishment to the developing embryo.

2.

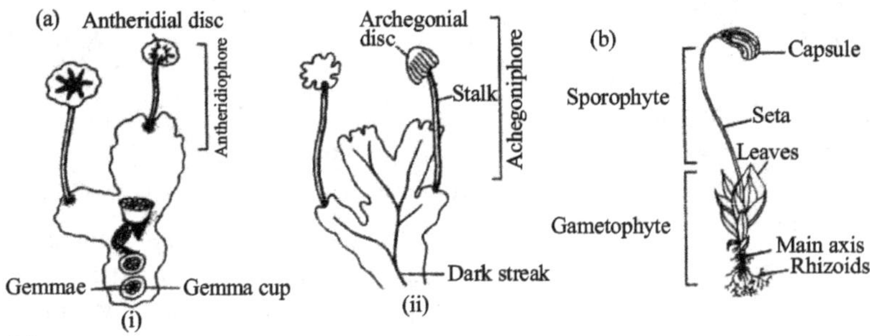

   (a) Liverworts
   (i) Male thallus of *Marchantia polymorpha*
   (ii) Female thallus of *Marchantia polymorpha*
   (b) Funaria
   (gametophyte and sporophyte)

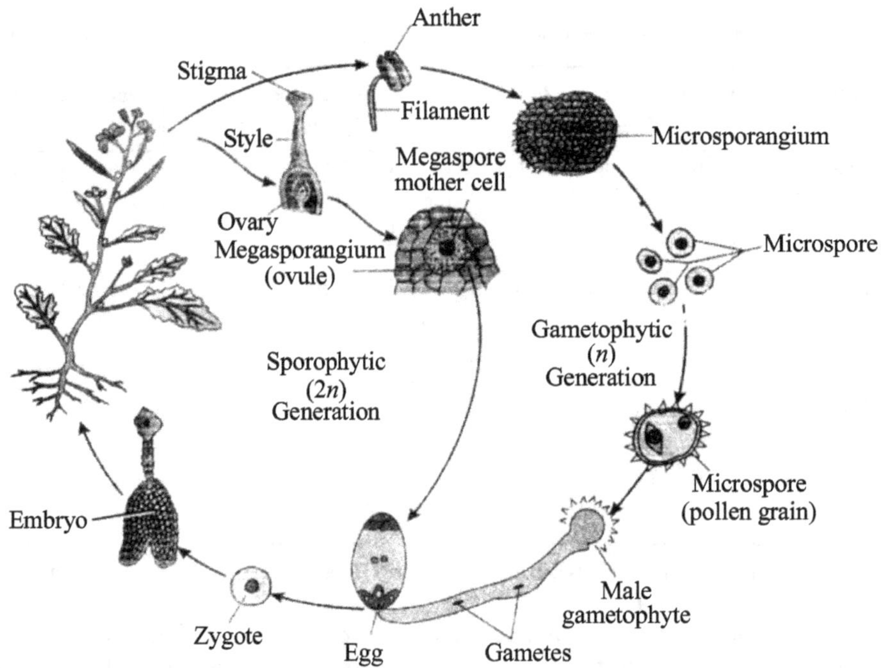

Life cycle of an angiosperm showing alteration of generation

Animal Kingdom

4.1 **What are the difficulties that you would face in classification of animals, if common fundamental features are not taken into account?**

Sol. If fundamental characters are not taken into account then the classification of animals is difficult due to difference in characters in different animals which are as following :
- (i) Grade of organisation
- (ii) Symmetry
- (iii) Coelom
- (iv) Segmentation
- (v) Notochord

Common fundamental features help in grouping animals in certain categories or sub-categories. For examples, all birds have fore-limbs modified to assist in flying. This gives us one clue to categorise a particular animals among aves.

4.2 **If you are given a specimen, what are the steps that you would follow to classify it?**

Sol. Classification of specimen deals according to a systematic plan on the basis of their similarities, differences and relationship.

We will take following steps
- (i) Level or grade of organisation :
  There are different types of cell which are organised into functional units of progressively increasing complexity. Such as acellular, cellular, tissue, organ and organ system.
- (ii) Pattern in organ system :
  Threre are different organ system in which specific group of organs work together to do a specific function. Such as digestive organs in digestive system. Respiratory organs in respiratory system, etc. in animal body.
- (iii) Symmetry :
  In animals, 4-types of symmetry are seen. These are spherical, radial, bilateral, Assymetrical species are classified according to symmetry.
- (iv) Diploblastic and triploblastic organisation:
  According to number of germ layers which differentiate at the time of gastrulation in developing embryo. Species are classified as diploblastic i.e. two germ layer and Triploblastic i.e. three germlayers.
- (v) Body cavity or coelom :
  According to types of coelom, species are classified into acoelom, pseudocoelom and eucoelom animals.
- (vi) Segmentation :
  Species are classified according to segmentation. It is of three types i.e. pseudometamerism or false segmentation, internal and external segmentation.
- (vii) Notochord :
  On the basis of notochord, animals or species are divided into chordates and non-chordates.

We will follow the above steps in classification of animal, then fair idea of that animal can be derived.

4.3 **How useful is the study of the nature of body cavity and coelom in the classification of animals?**

Sol. Coelom is the gap between gut and body wall. Coelom is the characterstic feature of complex or higher animals while lower animals like platyheminthes are acoelomate. The absence of coelom indicates that the animal is yet to develop a functional division of labour to carry out various activities. So the coelom characterises complexity of the animals and represents organic evolution.

There are three types of coelom
- (i) **Acoelom** – It means absence of body cavity which is due to the failure of mesoderm to cavitate during embryogency, so there is no coelom, no peritonium. ex– porifera, colenterata, etc.
- (ii) **Pseudocoelom** – It means presence of coelom that develops from the blastocoel but not lined by mesoderm. ex–nematodes, etc.
- (iii) **Eucoelom** – It means true coelom, which is lined by mesoderm resulting in tube within -tube design. ex- higher invertebrates, chordates, etc.

4.4 **Distinguish between intracellular and extracellular digestion?**

Sol. Intracellular digestion takes place inside the cells by cellular enzymes, which are secreted by the surrounding cytoplasm into the food vacuole and the digestive products are then diffused in cytoplasm. It mainly occurs in unicellular organism and also is a less efficient method. Extracellular digestion occurs with the help of digestive enzymes poured into gastrovascular cavity by secretory cells and then the digestive products are diffused across the intestinal wall into various parts of the body. It mainly occurs in multicellular organisms and is more efficient.

4.5 What is the difference between direct and indirect development?

Sol. In direct development young ones are formed directly from development of zygote whereas young ones are formed through an intermediate stage *i.e.* larval stage in the indirect development. There is no intermediate stage, indirect development and young one resembles the adult.

4.6 What are the peculiar features that you find in parasitic platyhelminthes?

Sol. Members of platyhelminthes possess following characteristics.
(i) These are mostly endoparasites of animals including human.
(ii) Hook and suckers are present for attachment to host body.
(iii) They absorb nutrient from the host directly through their body surface.
(iv) These are free living, parasitic forms. Tissue, organ, grade of body organization is seen.
(v) Digestive tract is incomplete or absent.
(vi) Respiration is anaerobic.
(vii) Reproductive system of parasitic forms is highly developed with enormous power of reproduction.
(viii) Well defined excretory organs such as flame cells are present.

4.7 What are the reasons that you can think of for the arthropods to constitute the largest group of the animal kingdom?

Sol. Arthropods are the most successful group of animals on the earth. Their success is due to
(i) Unique chitinous cuticle
(ii) Light weight exoskeleton
(iii) Omnivorous habit
(iv) Mouth parts adapted to various mode of feeding like biting, chewing, sucking etc.
(v) Adaptation to different climatic conditions

4.8 Water vascular system is the characteristic of which group of the following:
(a) **Porifera**   (b) **Ctenophora**
(c) **Echinodermata**   (d) **Chordata**

Sol. Echinodermata – Its vascular system with tube feet helps in locomotion. A perforated plate , madreporite, permits entry of water into ambulacral system which also help in food and gas transport system.

4.9 "All vertebrates are chordates but all chordates are not vertebrates". Justify the statement.

Sol. Phylum chordates includes two subphyla
(i) Protochordates (urochordates and cephalochordates) or Acraniata
(ii) Vertebrates or Craniata
All chordates have notochord present in some stage of life. In vertebrates the notochord is present in the embryonic stage. This is replaced by a vertebral column during the adult stages.
This confirms that all vertebrates are chordates but all chordates are not vertebrates, they may be protochordate.

4.10 How important is the presence of air bladder in Pisces?

Sol. Air bladder is a hydrostatic organ which regulates buoyancy. It also aids in swimming by reducing the weight of body. Hence, this means that members of Pisces don't have to keep on swimming to remain floating.

4.11 What are the modifications that are observed in birds that help them fly?

Sol. The birds are adopted for flying by reducing the weight and other modifications which are as follows :
(i) The fore limb modified into wings to assist in flight.
(ii) Left ovary absent or reduced
(iii) Presence of pneumatic or hollow bones for making a light weight skeleton.
(iv) Aerodynamic body helps in flying.
(v) Excretion of urine and faeces occurs through single opening.

4.12 Could the number of eggs or young ones produced by an oviparous and viviparous mother be equal? Why?

Sol. The number of eggs given by oviparous and young ones given by viviparous animals are not equal because the egg laying animals lay-more eggs to resist the environmental forces for survival so that the population remains constant or not declining while the viviparous animals nurture their young ones and give birth to less number of offsprings as parental care is shown in the viviparous animals.

4.13 Segmentation in the body is first observed in which of the following:
(a) **Platyhelminthes**   (b) **Aschelminthes**
(c) **Annelida**   (d) **Arthropoda**

Sol. (c) Annelida.

4.14 Match the following:

(a) **Operculum**	(i) **Ctenophora**		
(b) **Parapodia**	(ii) **Mollusca**		
(c) **Scales**	(iii) **Porifera**		
(d) **Comb plates**	(iv) **Reptilia**		
(e) **Radula**	(v) **Annelida**		
(f) **Hair**	(vi) **Cyclostomata and Chondrichthyes**		
(g) **Choanocytes**	(vii) **Mammalia**		
(h) **Gill slits**	(viii) **Osteichthyes**		

Sol.
(a) Operculum	(viii) Porifera	
(b) Parapodia	(v) Annelida	
(c) Scales	(iv) Reptilia	
(d) Comb Plates	(i) Ctenophora	
(e) Radula	(ii) Mollusca	
(f) Hair	(vii) Mammalia	
(g) Choanocytes	(iii) Porifera	
(h) Gill slits	(v) Cyclostomata and Chondrichthys	

4.15 Prepare a list of some animals that are found parasitic on human beings.

Sol.
(i) *Porktape worm solium*
(ii) *Faciola hepatica* (liver fluke)
(iii) *Schistosoma* (blood fluke)
(iv) *Wuchereria bancrafti* (filarial worm)
(v) *Ancylostoma duodenale* (hook worm)
(vi) *Ascaris lumbricoides* (The giant intestinal round worm)
(vii) *Loa loa* (eyeworm)
(viii) *Trichinella spiralis* (trichinia worm)

<table><tr><td>**SECTION B**</td><td># PRACTICE QUESTIONS</td></tr></table>

MULTIPLE CHOICE QUESTIONS

1. Which of the following is not the common fundamental feature for animal classification?
   (a) Germinal layers.
   (b) Pathway of water transport.
   (c) Pattern of organization of cells.
   (d) Serial repetition of the segments.
2. Which of the following is a fresh water sponge?
   (a) *Sycon*   (b) *Euspongia*
   (c) *Spongilla*   (d) *Pleurobrachia*
3. Which of the following statement(s) is/are correct regarding phylum coelenterata?
   (i) They are aquatic, mostly marine, sessile or free-swimming, radially symmetrical animals.
   (ii) They have a central gastro-vascular cavity with a single opening called hypostome.
   (iii) Digestion is extracellular and intracellular.
   (iv) Examples are *Sycon, Spongilla* and *Euspongia*.
   (a) (i) and (ii)   (b) (i) and (iv)
   (c) (i), (ii) and (iii)   (d) All of these
4. Identify the correct characteristics of porifera.
   (i) Commonly known as sea walnuts.
   (ii) Presence of ostia and collar cells.
   (iii) Exhibit tissue level of characteristics.
   (iv) It is the largest phylum of animal kingdom.
   (v) The body is supported by spicules and sponging fibers.
   (vi) Contains cnidocytes which is used for defense, anchorage and capturing of prey.
   (a) (ii), (v) only   (b) (i), (ii), (vi) only
   (c) (i), (ii), (iii), (iv) only   (d) All of these.
5. Identify the figures and select the correct option.

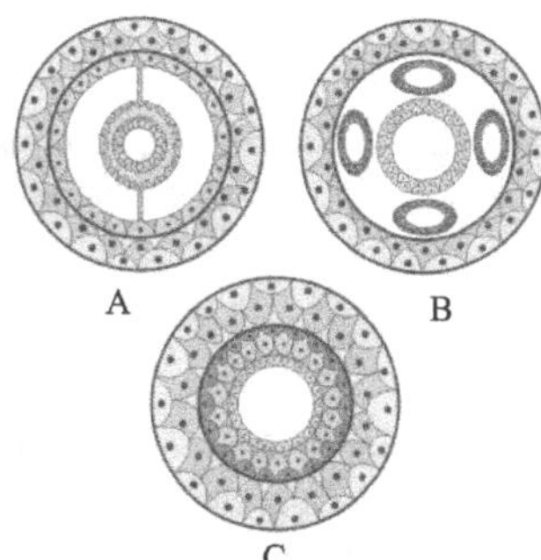

   (a) A - Pseudocoelomate; B - Coelomate, C-Acoelomate
   (b) A - Coelomate, B - Pseudocoelomate, C- Acoelomate
   (c) A - Coelomate; B- Acoelomate; C - Pseudocoelomate
   (d) A - Coelomate; B- Acoelomate; C-Eucoelomate
6. Which of the following belong to phylum arthropoda?
   (a) *Bombyx* and *Apis*   (b) *Laccifer* and *Anopheles*
   (c) *Locusta* and *Limulus*   (d) All of the above
7. Which of the following characteristic is probably most responsible for the great diversification of insects on land?
   (a) Segmentation   (b) Antennae
   (c) Bilateral symmetry   (d) Exoskeleton

8. Which of the following characters is absent in all chordates?
   (a) Diaphragm   (b) Coelom
   (c) Pharyngeal gill clefts (d) Dorsal nerve cord
9. Identify the correct characteristic feature shown by the given figure?

   (a) Diploblastic in nature.
   (b) Having radial symmetrical body.
   (c) Dioecious with direct development.
   (d) Presence of sensory tentacles on anterior head region.
10. An important characteristic that Hemichordates share with Chordates is :
    (a) Ventral tubular nerve cord
    (b) Pharynx with gill slits
    (c) Pharynx without gill slits
    (d) Absence of notochord

ASSERTION & REASON QUESTIONS

DIRECTION (Qs. 1-5) : *These questions consists of two statements. Answer these questions selecting the appropriate option given below:*
(a) Both Assertion (A) and Reason (R) are true and Reason (R) is the correct explanation of Assertion (A).
(b) Both Assertion (A) and Reason (R) are true, but Reason (R) is not the correct explanation of Assertion (A).
(c) Assertion (A) is true, but Reason (R) is false.
(d) Assertion (A) is false, but Reason (R) is true.

1. **Assertion :** Sponges have body organisation of "cellular level".
   Reason : There is some physiological division of labour.
2. **Assertion:** Coelenterates show alternation of generation.
   Reason: Asexual generation is followed by sexual generation in coelenterates.
3. **Assertion :** *Lumbricus* and *Nereis* both belong to annelida.
   Reason : They have nephridia.
4. **Assertion:** *Calotes, Crocodilus* and *Chelone* are members of class Reptilia.
   Reason: Heart is three chambered in *Calotes, Crocodilus* and *Chelone*.
5. **Assertion :** Tapeworm, roundworm and pinworm are endoparasites of human intestine.
   Reason : Improperly cooked food is the source of intestinal infections.

CASE/PASSAGE BASED QUESTIONS

DIRECTIONS (Qs. 1-5) : *Read the following passage and answer the questions that follows.*

Presence or absence of the cavity between the body wall and gut wall is very important in the classification of the animals. In the given diagram, sectional view of body cavity are shown. Observe diagram and answers the questions.

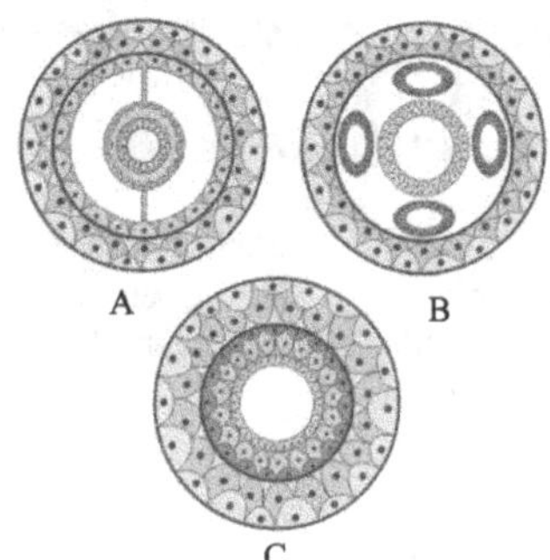

A   B

C

1. Which of the diagram represents the pseudocoelomate
   (a) B   (b) C
   (d) A   (d) All of them
2. What is shown by diagram A?
   (a) Pseudocoelomate   (b) Acoelomate
   (c) Coelomate   (d) None of them
3. Which of the following statement is true.
   (a) Annelids have pseudocoelomate body cavity.
   (b) Coelomate body cavity is present in arthropods.
   (c) Arthropods do not have any type of body cavity.
   (d) All organisms have same type of body cavity.
4. The body cavity which is lined by mesoderm is called
   (a) Intestine   (b) Coelom
   (c) Notochord   (d) None of them
5. A coelomatic body cavity is present in
   (a) Platyhlminthes   (b) Echinoderm
   (c) Both (a) and (b)   (d) None of them

Very Short Answer Questions

1. What is common name of *Euspongia* ?
2. Name the class which is characterised by pneumatic bones.
3. Give the characteristic feature of echinodermata.
4. Name the phyla which shows metamerism.
5. Name two animal groups with incomplete digestive tract.

6. Name a fresh water sponge and coelenterate.
7. What is radula ?
8. Name two characteristic organs of chordates.
9. To which phyla *Balanoglossus* belong ?
10. What is aestivation ?
11. Name two flightless birds.
12. Give one example each of ectothermal and endothermal animals.
13. Give one example of cephalochordata.
14. Why do lampreys and snakes lack girdles ?
15. What is the difference between epidermis of invertebrates and vertebrates ?
16. Mention modification of coelom in echinoderms.
17. What are setae ?
18. What are endothermic animals ?
19. Why is the *Ornithorhynchus* considered an exceptional mammal ?

Short Answer Questions

1. What are pneumatic bones ? Where do you find them ?
2. How do earthworm and leech differ with regard to their coelom?
3. Cite unique features of nematodes.
4. What is marsupium ?
5. Why is coelentron called gastrovascular cavity ?
6. What is the fate of notochord in higher chordate ?
7. State the two types of fishes. Give their examples.
8. What is metamerism?
9. Why are Urochordates called Tunicata?
10. Give an example of an organism showing.
    (1) Radial symmetry
    (2) Bilateral symmetry

Long Answer Questions

1. (i) What are different symmetry that exists in animal kingdom.
   (ii) Distinguish between diploblastic and triploblastic.
2. Describe economic importance of the largest phylum.

SOLUTIONS

Multiple Choice Questions

1. **(b)** Pathway of water transport is not the common fundamental feature for animal classification.
2. **(c)** Sponges are pore bearing animals belong to phylum porifera. They have a water transport or canal system. *Spongilla* is a fresh-water sponge.
3. **(c)** *Sycon, Spongilla* and *Euspongia* are examples of phylum Porifera. *Physalia, Adamsia, Pennatula, Gorgonia* and *Meandrina* are examples of phylum coelenterata (Cnidaria).
4. **(a)** Porifera is commonly referred to as sponges. They are multicellular organisms that have bodies full of pores and channels allowing water to circulate through them, consisting of jelly-like mesohyl sandwiched between two thin layers of cells.
5. **(b)** Acoelomates : The animals which do not have coelom *e.g.*, sponges, coelenterates, ctenophorans and flatworms. Pseudocoelomates : Body cavity is not lined by mesoderm continuously, but it is present as scattered pouches in between the ectoderm and endoderm. Aschelminthes (round worms) are pseudocoelomates.

Eucoelomates (Coelomates) : The animals which possess true coelom. True coelom is found in annelids, echinoderms and chordates.

6. **(d)** Phylum arthropoda is the most numerous phyla of all living organisms, both in number of species and in number of individuals.
7. **(d)** Exoskeleton is probably the most responsible for the great diversification of insects on land. An exoskeleton is the external skeletons that supports and protects an animal's body, in contrast to the internal skeleton (endoskeleton) of, for example, a human. Examples of exoskeleton animals include insects such as grasshoppers and cockroaches, and crustaceans such as crabs and lobsters.
8. **(a)** Diaphragm is a membrane that separates thoracic cavity from abdominal cavity. It is present only in mammals. All other chordates do not have diaphragm as their body cavity is not divided into thoracic and abdominal cavities.
9. **(d)** The given figure shows the examples of Mollusca. These animals are triploblastic and bilaterally symmetrical in nature. They are usually dioecious and oviparous with indirect development.

10. **(b)** Pharyngeal gill slits are present in hemichordates and in chordates. Notochord is present in chordates only. Ventral tubular nerve cord is present in non-chordates.

Assertion & Reason Questions

1. **(b)** Sponges are multicellular but they have cellular level of body organization *i.e.*, true tissue, movable parts, or appendages are not formed. Although, there is some physiological division of labour, accompanied with structural differentiation amongst body cells. But here, similar cells are arranged neither in permanent layer nor masses to form tissues.

2. **(a)** Alternation of generations may be defined as a phenomenon whereby, during the life history of an organism, a diploid asexual phase and a haploid sexual phase regularly alternates with each other. This type of true alternation of generations is also called metagenesis. In coelenterates, an asexual polypoid generation appears to alternate regularly with a sexual medusoid generation.

3. **(b)** *Lumbricus* belongs to class Oligochaeta and *Nereis* belongs to class Polychaeta of phylum Annelida.

4. **(c)** *Calotes, Crocodilus* and *Chelone* are members of class Reptilia. Heart is four chambered in *Crocodilus* while three chambered in *Calotes* and *Chelone*.

5. **(b)** Tapeworm, roundworm & pinworm are all endoparasites. The main cause of the intestinal infection is improperly cooked food. However, tapeworm infection occur by eating improperly cooked food, roundworm is transmitted by contaminated food & water and pinworm or ringworm is transmitted through food or improper sanitary condition.

Case/Passage Based Questions

1. **(a)** **2.** **(c)** **3.** **(b)**

4. **(c)** The body cavity which is lined by mesoderm is called notochord.

5. **(a)** A coelomatic body cavity is present in platyhlminthes.

Very Short Answer Questions

1. Bath sponge
2. Aves
3. Water vascular system
4. Annelida, Arthropoda and Chordata.
5. Cnidaria and platyhelminthes.
6. *Spongilla* and *Hydra*
7. Rasping organ of molluscs.
8. Notochord and gill slits.
9. Hemichordata
10. Ostrich, Kiwi
11. Reptiles, mammals.
12. *Branchiostoma* (Amphioxus)
13. Due to lack of limbs.
14. Epidermis is a stratified epithelium in vertebrates and a simple epithelium in invertebrates.
15. A part of the echinoderm coelom is modified into a water-vascular system for help in locomotion.
16. Locomotive organs of phylum annelida.
17. Endothermic animals (birds and mammals) generate most of their body heat by metabolism.
18. *Ornithorhynchus*, though a mammal, lays egg and has a cloacal aperture.

Short Answer Questions

1. Bones having air spaces in them are called pneumatic bones. Birds have such types of bones to make body light for flying.
2. Coelom is spacious in earthworm and greatly reduced in leech by formation of botryoidal tissue in it.
3. Syncytial epidermis, pseudocoel, non-muscular intestine and body wall musculature of longitudinal fibres only.
4. Marsupium is pouch on the females belly for rearing the young one in metatherian mammals. *e.g.* Kangaroo.
5. It is a cavity in which both digestion and circulation occur.
6. Notochord is replaced by vertebral column partly or fully in chordates.
7. The two types of fishes are
(1) Chrondrichthyes example Trygon, electric ray
(2) Osteichthyes example Rohu, Sea horse
8. It is a phenomenen found in organisms like earth worm that they have their bodies segmented and this parttern is called metameric segmentation.
9. As the adult bodies of Urochordata is covered by a tunic like cover to these are called Tunicata.
10. Radial symmetry : Star fish
Bilateral symmetry : Octopus, men.

Long Answer Questions

1. **(a) Asymmetrical symmetry**
   I. In many animals the body can not be divided in two equal halves on any plane.
   II. Ex. *Amoeba* being irregular in shape, some sponges with various branching. Gastropod molluscs (snails, conch) have no symmetry due to torsion in embryonic stage.

  (b) Radial symmetry
   I. Any plane passing through a central axis of the body divides the organism into two identical halves.
   II. Examples are Coelentrates, ctenophores and echinoderms.

  (c) Bilateral symmetry
   I. In most animals body can be divided into two equal halves on only one plane, hence body has left and right sides front and rear (back) sides; anterior and posterior ends; dorsal and ventral sides.
   II. Their advance symmetry and such animals are most mobile.

Diploblastic animals: Animals in which cells are arranged in two embryonic layers, an external ectoderm and internal endoderm are called diploblastic animals.

Triploblastic animals: Animals in which developing embryo has the third germinal layers, mesoderm, in between the ectoderm and endoderm are called triploblastic animals.

2. The largest phylum is Arhtropoda and its economic importance is as follows:
– They are major agents for cross pollination. Insects, like butterflies and honey bee facilitate cross pollination.
– Honey is an important food for human.

— Many crustaceans, like lobsters and prawns are art of cuisine around the world.

— The red dye cochineal, produced from a Central American species of insect, was economically important to the Aztecs and Mayans.

— The blood of horseshoe crabs a clotting agent Limulus Amebocyte Lysate which is now used to test that antibiotics and kidney machines are free of dangerous bacteria, and to detect spinal meningitis and some cancers.

— Maggots of housefly are used to treat those wounds which take time to heal because of absence of blood supply.

— The relative simplicity of the arthropods' body plan, allowing them to move on a variety of surfaces both on land and in water, have made them useful as models for robotics.

— They are carriers of many human parasite causing diseases like malaria, filaria and sleeping sickness.

— Cockroaches are one of the major nuisance as they contaminate food in kitchens.

— Termites are major causes of playing havoc with wooden furnitures.

— Scorpions are known for their deadly sting, which can kill human and livestock.

SECTION C   NCERT EXEMPLAR QUESTIONS 

Multiple Choice Questions

1. In some animal groups, the body is found divided into compartments with at least some organs. This characteristic feature is called
   (a) Segmentation   (b) Metamerism
   (c) Metagenesis   (d) Metamorphosis

2. Given below are types of cells present in some animals. Which of the following cells can differentiate to perform different functions?
   (a) choanocytes   (b) interstitial cells
   (c) gastrodermal cells   (d) nematocytes

3. Which one of the following sets of animals share a four chambered heart?
   (a) Amphibian, Reptiles, Birds
   (b) Crocodiles, Birds, Mammals
   (c) Crocodiles, Lizards, Turtles
   (d) Lizards, Mammals, Birds

4. Which of the following pairs of animals has non-glandular skin?
   (a) Snake and frog   (b) Chameleon and turtle
   (c) Frog and pigeon   (d) Crocodile and tiger

5. Birds and mammals share one of the following characteristics as a common feature.
   (a) Pigmented skin   (b) Pneumatic bones
   (c) Viviparity   (d) Warm blooded body

6. Which one of the following sets of animals belong to a single taxonomic group?
   (a) Cuttlefish, jellyfish, silverfish, dogfish, starfish
   (b) bat, pigeon, butterfly
   (c) Monkey, chimpanzee, man
   (d) Silkworm, tapeworm, earthworm

7. Which one of the following statements is incorrect?
   (a) Mesoglea is present in between ectoderm and endoderm in *Obelia*
   (b) *Asterias* exhibits radial symmetry
   (c) *Fasciola* is a pseudocoelomate animal
   (d) *Taenia* is a triploblastic animal

8. Which one of the following statements is incorrect?
   (a) In cockroaches and prawns excretion of waste material occurs through malpighian tubules.
   (b) In ctenophores, locomotion is mediated by comb plates.
   (c) In *Fasciola* flame cells take part in excretion
   (d) Earthworms are hermaphrodites and yet cross fertilisation take place among them.

9. Which one of the following is oviparous?
   (a) Platypus   (b) Flying fox (bat)
   (c) Elephant   (d) Whale

10. Which one of the following is not a poisonous snake?
    (a) Cobra   (b) Viper
    (c) Python   (d) Krait

11. Body cavity is the cavity present between body wall and gut wall. In some animals the body cavity is not lined by mesoderm. Such animals are called
    (a) Acoelomate   (b) Pseudocoelomate
    (c) Coelomate   (d) Haemocoelomate

Very Short Answer Questions

1. What is the importance of pneumatic bones and air sacs in Aves?

2. What is metagenesis? Mention an example which exhibits this phenomenon.

3. What is the role of feathers?

4. Which group of chordates posses sucking and circular mouth without jaws?

5. Mention two modifications in reptiles required for terrestrial mode of life.

6. What is the role of radula in molluscs?

7. Name the animal, which exhibits the phenomenon of bioluminescence. Mention the phylum to which it belongs.

8. Write one example for each of the following in the space providing.
   (a) Cold blooded animal ....
   (b) Warm blooded animal ....
   (c) Animal possessing dry and cornified skin ....
   (d) Dioecious animal ....

9. Differentiate between a diplobastic and triploblastic animal.

10. Give an example of the following
    (a) Roundworm
    (b) Fish possessing poison sting
    (c) A limbless reptile/amphibian
    (d) An oviparous mammal

11. Provide appropriate technical term in the space provided.
    (a) Blood-filled cavity in arthropods ....
    (b) Free-floating form of cnidaria ....
    (c) Stinging organ of jelly fishes ....
    (d) Lateral appendages in aquatic annelids ....

12. Match the following.

Animals	Locomotory Organ
A. Octopus	(i) Limbs
B. Crocodile	(ii) Comb plates
C. Catta	(iii) Tentacles
D. Ctenoplana	(iv) Fins

SHORT ANSWER QUESTIONS

1. Differentiate between
(a) Open circulatory system and closed circulatory system.
(b) Oviparous and viviparous characteristic.
(c) Direct development and indirect development.

2. There has been an increase in the number of chambers in heart during evolution of vertebrates. Give the names of the class of vertebrates having two, three or four chambered heart.

3. Fill up the blank spaces appropriately

Phylum/Class	Excretory Organ	Circulatory Organ	Respiratory Organ
Arthropoda			Lungs/Gills/Tracheal System
	Nephridia	Closed	
	Metanephridia	Open	Skin/Parapodia
Amphibia		Closed	Lung

4. Match the following

A.	Amphibia	(i)	Air bladder
B.	Mammals	(ii)	Cartilaginous notochord
C.	Chondrichtyes	(iii)	Mammary glands
D.	Osteichthyes	(iv)	Pneumatic bones
E.	Cyclostomata	(v)	Dual habitat
F.	Aves	(vi)	Sucking and circular mouth with out jaws.

5. Endoparasites are found inside the host body. Mention the special structure, possessed by these and which enables them to survive in those conditions.

6. Mention two similarities between
(a) Aves and mammals (b) A frog and crocodile
(c) A turtle and *Pila*

7. Name
(a) A limbless animal
(b) A cold blooded animal
(c) A warm blooded animal
(d) An animal possessing dry and cornified skin
(e) An animal having canal system and spicules
(f) An animal with cnidoblasts

8. Excretory organs of different animals are given below. Choose correctly and write in the space provided.

Animal	Excretory Organ/Unit
A. Balanoglossus	(i) Metanephridia
B. leech	(ii) Nephridia
C. Locust	(iii) Flame cells
D. Liver fluke	(iv) Absent
E. Sea urchin	(v) Malpighian tubule
F. Pila	(vi) Proboscis gland

A. ....
B. ....
C. ....
D. ....
E. ....
F. ....

LONG ANSWER QUESTIONS

1. What is the relationship between germinal layers and the formation of body cavity in case of coelomate, acoelomates and pseudocoelomates?

2. Comment upon the habitats and external features of animals belonging to class-Amphibia and Reptilia.

SOLUTIONS

Multiple Choice Questions

1. **(b) Metamerism** is the external and internal division of animal body into segments with a serial repetition of at least some organs. e.g., annelids (earthworm).
Segmentation refers to the division of animal's body into a series of repetitive segments. It is external in arthropods, and internal in vertebrates.
Metagenesis is the phenomenon in which one generation of certain animals and plants reproduce asexually, followed by a sexually reproducing generation, *i.e.*, alternation of generation (*e.g. Obelia*).
Metamorphosis is the developmental process in an organism through which it changes from one life form to another.

2. **(b) Interstitial cells** are the totipotent cells in the body of cnidarians that are capable of giving rise to any kind of specialised cells in order to perform different functions.
Choanocytes or collar cells are associated with filtering of nutrients in sponges.
Gastrodermal cells or the cnidocyst are used for attachment and defence in cnidarians.

Nematocyst are capsules that are the specialised cells in cnidarians, that act as a paralysing sting and are used for defence purpose.

3. **(b)** Crocodiles, birds, and mammals have four-chambered heart.
Heart is usually three chambered in reptiles with an exception in crocodiles, which possess four chambered heart. The division in their heart is due to the incomplete interventricular septum.
Heart in **birds** and **mammals** is four chambered and there is a complete division of interventricular septum. **Amphibians** possess a three chambered heart in which the ventricles are not divided thus 2 atria and one ventricle is present.

4. **(b)** Chameleon and turtle belong to class–Reptillia and possess dry and non-glandular skin with scales.
Frog, pigeon and tiger possess modifications in their skin according to the adaptations in their respective habitats.

5. **(d)** Warm blooded animals are capable of maintaining constant body temperature, irrespective of the surrounding environment, *i.e.*, their body temperature is fixed. Warm blooded body is the characteristic feature in birds and mammals. This characteristic was first evolved in higher reptiles. Birds and mammals have acquired this feature from higher reptiles during evolution.

Pigmented skin is the adaptive feature seen in mammals and not present in birds. Pneumatic bones are found only in birds as their flight adaptation. These reduce body weight for flight. Viviparity is shown by mammals and not by birds as they are oviparous (lay eggs).

6. **(c)** Monkey, chimpanzee and man belong to a single taxonomic group, *i.e.* mammals because all of them possess the following characters.
    (i)   Two pairs of limbs.
    (ii) Presence of external ears.
    (iii) Viviparity
    (iv) Skin possessing hair.
    (v) Milk producing mammary glands.

7. **(c)** *Fasciola* does not possess body cavity hence, it is an acoelomate.

8. **(a)** The statement (a) is incorrect because malpighian tubules are excretory structures in most of the insects, including cockroach, but green glands perform excretory functions in crustaceans like prawns, whereas all the other statements are true.

9. **(a)** Platypus is a primitive mammal which displays many characters of their reptilian descent, such as ovaparity. (they lay eggs.)

10. **(c)** **Except Python,** all other snakes are highly poisonous in nature. Python due to its large size, kills its prey by constriction of their body.

11. **(b)** Body cavity not completely lined by the mesoderm, instead present in the form of scattered pouches, in between ectoderm and endoderm, is called pseudocoelomate, *e.g.*, roundworm.

The animals in which coelom is completely absent, *e.g.*, flatworms are **acoelomates.**

Coelomates have their body cavity lined by mesoderm and hence have true coelom, *e.g.*, annelids, molluscs, arthropods, *etc.*

Haemocoelomates are the animals in which body cavity is filled with haemolymph, *e.g.*, arthropods, molluscs.

Very Short Answer Questions

1. Birds possess light weight bones that contain internal spaces filled with air, which are pneumatic bones. They are an adaptation for flight as they help in, reducing the body weight. Aerodynamic lungs with specialized air sacs are an additional feature that aids birds in flying (*e.g.*, bald eagle, pigeon).

2. The phenomenon in which one generation of certain plants and animals reproduce asexually, followed by the sexually reproducing generation is **metagenesis**. Both the forms in metagenesis are diploid hence, it is known as the false alternation of generation.

Coelenterates exhibit **metagenesis** (*e.g.*, *Obelia*) where in its life cycle polyp form alternates with medusa.

3. Feathers are the epidermal out growths that form distinctive outer covering or plumage in birds.
A variety of role are played by feathers which includes:
    (i)   They provide life and help in flight, by creating airfoil shape for wings.

    (ii) They help in maintaining body temperature.
    (iii) Feathers play a vital role in mating by providing secondary sexual that characters in both the sexes the colour and markings determine the alteractiveness of mate.

4. Class-Cyclostomata is comprised of living jawless fishes. They have a circular mouth and lack jaws, hence they are also called agnathans.

The mouth works like a sucker and is surrounded by tentacles (*e.g.*, lampreys and haglish). These also prosses rectroctable teeth that are horny.

5. Certain characters acquired by reptiles for the terrestrial adaptations include.
    (i)   Body is covered with dry and cornified skin and epidermal scales or scutes.
    (ii) Internal fertilisation.

6. The radula is a special rasping structure present many **molluscs**. It is used to scrape and scratch the food and to create depressions in rocks used as habitat.
It bears many rows of tiny teeth that are replaced as they wear down *e.g., Limplet* is a marine invertebrate that uses its radula for creating home by boring a shallow hole in the rock.

7. Bioluminescence is the phenomenon of production and emission of light by an organism as a result of chemical reaction during which chemical energy is converted to light energy.
The phenomenon of bioluminescence is exhibited by Ctenoplana from phylum-Ctenophora.

8. (a) A cold blooded animal is *Crocodilus* (crocodile)
    (b) *Elephas maximus* (elephant), (mammal) is a warm blooded animal.
    (c) *Testudo* (tortoise) bears dry and cornified skin.
    (d) *Ascaris* (roundworm) is a dioecious animal.

9. Diploblastic animals are animals in which the cells are arranged in two embryonic layers, an external ectoderm and an internal endoderm (*e.g.*, coelentrates). Animals in which the developing embryo has a third germinal layer, *i.e.*, mesoderm lying between the ectoderm and endoderm are called triploblastic animals. (*e.g.*, chordates).

10. (a) Roundworm - *Ascaris*
    (b) Fish possessing poison sting - *Trygon*
    (c) A limbless reptile/amphibian - *Ichthyophis*
    (d) An oviparous mammal – Duck billed platypus.

11. (a) The blood-filled cavity in arthropods containing haemolymph is haemocoel.
    (b) A form in cnidarians in which the body is shaped like an umbrella which can float freely in sed water is medusa.
    (c) Capsules of specialised cells in cnidarians which act as a paraylysing sting are nematocytes.
    (d) The paired unjointed lateral outgrowth in annelids bearing chaetae are parapodia.

12. (a) **Octopus** The appendages in invertebrates that are used for grasping food and for locomotion are tentacles.
    (b) **Crocodile** for locomotion, and swimming limbs are used.
    (c) **Catta** Fins are means of locomotion and are used to generation optimum thrust thus controlling the subsequent motion.
    (d) **Ctenoplana** Locomotory organs formed by strong cilia with fused bases are comb plates.

Short Answer Questions

1. *Differentiation between these are as below*

(a) Open circulatory system	**Closed Circulatory System**
Blood flows in spaces called sinuses in this type of circulation and the cells and tissues are directly bathed in it. *e.g.*, arthropods (grasshopper, cockroach), gastropods (snail).	Blood is circulated *via* a series of vessels (arteries, veins and capillaries) in this type of circulation. *e.g.*, annelids (earthworm) and vertebrates (birds, primates etc).
(b) Oviparous characteristic animals	**Viviparous characteristic animals**
The expulsion of undeveloped eggs rather than live young ones is oviparity. The animals that lay eggs are called oviparous. *e.g.*, fishes, reptiles, amphibians, birds, in sects and monotremes (mammals that lay eggs).	The retention and growth of fertilized egg within the material body until the young one is capable of independent existence is viviparity. The animals which give birth to their young ones and are called viviparous animals. *e.g.*, mammals.
(c) Direct development	**Indirect development**
The type of development in which there is no larval/nymphal or other intermediate stages in life, cycle between the egg (or birth) and the adult (*e.g.*, mammals) is direct development.	In lower animals mostly indirect development is observed. The adult individuals lay eggs, which develop passing into the adult after passing through few to several larval nymphal stages. (*e.g.*, echinoderms, arthropods)

2. (a) In organisms like fishes two chambered heart is present. Mixing of oxygenated and deoxygenated blood blood occurs as only one atria and one ventricle is present which are not separated.

(b) After division of auricle into right and left halves three chambered heart develops and in amphibian. In ventiricles mixing of oxygenated and deoxygenated blood occurs.

(c) In reptiles an intermidiary heart is present in which ventricles get partially divided through a septum which is incomplete thus having a false four-chambered heart *e.g.*, Crocodiles.

(d) Both the auricle and ventricle are divided into two halves in four chambered heart and so no mixing of oxygenated and deoxygenated blood occurs. *e.g.*, birds and mammals.

3. Excretion involves the elimination of metabolic waste products from the animal body. In the process of excretion in different animals different organs are involved.

(a) In arthropods excretory products from haemolymph are removed by the malpighian tubules.

(b) The excretory organ occurs as segmentally arranged coiled tubules called nephridia in annelids.

(c) Excretion occurs by paired structures called organ of Bojanus in molluscs also called metanephridia.

(d) Mesonephric kidneys are associated with excretion in amphibians.

The circulation of blood and lymph along with oxygen carbondioxide, hormones, blood cells, etc, within the body system for the nourishment of cells, fighting diseases, and for stabilising body temperature and pH is involved blood circulation.

Open Circulation	**Closed Circulation**
Blood is pumped out of the heart into sinuses which directly open into cells and tissues in open circulation *e.g.*, phylum-Arthropoda, and Mollusca.	Blood is circulated through a series of complexly arranged vessels and capillaries in closed circulation *e.g.*, phylum-Annelida and Class-Amphibia.

Respiratory organs are involved in the exchange of gases from the atmosphere.

Different respiratory organs in various animals.

(a) Lungs and skin in amphibians.

(b) Lung/gills/tracheal system in arthropoda and molluscs.

(c) Skin in annelids.

4. A. **Amphibians** are found in both aquatic and terrestrial habitat. Their large is completely aquatic while adult lives in terrestrial as well as in aquatic habitat.

B. **Mammals** produce milk in the **mammary glands** and feed their young one. The mammary glands are enlarged exocrine modified sweat glands functional in female mammals.

C. **Chondrichthyes** have (notochord) in the young stage which is gradually replaced by cartilage.

D. **Osteichthyes** possess **air bladder** which is a vesicle or sac containing air.

E. **Cyclostomes** have sucking and circular mouth without jaws which is surrounded by tentacles and the tongue bears teeth, *e.g.*, lamprey and hagfish.

F. **Aves** comprise of light weighted bones with internal spaces field with air called pneumatic bones and aerodynamic lungs with specialised air sacs. These are the adaptations which enable birds to fly.

5. Endoparasites such as *Taenia solium* and *Fasciola hepatica* (liver fluke), etc., are found inside body the host and survive due to the presence of certain characters.

Endoparasites special characters which include:

(i) The is respiration is anaerobic and the gaseous exchange in via general body surface.

(ii) They bear additional organs for the attachment to the host. *Taenia solium* posses hooks and suckers for the attachment with the host. *Fasciola hepatica* possesses acetabulum or posterior sucker for the attachment.

(iii) they have well developed reproductive organs. They are generally, harmaphrodite and self fertilisation occurs commonly.

(iv) They have a thick tegument (body covering) which is resistant to the host's digestive enzymes and antioxins.

(v) Locomotary organs are absent.

(vi) They lack digestive organs because digested and semidigested food of the host is directly absorbed through their body surface.

6. (a) Following are the similarities between aves and mammals

(i) Presence of four chambered heart.

(ii) The members of both the groups are homeotherms, *i.e.*, warm blooded. They are able to maintain constant body temperature.

(b) Similarities between frog and crocodile include:

(i) They are cold blooded animals. The members of both the groups are poikilotherms, *i.e.*, they lack the capacity to regulate their body temperature.

(ii) Frogs and crocodiles are oviparous animals.

(c) Similarities between turtle and Pila include

(i) Body is covered with dry and cornified skin in both animals. In turtle, the epidermal covering is known as scales whereas in case of Pila, it is known as calcareous shell.

(ii) Both animals are oviparous.

7. (a) *Ichthyophis* does not possess limbs.

(b) A cold blooded animal scoliodon (dog fish).

(c) warm blooded animal is Columba (pigeon).

(d) *Naja naja* (snake) possesses dry and cornified skin.

(e) *Sycon* (sponge) possesses canal system and bear spicules.

(f) *Obelia* bears cnidoblast.

8. **A.** *Balanogolossus* – Proboscis glands. This gland excretes brown granules and is present in front of central sinus.

B. Nephridia in Leech. It helps in osmoregulation and excretion.

C. Malpighian tubules in Locust open into gut and help in excretion.

D. The Flame cells of liver fluke are specialised cells in Platyhelminthes which helps in osmoregulation and excretion. These are also called protonephridia.

E. Sea urchin-absent Specialised excretory organs are absent in sea urchin.

F. It *Pila*-Metanephridia is a type of excretory gland or nephridium found in many types of invertebrates such as annelids, arthropods, and molluscs (in molluscus nephridia is also known as Bojanus organ).

Long Answer Questions

1. Multicellular organisms typically possess a concentric arrangement of tissues in the body. These tissues are derived from the three embrycnio cell, layers called germinal layers.

(i) The outer layer is the ectoderm, the middle layer is the mesoderm and the innermost layer is the endoderm.

(ii) Ectoderm is associated with the formation of CNS, eye lens, ganglia, nerves and glands.

(iii) Mesoderm forms the that in structural components of the body like the skeletal muscles the skeleton, the dermis of the skin connective tissue, etc.

(iv) Endoderm layer is associated with the formation of the stomach, colon, liver, pancreas urinary bladder and other vital organs is an organism.

(v) Coelom is the body cavity that is lined by mesoderm and the animals possessing coelom are called as ceolomates. *e.g.*, phylum-Annelida, Mollusca, Arthropoda, Echnidermata, Hermichordata and Chordata.

(vi) In some organisms, body cavity is not lined by mesoderm, instead mesoderm is present in the form of scattered pouches in between ectoderm and endoderm, Such body cavity is called pseudocoelom and animals possessing there stusturs are refered to as pseudocoelomates *e.g.*, *Ascaris*.

(vii) The animals in which there is complete absence of body cavity are called **acoelomates**. *e.g.*, *Platyhelminthes*.

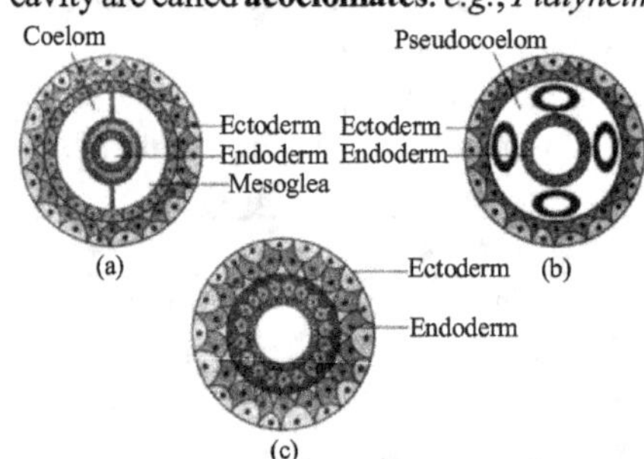

(a) Coelomate, (b) Pseudocoelomae and (c) Acoelomate

2. Amphibians

(i) They can dwell in aquatic as well as terrestrial habitats. They are ectothermic or (cold blooded).

(ii) They are tetrapods having (4 limbs) which facilitate movement on land.

(iii) Their limbs have evolved from the pectoral and pelvic fins.

(iv) Skin is thin, covered by mucus and remains mostly moist. It also serves as an accessory source of oxygen.

(v) They breathe through gills and lung gills usually appear in the larval stage, replaced by lungs in the adults stage.

(vi) Their heart is three chambered with two atria and one ventricle.

(vii) Females are oviparous and fertilisation is mostly external.

(viii) Larva is a tadpole, which metamorphose into adult *e.g.*, Rana frog, *Nectureus* (mud puppy), Salamandera (salamander).

(a) *Salamandra*　　　(b) Frog

Reptiles

(i) They are mostly terrestrial animals and their body is covered by dry, and cornified skin, epidermal scales or scutes.

(ii) In reptiles the mode of locomotion is creeping and crawling.

(iii) Lungs are well developed and present in all stages of life.

(iv) Claws are present in toes.

(v) Appendages are well adapted for land movement.

(vi) Heart possesses a partially divided ventricle and 2 atria.

(vii) They lay amniotic eggs which are inclubated on land.

(viii) They are poikilothermic or cold blooded animals.

5

Morphology of Flowering Plants

5.1 **What is meant by modification of root? What type of modification of root is found in the:**
(a) **Banyan tree**
(b) **Turnip**
(c) **Mangrove trees.**

Sol. When roots are modified to carry out some additional functions like storage of food, additional mechanical support, other than absorption of water, minerals and main support to plant then, they represent modification of roots.
(a) In banyan tree, adventitious roots are modified into hanging supporting roots for giant banyan tree. These roots develop from branches and provides additional support to reach down the ground. Hence this modification is prop root.
(b) Tap roots of turnip get swollen and modified for storage of food. Such roots are called napiform roots.
(c) In mangrove tree, roots come out from ground and grow vertically. Such roots are called pneumatophores or respiratory roots. They help to get oxygen for respiration, to get modified into pneumatic structures. Mangrove trees generally grow in marshy area.

5.2 **Justify the following statements on the basis of external features :**
(i) **Underground parts of a plant are not always roots.**
(ii) **Flower is a modified shoot.**

Sol. (i) Underground parts of a plant are not always roots as some perennial herbs develop their stems underground for the purpose of perennation, and food storage during unfavourable conditions. The stem produces aerial branches every year when conditions become favourable. The underground stems act as storage organs and also help in vegetative propagation by means of their buds. These stems are non-green and leafless like roots but differ from them on the basis of :
(a) presence of nodes and internodes, scale-leaves, and axillary and terminals buds
(b) absence of root hair and root cap.
(ii) Flower is highly modified and condensed shoot meant essentially for the sexual reproduction of the plant. Calyx, corolla, androecium and gynoecium are modifications of leaf for playing various role in reproduction.

5.3 **How is a pinnately compound leaf different from a palmately compound leaf?**

Sol. In pinnately compound leaf, a number of leaflets are present on rachis (*e.g.*, neem) whereas in palmately compound leaf, leaflets are attached at a common point *i.e.*, at the tip of petiole *e g.*, silk cotton.

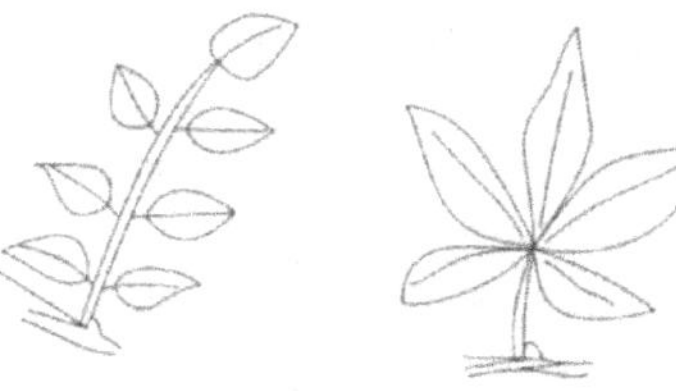

Pinnately compound leaf   Palmately compound leaf

5.4 **Explain with suitable examples the different types of phyllotaxy.**

Sol. Phyllotaxy is the pattern of arrangement of leaves at the stem or branch. This is usually of three types:
(i) **Alternate :** In this arrangement, a single leaf arises at each node in alternate manner. *e.g.*, in china rose, mustard & sunflower plants.
(ii) **Opposite :** A pair of leaves arise on each node in the manner that these lie opposite to each other. *e.g.* guava leaves.
(iii) **Whorl :** In this arrangement, more than two leaves arise at node and form a whorl. *e.g.*, in *Alstonia, Nerium* (Oleander).

5.5 **Define the following terms :**
(a) **Aestivation** (b) **Placentation**
(c) **Actinomorphic** (d) **Zygomorphic**
(e) **Superior ovary** (f) **Perigynous flower**
(g) **Epipetalous stamen.**

Sol. (a) **Aestivation :** It is the arrangement of sepals/petals in relation to one another in a floral buds. It is of four types open, valvate, twisted and imbricate.
(b) **Placentation :** The manner of arrangement of placentae inside the cavity of the ovary for providing cushions is called placentation.
(c) **Actinomorphic :** A flower that can be vertically divided in two equal halves by any vertical division passing through a centre is actinomorphic. Such flowers are radially symmetrical. *e.g.*, *Mustard.*

    (d)   **Zygomorphic :** A flower that can be vertically divided in two equal halves in one vertical plane only. Such flowers are bilaterally symmetrical. *e.g., Pea, Salvia.*

    (e)   **Superior ovary :** When the flower is hypogynous, it has ovary attached to the receptacle above the attachments of floral parts. ex.- berries, drupes etc.

    (f)   **Perigynous :** When the sepals, petals and stamens appear to be arising from middle of the ovary, the flower is described as perigynous. In these flowers, the ovary is **semi-inferior**, *e.g., Saxifraga.*

    (g)   **Epipetalous stamen :** Stamen are attached with petals.

5.6 Differentiate between

    (a) Racemose and cymose inflorescence

    (b) Fibrous root and adventitious root

    (c) Apocarpous and syncarpous ovary

Sol. The main difference between racemose and cymose inflorescence are as following:

(a)		Recemose inflorescence		Cymose inflorescence
	1.	The main axis has indefinite growth because there is no terminal flower.	1.	The growth of the main axis is definite because the growing point of peduncle is used up in the formation
	2.	The flowers are borne laterally in acropetal succession, i.e., oldest flowers are borne at the base and younger ones are borne near tip.	2.	The flower are borne in a basipetal succession i.e., the oldest flower is borne at the top and the younger ones are lateral.
	3.	The order of opening of flowers is centripetal	3.	The order of opening of the flowers is basipetal or centrifugal.

The main difference between fibrous root and adventitious root are as following :

(b)		Fibrous root		Adventitious root
	1.	These roots arise due to repeated branching or radicle.	1.	These roots do not arise from radicle.
	2.	They appear from base of stem.	2.	They may appear from parts like stem or leaves.
	3.	E.g., Wheat plant	3.	E.g., Grass, Banyan

The main difference between apocarpous ovary and syncarpous ovary are as following :

(c)		Apocarpous ovary		Syncarpous ovary
	1.	There are two or more carpels in the gynoecium which are free from each other.	1.	There are two or more carpels in the gynoecium which are fused to form a single compound ovary.
	2.	E.g., Lotus and Rose.	2.	E.g., Mustard and Tomato.

5.7 Draw the labelled diagram of the following:

    (i) Gram seed   **(ii) V. S. of maize seed**

Sol.

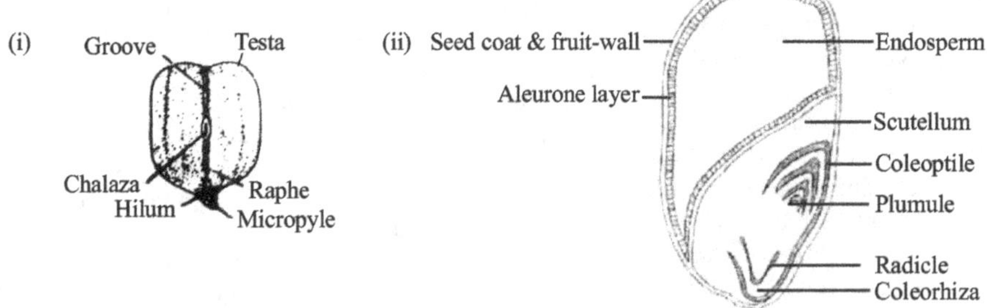

5.8 Describe modifications of stem with suitable examples.

Sol. **Modifications of Stem**

    Food Storage: Stems are modified to perform different functions. Underground stems of potato, ginger, turmeric, *Colocasia* are modified to store food in them. They also act as organs of perennation to tide over conditions unfavourable for growth.

    Tendrils Stem: Tendrils which develop from axillary buds, are slender and spirally coiled and help plants to climb, such as in gourds (cucumber, pumpkins, watermelon) and grapevines.

Thorns: Axillary buds of stems may also get modified into woody, straight and pointed thorns. Thorns are found in many plants such as *Citrus, Bougainvillea*. They protect plants from grazing animals.

Some plants of arid regions modify their stems into flattened (*Opuntia*), or fleshy cylindrical (*Euphorbia*) structures. They contain chlorophyll and carry out photosynthesis.

Vegetative Reproduction: Underground stems of some plants such as grass and strawberry, etc., spread to new niches and when older parts die, new plants are formed. In plants, like mint and jasmine a slender lateral branch arises from the base of the main axis and after growing aerially for some time arch downwards to touch the ground. A lateral branch with short internodes and each node bearing a rosette of leaves and a tuft of roots is found in aquatic plants like *Pistia* and *Eichhornia*. In banana, pineapple and *Chrysanthemum*, the lateral branches originate from the basal and underground portion of the main stem, grow horizontally beneath the soil and then come out obliquely upward giving rise to leafy shoots.

5.9 **Take one flower each of the families Fabaceae and Solanaceae and write its semi-technical description. Also draw their floral diagram after studying them.**

Sol. **Fabaceae:**This family was earlier called papilionoidae, a subfamily of family Leguminosae. It is distributed all over the world.

Example : *Pisum sativum*

Semi technical descritpion of *Pisum sativum* are as follows:

Vegetative characters :

Habit : An annual herb.

Root : Nodulated tap root.

Stem : Climber, leaflet tendrils

Leaves : Alternate, pinnately compound or simple; leaf base, pulvinate, stipulate, venation reticulate.

Floral characters :

Inflorescence : Racemose

Flower : Bisexual, zygomorphic, complete, irregular, hypogynous

Calyx : Sepal 5, gamosepalous, valvate aestivation.

Corolla : Petals 5, polypetalous, papilionaceous consisting of a posterior standard, two lateral wings, two anterior ones forming a keel. Thus, flower becomes zygomorphic, with descending imbricate aestivation *i.e.* vexillary aestivation.

Androecium : Stamen 10, diadelphous [1 + (9)], anther dithecous, introrse.

Gynoecium : Ovary superior, monocarpellary, unilocular with many ovules, marginal placentation.

Fruit : Legume

Seed : One to many, non-endospermic.

Floral formula : $\oplus \male\female K_{(5)} C_{1+2+(2)} A_{(9)} \underline{G_{(1)}}$

Economic importance

Many plants belonging to the family are sources of pulses (gram, arhar, sem, moong, soyabean, edible oil (soyabean, groundnut); fibres (sunhemp); fodder (*Sesbania, Trifolium*), ornamentals (lupin, sweet pea); medicine (muliathi).

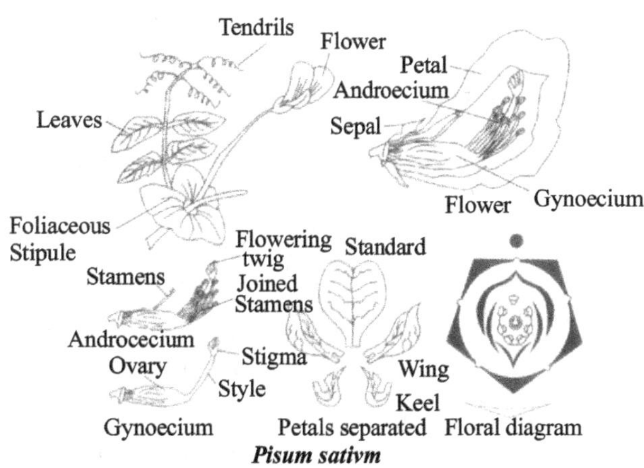

Pisum sativm

Solanaceae :

It is large family, commonly called as the potato family. It is widely distributed in tropics, subtropics and temperate zones.

Example : *Datura*

Semi technical description of *Solanum nigrum*.

Vegetative characters :

Habit : Annual herb

Stem : Erect, cylindrical, hairy, slightly fistular.

Leaves : Alternate, simple, petiolate, ovate with acute apex, venation reticulate.

Floral characters :

Inflorescence : Solitary, axillary

Flower : Ebracteate, actinomorphic, hypogynous

Calyx : Sepals 5, gamosepalous, persistent, valvate astivation.

Corolla : Petals 5, gamopetalous, valvate aestivation

Androecium : Stamen 5, epipetalous

Gynoecium : Bicarpellary, syncarpous, ovary superior, bilocular but four celled by formation of false septum, placenta swollen with many ovules.

Fruit : Spinous capsule with septifragal dehiscence.

Floral formula : $\oplus \male\female K_{(5)} \overarc{C_{(5)}} A_5 \underline{G_{(2)}}$

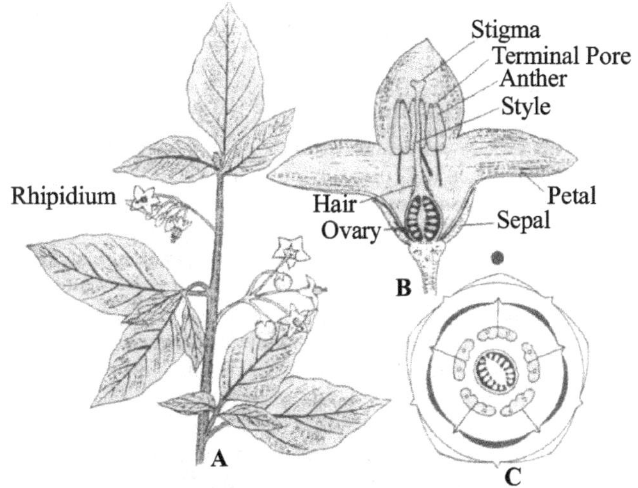

***Solanum nigrum* A, a flowering branch; B. V.S. flower; C. floral diagram**

5.10 Describe the various types of placentations found in flowering plants.

Sol. Placentation of flowering plants is the distribution of ovule bearing cushions or placentae inside the ovary. It is of the following types.

(i) **Marginal.** A monocarpellary unilocular ovary bears ovules longitudinally along the ventral suture in one or two alternate rows, *e.g.*, Pea.

(ii) **Parietal.** A syncarpous, unilocular ovary bears two or more placentae longitudinally along the wall, *e.g.*, *Fumaria, Viola*. A false septum occurs between two parietal placentae in Mustard. It makes the ovary falsely bilocular. In cucurbits, the three parietal placentae grow inwardly, meet in the centre and bend outwardly. The ovary becomes trilocular.

(iii) **Axile.** A syncarpous bilocular to multilocular ovary bears ovules on the central axile column where the septa meet, *e.g.*, *China rose, Petunia, Asphodelus*.

(iv) **Free central.** Polycarpellary syncarpous but unilocular, ovary bears ovules around a central column which is not connected to ovary wall.

(v) **Basal.** Unilocular ovary bears a single ovule from basal region, *e.g.*, *Ranunculus*, Sunflower.

(vi) **Apical.** Unilocular ovary bears a single ovule from the apical region, *e.g.*, *Cannabis*.

(vii) **Superficial.** Ovules are borne along the inner surface of ovary including the septa if present, *e.g.*, *Butomus* (unilocular), *Nymphaea* (multilocular).

5.11 What is flower? Describe the parts of a typical angiosperm flower.

Sol. Flower is a condensed shoot which is specialised to take part in sexual reproduction of angiosperms.

Part of Flower. A flower is generally raised above the point of origin by means of a stalk called **pedicel**. Base of flower is broadened to accommodate all the components. It is called **thalamus**. It has condensed nodes and internodes. The various parts of the flower are called **floral organs**. They are of four types – sepals, petals, stamens and carpels.

Sepal or Calyx. They are green, foliaceous outermost and lowermost floral organs. They can be free (polysepalous) or fused (gamosepalous). An extra whorl of green bracts called epicalyx occurs in many members of family malvaceae. The major function of sepals is protection and support to other floral organs.

Petals or Corolla. They are brightly coloured flat leaf like floral organs which lie inner to sepals and outside the stamens. Petals may be free (polypetalous) or fused (gamopetalous). Their major function is to attract pollinating animals.

Stamens or Androecium. They are male reproductive organs or microsporophylls of a flower. Stamens may be borne directly over the thalamus or attached to petals (epipetalous). Stamens can be free or fused by their filaments (adelphous condition), anthers (syngenesious) or both (synandrous). Each stamen has a thread like stalk or filament and knob-like anther. Anther is bilobed and tetrasporangiate. Pollen grains are formed inside the sporangia of anther.

Carpels or Gynoecium. They are mega-sporophylls or female reproductive organs of the flower. Carpels may be free (apocarpous) or fused (syncarpous). It has three parts – stigma, style and ovary. Stigma is the terminal part of the pistil which is specialized to receive and nourish the pollen grains. Style is a stalk that raises the stigma above the ovary. Ovary is the basal swollen part which internally bears ovules over the placenta. Ovules later ripen to form seeds while ovary develops into a fruit.

5.12 How do the various leaf modifications help plants?

Sol. Leaves are often modified to perform functions other than photosynthesis. They are converted into tendrils for climbing as in peas or into spines for defence as in cacti. The fleshy leaves of onion and garlic store food. In some plants such as *Australian acacia*, the leaves are small and short lived. The petioles in these plants expand, become green and synthesise food. Leaves of certain insectivorous plants such as pitcher plant, venus-fly trap are also modified leaves and get nitrogen from prey.

5.13 Define the term inflorescence. Explain the basis for the different types of inflorescence in flowering plants.

Sol. The arrangement and distribution of flowers on the floral axis is termed as inflorescence. Depending on whether the apex gets converted into a flower or continues to grow, two major types of inflorescences are defined – racemose and cymose. In racemose type of inflorescence, the main axis continues to grow, the flowers are borne laterally in an acropetal succession, *i.e.*, older flower are at the base and younger flowers are at the top.

In cymose type of inflorescence, the main axis terminates in a flower, hence is limited in growth. The flowers are borne in a basipetal order, *i.e.*, younger flowers are near the base and older flower are at the apex.

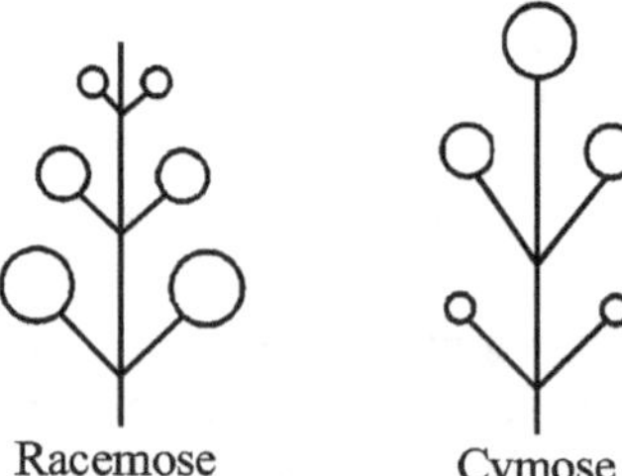

Racemose   Cymose

5.14 Write the floral formula of a actinomorphic, bisexual, hypogynous flower with five united sepals, five free petals, five free stamens and two united carples with superior ovary and axile placentation.

Sol. Floral formula : $\oplus \female K_{(5)} C_5 A_5 \underline{G}_{(2)}$

5.15 Describe the arrangement of floral members in relation to their insertion on thalamus. Calyx, corolla, androecium and gynoecium.

Sol. Based on the position of calyx, corolla and androecium in respect of the ovary on thalamus, the flowers are described as hypogynous, perigynous and epigynous.

In the hypogynous flower, the gynoecium occupies the highest position while the other parts are located below it. The ovary in such flowers is said to be superior, *e.g.*, Mustard, China rose etc.

If gynoecium is situated in the centre and other parts of the flower are located on the rim of thalamus almost at the same level, it is called perigynous. The ovary here is said to be half inferior *e.g.*, Pea (disc shaped perigynous), Plum (cup-shaped perigynous).

In epigynous flower, thalamus grows upward enclosing the ovary completely and getting fused with it, the other parts of flower arise above the ovary. Hence, the ovary is said to be inferior as in flowers of guava and cucumber and the ray florets of sunflower.

SECTION B	**PRACTICE QUESTIONS**

MULTIPLE CHOICE QUESTIONS

1. Fibrous root system is found in
   (a) monocotyledonous plants.
   (b) dicotyledonous plants.
   (c) bryophytes.
   (d) gymnosperms.
2. The region of the root-tip whose cells undergo rapid elongation and enlargement and are responsible for the growth of the root in length is called the:
   (a) region of maturation.
   (b) region of elongation.
   (c) region of meristematic activity.
   (d) root hairs.
3. When the anthers mature earlier than the stigma of ones own flower, the condition is known as
   (a) herkogamy   (b) protandry
   (c) heterostyly   (d) heterogamy
4. Which of the following option shows the correct labelling of the parts of leaf marked as A, B, C and D.

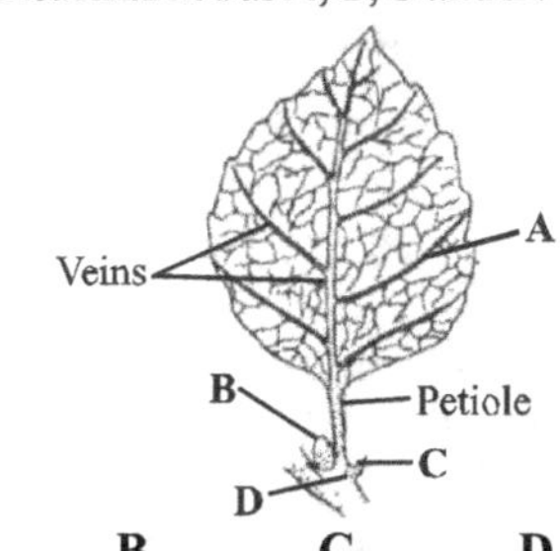

	A	B	C	D
(a)	Lamina	Axillary bud	Stipule	Leaf base
(b)	Lamina	Stipule	Axillary bud	Leaf base
(c)	Lamina	Axillary bud	Stipule	Pedicel
(d)	Leaflet	Axillary bud	Stipule	Leaf base

5. Which of the following plant parts is generally green when young and later often becomes woody and dark brown?
   (a) stem   (b) seed
   (c) leaves   (d) flower
6. In floral formula, 'Q' and 'G' is respectively used for
   (a) superior ovary, inferior ovary
   (b) intermediate ovary, inferior ovary
   (c) superior ovary, intermediate ovary
   (d) inferior ovary, superior ovary
7. Gynoecium in the members of family—leguminosae is composed of
   (a) two carpels   (b) one carpel
   (c) five carpels   (d) three carpels
8. Diadelphous stamens are the characteristic features of
   (a) ranunculaceae   (b) fabaceae
   (c) poaceae   (d) malvaceae
9. Trimerous flower, superior ovary and axile placentation is characteristics of
   (a) liliaceae
   (b) cucurbitaceae
   (c) solanaceae
   (d) compositae
10. It is a proteinous layer and the outer covering of endosperm which separates the embryo. Identify the layer.
   (a) Tegmen
   (b) Scutellum
   (c) Hyaline layer
   (d) Aleurone layer

ASSERTION & REASON QUESTIONS

DIRECTION (Qs. 1-5) : *These questions consists of two statements. Answer these questions selecting the appropriate option given below:*
(a) Both Assertion (A) and Reason (R) are true and Reason (R) is the correct explanation of Assertion (A).
(b) Both Assertion (A) and Reason (R) are true, but Reason (R) is not the correct explanation of Assertion (A).
(c) Assertion (A) is true, but Reason (R) is false.
(d) Assertion (A) is false, but Reason (R) is true.

1. **Assertion :** Apical meristem of root is subterminal.
   Reason : At the terminal end of root, root cap is present.
2. **Assertion :** A simple leaf has undivided lamina.
   Reason : Leaves showing pinnate and palmate venation which have various types of incisions.
3. **Assertion :** Many plants are propagated vegetatively even though they bear seeds.
   Reason : Potatoes multiply by cutting, apple by tuber etc.
4. **Assertion:** Fruit is a mature or ripened ovary.
   Reason: Flower is a reproductive organ of the flowering plants.
5. **Assertion:** Maize is a type of grain that is dicotyledonous in nature.
   Reason: A dicotyledonous seed contains two seed coats.

CASE/PASSAGE BASED QUESTIONS

DIRECTIONS (Qs. 1-5) : *Read the following passage and answer the questions that follows.*

Leaf is flattened green outgrowth from the stem of a vascular plant. As the primary sites of photosynthesis, leaves manufacture food for plants, which in turn ultimately nourish and sustain all land animals, leaves are an integral part of the stem system. They are attached by a continous vascular system to the rest of the plant, so that free exchange of nutrients, water, and products of photosynthesis (oxygen and carbohydrates in particular) can be carried to its various parts. Leaves are initiated in the apical bud (growing tip of a stem) along with the tissues of the stem itself. Certain organs that are superficially very different from the usual green leaf are formed in the same manner and are actually modified leaves.

1. Which among the following is incorrect about different parts of the leaf?
   (a) Lamina contains veins and veinlets that transmit water to different regions of the leaf.
   (b) Petiole is long thick structure that helps in flattering of leaves in the air.
   (c) Grass is an example of petiolate plants.
   (d) Legumes have a swollen leaf base called Pulvinus.
2. Which amount the following is incorrect about reticulate and parallel venation?
   (a) In reticulate venation, veins are arranged haphazardly
   (b) In parallel venation, veins are arranged in a parallel manner
   (c) In palmate venation, only one strong mid-rib is present
   (d) Rice is an example of concergent palmate parallel venation.
3. Which among the following statements is incorrect show leaves?
   (a) Simple leaves are those leaves that are either entire or incised without touching the mid-rib
   (b) Compound leaves are those leaves in which incisions reach the mid-rib breaking the lamina into leaflets called as 'pinnate'
   (c) In palmate compound leaves, leaflets are attached at a common point.
   (d) An axillary bud is present at the end of every leaflet
4. Which among the following is incorrect about phyllotaxy?
   (a) The arrangement of leaves in the plant is called phyllotaxy
   (b) In alternate phyllotaxy, a single leaf is present at each node.
   (c) Opposite phyllotaxy is present in China rose
   (d) In whorled phyllotaxy, multiple leaves are present at each node
5. Scale leaves are present in_________.
   (a) Cactus   (b) Potato
   (c) Cucumber   (d) Tomato

Very Short Answer Questions

1. What does take over the function of photosynthesis in *Opuntia*?
2. Which plant part has transformed into the following different modifications (i) tendril of pumpkin (ii) thorn of Citrus.
3. Name a cultivated plant in which neither fruits nor seeds are formed.
4. What term is given to arrangement of leaves on stem?
5. Give one example where epigynous type of flower is present.
6. Which type of placentation is present in *Lathyrus*?
7. Why are potato and sweet potato called tubers?
8. What is phyllode? Give one example of it.
9. Distinguish between alternate and whorled phyllotaxy.
10. What is tetradynamous condition of stamens?
11. Describe the corolla of family – Fabaceae.
12. What is a floral diagram?
13. Give any two reasons to justify that onion bulb is a modified stem.
14. What are the main characters of family Brassicaceae?
15. Name the food yielding plants of Liliaceae.
16. What is meant by maturation zone?
17. What type of function is performed by the fleshy leaves of onion and garlic?

Short Answer Questions

1. What is a fruit ? Describe the parts of a fruit.
2. Distinguish between prop roots and stilt roots.
3. What are pneumatophore ? How do they help the plant ? Name an example.
4. What is the function of leaf?
5. What is the main function of root system?
6. What is aleurone layer?

Long Answer Questions

1. Mention the diagnostic characters of family fabaceae and write the floral formula.
2. Describe placentation in flower:

SOLUTIONS

Multiple Choice Questions

1. **(a)** Fibrous root system is found in monocotyledonous plants. In monocotyledons, primary root is short lived and replaced by a large number of roots which originate from the base of the stem and constitute the fibrous root system.
2. **(b)** Region of elongation lies above the region of meristematic activity. Cells in this region undergo rapid elongation and enlargement and are responsible for the growth of the root in length.
3. **(b)**
4. **(a)** Leaf is the main photosynthetic organ of plants. In the given figure of leaf, the part marked as A, B, C and D are lamina, axillary bud, stipule and leaf base, respectively. Lamina or leaf blade is green and expanded portion of the leaf. In the middle of the lamina, a strong vein called midrib is present which extends from its base or apex. Axillary bud is borne at the axil of a leaf and is capable of developing into a branch shoot or flower cluster. Stipule is a small leaf-like appendage to a leaf, typically borne in pairs at the base of the leaf stalk. Leaf base is the lower part of the lamina, and is attached to petiole or stem.
5. **(a)** Stem is generally green when young and later often become woody and dark brown.
   The stem bears buds which may be terminal or axillary.
6. **(a)** $\underline{G}$ = Superior ovary (Hypogynous flower) = $\overline{G}$ Inferior ovary (epigynous flower)
7. **(b)**   8. **(b)**   9. **(a)**
10. **(d)** The aleurone layer is the outermost layer of the endosperm, followed by the inner starchy endosperm. This layer of cells is sometimes referred to as the peripheral endosperm. It lies between the pericarp and the hyaline layer of the endosperm.

Assertion & Reason Questions

1. **(a)**
2. **(b)** A leaf having a single or undivided lamina is called simple leaf, the lamina can have different types of incisions, which may reach upto half, more than half or near the base or midrib. Depending upon the pinnate or palmate venation, the incisions are known as pinnatifid, palmatifid, pinnatipartite, palmatipartite, pinnatisect and palmatisect, etc.
3. **(c)** Plants do propagate more by vegetative means since they multiply faster vegetatively. Potato tubers have nodes or eyes from which the new growth begins. Apple trees are mainly propagated by grafting, layering and budding.
4. **(b)** Flower is called as the reproductive organ of the plants because it is involved in reproduction process. When ovary becomes fully mature then it changes into fruit.
5. **(d)** Maize is monocotyledonous plants. Dicotyledonous seed contains two seed coats.

Case/Passage Based Questions

1. **(b)** The petiole help hold the blade to light. Long thin flexible petioles allow leaf blades to flatter in wind, thereby, cooling the leaf and bringing fresh air to leaf surface.
2. **(c)** In palmate venation leaflets are attached at a common point, and mid rib is divided into each leaves.
3. **(d)** Axillary bud is present at the junction between a leaf and the stem.
4. **(c)** China rose is an example of alternate phyllotaxy. Opposite phyllotaxy appears in calotropis.
5. **(b)**

Very Short Answer Questions

1. Stem
2. Stem (Axillary buds)
3. Sugarcane.
4. Phyllotaxy
5. Sunflower
6. Marginal
7. Potato and sweet potato are called tubers because they are irregularly shaped swollen stem that stores plenty of food.
8. Petiole and rachis modified into leaf like structures are called phyllodes. *e.g., Parkinsonia Australian Acacia.*
9. In alternate phyllotaxy, only one leaf is borne at each node whereas in whorled phyllotaxy, more than two leaves are borne at each node.
10. Two out of six stamen are short while remaining four are long.
11. Corolla of family fabaceae is papilionaceous *i.e.*, consisting of posterior standard or vexillum, two lateral wings and anterior petals fused along margin to form keel or carina.
12. Floral diagram is an illustration of the relative and number of parts in each of the sets of organs comprising a flower.
13. It bears a large number of fibrous adventitious roots at its base. It bears several fleshy sheathing leaf bases and a terminal bud.
14. Tetramerous flowers, six stamens, bicarpellary gynoecium, siliqua type fruit.
15. *Allium cepa, A. sativum and Asparagus racemosus.*
16. The part of the root which is most active in water absorption is called maturation zone.
17. The function of fleshy leaves of onion and garlic is storage.

Short Answer Questions

1. The fruit is a characteristic feature of the flowering plants. It is a mature or ripened ovary, developed after fertilisation. The fruit consists of a wall or **pericarp** and seeds. The pericarp may be dry or fleshy. When pericarp is thick and fleshy, it is differentiated into the outer **epicarp**, the middle **mesocarp** and the inner **endocarp**.

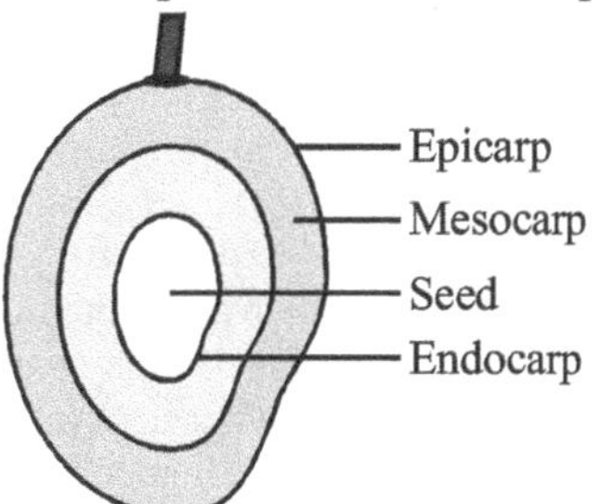

Fig. Parts of a fruit : Mango
In mango, the fruit is known as a drupe.

2. The main differences between prop roots and stilt roots are as following :

	Prop roots		Stilt roots
1.	Arise from horizontal aerial branches.	1.	Arise from basal nodes of stem.
2.	Long and provide support to the plants like pillars e.g., Banyan tree.	2.	Short roots and grow downwards obliquely to provide support to stem like ropes of a tent e.g., maize, jowar.

3. **Pneumatophores :**
   * These are the roots that grow vertically upwards and come above the soil surface; they bear opening called pneumathodes, for exchange of gases.
   * This feature is an adaptation for plants growing in marshy/ swampy areas, where oxygen is deficient in the soil.
   * These roots help the plants to get oxygen from the air for respiration e.g., *Rhizophora.*

4. Leaf is a green, flattened outgrowth of the plant arising from the node of the stem and is specialized to perform the process of photosynthesis. Therefore, leaf is also known as the kitchen or food factory of the plant.

5. Root system generally grows beneath the ground into the soil, functions of root system are as follows:-
   – It provides great anchorage and support to the plant. Huge trees such as mango, red wood stand erect due to the root.
   – The root hair absorbs nutrients, water and oxygen from the soil and conduct them to the upper parts of the plants.
   – some of the tap roots are specially modified for storage of carbohydrates and water.

6. The major part of the grain is occupied by large endosperm which is rich in starch. The endosperm has one to three layered peripheral protein layer called aleurone layer which separates the embryo with endosperm.

Long Answer Questions

1. Diagnostic characters of family fabaceae are :

(i) Presence of nodulated roots.

(ii) Inflorescence racemose.

(iii) Perigynous ovary.

(iv) Flower zygomorphic and papilionaceous.

(v) Calyx 5, gamosepalous.

(vi) Corolla 5, petals unequal and differentiated into standard, 2 lateral wings and two smallest anterior petals (keel).

(vii) Androecium commonly diadelphous (1 + 9 or 5 + 5) or monoadelphous (10 or 9)

(viii) Gynoecium monocarpellary, ovary unilocular with marginal placentation.

(ix) Fruit legume.

Floral Formula : $\% \oplus K_{(5)} C_{1+2+(2)} A_{(9)+1} \underline{G}_1$

2. The arrangement of placenta in the ovary of the flower is known as placentation. Its main function is to transfer nutrients from material tissue to growing embryo.

(A) Marginal placentation: It is found in monocarpellary ovary. In this, ovary is unilocular and ovules are arranged along margin of unilocular ovary. Ex- Pea, Clitoria, etc.

(B) Axile placentation : It is found in bi or multicarpellary and multilocular ovary. Ovules are arranged along the central axis of placenta and the number of chambers corresponds to the number of carpels. Ex-Lemon, Tomato, Hibiscus, Cotton, etc.

(C) Parietal placentation : It is found in bi or multicarpellary ovary but unilocular. Ovules are arranged along periphery or the inner walls of ovary and the number of placenta corresponds to the carpels. Ex - Cucurbita, Argemone, etc.

(D) Free central placentation : It is found in multicarpellary syncarpous ovary. Ovules are borne along the central axis. Which is not connected with the ovary wall by septum.

Ex- Dianthus rome primrose, etc.

(E) Basal placentation : It is found in monocarpellary but unilocular. In this placentation, the placenta develops at the base of the ovary and a single ovule is attached to it.

Ex - Sunflower, etc.

SECTION C   NCERT EXEMPLAR QUESTIONS

Multiple Choice Questions

1. Rearrange the following zones as seen in the root in vertical section and choose the correct option.

A. Root hair zone

B. Zone of meristems

C. Root cap zone

D. Zone of maturation

E. Zone of elongation

(a) C, B, E, A, D   (b) A, B, C, D, E

(c) D, E, A, C, B   (d) E, D, C, B, A

2. In an inflorescence where flowers are borne laterally in an acropetal succession, the position of the youngest floral bud shall be

(a) proximal   (b) distal

(c) intercalary   (d) anywhere

3. The mature seeds of plants such as gram and peas possess no endosperm, because

(a) these plants are not angiosperm

(b) there is no double fertilisation in them

(c) endosperm is not formed in them

(d) endosperm gets used up by the developing embryo during seed development

4. Roots developed from parts of the plant other than radicle are called

(a) tap roots   (b) fibrous roots

(c) adventitious roots   (d) nodular roots

5. Venation is a term used to describe the pattern of arrangement of

(a) floral organs

(b) flower in infloresence

(c) veins and veinlets in a lamina

(d) all of them

6. Endosperm, a product of double fertilisation in angiosperms is absent in the seeds of

(a) Coconut   (b) Orchids

(c) Maize   (d) Castor

7. Many pulses of daily use belong to one of the families below.

(a) Solanaceae   (b) Fabaceae

(c) Liliaceae   (d) Poaceae

8. The placenta is attached to the developing seed near the

(a) testa   (b) hilum

(c) micropyle   (d) chalaza

9. Which of the following plants is used to extract the blue dye?

(a) Trifolium   (b) Indigofera

(c) Lupin   (d) Cassia

Very Short Answer Questions

1. Roots obtain oxygen from air in the soil for respiration. In the absence or deficiency of O_2, root growth is restricted or completely stopped. How do, the plants growing in marsh lands or swamps obtain their O_2 required for root respiration?

2. In *Opuntia*, the stem is modified into a flattened green structure to perform the function of leaves, (*i.e.*, photosynthesis). Cite some other examples of modifications of plant parts for the purpose of photosytnthesis.

3. In swampy areas like the sunderbans in West Bengal, plants bear special kind of roots called ....

4. In aquatic plants like *Pistia* and *Eichhornia*, leaves and roots are found near ....

5. Which parts in ginger and onion are edible?

6. In epigynous flower, ovary is situated below the ....

7. Add the missing floral organs of the given floral formula of Fabaceae.

$$\% \oplus K_{()} ... C_{()} A_{(9+...)} G_{(1)}$$

SHORT ANSWER QUESTIONS

1. Give two examples of roots that develop from different parts of the angiospermic plant other than the radicle.
2. The essential functions of roots are anchorage and absorption of water and minerals in the terrestrial plant. What functions are associated with the roots of aquatic plants. How are roots of aquatic plants and terrestrial plants different?
3. Draw diagrams of a typical monocot and dicot leaves to show their venation pattern.
4. A typical angiosperm flower consists of four floral parts. Give the names of the floral parts and their arrangements sequentially.
5. Reticulate venation is found in dicot leaves while in monocot leaves venation is of parallel type. Biology being a 'Science of exceptions', find out any exception to this generalisation.
6. You have heard about several insectivorous plants that fee on insects. *Nepenthes* or the pitcher plant is one such example, which usually grows in shallow water or in march lands. What part of the plant is modified into a pitcher? How does this modification help the plant for food even though it can photosynthesise like any other green plant?
7. How can you differentiate between free central and axile placentation?
8. Why is maize grain usually called as a fruit and not a seed?
9. Tendrils of grapevins are homologous to the tendril of pumpkins, but are analogous to that of pea. Justify the above statement.
10. Rhizome of ginger is like the roots of other plants that grows underground. Despite this fact ginger is a stem and not a root. Justify.

LONG ANSWER QUESTIONS

1. Distinguish between families – Fabaceae, solanaceae, Liliaceae on the basis of gynoecium characteristics (with figures). Also write economic importance of any one of the above family.
2. Describe various stem modifications associated with food storage climbing and protection.

SOLUTIONS

Multiple Choice Questions

1. **(a) Root Cap Zone** provides protective covering at the root apex, secretes mucilage to soften the hard soil for the growth of root.
   Zone of Meristem is the region of actively dividing, densely packed cells resulting in root growth.
   Zone of Elongation comprises of divided cells growing in size and elongating, increasing the length of root. They cannot divide further.
   Root Hair Zone: root hair arises and grows in this region, helps in water and mineral absorption from the soil.
   Zone of Maturation: the cells of root at this region are fully differentiated and mature, performing different functions of root.
2. **(b)** In racemose inflorescence, younger flowers are borne, at the apex or distal end while older flowers are at the base, this type of succession is acropetal succession. Thus, the position of youngest floral bud would be distal.
3. **(d)** Endosperm is a nourishing tissue of seed which provides nourishment to the developing embryo either before or after germination. In gram and peas, the endosperm is consumed at the time of seed development. So, seed is non-endospermic, *i.e.*, endosperm is not present in the mature seed.
4. **(c)** Roots developed from parts of plant other than the radicle are called adventitious roots. They branch like tap roots and may be underground or aerial, and may develop from nodes, internodes or leaves, *etc.*
   Tap roots develop from the radicle of embryo and persist and grow directly into primary root.
   Fibrous roots are thin, thread-like branched roots developing from the base of stem. These are modifications of tap root, found in monocots.
   Nodular roots are modifications of tap roots in which root branches develop small or large swellings called nodules. They help in nitrogen fixation.

5. **(c) Venation :** The veins are the part of leaf which possess vascular tissues, *i.e.*, xylem and phloem. They are meant for the conduction of water, minerals and food, to and from in the leaf. The special arrangement of veins in a leaf is called as venation.
6. **(b)** Orchid is a non-endospermic seed, endosperm is absent in it. Endosperm is a nourishing tissue present in the seed which nourishes the developing embryo. In orchid seed endosperm is absent because it is used up during seed development. Nourishment for germinating seed is provided by the food material present in cotyledons.
7. **(b) Fabaceae** is the new name of Leguminosae. Plants of this family are the source of pulses and edible oils. Pulses are rich in protein contents.
8. **(b)** The placenta is attached to the developing seed near the hilum . It is the scar present near the edge where seed breaks from stalk of funiculus, connecting the seed with fruit wall and placenta.
   Testa is the outer most covering of seed, micropyle is a small opening in the seed coat through which water enters the seed and chalaza is a tissue where nucellus and integument joins.
9. **(b)** *Indigofera tinctoria* and *I. suffruticosa* are the two plants that belong to the family-Fabaceae, that produce blue indigo dye.
   The other options are incorrect because
   Trifolium is used as fodder. *Lupin* is an ornamental plant. *Cassia* is a shrub usually grown on the roadside as an ornamental plant.

Very Short Answer Questions

1. The roots of the plants as *Rhizophora* that grow in marsh/swamp areas become negatively geotropic. They grow vertically upwards in air, above the soil level and respire. They are thus called respiratory roots or pneumatophores.

2. In *Opuntia* a xerophytic plant leaves are modified into spine to reduce the rate of transpiration and they do not perform the photosynthesis at all.

   The function of photosynthesis in *Opuntia* plant is performed by stem which is thick fleshy and flattened structure containing chlorophyll and stores food and known as phylloclade.

   In some plants similarly roots become assimilatory *e.g.*, case of *Trapa* and *Tinospora*. These roots grow outside the soil, develop chlorophyll in them and perform photosynthesis.

3. **Pneumatophores Roots** are meant for the absorption of water and minerals from the soil. Cells of roots require O_2 to respire. In swampy areas, soil does not have air, so no O_2 is available to them.

   In such cases, roots come out of the soil showing negative geotropism and breathe after coming in contact with air, *e.g.*, *Rhizophora*. Such roots are called pneumatophores or respiratory roots.

4. In *Pistia* and *Eichhonia*, the stem is like a runner where it branches to form leaves at the apex and roots below. Both the plants are hydrophytes and thus the roots are found near the surface of water.

5. The edible part of ginger is rhizome the modified stem which stores food material whreas the edible part in onion is fleshy leaves, where the internode becomes shortened, leaves get condensed to form a tunic and store food material.

6. Ovary is situated below the thalamus (inferior) in epigynous flower while the other whorls of flower like sepals, petals and androecium grows above the ovary (superior), *e.g.*, carrot, guava, *Cucurbita*, sunflower, etc.

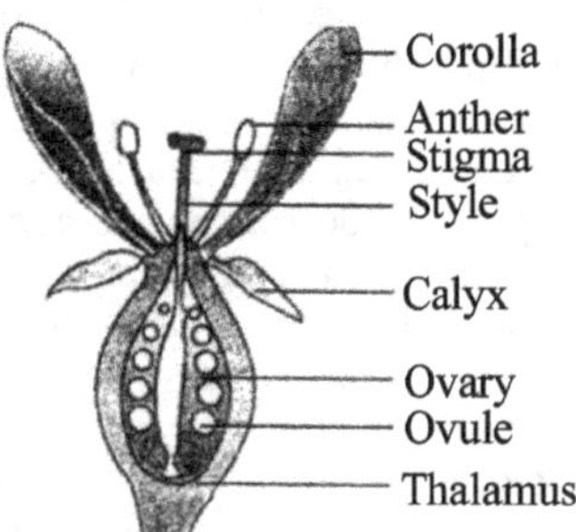

Epigynous flower

7. The floral formula of fabaceae family is

$$= \% \, \male\female \, K_5 \, C_{1+2+(2)} \, A_{(9)+1} \, \underline{G}_{(1)}$$

Short Answer Questions

1. Prop roots are meant for support. Prop roots develop from the lower nodes of stem of banyan tree. They grow downwards and touch the soil.

   Stilt roots arise from the lower nodes of stem in sugarcane and enter the soil to provide strength to the plant. These protect the plant against winds.

2. Usually the terrestrial roots show a branched network that helps in anchorage and absorption of water and minerals from soil to the plant. While in aquatic plants, roots show modification and deviation from their normal function.

   Ex - in plants like *Trapu*, *Tinospora* the roots are green and highly branched to increase the photosynthetic area, whereas

in plants like *Jussiaeca* they get inflated due to air project out of water so a to help the plant in floating and exchange of gases. Difference between roots of aquatic plants and terrestrial plants are as:

	Aquatic plants	Terrestrial plants
(a)	Roots may be absent e.g, Wolffia. If roots are present they are not well developed. Usually thin adventitious roots are present.	Roots are well developed with root cap and root hairs and branches.
(b)	Vascular strands are poorly developed.	Vascular bundles are well developed.
(c)	Modified to carry out photosynthesis food storage and exchange of gases.	Provide anchorage and help in absorption of nutrients from soil.

3. The pattern of distribution of veins and veinlets in the lamina of leaf is called **Venation**. It's pattern is different in monocot and dicot leaf.

Monocot leaf	Dicot leaf
In monocot leaf the veins run parallel to each other within a lamina. It is called parallel venation.	Veins and veinlets form a network in the lamina in dicot leaf. It is called reticulate venation.
e.g., grasses, wheat, maize, etc., (usually found in monocots).	*e.g.*, *Hibiscus*, bean, pear etc., (usually found in dicots).

4. Following are the four floral parts of typical angiospermic flower.

   Calyx is the outermost whorl of the flower and comprised of sepals. These are usually green and (in bud stage) are protective in function.

   Corolla is composed of petals, usually bright coloured to attract insects for pollination.

   Androecium is composed of stamens, the male reproductive organ. Each stamen consists of stalk or filament and anther (containing pollen sac and pollen grains).

   Gynoecium is the female reproductive part and comprised of one or more carpels. Each carpel has stigma, style and ovary.

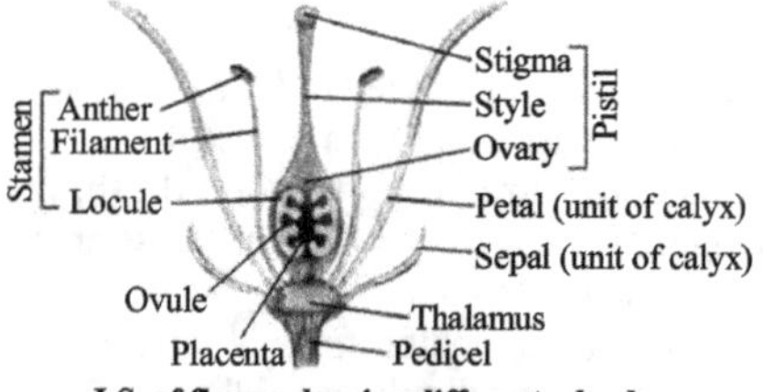

LS. of flower showing different whorls

5. Reticulate venation is a characteristic of dicots and parallel venation is of monocots. But few exceptions are also seen in this generalisation, parallel venation is also found in dicot plants, e.g, Calophyllum, Corymbium, etc and reticulate venation is also found in monocot plants such as *Alocasia, smilax*, etc.

6. In insectivorous plant like *Nepenthes*, the leaf lamin is modified to form a pitcher and anterior part of petiole coils like **tendril** which keeps the pitcher in a vertical direction. Posterior part of the petiole remains flattened like a leaf. The apex of lamina forms a lid. Pitcher contains digestive enzyme for digesting trapped insects.

All these modifications and adaptations are developed to make up for the nitrogen deficiency in the plant because these plants are found in N_2 deficient soil, (marshy/swamp soils).

7. The arrangement of ovules on the walls of ovary with the help of special kind of tissue called placenta is **placentation**. Plants show different types of placentation. Difference between free central placentation and axile placentation include:

Free Central Placentation	Axile Placentation
In this type of placentation Ovary contains only one chamber. The placenta bearing the ovules are borne on the central axis and lies free inside the ovary. The septa are absent.	Ovary is syncarpous and multi-carpellary, *i.e.*, contains many chambers in axile placentation. Placenta arises from the central axis where the septa fuse to form axile column to which ovules are attached.

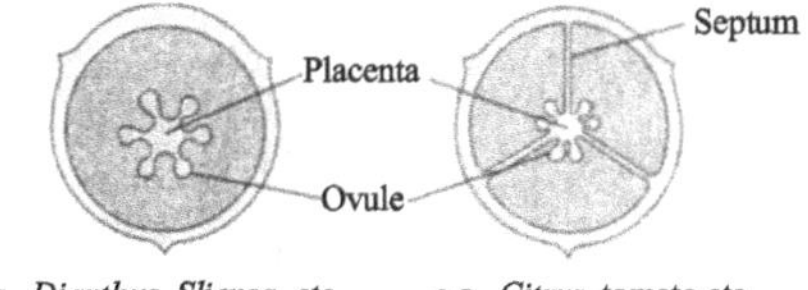

e.g., Dianthus, Sliensa, etc.   *e.g., Citrus,* tomato etc.

8. The maize grain is usually known as fruit because it is a ripened ovary which contains a ripened ovule, *e.g.*, a single seed. This fruit is known as caryopsis in which the pericarp is fused with the seed coat. The maize grain occurs attached to a thick cob or peduncle.

9. Homologous organs are organs that have similar origin but they differ functionally. Axillary bud of stem gives rise to tendril of both grapevine and pumpkins so they have same origin, *i.e.*, homologous, whereas analogous organs are organs having different origin, but perform same function. The tendril of pea arises from the leaf and helps the plant to climb.

10. **Rhizome of Ginger** is a type of modified underground stem which grows horizontally underground and bears nodes, internodes and scaly leaves and buds, which gives rise to aerial shoots.

The adventitious root arises from the lower surface of nodes. It is not a true root because root does not have nodes and internodes. The rhizome does not perform the function of anchorage and absorption, rather serve as reservoir for food storage. All these characteristics support the fact that ginger is a stem and not a root.

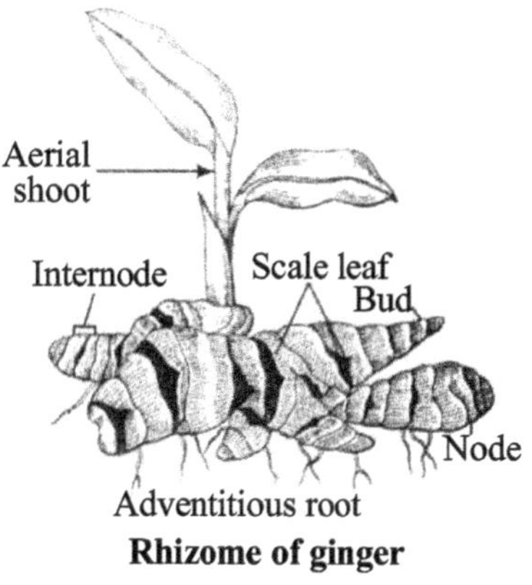

Rhizome of ginger

Long Answer Questions

1. The families in plant kingdom mainly differ from each other in their reproductive structures.

Based on characteristics of gynoecium the difference between the three families include the following:

Gynoecium Characteristics	Fabaceae	Solanaceae	Liliaceae
Carpels	Monocarpellary free, single	Bicarpellary Syncarpous	Tricarpellary syncarpous
Ovary	Superior unilocular	Superior bilocular (2-4 locular in tomato)	Superior
Ovules	Margin in two alternate rows	Many in each locular	Trilocular
Placentation	Marginal	Axile	2-many ovules in each locules
Style	Bent, single	Simple	Simple but may be united or separate
Stigma	Simple and capitate	Simple and lobeb	Free or fused trilobed
Floral formula	Br % $K_{(5)}\ G_{1+2\,(2)}A_{1+9+1}G_1$	– Br $\oplus\ K_{(5)}\ G_5A_5\ \underline{G}_{(2)}$	Br $\oplus\ P_{3+3}A_{3+3}\ \underline{G}_{(3)}$

Gynoecium Characteristics	Fabaceae	Solanaceae	Liliaceae
Diagram of gnoecium	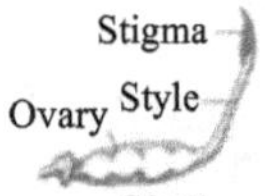 Stigma, Style, Ovary, **Pistil**	 Stigma, Style, Ovary, **Pistil**	 **Pistil**
T.S. of Ovary	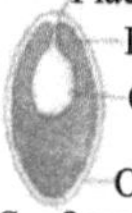 Placenta, Locule, Ovule, Ovary wall — **T.S. of ovary**	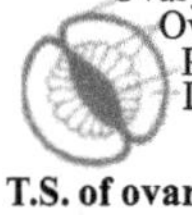 Ovary wall, Ovules, Placenta, Locule — **T.S. of ovary**	 Ovary wall, Locule, Ovules, Placenta — **T.S. of ovary**
Examples	Garlic, onion, *Colchicum*	Potato, tomato, brinjal, datura, etc	All pules, Sunhemp, *Lupin*, Indigo, *Cassia*

2. The aerial part of plant bearing nodes, internodes, buds, flowers, fruits and seeds is stem. Besides these functions and forms, it gets modified and perform under special conditions.

The various stem modifications include:

Stem	Modification of Stem for Stroge of Food
Rhizome	The stem becomes underground and grows horizontally, stores food material. It bears nodes, intermodes and buds which give rise to aerial shoots, e.g., ginger, banana, turmeric. 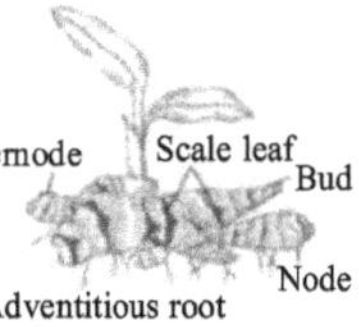 Internode, Scale leaf, Bud, Node, Adventitious root **Rhizome of ginger**
Corm	Stem is underground, grows vertically and bears nodes as well as internodes *e.g. Colocasia*. 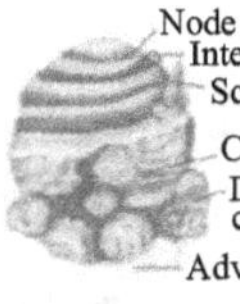 Node, Internode, Scale leaf, Corm, Daughter com, Adventitious roots **Corm of *Colocasia***
Bulb	The stem becomes underground, the internode is shortened in a manner that the leaves are condensed and these leaves become thick and fleshy and store food material *e.g.*, onion. 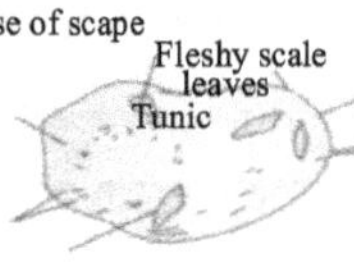 Base of scape, Fleshy scale leaves, Tunic, Terminal bud, Axillary bud, Bulb **Tunicated bulb of and L.S. of bulbs**
Tuber	A special kind of stem modification, which arises at the tips of special narrow underground branches. They have nodes, internodes apical buds, scale leaf in the form of ridge. They have numbers of eyes which represent nodes. It is meant for storing food material, *e.g.*, potato 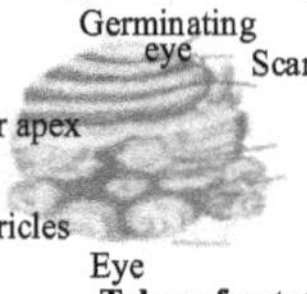 Germinating eye, Scar or scale leaf, Bud, Sucke, Tuber apex, Ventricles, Eye **Tuber of potato**
Stem tendrils	**It is a modification of Stems for climbing** These are found in cucurbits and grapevine. The axillary buds of the stem become elongated and spirally coiled and twine around a support for the plant to grow as the stem is weak and herbaceous.
Stem thorns	**It is a modification of stem for protection** These are present in the axil of leaf or apex of stem performing the function of either climbing or defence, *e.g.*, *Duranta, Calamus* and also reduce transpiration.

Anatomy of Flowering Plants

 NCERT EXERCISES 

6.1 State the location and function of different types of meristems.

Sol.

Types of meristems	Location	Function
Apical meristem	Root tips and shoot tips	Growth in length
Intercalary meristems	Between mature tissues	Repair
Secondary meristem	On the periphery of stems and roots	Secondary growth, i.e., growth in thickness

6.2 Cork cambium forms tissues that form the cork. Do you agree with this statement? Explain.

Sol. Cork cambium : As the stem continues to increase in girth due to the activity of vascular cambium, the outer cortical and epidermal layers get broken and need to be replaced to provide new protective cell layers. Hence, sooner or later, another meristematic tissue called cork cambium or phellogen develops, usually in the cortex region. Phellogen is a couple of layers thick. It is made of narrow, thin-walled and nearly rectangular cells. Phellogen cuts off cells on both sides. The outer cells differentiate into cork or phellem while the inner cells differentiate into secondary cortex or phelloderm. This is clear how cork cambium forms tissues that form the cork. Cork is formed and outer tissues removed.

6.3 Explain the process of secondary growth in the stems of woody angiosperms with the help of schematic diagrams. What is its significance?

Sol.

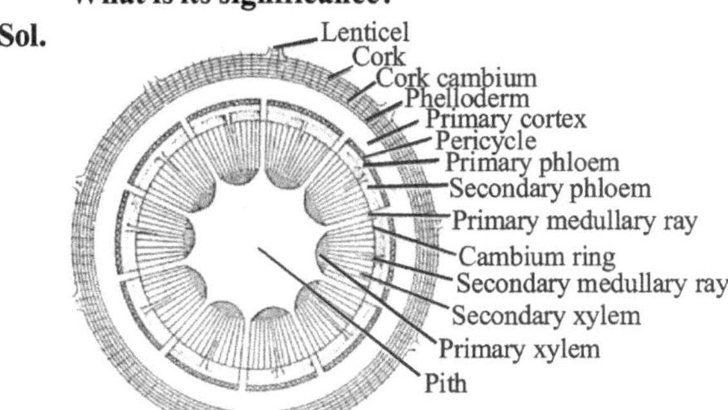

Fig. Diagrammatic T.S. of Dicotyledonous stem showing secondary growth.

Secondary growth in dicot stem: It is "permanent increase in thickness due to the activity of vascular cambium and cork cambium in stelar and extrastelar regions". In dicot stem intra fascicular cambium is present. The cells of medullary ray become meristematic and form interfascicular cambium. These two cambiums unite and make a complete cambial ring. The cells of it divide and produce new cells both on its outer and inner sides. The cells formed on the outer side differentiate into secondary phloem while the cells of inner side form secondary xylem. The epidermis is replaced by a secondary protective tissue by increase in growth of the stem of the plant. It is made of phellogen (cork cambium). It arises from the peripheral cells of cortex. The phellogen forms new cells on the outer side which make phellem (cork) and phelloderm on its inner side also.

Significance : Secondary growth increases girth or thickness of plant.

Annual rings of woody angiosperms are very distinct and thus helps in determining the age of plant.

6.4 Draw illustrations to bring out the anatomical difference between

(a) Monocot root and dicot root

(b) Monocot stem and dicot stem

Sol. (a)

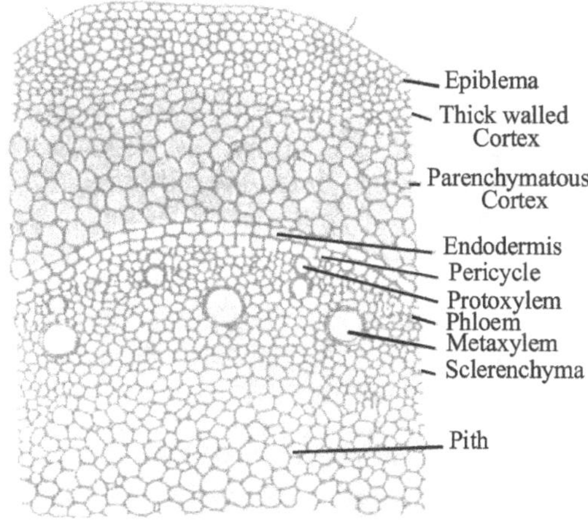

Fig. A part of T.S. of monocot root of maize (zea mays)

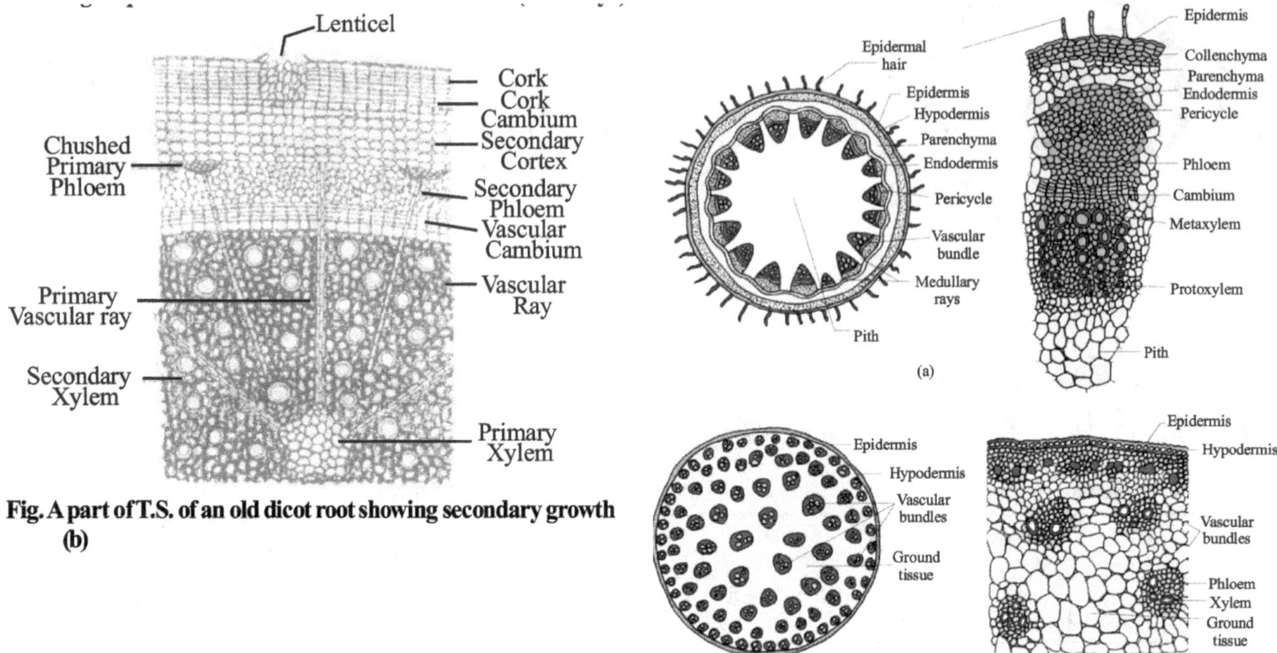

Fig. A part of T.S. of an old dicot root showing secondary growth
(b)

Fig. (a) T.S. of primary dicot stem of Sunflower (Diagrammatic)
(b) Detailed structure of a part of T.S. stem of Sunflower.

6.5 Cut a transverse section of young stem of a plant from your school garden and observe it under microscope. How would you ascertain whether it is a monocot stem or a dicot stem? Give reasons.

Sol. After observing the transverse section of the stem we can differentiate that stem is monocot or dicot on the basis of following characters :

	Monocot stem		Dicot stem
1.	Multicellular hairs are absent on the epidermis.	1.	Multicellular hairs may be present on the epidermis.
2.	Sclerenchmatous hypodermis present.	2.	Collenchymatous hypodermis present.
3.	There is no differentiation of ground tissue into cortex, endodermis and ground tissue.	3.	There are three parts of ground tissue- cortex, endodermis and pericycle.
4.	Vascular bundles are more. They are scattered. They are collateral and closed.	4.	There are few vascular bundles. They are open and collateral. They are arranged in a ring.
5.	Lysigenous cavity present.	5.	Lysigenous cavity absent.

6.6 The transverse section of a plant material shows the following anatomical features – (a) the vascular bundles are conjoint, scattered and surrounded by a sclerenchymatous bundle sheaths. (b) phloem parenchyma is absent. What will you identify it as?

Sol. Monocotyledonous stem.

6.7 Why xylem and phloem are called complex tissues?

Sol. Complex tissue is collection of different types of cells that help in the performance of a common function. Xylem and phloem are made up of different types of cells. Xylem is made of four types of cells *i.e.*, tracheids, tracheae (vessels), xylem fibres and xylem parenchyma and phloem also consists of four kinds of cells *i.e.*, Sieve elements, companion cells, phloem fibres, phloem parenchyma. Both xylem and phloem form conducting tissue of plant.

6.8 What is stomatal apparatus? Explain the structure of stomata with a labelled diagram.

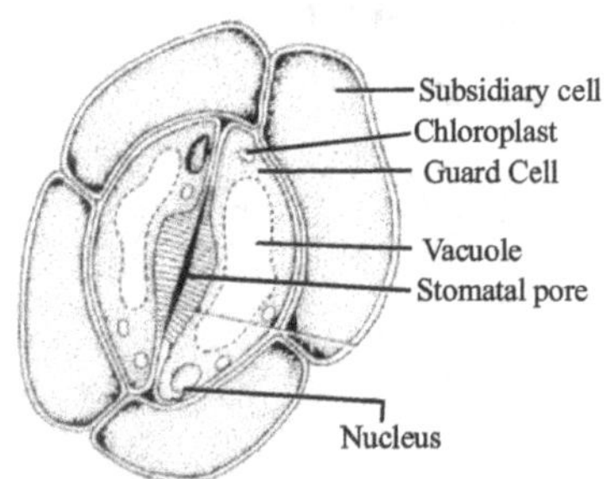

Fig. Structure of Stomata

Sol. Several minute openings or stomata are found on the epidermis of all the green aerial parts of plants, but are abundant on the lower surface on the leaves as they regulate the process of transpiration. A large number of stomata occur on the upper surface of leaves of aquatic plants. Each stomata is surrounded by two cells known as the guard cells. In the dicotyledons plants these are bean shaped, but in sedges and grasses these are dumb-bell shaped. The guard cell are living. Their outer walls are thin where as inner ones surrounding the aperture are highly thickened. Due to this variation in the thickening, the guard cell may becomes turgid and flaccid, depending upon the supply of water in them, which makes the opening and closing of stomata possible. Some times a few neighbouring epidermal cells in vicinity of guard cells become specialized in their shape and size and contents. These are known as subsidiary cells. The stomatal aperture, guard cells and the surrounding subsidiary cell are together called stomatal apparatus.

6.9 Name the three basic tissue systems in the flowering plants. Give the tissue names under each system.

Sol. There are three basic tissue systems viz., epidermal, ground and vascular tissue system.
   (i) Epidermal tissue system–Epidermis, stomata and epidermal appendages.
   (ii) Fundamental or ground tissue system – Cortex (hypodermis, general cortex and endodermis), pericycle and pith.
   (iii) Vascular tissue system – Xylem and phloem.

6.10 How is the plant anatomy useful to us?

Sol. 1. Study of anatomy helps in solving taxonomic problems.
   2. It helps in tracing inferior woods as compared to certified and standard wood required for construction, ship building, *etc.*
   3. Anatomical studies are also helpful for medicinal purposes.

6.11 What is periderm? How does periderm formation take place in the dicot stems?

Sol. As the stem continues to increase in girth due to activity of vascular cambium, the outer cortical and epidermis layers get broken and need to be replaced to provide new protective cell layers. Hence, sooner or later, another meristematic tissue called cork cambium or phellogen develops, usually in the cortex region. Phellogen is made of thinwalled rectangular cells. Its cuts off cells on both side. The outer cell differentiate into cork or phellem while inner cells differentiate into secondary cortex or phelloderm. Phelloderm, phellem and phelloderm are collectively called as periderm.

6.12 Describe the internal structure of a dorsiventral leaf with the help of labelled diagrams.

Sol. **Dorsiventral (dicotyledonous) leaf :** The vertical section of a dorsiventral leaf through the lamina shows three main parts, namely, epidermis, mesophyll and vascular system.
Epidermis : The epidermis which covers both the upper surface (adaxial epidermis) and lower surface (abaxial epidermis) of the leaf has a conspicuous cuticle. The abaxial epidermis generally bears more stomata than the adaxial epidermis. The latter may even lack stomata.
Mesophyll : The tissue between the upper and the lower epidermis is called the mesophyll. It possesses chloroplasts and carries out photosynthesis, is made up of parenchyma. It has two types of cells – the palisade parenchyma and the spongy parenchyma. The adaxially placed palisade parenchyma is made up of elongated cells, which are arranged vertically and parallel to each other. The oval or round and loosely arranged spongy parenchyma is situated below the palisade cells and extends to the lower epidermis.

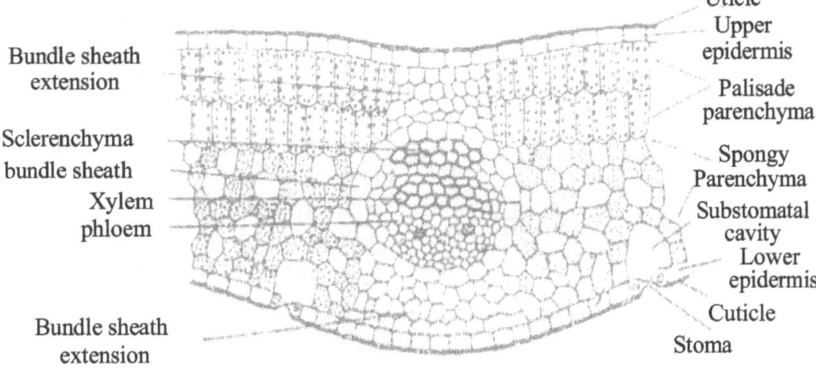

Fig. V. S. of dorsiventral leaf

There are numerous large spaces and air cavities between these cells.

Vascular system : This includes vascular bundles, which can be seen in the veins and the midrib. The size of the vascular bundles is dependent on the size of the veins. The veins vary in thickness in the reticulate venation of the dicot leaves. The vascular bundles are surrounded by a layer of thick walled bundle sheath cells.

SECTION B

PRACTICE QUESTIONS 

MULTIPLE CHOICE QUESTIONS

1. Which of the following is not a characteristics of spring wood?
  (a) Lesser number of xylary elements.
  (b) Density is less.
  (c) Cambium is active.
  (d) Colour of the wood is light.

2. A transverse section of a young dicot root can be distinguished from that of a young dicot stem by the presence of
  (a) collateral arrangement of xylem and phloem
  (b) radial arrangement of xylem and phloem
  (c) intrafascicular cambium
  (d) interfascicular cambium

3. Stem grows in girth due to
  (a) phelloderm   (b) epidermis
  (c) vascular cambium   (d) outer cortical

4. Which of the following helps in the curling of the leaf surface to minimise water loss?
  (a) Palisade parenchyma   (b) Xylem tissue
  (c) Bulliform cells   (d) Bundle sheath cells

5. The xylem Vessels is differ from Tracheids
  (a) it interconnected through perforations in their common walls.
  (b) in being derived from a single cell
  (c) in being living
  (d) in conducting water and minerals

6. Layer need to be replaced to provide new protective cell layers
  (a) Endodermis   (b) Outer cortical
  (c) Epidermis   (d) Both (b) and (c)

7. Phloem in gymnosperms lacks:
  (a) Both sieve tubes and companion cells
  (b) Albuminous cells and sieve cells
  (c) Sieve tubes only
  (d) Companion cells only

8. Stomata in grass leaf are
  (a) Dumb-bell shaped   (b) Kidney shaped
  (c) Rectangular   (d) Barrel shaped

9. Casparian strips occur in
  (a) Epidermis   (b) Pericycle
  (c) Cortex   (d) Endodermis

10. Identify the wrong statement in the context of heartwood:
  (a) It is highly durable
  (b) It conducts water and minerals efficiently
  (c) It compromises dead elements with highly lignified walls
  (d) Organic compounds are deposited in it.

ASSERTION & REASON QUESTIONS

DIRECTION (Qs. 1-5) : *These questions consists of two statements. Answer these questions selecting the appropriate option given below:*
  (a) Both Assertion (A) and Reason (R) are true and Reason (R) is the correct explanation of Assertion (A).
  (b) Both Assertion (A) and Reason (R) are true, but Reason (R) is not the correct explanation of Assertion (A).
  (c) Assertion (A) is true, but Reason (R) is false.
  (d) Assertion (A) is false, but Reason (R) is true.

1. **Assertion:** Higher plants have meristematic regions for indefinite growth.
  Reason: Higher plants have root and shoot apices.

2. **Assertion:** The cells of the parenchyma are generally isodiametric.
  Reason: the walls of parenchyma are thick and made up of lignin.

3. **Assertion:** A simple tissue is made of only one type of cells.
  Reason: Various simple tissues in plants are parenchyma, collenchyma and sclerenchyma.

4. **Assertion:** Sclerenchyma are usually dead and without protoplasts.
  Reason: It consists of long, narrow cells with thick and lignified cell walls

5. **Assertion:** endodermis lies a single layers of thin walled parenchyomatous cells referred to as casparian strips.
  Reason: Initiation of lateral roots and vascular cambium during the secondary growth takes place in parenchyomatous cells.

CASE/PASSAGE BASED QUESTIONS

DIRECTIONS (Qs. 1-5) : *Read the following passage and answer the questions that follows.*

The epidermal tissue system forms the outer-most covering of the whole plant body and comprises epidermal cells, stomata and the epidermal appendages- the trichomes and hairs. The epidermis is the outermost layer of the primary plant body. It is made up of elongated, compacity arranged cells, which form a continuous layer. Epidermis is usually single layered. Epidermal cells are parenchymatous with a small amount of cytoplasm lining the cell wall and a large vacuole. The outside of the epidermis is often covered with a waxy thick layer called the cuticle which prevents the loss of water. Cuticle is absent in roots. Stomata are structures present in the epidermis of leaves. Stomata regulate the process of transpiration and gaseous exchange. Each stoma is composed of two bean shaped cells known as guard cells which enclose stomatal pore. In grasses, the guard highly thickened. The guard cells possess chloroplasts and regulate the opening and closing of stomata. Sometimes, a few epidermal cells, in the vicinity of the guard cells become specialised in their shape and size and are known as subsidiary cells. The stomatal aperture, guard cells and the surrounding subsidiary cells are together called stomatal apparatus.

The cells of epidermis bear a number of hairs. The root hairs are unicellular elongations of the epidermal cells and help absorb water and minerals from the soil. On the stem the epidermal hairs are called trichomes. The trichomes in the shoot system are usually multicellular. They may be branched or unbranched and soft or stiff. They may even be secretory. The trichomes help in preventing water loss due to transpiration.

1. Which of the following cell regulates the opening and closing of guard cell?
   (a) Epidermal cell   (b) Guard cell
   (c) Subsidiary cell   (d) Trichomes
2. Which of the following components are knwon as epidermal appendages?
   (a) Trichomes   (b) Hairs
   (c) Trichomes & Hairs   (d) Stomata
3. In grass, the shape of guard cell is
   (a) bean shaped   (b) dumb-bell shaped
   (c) crescent-shaped   (d) kidney-shaped
4. Define cuticles and give its function.
5. What is trichomes?

VERY SHORT ANSWER QUESTIONS

1. Vascular bundles having cambium are known as.
2. Name the two types of sclerenchyma.
3. From where do the secondary meristerms originate?
4. What does make the root apical meristem subterminal?

5. Where are companion cells located in flowering plants? What are their functions?
6. What is the advantage of lignocellulose in wall of xylem?
7. A cross-section of a plant material shows the following features under the microscope: vascular bundles are radially arranged. These are found xylem strands showing exarch condition. What type plant part of is this?
8. Based on position, classify various types of meristems.
9. Name the various component cells of xylem. Which of them does not have a nucleus?
10. Give example of secondary meristem.
11. Name the tissue involved in linear and lateral growth in plants.
12. Heart wood is more durable than spring wood. Why?
13. Where these present :
    (1) Hypodermis layer   (2) Mesophyll tissue
    (3) Stomata   (4) Cambium

SHORT ANSWER QUESTIONS

1. What are the differences between root hairs and stem hairs?
2. Draw well labelled diagrams of the T.S. of dicotyledonous leaf.
3. Why is cambium considered to be a lateral meristem?
4. Name the plant part in which endodermis is absent. Give one basic difference between endodermis and epidermis.
5. What are casparian strips?
6. Which tissue is most abundantly found in plants? Where all is it present in plants?
7. What is present in phloem of leaves besides seive elements and is it living or dead? How are these functional & used?

LONG ANSWER QUESTIONS

1. Describe the structure and functions of xylem tissues in an angiospermic plants.
2. Describe the structure of a monocotyledonous leaf.

SOLUTIONS

Multiple Choice Questions

1. (a) Spring season produces a wood which has large number of xylary elements having vessels with wider cavities.
2. (b) Young dicot root can be distinguished from that of a young dicot stem by the presence of radial arrangement of xylem and phloem.
3. (c) The stem continues to increase in girth due to the activity of vascular cambium, the outer cortical and epidermis layers get broken and need to be replaced to provide new protective cell layers.
4. (c) The bulliform cells in the leaves have absorbed water and are turgid, the leaf surface is exposed. When they are flaccid due to water stress, they make the leaves curl inwards to minimise water loss.

5. (a) The vessel cells are also devoid of protoplasm. Vessel members are interconnected through perforations in their common walls. Tracheids are dead and are without protoplasm.
6. (d) The outer cortical and epidermis layers get broken and need to be replaced to provide new protective cell layers.
7. (a) Gymnosperms have albuminous cells and sieve cells. They lack sieve tubes and companion cells.
8. (a) In grasses, the guard cells are dumb-bell shaped.
9. (d) The tangential as well as radial walls of the endodermal cells have a deposition of water-impermeable, waxy material suberin in the form of casparian strips.
10. (b) The heartwood does not conduct water but it gives mechanical support to the stem.

Assertion & Reason Questions

1. **(a)** The root apex and shoot apex are meristematic in nature. These meristematic tissues are embryonic in origin. They are primary in origin because it develops from embryonic tissues and primary in function because they form the primary structure of the plant cell, the root apex and shoot apex, that live till the death of the whole plant. Hence, plants have the feature of indefinite growth.

2. **(c)** The cells of the parenchyma are generally isodiametric. They may be spherical, oval, round, polygonal or elongated in shape. Their walls are thin and made up of cellulose. They may either be closely packed or have small intercellular spaces.

3. **(b)** The tissues in which the cells of which have lost the capacity to divide and have attained a permanent shape, size and function due to morphological, biochemical and physiological differentiation are permanent tissues. Permanent tissues can be classified as simple, complex and special on the basis of composition. A simple permanent tissue is that tissue which is made up of similar permanent cells that carry out the same function or have the same structure. Simple permanent tissues are of three types-parenchyma, collenchyma and sclerenchyma.

4. **(a)** Sclerenchyma consists of long, narrow cells with thick and lignified cell walls having a few or numerous pits. Due to the excessive secondary cell wall thickening composed of lignin. Due to this, the cell wall becomes hard & impermeable to water & other components essential for cell metabolism. They are usually dead and without protoplasts.

5. **(d)** The tangential as well as radial walls of the endodermal cells have a deposition of water-impermeable, waxy material suberin in the form of casparian strips. Next to endodermis lies a few layers of thick-walled parenchyomatous cells referred to as pericycle. Initiation of lateral roots and vascular cambium during the secondary growth takes place in these cells.

Case/Passage Based Questions

1. **(b)** Guard cell regulates the opening and closing of guard cell.

2. **(c)** Trichomes & Hairs components are known as epidermal appendages.

3. **(b)** In grasses, the guard cells are dumb-bell shaped.

4. Cuticle- The outside of the epidermis is often covered with a waxy thick layer called the cuticle.
Function of cuticle- prevents the loss of water.

5. The cells of epidermis bear a number of hairs. Epidermal hairs present on the stem are called as trichomes.

Very Short Answer Questions

1. Open, Vascular bundle
2. Sclerenchyma fibres and stone cells.
3. Permanent tissue.
4. Presence of root cap makes the root apical meristem subterminal.
5. Companion cells are located in phloem cells of vascular tissues, they support the sieve tubes in water conduction.
6. It provides rigidity, thickness and resistance.
7. Dicot root.
8. Apical, intercalary and lateral meristems.
9. Tracheids, vessels, xylem parenchyma and xylem fibres. Only xylem parenchyma have nucleus and living.
10. Examples of secondary meristem are cork cambium and interfascicular cambium.
11. Linear growth is caused by apical meristem and lateral growth is caused by lateral meristem.
12. Heart wood is more durable than spring wood due to its little susceptibility to the attack of pathogens and insects.
13. (1) Hypodermis layer - is found in stems
    (2) Mesophyll tissue - in leaves
    (3) Stomata - lower epidermis in leaves
    (4) Cambium :- In vascular bundles which are open

Short Answer Questions

1. The main difference between stem hairs and root hairs are :

	Stem hairs		Root hairs
I.	They are generally multicellular.	I.	Root hairs are unicellular.
II.	Stem hairs are additional cells. They do not arise as outgrowths of the epidermal cells.	II.	Root hairs are tubular outgrowths of epiblema.
III.	They may be branched or unbranched.	III.	Root hair are always unbranched.
IV.	They are spread all over the stem.	IV.	They are found in clusters in young roots near their tips. It is known as root hair zone.
V.	Stem hairs are heavily cutinised.	V.	Root hairs are not cutinised.
VI.	They are long-lived.	VI.	They are short lived.
VII.	Stem hairs prevent or reduce the rate of transpiration.	VII.	Root hairs take part in absorption of water from the soil.

2.

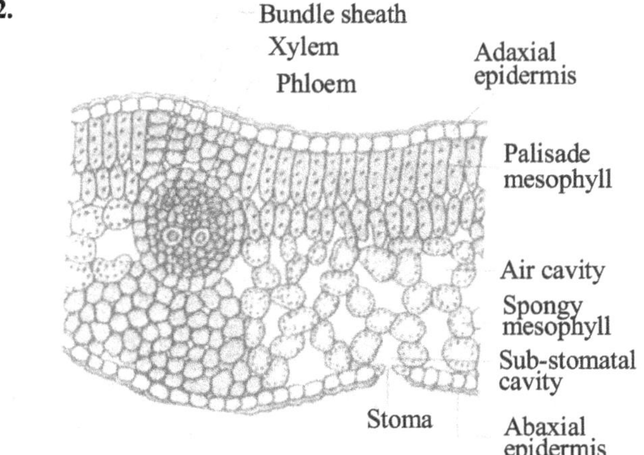

Fig. T.S. of leaf : Dicot

3. Cambium is responsible for increase in thickness of stems and roots as a result of addition of secondary tissues (secondary cortex, secondary phloem and secondary xylem). They are located at the lateral position so known as lateral meristems.

4. Endodermis is absent in leaves. Cells of endodermis posses casparian strips or bands in their radial and transverse walls which is not found in epidermis.

5. These are thickenings of lignin and suberin formed around the lateral walls of endodermis to prevent plasmolysis.

6. The tissue most abundantly found in plants is parenchyma. It is found in pith, cortex and in the entire mesophyll of the leaves.

7. Besides seive elements, in phloem parenchyma, living cells are present. These store food other cells are phloem fibres that are dead and provide mechanical strength. These are also used in making ropes and coarse textiles.

Long Answer Questions

1. Xylem is a complex tissue. It forms a part of the vascular bundle. It is mainly concerned with the conduction of water and minerals. It also provides mechanical support to the plant. As a conducting strand, xylem forms a continuous channel through the roots, stem, leaves and other aerial parts. It consists of four different types of cells—xylem vessels, trachieds, xylem fibres and xylem parenchyma. Xylem vessels and tracheids are concerned with the conduction of water and minerals from roots to aerial parts of the plant. Xylem fibres provide mechanical strength to the plant body. Xylem parenchyma are the only living components of xylem. These are concerned with the storage of food and other vital functions.

2. **Anatomy of Monocot/isobilateral leaf :** The upper and lower surfaces are covered by single-layered epidermis.

The upper epidermis has some cells larger than the others; such large cells are known as **bulliform/motor cells**.

Stomata are found on both upper and lower epidermal layers. The mesophyll is not differentiated into palisade and spongy parenchyma.

Mesophyll cells are isodiametric and are arranged compactly; they contain a number of chloroplasts. Since monocot leaves have parallel veins, a number of vascular bundles can be seen in a row in the section.

Each vascular bundle has sclerenchyma cells (caps) on its upper and lower edges. The xylem is on the upper side and phloem on the lower side. There is a parenchymatous bundle sheath, which often contains chloroplasts and perform the function of photosynthesis.

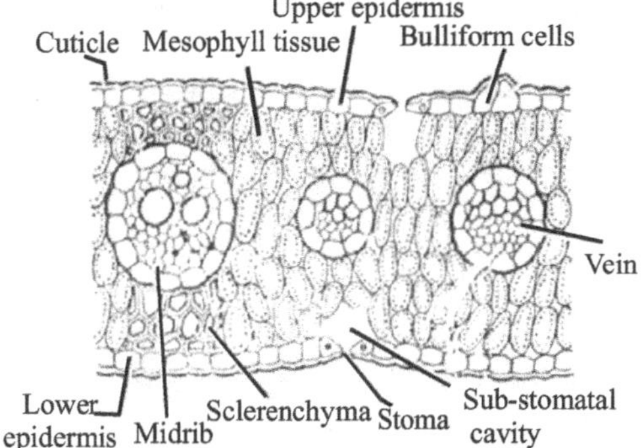

Fig.(b) : T.S. of maize leaf

SECTION C — NCERT EXEMPLAR QUESTIONS

MULTIPLE CHOICE QUESTIONS

1. A transverse section of stem is stained first with safranin and then with fast green following the usual schedule of double staining for the preparation of a permanent slide. What would be the colour of the stained xylem and phloem?

(a) Red and green
(b) Green and red
(c) Orange and yellow
(d) Purple and orange

2. Match the followings and choose the correct option from below.

A.	Meristem	(i)	photosynthesis, storage
B.	Parenchyma	(ii)	mechanical support
C.	Collenchyma	(iii)	actively dividing cells
D.	Sclerenchyma	(iv)	stomata
E.	Epidermal tissue	(v)	sclereids

(a) A-(i), B-(iii), C -(v), D-(ii), E-(iv)
(b) A-(iii), B-(i), C-(ii), D-(v), E-(iv)
(c) A-(ii), B-(iv), C-(v), D-(i), E-(iii)
(d) A-(v), B-(iv), C-(iii), D-(ii), E-(i)

3. Match the following and choose the correct option from below.

A.	Cuticle	(i)	guard cells
B.	Bulliform cells	(ii)	single layer
C.	Stomata	(iii)	waxy layer
D.	Epidermis	(iv)	empty colourless cell

Options:
   (a) A-(iii), B-(iv), C-(i), D-(ii)
   (b) A-(i), B-(ii), C-(iii), D-(iv)
   (c) A-(iii), B-(ii), C-(iv), D-(i)
   (d) A-(iii), B-(ii), C-(i), D-(iv)

4. Identify the simple tissue from among the following.
   (a) Parenchyma   (b) Xylem
   (c) Epidermis   (d) Phloem

5. Cells of this tissue are living and show angular wall thickening. They also provide mechanical support. The tissue is
   (a) xylem   (b) sclerenchyma
   (c) collenchyma   (d) epidermis.

6. Epiblema of roots is equivalent to
   (a) pericycle   (b) endodermis
   (c) epidermis   (d) stele

7. A conjoint and open vascular bundle will be observed in the transverse section of
   (a) monocot root   (b) monocot stem
   (c) dicot root   (d) dicot stem

8. Interfascicular cambium and cork cambium are formed due to
   (a) cell division   (b) cell differentiation
   (c) cell dedifferentiation (d) redifferentiation

9. Phellogen and phellem respectively denote
   (a) cork and cork cambium
   (b) cork cambium and cork
   (c) secondary cortex and cork
   (d) cork and secondary cortex

10. In which of the following pairs of parts of a flowering plant is epidermis absent?
   (a) Root tip and shoot tip
   (b) Shoot bud and floral bud
   (c) Ovule and seed
   (d) Petiole and pedicel

11. How many shoot apical meritsems are likely to be present in a twig of a plant possessing, 4 branches and 26 leaves?
   (a) 26   (b) 1
   (c) 5   (d) 30

12. In conifers fibres are likely to be absent in
   (a) secondary phloem (b) secondary xylem
   (c) primary phloem   (d) leaves

13. When we peel the skin of a potato tuber, we remove
   (a) periderm   (b) epidermis
   (c) cuticle   (d) sapwood

14. A vessel less piece of stem possessing prominent sieve tubes would belong to
   (a) Pinus   (b) Eucalyptus
   (c) Grass   (d) Trochodendron

15. Which one of the following cell types always divides by anticlinal cell division?
   (a) Fusiform initial cells (c) Protoderm
   (b) Root cap   (d) Phellogen

16. What is the fate of primary xylem in a dicot root showing extensive secondary growth?
   (a) It is retained in the centre of the axis
   (b) It gets crushed
   (c) May or may not get crushed
   (d) It gets surrounded by primary phloem

VERY SHORT ANSWER QUESTIONS

1. Product of photosynthesis is transported from the leaves to various parts of the plants and stored in some cell before being utilised. What are the cells/tissues that store them?

2. Protoxylem is the first formed xylem. If the protoxylem lies next to pholem what kind of arrangement of xylem would you call it?

3. What is the function of phloem parenchyma?

4. What is present on the surface of the leaves which helps the plant prevent loss of water but is absent in roots?

5. What is the epidermal cell modification in plants which prevents water loss?

6. What constitutes the cambial ring?

7. Give one basic functional difference between phellogen and phelloderm.

8. Arrange the following in the sequence you would find them in a plant starting from the periphery-phellem, phellogen, phelloderm.

9. If one debarks a tree, what parts of the plant is being removed?

SHORT ANSWER QUESTIONS

1. While eating peach or pear it is usually seen that some stone like structures get entangled in the teeth, what are these stone like structures called?
   The edible part of the peach or pear pome fruit for the fleshy thalamus.

2. What is the commercial source of cork? How is it formed in the plant?

3. Below is a list of plant fibres. From which part of the plant these are obtained.
   (a) Coir   (b) Hemp
   (c) Cotton   (d) Jute

4. Epidermal cells are often modified to perform specialised functions in plants. Name some of them and function they perform.

5. The lawn grass (*Cyandon dactylon*) needs to be mowed frequently to prevent its overgrowth. Which tissue is responsible for its rapid growth?

6. Plants require water for their survival. But when watered excessively, plants die. Discuss.

7. A transverse section of the trunk of a tree shows concentric rings which are known as growth rings. How are these rings formed? What is the significance of these rings?

8. Trunks of some of the aged tree species appear to be composed of several fused trunks. Is it a physiological or anatomical abnormality? Explain in detail.

9. What is the difference between lenticels and stomata? The gaseous exchange in all plants. Occurs by means of several openings present in the plant body.

10. Write the precise function of
(a) sieve tube
(b) interfascicular cambium
(c) collenchyma
(d) aerenchyma

11. The stomatal pore is guarded by two kidney shaped guard cells. Name the epidermal cells surrounding the guard cells. How does a guard cell differ from an epidermal cell? Use a diagram to illustrate your answer.

LONG ANSWER QUESTIONS

1. Is *Pinus* an evergreen Tree? Comment.

2. Assume that a pencil box held in your hand, represents a plant cell. In how many possible planes can it be cut? Indicate these cuts with the help of line drawings.

3. Each of thefollowing terms has some anatomical significance. What do these terms mean? Explain with the help of line diagrams.
(a) Plasmodesmata   (b) Middle Lamella
(c) Secondary wall

SOLUTIONS

Multiple Choice Questions

1. **(a)**

2. **(b)** A meristem is a simple tissue made of a group of similar and immature cells (meristematic cells) which can divide and form new cells.
Parenchyma cells having chloroplasts are termed as chlorenchyma. It helps in the manufacture of food (photosynthesis). Storage parenchyma is made of large sized vacuolated cells which are used to store water, mucilage and food,
e.g., Aloe, Opuntia, potato tuber.
Collenchyma gives mechanical strength to young dicot stems, petioles and leaves.
Sclerenchyma is of two types, sclerenchyma fibres and sclereids.
Epidermal tissue system make the outermost covering of plant body. It mainly consists of epidermis and epidermal appendages. Epidermis is made of epidermal cells and stomata.

3. **(a)**

4. **(a)** Simple permanent tissue found in plants is Parenchyma and, xylem and phloem are complex permanent tissues. Epidermis is a part of epidermal tissue system.

5. **(c)**

6. **(c)** Epiblema (rhizodermis) is the outermost layer of young root which has thin-walled cells. Some of the cells give rise to root hairs which take part in the absorption of water and mineral salts. Epidermis is also outer most layer. Therefore epiblema of root is equivalent to epidermis.

7. **(d)**

8. **(c)** Dedifferentiation is the phenomenon of regeneration of permanent tissue to become meristematic. Cork cambium, wound cambium and interfascicular vascular cambium are the examples of secondary meristems which are always produced through dedifferentiation.

9. **(b)** Cork cambium is also called phellogen and cork cells is called cork or phellem.

10. **(a)**

11. **(c)** The shoot apical meristems are present at the tips of the stem, and its branches. They produce growth in length. As the twig possesses 4 branches, number of shoot apical meristems are likely to be 5 including one of the twig itself.

12. **(b)** Fibres occur in all those parts of plants where mechanical strength is required i.e., leaves, petioles, cortex, xylem, phloem, etc. In conifers, they are likely to be absent in secondary xylem.

13. **(a)** Periderm is a tissue of secondary origin that replaces damaged epidermis. It can be found in underground plant organs. In potato, a model for periderm studies, periderm replaces the epidermis early in tuber development and suberized phellems constitute tuber's skin. Thus when we peel off a potato tuber we will remove periderm.

14. **(d)** **15.** **(c)** **16.** **(a)**

Very Short Answer Questions

1. The first product of photosynthesis is glucose. It is highly reactive molecule and gets converted into a disaccharide-sucrose for storage.
The food gets stored in specialised prarenchymatous cells present either in roots and stems or in their modifications in the form of a polysaccharide called starch.

2. The condition of the xylem arrangement if protoxylem lies next to phloem is called as exarch. It is found in roots.

3. The main function of phloem parenchyma is to store food and other substances like resins, latex and mucilage. They help in transport of food as well.

4. Cuticle is a waxy coating covering the entire surface of the plant body. It is absent in roots, it prevents the loss of water through the surface of the plant.

5. Bulliform or motor cells are modified epidermal cells meant for checking water loss present in monocots or grasses. They help in shutting down stomata and thus reduce water loss through transpiration under stressed conditions.

6. The cambium present in between the xylem and phloem is called fasicular or intrafasicular cambium and the newly formed cambium between the two vascular bundle is known as interfascular cambium. Both type of cambium combine to form the cambial ring.

7. Phelloderm is a permanent tissue while phellogen is a meristematic tissue. Phellogen (cork cambium) develops from the cortical cells, sometimes from pericycle cells. These cells actively divide and forms phellem on outerside and phelloderm (cortex cells) innerside so phelloderm originates from phellogen.

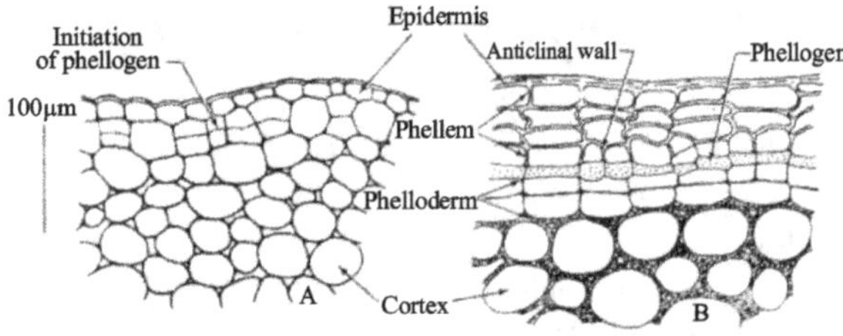

Formation of phellogen and phelloderm

8. The outer most layer is phellem or cork followed by phellogen (cork cambium) which in turn is followed by phelloderm (secondary cortex.

9. Debarking refers to removal of bark, *i.e.*, all tissues exterior to the vascular cambium, including secondary phloem. Bark includes periderm (phellogen, phellem and phelloderm) and secondary phloem.

Short Answer Questions

1. The stone cells are present in the pulpy part of fruit of peach and pear. These are sclerenchymatous cells and which are dead in nature. They provide mechanical support to the soft tissue.

2. The source of commercial cork is the cork tissue of *Quercus suber*, which yields bottle cork. Cork is formed by cork cambium or phellogen cell. cells of cork cambium divide periclinally, cutting cells towards the inside and outside. The cells that cut off towards the outside become suberised and dead.

   These are compactly packed in radial rows without intercellular spaces and form cork of phellem. Cork is impervious to water due to presence suberin and provides protection to the underlying tissues.

3. (a) **Coir** is a natural fibre obtained from coconut husk. It is the fibrous mesoderm of the fruit of *Cocos nucifera* (coconut).

   (b) **Hemp** fibre is obtained from the stems of *Cannabis sativa*. It is the bast fibre (soft or stem fibre) obtained from secondary phloem.

(c) **Cotton** fibre is the epidermal growth in cotton (*Gossypium hirsutum*) seed. It is an elongated structure made up of cellulose.

(d) **Jute** is a natural bast fibre made up of cellulose and lignin obtained from *Corchorus capsularis*.

4. The epidermal tissue system comprises of one cell thick layer of epidermal tissue and forms the outer most covering of the whole plant body.

Modification of Epidermal Cells

Following are the modifications of the epidermal tissue

(i) **root hair**

Structure

These unicellular hairs are the extensions of epidermal cell of roots in the root hair zone.

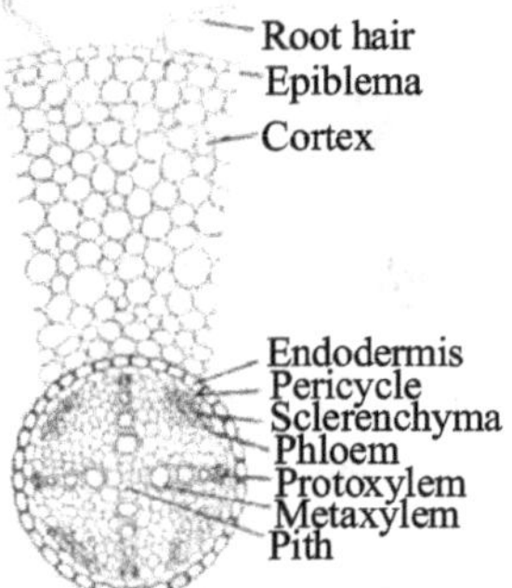

Function

They increase the surface area for absorption of water and minerals.

(ii) **Epidermal Appendages**

Structure

These are called trichomes and are epidermal cell modifications. There any be unicellular or multicellular.

Appendages of epidermis of leaves

A-Stellate hair of a Alyssum

B-Glandular hair of Pelargonium

C-Short glandular hair of Lavandula

D-Floccose hair of Malva

E-Glandular hair of solanum

F-Urtivating hair of Verbascum

Function

They produce some glandular secretions.

5. The rapid growth of mowed lawn grass is due to meristematic tissue. When the apex of grass is cut frequently, it leads to the growth of the lateral branches, that makes it more bushy.

6. Plants use water for several metabolic process as photosynthesis, transpiration and respiration. Plants when watered in excess die because excess water removes the air trapped between the soil particles.

   The plant roots do not get O_2 for respiration. Once cells of root die, water and mineral absorption is stopped and this leads to gradual death of a plant.

7. The concentric growth rings are called annual rings. These rings are formed due to the secondary growth. Secondary growth occurs due to the activity of cambium which is a meristermatic tissue in dicot trees.

The rate of activity of cambium is more in spring so wood formed has larger wider xylem cells, whereas wood formed in autumn has narrower and smaller xylem elements. This results in the formation of two rings called growth rings. By counting these rings, age of the tree can be determined. This branch of science is known as dendrochronology or growth ring analysis.

8. The appearance of several fused trunks is anatomical abnormality. It is an abnormal type of secondary growth where a regular vascular cambium or cork cambium is not formed in its normal position. Anomalous secondary growth produces cortical and medullary vascular bundles in case of old tree trunks.

Thus, the additional or accessory vascular bundles given appurtenance of several fused trunks.

9.

Lenticels	Stomata
Lenticels are formed due to loosening of the tissues epidermis.	Stomata are specialised structure on epidermis.
Lenticels do not have guard cells. These are mostly found on the stem region.	Stomata posses guard cells and are mostly found on lower surface of leaves.
They are used for removal of waste. These openings are not regulated.	They are involved in gaseous exchange, removal of extra water. Opening and closing are its highly regulated mechanism

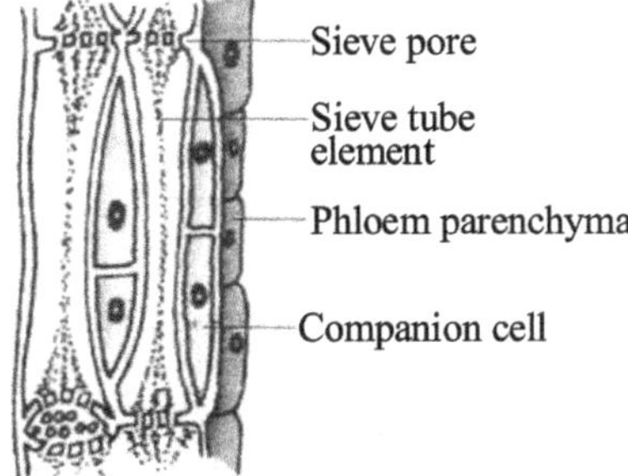

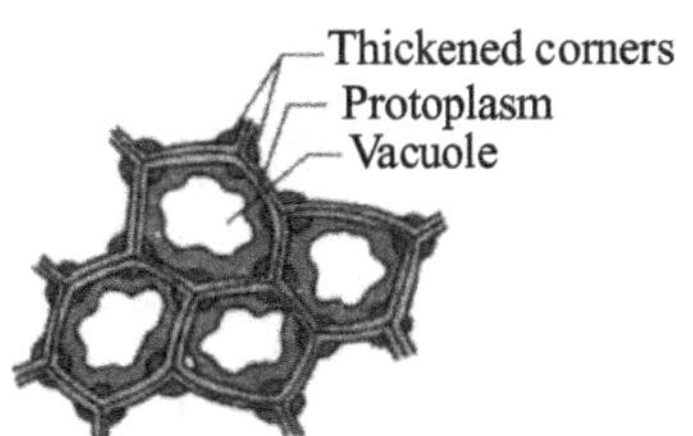

10. **Sieve tube** It's function is to transport of synthesised food throughout the plant. It is present in the phleom tissue.

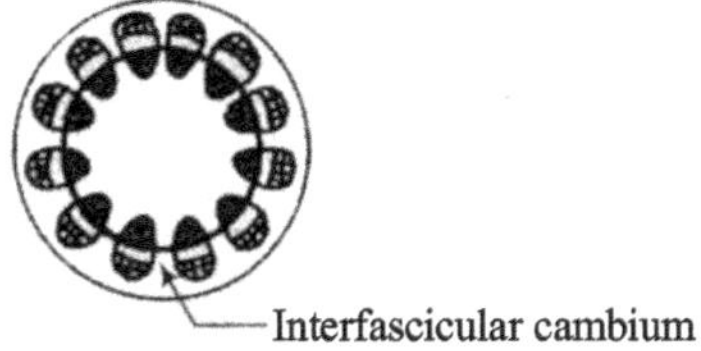

Structure of phloem tissue

Interfascicular Cambium It is a kind of secondary meristermatic tissue present in between two vascular bundles. It is function is to bring about secondary growth in the dicot stem and root.

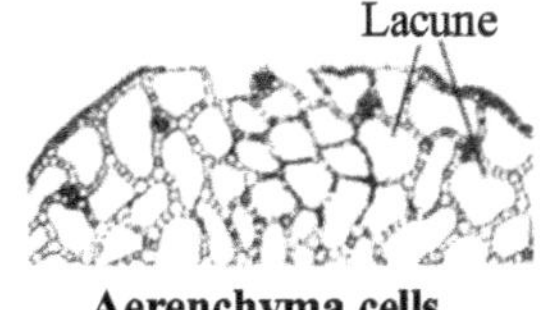

TS of stem of dicot plant

Collenchyma cells have angular thickening at corners. There function is to provide mechanical support to young growing herbaceous stem.

Collenchyma cells

Aerenchyma is a specilised parenchyma having large air spaces. It provides buyoncy to the hydrophytic plants.

Aerenchyma cells

11. Stomatal apparatus is a special modification of epidermal tissue present over leaf area. The epidermal cells surrounding the guard cells of stomata are called subsidiary cells include. Differences between guard cells and epidermal cells include:

Guard Cells	Epidermal Cells
They are bean or kidney shaped	They are barrel shaped.
They possess chloroplasts.	They lack chloroplasts.
They are smaller in size.	
Cell walls of guard cells are not uniforms in size.	They are bigger in size. Epidermal cells are uniformly thin.

Long Answer Questions

1. The plants which have persistent leaves in all the four seasons are evergreen. Deciduous plants in contrast completely loose their foliage during winter or dry season. *Pinus* belonging to gymnosperms is an evergreen tree. Under conditions of extreme cold the flowering plants shed their leaves and become dormant. In *Pinus* due to the presence of a thick bark thick needle-like leaves and sunken stomata to reduce the rate of transpiration the leaves we not shed. The cold areas are both physiologically and physically dry due to scanty rainfall, precipitation as snow, decreased root absorption at low temperature and exposed habitats.

Pinus however is well adapted to such conditions. It continues to manufacture food during this period and grows to domiante other plants. This show that *Pinus* is an evergreen tree. It does not shed its leaves or needles under any condition.

2. **A.** If a plant cell is cut in different plane if result, in radial symmetry.

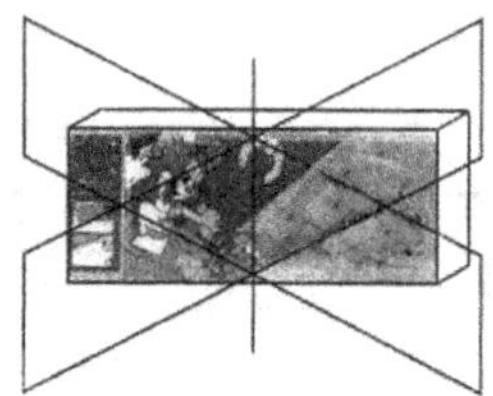

B. If a plant cell is cut in two equal halves it result in bilateral symmetry.

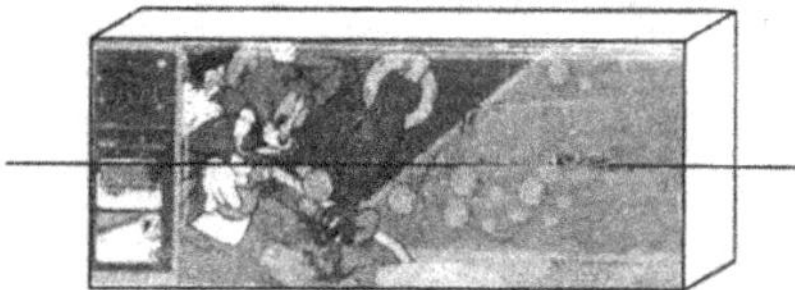

3. The given terms and their functions includes:

Structure	Function	Diagram
Plasmodesmata are microscopic connecting channels between the two cells through the cell wall.	It allows communication and transport between two neighbouring cells. Plasmodesmata also facilitates molecules to travel between plant cells through the symplastic pathway.	
Middle lamella is a layer in the cell wall mainly made of calcium pectate.	It performs the function of cementing between the two neighbouring cells.	
Secondary wall is a non-extensible layer made of hemicellulose fibres, in the cell wall of plant cells.	It provides rigidity to the cell wall in plant cell.	

7

Structural Organisation in Animals

7.1   Answer in one word or one line.
   (i)   Give the common name of *Periplanata americana.*
   (ii)   How many spermathecae are found in earthworm ?
   (iii)   What is the position of ovaries in cockroach ?
   (iv)   How many segments are present in the abdomen of cockroach ?
   (v)   Where do you find malpighian tubules?

Sol. (i)   Cockroach
   (ii)   Four pairs of spermathecae are found in the 6th to 9th segments (one pair in each segments).
   (iii)   Cockroach includes a pair of ovaries, that lie laterally in the 2nd to 6th abdominal segments of abdomen.
   (iv)   Ten
   (v)   At the junction of midgut and hindgut. 100-150 yellow coloured thin filamentous ring is present in earthworm, which is called malpighian tubules.

7.2   Answer the following :
   (i)   What is the function of nephridia ?
   (ii)   How many types of nephridia are found in earthworm based on their location?

Sol. (i)   Nephridia are the minute openings found in all segments excepts the first two and their function is to discharge of nitrogenous waste.
   (ii)   There are three types of nephridia -
      (i)   **Septal nephridia** - Present on both the sides of intersegmental septa of segment 15 to the last that open into intestine.
      (ii)   **Integumentary nephridia** - Attached to the lining of the body wall of segment 3 to the last that open on the body surface.
      (iii)   **Pharyngeal nephridia** - Present as three paired tufts in the 4th, 5th and 6th segments.
   These three different types of nephridia are almost similar in structure.

7.3   Draw a labelled diagram of the reproductive organs of an earthworm.

Sol.

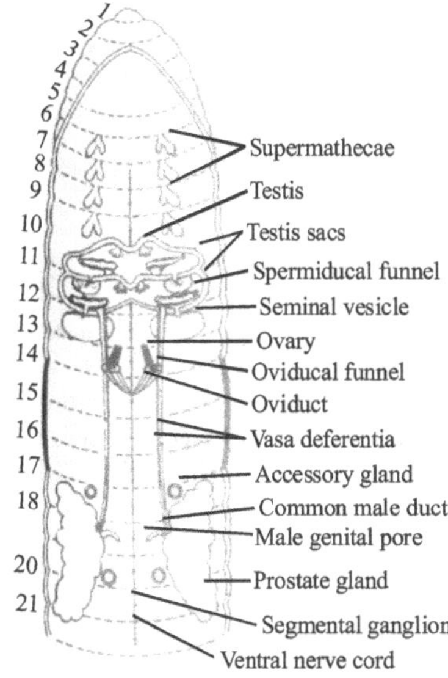

Fig. Reproductive system of earthworm

7.4   Draw a labelled diagram of alimentary canal of a cockroach.

Sol.

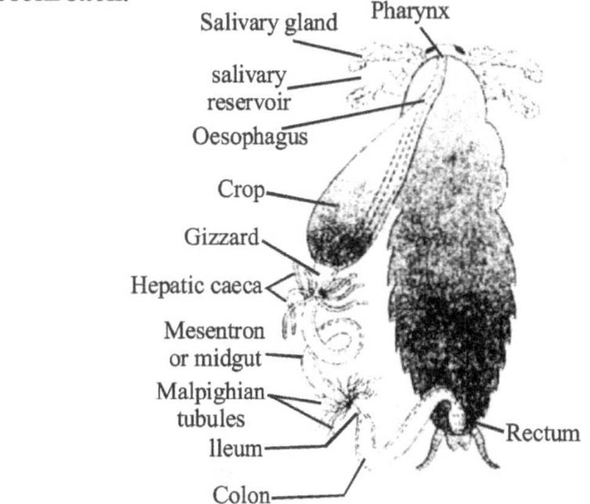

Fig. Alimentary canal of cockroach

7.5 **Distinguish between the followings :**
    (a) **Prostomium and peristomium**
    (b) **Septal nephridium and pharyngeal nephridium**
Sol. **(a)** The main difference between prostomium and peristomium are :

Prostomium	Peristomium
It is a small lobe/projection that hangs over the crescent shaped mouth.	It is the first anterior segment in which the mouth is present.

    (b) The main difference between septal nephridium and pharyngeal nephridium are:

Septal nephridium	Pharyngeal nephridium
These are present on either side of the intersegment septa from 15th segment to the last.	These are present as three paired tufts in the 4th, 5th and 6th segments
These open into the	These open into the pharynx.

7.6 **What are the cellular components of blood?**
Sol. Blood consists of plasma, red blood cells (RBCs), white blood cells (WBCs) and platelets.

7.7 **What are the following and where do you find them in animal body.**
    (a) **Chondrocytes**
    (b) **Axons**
    (c) **Ciliated epithelium**
Sol. **(a)** **Chondrocytes :**
        These are the cells found in cartilage connective tissue. The number of chondrocytes found in cartilage determine how bendy the cartilage is chondrocytes produce and maintain the cartilage matrix. It is present in the tip of the nose, pinna of ear, joints between vertebral column, etc.
    (b) **Axon :**
        It is the longest processes of a neuron, that conducts the impulse away from the cell body. They are present in all nerve fibres.
    (c) **Ciliated epithelium :**
        When cuboidal or columnar epithelial cells bear cilia, they are called as ciliated epithelium.
        Ciliated epithelium is found in the living of respirator tract, bronchioles and fallopian tube. It contains goblet cells, which secretes mucus.

7.8 **Describe various types of epithelial tissues with the help of labelled diagrams.**
Sol. **Epithelial tissues**
    Epithelial tissues provide covering to the inner and outer lining of various organs. The cells of epithelial tissues are compactly packed with little intercellular matrix.
    There are two types of epithelial tissues :
    (i) **Simple epithelium**
    (ii) **Compound epithelium**
    (i) **Simple epithelium :**
        Composed of single layer of cells and functions as a lining for body cavities ducts and tubes. It is further divided into three types on the basis of structure modifications-

    (a) **Squamous epithelium** - It is made of a single layer of flattened cells with irregular boundaries.
        It is found as a lining for body cavities, ducts and tubes such as in the walls of blood vessels and air sacs of lungs.
        Functions - It helps in forming a diffusion boundaries.
    (b) **Cuboidal epithelium** - It is made of single layer of cube-like cells.
        It is commonly found in ducts of glands and tubular parts of nephrons in kidneys. Specialized cuboidal cells are capable of producing gametes found in gonads called germinal epithellium.
        Functions - It helps in secretion and absorption and also in moving particles or mucus in a specific direction over the epithellium.
    (c) **Columnar epithelium** - It is composed of a single layer of tall and slender cells.
        Nuclei are located at base.
        Its free surface may have microvilli.
        It is found in lining of stomach and intestine.
        Functions - It helps in secretion and absorption.

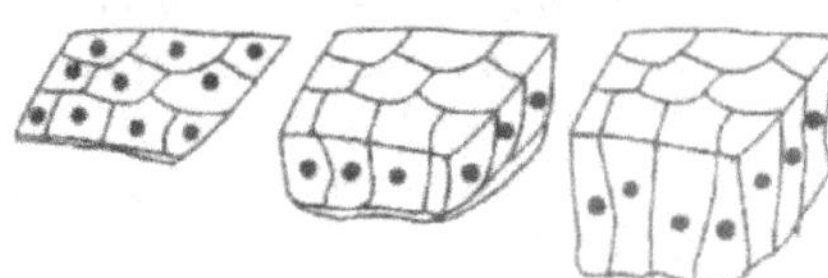

    (ii) **Compound epithelium :**
        It is made of more than one layer (multi-layered) of cells and thus it has very limited role in secretion and absorption.
        It is located at dry surfaces of the skin, moist surface of buccal cavity, pharynx inner lining of ducts of salivary glands and of pancreatic ducts.
        Functions - To provide protection against chemical and mechanical stresses.

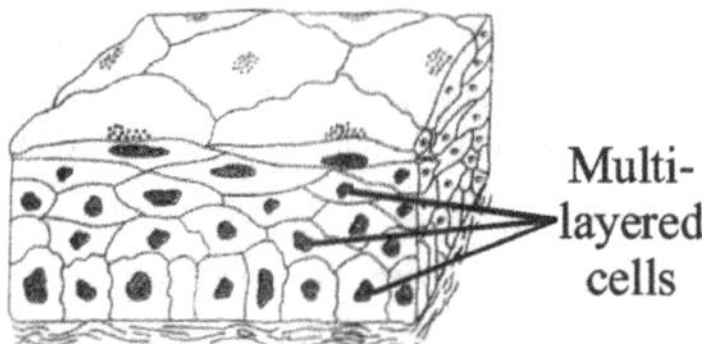

Compound epithelium

7.9 **Distinguish between**
    (a) **Simple epithelium and compound epithelium**
    (b) **Cardiac muscle and striated muscle**
    (c) **Dense regular and dense irregular connective tissues**
    (d) **Adipose and blood tissue**
    (e) **Simple gland and compound gland**

Sol. The main difference between simple epithelium and compound epithelium are as following.

(a)	**Simple epithelium**		**Compound epithelium**
1.	It is formed of a single layer of cells.	1.	It is formed of more than one layer of cells.
2.	All the cells rest on the basement membrane.	2.	Only the cells of the deepest layer membrane.
3.	They are not effective in protecting the underlying tissues.	3.	They give protection against mechanical, chemical osmotic and thermal stresses.

The main difference between Cardiac muscles and striated muscle are as following.

(b)	**Cardiac muscles**		**Striated muscles**
1.	They are present in the wall of the heart, pulmonary viens and superior vena cava	1.	They are present in the limbs, body walls, tongue, pharynx and beginning of oesophagus.
2.	Fibres branched	2.	Fibres unbranched
3.	Uninucleate	3.	Multinucleate
4.	Oblique bridges and intercalated discs present.	4.	No oblique bridges and intercalated discs present.
5.	Nerve supply from the brain and autonomic nervous system	5.	Nerve supply from central nervous system.
6.	Rapid contraction	6.	Very rapid contraction
7.	They never get fatigued	7.	They soon get fatigued.
8.	Involuntary	8.	Voluntary.

The main difference between dense regular connective tissues and dense irregular connective tissues are as following.

(c)	**Dense regular connective tissues**		**Dense irregular connective tissues**
1.	The cells and fibres are arranged compactly and the orientation of fibres shows a regular pattern.	1.	Cell fibres are arranged compactly but the fibres are not oriented in any irregular pattern.
2.	The collagen fibre bundles are in parallel rows, with the cells is between the rows.	2.	The fibres run in different direction with cells scattered between them.

The main difference between adipose tissue and blood tissue are as following.

(d)	**Adipose tissue**		**Blood tissue**
1.	It is a loose connective tissue.	1.	It is a fluid connective tissue.
2.	The matrix has fibres.	2.	The matrix does not have any fibres.
3.	It is meant for storage and metabolism of fats.	3.	It is meant for circulation of various substances and respiratory gases.

The main difference between simple gland and compound gland are as following.

(e)	**Simple gland**		**Compound gland**
1.	It is an exocrine gland with a single unbranched duct. *e.g.* - intestinal glands.	1.	It is an exocrine gland with a branched system of ducts. *e.g.*- pancreas.
2.	the grandular cells are arranged in the form of tubes or sweat gland, etc.	2.	The grandular cells are present in separate pockets when discharge their secretion in duct.

7.10 Mark the odd one in each series :
(a) Areolar tissue; blood; neuron; tendon
(b) RBC; WBC; platelets; cartilage
(c) Exocrine: endocrine; salivary gland; ligament
(d) Maxilla; mandible; labrum; antennae
(e) Protonema; mesothorax; metathorax; coxa

Sol. (a) Neuron   (b) Cartilage
(c) Ligament   (d) Antennae
(e) Protonema

7.11 Match the terms in column I with those in column II :

	Column I			Column II
(a)	Compound epithelium	–	(i)	Alimentary canal
(b)	Compound eye	–	(ii)	Cockroach
(c)	Septal nephridia	–	(iii)	Skin
(d)	Open circulatory system	–	(iv)	Mosaic vision
(e)	Typhlosole	–	(v)	Earthworm
(f)	Osteocytes	–	(vi)	Phallomere
(g)	Genitalia	–	(vii)	Bone

Sol.

(a)	Compound epithelium	–	(iii)	Skin
(b)	Compound eye	–	(iv)	Mosaic vision
(c)	Septal nephridia	–	(v)	Earthworm
(d)	Open circulatory system	–	(ii)	Cockroach
(e)	Typhlosole	–	(i)	Alimentary canal
(f)	Osteocytes	–	(vii)	Bone
(g)	Genitalia	–	(vi)	Phallomere

7.12 Mention briefly about the circulatory system of earthworm.

Sol. **Circulatory system of earthworm -**
- Earthworm consists of a closed circulatory system, which consists of heart, blood vessels and blood.
- Blood glands are present into the 4th, 5th and 6th segments of the body, they produce blood cells and haemoglobin which remains dissolved in plasma.
- 7th, 9th, 12th and 13th segments contains four pairs of pulsatile hearts.
- Blood circulates in one direction, which is maintained by contractions of the heart.
- Alimentary canal, nerve cord and body wall gets blood by smaller blood vessels.
- Blood cells are phagocytic in nature.

7.13 Draw a neat diagram of digestive system of frog.

Sol. **Digestive system of frog :**

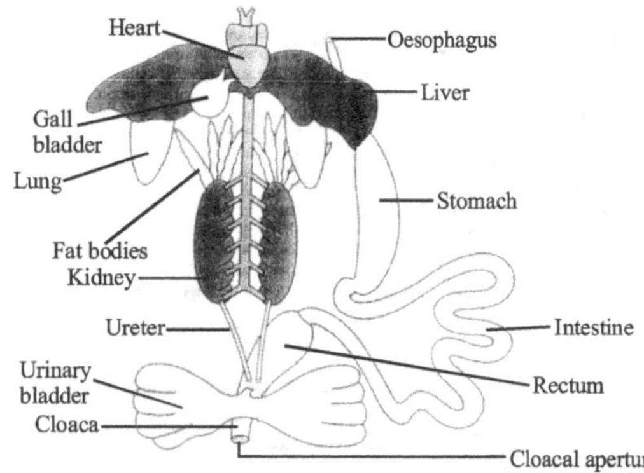

Diagrammatic representation of internal organs of frog showing complete digestive system

7.14 Mention the function of the following :
- **(a) Ureters in frog**
- **(b) Malpighian tubules**
- **(c) Body wall in earthworm**

Sol. **Functions :**
1. **Ureters in frog :**
   - They carry the urine from the kidneys to the cloaca. In males, it also conducts the sperm as it is urinogenital duct. In females the ureters and oviduct open-separately in the cloaca.
2. **Malphigian tubules :**
   - They are the excretory organs of a cockroach.
   - They collect the nitrogenous wastes from the haeomolymph and send them into the intestine.
   - Each tubule is lined by glandular and ciliated cells. They absorb nitrogenous waste products and convert them into uric acid which is excreted out through the hindgut.
3. **Body wall of earthworm :**
   The body wall of the earthworm is covered externally by a thin non-cellular cuticle below which is the epidermis, two muscle layers (circular and longitudinal) and an innermost coelomic epithelium. The epidermis is made up of a single layer of columnar epithelial cells which contain secretory gland cells.

SECTION B   **PRACTICE QUESTIONS** ◆

MULTIPLE CHOICE QUESTIONS

1. Compound squamous epithelium is found in
   - (a) stomach   (b) intestine
   - (c) trachea   (d) pharynx
2. Tendons and ligaments are the examples of
   - (a) areolar connective tissue
   - (b) adipose tissue
   - (c) dense regular connective tissue
   - (d) loose connective tissue
3. The protein present in the matrix of cartilage is
   - (a) Chitin   (b) Chondrin
   - (c) Ossein   (d) Chondriotin
4. Neuroglia are
   - (a) excitable cells of neural tissue.
   - (b) supporting and non-excitable cells of neural tissue.
   - (c) two to three times in volume of neural tissue.
   - (d) protective and excitable cells of neural tissue.
5. Lack of blood supply and presence of the noncellular basement membrane are the characteristics of the
   - (a) muscular tissue   (b) fluid connective tissue
   - (c) epithelial tissue   (d) nervous tissue
6. Gizzard (proventriculus) in cockroach lies between
   - (a) oesophagus and stomach
   - (b) crop and mesenteron
   - (c) mesenteron and ileum
   - (d) oesophagus and crop
7. In cockroach, the testes are present in
   - (a) 3, 4, 5 abdominal segments
   - (b) 4, 5, 6 abdominal segments
   - (c) 5, 6, 7 abdominal segments
   - (d) 6, 7, 8 abdominal segments
8. The faecal deposits of earthworm are known as:
   - (a) worm blastings   (b) worm pellets
   - (c) worm castings   (d) vermicomposts
9. The sensory papillae in frogs are associated with
   - (a) smell   (b) hearing
   - (c) respiration   (d) touch
10. The following are required for blood clotting in mammals
    - (a) K^+ and vitamin K
    - (b) Ca^{2+} and vitamin A
    - (c) Ca^{2+} and vitamin K
    - (d) K^+ and vitamin E

ASSERTION & REASON QUESTIONS

DIRECTION (Qs. 1-5) : *These questions consists of two statements. Answer these questions selecting the appropriate option given below:*
(a) Both Assertion (A) and Reason (R) are true and Reason (R) is the correct explanation of Assertion (A).
(b) Both Assertion (A) and Reason (R) are true, but Reason (R) is not the correct explanation of Assertion (A).
(c) Assertion (A) is true, but Reason (R) is false.
(d) Assertion (A) is false, but Reason (R) is true.

1. **Assertion:** Tissue is a group of similar cells that perform a specific function.
   Reason: Animals are made up of four different types of tissues.
2. **Assertion:** Smooth muscle are present in blood vessels and intestine.
   Reason: Smooth muscles are voluntary in nature because their functions are controlled.
3. **Assertion:** Neuroglial cells produce electrical signals in the body.
   Reason: Neurons having ability to transmit the electrical signals.
4. **Assertion:** Earthworms are known as hermaphrodites.
   Reason: They have both male and female sex organs in a single organism.
5. **Assertion:** Cockroach contains open type blood vascular system.
   Reason: The blood of cockroach contains blood pigment.

CASE/PASSAGE BASED QUESTIONS

DIRECTIONS (Qs. 1-5) : *Read the following passage and answer the questions that follows.*

Cockroaches are insects in which sexual dimorphism is prominent. The male and female individuals can be identified externally. In the given figure, female reproductive system of cockroach is shown. Observe the diagram and answer the questions.

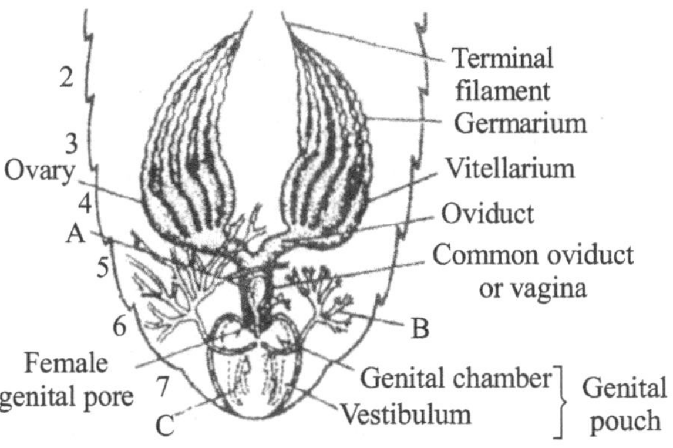

1. In the given figure, spermatheca is shown by labelling
   (a) B   (b) C
   (c) A   (d) None of them
2. What is represented by labelling C?
   (a) Spermatheca   (b) Gonapophyses
   (c) Tegmina   (d) Phallic gland
3. Which of the following statement is true for Sexual dimorphism-
   (a) Individuals having different sexes but belong to the same species.
   (b) Single organism of a species contain both sexes.
   (c) Individuals having different sexes and belong to the different species.
   (d) None of the above statements is correct.
4. Labelling B represents
   (a) Collaterial glands   (b) Tegmina
   (c) Seminal vesicle   (d) Spermatheca
5. Cockroaches are
   (a) Monoecious   (b) Dioecious
   (c) Both (a) and (b) (d) None of them

VERY SHORT ANSWER QUESTIONS

1. Name the protein found in white fibres.
2. State the function of setae.
3. What is the functional unit of cockroach eye?
4. Name the unit of neural or nervous system.
5. What is worm casting ?
6. Which cell covers the exposed surfaces of the body (skin) and internal passage ways (digestive tract and glands) ?
7. Name the type of epithelium that lines the inner surface of stomach.
8. Name the type of epithelium that lines the buccal cavity.
9. Name of type of tissue that is the most abundant in animal body.
10. What is the other name given to the gizzard of cockroach?
11. Name the larva of a frog.
12. What is the scientific name of Indian (bull) frog?

SHORT ANSWER QUESTIONS

1. What are the neuroglia cells?
2. What is vermicompositing?
3. What are exocrine glands? Name any two secretions of them.
4. Write four functions of bones.
5. Describe the three types of cell junctions present in the epithelium and other tissues.
6. How is the gizzard in the alimentary canal of a cockroach suitable for grinding the food?
7. What is a typhlosole in an earthworm? Where is it found? What is its function?

LONG ANSWER QUESTIONS

1. Describe the female reproductive organs of frog.
2. Describe with examples, various types of connective tissues.

SOLUTIONS

Multiple Choice Questions

1. **(d)** Compound epithelium covers the dry surface of the skin, the moist surface of buccal cavity, pharynx, inner lining of ducts of salivary glands and pancreatic ducts.

2. **(c)** Tendons, which attach skeletal muscles to bones and ligaments which attach one bone to another are examples of dense regular connective tissues in which collagen fibres are present in rows between many parallel bundles of fibres.

3. **(b)**

4. **(b)** Neurons forms the structural and functional unit of nervous tissue. They are excitable cells. While the neuroglial cells constitute the rest of the neural system that protect and support neurons and are non-excitable.

5. **(c)** Epithelial tissue covers the body surface, or lines the body cavity. The cells rest upon a non-cellular basement membrane which is secreted by epithelial cells. It is not nourished by blood, so non-vascularized.

6. **(b)** Gizzard has an outer layer of thick circular muscles and thick inner cuticle forming six highly chitinous plate called teeth. It helps in grinding food particles.

7. **(b)** Testes are paired, 3-4 lobed, situated dorsolaterally in the 4th, 5th, 6th abdominal segments.

8. **(c)** Earthworm is a reddish brown terrestrial invertebrate, inhabits the upper layer of the moist soil. It can be traced by their faecal deposits known as **worm castings**.

9. **(d)** Frog has different types of sense organs like organs of touch (sensory papillae), taste (taste buds), smell (nasal epithelium), vision (eyes) and hearing (tympanum with internal ears).

10. **(c)**

Assertion & Reason Questions

1. **(b)** When similar cells are grouped and perform a specific functions then such type of a group of cells is known as tissue. Animals have four type of tissues such as epithelial tissue, connective tissue, muscle tissue and neural tissue.

2. **(c)** Smooth muscles are present in the wall of internal organs such as intestine, blood vessels. They are involuntary in nature.

3. **(d)** Neuroglial cells are non-neuronal cells of the central nervous system and they are not involved in the production of electrical signals. They maintain homeostasis condition. Neurons are the neuronal cells in the central nervous system and play important role in the production of electrical signals or impulses.

4. **(a)** Male and female sex organs are present in a single body of earthworm so it is called as hermaphrodite.

5. **(c)** The blood of cockroach is called as haemolymph in which blood pigment is absent. Cockroach has open circulatory system.

Case/Passage Based Questions

1. **(c)**

2. **(b)** The external genitalia are represented by male gonapophysis or phallomer.

3. **(a)** Sexual dimorphism can be define as the systematic diference in form between individuals of different sex in the same species.

4. **(a)**

5. **(b)** Cockroaches are dioecious and both sexes have well developed reproductive organs.

Very Short Answer Questions

1. Collagen.

2. It helps in locomotion by gripping the earth.

3. Ommatidium.   4. Neurons.

5. It is the insoluble and undigested food that is given out along with soil through anus.

6. Squamous epithelium   7. Columnar epithelium

8. Stratified squamous epithelium.

9. Connective tissue.   10. Proventriculus.

11. Tadpole.   12. *Rana tigrina*.

Short Answer Questions

1. Cells which holds the neuron together are known as neuroglia cells.

2. The process of increasing soil fertility by earthworms is known as vermicomposting.

3. **Exocrine glands :** Those glands which have ducts to pour their secretion(s) into the respective site of action, are called exocrine. *e.g.,*
   (i) Salivary glands secrete saliva into the buccal cavity.
   (ii) Liver secretes bile into the duodenum.

4. **Functions of bones :**
   (i) They provide place for attachment of muscles and help in movement and locomotion.
   (ii) Bone marrow is the site of manufacture of blood cells.
   (iii) Bones provide protection to the internal organs.
   (iv) The long bones of the limbs serve the weight-bearing function.
   (v) They act as the depot of calcium and phosphorus.

5. **Cell junctions**
   (i) Tight junctions – They check leaking of substances across a tissue.
   (ii) Adhering junctions – They help in cementing the neighbouring cells together.
   (iii) Gap junctions – They facilitate the cells to communicate with each other by cytoplasmic connections, for rapid transfer of ions, small molecules, etc.

6. **Gizzard of cockroach has following characteristics:**
   (i) The gizzard has an outer layer of thick circular muscles.
   (ii) The inner thick layer of cuticle forms six plate like teeth.
   (iii) The movement with the help of muscles and the teeth-like structures help in grinding the food.

7. **Typhlosole :** It is an internal median fold of the dorsal wall of the intestine. It is found in the intestine between 26th and 35th segments of the body.
   It increases the effective area of absorption.

Long Answer Questions

1. The female reproductive organs include a pair of ovaries. The ovaries are situated near kidneys and there is no functional connection with kidneys. A pair of oviduct arising from the ovaries opens into the cloaca separately. A mature female can lay 2500 to 3000 ova at a time.

Fertilisation is external and takes place in water. Development involves a larval stage called tadpole. Tadpole undergoes metamorphosis to form the adult.

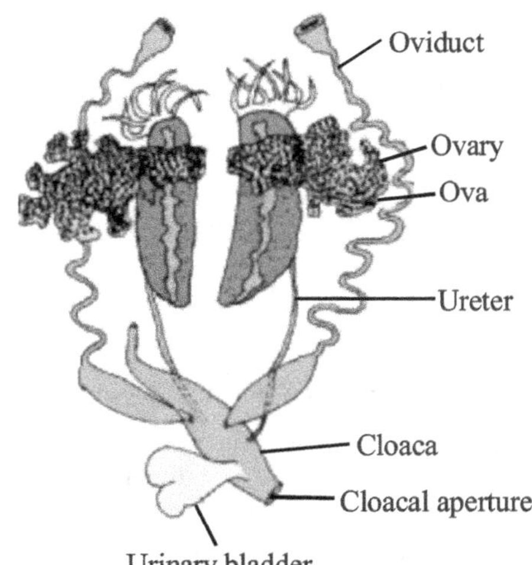

Female reproductive system

2. Connective tissues are most abundant and widely distributed in the body of complex animals. They are named connective tissues because of their special function of linking and supporting other tissues/organs of the body. Connective tissues are classified into three types: (i) Loose connective tissue, (ii) Dense connective tissue and (iii) Specialised connective tissue.

(i) Loose connective tissue: It has cells and fibres loosely arranged in a semi-fluid ground substance, for example, **areolar tissue** present beneath the skin. Often it serves as a support framework for epithelium. It contains fibroblasts (cells that produce and secrete fibres), macrophages and mast cells. Adipose tissue is another type of loose connective tissue located mainly beneath the skin. The cells of this tissue are specialised to store fats.

(ii) Dense connective tissue : Fibres and fibroblasts are compactly packed in the dense connective tissues. Orientation of fibres show a regular or irregular pattern and are called **dense regular** and **dense irregular tissues**. In the dense regular connective tissues, the collagen fibres are present in rows between many parallel bundles of fibres. Tendons, which attach skeletal muscles to bones and ligaments which attach one bone to another are examples of this tissue.

Dense irregular connective tissue has fibroblasts and many fibres (mostly collagen) that are oriented differently. This tissue is present in the skin.

(iii) Specialised connective tissue : Cartilage, bones and blood are various types of specialised connective tissues.

The intercellular material of cartilage is solid and pliable and resists compression. Cells of this tissue (chondrocytes) are enclosed in small cavities within the matrix secreted by them. Cartilage is present in the tip of nose, outer ear joints, between adjacent bones of the vertebral column, limbs and hands in adults.

Bones : It has a hard and non-pliable ground substance rich in calcium salts and collagen fibres which give bone its strength. It is the main tissue that provides structural frame to the body.

Blood : It is a fluid connective tissue containing plasma, red blood cells (RBC), white blood cells (WBC) and platelets. It is the main circulating fluid that helps in the transport of various substances.

SECTION C — NCERT EXEMPLAR QUESTIONS 

Multiple Choice Questions

1. Which one of the following types of cell is involved in making of the inner walls of large blood vessels?
  (a) Cuboidal epithelium (b) Columnar epithelium
  (c) Squamous epithelium (d) Stratified epithelium

2. To which one of the following categories does adipose tissue belong?
  (a) Epithelial (b) Connective
  (c) Muscular (d) Neural

3. Which of the following is not a connective tissue?
  (a) Bone (b) Cartilage
  (c) Blood (d) Muscles

4. The clitellum is a distinct part in the body of earthworm, it is found in?
  (a) segments 13-14-15 (b) segments 14-15-16
  (c) segments 12-13-14 (d) segments 15-16-17

5. Setae help in locomotion in earthworm but are not uniformly present in all the segments, They are absent in
  (a) First (b) Last segment
  (c) Both (a) & (b) (d) Neither (a) nor (b)

6. Which one of the following statements is true for cockroach?
  (a) The number of ovarioles in each ovary are ten.
  (b) The larval stage is called caterpillar.
  (c) Anal styles are absent in females.
  (d) They are ureotelic.

Very Short Answer Questions

1. State the number of segments in earthworm which are covered by a prominent dark band or clitellum.

2. Where are sclerites present in cockroach?

3. How many times do nymphs moult to reach the adult form of cockroach?

4. Identify the sex of a frog in which sound producing vocal sacs are present.
5. A muscle fibre tapers at both ends and does not show striations. Name the muscle fibre.
6. Name the different cell junctions found in tissues.
7. Give two identifying features of an adult male frog.
8. Which mouth part of cockroach is comparable to our tongue?
9. The digestive system of frog is made of the following parts. Arrange them in an order beginning from mouth. Mouth, oesophagus, buccal cavity, stomach, intestine, cloaca, rectum, cloacal aperture.
10. What is the difference between cutaneous and pulmonary respiration?
11. Special venous connection between liver and intestine and between kidney and intestine is found in frog, what are the called?

SHORT ANSWER QUESTIONS

1. Stratified epithelial cells have limited role in secretion. Justify their role in our skin.
2. How does a gap junctions facilitate intercellular communication ?
3. Why are blood, bone and cartilage called connective tissue?
4. How do you distinguish between dorsal and ventral surface of the body of earthworm?

5. Complete the following statement.
   (a) In cockroach grinding of food particle is performed by ....
   (b) malpighian tubules help in removal of ....
   (c) Hind gut of cockroach is differentiated into ....
   (d) In cockroach blood vessels open into spaces called ....
6. Mention special features of eye in cockroach. Discuss compound eye in arthropods and mention its structural features.
7. Frog is a poikilotherm, exhibits camouflage and undergoes aestivation and hibernation, how are all these benficial to it?
8. Write the functions in brief in Column II, appropriate to the structures given in column I.

	Column I		Column II
A	Nictitating membran	1	....
B	Tympanum	2	....
C	Copulatory pad	3	....

9. Using appropriate examples, differentiate between false and true body segmentation.
10. What is special about tissue present in the heart?

LONG ANSWER QUESTIONS

1. Write down the common features of the connective tissue. On the basis of structure and function, differentiate between bones and cartilages.
2. Draw a neat and well labelled diagram of male reproductive system of a frog.

SOLUTIONS

Multiple Choice Questions

1. **(c)** Simple squamous epithelium forms the inner walls of blood vessels. It is composed of large flat cells which rest on a thin basement membrane.
2. **(b)** Adipose tissue is a fat-storing loose connective tissue found subcutaneously, around the heart, kidney, eyeballs, mesenteries, etc.
3. **(d)** It is a muscular tissue. Muscle fibres is not a connective tissue.
4. **(b)** In a mature earthworm segments 14-16 are covered by a prominent dark band of glandular tissue called clitellum.
5. **(d)** In each body segment of earthworm, except the first, last and clitellum, there are rows of setae, embedded in the epidermal pits in the middle of each segment.
6. **(c)** Anal styles are paired, thin, unjointed outgrowths, projecting backwardly from the sides of 9th sternum of the male cockroach only. They are absent in females. The number of ovarioles in each ovary are eight. The larval stage of cockroach is called nymph. Cockroach is uricotelic.

Very Short Answer Questions

1. **Segments 14-16** bare covered by a prominent dark band of glandular tissue called clitellum in a mature earthworm. It secretes mucus and albumen that help in formation of cocoon.

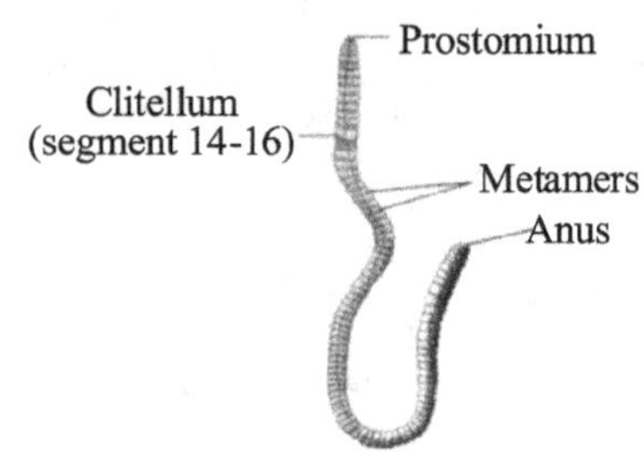

Dorsal view of earthworm showing clitellum and metamer

2. In all the body segments of cockroach sclerites are present. They are of two types **dorsal sclerites** often known as tergites, and **ventral sclerites** which are referred to as **sternites**.
3. The nymph grows by moulting about 13 times to reach. In cockroach', the development is indirect and paurometabous adult form has three stages, i.e., egg, nymph and adult. The nymph resembles adult except/or undeveloped wings and genitalia.
4. Sex of frogs can be distinguished on the basis of presence of sound producing vocal sacs. These organs are present in males which make them crock lauder than females, so as to attract females for mating.
5. Muscle fibres that taper at both the ends (fusiform) and do not show striations are smooth muscle fibres. They are also called involuntary muscles.

6. The different cell junctions found in tissue include:
   (i) **Tight junctions** are regions where plasma membrane of adjacent epithelial cells are held close together. They check the movement of material between then.
   (ii) **Gap junctions** are meant for chemical exchange between adjacent cells.
   (iii) **Adhering junctions** function to keep neighbouring cells together.
7. The two identifying features of an adult male frog include
   (a) **Nuptial Pad** is a copulatory pad present on the first digit of the forelimb of male frog and helps in closing female during amphelexus.
   (b) **Vocal Sacs** are loose skin folds on throat of male frogs for producing louder croak to attract females for mating purposes.
8. In cockroach, **hypopharynx** acts as a tongue and lies within cavity enclosed by the mouth parts.
9. The correct arrangement of the part of digestive system in frog is
   Mouth → Buccal cavity → Oesophagus → Stomach → Intestine → Rectum → Cloaca → Cloacal aperture.
10. In frog respiration takes place *via* the skin as well lungs. Pulmonary respiration and occurs outside the water through lungs. Cutaneous respiration takes place in water as well as land, occurs through highly vascularised moist skin.
11. In frog, venous connection between liver and intestine is called hepatic portal system and venus connection between the kidney and the lower parts of the frog is called **renal portal system**.

Short Answer Questions

1. **Stratified epithelium** consists of epithelial cells in which the innermost layer is made up of columnar or cuboidal cells. It is a type of compound epithelium and a waterproof protein called keratin is present few outer layers.
   These layers of dead cells is called horny layer which is shed at intervals due to frictions and thus has a limited role in secretions and absorption. The main function of stratified epithelium is to provide protection to the body against mechanical and chemical stresses.
2. Intercellular communication is facilitated by gap junction allowing small signaling molecules to pass from cell to cell. These are fine hydrophilic channels, between two adjacent animal cells that are formed with the help of two protein cylinders called connexus.
   Each connexus consists of six proteins subunits that surround a hydrophilic channel. Opening or closing of channel is controlled by pH and Ca^{2+} ion concentration.
3. Connective tissue provides the structural framework and support to different organs forming tissue. Blood is a fluid or vascular connective tissue, which connects various organs and transports substances from one place to another.

Bone is a solid, rigid and strong skeletal connective tissue, which supports the body and helps in locomotion. Cartilage is also a skeletal connective tissue, not as rigid bone but piable and resists compression. It plays role in support and protection and present in tip of nose, outer ear joints etc.

4. The body of an earthworm can be distinguished into dorsal and ventral sides due to the presence of certain peculiar feature in it which include the following.
   (i) The dorsal surface is darker than ventral surface because it is marked by a **dark median mid dorsal** line along the longitudinal axis of body. This is due to dorsal blood vessel, seen through integument.
   (ii) **Genital openings** (pores), are present in the ventral surface of both male and female.
   (iii) On vental surface genital papilla is located and helps in copulation.

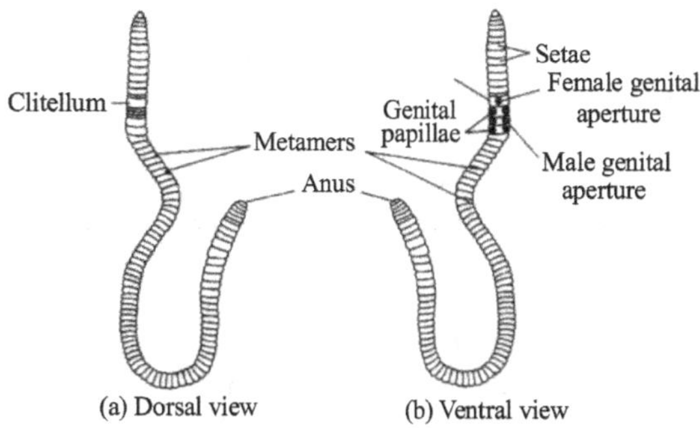

Body of the earthworm

5. (a) **Gizzard** is a muscular and greatly folded structure which marks the end of foregut in cockroach and bears six plates with teeth for crushing and grinding the food.
   (b) **Malpighian tubules** are excretory in function as they help in the removal of nitrogenous wastes in arthropods.
   (c) **Ileum, colon and rectum** and rectum opens and through anus.
   (d) **Haemocoel** is the body cavity of cockroach divided into sinuses and contains visceral organs of cockroach floating in haemolymph.
6. In cockroach the eyes are large sessile, paired bean-shaped and present on either side of head. The are compound in nature. Each compound eye consists of a large number of visual elements called **ommatidia**.
   Each ommatidium is composed of a diopteric region and reticular (receptor) region. It is capable of producing a separate image of a small part of object seen.
   Thus, the image of the object viewed consists of several pieces and is known as **mosaic image**. Fine nerve fibres arise from the inner end of each ommatidium all of which combine to form one **optic nerve** connected to the brain.

7. A trait with a current functional role in the life history of an organism that is maintained and evolved by means of natural selection and evolution and help organism in its survival is an adapture triat.

    Frog is a poikilotherm or a (cold blooded animal). It regulates its body temperature according to its environment.

    It undergoes winter sleep (hibernation) for withstanding very cold temperatures and summer sleep in hot temperatures (aestivation). During this period, it lives in a dormant stage with very minimal vital body activities.

    Frog is capable of changing its body colour as well, though gradually, with the change in its surrounding and climatic conditions. This capability in frog is called as camouflage which lets it escape from the predators, an essential survival parameter for living.

8. (a) **Nictitating Membrane** in frog protects the eye from water and any damage by covering the eye ball of frog.

    (b) **Tympanum** is present on each side of the frog head and is involved in the hearing process.

    (c) **Copulatory Pad** present in the limbs of the male frog and helps in copulation by holding the female during its sexual activity.

9. The serial repetition of similar body parts along the length of an animal is **segmentation**. The body of animals can be truely segmented or pseudo/false segmented.

    True segmentation is found in annelids, arthropods and some chordates. In these organisms there is a linear repetition of body parts and each repeated unit is called somite (metamere). In earthworms, the successive somites are externally and internaly.

    Pseudosegmentation is seen when body is divided into number of **false segments** which are independent of each other. Each segment is able to perform all the vital function of body. Growth occurs by the addition of new segments from the anterior end, *e.g.*, tapeworm.

10. Special tissue present in heart is called cardiac muscle, which has the following features

    (i)   Cardiac muscle fibres are supplied with both central and autonomic nervous system and are not under the control of will of animal.

    (ii) These muscles show rhythmicity and are immune to fatigue.

    (iii) They have a rich supply of blood.

    (iv) They are myogenicas. They possess the property of contraction even if completely isolated from the body.

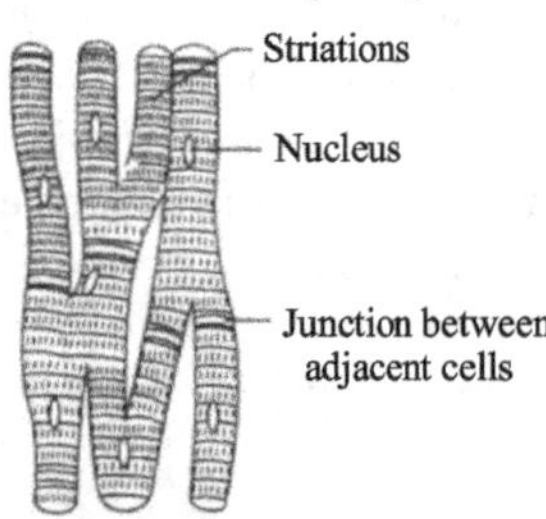

Cardiac muscle fibres

1. **Features of connective tissue:**
    Connective tissues are most abundant and widely distributed in the body of complex animals. They are named connective tissues because of their special function of linking and supporting other tissues/organs of the body. They range from soft connective tissues to specialised types, which include cartilage, bone, adipose, and blood. In all connective tissues except blood, the cells secrete fibres of structural proteins called collagen or elastin. The fibres provide strength, elasticity and flexibility to the tissue. These cells also secrete modified polysaccharides, which accumulate between cells and fibres and act as matrix (ground substance).

    Difference between Bone and cartilage:
    The intercellular material of cartilage is solid and pliable and resists compression. Cells of this tissue (chondrocytes) are enclosed in small cavities within the matrix secreted by them. Most of the cartilages in vertebrate embryos are replaced by bones in adults. Cartilage is present in the tip of nose, outer ear joints, between adjacent bones of the vertebral column, limbs and hands in adults.

    •   Bones have a hard and non-pliable ground substance rich in calcium salts and collagen fibres which give bone its strength. It is the main tissue that provides structural frame to the body. Bones support and protect softer tissues and organs. The bone cells (osteocytes) are present in the spaces called lacunae. Limb bones, such as the long bones of the legs, serve weight-bearing functions. They also interact with skeletal muscles attached to them to bring about movements. The bone marrow in some bones is the site of production of blood cells.

2.

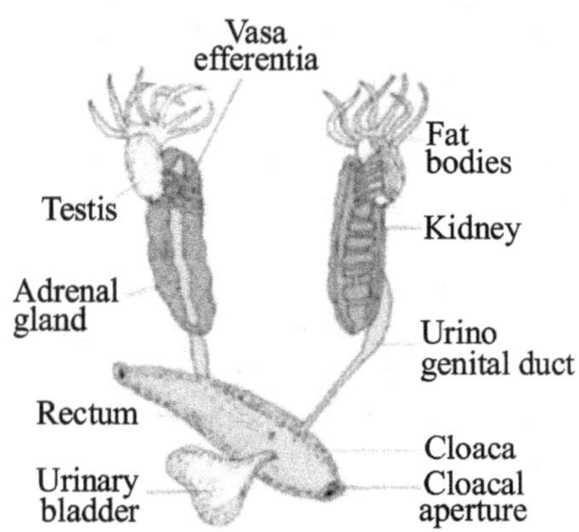

8. Cell: The Unit of Life

8.1 Which of the following is not correct?
(a) Robert brown discovered the cell.
(b) Schleiden and Schwann formulated the cell theory.
(c) Virchow explained that cells are from pre- existing cells.
(d) A unicellular organism carries out its life activities within single cell.

Sol. (a)

8.2 New cells generate from
(a) bacterial fermentation
(b) regeneration of old cells
(c) pre-existing cells
(d) abiotic material

Sol. (c)

8.3 Match the following

Column A		Column B
(a) Cristae	(i)	Flat membranous sac in stroma
(b) Cisternae	(ii)	Infoldings in mitochondria
(c) Thylakoids	(iii)	Disc-shaped sacs in Golgi apparatus

Sol. (a)(ii) (b)(iii) (c)(i)

8.4 Which of the following is correct
(a) Cells of living organisms have a nucleus.
(b) Both animals and plant cells have a well defined cell wall.
(c) In prokaryotes, there are no membrane bound organelles.
(d) Cells are formed *de novo* from abiotic materials.

Sol. (c)

8.5 What are mesosomes in prokaryotic cell? Mention the function that it performs.

Sol. Mesosome is infold of plasma membrane of a Gram positive bacterium. It increases the surface area of respiratory membrane and also helps in replication of DNA and their separation.

8.6 How do neutral solutes move across the plasma membrane? Can the polar molecules also move across it in the same way? If not, then how are these transported across the membrane?

Sol. Neutral solutes move across plasma membrane by simple diffusion along concentration gradient (from higher concentration to the lower). Water moves like this way. Osmosis is the movement of water by diffusion. The polar molecules may not pass through non-polar bilipid layer, they require a carrier protein of membrane for transport across it. Few ions are transported by Na^+/K^+ pump by active transport. Such a transport is an energy dependent process, in which ATP is utilized and is called active transport.

8.7 Name two cell-organelles that are double membrane bound. What are the characteristics of these two organelles? State their functions and draw labelled diagram of both.

Sol. Two double membrane bound cell organelles:
(a) **Mitochondria :** It has finger like folds in the inner membrane called cristae. Mitochondria is the place for aerobic respiration.

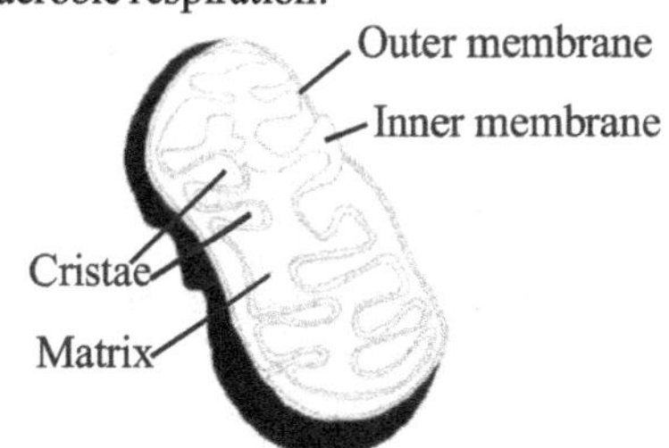

Mitochondria

(b) **Chloroplast :** Chloroplast is responsible for converting light energy into chemical energy. Chloroplast contains stacked thylakoid in its matrix.

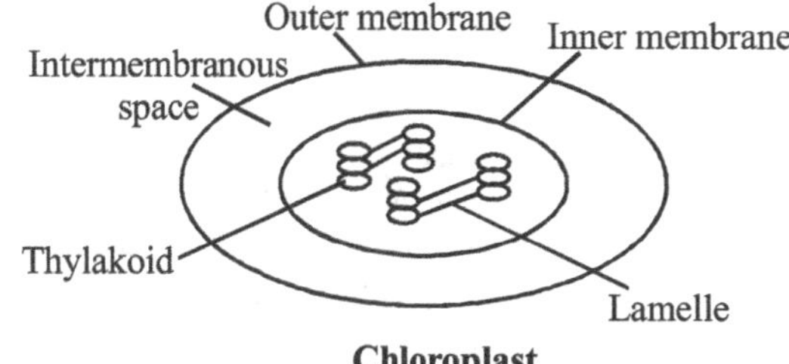

Chloroplast

Functions of mitochondria : The double membrane mitochondria are actively associated with aerobic respiration and the release of energy for cellular activity. The biological oxidation of the fats and carbohydrate release much amount of energy which is utilised by mitochondria for ATP synthesis. Required energy is released from ATP molecules for various cell processes in cells so they are termed as *"the powerhouse of the cell"*

Functions of chloroplast :

(i) Their main function of chloroplast is to trap sun's energy and to convert it into chemical energy of food by **photosynthesis.**

(ii) Storage of starch.

(iii) Chloroplast in fruits and flowers change into **chromoplasts.**

8.8 What are the characteristics of prokaryotic cells?

Sol. Characteristic of prokaryotic cells :

(i) These are represented by PPLO, Mycoplasma, BGA and bacteria.

(ii) These are smaller in size and multiply more rapidly.

(iii) Vary greatly in size and shape.

(iv) All prokaryotes have cell wall enclosing cell membrane, cytoplasm and circular DNA (plasmid/ naked chromosome) that is not bounded by nuclear membrane.

8.9 Multicellular organisms have division of labour. Explain.

Sol. In unicellular organisms, there is no division of labour. The single cell of the organisms is capable of performing all the vital activities of life i.e., respiration, movement, digestion and reproduction, etc. Respiration, nutrition and excretion in most of these unicellular organisms takes place through general body surface. No special organs for these are present in them because they are too small to need them. Most of these unicellular organisms reproduce by simple binary division, to maintain their continuity. However in some, sexual reproduction has also been observed.

8.10 Cell is basic unit of life. Discuss in brief.

Sol. Cell : The Basic Unit of life : All the living organism are composed of small, tiny structure or compartments called cells. These cells are called the '**building blocks**' of life. The cells in true sense are considered as the basic unit of life because all the life processes i.e., metabolism, responsiveness, reproduction are carried out by the cells. Respiration, nutrition, release of energy for the body are carried out within the cells only. Even the animals and plants reproduce because the cells reproduce individually. Growth occurs because cell grow and multiply.

In *Amoeba* all the life processes are performed within the boundaries of the single cell. This is true of all other multicellular organisms. The only difference in the multicellular organisms is that the body of these organisms is made up of many cells. In these organisms, the cell do not behave independently, but get organized into tissues. Each tissue is specialized to perform specific functions. Different tissues then get organised into tissues. Each tissue is specialized to perform specific functions. Different

tissues then get organised into organs which perform certain specific functions. Different organs are finally organised to form organ systems. Now it must be very clear that the basic structure to tissues, organs and organ system are the cells only. These tissues, organs and organ system of the organisms work because the cells work. Thus *"the cells are structural and functional unit of the living beings"* hence it is the basic unit of life.

8.11 What are nuclear pores? State their function.

Sol. Nuclear pores : Electron microscopy has revealed that nuclear envelope contains two parallel membranes and the space (10 nm–50 nm) between them. Outer membrane has small pores called the nuclear pores formed by fusion of two membrane.

Function : Nuclear pores are the passages through which the movement of RNA and protein molecules occur in both the directions between nucleus and cytoplasm.

8.12 Both lysosomes and vacuoles are endomembrane structures, yet they differ in terms of their functions. Comment.

Sol. Lysosomes are filled with hydrolytic enzymes that are capable of digesting carbohydrates, proteins, lipids and nucleic acids whereas vacuoles contain water, sap , excretory product and other materials not useful for cell.

8.13 Describe the structure of the following with the help of labelled diagrams.

(i) Nucleus (ii) Centrosome

Sol.

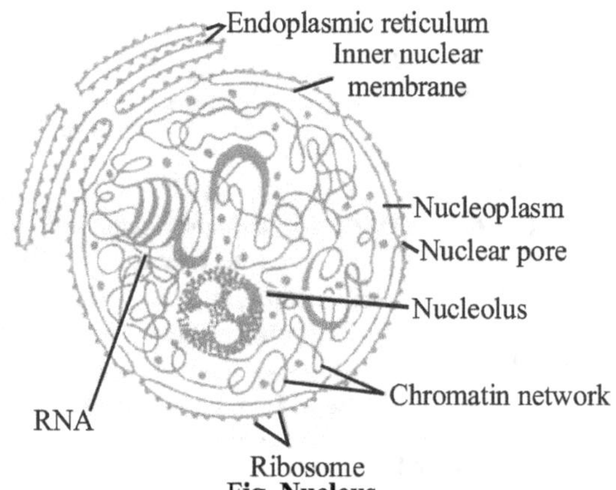

Fig. Nucleus

(i) Nucleus : The nucleus is a large organelle controlling all the activities of the eukaryotic cells. The nucleus is bounded by two membranes, which make the nuclear envelope. The outer and inner membranes are separated by a narrow space, perinuclear space. The outer membrane remains in continuation with endoplasmic reticulum (ER) and the inner one surrounds the nuclear contents. At some points, the nuclear evelope is interrupted by the presence of small structures called nuclear pores. These pores help in exchange of materials between nucleoplasm and cytoplasm.

The nucleoplasm contains chromatin and nucleolus. The nucleolus is a rounded structure. It is not separated from the rest of the nucleoplasm by membrane. Nucleolus is the *"site for ribosomal RNA synthesis"*.

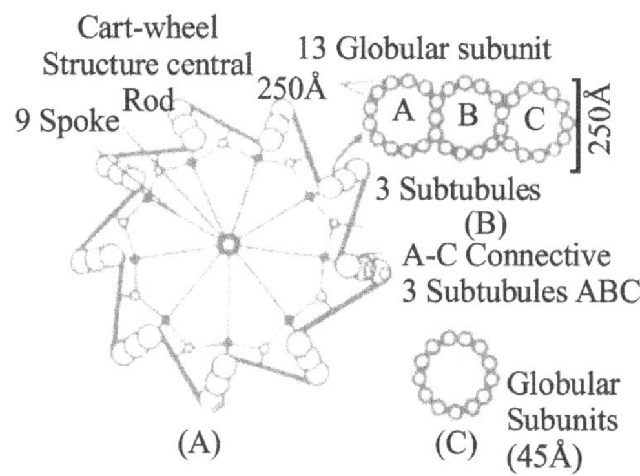

Fig. Centrosome

(ii) Centrosome : Under the electron microscope, each centriole is seen to be formed of nine sets of tubular structures arranged in circular fashion. Each of these sets is a triplet composed of three microtubules. Each microtubule has a diameter of about 250Å. The triplets are found in the matrix. Sometimes delicate strands appear to connect sets of the triplet to each other. Also can be seen radiating from the central core of the cylinder, delicate strands which connect sets of the triplets to each other giving a cartwheel appearance. Basal bodies are structures similar to the centrioles. They produce cilia and flagella.

8.14 What is a centromere? How does the position of centromere form the basis of classification of chromosomes? Support your answer with a diagram showing the position of centromere on different types of chromosomes.

Sol. Eukaryotic chromosomes : The chromosomes are uncoiled in a loose, indistinct network called the chromatin that contains DNA, RNA and protein in interphase. The types of protein present and associated with DNA are histone and non-histone proteins. Chromosomes are thread-like structures. They become visible (under light microscope) during cell division. In higher organisms, the well developed nucleus contains a definite number of chromosomes of definite size and shape.

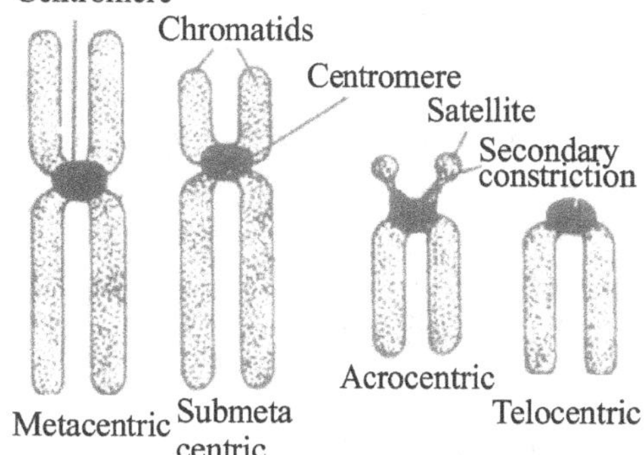

Fig. : Types of chromosomes

The shape of a chromosome is usually observable at metaphase and anaphase, when the position of primary constriction (*centromere*) is clearly seen. Based on the position of centromere, chromosomes are of 3 types:

(i) **telocentric** - with terminal centromere,

(ii) **acrocentric** - terminal centromere is capped by a telomere,

(iii) **submetacentric** - the centromere is subterminal in position, and

(iv) **metacentric** - these have median centromere.

SECTION B # PRACTICE QUESTIONS 

Multiple Choice Questions

1. In prokaryotes, chromatophores are
 (a) specialized granules responsible for colouration of cells.
 (b) structures responsible for organizing the shape of the organism.
 (c) inclusion bodies lying free inside the cells for carrying out various metabolic activities.
 (d) internal membrane system which becomes extensive and complex in photosynthetic bacteria.

2. Polysome is a chain of
 (a) oxysomes (b) sphaerosomes
 (c) ribosomes (d) dictyosomes

3. Basal bodies are associated with the formation of
 (a) phragmoplast (b) cilia and flagella
 (c) cell plate (d) kinetochore

4. Which of the following lacks cell wall?
 (a) Gametes (b) *Amoeba*
 (c) *Mycoplasma* (d) All of these

5. An organalle devoid of membrane covering is
 (a) vacuole (b) ribosome
 (c) peroxisome (d) lysosome

6. Microtubules are absent in
 (a) mitochondria (b) centriole
 (c) flagella (d) spindle fibres

7. Microtubules, motor proteins, and actin filaments are all part of the
 (a) mechanism of photosynthesis that occurs in chloroplasts.
 (b) rough ER in prokaryotic cells.
 (c) cytoskeleton of eukaryotic cells.
 (d) process that moves small molecules across cell membranes.

8. Mitochondria are numerous and densely packed in
 (a) inactive tissues (b) less active tissues
 (c) very active tissues (d) damaged tissues

9. In polytene chromosomes dark bands are visible. These bands are formed by
 (a) protein particles (b) chromomeres
 (c) nucleosomes (d) none of the above

10. Organelle important in spindle formation during nuclear division is
 (a) Golgi body (b) chloroplast
 (c) centriole (d) mitochondrion

ASSERTION & REASON QUESTIONS

DIRECTION (Qs. 1-5) : *These questions consists of two statements. Answer these questions selecting the appropriate option given below:*
(a) Both Assertion (A) and Reason (R) are true and Reason (R) is the correct explanation of Assertion (A).
(b) Both Assertion (A) and Reason (R) are true, but Reason (R) is not the correct explanation of Assertion (A).
(c) Assertion (A) is true, but Reason (R) is false.
(d) Assertion (A) is false, but Reason (R) is true.

1. **Assertion:** A cell is a structural and functional unit of a living organism.
   Reason: All living organisms are made up of cells, their products and all the metabolic reactions take place in the cell.

2. **Assertion:** Ribosome plays important role in the process of protein synthesis.
   Reason: Ribosome is a single membrane organelle of the cell.

3. **Assertion:** In Amoeba, the process of excretion takes place by contractile vacuole.
   Reason: The vacuoles of plant cells are larger than the animal cells.

4. **Assertion:** Mitochondria and chloroplast are surrounded by the double membrane.
   Reason: Both organelles are present only in eukaryotic cells.

5. **Assertion:** Chromosomes are present only in animal cells.
   Reason: Animals cells contain more than one DNA.

CASE/PASSAGE BASED QUESTIONS

DIRECTIONS (Qs. 1-5) : *Read the following passage and answer the questions that follows.*

The fluid mosaic model of the plasma membrane explains about the fluid nature of the membrane. The given diagram labelled as A, B, C and D. It represents a fluid mosaic model of the cell membrane. Observe the diagram and answer the questions.

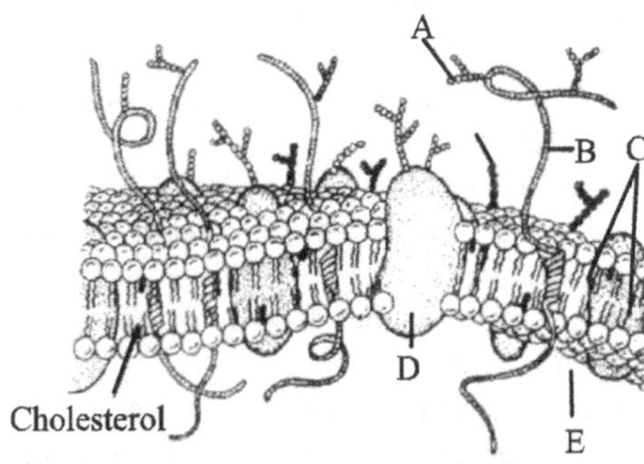

1. Which of the labelling represents the sugar ?
   (a) D   (b) C
   (c) A   (d) E

2. What is indicated by labelling E ?
   (a) Sugar   (b) Protein
   (c) Cytoplasm   (d) Lipid

3. In the given diagram, labelling D represents
   (a) Lipid bilayer of the membrane
   (b) Integral protein of the cell membrane
   (c) Cholesterol that are attached with the membrane

4. Fluidity of the cell membrane is due to
   (a) Protein   (b) Lipid
   (c) Carbohydrate   (d) All of them

5. The bilayer of the plasma membrane is made up of
   (a) Phospholipid   (b) DNA and RNA
   (c) Only protein   (d) None of them

VERY SHORT ANSWER QUESTIONS

1. Who discovered Golgi body?
2. Give the location of 70S ribosomes.
3. Name the cell organelle rich in acid hydrolases.
4. Who proposed the cell theory?
5. Expand PPLO.
6. Name the organelle responsible for protein synthesis in a cell.
7. Give the full form of SER and RER.
8. Name the membrane which surrounds the vacuole in cell.
9. Name two types of constituents of the plasma membrane.
10. Name two processes of passive transport.
11. What is plasmodesmata? What is its function?

SHORT ANSWER QUESTIONS

1. Why fluid-mosaic model is more accepted over other models of plasma membrane?
2. Name three types of elements in Golgi body. List two major functions of Golgi body.
3. What is peculiar about mitochondrial DNA?
4. How does cytokinesis take place in plant and animal cells?
5. Differentiate between prokaryotic and eukaryotic cells.
6. Differentiate between active and passive transport across the membrane.
7. Describe the different methods of transport of nutrients in cell.
8. Why are ribosomes of prokaryotes different from eukaryotes?
9. What is the function of
   (1) Nuclear Pores   (2) Slimy Capsule in Bacteria
   (3) Golgi Bodies :   (4) Centrosome with Centrioles

LONG ANSWER QUESTIONS

1. Describe the fluid mosaic model of membrane.
2. What are plastids? How are they classified on the basis of the type of pigments? Name them and their pigments and mention their functions.

Multiple Choice Questions

1. **(d)** In some prokaryotes like cyanobacteria, there are membranous extensions into the cytoplasm called chromatophores which contain pigments.
2. **(c)** Several ribosomes may attach to a single mRNA and forms a chain called polysomes. The ribosomes of a polysome translate the mRNA into proteins.
3. **(b)** Basal body is a short cylindrical array of microtubules. It is formed from a centriole and associated with the formation of cilia and flagella. It is located at the base of eukaryotic cilia and flagella, which is a continuation of the 9 outer-axonemal microtubule doublets, but with the addition of a C tubule to form a centriole-like triplet. Basal bodies may be self-replicating and serve as a nucleating centre for axonemal assembly, which are anchored in the cytoplasm by rootlets.
4. **(d)** Cell wall is a characteristic feature to cells of plants, bacteria, fungi, algae and some archaea. It is located outside the cell membrane. The major function of the cell wall is to provide rigidity, tensile strength, structural support, protection against mechanical stress and infection. It also help in diffusion of gases in and out of the cell. Gametes, *Amoeba* and Mycoplasma lack cell wall.
5. **(b)** Ribosome is sub-spherical granular structure which is devoid of any covering membrane.
6. **(a)** Microtubules occur in the cytoplasm of all eukaryotic cells. Besides cytoplasm, microtubules occur in many specialized cellular structures like cilia, flagella, basal bodies, centrioles, astral rays, spindle apparatus, chromosome fibres etc.
7. **(c)** The cytoskeleton supports the cell and allows movement of the entire cell and microtubules, motor proteins and actin filaments are part of the cytoskeleton.
8. **(c)** 9. **(b)** 10. **(c)**

Assertion & Reason Questions

1. **(a)** All the organisms that may be unicellular or multicellular are made up of one or more cells and all the metabolic functions occur in the cells. So a cell is called as the structural and functional unit of the living organisms.
2. **(c)** Ribosomes are involved in the process of protein synthesis but they are not membrane bounded.
3. **(b)** Contractile vacuoles are spherical in shape in the protozoans like amoeba and expel the excess liquid or nitrogenous waste from the body.
4. **(b)** Mitochondria, chloroplast are cell organelles that are surrounded by a double membrane. These organelles are not present in the prokaryotic cells. So they are only present in the eukaryotic cells.
5. **(d)** A chromosome is a thread like structure that are present in all types of the cells or the organisms. More than one number of chromosomes are present in animals cells as they are diploid.

Case/Passage Based Questions

1. **(c)** 2. **(c)** 3. **(a)**
4. **(b)** Fluidity of the cell membrane is due to lipid.
5. **(a)** The bilayer of the plasma membrane is made up of phospholipid.

Very Short Answer Questions

1. Camillo Golgi (1898).
2. Prokaryotic cells, plastids and mitochondria
3. Lysosomes
4. Schleiden and Schwann.
5. PPLO (Pleuro Pneumonia Like Organisms)
6. Ribosome
7. (i) SER – Smooth endoplasmic reticulum.
   (ii) RER – Rough endoplasmic reticulum.
8. Tonoplast
9. Proteins and lipids.
10. (i) Osmosis
    (ii) Diffusion
11. **Plasmodesmata :** Adjoining the cells and the linking gap of cycoplasmic protoplasmic presence is called Plasmodesmata. It links the neighbouring cells together.

Short Answer Questions

1. Fluid mosaic model explains (i) quasifluid state of plasma membrane, (ii) It differentiates two types of proteins (iii) It explains functional specificity and variability in two surfaces of PM.
2. Three types of elements in golgi body are cisternae, vesicles and vacuoles. The main function of golgi bodies are cellular secretion and acrosome formation.
3. Mitochondrial DNA is a circular double stranded and not associated with histone proteins.
4. In plant cell cytokinesis take place by cell plate formation and in animal cells it occurs by constriction.
5. The main differences between prokaryotic cell and eukaryotic cell are

	Prokaryotic cells		Eukaryotic cells
I.	These cells lack a nuclear membrane and other membrane-bound organelles.	I.	These cells have a nuclear membrane and other membrane-bound organelles.
II.	They have 70 S ribosomes.	II.	They have 80 S ribosomes.
III.	Gas vacuoles are present.	III.	Sap/food/contract-ile vacuoles are present.
IV.	Cell wall is always present and made of peptidoglycan (murein)	IV.	Cell wall is present in plant cells (cellulose), fungal cells (chitin) and some protists (cellulose) but absent in animal cells.

6. The main differences between active transport and passive transport are

	Active transport		Passive transport
I.	It refers to transport of substances with the expenditure of energy.	I.	It refers to the transport of substances without the utilisation of energy.
II.	It is more rapid.	II.	It is slow.
III.	It occurs even against concentration gradient.	III.	It occurs along the concentration gradient.
IV.	It is affected by cyanides and lack of oxygen.	IV.	It is not affected by cyanides or absence of oxygen.

7. Different methods of transport of nutrients in the cell are:

(i) **Simple diffusion :** It is the movement of ions/molecules of any substance from a region of higher concentration to the region of lower concentration, until equilibrium is reached.

Many neutral solutes move by diffusion.

(ii) **Osmosis :** It is the movement of solvent molecules across a semipermeable membrane, from the region of higher concentration to the region of lower concentration, until equilibrium is reached. Water moves by osmosis from one cell to the other.

(iii) **Facilitated diffusion :** It refers to the movement of ions/molecules across the membrane with the help of trans-membrane proteins.

8. The type of ribosomes of prokaryotes is different from eukaryotes because the prokaryotes were primitive, simpler and have remained intact during evolution while at the base level eukaryotes have adapted with the environment and are retaining their kind of entities for the complex structure. Prokaryotes have 70S ribosomes with 30S and 50S subunit and eukaryotes have 80S ribosome with 40S subunit and 60S sub unit.

9. **(1) Nuclear Pores :** There is exchange of RNA and proteins through the nuclear pores

(2) Slimy Capsule in Bacteria : A slimy capsule is the outer covering of cell wall of bacteria and is an additional protection for the bacteria.

(3) Golgi Bodies :

(i) It takes part in packaging materials delivered either to the intra-cellular targets or secteted outside the cell.

(ii) It is also a important site of formation of glycoproteins and glycolipids.

(4) Centrosome with Centrioles

(i) Centrioles help in organising the spindle fibres and astral rays during cell division.

(ii) It also provides basal bodies which give rise to cilia and flagella.

1. **The characteristic features of fluid mosaic model**

- This model was proposed by Singer and Nicholson.
- According to this model, there is a central bilipid layer (of phospholipids) with their polar head group toward the outside and the non-polar tails pointing inwards.
- Some proteins which are embedded in the lipid layer are called integral proteins and they cannot be separated from the membrane easily.
- Some large globular integral proteins which project beyond the lipid layer on both the sides are believed to have channels through which water soluble materials can pass across.
- Those proteins which are superficially attached are called peripheral (extrinsic) proteins and they can be easily removed.
- Some membrane lipids and integral proteins remain bound to oligosaccharides; such oligosaccharides project into the extracellular fluid and they influence the manner in which cells interact with the other cell.
- There are also certain specific proteins called membrane receptors, which mediate the flow of materials and information into the cell.

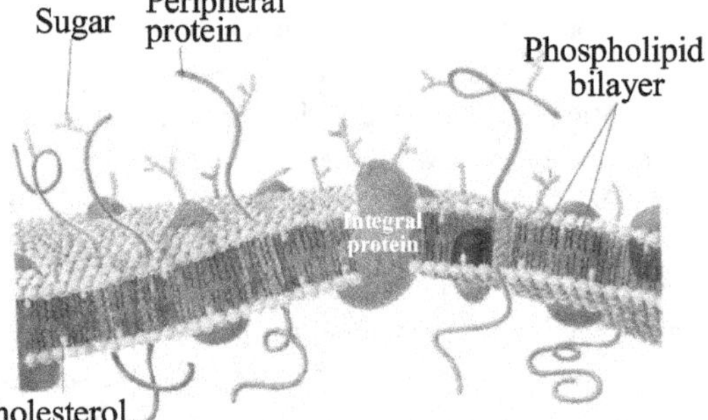

2. Plastids are double-membrane bound organelles of different shapes, that are found only in plant cells and contain pigments and storage products.

They are of three types :

(i) **Leucoplasts**

- These are the oval, spherical, rod-like or filamentous colourless plastids which are found in storage organs. Their main function is to store reserve materials like starch (amyloplasts), proteins (aleuroplasts) and fats (elaioplasts).

(ii) **Chromoplasts**

- These are coloured plastids containing mainly the yellow, red and orange pigments (carotene and xanthophyll).
- These are found in petals of flowers and skin of fruits.
- They attracts agents for pollination and dispersal of fruits/seeds.

(iii) **Chloroplasts**

- These are the green plastids containing mainly chlorophylls and very little carotene and xanthophyll.
- Their main function is photosynthesis and formation of starch.

SECTION C — NCERT EXEMPLAR QUESTIONS 

MULTIPLE CHOICE QUESTIONS

1. A common characteristic feature of plant sieve tube cells and most of mammalian erythrocytes is
   (a) absence of mitochondria
   (b) presence of cell wall
   (c) presence of haemoglobin
   (d) absence of nucleus

2. Select one which is not true for ribosomes.
   (a) Made of two subunits
   (b) Form polysome
   (c) May attach to mRNA
   (d) Have no role in protein synthesis

3. Which one of these is not a eukaryote?
   (a) *Euglena*   (b) *Anabaena*
   (c) *Spirogyra*   (d) *Agaricus*

4. Which of the following stains is not used for staining chromosomes?
   (a) Basic Fuchsin   (b) Safranin
   (c) Methylene green   (d) Carmine

5. Different cells have different sizes. Arrange the following cells in an ascending order of their size and select the correct option.
   (i) Mycoplasma
   (ii) Ostrich eggs
   (iii) Human RBCs
   (iv) Bacteria
   (a) (i)-(iv)-(iii)-(ii)   (b) (i)-(iii)-(iv)-(ii)
   (c) (ii)-(i)-(iii)-(iv)   (d) (iii)-(ii)-(i)-(iv)

6. Which of the following features is common to prokaryotes and many eukaryotes?
   (a) Chromosome present
   (b) Cell wall present
   (c) Nuclear membrane present
   (d) Subcellular organelles present

7. Who proposed the fluid mosaic model of plasma membrane?
   (a) Camillo Golgi
   (b) Schleiden and Schwann
   (c) Singer and Nicolson
   (d) Robert Brown

8. Which of the following options is true for a secretory cell?
   (a) Golgi apparatus is absent.
   (b) RER is easily observed in the cell.
   (c) Only SER is present
   (d) Secretory granules are formed in nucleus

9. What is a tonoplast?
   (a) Outer membrane of mitochondria
   (b) Inner membrane of chloroplast
   (c) Membrane boundry of the vacuole of plant cells
   (d) Cell membrane of a plant cell

10. Which of the following is not true for a eukaryotic cell?
    (a) It has 80S type of ribosome present in the mitochondria.
    (b) It has 80S type of ribosome present in the cytoplasm.
    (c) Mitochondria contain circular DNA.
    (d) Membrane bound organelles are present.

11. Which of the following statements is not true for the cell membrane?
    (a) It is present in both plant and animal cells.
    (b) Lipids are present in it as bilayer.
    (c) Proteins may be peripheral or integral in it.
    (d) Carbohydrates are never found in it.

12. Plastids differ from mitochondria on the basis of which of the following features?
    (a) Presence of two layers of membrane
    (b) Presence of ribosome
    (c) Presence of thylakoids
    (d) Presence of DNA

13. Which of the following is not a function of cytoskeleton in a cell?
    (a) Intracellular transport
    (b) Maintenance of cell shape and structure
    (c) Support of the organelles
    (d) Cell motility

14. The stain used to visualise mitochondria is
    (a) fast green   (b) safranin
    (c) acetocarmine   (d) janus green.

VERY SHORT ANSWER QUESTIONS

1. Mention a single membrane bound organelle which is rich in hydrolytic enzymes.

2. What are gas vacuoles? State their functions.

3. What is the function of a polysome? (Gk. Poly – many, Soma = body).

4. What is the feature of a metacentric chromosome?

5. What is referred to as satellite chromosome?

SHORT ANSWER QUESTIONS

1. Discuss briefly the role of nucleous in the cells activity involved in protein synthesis.

2. Explain the association of carbohydrate to the plasma membrane and its significance.

3. Briefly describe the cell theory.

4. Give the biochemical composition of plasma membrane. How are lipid molecules arranged in the membrane?

5. What are plasmids? Describe their role in bacteria.

LONG ANSWER QUESTIONS

1. Is there a species specific or region specific type of plastids? How does one distinguish one from the other?

2. Write the functions of the following
   (a) Centromere   (b) Cell wall
   (c) Smooth ER   (d) Golgi apparatus
   (e) Centrioles

SOLUTIONS

Multiple Choice Questions

1. **(d)** The mammalian RBCs lose their nuclei at maturity and live for a few months only. The food conducting phloem cells known as sieve tubes, of flowering plants also lose their nuclei at maturity but they remain functional for many years.

2. **(d)** Ribosomes are cell organelles that are formed of two subunits. Cytosolic eukaryotic ribosomes (80S) consists of 60S and 40S subunits, while prokaryotic ribosomes (70s) consists of 50S and 30S subunits.

3. **(b)** Anabaena is a cyanobacterium belonging to the kingdom *Monera*. Cyanobacteria are prokaryotes.

4. **(b)** Safranin in red colour biological stain used to strain cell wall, cell membrane and endomembranous cell organells.

5. **(a)** The smallest cells is *Mycoplasma* (0.1 - 0.5 μm). Bacterial cells are 3 - 5 μm in length. Erythrocytes are 6 - 8 μm in diameter. The largest cell is the egg of Ostrich.

6. **(b)** Cell wall is found in bacteria (prokaryotes), fungi, algae and plants (eukaryotes). Bacterial cell walls are formed of peptidoglycan. Algal cell walls are formed of glycoproteins and polysaccharides. The cell walls of fungi are formed of chitin. Plant cell walls have variety of polysaccharides, lipids, proteins, *etc*. In prokaryotes nuclear membrane, and membrane bound subcellular organelles are absent. Genetic material is naked called nucleoid.

7. **(c)** Fluid mosaic model of lipid membrane was given by Singer and Nicolson, 1972. As per to this model, the membrane does not have a uniform disposition of lipids and proteins but is instead a mosaic of the two. The membrane is not solid but is quasifluid. This nature is responsible for properties like repair, dynamic nature, ability to fuse, endocytosis *etc*.

8. **(b)** Rough endoplasmic reticulum (RER) mainly consists of cisternae. Ribosomes are attached on its cytoplasmic surface. This makes the surface look rough or granular. The RER often occurs deep in the cytoplasm. It is used to synthesize and secrete proteins.

9. **(c)** Tonoplast is a single membrane that bounds the vacuoles and separates it from cytoplasm. In plants tonoplast is a stretchy membrane, and its main function is to protect the vacuole and isolate it from harmful substances. It controls ionic movement in and around the cell.

10. **(a)** Mitochondria are semi autonomous organelles, which are double membrane-bound and have their own ribosomes (70S) and DNA (circular). A eukaryotic cell has 80S ribosomes present in the cytoplasm. Membrane-bound organelles are present, like, mitochondria, ER, Golgi apparatus, chloroplasts, etc. inside the cell. Cell wall, if present, do not contain muramic acid (therefore, peptidoglycan).

11. **(d)**

12. **(c)** Thylakoids are present in chloroplasts and absent in mitochondria. Hence, mitochondria cannot take part in converting light energy to chemical energy. Ribosomes, DNA and double membranes are present in both chloroplasts and mitochondria as they are semi-autonomous organelles. Also refer answer 6.

13. **(d)** Cytoskeletal structures are externally minute, fibrous and tubular structures which maintain cell shape and support the organelles. They also help in intracellular transport and cell mobility.

14. **(d)** Janus green is a super vital stain which is used to show that mitochondria are oxidation-reduction sites in the cell.

Very Short Answer Questions

1. The membrane bound vesicular structures formed by Golgi apparatus are Lysosomes. These vesicles have been found to be rich in all types of hydrolytic enzymes as hydrolase, lipases, proteases and carbohydrases which digest carbohydrates proteins, lipids and nucleic acid at an acidic pH.

2. Gas vacuoles also known as pseudovacuoles or air vacuoles are the characteristic feature of prokaryotes. They store metabolic gases and take part in regulation of buoyancy.

3. A polysome consists a cluster of ribosomes that are held simultaneously by a strand of messenger RNA in rosette or helical group. They contain a portion of the genetic code that each ribosome is translating and are used in formation of multiple copies of same polypeptide. They are found in the cyloplasm during the process of active protein synthesis.

4. The centromere is median, in metacentric chromo-some. The centromere lies in the middle portion and forms two equal arms of chromosome.

5. Additional constriction or secondary constriction at the chromosomal ends as distal part of the arm formed by chromatin thread are known satellite chromosomees. These constriction gives appearance of an outgrowth or a small fragment.
   These are also known as (sat) chromosomes or marker chromosomes. Chromosomes 13, 14, 15, 16, 21 and 21 satellite chromosomes.

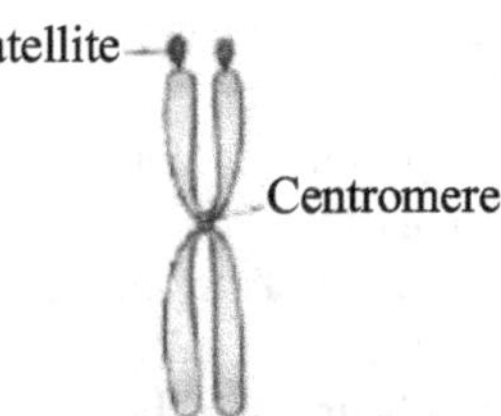

Diagram representing satellite chromosomes

Short Answer Questions

1. The round, naked and a slightly irregular structure, which is attached to the chromatin at a specific region called as **Nucleolar Organizer Region** (NOR). **Nucleous** was first discovered by Fontana (1781).

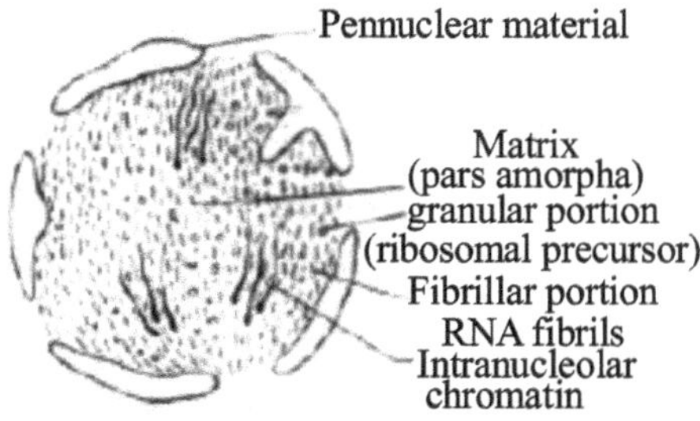

Ultrastructure of nucleolus

The role of nucleolus can be described as:

(i) Nucleolus is the chief site for the synthesis of ribosomal RNA.

(ii) It is the centre for the formation of ribosome components.

(iii) It is the colloidal complex that fills the nucleus.

(iv) It combines rRNA with proteins to produce ribosomal sub-units. The ribosomes sub-units after their formation pass out and get established in the cytoplasm.

(v) It also receives and stores ribosomal proteins formed in the cytoplasm.

(vi) These ribosomal proteins formed are the sites for protein synthesis in the cell.

(vii) Nucleolus is essential for spindle formation during nuclear division as well.

2. The plasma membrane, surrounds th cell. It consists of lipids, proteins and carbohydrates that are imperative in both structure and function of the cell.

Carbohydrates attach either with proteins or lipids usually making up less than 10% of the membrane weight. They can give rise to a wide variety of structures in relatively short chains. They give distinguishing features to individual cell types and thus they may be involved.

Cell Recognition like RBC surfaces have carbohydrates arranged in branched chains: difference in the arrangement give rise to different blood group antigens (i.e., A, B and O). Cell surface differences are also responsible for the specificity of action of cells with hormones, drugs, viruses or bacteria. The cause of difference of cell surface is related to characteristic surface due to carbohydrate component.

3. Schleiden and Schwann formulated the cell theory, in 1938-39 which stated

(i) All living beings are made up of cells and products formed by the cells.

(ii) Cells are the structural and functional units of life

The cell theory stated by Schleiden and Schwann failed to explain the question of origin of cells. A major expansion of the cell theory was expressed by Virchow in his statment 'Omnis cellula e cellula' (all cells arise from pre-existing cells) in 1855. This concept, was the actual idea of Nagelli (1846), which later on was elaborated by Virchow, along with considerable evidences in its support. The work of Nagelli and Virchow established cell division as the central pehnomenon in the continuity of life.

The modern cell theory is thus based on two facts

(i) All living organisms are composed of cells and products of cells.

(ii) Cells are the basic structural and functional units of life.

(iii) All cells arise from pre-existing cells.

Viruses are exception to cell theory as they are not composed of cell. They consist of a nucleic acid (DNA or RNA) surrounded by a protein sheet and are incapable of independant existence, self regulation and self reproduction.

4. Chemcial composition of plasma membrane includes

Component	Composition
Lipids	(20-79%)
Proteins	(20-70%)
Carbohydrates	(1-5%)
Water	20%

Lipids form the continuous structural frame of the cell membrane and hence are the major components of the cell membrane. Lipids such as phospholipids, glycolipids, and steroids are found in membranes.

The lipid molecule possess both polar hydrophilic (water loving) and non-polar hydrophobic (water repelling) ends. The hydrophilic region is in the form of a head, while the hydrophobic part contains fatty acid tails.

Hydrophobic tail is present towards the centre of the membrane. This structures results is the formation of lipid bilayer known as unit membrane/biological membrane/cell membrane. Proteins are embedded within the lipid bilayer - Carbohydrates are structure upon proteins.

5. A plasmid is usually a circular (sometimes linear), double stranted DNA that can autonomously replicate. These are found in the cytoplam of the bacterial cell. Plasmids normally remain separated from the chromosome, but sometimes may temporarily integrate into it and replicate with it incidentally.

Role and Plasmids in Bacteria

Plasmids are the extra chromosomal circular, independently replicating unit besides nucleoid in the bacterial cell. Plasmids are used to transfer information from one cell to another, i.e., transfer of important genes, enabling to metabolise a nutrient, which normally a bacteria is unable to. It also helps in conjugation of bacteria. These days plasmids are used in a variety of recombination experiments, as cloning vectors.

Long Answer Questions

1. Plastids are specific to different species and are found in all plant cells and in euglenoids. They bear certain pigments that impart specific colours to the part of the plant possesing them. Plastids ar classified into three main types, based on the type of pigments- leucoplasts, chromoplast and chloroplast.

   Leucoplasts are colourless plastids which store food material. They are of three types based on their storage products.

   (a) **Amyloplasts** store starch, e.g., tuber of potato, grain of rice, grain of wheat.

   (b) **Elaioplasts** store fats, e.g., rose

   (c) **Aleuroplasts** are protein storing plastids, e.g., castor endosperm.

   Chromoplast are non photosynthetic coloured plastids which synthesise and store carotenoid pigments. They appear orange, red or yellow. These mostly occur in ripe fruits (tomato and chilies) carrot roots, etc.

   Chloroplasts are green color plastids which help in synthesising food material by photosyntheis. They contain chrophyll and carotenoid pigments which trap light energy. Each chloroplast is oval or spherical, double membrane bound cell organelle.

   The space present inside inner membrane is called stroma. A number rof organised flattened membranous sacs called thylakoids are present in the stroma. Thylakoids are arranged in stacks called grana.

   The thylakoids of different grana are connected by membranous tubules called the stroma lamellae. The stroma of the lamellae contain the enzymes that are required for the synthesis of carbohydrates and proteins.

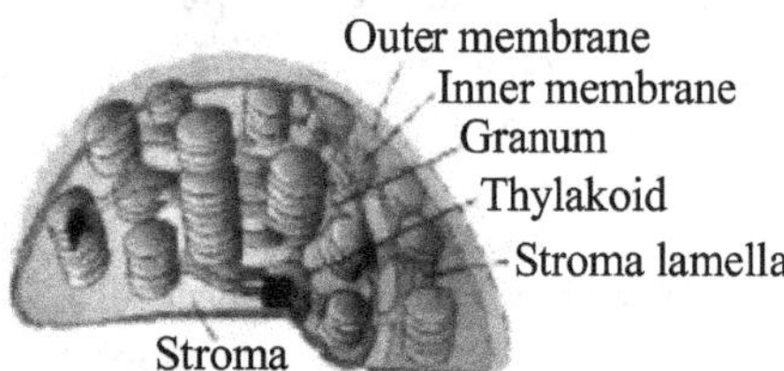

   Structure of chloroplast

2. (a) Centromere is required for proper chromosome segregation. The centromere consists of two sister chromatids. It is also necessary for attachment of chromosomes to the spindle apparatus during mitosis and meiosis.

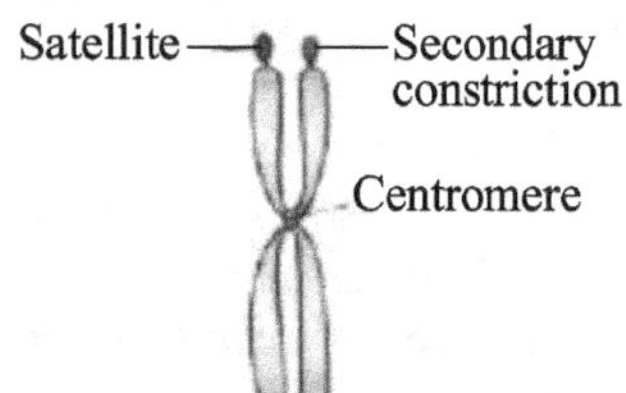

   Centromeres

   (b) **Cell wall** gives a definite shape to the cell and protects the cell from mechanical injury and infections. It also aids in cell to cell interaction and acts as a barrier for undesirable macromolecules.

   (c) **Smooth ER** helps in synthesis of lipids, metabolism of carbohydrates, regulation of calcium concentration, drug detoxification and attachment of receptors on cell membrane proteins.

   The smooth ER also contains enzymes-glucose 6 phosphatase, which converts glucose 6 phosphate to glucose essential in glucose metabolism.

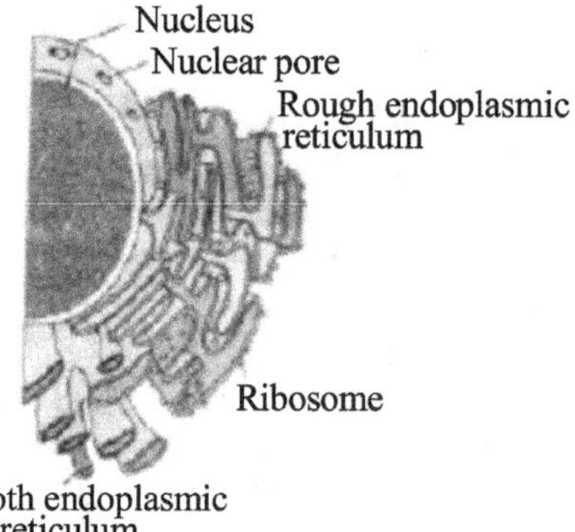

   (d) **Golgi apparatus** is an important site for the formation of glycoprotein and glycolipids also involved in the synthesis of cell wall materials and plays an important role in formation of cell plate during cell divisionas well.

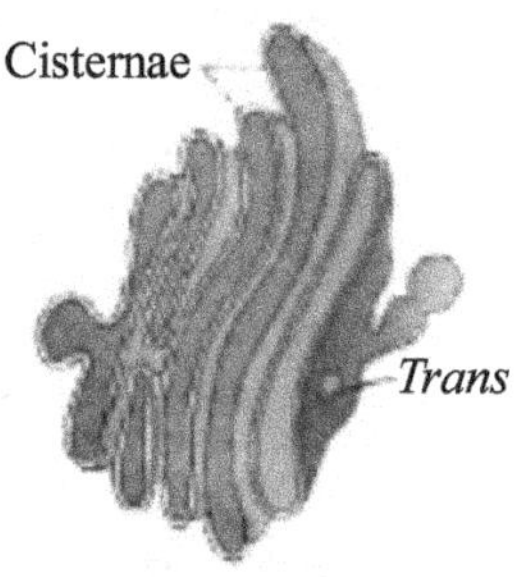

   Structure of Golgi body

   (e) **Centrioles** form the base body of cilla and flagella and spindle fibres that gives rise to spindle apparatus during cell division in animal cells. They help in formation of microtubules and sperm tail. They also help in cell division by forming asters, which acts as spindle pole.

Biomolecules

9.1 **What are macromolecules? Give examples.**

Sol. Biomacromolecules are found in acid insoluble fraction. They are polymeric compounds *e.g.,* polysaccharides, proteins and nucleic acids. They have high molecular weight more than 1000 Daltons.

9.2 **Illustrate a glycosidic, peptide and a phospho-diester bond.**

Sol. **Peptide bond :** In a polypeptide or a protein, amino acids are linked by a peptide bond which is formed when the carboxyl (COOH) group of one amino acid reacts with the amino (NH_2) group of the next amino acid with the removal of water molecule.

Glycosidic bond : In a polysaccharide the individual monosaccharides are linked by glycosidic bond. This bond is also formed by dehydration. This bond is formed between two carbon atoms of two adjacent monosaccharides.

Phosphodiester bond : In a nucleic acid, a phosphate moiety links the 3'-carbon of one sugar of one nucleotide to the 5'-carbon of the sugar of the succeeding nucleotide. The bond between phosphate and hydroxyl group of sugar is an ester bond. As there is one such ester bond on either side, it is called phosphodiester bond.

9.3 **What is meant by tertiary structure of proteins?**

Sol. **Tertiary structure of protein :** When the individual peptide chains of secondary structure of protein are further extensively coiled and folded into sphere like shapes with the hydrogen bonds between the amino and carboxyl group and various other kinds of bonds cross linking on chain to another they form tertiary structure.

The ability of proteins to carry out specific reactions is the result of their primary, secondary and tertiary structure.

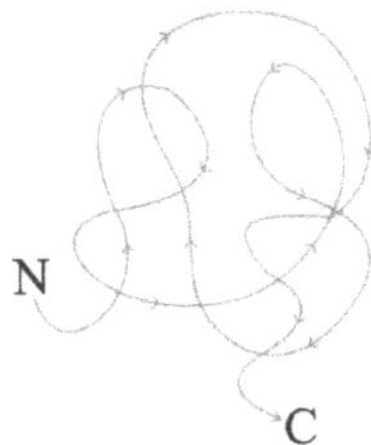

Fig. A tertiary structure of proteins

9.4 **Find and write down structures of 10 interesting small molecular weight biomolecules. Find if there is any industry which manufactures the compounds by isolation. Find out who are the buyers?**

Sol. (1)

Glucose ($C_6H_{12}O_6$)

(2) Ribose ($C_5H_{10}O_5$)

(3)
$$H - \overset{\overset{COOH}{|}}{\underset{\underset{H}{|}}{C}} - NH_2$$
Glycine

(4)
$$H - \overset{\overset{COOH}{|}}{\underset{\underset{CH_2}{|}}{C}} - NH_2$$
Alanine

(5)
$$H - \overset{\overset{COOH}{|}}{\underset{\underset{CH_2OH}{|}}{C}} - NH_2$$
Serine

(6)
$$R_2 - \overset{O}{\overset{||}{C}} - O - CH \begin{matrix} CH_2 - O - \overset{O}{\overset{||}{C}} - R_1 \\ CH_2 - O - \overset{\underset{OH}{|}}{\overset{O}{\overset{||}{P}}} - O - CH_2 - CH_2 - N^+(CH_3)_3 \end{matrix}$$
Phospholipid

(7) CH_2-OH
      $|$
      $CH-OH$
      $|$
      CH_2-OH
      Glycerol

(8) $CH_3-(CH_2)_{14}-COOH$
      Fatty acid
      (Palmitic acid)

(9)   HOH$_2$C ... O ... Adenine
      OH   OH
      Adenosine

(10) $HO-\overset{O}{\underset{O}{P}}-O-CH_2$ ... O ... Adenine
      OH   OH
      Adenylic acid
      Nucleotide

Fat is being manufactured by many companies in pharmaceuticals business as well as in food business. Vitamins come in many combination and are being used as supplementary medicines. Lactose is made by companies in manufacturing baby food. All of us are buyers of fat, protein and lactose.

9.5 **Proteins have primary structures. If you are given a method to know which amino acid is at either of two termini (ends) of a protein, can you connect this information to purity or homogeneity of a protein?**

Sol. In primary structure proteins have linear arrangement of aminoacids. Because proteins are made up of 20 different types of amino acids we can not make statement of purity or homogeneity only by knowing the terminal amino acids.

9.6 **Find out and make a list of protein used as therapeutic agents. Find other applications of proteins (e.g., Cosmetics etc.)**

Sol. **Therapeutic Agents :**

Contraceptive pills : As they are hormones so they are made up of protein.

Nutritional Supplements : Many brands are available as protein supplements.

Example : Protinex

Other use : Chicken cubes are used in making soups and dishes.

9.7 **Explain the composition of triglyceride.**

Triglycerides are esters of three molecules of fatty acids and one molecule of glycerol.

$$R_2-\overset{O}{\overset{||}{C}}-O-\overset{CH_2-O-\overset{O}{\overset{||}{C}}-R_1}{\underset{CH_2-O-\overset{O}{\overset{||}{C}}-R_3}{CH}}$$

Triglyceride

(R_1, R_2 and R_3 are fatty acid)

9.8 **Can you describe what happens when milk is converted into curd or yoghurt, from your understanding of proteins.**

Sol. When milk is converted into yoghurt or curd then coagulation of milk protein *i.e.*, casein occurs. Casein is converted to paracaesin in the formation of curd.

9.9 **Can you attempt building models of biomolecules using commercially available atomic models (Ball and Stick model).**

Sol. Yes, Three dimensional structure of cellulose can be made using balls and sticks. Similarly, models of other bimolecular can be made.

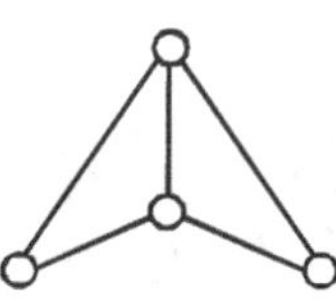

Ball and stick model

9.10 **Attempt titrating an amino acid against a weak base and discover the number of dissociating (ionizable) functional groups in the amino acid.**

Sol. When an amino acid is titrated with weak base then its-COOH group also acts as weak acid. So it forms a salt with weak base then the pH of the resulting solution is near 7, so there is no sudden change. Number of dissociating functional groups are two, one is amino group (NH_2) and another is carboxylic group (–COOH). In the titration amino acid acts as indicator. Amino acids in solution acts as basic or acidic as situation demands. So these are also called amphipathic molecules.

9.11 **Draw the structure of the amino acid, alanine.**

Sol.

$C^{\alpha}H_3$
$|$
$H^{\alpha}C^{\alpha}$
^+H_3N COO^-
L-α-alanine

$^+H_3N\diagdown C^{\beta}H_2$
$H^{\alpha2}C^{\alpha}$
$H^{\alpha1}$ COO^-
β-alanine

Structure of alanine

9.12 **What are gums made of? Is fevicol different?**

Sol. The gums are made of lignocellulose which is secreted in the form of resin from resin ducts of plant. It is an adhesive substance which is used in artificial adhesion of different substances. It is capable of causing a large viscosity in solution. Fevicol is different from gums as it is a artificial substance. Fevicol is a synthetic glue. These adhesives are a mixture of ingredients (typically polymers) dissolved in a solvent. As the solvent evaporates, the adhesive hardens. Depending on the chemical composition of the adhesive, they will adhere to different materials to greater or lesser degrees. These adhesives are typically weak and are used for household applications.

9.13 **Find out a qualitative test for proteins, fats and oils, amino acid and test any fruit juice, saliva, sweat and urine for them.**

Sol. Qualitative Tests for proteins, amino acids and fats :

Biuret Test : Biuret test for protein indentifies presence of protein by producing violet colour of solution. Biuret $H_2NCONHCONH_2$, reacts with copper ion in a basic solution and gives violet colour.

Liebermann-Burchard Test for cholesterol: This is a mixture of acidic anhydride and sulphuric acid. This gives a green colour when mixed with cholesterol.

Grease Test for oil : Certain oils gives a translucent stain on clothes. This test can be used to show presence of fat in vegetable oils.

These tests can be performed to check presence of proteins and amino acids and fats in any of the fluid mentioned in the question.

9.14 Find out how much cellulose is made by all the plants in the biosphere and compare it with how much of paper is manufactured by man and hence what is the consumption of plant material by man annually. What a loss of vegetation?

Sol. According to a 2006 report from the UN, forests store about 312 billion tons of carbon in their biomass alone. If you add to that the carbon in deadwood, litter, and forest soil, the figure increases to about 1.1 trillion tons! The UN assessment also shows that the destruction of forests adds almost 2.2 billion tons of carbon to the atmosphere each year, the equivalent of what the U.S. emits annually. Many climate experts believe that the preservation and restoration of forests offers one of the least expensive and best ways to fight against climate change.

Although it is difficult to get exact data about the quantum of cellulose produced by plants, but above information can give some idea. About 10% of cellulose is used in paper making. The percentage is less but wrong practice of cutting wood and re-plantation makes the problem complicated. Usually older trees are cut for large quantity of cellulose and re-plantation is limited to selected species of plants. Selected species disturbs the biodiversity as it leads to monoculture.

Add to this the problem of effluents coming out of a paper factory and the problem further aggravates.

9.15 Describe the important properties of enzymes.

Sol. Properties of enzymes are as following
- Lowering the activation energy
- Lowering the energy of the transition state
- Providing an alternative pathway
- Reducing the reaction entropy change
- Increases in temperatures speed up reactions
- Unique enzyme for unique substance
- Small quantity is enough to facilitate faster reaction.

SECTION B — PRACTICE QUESTIONS

MULTIPLE CHOICE QUESTIONS

1. The acid used for preliminary separation of biomolecule in a living tissue is
   (a) trichlorobenzoic acid   (b) benzoic acid
   (c) trichloroacetic acid   (d) acetic acid
2. Building block of nucleic acid is __________ .
   (a) nucleotide   (b) nucleoside
   (c) amino acid   (d) fatty acid
3. All the following amino acids are aromatic, except
   (a) tyrosine   (b) phenylalanine
   (c) tryptophan   (d) valine
4. Unsaturated fatty acids have
   (a) palmitic acid   (b) oleic acid
   (c) high melting point   (d) one or more double bonds
5. In the composition of cellular mass, arrange the components- proteins(P), carbohydrates (C), lipids(L) and nucleic acids(N) in decreasing order of mass percentage.
   (a) $C > N > P > L$ (b) $P > N > C > L$
   (c) $P > C > L > N$ (d) $P > N > L > C$
6. Inulin is a polymer of
   (a) glucose   (b) galactose
   (c) fructose   (d) arabinose
7. Which of the following sets contains polysaccharides?
   (a) Glucose, fructose, lactose
   (b) Starch, glycogen, cellulose
   (c) Sucrose, maltose, cellulose
   (d) Galactose, starch, sucrose
8. Which of the following statement is wrong regarding chitin?
   (a) It is a storage polysaccharide.
   (b) It is a heteropolysaccharide.
   (c) It is a constituent of arthropods and fungal cell wall.
   (d) It is a second most abundant carbohydrate on earth.

9. The catalytic efficiency of two different enzymes can be compared by the
   (a) Km value.
   (b) pH optimum value.
   (c) formation of the product.
   (d) molecular size of the enzyme.
10. At temperature near freezing point, the enzymes are
   (a) inactivated
   (b) activated
   (c) slightly activated
   (d) slightly inactivated

ASSERTION & REASON QUESTIONS

DIRECTION (Qs. 1-5) : *These questions consists of two statements. Answer these questions selecting the appropriate option given below:*
(a) Both Assertion (A) and Reason (R) are true and Reason (R) is the correct explanation of Assertion (A).
(b) Both Assertion (A) and Reason (R) are true, but Reason (R) is not the correct explanation of Assertion (A).
(c) Assertion (A) is true, but Reason (R) is false.
(d) Assertion (A) is false, but Reason (R) is true.

1. **Assertion:** A fatty acid has a carboxyl group attached to an R group.
   Reason: Glycerol is a simple lipid, which is chemically trihydroxy methane.
2. **Assertion:** Phenyalanine and tryptophan are aromatic amino acids.
   Reason: Aromatic groups are present in the side chain of phenylalanine and tryptophan.

3. **Assertion:** Starch and cellulose are type of homopoly-saccharides.
   Reason: They are made up of same type of mono-saccharides.
4. **Assertion:** Protein part of enzyme is called as cofactor.
   Reason: Coenzyme is small organic molecule.
5. **Assertion:** Rate of reaction is increased by an enzyme.
   Reason: Enzyme decreases the activation energy of reaction.

CASE/PASSAGE BASED QUESTIONS

DIRECTIONS (Qs. 1-5) : *Read the following passage and answer the questions that follows.*

All molecules require some amount of energy to overcome energy barrier before they can react. Enzymes lowes the activation energy and speed up the reaction. The given figure labelled as A, B, C and D and represents the conversion of a substrate into product by the action of an enzyme. Observe the diagram and answers the questions.

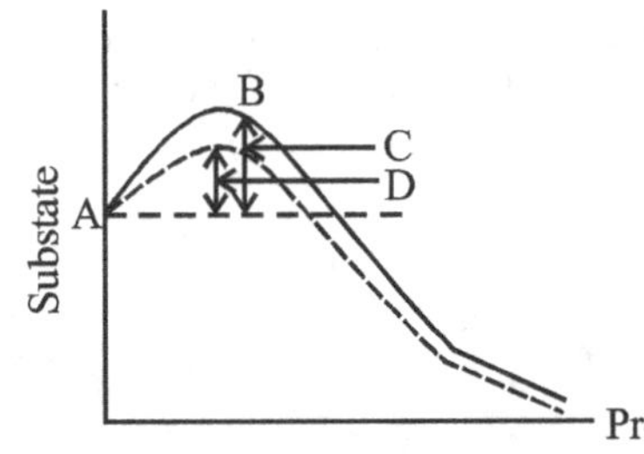

1. Which of the labelling represent the activation energy with enzyme?
   (a) A   (b) B & C   (c) D   (d) B
2. What is indicated by the labelling B?
   (a) Potential energy   (b) Transition state
   (c) Activation energy   (d) None of them
3. Which of the following statement is true about Activation energy ?
   (a) The minimum amount of energy that requires to initiate a reaction.
   (b) The energy which slow the reaction.
   (c) The amount of energy that stop the reaction.
   (d) All of them
4. Activation energy without enzyme is indicated by labelling
   (a) B   (b) D   (c) A   (d) C
5. What is represent by the given diagram?
   (a) Conversion of a substrate into product
   (b) Dissociation of product
   (c) No reaction takes place
   (d) All of them

VERY SHORT ANSWER QUESTIONS

1. Which organic compound is commonly called animal starch?
2. What are building blocks of nucleic acids?
3. Name one basic amino acid.
4. Name one heteropolysaccharide.
5. Name the biomolecules present in the acid insoluble fraction.
6. Which protein molecule does catalyse biochemical reactions?
7. Name three pyrimidines.
8. Which enzyme does catalyse covalent bonding between two molecules to form a large molecule?
9. On reaction with iodine starch turns blue black, why ?
10. Which type of bonds are found in proteins and polysaccharides?
11. Name one neutral amino acid.
12. Name one phospholipid found in cell membrane.
13. Name two different kinds of metabolism.

SHORT ANSWER QUESTIONS

1. Which type of bonds are found in nucleic acids?
2. What are triglycerides?
3. What are fatty acids ? Give two examples.
4. What are co-enzymes ? Give two examples.
5. (i)   What is meant by complementary base pairing ?
   (ii) What is the distance between two successive bases in a strand of DNA?
   (iii) How many base pairs are present in one turn of the helix of a DNA strand?
6. Differentiate between DNA and RNA.
7. Where are the following found ?
   Glycosidic bonds, ester bonds, peptide bonds, energy rich bonds, double bonds.
8. Differentiate between essential amino acids and non essential amino acids
9. Differentiate between Structural Proteins and Functional Proteins
10. What is activation energy ?
11. What is competitive inhibition?

LONG ANSWER QUESTIONS

1. Distinguish between primary, secondary and tertiary structure of proteins.
2. Explain the effect of following factors on enzyme activity:
   (i) Temperature (ii) pH.
3. What are the different kind of enzymes? Mention with enzymes examples.

SOLUTIONS

Multiple Choice Questions

1. **(c)** In order to study the various biomolecules found in living tissues, the living tissues are ground in trichloroacetic acid using a mortar and a pestle to form a thick soup. It is then strained to obtain two fractions : acid soluble and acid insoluble fraction. Chemicals present in both the fractions are further separated by various analytical techniques and identified.

2. **(a)** DNA and RNA are made up of nucleic acids. They are the vehicles of genetic inheritance. Building blocks of nucleic acids are called nucleotides. Each nucleotide consists of three parts: a sugar (ribose for RNA and deoxyribose for DNA), a phosphate, and a nitrogenous base. These nucleotides linked together with covalent bonds to form a sugar-phosphate backbone with extended nitrogenous bases.

3. **(d)** Aromatic amino acid possess cyclic structure with a straight side chain bearing carboxylic and amino group. Valine is a neutral amino acid. It contains equal number of amino and carboxylic groups.

4. **(d)** Saturated fatty acids do not have any double bond while unsaturated fatty acids have one or more double bonds.

5. **(b)** In the comparison of cellular mass, the decreasing order of the components is:
P (Protein):10 – 15% >N (Nucleic acid): 5 – 7 % > C (Carbohydrates): 3% > L (Lipid): 2%

6. **(c)** Inulin is a heterogeneous collection of fructose polymers. It consists of glucosyl moiety and fructosyl moiety, which are linked by β (2, 1) bonds. It is a soluble dietary fibre which is a naturally occurring oligosaccharide belonging to a group of carbohydrates known as fructans. Unlike most carbohydrates, inulin is non-digestible.
Inulin is naturally present in many different foods such as asparagus, leek, onions, banana, wheat and garlic. Higher concentrations exist in herbs.

7. **(b)**

8. **(a)** Chitin is a long-chain polymer of a Nacetylglucosamine, a derivative of glucose. It is a characteristic component of the cell walls of fungi, exoskeletons of arthropods such as crustaceans (e.g., crabs, lobsters and shrimps) and insects, the radulae of molluscs, and the beaks and internal shells of cephalopods, including squid and octopuses.

9. **(a)** The catalytic efficiency of two different enzymes can be compared by the Km value. Km is the Michaelis-Menten constant. It is the substrate concentration at which an enzyme attains half its maximal velocity.

10. **(a)** Temperature affects activity of enzyme. At very low temperature (almost near freezing point) the enzymes are inactivated whereas high temperature denatures enzymes permanently. Temperature ranges for maximum functioning of enzyme is 25 – 40 degree Celsius.

Assertion & Reason Questions

1. **(c)** Lipids are simple fatty acids. They contain carboxyl group that is attached to an - group. Glycerol is a simple lipid that is made of trihydroxypropane.

2. **(a)** Phenyalanine, tryptophan and tyrosine contain a benzene ring in the side chain. So they are called as aromatic amino acids.

3. **(a)** Starch and cellulose are polysaccharides that are made up of same type of monosaccharides that are glucoses.

4. **(d)** The proteinous part of the enzyme is called as apoenzyme. Co-enzyme is a type of cofactor in which small organic molecule is present.

5. **(b)** Enzyme is a type of biological catalyst that increases the rate of reaction by reducing the activation energy.

Case/Passage Based Questions

1. **(c)** Labelling D represent activation energy with enzyme.
2. **(b)** Transition state incidate by labelling B.
3. **(a)**
4. **(d)** Labelling C indicated the activation energy without enzyme.
5. **(a)**

Very Short Answer Questions

1. Glycogen
2. Nucleotides.
3. Lysine.
4. Chitin
5. Protein, polysaccharide, nucleic acid and lipids.
6. Enzymes.
7. Thymine, cytosine and uracil
8. Ligases.
9. Appearance of blue colour with the addition of iodine is due to its reaction with amylose fraction of starch.
10. Peptides bonds in protein and glycosidic bonds in polysaccharides.
11. Valine.
12. Lecithin
13. Anabolism and catabolism.

Short Answer Questions

1. Phosphodiester bond.
2. In a triglyceride three similar or different fatty acids are attached to three hydroxyl groups of glycerol by ester bond.
3. Fatty acids are compounds which have a carboxyl group attached to an R-group, which could be a methyl (CH_3), or ethyl (C_2H_5) group or a higher number of CH_2 groups *e.g.*, Linoleic acid, Palmitic acid.
4. Coenzymes are the non-protein organic compounds bound to the apoenzyme in a conjugate enzyme, their association with the apoenzyme is only transient. *e.g.*, Nicotinamide adenine dinucleotide (NAD). Flavin adenine dinucleotide (FAD), Nicotinamide adenine dinucleotide phosphate (NADP).
5. (i) Complementary base pairing is the type of pairing in DNA, where a purine always pairs with a pyrimidine, i.e., adenine pairs with thymine (A=T) and guanine pairs with cytosine (G≡C).
   (ii) 0.34 nm or 34 Å is distance between two successive bases in the strand of DNA
   (iii) 10 base pairs
6. The main differences between DNA and RNA are as following

	DNA		RNA
1.	It is a double-standed molecule	1.	It is a single-standed molecule.
2.	It has thymine and cytosine as pyrimidine bases.	2.	It has uracil and cytosine as pyrimidine bases.
3.	It has deoxyribose sugar.	3.	It has ribose sugar.

7. (i) **Glycosidic bonds :** Disaccharides.
   (ii) **Ester bond :** Between glycerols and fatty acids.
   (iii) **Peptide bond :** Proteins
   (iv) **Energy rich bond :** ATP
   (v) **Double bond :** Unsaturated fatty acids.

8. **Essential Amino Acids**
   The amino acids that are not synthesized in the body and required in our diet are essential amino acids Examples are : Alanine Tyrosine, Valine, Histidine

   Non Essential Amino Acids
   The amino acids present in the body, not required in our diet are non-essential amino acids. Examples are : Serine, aspartic acid.

9. **Structural Proteins**
   The Building materials needed for growth, repair reproduction and function are structural proteins Example : Keratin, Collagen

   Functional Proteins
   Proteins that act as regulator of the body functions and metabolism are functional proteins Example : enzymes and homones (Insulin)

10. Activation Energy : An energy barrier is required for the reactant molecules for their activation. So this energy with enzyme substrate reaction is called Activation energy.

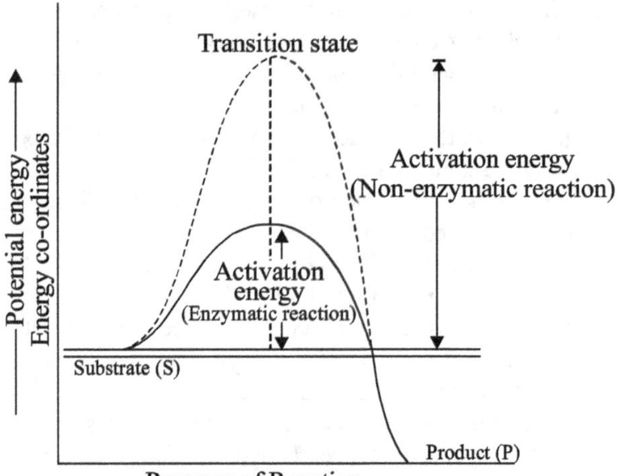

The activation energy is low for reactions with catalysts [enzymes] than those with Non enzymatic reactions.

11. Competitive Inhibition :
    When in a biochemical reaction an inhibitor has close structure with the substrate and it binds to the enzyme rather then the other substrate.
    This process of competition between the inhibitor substrate for the active site is called competitive inhibition.
    e.g. in kreb's Cycle, malonale completes with Suecinate for the active site of suecinate dehydrobenase.

Long Answer Questions

1.

Primary structure of protein		Secondary structure of protein		Tertiary structure of protein
1.	Proteins are made of amino acids which have carboxyl group(COOH) and amino (group) (NH_2). The COOH end of an amino acid is joined to NH_2 end of the other amino acid. Many amino acids are joined by peptide bonds which held them together in a particular sequence and constitute the primary structure of proteins. This structure does not make a protein functional.	1. A functional protein has 3-dimensional configuration. It has one or more polypeptide chains. The sequence of amino acids determines where the chain will bend through the formation of H-bonds peptide chains assume secondary structure of proteins may be in the form of twisted helix or pleated sheet.		1. When individual peptide chains of secondary structure of protein are further coiled and folded into sphere like shapes with the H-bonds between NH_2 and COOH groups and various other kinds of bonds cross linking on chain to another they form tertiary structure.
2.	It is linear sequence of amino acids.	2. Have α helices and β-sheets held in place of amino acids.		2. Final folding and twisting of polypeptide.

2. **Temperature :** An enzyme is active within a narrow range of temperature. The temperature at which an enzyme shows its highest activity is called optimum temperature.
   It generally corresponds to the body temperature of warm blood animals *e.g.*, 37°C in human beings. Enzyme activity decreases above and below this temperature. Enzyme become inactive below minimum temperature and beyond maximum temperature. Low temperature present inside cold storage prevents spoilage of food. High temperature destroys enzymes by causing their denaturation.

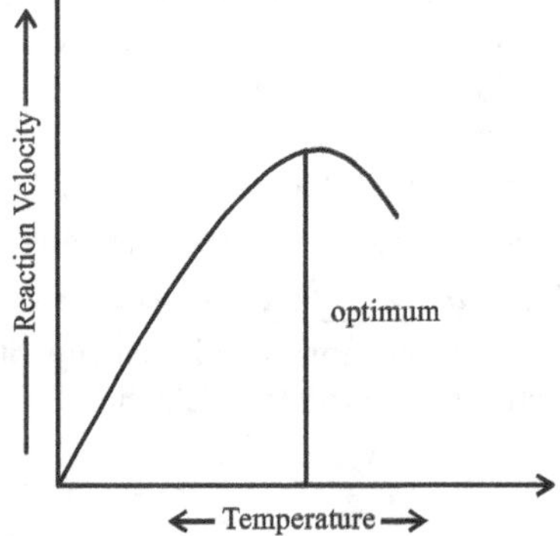

Relation between temperature and enzyme controlled reaction velocity

pH – Every enzyme has an optimum pH when it is most effective. A rise or fall in pH reduces enzyme activity by changing the degree of ionisation of its side chains. A change on pH may also reverse reaction. Most of the intracellular enzymes function near neutral pH with the exception of several digestive enzymes which work either in acidic range of pH or alkaline range of pH. pH for trypsin is 8.5.

3. Enzymes with substrate bonds are broken and changed to different kinds as :–

(1) **Oxidoreductases :** eg Alcohol dehydrogenase, oxidation, Reduction occurs
(2) **Transferases :** transfer a particlar group to another substrate. eg. transavninase
(3) **Hydrolases :** cleave their substrates by hydrolysis of a covalent bond e.g. Urease, amylase.
(4) **Lyases :** break the covalent bond eg. Diaminase
(5) **Isomerase :** by changing the bonds they make isomers. eg: Aldolase.
(6) **Ligase :** These bind two substrate molecules eg : DNA ligase, RNA ligase

SECTION C — NCERT EXEMPLAR QUESTIONS 

MULTIPLE CHOICE QUESTIONS

1. It is said that elemental composition of living organisms and that of inanimate objects (like earth's crust) are similar in the sense that all the major elements are present in both. Then what would be the difference between these two groups? Choose a correct answer from the following.
   (a) Living organisms have more gold in them than inanimate objects.
   (b) Living organisms have more water in their body than inanimate objects.
   (c) Living organisms have more carbon, oxygen and hydrogen per unit mass than inanimate objects.
   (d) Living organisms have more calcium in them than inanimate objects.

2. Many elements are found in living organisms either free or in the form of compounds. One of the following is not found in living organisms.
   (a) Silicon   (b) Magnesium
   (c) Iron   (d) Sodium

3. Amino acids, as the name suggests, have both an amino group and a carboxyl group in their structure. In addition, all naturally occurring aminoacids (those which are found in proteins) are called L-amino acids. From this, can you guess from which compound can the simplest amino acid be made?
   (a) Formic acid   (b) Methane
   (c) Phenol   (d) Glycine

4. Many organic substances are negatively charged e.g., acetic acid, while others are positively charged e.g., ammonium ion. An amino acid under certain conditions would have both positive and negative charges simultaneously in the same molecule. Such a form of amino acid is called
   (a) Positively charged form
   (b) Negatively charged form
   (c) Neutral form
   (d) Zwitterionic form

5. Which of the following sugars have the same number of carbon as present in glucose?
   (a) Fructose   (b) Erythrose
   (c) Ribulose   (d) Ribose

6. When you take cells or tissue pieces and grind them with an acid in a mortar and pestle, all the small biomolecules dissolve in the acid. Proteins, polysaccharides and nucleic acids are insoluble in mineral acid and get precipitated. The acid soluble compounds include amino acids, nucleosides, small sugars etc. When one adds a phosphate group to a nucleoside one gets another acid soluble biomolecule called
   (a) Nitrogen base   (b) Adenine
   (c) Sugar phosphate   (d) Nucleotide

7. When we homogenise any tissue in an acid the acid soluble pool represents
   (a) cytoplasm   (b) cell membrane
   (c) nucleus   (d) mitochondria.

8. The most abundant chemical in living organisms could be
   (a) protein   (b) water
   (c) sugar   (d) nucleic acid.

9. A homopolymer has only one type of building block called monomer repeated 'n' number of times. A heteropolymer has more than one type of monomer. Proteins are heteropolymer usually made of
   (a) 20 types of monomers (b) 40 types of monomers
   (c) 30 types of monomers (d) only one type of monomer.

10. Proteins perform many physiological functions. For example some proteins function as enzymes. One of the following represents an additional function that some protein discharge
   (a) antibiotics
   (b) pigment conferring colour to skin
   (c) pigment making colours of flowers
   (d) hormones.

11. Glycogen is a homopolymer made up of
   (a) glucose units   (b) galactose units
   (c) ribose units   (d) amino acids.

12. The number of 'ends' in a glycogen molecule would be
  (a) equal to the number of branches plus one
  (b) equal to the number of branch points
  (c) one
  (d) two, one on the left side and another on the right side.

13. The primary structure of a protein molecule has
  (a) two ends   (b) one end
  (c) three ends   (d) no ends.

14. Enzymes are biocatalysts. They catalyse biochemical reactions. In general they reduce activation energy of reactions. Many physico-chemical processes are enzyme mediated. Some examples of enzyme mediated reactions are given below. Tick the wrong entry
  (a) Dissolving CO_2 in water
  (b) Unwining the two strands of DNA
  (c) Hydrolysis of sucrose
  (d) Formation of peptide bond

VERY SHORT ANSWER QUESTIONS

1. Medicines are either man made (i.e. synthetic) or obtained from living organisms like plants, bacteria, animals, etc., and hence, the latter are called natural products. Sometimes, natural products are chemically altered by man to reduce toxicity or side effects. Write against each of the following whether they were initially obtained as a natural product or as 3 synthetic chemical.
  (a) Penicillin   (b) Sulphonamide
  (c) Vitamin-C   (d) Growth hormone

2. Write the name of any one amino acid, sugar, nucleotide and fatty acid.

3. Reaction given below is catalysed by oxidoreductase between two substrates A and A', complete the reaction.
A reduced + A' oxidised →

4. How are prosthetic groups different from co-factors?

5. Glycine and alanine are different with respect to one substituent on the α-carbon. What are the other common substituent groups?

SHORT ANSWER QUESTIONS

1. Enzymes are proteins. Proteins are long chains of amino acids linked to each, other by peptide bonds. Amino acids have many functional groups in their structure.

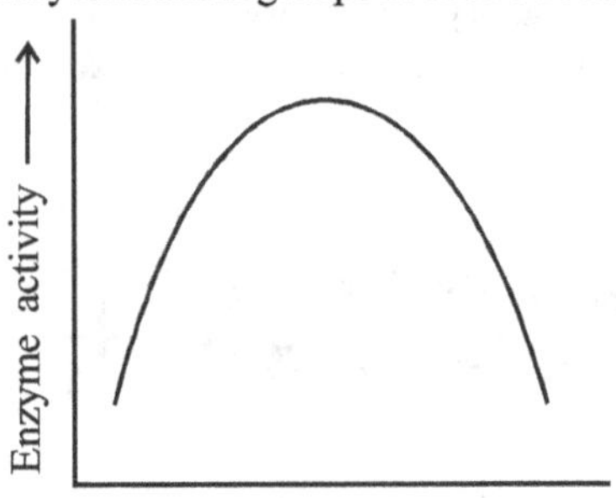

These functional groups are many of them at least, ionisable. As they are peak acids and bases in chemical nature, this ionisation is influenced by pH of the solution. For many enzymes, activity is influenced by surrounding pH. This is depicted in the curve below, explain briefly.

2. Is rubber a primary metabolite or a secondary metabolite? Write four sentences about rubber.

3. Nucleic acids exhibit secondary structure, justify with example.

4. Comment on the statement 'living state is a non-equilibrium steady state to be able to perform work'.

LONG ANSWER QUESTIONS

1. What are different classes of enzymes? Explain any two with the type of reactions they catalyse.

SOLUTIONS

Multiple Choice Questions

1. **(c)** A comparison of elements present in non-living and living matter is given in the table below:

Element	% weight of	
	Earth crust (non living matter)	Human body (living matter)
Hydrogen	0.14	0.5
Carbon	0.03	18.5
Oxygen	46.6	65.5
Nitrogen	very little	3.3
Sulphur	0.03	0.3
Sodium	20.8	0.2
Calcium	30.6	1.5
Magnesium	2.1	0.1
Silicon	27.7	negligible

2. **(a)** Various mineral elements present in living organisms include (i) major minerals (macro minerals)- Calcium (Ca), Chlorine (Cl), Magnesium (Mg), Phosphorus (P), Sodium (Na), Potassium (K), Sulphur (S) and (ii) trace minerals (micro minerals)- Chromium (Cr), Cobalt (Co), Copper (Cu), Fluorine (F), Iodine (I), Iron (Fe), Manganese (Mn), Molybdenum (Mo), Selenium (Se) and Zinc (Zn).

3. **(d)** Glycine is the simplest amino acid with hydrogen as R group. Formic acid is simplest carboxylic acid molecule. It is chemically HCOOH. Glycerol is a polyol compound, which is chemically propane-1, 2, 3-triol and glycolic acid is chemically, 2-hydroxyethanoic acid.

4. **(d)**

$$R - \overset{\overset{\displaystyle H}{|}}{\underset{\underset{\displaystyle NH_3^+}{|}}{C}} - COO^-$$

Zwitterion (isoelectric pH)

In neutral solution, an amino acid molecule exists as a dipolar ion (zwitter ion) i.e., molecule containing positive and negative ionic groups. The charge on the ion changes with pH. In an acid solution (low pH) the amino acid picks up H^+ ions and becomes positively charged. In alkaline solution (high pH) the amino acid donates H^+ ions to the medium and becomes negatively charged. The pH at which the amino acid is electrically neutral or the molecule exists as a zwitterion is called the isoelectric pH.

5. **(a)** Fructose and glucose, both are six carbon sugars having formula $C_6H_{12}O_6$. Erythrose is a four carbon sugar. Ribulose and Ribose are both five carbon sugars.

6. **(d)** Nucleoside is basically sugar + nitrogenous base. Nucleotide is sugar + nitrogenous base + phosphate. DNA and RNA are composed of nucleotides.

7. **(a)** The acid soluble pool has roughly similar composition as of cytoplasm. Biomolecules with molecular weights in the range of 18 - 800 Daltons come in acid-soluble fraction (with the exception of lipids). Though, the macromolecules from cytoplasm and organelles represent the acid-insoluble fraction.

8. **(b)** Approx 70% of living orgamisms' body weight is water.

9. **(a)** The function and shape of a protein is affected by sequence of 20 types of amino acids, each having an amino group $–NH_2$, a carboxylic acid group $–COOH$, a hydrogen atom each attached to carbon located next to $–COOH$ group and a side chain R which varies from one amino acid to other. (It can be hydrogen or an aliphatic group, an aromatic or heterocyclic group).

$$H_2N - \overset{\overset{\displaystyle H}{|}}{\underset{\underset{\displaystyle R}{|}}{C}} - COOH$$

10. **(d)** Most of the body functions are regulated by hormone: like growth, vegetative and sexual development, thermo-regulation, cellular oxidation, metabolism of carbohydrates, proteins, fats, *etc.* Hormones are needed in very small quantity to carry out these functions. Some hormones are proteinaceous, e.g., insulin (regulates sugar metabolism) growth hormone of pituitary, parathyroid hormone: parathormone (regulates Ca and phosphate transport).

11. **(a)** Glycogen is a branched polymer of glucose. It is readily soluble in water. It consists of α-D glucose units, mostly linked by 1- 4 glycosidic linkage, and is highly branched *via* frequent 1 - 6 linkages. Glycogen is found mostly in muscle and liver of animals and is also called animal starch. It gives red colour with iodine solution. It has about 30,000 glucose. residues and a molecular weight of about 4.8 million. The straight part is helically twisted with each turn having six glucose units. The distance between two branching point is 10 - 14 glucose residues. In a polysaccharide chain of glycogen, the right end is called reducing end and the left end is called non-reducing end.

12. **(a)** All the branches of glycogen ends in non-reducing end, while the right end is reducing.

13. **(a)** Primary structure of a protein is simply the amino acid sequence of it which has two ends the carboxyl and amino terminals.

14. **(a)** Dissolving CO_2 in water does not require any enzyme CO_2 has higher solubility in water than O_2. Solubility of CO_2 in water can be increased with decrease in temperature, a principle used in carbonated drinks.

Very Short Answer Questions

1. (a) Penicillin is a group of antibiotics derived from fungi *Penicillium* obtained naturally.

   (b) Sulphonamide an antimirobial agent is a synthetic chemical.

   (c) Vitamin-C or L-ascorbic acid or ascorbate is a natural product and an essential nutrient for humans. It is present in citrus fruits.

   (d) Growth hormone also known as somatotropin or somatropin is a peptide hormone occurring naturally in the body it stimulates growth.

2. (a) Amino acid — Leucine

   (b) Sugar — Lactose

   (c) Nucleotide — Adenosine triphosphate

   (d) Fatty acid — Palmitic acid

3. Oxidoreductase is an enzyme that catalyses oxidation reduction reactions. This enzyme is associated in catalysing the transfer of electron from one molecule (the reduction), also called as electron donor, to another molecule (the oxidant), also called as electron acceptor. The complete reaction is

A reduced + A' oxidised $\rightarrow$ A oxidised + A' reduced

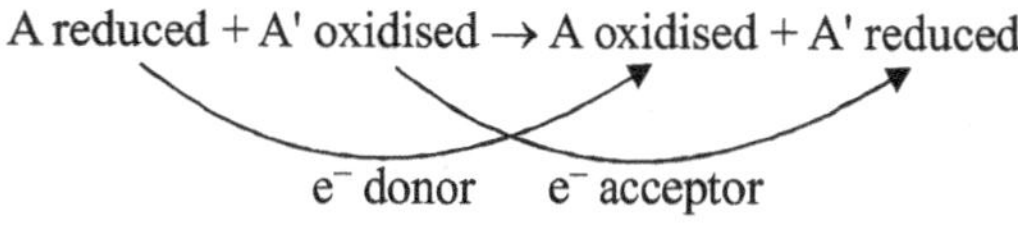

4. Organic compounds that are tightly bound to the apoenzyme, (an enzyme without cofactor) by covalent or non-covalent bonds are **prosthetic groups** e.g., peroxidase and catalase catalyse the breakdown of hydrogen peroxide to water and oxygen where haeme is the prosthetic group and it is a part of the active site of the enzyme.

Co-factor is small, heat stable and non-protein part of conjugate enzyme. It may be inorganic or organic in nature. Co-factors when loosely bound to an enzyme is called coenzyme and when tightly bound to apoenzyme is called prosthetic group.

5. The common substitutent groups in both the amino acids are NH_2 COOH and H.

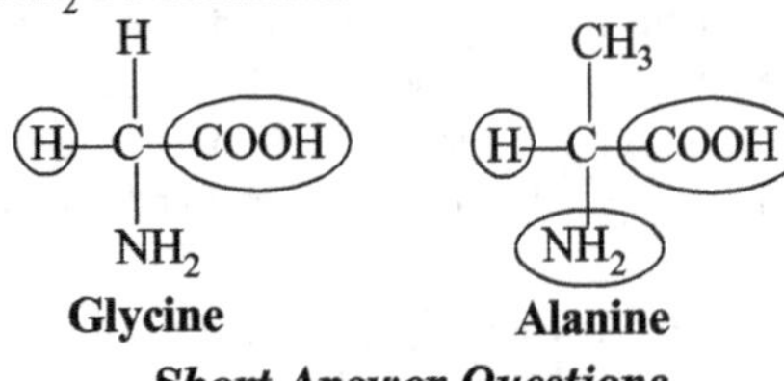

Short Answer Questions

1. Enzymes, generally function in a narrow range of pH. Most of the enzymes show their highest activity at a particular pH called optimum pH-activity declines below and above this value.

Extremely high or low pH values generally results in complete loss of activity for most enzymes. The given graph represents the maximum enzyme activity at the optimum pH.

2. Secondary metabolites are chemicals produced by plants which do not play any [role] in growth, photosynthesis reproduction or other primary functions of the plant. Rubber (cis 1, 4-polyisopyrene) is a secondary metabolite.

(i) Rubber is extracted from *Hevea brasiliensis* (rubber tree)

(ii) It is a byproduct of the lactiferous tissue of the vessels that are in the form of latex.

(iii) It contains over 400 isoprene units and thus is the largest of the terpenoids.

(iv) It is elastic, water proof and a good conductor of electricity.

3. Nucleic acids are large biological molecules, essential for all known forms of life. The secondary structure of a nucleic acid molecule refers to the base pairing interactions within a single molecule or set of interacting molecules. DNA and RNA represent two main nucleic acids, their secondary structures however differ the secondary structure of DNA comprises of two complementary strands of polydeoxyribonucleotide, spirally coiled on a common axis forming a helical structure.

This double helical structure of DNA is stabilized by phosphodiester bonds (between 5' of sugar of one nucleotide and 3 sugar of another nucleotide), hydrogen bonds (between bases, and ionic interactions.

4. Living organism are not in equilibrium because work cannot be performed by a system at equilibrium. The living organisms exist in a steady state characterised by concentration of each of the biomolecules.

These biomolecules are in a metabolic flux. Any chemical or physical process moves simultaneously to equilibrium. Living organisms work continuously and they cannot afford to reach equilibrium. The living state thus is an a non-equilibrium steady-state to be able to perform work. This achieved by energy input provided by metabolism.

Long Answer Questions

1. Enzymes are divided into six classes each with 4-13 sub-classes and named accordingly by a number comparising of four digits.

(i) Oxidoreductases/dehydrogenases : These enzymes take part in oxidation, reduction or transfer of electrons.

(ii) Transferase : These enzymes transfer a functional group (other than hydrogen). from one molecule to another. The transfer chemical group does not occur in free state.

(iii) Hydrolases : These enzymes catalyse the hydrolysis of bonds like ester, ether, peptide, glycosidic C-C, C-halide, P-N etc.

$$C_{12}H_{22}O_{11} + H_2O \xrightarrow{\text{Maltase}} 2C_6H_{12}O_6$$

(iv) Lyases cause cleavage, removal of groups without hydrolysis and addition of groups to double bonds or removal of groups producing double bonds.

$$\begin{array}{cc} X & Y \\ | & || \\ C & — C \end{array} \xrightarrow{\text{lyase}} X — Y + C = C$$

(v) Isomerases : These enzymes cause rearrangement of molecular structure to effect isomeric changes. They are of three types isomerases, epimerases and mutases.

Glucose-6-phosphate $\xrightarrow{\text{Isomerase}}$ Fructose 6-phosphate

(Aldose to ketose group or vice-versa)

Glucose-6-phosphate $\xrightarrow{\text{Mutase}}$ Glucose-1-phosphate

(Shifting the position of side group)

Xylulose 5-phosphate $\xrightarrow{\text{Epimerase}}$ Ribulose-5-phosphate

(vi) Ligases catalyse bonding of two chemicals with the help of energy obtained from ATP resulting formation of bonds such as C—O, C—S, C—N and P—O e.g., pyruvate carboxylase

Pyruvic acid $+ CO_2 + ATP + H_2O$

$$\left[\xrightarrow{\text{pyruvate carboxylase}} \text{Oxaloacetic} + ADP + Pi — \right]$$

10 — Cell Cycle and Cell Division

10.1 What is the average cell cycle span for a mammalian cell?

Sol. About 24 hours.

10.2 Distinguish cytokinesis from karyokinesis.

Sol. Karyokinesis is division of nucleus (mitosis or meiosis) while cytokinesis is division of cytoplasm. Cytokinesis in animal cell is achieved by the appearance of a furrow in the plasma membrane. The furrow gradually deepens and ultimately joins in the center dividing the cell cytoplasm into two. In plant cells cell wall formation starts in the center of the cell and grows outward to meet the existing lateral walls. The formation of new cell wall begins with the formation of simple precursor, called the cell plate that represents the middle lamella between the walls of two adjacent cells. It is the time of cytoplasmic division, organelles like mitochondria and plastids get distributed between the two daughter cells. In some organisms karyokinesis is not followed by cytokinesis as a result of which multinucleate condition arises leading to formation of syncytium (liquid endosperm of coconut).

10.3 Describe the events taking place during interphase.

Sol. Interphase is divided into three phases viz. G_1 phase, S phase and G_2 phase.

G_1 phase (Gap 1) : G_1 phase corresponds to the interval between mitosis and initiation of DNA replication. During G_1 phase the cell is metabolically active and continuously grows but does not replicate its DNA.

S phase (Synthesis) : S or **synthesis** phase marks the period during which DNA synthesis or replication takes place. During this time the amount of DNA per cell doubles. If the initial amount of DNA is denoted as 2C then it increases to 4C. However, there is no increase in the chromosome number; if the cell had diploid or 2n number of chromosomes at G_1, even after S phase the number of chromosomes remains the same *i.e.*, 2n.

G_2 phase (Gap 2) : In animal cells, during the S phase, DNA replication begins in the nucleus, and the centriole duplicates in the cytoplasm. During the G_2 phase, proteins are synthesised in preparation for mitosis while cell growth continues.

10.4 What is G_0 (quiescent phase) of cell cycle?

Sol. Some cells in adult animals do not appear to exhibit division (e.g., heart cell, nerve cell). These cell become inactive and become specialized by differentiate and do not further exit G_1 phase, and enter a stage but divide occasionally called quiescent stage (G_0) of the cell-cycle.

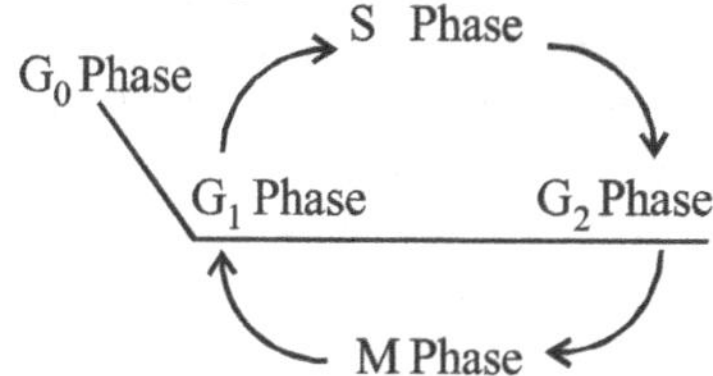

Cell Cycle

Cell in this stage remain metabolically active but no longer proliferate unless called to do so depending on the requirement of the organism.

10.5 Why is mitosis called equational division?

Sol. Mitosis called equational division because it keeps the chromosome number constant and genetic stability in daughter cells.

10.6 Name the stage of cell cycle at which one of the following events occur:

i. Chromosomes are moved to spindle equator.

ii. Centromere splits and chromatids separate.

iii. Pairing between homologous chromoso-mes takes place.

iv. Crossing over between homologous chromosomes takes place.

Sol. i. Metaphase

ii. Anaphase II

iii. Zygotene

iv. Pachytene

10.7 Describe the following:

(a) synapsis (b) bivalent (c) chiasmata

Draw a diagram to illustrate your answer.

Sol. (a) During zygotene of prophase I of meiosis homologous chromosomes pair together. This pairing is called synapsis.

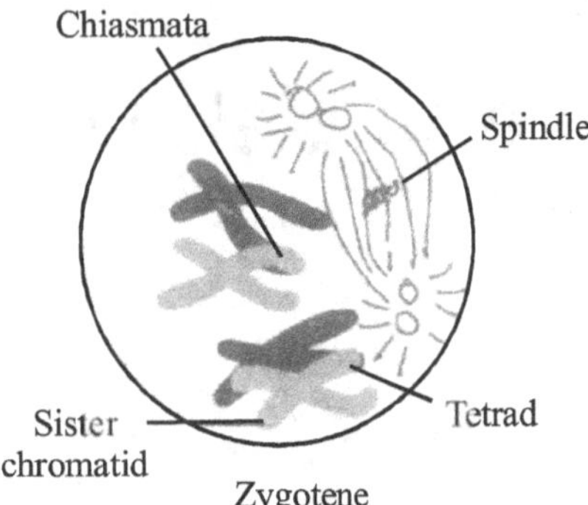

(b) Bivalent : The complex formed by homologous chromosomes during zygotene is called a bivalent.

(c) Chiasmata : During diplotene the paired chromosomes make a X-shaped structure. This is called chiasmata.

10.8 How does cytokinesis in plant cells differ from that in animal cells?

Sol. Due to the presence of a cell wall, cytokinesis in plant cell is significantly different from that in animal cells. Rather than forming a contractile ring, plant cells construct a cell plate in the middle of the cell. The golgi apparatus releases vesicles containing cell wall materials. These vesicles fuse at the equatorial plane and form a cell plate that represents the middle lamella between the walls of two adjacent cells.

10.9 Find examples where the four daughter cells from meiosis are equal in size and where they are found unequal in size.

Sol. The four daughter cells produced may be equal in size in the sperm of animals. They may be unequal in size as gametes in plants-pollen grains and egg in ovules.

10.10 Distinguish anaphase of mitosis from anaphase I of meiosis.

Sol. The main difference between anaphase of mitosis and anaphase I of meiosis are as follows:

	Anaphase of Mitosis		**Anaphase I of Meiosis**
(i)	During the anaphase of mitosis, the sister chromatids of each chromosome separate from one an other and pass to the opposite poles of the spindle as daughter chromosomes.	(i)	During this process, the two chromosomes of each bivalent separate from one another and pass to the opposite poles of the spindle. But the two chromatids of each chromosome still continue to remain joined with each other at the centromere. Thus only one chromosome of each homologous pair reaches their respective pole.
(ii)	This is caused by the division of the centromere and the contraction of the spindle fibres. As a result of this the **original diploid** number is maintained in the daughter cells.	(ii)	It is because of this that the nucleus of each daughter cell gets only half of the number of (*haploid*) chromosome present in the original cell.

10.11 List the main differences between mitosis and meiosis.

Sol. The main differences between mitosis and meiosis are as follows :

	Mitosis		**Meiosis**
I.	Mitosis occurs continuously in the body or somatic cells.	I.	Meiosis occurs in the germ cells (the cells of the testes or ovaries during the process of gametogenesis)
II.	Each replication cycle is followed by one cell division.	II.	Each replication cycle is followed by two cell divisions.
III.	Genetic material remains constant.	III.	Genetic variability is one of the main consequences of meiosis.
IV.	Daughter cell contains same amount of DNA as each parent cell.	IV.	Daughter cell contains half the amount of DNA as the parent cell.
V.	DNA synthesis occurs in S-phase, which is followed by G_2 phase.	V.	There is premeiotic DNA synthesis. G_2 phase is short and non-existent.
VI.	The prophase is of short duration and no substage.	VI.	The prophase is of longer duration and it includes completes in five successive stages, *viz.*, leptotene, zygotene, pachytene, diplotene and diakinesis.
VII.	The chromatids occur in the form of dyads.	VII.	The chromatids of two homologous chromosomes occur as the tetrads.
VIII.	The centromeres of the chromosomes remain directed towards the equator and the arms of the chromosomes remain directed towards the poles.	VIII.	The centromeres of the chromosomes remain directed towards the poles and the chromosomal arms remain directed towards the equator.
IX.	The chromosomes are the monads, *i.e.*, having single chromatid.	IX.	The chromosomes are the biads, *i.e.*, having two chromatids and single centromere.

X. The chromosomes are long and thin.	X. The chromosomes are short and thick.
XI. The telophase always occurs.	XI. The first telophase is some times omitted.
XII. The chromosome number in each daughter cell remains the same like the parent cell.	XII. In meiotic division the chromosome number reduced to half in the daughter cells thanis the parental cells.
XIII. A diploid cell produces two diploid cells by a mitotic division.	XIII. A diploid cell produces four haploid cells by a meiotic division.

10.12 What is the significance of meiosis?

Sol. **The significance of meiosis :**

1. It reduces the number of chromosomes to half in the daughter cells.

2. It is very essential phenomenon in the life cycle of sexually reproducing animals as it restores the fixed number of chromosomes present in the somatic cells, characteristic of the species.

3. Gametes are formed as a result of meiosis. Each gamete possesses half the number of chromosomes present in the somatic cells.

4. It avoids the multiplication of chromosomes and thus maintains the stability and constant number of chromosomes of the species.

5. During the crossing over exchange of nuclear material (genes) cause genetic variations within the species. As a result new combinations of hereditary material are formed.

10.13 Discuss with your teacher about

(i) haploid insects and lower plants where cell-division occurs and

(ii) some haploid cells in higher plants where cell-division does not occur.

Sol. (i) Some insects like honey bee drones are haploid. They are not fertile.

(ii) In lower plant, main plant body is haploid produces haploid microspores by mitosis. The gametes of *Chlamydomonas* fuse to form diploid zygotes. Meiosis take place at this stage in lower plants forming haploid spous which give rise to new plant.

10.14 Can there be mitosis without DNA replication in S-phase?

Sol. DNA replication is necessary for cell division and cell division cannot happen without DNA replication.

10.15 Can there be DNA replication without cell division?

Sol. DNA replication takes place in order to prepare cell for division. Cell division is the next logical step after DNA replication.

10.16 Analyse the events during every stage of cell cycle and notice how the following two parameters change

i   Number of chromosomes (N) per cell

ii   Amount of DNA content (C) per cell

Sol. G_1 Phase – 2N 2C
S Phase   – 2N 2C
G_2 Phase – 4N 4C
M Phase   – 2N 2C

2N corresponds to diploid chromosomes where as 2C corresponds to diploid.

(i) Number of chromosomes doubles after mitotic cell division and becomes half after meiotic cell division.

(ii) During S phase the DNA content doubles, but number of chromosomes remains the same.

SECTION B	PRACTICE QUESTIONS 

MULTIPLE CHOICE QUESTIONS

1. In cell cycle, DNA replication takes place in ______
   (a) G_1 phase (b) G_2 phase
   (c) Mitotic metaphase (d) S phase

2. In which stage of the cell cycle, histone proteins are synthesized in a eukaryotic cell?
   (a) During G_2 stage of prophase.
   (b) During S-phase.
   (c) During entire prophase.
   (d) During telophase.

3. Which of the following is responsible for the formation of the new cell wall and also represents the middle lamella between the walls of two adjacent cells?
   (a) Cell plate (b) Cell inclusion
   (c) Cell membrane (d) None of these

4. The separation of two chromatids of each chromosome at early anaphase is initiated by
   (a) the interaction of centromere with the chromosomal fibres.
   (b) the elongation of metaphasic spindle.
   (c) the force of repulsion between the divided kinetochores.
   (d) All of the above.

5. What is the stage of mitosis in which chromosomes are arranged on the equator of spindle?

    (a) Anaphase   (b) Prophase

    (c) Metaphase   (d) Telophase

6. In meiosis, division is

    (a) Ist reductional and IInd equational.

    (b) Ist equational and IInd reductional.

    (c) both reductional.

    (d) both equational.

7. The synaptonemal complex appears

    (a) between homologous chromosomes.

    (b) in zygotene stage.

    (c) composed of DNA + protein.

    (d) All of the above

8. The number of chromosome groups at the equatorial plate in metaphase-I of meiosis in a plant with $2n = 50$ shall be

    (a) 50   (b) 25

    (c) 30   (d) 100

9. At which stage, the homologous chromosomes separate due to repulsion, but are yet held by chiasmata ?

    (a) Zygotene   (b) Pachytene

    (c) Diplotene   (d) Diakinesis

10. Significance of meiosis lies in

    (a) reduction of chromosome number to one half.

    (b) maintaining consistancy of chromosome number during sexual reproduction.

    (c) production of genetic variability.

    (d) all of the above.

Assertion & Reason Questions

DIRECTION (Qs. 1-5) : *These questions consists of two statements. Answer these questions selecting the appropriate option given below:*

(a) Both Assertion (A) and Reason (R) are true and Reason (R) is the correct explanation of Assertion (A).

(b) Both Assertion (A) and Reason (R) are true, but Reason (R) is not the correct explanation of Assertion (A).

(c) Assertion (A) is true, but Reason (R) is false.

(d) Assertion (A) is false, but Reason (R) is true.

1. **Assertion :** Interphase is resting stage.

    Reason : The interphase cell is metabolically inactive.

2. **Assertion:** The period required to complete one cell cycle is called generation time.

    Reason: Cell cycle is complex in prokaryotes.

3. **Assertion:** DNA synthesis occurs during G_0 phase.

    Reason: During G_2 phase protein are synthesised.

4. **Assertion:** Meiosis results in production of haploid cells.

    Reason: Synapsis occurs during leptotene.

5. **Assertion :** Diplotene is characterised by the presence of chiasmata.

    Reason : Diplotene can last for months and years in oocytes of some vertebrates.

Case/Passage Based Questions

DIRECTIONS (Qs. 1-5) : *Read the following passage and answer the questions that follows.*

A number of electron dense bodies about 100 nm in diameter are seen at irregular intervals within the centre of the synaptonemal complex, known as recombination *nodules*. They are believed to be sites having multienzyme recombinase complex required for crossing over. Observe the diagram and answer the questions.

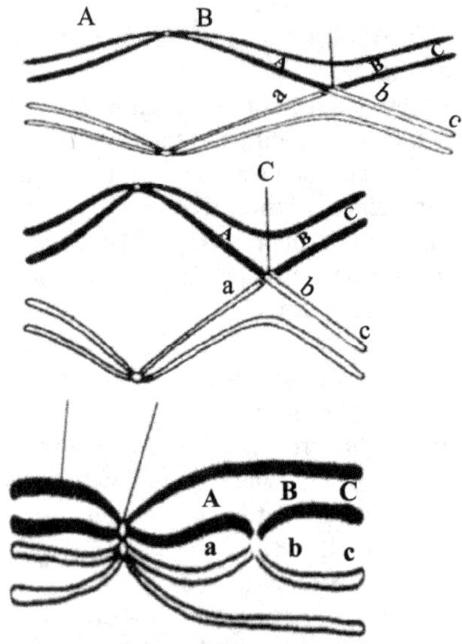

1. Crossing over occurs between

    (a) sister chromatids of homologous chromosomes.

    (b) non-sister chromatids of homologous chromosomes.

    (c) sister chromatids of non-homologous chromosomes.

    (d) non-sister chromatids of non-homologous chromosomes.

2. Which of the following labelling represents chiasma?

    (a) A   (b) C

    (c) B   (d) None of them

3. Which of the following statement is true?

    (a) Crossing over takes place during G_2 phase of mitosis

    (b) Crossing over occurs in both meiosis as well as mitosis.

    (c) Crossing over occurs only during meiosis.

    (d) During crossing over number of chromosomes decreases.

4. The centre of the synaptonemal complex is called as

    (a) Recombination nodules

    (b) Recombinant DNA

    (c) Recombinant RNA

    (d) None of them

5. What is represented by labelling B?

    (a) Chromatid   (b) Centromere

    (c) Chiasma   (d) All of them

Very Short Answer Questions

1. What is karyokinesis?

2. Name the phase in which chromatids move apart.

3. In which phase DNA replication takes place?

4. Name the cell divisions which help recombination of genes.
5. Which type of cell division occurs in meristematic cell of root apex?
6. Name the stage during which astral and spindle fibres disappear and nuclear membrane and nucleoli reappear.
7. Name the sub-phases of prophase-I of Meiosis.
8. In which stage, actual reduction of chromosome number occurs in meiosis?
9. What is kinetochore?
10. What is peculiarity of zygotene?
11. Define crossing over. Give its significance.
12. What is interkinesis?

Short Answer Questions

1. Differentiate between :
   (a) S-phase and G_2 phase.
   (b) G_1 and G_2 phase
2. Write the three processes which take place in interphase.
3. Mention the events that occur during diakinesis.
4. When and why does reduction in the number of chromosomes take place in meiosis?
5. Differentiate between prophase I and prophase of mitosis.
6. Imagine a situation if there was no meiosis. Then what would have happened to the next generation?
7. Which stage in meiosis is marked with genetic recombination? How
8. What is Synapsis and Synaptonemal Complex? In which stage do these occur?

9. What is the role of centrosome with centriole?
10. Diagramatically show the cell cycle and answer the following questions.

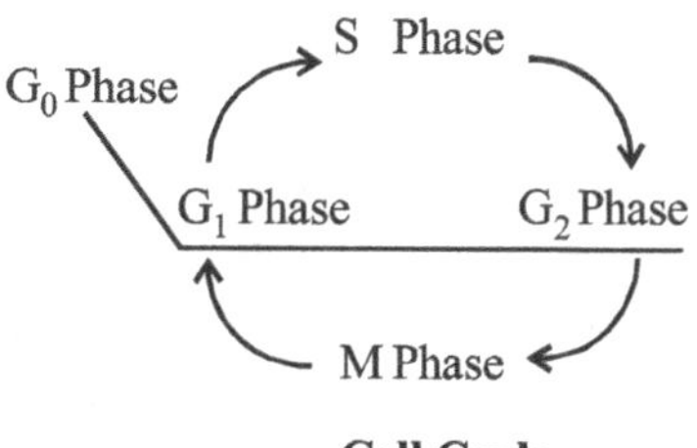

Cell Cycle

(a) Which is the resting stage __________ .
(b) Which is the stage where replication takes palce __________ .
(c) Which is the stage where mitosis takes place __________ .
(d) Which is the post cell synthetic but pre cell division stage __________ .

11. How and why chromosome number is maintained the same in the cell mitotic division.

Long Answer Questions

1. Describe briefly cytokinesis in animal cells and plant cells.
2. Mention the significance of mitosis.
3. Describe meiosis II with the help of suitable diagrams.

SOLUTIONS

Multiple Choice Questions

1. **(d)** S-phase is a synthetic phase in which DNA molecules replicate and synthesis of histone proteins occurs.
2. **(b)** During S phase, replication of chromosomal DNA and synthesis of histone proteins takes place. During this time, the amount of DNA for cell doubles.
3. **(a)** The formation of new cell wall begins with the formation of a simple precursor, called cell plate that represents the middle lamella between the walls of two adjacent cells.
4. **(c)** The separation of two chromatids of each chromosome at early anaphase is initiated by the force of repulsion between the divided kinetochores.
5. **(c)** In metaphase of mitosis, centromeres of all the chromosomes lie over the equator to form an apparent plate called equatorial plate.
6. **(a)** Meiosis I is known as reductional division due to reduction in the number of chromosomes. Meiosis II is called equational division because of maintaining the same number of chromosomes.
7. **(d)** The synaptonemal complex is formed at the region of synapsis. It is a protein structure that forms between homologous chromosomes (two pairs of sister chromatids)

during meiosis and is thought to mediate chromosome pairing, synapsis, and recombination. This stage appears in zygotene stage of prophase I of meiosis I.

8. **(b)**
9. **(c)** Diplotene is the longest and the most active sub-phase of prophase I of meiosis. In diplotene, the homologous chromosomes separate due to repulsion as the nucleoprotein complex of synapsed chromosomes dissolves, but are yet held by chiasmata.
10. **(d)** Meiosis results in four daughter cells and each with having half the number of chromosomes of the parent cell. Meiosis begins with a parent cell that is diploid, *i.e* it has two copies of each chromosome. The parent cell undergoes one round of DNA replication followed by two separate cycles of nuclear division. The process leads to production of four daughter cells that are haploid, which means that they contain half the number of chromosomes of the diploid parent cell. The significance of meiosis are:
   (i) It maintains the same chromosome number in the sexually reproducing organisms. From a diploid cell, haploid gametes are produced which in turn fuse to form a diploid cell.

(ii) It restricts the multiplication of chromosome number and maintains the stability of the species.

(iii) Maternal and paternal genes get exchanged during crossing over which results in variations among the offspring.

(iv) All the four chromatids of a homologous pair of chromosomes segregate and go over separately to four different daughter cells. This leads to variation in the daughter cells genetically.

Assertion & Reason Questions

1. **(c)** Previously interphase is called resting stage because there is no apparent activity related to cell division. The interphase cell is metabolically quite active. Interphase consist of three subphases (G_1, G_2 and S). Synthesis of DNA occurs in S phase. G_1 is the period between the end of mitosis and the start of S phase. G_2 is the phase between S phase and the next mitosis. As the synthesis of DNA and proteins occurs in interphase, so it is considered as metabolically active phase.

2. **(c)** The period in which one cell cycle is completed is called as generation time. Cell cycle is simple in prokaryotes and complex in eukaryotes.

3. **(d)** In cell cycle, the synthesis of the DNA occurs during S-phase. During G_2 phase synthesis of proteins and organelles take place.

4. **(c)** Synapsis occurs during zygotene stage. Synapsis is the pairing of homologous chromosomes which leads to formation of bivalents.

5. **(b)** Diplotene is the longest and most active subphase of prophase I of meiosis. The beginning of diplotene is recognised by the dissolution of synaptonemal complex and the tendency of the recombined homologous chromosomes of the bivalents to separate from each other except at the sites of crossovers. These X-shaped structures are called chiasmata. Diplotene can last for months and years in oocytes of some vertebrate.

Case/Passage Based Questions

1. **(b)** Crossing over is exchange of chromosomes segments between non-sister chromatids of homologous pair. It brings about gene recombination and also produces genetic variation. The chromatids are the unit of crossing over.

2. **(b)** 3. **(c)**

4. **(a)** The centre of the synaptonemal complex is called as recombination nodules.

5. **(b)**

Very Short Answer Questions

1. Division of nucleus is known as karyokinesis.
2. Anaphase.
3. S or synthetic phase.
4. Meiosis.
5. Mitosis
6. Telophase.
7. Leptotene, Zygotene, Pachytene, Diplotene and Diakinesis.
8. Anaphase I
9. Kinetochore is a discoidal area on chromatid which is site of attachment of spindle fibre.

10. In zygotene phase pairing of homologous chromosomes or synapsis takes place.

11. It is exchange of genes between non-sister chromatids of homologous chromosomes. It produces new combination of genes and variation.

12. Interkinesis is interphase between meiosis I and meiosis II.

Short Answer Questions

1. (a) Difference between S-phase and G_2 phase:

	S-phase	**G_2 phase**
(i)	It is called synthetic phase.	It is called pre-mitotic phase.
(ii)	Replication of DNA occurs	RNA of all three types and proteins for asters and spindle are synthesized in it.
(iii)	It lasts for 6-8 hours	It lasts for 2-5 hours.

(b) Difference between G_1 and G_2 phase

	G_1 phase	**G_2 phase**
(i)	It is called first growth period.	It is post-synthesis or 'S' phase.
(ii)	Its duration is variable.	It lasts for 2-5 hours.
(iii)	Cells grow in size.	Cell prepares to go into mitotic phase.

2. Three processes which take place in interphase are :
   (i) The replication of DNA and the synthesis of histones and nuclear proteins.
   (ii) Division of centriole to form two new centrioles which lie at right angle to each other.
   (iii) The synthesis of energy-rich compound to provide energy for mitosis.

3. The events occurs during diakinesis :
   (i) There is terminalisation of chiasmata.
   (ii) The chromosomes are fully condensed.
   (iii) The assembling of meiotic spindle is initiated.
   (iv) The nucleolus and nuclear membrane break down and disappear completely by the end of diakinesis.

4. Actual reduction in the number of chromosomes takes place in anaphase I.
   This is because in anaphase I, one member from each homologous pair moves to one pole; the two chromatids of the chromosomes do not separate as the centromeres do not divide at this stage.

5. Difference between prophase I and prophase of mitosis are :

	Prophase I	**Prophase**
(i)	Pairing of homologous chromosomes (synapsis) takes place.	There is no synaptic pairing of homologous chromosomes.
(ii)	Crossing over and recombination occur.	There is no crossing over or recombination.
(iii)	It is comparatively a long phase.	It is relatively short.

6. In the absence of meiosis the next generation would have double the number of chromosomes after fusion of gametes. This would have resulted in the birth of an altogether new species. The maintenance of characters set would have been possible only through asexual reproduction.

7. In pachytene stage of meiosis I the chromosomes appear as tetrads of homo logous chromosomes and crossing as the genetic material exchange takes place. Thus this stage is marked with genetic recombination.

8. The pairing of chromosomes is called Synapsis. In the chromosomal synapsis a complex structure is made known as **Synaptonemal complex** These occur in zygotene stage of mieosis I.

9. The centrosome with centriole play a very important role in mitosis and meiosis. It forms spindle shaped fibres attached 10 chromosome and these place chromosomes to equater and then to the poles. Without the centrosome with centriole these processes were not able to be performed in the cell.

10. (a) Go Phase   (b) S Phase
    (c) M Phase   (d) G_2 Phase

11. The chromosomes in prophase stage of mitosis is 2N, which later becomes 4N. Then in anaphase I, the chromosomes seggregate, followed by nuclear and cell division. Which restores the chromosome number to 2N.

Long Answer Questions

1. (a) **Cytokinesis in animals cells :** In the animal cells, cytoplasm divides by constriction. It appears on equator and slowly deepens. The constriction converges on all the sides and pinches off parent cell into 2 daughter cells. Constriction is the result of a peripheral band of microfilaments. This constriction divide the cytoplasm finally.

    (b) **Cytokinesis in plant cells :** Plant cells have rigid cell wall and this cannot undergo cytokinesis by invaginating cleavage furrow. Therefore, in them the cytokinesis is accomplished by formation of **phragmo-plast** from carbohydrate and lipid-containing vesicles of Golgi apparatus and endoplasmic reticulum vesicles. A **cell plate** at equator of the dividing cell is formed and divide the cytoplasm.

2. **Significance of mitosis:** Mitosis or the equational division is usually restricted to the diploid cells only. However, in some lower plants and in some social insects haploid cells also divide by mitosis. It is very essential to understand the significance of this division in the life of an organism.

Mitosis results in the production of diploid daughter cells with identical genetic complement usually. The growth of multicellular organisms is due to mitosis. Cell growth results in disturbing the ratio between the nucleus and the cytoplasm. It therefore becomes essential for the cell to divide to restore the nucleo-cytoplasmic ratio. A very significant contribution of mitosis is cell repair. The cells of the upper layer of the epidermis, cells of the lining of the gut, and blood cells are being constantly replaced. Mitotic divisions in the meristematic tissues – the apical and the lateral cambium, result in a continuous growth of plants throughout their life.

3. **Meiosis II** is divided into four phases.

Prophase II. Meiosis II is initiated immediately after cytokinesis, usually before the chromosomes have fully elongated. In contrast to meiosis I, meiosis II resembles a normal mitosis. The nuclear membrane disappears by the end of prophase II. The chromosomes again become compact.

Metaphase II- At this stage the chromosomes align at the equator and the microtubules from opposite poles of the spindle get attached to the kinetochores of sister chromatids.

Anaphase II- It begins with the simultaneous splitting of the centromere of each chromosome (which was holding the sister chromatids together), allowing them to move toward opposite poles of the cell.

Telophase II- Meiosis ends with telophase II, in which the two groups of chromosomes once again get enclosed by a nuclear envelope; cytokinesis follows resulting in the formation of tetrad of cells i.e., four haploid daughter cells.

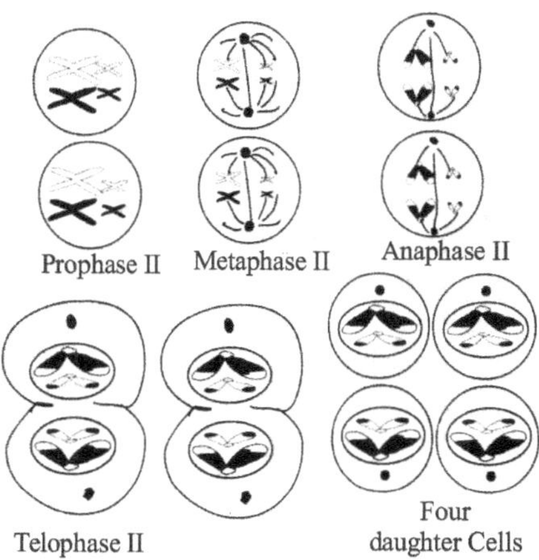

SECTION C — NCERT EXEMPLAR QUESTIONS

MULTIPLE CHOICE QUESTIONS

1. Meiosis in diploid organisms results in
   (a) production of gametes
   (b) reduction in the number of chromosomes
   (c) introduction of variation
   (d) All of the above

2. At which stage of meiosis does the genetic constitution of gametes is finally decided.
   (a) Metaphase-I   (b) Anaphase-II
   (c) Metaphase-II   (d) Anaphase-I

3. Meiosis occurs in organisms during
   (a) sexual reproduction   (b) vegetative reproduction
   (c) Both (a) and (b)   (d) None of these

4. During Anaphase-I of meiosis
   (a) homologous chromosomes separate
   (b) non-homologous autosomes separate
   (c) sister chromatids separate
   (d) non-sister chromatids separate

5. Mitosis is characterised by
   (a) reduction division
   (b) equal division
   (c) Both (a) and (b)
   (d) pairing of homologous chromosomes

6. A bivalent meiosis-I consists of
   (a) two chromatids and one centromere
   (b) two chromatids and two centromeres
   (c) four chromatids and two centromeres
   (d) four chromatids and four centromeres

7. Cells which are not dividing are likely to be at
   (a) G_1 (b) G_2
   (c) G_0 (d) S-phase

8. Which of the events listed below is not observed during mitosis?
   (a) Chromatin condensation
   (b) Movement of centrioles to opposite poles
   (c) Appearance of chromosomes with two chromosome joined together at the centromere
   (d) Crossing over

9. Identify the wrong statement about meiosis
   (a) Pairing of homologous chromosomes
   (b) Four haploid cells are formed
   (c) At the end of meiosis the number of chromosomes are reduced to half
   (d) Two cycle of DNA replication occurs

10. Select the correct statement about G_1 phase
   (a) cell is metabolically inactive
   (b) DNA in the cell does not replicate
   (c) it is not a phase of synthesis of macromolecules
   (d) cell stops growing

VERY SHORT ANSWER QUESTIONS

1. Between a prokaryote and a eukaryote, which cell has a shorter cell division time?

2. Name a stain commonly used to colour chromosomes.

3. Which tissue of animals and plants exhibits meiosis?

4. Which part of the human body should one use to demonstrate stages in mitosis?

5. The diagram shows a bivalent at prophase-I of meiosis. Which of the four chromatids can cross over?

Prophase-I

6. If a tissue has at a given time 1024 cells, how many cycles of mitosis had the original parental single cell undergone?

7. An anther has 1200 pollen grains. How many pollen mother cells must have been there to produce them?

8. At what stage of cell cycle does DNA synthesis take place?

9. It is said that the one cycle of cell division in human cells (eukaryotic cells) takes 24 hours. Which phase of the cycle, do you think occupies the maximum part of cell cycle?
   Cell cycle is under genetic control and is a sequential event. Every cell prepares itself before it starts dividing. This preparation takes place in interphase stage of the cell cycle.

10. It is observed that heart cells do not exhibit cell division. Such cells do not divide further and exit... phase to enter in inactive stage called .... of cell cycle. Fill in the blanks.

SHORT ANSWER QUESTIONS

1. State the role of centrioles other than spindle formation.

2. Label the diagram and also determine the stage at which this structure is visible.

3. A cell has 32 chromosomes. It undergoes mitotic division. What will be the chromosome number (n) during metaphase? What would be the DNA content (C) during anaphase?

4. While examining the mitotic stage in a tissue, one finds some cells with 16 chromosomes and some with 32 chromosomes. What possible reasons could you assign to this difference in chromosome number. Do you think cells with 16 chromosomes could have arisen from cells with 32 chromosomes or vice-versa?

5. The following events occur during the various phases of the cell cycle. Name the phase against each of the events.
    (a)   Disintegration of nuclear membrane ....
    (b)   Appearance of nucleolus ....
    (c)   Division of centromere ....
    (d)   Replication of DNA ....

6. Mitosis results in producing two cells which are similar to each other. What would be the consequence if each of the following irregularities occur during mitosis?
    (a)   Nuclear membrane fails to disintegrate
    (b)   Duplication of DNA does not occur
    (c)   Centromeres do not divide
    (d)   Cytokinesis does not occur

7. Both unicellular and multicellular organisms undergo mitosis. What are the difference, if any, observed in the process between the two?

8. Comment on the statement-meiosis enables the conservation of specific chromosome number of each species even through the process per se results in reduction of chromosome number.

9. Name a cell that is found arrested in diplotene stage for months and years. Comment in 2-3 lines how it completes cell cycle?

10. How does cytokinesis in plant cells differ from that in animal cells?

Long Answer Questions

1. Comment on the statement- Telophase is reverse of prophase.

2. An organisms has two pair of chromosomes (i.e., chromosome number = 4). Diagrammatically represent the chromosomal arrangement during different phases of meiosis-II.

SOLUTIONS

Multiple Choice Questions

1. **(d)** Meiosis is a reduction division in which the chromosomes number is reduced to half in gametes. It is a special kind of cell division in which exchange of genetic material takes place, that brings about variation in next generations. Thus all the given options are characteristic features of meiotic cell division.

2. **(d)** The genetic constitution of gametes is finally decided at the anaphase-I after which each cell receives half the chromosome number, (from '$2n$' in parent cell it changes to 'n' in daughter cells.) During this phase, the two homologous pair of each chromosome separate and move toward opposite poles attached by microtubule of the spindle apparatus.
These are further separated in anaphase-II, wherein the sister chromatids of each chromosome separate and move towards opposite poles. It cannot be metaphase-I or metaphase-II because during these stages, the chromosomes or chromatids, merely arrange themselves at the metaphasic plate.

3. **(a)** Meiosis occurs in sexually reproducing organisms to reduce the chromosome number to half, before their gametes unite, so as to maintain the constant chromosome number ($2n$) in the progeny.
Vegetative reproduction is a kind of asexual reproduction occurring in plants and does not involve the formation and fusion of gametes.

4. **(a)** During Anaphase-I, homologous chromosomes separate, while sister chromatids remain associated at their centromeres.

5. **(b)** Mitosis is characterised by equal division because the chromosome numbers in the daughter cells remains same as that of the parent cell. Reduction division is the characteristic of meiosis.

6. **(c)** The complex formed by a pair of synapsed homologous chromosome is called bivalent or a tetrad. It has two centromeres and four chromatids.

7. **(c)** In G_0 stage, no growth takes place. It is also called the quiescent stage. Some cells of the body like heart cells, neuron which do not divide, exit at G_1 stage and enter G_0 of the cell cycle an inactive stage.
The cells in this stage remain metabolically active but no longer proliferate unless called on to do so depending up on the requirement of the organism.
G_1 phase is the first growth phase in post mitotic gap phase that lasts from the end of mitotic cycle to the initiation of DNA replication.
G_2 phase is the second growth phase or premitotic gap phase in which cell prepares itself to enter cell division, or mitosis.
S-phase is the synthetic phase in which chromosomes replicate.

8. **(d)** **Crossing Over** is the phenomenon of genetic exchange between homologous pair of chromosomes and is a characteristic feature of meiotic cell division. It does not occur in mitosis.

9. **(d)** Two cycles of DNA replication do not occur in meiosis.

10. **(b)** G_1 phase means gap 1 phase. It is the interval between mitosis and initiation of DNA replication. The cell is metabolically active and grows continuously but the DNA does not replicate. The cell also synthesizes proteins that are required for DNA replication.

Very Short Answer Questions

1. Prokaryotic cell has simple cell structure and cellular organisation. It's nucleus does not contain nuclear membrane. Prokaryotic cell thus has shorter cell cycle than the eukaryotic cell.

2. The chromosomes are the thickest and the shortest at metaphase. Acetocarmine and Giemsa stain can be used to stain the chromosomes. They are stained for karyotyping for further study of chromosomes.

3. Meiosis is also called as reduction division, it is a special kind of cell division which occurs in germ cells or sex cells of male and female reproductive organs of plants and animals. They produce male ($\male$) and female ($\female$) gametes that take part in sexual reproduction.

4. All the cells in the human body except germinal cells in the male and female reproductive organs are somatic cells. The somatic cells divide by mitotic cell division for growth and regeneration and can be used to demonstrate mitosis.

5. In prophase-I of meiosis, the homologous chromosomes lie parallel to each other in leptotene stage. Each chromosome has four chromatids and are bivalent. The non-sister chromatids of homologous chromosomes cross over in pachytene stage of prophase-I.

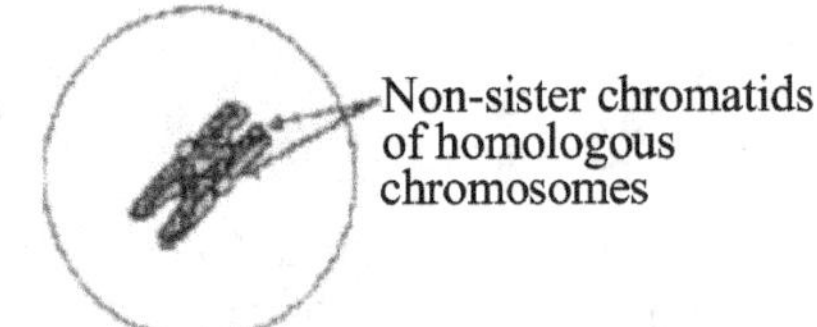

Pachytene of prophase-I of meiosis

6. To give 1024 cells the parental cell undergoes 10 divisions of mitotic cycle.

7. The pollen mother cell (2n) undergoes meiotic cell divisions, each such cell produces four daughter cells with haploid (n) number of chromosomes. Three hundred pollen mother cells would have to be there to produce 1200 pollen grains, because one pollen mother cell will produce four pollen grains.

8. The stage of cell cycle where DNA synthesis or replication takes place is Synthetic phase or S-phase of interphase.

9. If a cell takes 24 hours to divide, it spends 18-20 hours time in interphase stage to prepare itself to undergo cell division.

10. It is observed that heart cells do not exhibit cell division. Such cells do not divide further and exit G_1 phase to enter an inactive stage called **quiescent stage** (G_0) of cell cycle. Muscle cells when reach a level of maturity, no longer divide and just perform their function all through it life.

Short Answer Questions

1. The animal cell are present in few membrane less cell organelles. Centrosome is one of them. Two cylindrical structures called centrioles are the part of centrosome.
In the centrosome the two centrioles lie perpendicular to each other. Each has organisation lie a cart wheel. These form the basal body of cilia and flagella of plant/animal cells besides forming spindle fibre in animal cell division. It also helps in the formation of microtubules and sperm tail.

2. The transition stage between prophase and metaphase stage of mitotic cell division is shown in the diagram.

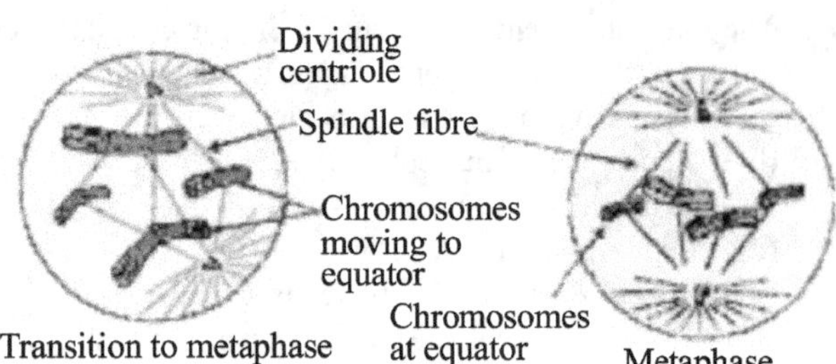

3. Mitosis helps in the growth of organism and its development. It also plays a vital role in a sexually reproducing organisms. The mitotic cell division occurs in somatic cells of an organism. The chromosome number in the daughter cells remains same as that of the parent (dividing) cell, so even at metaphase or anaphase, the chromosome number does not change. The DNA content gets doubled at the synthetic phase of interphase and gets divided at anaphase but the chromosome number remains same.

4. A condition as such, may arise in case of a mosaic, which denotes presence of two or more populations of cells in one individual with varying genotypes.
It can result from various mechanisms including non-disjunction, anaphase lagging and end replication. It may also result from a mutation during development, which is propagated to only a subset of the adult cells. In this case, cells with 16 chromosomes could have arisen from cells with 32 chromosomes.

5. (a) Prophase   (b) Telophase
   (c) Anaphase   (d) S-phase

6. (a) The spindle fibres would not be able to reach chromosomes if nuclear membrane fails to disintegrate and they would not move towards opposite poles of the cell. In certain protozoans, such as Amoeba, the spindle is formed within the nucleus and this is called intra nuclear mitosis or pre-mitosis.

   (b) The cell might not be able to surpass S-phase of cell-cycles. If DNA duplication does not occur as no chromosome formation will take place, and cell will not be able to enter M-(mitotic phase) in case it enters mitosis, the cycle will cease.

   (c) If the centromeres do not divide as it may result in trisomy. one of the daughter cell will receive a complete pair of chromosomes and other cell would not get any of them.

   (d) Multinucleate condition called coenocyte, syncytium is produced. If cytokinesis does not occur as in Rhizopus and Vaucheria, etc.

7. The type of cell divisions in unicellular organisms is known as amitosis in which somatic cell is directly divided into the parts. Occurs an indirect process occurs. In multicellular organisms.
In both unicellular and multicellular organisms. The difference between mitosis include:

Cell Division in Unicellular Organism (Amitosis)	Cell Division in Multicellular Organism (Mitosis)
Direct division of cellular and nuclear content, without the formation of chromosomes. Phases of cell divisions are not observed. **Stage 1** Specialised proteins speed up change **Stage 2** Nucleus divides **Stage 3** Cytoplasm divides having each one of the two nuclei	Involves formation of chromosomes as nucleus and cellular content do not divide directly Involves different phase of cell division. Parent cell — Prophase — Metaphase — Anaphase — Two daughter cells

8. Meiosis is the mechansim of conservation of specific chromosome number of each species across generations in organisms reproducing sexually. The process results in reduction of chromosome number by half, which is gradually conserved by union of male gamete 9n) and female gamete (n) in next generation. Meiosis also increases the genetic variability in the population of organisms from one generation to the next.

9. In mammalian occytes, meiotic arrest at diplotene stage usually occurs. In females, meiosis starts in the embryo and proceeds as for as diplotene, when the chromosomes become diffused and the cells are referred to as being in the dictyate stage. This arest is under hormonal control.

   In many amphibian oocyles, birds and insects with a long period of immaturity, the oocyte may be arrested in the dictyate stage for many years and spend a prolonged period in diplotene.

   This stage is characterised by formation of lampbrush chromosomes where intense RNA synthesis occurs and most of the genes in the DNA loops are actively transcribed and expressed.

10. Difference between cytokinesis in plant cell and animal cell is as follows.

Cytokinesis in Plant Cell	Cytokinesis in Animal Cell
In plant cell division of cytoplasm takes place by cell plate formation. The cell plate formation starts at the centre of the cell and grows outward, toward the lateral walls. Cell plate **Plants cell**	The division of cytoplasm takes place by cleavage in animal cells. Cleavage starts at the periphery and then moves inward, dividing the into two parts. Furrow **Animals cell**

Long Answer Questions

1. The following contrasting differences reveals that telophase is reverse of prophase, in cell division.

Prophase	Telophase
It is the first stage of (karyokinesis) in cell division, Viscosity of cytoplasm increases.	It is the last stage of karyokinesis in cell division. Viscosity of cytoplasm decreases.
The indistinct DNA condense to form elongated chromosomes.	Chromosome groups reorganizes themselves into nuclei.
Chromatin disappears and chromosome fibres get shortened and thickened.	Chromosomes elongate and overlap each other to form chromatin.
Spindle fibres appear (towards the poles from the centriole connected in animals with astral rays and in plants without asters).	Spindle fibres disappear around the poles.
Nucleolus degenerate completely.	Nuclear envelope appears and two daughter nuclei are formed at the poles.
Cell organelles such as ER, Golgi complex disorganise, and there is to difference between cytoplasm and nucleoplasm.	Cell organelles as ER and Golgi complex are reformed in the cell. Nucleoplasm also appears in the chromatin area making it distinct from rest of cytoplasmic area.

2. Meiosis is reduction division in which chromosome number reduces to half in daughter cells. The number reduces as half set of chromosomes move to 2 daughter cells in meiosis-I. Thus two cells with half set of chromosomes again re-enter meiosis-II which is similar to mitotic cell division.

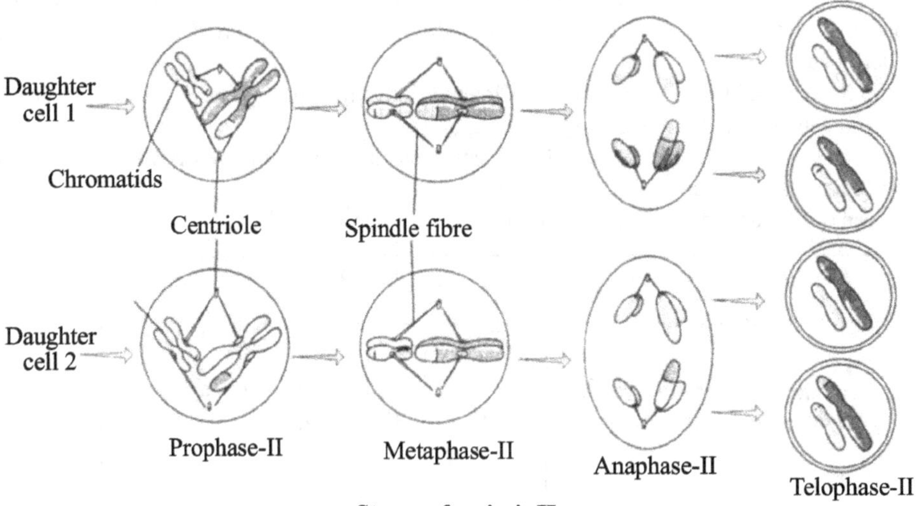

Stages of meiosis II

11 Transport in Plants

11.1 What are the factors affecting the rate of diffusion?

Sol. Factors affecting the rate of diffusion are :
- Gradient of concentration
- Permeability of membrane
- Temperature
- Pressure

11.2 What are porins? What role do they play in diffusion?

Sol. Porins are proteins that form huge pores in outer membranes of plastids, mitochondria and some bacteria, allowing molecules upto the size of small proteins to pass through. Thus porins facilitate diffusion.

11.3 Describe role played by protein pumps during active transport in plants.

Sol. In active transport, the movable carrier proteins are called pumps. They performs transport across the membrane against concentration gradient by using ATP as energy.

11.4 Explain why pure water has maximum water potential?

Sol. Water potential of pure water at normal temperature and pressure is zero. Due to interaction of water molecules with the solute particle the free energy of water molecule decreased. In solution value of water potential is always negative or less than zero. Thus pure water has maximum water potential.

11.5 Differentiate between the following:

  (a) **Diffusion and Osmosis**

  (b) **Transpiration and Evaporation**

  (c) **Osmotic Pressure and Osmotic Potential**

  (d) **Imbibition and Diffusion**

  (e) **Apoplast and Symplast pathways of movement of water in plants**

  (f) **Guttation and Transpiration**

Sol. (a) The differences between diffusion and osmosis are as following:

	Diffusion		Osmosis
1.	It is the movement of ions or molecules of any substance (liquid, solid or gas) from a region of its higher concentration to the region of its lower concentration.	1.	It is the movement of only solvent molecules from a region of its higher concentration to the region of its lower concentration through membrane.
2.	No membrane is requires.	2.	Movement occurs through semi-permeable membrane.
3.	It occurs in different medium, gas, liquid or solid.	3.	It occurs in liquid medium only.

(b) The differences between transpiration and evaporation are as following :

	Transpiration		Evaporation
1	It is a physiological process.	1	It takes place at the surface of non-living objects.
2	It occurs at the exposed surface of plants.	2	It is a physical process.
3	It is influenced by the rate of water absorption, osmotic pressure of cell, thickness of cuticle, number, position and opening of stomata.	3	It is influenced by relative humidity and air current.
4	Transpiration is slow process.	4	Evaporation is comparatively faster.
5	Transpiration is affected by pH, CO_2 and hormones.	5	CO_2, pH and hormones have no effect on evaporation.

(c)   The main differences between osmotic pressure and osmotic potential are as following :

	Osmotic pressure		Osmotic potential
1.	It is the hydrostatic pressure required to stop the movement of water molecules through semipermeable membrane.	1.	It is decrease in water potential of pure water due to the presence of solutes.
2.	Expressed in bars with positive sign though numerically equal to osmotic potential.	2.	Expressed in bars with negative sign though numerically equal to osmotic pressure.
3.	The value of O. P. increase by increasing concentration of solute particles.	3.	More negative value of osmotic potential means greater the concentration of solute particles.
4.	It develops only in a confined system.	4.	Osmotic potential is present whether the solution occur in a confined system or an open system.

(d)   The main differences between imbibition and diffusion are as following :

	Imbibition		Diffusion
1.	Absorption of water by solid substance.	1.	It is flow of substance from higher concentration to lower concentration.
2.	Solid substance undergo swelling volume is increased.	2.	Total volume remains same.
3.	Pressure created is called imbibitional pressure.	3.	Takes place due to DPD.

(e)   The main differences between apoplast and symplast pathways of movement of water in plants are as following :

	Apoplast		Symplast
1.	Apoplast pathway is the movement of water through adjacent cell walls.	1.	In this pathway water moves from one cell to another through plasmodesmata.
2.	Movement through apoplast does not involve crossing the cell membrane.	2.	During symplast movement, the water travels through cells.
3.	Apoplast movement is fast.	3.	Symplast movement is relatively slower.
4.	The apoplast does not provide any barrier to water movement.	4.	In symplast water molecule are unable to penetrate casparian strip.

(f)   The main differences between guttation and transpiration are as following :

	Guttation		Transpiration
1.	It is loss or excretion of water in form of liquid droplet.	1.	It is loss of water in the form of vapour.
2.	Occurs through hydathodes.	2.	Occurs through stomata, lenticle or cuticle.
3.	Commonly occurs in night or early in the morning.	3.	Commonly occurs in day time.
4.	It is restricted to about 345 genera of herbaceous and some woody plants.	4.	It occurs in all higher terrestrial plants.
5.	It takes place due to root pressure.	5.	Root pressure is not involved.
6.	It has no relation with the temperature.	6.	Transpiration maintains the temperature of plants.

11.6 Briefly describe water potential. What are the factors affecting it?

Sol.   **Water potential :** Free energy per mole of water molecule is called water potential. It is represented by Greek letter 'ψ' (Psi). Water potential of pure water is zero and addition of solute, decreases its free energy or water potential.

Factors affecting water potential are as following :

(i)   Matric potential (ψ_m) causes by adsorbent or colloidal particles (always negative and almost negligible).

(ii)   Solute potential (ψ_s) caused by presence of solute particles (decreases the water potential).

(iii)   Pressure potential (ψ_p) caused by entry or exit of water (increases the water potential).

$$\psi_w = \psi_p + \psi_s + \psi_m$$

11.7   What happens when a pressure greater than the atmospheric pressure is applied to pure water or a solution?

Sol.   Under constant temperature the volume of liquid varies inversely to pressure. Moreover, if greater pressure is applied then it will change the state of the matter from liquid to solid at a given temperature. Any liquid will abide by these laws.

11.8 (a)   With the help of well-labelled diagrams, describe the process of plasmolysis in plants, giving appropriate examples.

(b)   Explain what will happen to a plant cell if it is kept in a solution having higher water potential.

Sol.   (a)   Plasmolysis is shrinkage of protoplast of a cell from its cell wall under the influence of a hypertonic solution (solution of higher concentration).

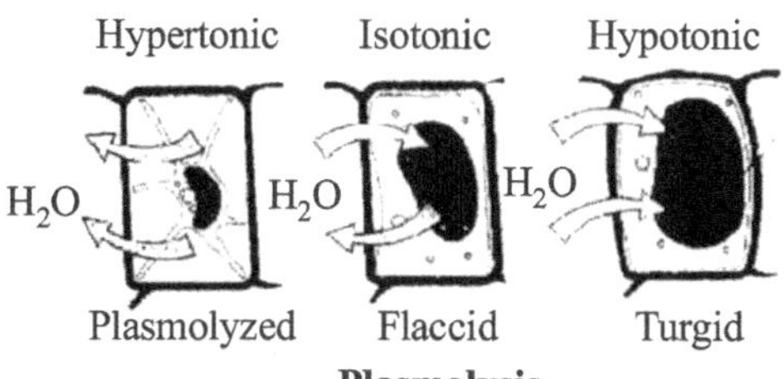

Plasmolysis

(b) The process of plasmolysis is usually reversible. When the cells are placed in hypotonic solution (solution with low concentration), water diffuses into the cell causing the cytoplasm swelling up. Swelling of shrunken protoplast is called as deplasmolysis.

11.9 How is the mycorrhizal association helpful in absorption of water and mineral in plants?

Sol. In conifers (*e.g. Pinus*) the root hairs (helps in water absorption) are either very poorly developed or entirely absent. Such roots are associated with fungal hyphae is called as mycorrhiza. The fungal filaments form a network around the young roots. The hyphae have a very large surface area that absorb mineral ions and water from the soil and handed over them to root.

11.10 What role does root pressure play in water movement in plants?

Sol. As various ions from the soil are actively transported into the vascular tissues of the roots, water follows (its potential gradient) and increases the pressure inside the xylem. This positive pressure is called root pressure, and can be responsible for pushing up water to small heights in the stem.

Root pressure can, at best, only provide a modest push in the overall process of water transport. They obviously do not play a major role in water movement up tall trees. The greatest contribution of root pressure may be to re-establish the continuous chains of water molecules in the xylem which often break under the enormous tensions created by transpiration. Root pressure does not account for the majority of water transport; most plants meet their need by transpiratory pull.

11.11 Describe transpiration pull model of water transport in plants. What are the factors influencing transpiration? How is it useful to plants ?

Sol. **Transpiration pull theory :** The theory was put forward by Dixon and Jolly.

The main features of the theory are :

(i) There is a continuous column of water (present in tracheary element) from root through the stem and into the leaves.

(ii) Water molecule attached to one another, by cohesion force, adhesion force (between their walls and water molecules) and surface tension.

(iii) The water in tracheary element would, come under tension, due to transpiration also called as transpiration pull.

- **Factor affecting transpiration :** External factor *e.g.* atmospheric pressure, temperature, humidity, CO_2, sunlight, wind velocity, etc. Thickness of cuticle, number, position and closing and opening of stomata, pH and hormones are internal factors which affects transpiration.

   Significance of transpiration :
- Ascent of sap
- Removal of excess of water
- Cooling effect
- Distribution of minerals.
- Transpiration supplies water for photosynthesis.

11.12 Discuss the factors responsible for ascent of xylem sap in plants.

Sol. Ascent of xylem sap is supported by following factors.

(i) Root pressure (positive pressure that develops in the xylem sap of root).

(ii) Cohesion (adhesion of water molecules due to hydrogen bonding).

(iii) Adhesion (force between tracheary wall and water molecule).

(iv) Transpiration pull (tension develops due to transpiration) is the main cause of ascent of xylem sap.

11.13 What essential role does the root endodermis play during mineral absorption in plants?

Sol. Water flowing through apoplast contains minerals useful to plants and also toxins.

Endodermal cells have many transport proteins embedded in their plasma membrane; they let some solutes cross the membrane, but not others. Transport proteins of endodermal cells are control points, where a plant adjusts the quantity and types of solutes that reach the xylem.

11.14 Explain why xylem transport is unidirectional and phloem transport bidirectional.

Sol. The plant part which synthesise the food, *i.e.* leaf known as source and part that needs or stores the food called as sink. Food, primarily sucrose, is transported by vascular tissue phloem, from a source to a sink. But depending on season or plants need, the source sink may be reversed. Sugar stored in roots may be mobilised to become a source of food source in early spring when buds of trees require energy for their growth and development and act as sink. Since the source - sink relationship is bidirection in phloem while in xylem it is unidirection.

11.15 Explain pressure flow hypothesis of translocation of sugars in plants.

Sol. Mass flow or Pressure Flow Hypothesis : It was put forward by Munch (1927, 1930). According to this hypothesis organic substance move from region of high osmotic pressure to low osmotic pressure due to turgor pressure. A high osmotic concentration is present in source *e.g.* mesophyll cells (due to photosynthesis). Sugar present in them passed into sieve tube therefore high osmotic concentration develops and it absorbs water from xylem and develop a high turgor pressure. It causes flow of sugar towards area of low turgor pressure or sink.

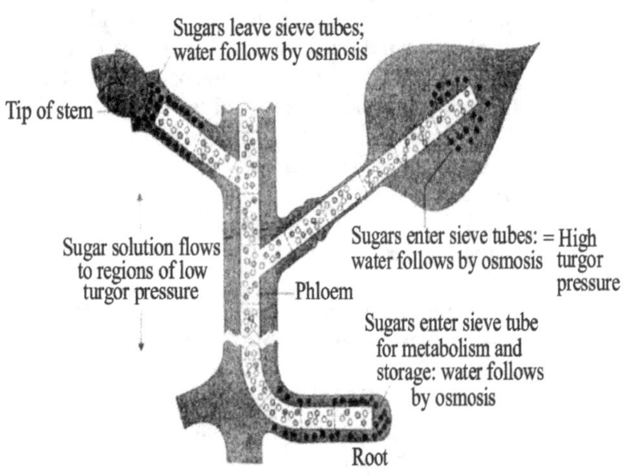

Fig. Diagrammatic presentation of mechanism of translocation

11.16 What causes the opening and closing of guard cells of stomata during transpiration?

Sol. The opening and closing of stomata depend upon the turgid or flaccid state of the guard cells. The inner wall of guard cells (towards pore) is thick and outer wall (towards other epidermal cells) is thin. When the turgor pressure of the guard cells in increased the outer thinner wall of the guard cell is pushed out (towards the periphery) thus pulling the inner thicker wall leading to the opening of stomatal pore. When the guard cells are in a flaccid state the outer thinner wall of guard cells returns to original position (moves towards pore) due to which tension on the inner wall is released and stomatal aperture gets closed.

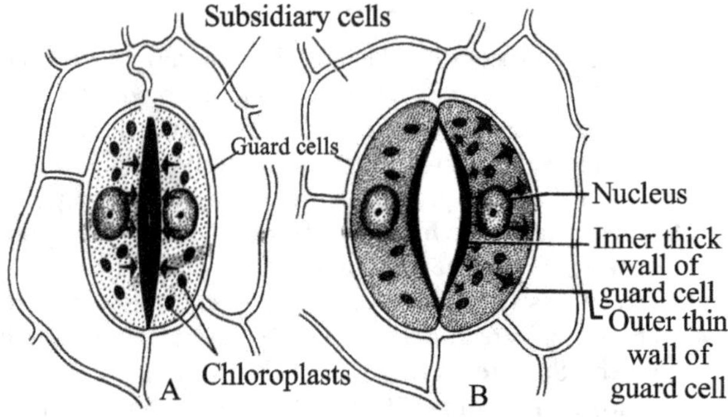

Fig. The cell wall bordering the stomatal pore is thicker than that of next to the surrounding cells
A. Aperture closed, B. Aperture open

SECTION B — PRACTICE QUESTIONS 

MULTIPLE CHOICE QUESTIONS

1. Which of the following is the unit of ψ (psi)
   (a) Pascal (b) Joule
   (c) Newton (d) Electron volt

2. The process responsible for facilitating loss of water in liquid form from the tip of grass blades at night not early morning is:
   (a) Root pressure (b) Imbibition
   (c) Plasmolysis (d) Transpiration

3. The water potential of pure water is
   (a) Less than zero
   (b) More than zero but less than one
   (c) More than one
   (d) Zero

4. Which of the following is decreased during increase in humidity in the atmosphere?
   (a) Transpiration (b) Photosynthesis
   (c) Respiration (d) Glycolysis

5. Two types of molecules cross the membrane in the same direction, it is called as
   (a) Uniport (b) Symport
   (c) Antiport (d) Multiport

6. Diffusion rate is affected by
   (a) temperature (b) membrane permeability
   (c) gradient of concentration (d) all of these

7. Which of the following is true about diffusion?
   (a) There is no expenditure of energy.
   (b) Molecules move in Brownian motion.
   (c) Substances moves from the region of higher concentration to the region of lower concentration.
   (d) Diffusion depends on the type of living system.

8. If pressure greater than atmospheric pressure is applied to pure water, the water potential
   (a) increases
   (b) decreases
   (c) remains same
   (d) atmospheric pressure does not affect water potential.

9. Wilting of a plant results from excessive
   (a) respiration (b) photosynthesis
   (c) absorption (d) transpiration

10. When a plant is girdled (ringed)
   (a) the root and shoot die at the same time
   (b) the shoot dies first
   (c) the root dies first
   (d) neither root nor shoot will die

ASSERTION & REASON QUESTIONS

DIRECTION (Qs. 1-5) : *These questions consists of two statements. Answer these questions selecting the appropriate option given below:*
(a) Both Assertion (A) and Reason (R) are true and Reason (R) is the correct explanation of Assertion (A).
(b) Both Assertion (A) and Reason (R) are true, but Reason (R) is not the correct explanation of Assertion (A).
(c) Assertion (A) is true, but Reason (R) is false.
(d) Assertion (A) is false, but Reason (R) is true.

1. **Assertion:** In symport transport both molecules cross the membrane at the same time in the same direction.
   Reason: In antiport transport, both molecules move in opposite direction.

2. **Assertion:** Turgor pressure is the positive pressure that develops in the plant cell due to entry of water.
   Reason: During growth of cells, the turgor pressure is responsible for enlargement and extension.
3. **Assertion:** Pure water has maximum water potential.
   Reason: The osmotic potential is zero in pure water.
4. **Assertion:** When the ambient temperature is high and soil contains excess of water, the plants tend to lose water in the form of droplets from lenticels.
   Reason: Root pressure not regulates the rate of loss of water form lenticels.
5. **Assertion:** In phloem the movement is always bidirectional.
   Reason: The direction of movement in the phloem can be upwards or downwards.

CASE/PASSAGE BASED QUESTIONS

DIRECTIONS (Qs. 1-5): *Read the following passage and answer the questions that follows.*

Transpiration is the evaporative loss of water by plants. It occurs mainly through stomata. Besides the loss of water vapour in transpiration, exchange of oxygen and carbon dioxide in the leaf also occurs through these stomata. Normally stomata are open in the day time and close during the night. The immediate cause of the opening or closing of stomata is a change in the turgidity of the guard cells.

The transpiration driven ascent of xylem sap depends mainly on the following physical properties of water:

Cohesion – mutual attraction between water molecules.

Adhesion – attraction of water molecules to polar surfaces.

Surface Tension – water molecules are attracted to each other in the liquid phase more than to water in the gas phase.

These properties give water high tensile strength, i.e., an ability to resist a pulling force, and high capillarity, i.e., the ability to rise in thin tubes. In plants capillarity is added by the small diameter of the tracheary elements – the tracheids and vessel elements. As water evaporates through the stomata, since the thin film of water cover the cells is continuous, it results in pulling of water, molecule by molecule, into the leaf from the xylem. Also, because of lower concentration of water vapour in the atmosphere as compared to the substomatal cavity and intercellular spaces, water diffuses into the surrounding air.

1. __________ is the site for gaseous exchange and evaporation of water in the form of vapours i.e. transpiration.
   (a) Leaf   (b) Leaf surface
   (c) Stomata   (d) All of the above
2. Hydrophilic mutual attraction between water molecules is termed as
   (a) Cohesion   (b) Adhesion
   (c) Surface tension   (d) Both (a) and (c)
3. Identify the correct statement
   (i) Cohesion is mutual attraction between water molecules.
   (ii) Adhesion is attraction of water molecules to polar surfaces.
   (iii) Transpiration is the evaporative loss of water by plants.
   (iv) Water molecules are attracted to each other in the liquid phase more than to water in the gas phase.
   (a) Only (i)   (b) Only (ii)
   (c) Only (iii) & (iv)   (d) All of the above
4. What is the reason behind immediate opening or closing of stomata?
5. Enlist the properties that give water high tensile strength.

VERY SHORT ANSWER QUESTIONS

1. What fraction of soil water is readily available to plants?
2. A plant cell when kept in a certain solution got plasmolysed. What was the nature of this solution?
3. What is the chemical potential of pure water at normal temperature and pressure?
4. What is transmembrane pathway?
5. Define transpirational pull.
6. Identify a type of molecular movement which is highly selective and requires special membrane proteins, but does not require energy.
7. How can you revert a freshly plasmolysed plant cell to its normal state?
8. What is meant by uniport?
9. What is the use of imbibition pressure to plants?
10. What is a casparian strip?
11. Name the form in which cabohydrates are transported in plants and the tissue through which it is transported.
12. What is the pressure potential of a plasmolysed cell?
13. In which plant there will be no transpiration?
14. If water enters a cell what is the pressure exerted by its swollen protoplasts?

SHORT ANSWER QUESTIONS

1. List any four mechanisms that contribute to the ascent of sap in tall trees.
2. Mention two advantage of transpiration.
3. How do rise in temperature and wind velocity affect transpiration? Write any three adaptations shown by plants to reduce transpiration.
4. What is meant by apoplast pathway? Why does it occur in cortex and not in endodermis?
5. What is the significance of osmosis?
6. Describe the apoplastic and symplastic movements of water in plants.
7. Sugar crystals do not dissolve easily in ice cold water. Explain.
8. What is imbibition pressure? What is the usefulness of imbibition pressure to seed germination?
9. Differentiate between active and passive transport.
10. Differentiate between diffusion and facilitated diffusion.
11. What is meant by source and sink in plants, with regard to translocation?
12. Differentiate between transportation of water and translocation of Food.

LONG ANSWER QUESTIONS

1. Describe with the help of labelled diagrams, the closing and opening of stomata in plants.
2. Describe the root pressure theory and its demerits.
3. Differentiate the following :-
   - (a) Simple diffusion and active transport
   - (b) Turgid cell and flaccid cell
   - (c) Isotonic solution and hypotonic solution

SOLUTIONS

Multiple Choice Questions

1. (a) Psi or ψ is expressed in pressure units e.g. pascals.
2. (a) The process responsible for facilitating loss of water in liquid forms from the tip of grass blades at night and early morning is root pressure.
3. (d) The water potential of pure water is zero.
4. (a) With the increase in humidity in atmosphere, rate of transpiration decreases.
5. (b) In symport, two types of molecules cross the membrane in the same direction.
6. (d) Diffusion rate is affected by the gradient of concentration, permeability of the membrane separating them, temperature and pressure.
7. (d) Diffusion depends on the type of living system. Diffusion is a slow process, it is not dependent on the living systems.
8. (a) If a pressure greater than atmospheric pressure is applied to pure water, the water potential increases.
9. (d) Wilting of a plant results from excessive transpiration.
10. (c) When a plant is girdled (ringed) the root dies first.

Assertion & Reason Questions

1. (b) Some carrier proteins allow transport only if two types of molecules move together. This is known as co-transport. Symport and antiport are two types of co-transport. Symport allows both the molecules to move in same direction and antiport allows both the molecules to move in opposite direction.
2. (b) Due to entry of water into it, a positive pressure develops in a plant cell or system. This positive hydrostatic pressure is also known as turgor pressure. Turgor pressure keeps the cells and their organelles stretched, this is essential for proper functioning of a cell. It gives support to non-woody tissues like parenchyma. During growth, turgor pressure is essential for cell enlargement.
3. (c) Water potential is the potential energy of water relative to pure water in reference conditions. Pure water has maximum water potential, whereas, addition of solutes to water lowers the water potential. Osmosis is a special type of diffusion in which water diffuses from its pure state i.e., higher water potential to concentrated solution i.e., lower chemical potential through a semi-permeable membrane. Since pure water has no difference in chemical potential, it has zero osmotic potential.

4. (d) Lenticels are the small pores which are present on the stem of the plant and they helps in the process of gaseous exchange.
   - The lenticels are not involved in the process of the loss of water in the form of droplets. The regulation of the water is done by the process of imbibition which shows that the session is incorrect
   - The root pressure does not regulate the rate of loss of water from the lenticels because the regulation of the water is done by imbibition which is a special type of diffusion process.
5. (a) The source-sink relationship is variable, the direction of movement in the phloem can be upwards or downwards, i.e., bi-directional. Hence, unlike one-way flow of water in transpiration, food in phloem sap can be transported in any required direction so long as there is a source of sugar and a sink able to use, store or remove the sugar.

Case/Passage Based Questions

1. (c) Stomata is the site for gaseous exchange and evaporation of water in the form of vapours i.e. transpiration.
2. (a) Hydrophilic mutual attraction between water molecules is termed as cohesion.
3. (d) All the above statements are correct.
4. The reason behind immediate opening or closing of stomata is the turgidity of the guard cells. A change in the turgidity of the guard cells cause immediate opening or closing of stomata.
5. Properties that give water high tensile strength;
   - Cohesion
   - Adhesion
   - Surface Tension

Very Short Answer Questions

1. Capillary water.
2. Hypertonic solution.
3. Zero.
4. The movement of water through the cell membrane is called transmembrane pathway or symplast pathway.
5. The tension develops due to transpiration which helps in pulling of water from soil to leaves, is called transpirational pull.
6. Facilitated diffusion.
7. By placing it in aqueous solution.
8. A molecule moves across the membrane independent of other molecule called as uniport.
9. Responsible for the seedling to emerge out of the soil.

10. Casparian strip is band of suberin on the tangential and radial walls of endodermal cells.
11. Sucrose, phloem.
12. Pressure potential of a plasmolysed cell is negative.
13. In aquatic submerged plant their will be no transpiration.
14. The pressure exerted will be turgor pressure.

Short Answer Questions

1. Mechanisms that contribute to the ascent of sap in tall trees are :
   (1) Adhesion   (2) Cohesion
   (3) Transpirational pull   (4) Root pressure.
2. Advantages of transpiration :
   (1) It helps in mineral absorption and ascent of sap.
   (2) Transpiration, by evaporating of water causes a cooling effect of plant body.
3. Rise in temperature, wind velocity increases the rate of transpiration.
   Three adaptations shown by plants to reduce transpiration are:
   (a) leaves with thick cuticle
   (b) sunken stomata
   (c) modification of leaves into scales or spines and stem into phylloclades.
4. The movement of water exclusively through cell wall without crossing cell membrane, is called apoplast pathway. It occurs in cortex due to the absence of casparian strip and presence of loosely packed cells. It does not occur in endodermis due to the presence of suberin in casparian strip.
5. Significance of osmosis :
   (1) Osmosis is important in the absorption of water by plants.
   (2) Helps in cell to cell movement of water.
   (3) Provides rigidity to the plant organs.
   (4) Helps in opening and closing of stomata.
6. Apoplastic movement of water occurs exclusively through the non-living cell wall without crossing any membrane. Symplastic movement of water occurs from one cell to the other through plasmodesmata it passes across membrane and *i.e.* living components.
7. Rate of diffusion is increased when temperature increase. So, sugar crystal do not dissolve easily in ice cold water.
8. Imbibition pressure is the pressure developed in an adsorbent due to diffusion of water into it.
   This pressure makes the seedlings to emerge above the ground during seed germination.
9. The main difference between active transport and passive transport are :

Active transport		Passive transport	
1.	It is the process that involves expenditure of energy.	1.	It is the process that does not involve expenditure of energy.
2.	It occurs even against concentration gradient.	2.	It occurs following concentration gradient.
3.	It is rapid.	3.	It is slow.

10. The main difference between diffusion and facilitated diffusion are :

Diffusion		Facilitated diffusion	
1.	Diffusion is the movement of any ions/substances from the region of higher concentration to the region of lower concentration.	1.	It is the movement of substances across the membrane with the help of membrane proteins.
2.	It may not involve any living system.	2.	It involves the membrane, a living system.

11. **Source :** Source is the part of the plant which synthesises the food, they are the leaves.
    Sink : Sink is the part of the plant that needs or stores the food like roots, tubers, any storage organ etc.

12.

Transportation of Water		Translocation of Food	
1.	Xylem transports water to all parts	1.	Phloem transports food to all parts of the plant
2.	Roots take up water from soil	2.	Food is made in leaves.
3.	It is unidirectional upwards	3.	It is bidirectional both upwards and downwards.

Long Answer Questions

1. Stomata are minute openings formed in the epidermis of leaves, stem and in (some cases) even flowers. Each stomata contains pore surrounded by two guard cells. The guard cells are joined at both ends but separate in the mid-region of their length. Stomata are mostly present on the lower epidermis of the leaf.
   The open stomata account for diffusion of water vapour through them. During the day, the cell-sap concentration becomes high due to accumulation of sugar as a result of photosynthesis. This results into endosmosis and the water is withdrawn into guard cells from the neighboring cells. This makes the guard cells turgid and stomata open. If the availability of water is reduced, the guard cells lose their turgidity and they become flaccid by exosmosis of water from guard cells. This leads to the closing of stomata and transpiration stops.
   Diagram Refer to Q. 11.16 NCERT Exercise
2. **Root pressure theory :** The theory was put forward by Priestley (1916). Root pressure refers to positive hydrostatic pressure which is develops in xylem sap, when rate of water absorption is more than the rate of transpiration and as a result of which water is pushed up in tracheary element of root.

Demerits of root pressure concept :

(1) Magnitude of root pressure is maximum upto 2 atmosphere which can raise water upto 64ft. only. It can't drive water in tall trees (300-400 feet) there is need of 20 atmosphere root pressure.

(2) No root pressure in conifers.

(3) Root pressure is low in summer when transpiration is high and high in spring when transpiration is low

(4) Root pressure is not seen in rapidly transpiring plants.

3. (a) The main difference between simple diffusion and active transport are :

	Simple diffusion	Active transport
1.	It is the movement of substances/ions from region of higher concentration to region of lower concentration.	It is the movement of substances even against concentration gradient.
2.	It does not involve expenditure of energy.	It makes use of metabolic energy.
3.	It is a slow process.	It is a rapid process
4.	It does not involve any living system.	In involves living systems like membranes.

(b) The main difference between turgid cell and flaccid cell are :

	Turgid cell	Flaccid cell
1.	A cell becomes turgid due to endosmosis or entry of water molecules into it.	A cell becomes flaccid due to exosmosis or exit of water molecules from the cell.
2.	The cell has a higher water potential and turgor pressure / pressure potential.	The cell has a lower water potential and lower turgor pressure / pressure potential.

(c) The main difference between isotonic solution and hypotonic solution are :

	Isotonic solution	Hypotonic solution
1.	When the external solution balances the atmospheric pressure of the cell, it is said to be isotonic.	When the external solution is more dilute compared to the cytoplasm, it is called hypotonic.
2.	There is no net movement of the water molecules.	Water moves into the cells and causes its swelling.

SECTION C — NCERT EXEMPLAR QUESTIONS 

MULTIPLE CHOICE QUESTIONS

1. Which of the following statements does not apply to reverse osmosis?
(a) It is used for water purification
(b) In this technique, pressure greater than osmotic pressure is applied to the system
(c) It is a passive process
(d) It is an active process

2. Which one of the following will not directly affect transpiration?
(a) Temperature
(b) Light
(c) Wind speed
(d) Chlorophyll content of leaves

3. The form of sugar transported through phloem is
(a) glucose   (b) fructose
(c) sucrose   (d) ribose

4. When a plant undergoes senescence, the nutrients may be
(a) exported
(b) withdrawn
(c) translocated
(d) None of the above

5. Water potential of pure water at standard temperature is equal to
(a) 10   (b) 20
(c) zero   (d) None of these

6. Based on the figure given below which of the following statements is not correct?

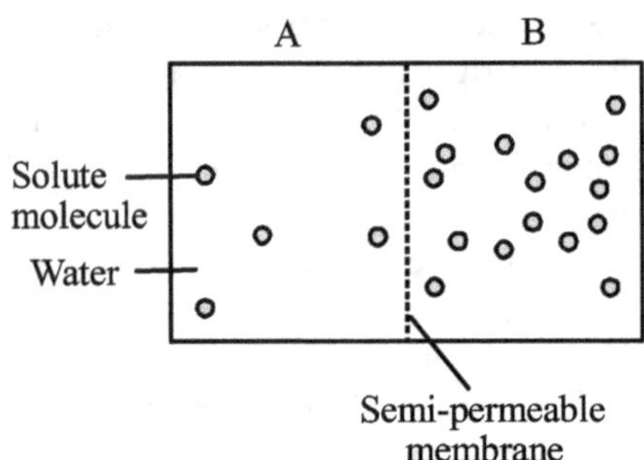

(a) Movement of solvent molecules will take place from chamber A to B
(b) Movement of solute will take place from A to B
(c) Presence of a semipermeable is a pre-requisite for this process to occur
(d) The direction and rate of osmosis depends on both the pressure gradient and concentration gradient

7. Choose the correct option mycorrhiza is a symbiotic association of fungus with root system which helps in
A. absorption of water   B. mineral nutrition
C. translocation   D. gaseous exchange
(a) Only A   (b) Only B
(c) Both A and B   (d) Both B and C

Very Short Answer Questions

1. Smaller, lipid soluble molecules diffuse faster through cell membrane, but the movement of hydrophilic substances are facilitated by certain transporters which are chemically ....

2. In a passive transport across a membrane. When two protein molecules move in opposite direction and independent of each other, it is called as ....

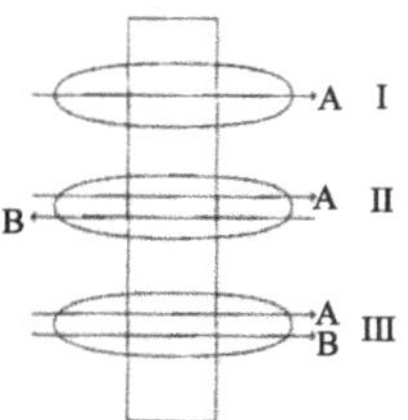

3. Osmosis is a special kind of diffusion, in which water diffuses across the cell membrane. The rate and direction of osmosis depends upon both ....

4. A flowering plant is planted in a earthen pot and irrigated. Urea is added to make the plant grow faster, but after sometime the plant dies. This may be due to ....

5. Absorption of water from soil by dry seeds increases the .... , thus helping seedlings to come out of soil.

6. Water moves up against gravity and even for a tree of 20 m height, the tip receives water within two hours. The most important physiological phenomenon which is responsible for the upward movement of water is ....

7. The plant cell cytoplasm is surrounded by both cell wall and cell membrane. The specificity of transport of substances are mostly across the cell membrane, because ....

8. The C_4 plants are twice as efficient as C_3 plants in terms of fixing CO_2 but lose only .... as much water C_3 plants for the same amount of CO_2 fixed.

9. Movement of substances in xylem is unidirectional while in phloem it is bidirectional. Explain

10. Define water potential and solute potential.

11. An onion peel was taken and
    (a) placed in salt solution for five minutes.
    (b) after that it was placed in distilled water.
    When seen under the microscope what would be observed in (a) and (b) ?

12. How does most of the water moves within the root?

13. Transpiration is a necessary evil in plants. Explain.

14. Describe briefly the three physical properties of water which helps in ascent of water in xylem.

15. Identify a type of molecular movement which is highly selective and requires special membrane proteins, but does not require energy.

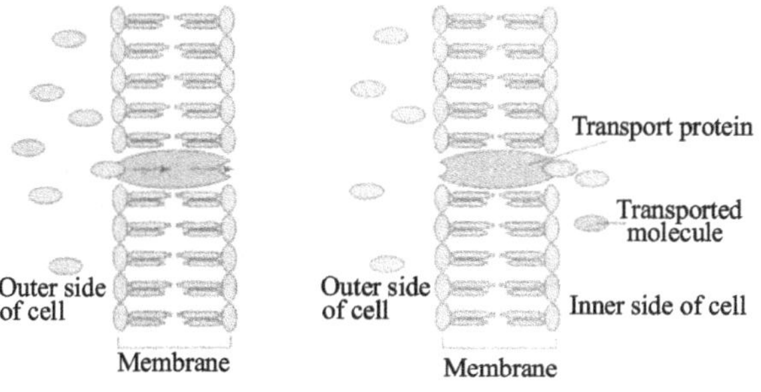

16. Correct the statements.
    (a) Cells shrink in hypotonic solutions and swell in hypertonic solutions.
    (b) Imbibition is special type of diffusion when water is absorbed by living cells.
    (c) Most of the water flow in the roots occurs via the symplast.

Short Answer Questions

1. Minerals absorbed by the roots travel up the xylem. How do they reach the parts where they are needed most? Do all the parts of the plant get the same amount of the minerals?

2. Water is indispensable for life. What properties of water make it useful for all biological process on the earth?

3. How is it that the intracellular levels of K^+ are higher than extracellular levels in animal cells?

4. In a girdled plant, when water is supplied to the leaves above the girdle, leaves may remain green for sometime then wilt and ultimately die. What does it indicate?

5. Various types of transport mechanisms are needed to fulfil the mineral requirements of a plant. Why are they not fulfilled by diffusion alone?

6. Will the ascent of sap be possible without the cohesion and adhesion of the water molecules? Explain.

7. When a freshly collected Spirogyra filament is kept in a 10% potassium nitrate solution, it is observed that the protoplasm shrinks in size
    (a) What is this phenomenon called?
    (b) What will happen if the filament is replaced in distilled water?

8. What are 'aquaporins'? How does presence of aquaporins affect osmosis?

9. ABA (Abscicis Acid) is called a stress hormone.
    A. How does this hormone overcome stress conditions?
    B. From where does this hormone get released in leave?

10. How is facilitated diffusion different from diffusion?

11. Observe the diagram and answer the following.

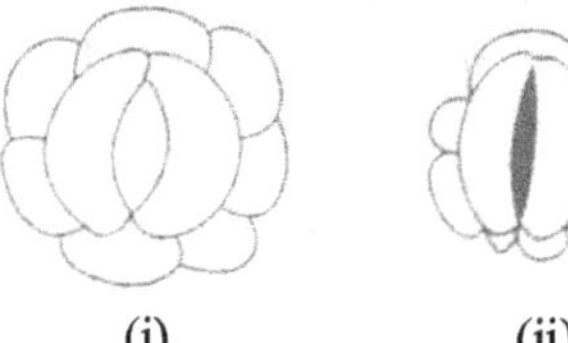

    (a) Are these types of guard cells found in monocots or dicots?
    (b) Which of these shows a higher water content (i) or (ii)?
    (c) Which element plays an important role in the opening and closing of stomata?

12. Define uniport, symport and antiport. Do they require energy?

Long Answer Questions

1. Minerals are present in the soil in sufficient amounts. Do plants need to adjust the type of solutes that reach the xylem? Which molecules help to adjust this? How do plants regulate the type and quantity of solutes that reach xylem?

2. Plants show temporary and permanent wilting. Differentiate between the two. Do any of them indicate the water status of the soil?

SOLUTIONS

Multiple Choice Questions

1. **(c)** Reverse osmosis is an active process as it consume ATP, or external pressure is applied in order to carry out osmosis in a reverse direction (lower to higher).

2. **(d)** The rate of transpiration will not be affected by chlorophyll content.
   Temperature increases the rate of transpiration.
   Light quality and intensity also play a role in transpiration.
   Wind speed: higher the wind speed, more will be the rate of transpiration.

3. **(c)** Sucrose a disaccharide sugar transported through phloem. It comprises of 2 units of glucose joined by α–1–4 glycosidic linkage. It is the most inactive form of sugar so used in the transport of food.
   Glucose is a reactive sugar because of presence of CHO group. Fructose is found in fruits and ribose is present in nucleic acids.

4. **(c)** Senescence is the programmed death of a plant. At the time of senescence, translocation of nutrients to different parts of the plant are withdrawn.

5. **(c)** Water potential of pure water at standard temperature is zero. It is the highest value of water potential.

6. **(b)** Movement of water will take place from chamber A to B because osmosis is a process in which solvent molecules moves from a region of higher concentration to a region of lower concentration through a semi-permeable membrane.

7. **(c)** Symbiosis is an association in which two organisms are associated with each other in such a way that both of them derive benefit from each other.
   Mycorrhiza is an association of fungi with roots of plants. Fungi take shelter in roots and in return help in absorption of water and minerals from the soil

Very Short Answer Questions

1. The movement of hydrophilic substances are facilitated by transporters which are chemically proteins. These proteins form porins, which are huge pores in the outer membranes of the plastids, mitochondria and some bacteria. These porins allow passage of small molecules through the membrane.

2. Antiport which facilitates transport of molecules in both the directions across the membrane and their movement is independent of each other.

3. The rate and direction of osmosis is dependent upon the pressure and concentration gradient.

4. The solution outside the plant is an hypertonic solution, and the plant cells are hypotonic in nature, so there is a gradual movement of water from plant cell to outside urea solution leading to plasmolysis of root cells and plant dies gradually due to exosmosis.

5. Imbibition of water by seed materials as starch and protein, pushes the seedlings out of the soil causing the seed to swell and increase of imbibition pressure inside the seed, contributes for germination of seeds.

6. Transpiration pull is the physiological phenomenon which is responsible for the upward movement of water in tall trees the water molecules transpire from stomata, which pulls water molecules upward to the leaf from the continuous chain of water molecules carried by xylem.

7. The transport takes place by the cell membrane because cell membrane as it is semi-permeable and composed of lipids that are arranged in bilayer structure along with proteins and carbohydrate.

8. C_4 plants are twice as efficient as C_3 plants in terms of fixing carbon in the form of glucose, but lose only half as much water as a C_3 plant for the same amount of C_2 fixed.

9. Xylem is involved in the one way transport of water and minerals from soil to root' $\to$ stem $\to$ leaves. Several forces like imbibition, root pressure and finally transpiration pull. Act in this mechanism, It is a undirectional process as there is continuous loss of water at the body surface of plants.
   The main function of Phloem is to transport food from source to sink where source is the part of plant responsible for food synthesis and sink are the organs requiring food for their growth and development. These source and sink parts of a plants may vary in different phases of growth, thus the food needs to travel in both upwards and downward direction. So, phloem shows bidirectional movement of substances.

10. Water potential is a measure of free energy associated with water per unit volume (JM^{-3}). The water potential of pure (ψ_w) at atmosp-heric Pressure is zero.
    Additional of solutes reduce water potential (to a negative value). This reduces the of water concentration. Solutions thus have a lower water potential than pure water, the magnitude of this lowering due to dissolution of solute is called solute potential of ψ_s

11. (a) When placed in salt solution an onion peel shrinks as water from cytoplasm of cell moves out of the cell to wards hypertonic solution.
    (b) When again placed back in distilld water, cell regains it's shape and absorbs water and become turgid.

12. Water mostly flows in the roots via the apoplast pathway as the cortical cells are loosly packed and hence offer no resistance to water movement, through mass flow. This mass flow of water occurs due to adhesive and cohesive properties of water.
    Like, symplast pathway is also involved in the movement of water molecules within the root (like, via endodermis to xylem).

13. Loss of water in the form of water vapours from the surface of leaves of plant is called transpiration.
    Transpiration a necessary evil because the plant continuously lose water in the vapour form from its body surfaces, Which creates a transpiration pull to absorb more and more water from soil through roots.
    If water is not available to plants in soil, even then loss through transpiration does not ceasle, so plants sometimes shows wilting.

14. The following are physical properties of water that helps in ascent up to xylem.

Cohesive properties	– Provider mutual attraction between molecules
Adhesive properties	– Causes attraction of water molecules to polar surfaces (of tracheids)
Surface tension	– Water molecules get attracted to each other more in liquid phase than in gas phase.

15. Facilitated diffusion's is a highly selective passive process. Facilitated diffusion cause net transport of molecules from a low to high concentration. In facilitated diffusion special proteins help in movement of substances across the membrane without expenditure of ATP energy.

16. (a) The cell swell in hypotonic solution and shrink in hypertonic solution.
    (b) Imbibition is a special type of diffusion when water is adsorbed by living cells.
    (c) Most of the water flow in roots occurs via the apoplast way.

Short Answer Questions

1. The sabsorbed mineral are transported through the transpiration steam up the stem, to all parts of plant. The growing region of the plant, such as the apical and lateral meristems, young leaves, developing flowers, fruits, seeds and the storage organs are the chief sinks for the mineral elements.

   Uploading of the mineral ions occurs via fine vein endings through diffusion and active uptake by the cells. Xylem are involved in transport of inorganic nutrients where phloem transport only organic materials in plants.

   Mineral ions are frequently remobilised from older parts of plant like leaves to the younger regions. Most readily mobilised elements are phosphorus, sulphur, nitrogen, potassium, and some elements like calcium that forms the structural component are not remobilised.

2. Following are the properties of water that make it useful for all biological processes.
   (i) Water is the major solvent through which mineral nutrients enter a Plant from the soil solution.
   (ii) It is an ideal solvent with neutral pH.
   (iii) Water is the major constituent of protoplasm. it constitutes approximately 90% of the protoplasm.
   (iv) Water acts as a medium for translocation of nutritive substances. Mineral nutrients are absorbed by the roots. Carbohydrates that are formed during photosynthesis are transported by water from cell to cell, tissue to tissue and organ to organ.
   (v) Water is involved in photosynthesis in plants, as it incorporates hydrogen atom into carbohydrate and releases oxygen atoms as O_2.
   (vi) Water acts as an agent for temperature control. The specific heat of water helps plant in maintaining a relatively stable internal temperature.
   (vii) Water is necessary for pollination in some plants in bryophytes and pteridophytes, water are essentially requires for the fertilisation process.

3. The excitability of sensory cells, neurons and muscles is dependent on ion channels, signal transducers that provide a regulated path for the movement of inorganic ions such as Na^+, K^+, Ca^{2+}, and Cl^- across the plasma membrane in response to various stimuli.

   Ion channels are 'gated' mplying that they may be open or closed. The Na^+, K^+, ATPase create a charge imbalance across the plasma membrane by carrying $3Na^+$ out of the cell for every $2K^+$ ion carried inside making the inside relatively negative outside.

   The membrane is said to be polarised. That is the reason the intracellular levels of K+ are higher than extracellular levels in animals cells.

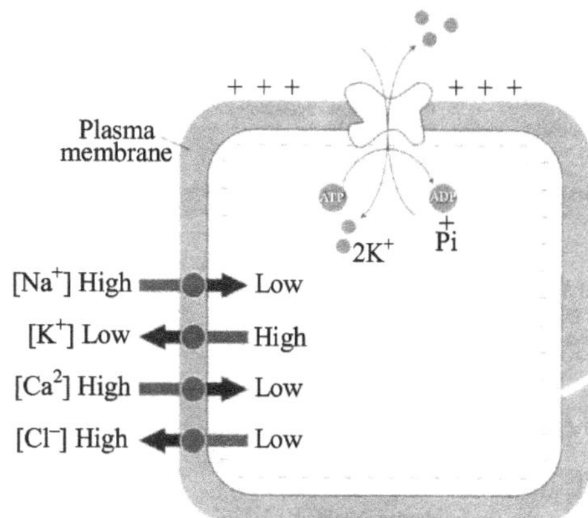

ion balance as in an animal cell

4. When water is supplied in a girdle plant to the leaves above the girdle, leaves may remain green for sometime because leaves can synthesise their own carbohydrate food through photosynthesis, they however, gradvally wilt due to non-availability of water.

   The system of xylem vessels from root to the leaf vein can supply the needed water during girding there is a possible loss of xylem vessels and the water supply is cut off, resulting in death of the plant.

5. Ions, minerals and organic compound are transported in plants in various ways which include.
   (i) Food substances ways which include synthesised in leaves are translocated downward towards root and stem.
   (ii) Food is translocated upwards to the developing leaves, buds and fruits.
   (iii) Radial transport of food occurs across the stem from the cells of pith, from cortex etc, towards epidermis.
   (iv) Ions and minerals are transported upwards through xylem.

   Diffusion is a slow process and allows movement of molecules only for short distances, so it cannot carry out the movements of organic and inorganic substances mentioned above. Therefore, a need arises for special long distance transport systems that permits and moves substances at a much faster rate, i.e., mas of bulk flow system through conducting tissues (translocation).

6. Ascent of sap is not possible without the cohesive and adhesive properties of water they play an important role in transport of water due to the following reasons
   (i) Cohesion forces hold the water molecule together in the conducting channels, so vaccum is not created.
   (ii) Adhesive forces acting between the water molecule and cellulose of cell wall make a thin film of water along the channels so that this film is pulled up by transpiration pull drawing more and more water upwards in the conducting channels from the root.

7. (a) The phenomenon, occurring is Spirogyra filament when placed in 10% potassium nitrate solution (hypertonic solution) is Plasmolysis. It occurs as water from the cell is drawn out to extracellular fluid causing the protoplast to shrink away from cell wall.
   (b) The Spirogyra upon reabsorption of water, causes the protoplast to regain its original shape. This phenomenon is known as deplasmolysis.

8. Aquaporins are integral membrane proteins which form pores or channels in the membrane. The water flows is more rapid through these pores to inside of the cell, as compared to the process of diffusion.
   These are plumbing systems of the cells. They selectively conduct water in and out of the cells, while preventing the passage of ions and other solutes.

9. A. Stress hormone ABA (Abscisic Acid) induces closing of stomata, whenever there is scarcity of water available to the plant. This prevents the loss of water through transpiration by leaves. It also increases the tolerance of plants to various kinds of stresses.

   B. (ABA) is released or transported from the stem apices to leaves.

10. Difference between diffusion and facilitated diffusion include

Diffusion	Facilitated Diffusion
The molecules move in a random fashion, the net result being substances moving from regions of higher concentration to regions of lower concentration.	Facilitated diffusion is the diffusion of substance against a concentration gradient, which is facilitated by the proteins without energy expenditure.
It is a slow process and is not dependent on a 'living system'. There is no expenditure of energy.	The porins proteins forming huge pores in the outer membranes of the plastids, mitochondria and some bacteria allow molecules up to the size of small proteins to pass through.

11. (a) The guard cells that are bean-shaped are found in dicot plants.

    (b) The guards cells in figure (i) are turgid as, they pull the inner wall of the cell outside thus, they have more water in figure (ii) cells are flaccid, this condition results when cells lose water and close stomatal pore.

    (c) The K^+ ions move from neighbouring cells to guards cells, lowering their water potential and as a result the water moves inside making them turgid and thus opening stomata.

12. For movement of substances the biological membranes have many mechanism. Some are active and some are passive. Specific membrane proteins are also involved for special types of transport mechanisms. These mechanisms include: Uniport is a membrane transport system by an integral membrane protein that is involved in facilitated diffusion. These channels open in response to a stimulus for free flow of specific molecules in a specific direction. These channels transport molecule with a solute gradient without energy expenditure.

    Symport involves the movement of two or more different molecules or ions, across the membrane in the same direction, with no expenditure of energy.

    Antiport is called exchanger. This integral membrane protein is involved in secondary active transport of two or more different molecules or ions across the membrane in opposite directions, without affecting the transport of other molecules.

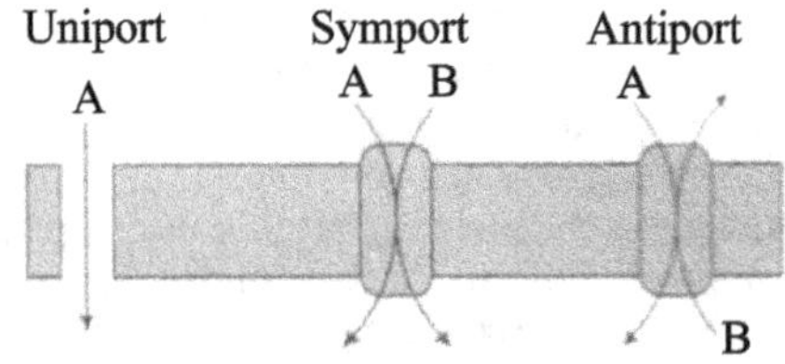

Long Answer Questions

1. Plants do need to adjust the type and quantity of solutes that reach the xylem. The transport of proteins in endodermal cells help in maintaining and adjusting solute movement. The minerals are present in soil as charged particles with a very low concentration compared to that of roots, and thus cannot be completely transported passively across the cell membranes of roots hairs.

   Minerals are thus transported both by active and passive processes, to the xylem. Upon reaching xylem, they are further transported, upwards to sinks through transpiration stream. At the sink regions mineral ions are unloaded through diffusion and active uptake by receptor cells.

   The mineral ions moving frequently through xylem include.

   (i) **Sulphur and Phosphorus** in small amounts are carried in organic forms.

   (ii) Nitrogen travels in plants as inorganic ions NO_2 and NO_3 but much of the nitrogen moves in the form of amino acids and related organic compounds.

   (iii) Mineral ions are frequently remobilised particularly from older senescing parts. Older dying leaves export much of their mineral content to younger leaves. Similarly, before leaf fall in deciduous plants, minerals are removed to other parts.

   The most readily mobilised elements are phosphorus, sulphur, nitrogen and potassium. Structural components elements like calcium are not remobilised.

2. The loss of turgidity of leaves and other soft aerial parts of a plant causing dropping, folding and rolling of non-woody plants is wilting. It occurs when rate of loss of water is higher than the rate of absorption.

Temporary Wilting	Permanent Wilting
It is temporary drooping of young leaves and shoots due to loss of turgidity especially during noon.	It is state of permanent loss of turgidity in leaves and other parts of plant.
It occurs when rate of transpiration is more than water absorption due to shrinkage of roots.	The rate of transpiration is more than rat of absorption but difference is below critical level.
Wilting recovers as soon as water is replenished in the soil around root hairs.	Wilting is not recovered as cells do not regain their turgidity even in presence of plentiful water and atmosphere.
Plant regains its normal growth.	Plant eventually dies.

Mineral Nutrition

12.1 "All elements that are present in a plant need not be essential to its survival". Comment.

Sol. The criteria for essentiality of an element are given below:

(a) The element must be absolutely necessary for supporting normal growth and reproduction.

(b) The requirement of the element must be specific and not replaceable by another element.

(c) The element must be directly involved in the metabolism of the plant.

All elements that are present in a plant do not fulfill these criteria hence cannot be essential for plant survival.

12.2 Why is purification of water and nutrient salts so important in studies involving mineral nutrition using hydroponics?

Sol. The technique of growing plants in a nutrient solution is known as hydroponics. Since a number of improvised methods have been employed to try and determine the mineral nutrients essential for plants. The essence on all these methods involves the culture of plants in a soil-free, defined mineral solution. These method require purified water and mineral nutrients salts. Purification of water and nutrient salt is important to find out other influencing factors.

12.3 Explain with example : Macronutrients, micronutrients, beneficial nutrients, toxic elements and essential elements.

Sol. (1) **Macronutrients :** It must generally be present in plant tissue in concentration of 1 to 10 mg /gm of dry matter. Examples are, carbon, hydrogen, oxygen, nitrogen, phosphorus, sulphur, potassium, calcium and magnesium.

(2) **Micronutrients :** There are needed in very small quantity *i.e.* less than 0.1 mg/gm of dry matter. Examples are iron, manganese, copper, molybdenum, zinc, boron, chlorine and nickel.

(3) **Beneficial elements** in addition to the 17 essential elements some elements which are needed by some higher plants. Examples sodium, silicon, cobalt and selenium.

(4) **Toxic elements :** Some micronutrients when moderately increase in plant body cause toxicity. Example manganese.

(5) **Essential element :** These elements are absolutely necessary for normal growth and reproduction of plants. They are categorized as micronutrients and macronutrients.

12.4 Name at least five different deficiency symptoms in plants. Describe them and correlate them with the concerned mineral deficiency.

Sol. (1) **Chlorosis :** Chlorosis is the loss of chlorophyll leading to yellowing in leaves. It is caused by deficiency of N, K, Mg, S, Fe, Mn, Zn and Mo.

(2) **Necrosis:** It is the death of tissue. It occurs due to deficiency of Ca, Mg, Cu, K.

(3) **Inhibition of cell division :** It occurs due to deficiency of N, K, S, Mo.

(4) **Stunted plant growth :** It occurs due to deficiency of Ca, N, etc.

(5) **Premature fall of leaf and buds :** It occurs due to deficiency of calcium, magnesium.

12.5 If a plant shows a symptom which could develop due to deficiency of more than one nutrient, how would you find out experimentally, the real deficient mineral element ?

Sol. The deficiency symptoms can be distinguished on the basis of the region of occurrence, presence or absence of dead spots, and chlorosis of entire leaf or interveinal chlorosis.

The region of appearance of deficiency symptoms depends on mobility of nutrient in plants. The nutrient deficiency symptoms of N, P, K, Mg and Mo appear in lower leaves. Zinc is moderately mobile in plants and deficiency symptoms, therefore, appear in middle leaves.

The deficiency symptoms of less mobile elements (S, Fe, Mn and Cu) appear on new leaves.

- Ca and B are immobile in plants, deficiency symptoms appear on terminal buds.
- Chlorine deficiency is less common in crop.

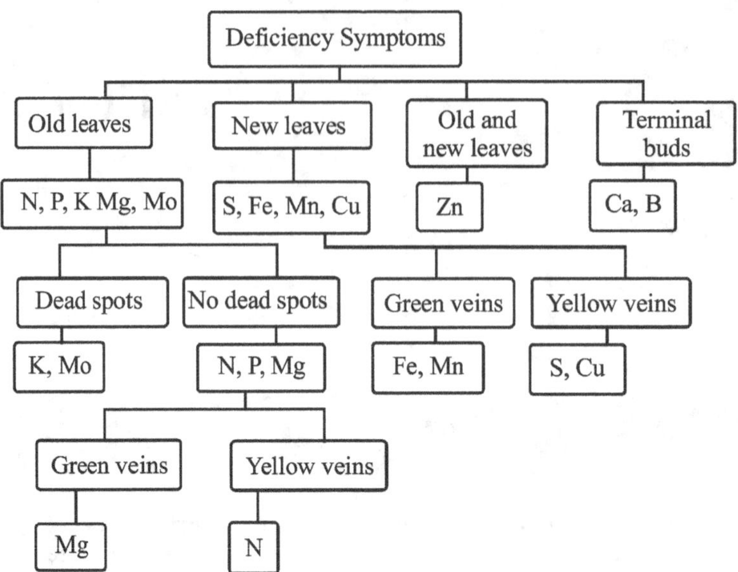

12.6 Why is that in certain plants deficiency symptoms appear first in younger parts of the plant while in other they do so in mature organs?

Sol. Deficiency symptoms depend on the mobility of the element in plants. Here, elements which are actively mobilised within the plants and exported to young developing tissue, the deficiency symptom tend to first appear in older tissues. For example, deficiency symptoms of nitrogen, potassium and magnesium.

The deficiency symptoms tend to appear first in the young tissues whenever the elements are relatively immobile and are not transported out of the mature organs. For example, sulphur and calcium.

12.7 How are the minerals absorbed by the plants?

Sol. Uptake of mineral ions, by plants occurs through two main phases.

Passive Absorption : It is the process of absorption of minerals through it's outer space (Intercellular space and cell wall) by physical process. Direct expenditure of metabolic energy is not involved. A substance moves from a region of higher chemical potential to lower chemical potential. It occurs through ion channels (transmembrane protein). The theories to explain the movement of ions :

(a) **Ion exchange :** Both cation and anion gets absorbed on the surface of cell wall. The absorbed ions are exchanged with ions present in soil solution.

(b) **Mass flow hypothesis :** According to this hypothesis mass flow of ions occur along with absorption of water as a result of transpirational pull.

Active Absorption : It is the process of movement of ions against concentration gradient, by utilizing ATP as energy. Both influx and efflux of ions are carried out by carrier mechanism. The activated ions combine with carrier proteins and form ion carrier complex. This complex moves across all the membrane and reaches inner surface, where it breaks and releases ions into cytoplasm.

12.8 What are the conditions necessary for fixation of atmospheric nitrogen by *Rhizobium*? What is their role in nitrogen fixation?

Sol. **Conditions for N_2 Fixation.** (i) Presence of enzyme nitrogenase (= dinitrogenase) (ii) Occurrence of anaerobic conditions in the area of nitrogenase activity. (iii) ATP. (iv) Source of hydrogen, NADPH or $FMNH_2$. (v) Source of electron donor, ferredoxin. (vi) Deficient occurrence of nitrate in the soil. (vii) Source of organic carbon in the form of ketoacids.

Role in Nitrogen Fixation. ATP provides energy to enzyme nitrogenase while ferredoxin supplies electrons from respiratory substrate.

Atmospheric nitrogen attaches to Fe-Mo component of dinitrogenase. Bonds between its two atoms are weakened by this attachment. In the presence of energy and electrons, hydrogen combines with nitrogen atoms to form N_2H_2 (dimide), N_2H_4 (hydrazine) and $2NH_3$ (ammonia). A reducing environment is essential for this. It is provided by leghaemoglobin which stores excess oxygen and sends only small limited quantities of oxygen inside the bunch of bacteriods. NH_3 is immediately assimilated with the help of organic acids.

12.9 What are the steps involved in the formation of root nodule?

Sol. Nodule formation involves a sequence of multiple interactions between *Rhizobium* and roots of the host plant. Stages in the nodule formation are summarised as follows: Steps in the development of root nodules :

(a) When a root hair of a leguminous plant comes in contact with *Rhizobium*, it is deformed due to the secretion from the bacterium.

(b) At the site of curling *Rhizobia* invades the root tissue and proliferate within root hairs.

(c) Some bacteria enlarge to form membrane bound structure, bacteroids which cannot divide.

(d) The plants form the infection thread, made up of plasma membrane that grows inward, separating the infected tissue from the rest of the plant.

(e) Cell division is stimulated in the infected tissue and more bacteria invade the newly formed tissues.
(f) It is believed that a combination of cytokinin produced by invading bacteria and auxins produced by plant cells, promote cell division and extension, leading to nodule formation.

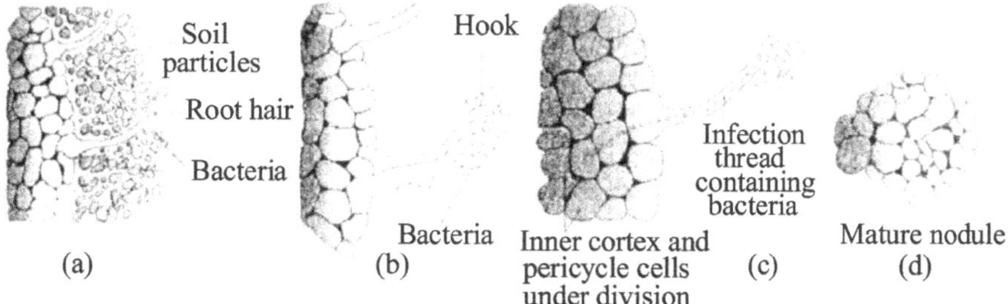

Fig. Development of root nodules in soyabean

12.10 Which of the following statements are true? If false correct them:
(a) Boron deficiency leads to stout axis.
(b) Every mineral element that is present in a cell is needed by the cell.
(c) Nitrogen as a nutrient elements, is highly immobile in the plants.
(d) It is very easy to establish the essentiality of micronutrients because they are required only in trace quantities.
Sol. (a) True
(b) False
Correct sentence : Every mineral element that is present in cell is not needed by cell.
(c) False
Correct sentence : Nitrogen as a nutrient element is highly mobile in the plants.
(d) False
Correct sentence : It is very difficult to establish the essentiality of micronutrients because they are required only in trace quantities.

SECTION B	PRACTICE QUESTIONS 

MULTIPLE CHOICE QUESTIONS

1. Which of the following is a group of micronutrients?
   (a) Ca, Zn, B
   (b) Fe, Mn, Cu
   (c) Cl, C, Ca
   (d) Ni, Mo, H

2. The process of conversion of NO_2^- to N_2 is called
   (a) nitrification
   (b) ammonification
   (c) denitrification
   (d) nitrogen fixation

3. The formation of first stable product of nitrogen fixation is catalysed by enzyme
   (a) dehydrogenase
   (b) nitrogenase
   (c) isomerase
   (d) none of these

4. Manganese toxicity leads to deficiency of
   (a) iron   (b) calcium
   (c) magnesium   (d) all of the above

5. Chlorosis will occur if a plant is grown in
   (a) dark
   (b) shade
   (c) strong light
   (d) Fe - free medium

6. Mineral salts which are absorbed by the roots from soil are in the form of
   (a) Dilute solution
   (b) Very concentrated solution
   (c) Concentrated solution
   (d) Very dilute solution

7. Oxygen scavangers present in root nodules of legumes is
   (a) haemoglobin
   (b) leg haemoglobin
   (c) cyano haemoglobin
   (d) none of these

8. Insectivorous plants grow where
   (a) There is carbohydrate deficient soil
   (b) There is nitrogen deficient soil
   (c) Vitamin c is required
   (d) Hormones are required

9. *Thiobacillus* is a group of bacteria helpful in carrying out:
   (a) Denitrification
   (b) Nitrogen fixation
   (c) Chemoautotrophic fixation
   (d) Nitrification

10. Select the mismatch:
    (a) Rhodospirillum - Mycorrhiza
    (b) Anabaena - Nitrogen fixer
    (c) Rhizobium - Alfalfa
    (d) Frankia - Alnus

ASSERTION & REASON QUESTIONS

DIRECTION (Qs. 1-5) : *These questions consists of two statements. Answer these questions selecting the appropriate option given below:*
(a) Both Assertion (A) and Reason (R) are true and Reason (R) is the correct explanation of Assertion (A).
(b) Both Assertion (A) and Reason (R) are true, but Reason (R) is not the correct explanation of Assertion (A).
(c) Assertion (A) is true, but Reason (R) is false.
(d) Assertion (A) is false, but Reason (R) is true.

1. **Assertion:** Chlorosis is the loss of chlorophyll leading to yellowing in leaves.
   Reason: Some plant disease is caused due to the deficiency of elements N, K, Mg, S, Fe, Mn, Zn and Mo.
2. **Assertion:** Manganese inhibits calcium translocation in shoot apex.
   Reason: The prominent symptom of manganese toxicity is the appearance of brown spots surrounded by chlorotic veins.
3. **Assertion:** Nitrate present in the soil is reduced to nitrogen by the process of denitrification.
   Reason: Denitrification is carried by bacteria *Pseudomonas* and *Azotobacter.*
4. **Assertion:** Leguminous plants are nitrogen fixers.
   Reason: These plants have *Rhizobium* in their root nodules.
5. **Assertion:** The enzyme nitrogenase is a Mo-Fe protein and catalyses the conversion of atmospheric nitrogen to ammonia.
   Reason: The enzyme nitrogenase is highly sensitive to the molecular oxygen.

CASE/PASSAGE BASED QUESTIONS

DIRECTIONS (Qs. 1-5) : *Read the following passage and answer the questions that follows.*

Nitrogen is the essential nutrient element required by plants in the greatest amount. It is absorbed mainly as NO_3^- though some are also taken up as NO_2^- or NH_4^+. Nitrogen is required by all parts of a plant, particularly the meristematic tissues and the metabolically active cells. Nitrogen is one of the major constituents of proteins, nucleic acids, vitamins and hormones. Phosphorus is absorbed by the plants from soil in the form of phosphate ions. Phosphorus is a constituent of cell membrane, certain proteins, all nucleic acids and nucleotides, and is required for all phosphorylation reactions.

Potassium is absorbed as potassium ion (K^+). In plants this is required in more abundant quantities in the meristematic tissues, buds, leaves and root tips. Potassium helps to maintain an anion-cation balance in cells and is involved in protein synthesis, opening and closing of stomata, activation of enzymes and in the maintenance of the turgidity of cells.

Plants obtain iron in the form of ferric ions (Fe^{3+}). It is required in larger amounts in comparison to other micronutrients. It is an important constituent of proteins involved in the transfer of electrons like ferredoxin and cytochromes. It is reversibly oxidised from Fe^{2+} to Fe^{3+} during electorn transfer. It activates catalase enzyme, and is essential for the formation of chlorophyll.

1. Nitrogen is absorbed as
   (a) NO3–, NO2+ or NH4+
   (b) NO3–, NH3– or NH4+
   (c) NO3–, NO2– or NH4 +
   (d) NO3+, NO2– or NH4–
2. Phosphorus is absorbed by the plants from soil in the form of
   (a) Phosphorus ions
   (b) Phosphate ions
   (c) Phosulphate ions
   (d) Phosphoric ions
3. Name the element which required by plant in highest amount.
4. Name the element which is an important constituent of electron acceptor proteins involved in the transfer of electrons.
5. Name the element which plays an important role in stomata functioning.

VERY SHORT ANSWER QUESTIONS

1. Name the enzymes that reduces nitrogen in the root nodules of a bean plant.
2. Name the enzymes used in biologically nitrogen fixation. What are the two mineral elements needed for the activity of the enzyme?
3. What are bacteroids?
4. What is the importance of phosphorus for plants?
5. Name two crops that are commonly produced by hydroponics.
6. Mention the two ways in which Ca^{++} is involved in cell division in plants.
7. Define critical concentration of elements with reference to plant nutrition.
8. Name the element which is a limiting nutrient for both natural and agricultural ecosystems.
9. Name two bacteria that oxidise ammonia into nitrite.
10. Which kind of plants harbour nitrogen fixing bacteria in their root nodules?
11. What is hydroponics (Tank farming)?
12. What are the framework elements of a plant?
13. What type of condition is created by leghaemoglobin in the root nodules of legumes?
14. What is meant by active absorption?
15. Which are the two macronutrients that usually play the most important role in limiting plant growth globally?
16. What is the function of enzyme nitrite reductase?
17. Name two free living micro-organism which can fix nitrogen.

SHORT ANSWER QUESTIONS

1. What is nitrification?
2. Prior to sowing rice, a legume crop was cultivated and ploughed back in this field. Why? Explain.
3. Name the nitrifying bacteria of the soil. Why are they called chemoautotrophs?
4. Bring out at similarity and difference between leghaemoglobin and haemoglobin.
5. Give main function importance and deficiency symptoms for each of the following in plants; iron, zinc, phosphorus.
6. List the macronutrients and mention three major function. (any three)
7. What are the general functions of mineral elements in plants?
8. In what form is boron absorbed by plants from the soil? Mention its two uses in the plants and give two deficiency symptoms of boron in them.
9. Distinguish between micronutrients and macronutrients.

LONG ANSWER QUESTIONS

1. With the help of suitable diagram describe nitrogen cycle.
2. Describe the process of symbiotic biological nitrogen fixation.
3. Write notes on :
   (a) Reductive amination
   (b) Transamination

SOLUTIONS

Multiple Choice Questions

1. **(b)** Iron, mangenese and copper are micronutrients
2. **(c)** The process of conversation of NO_2^- to N_2 is called denitrification.
3. **(b)** The first stable product of nitrogen fixation is ammonia obtained from atmospheric nitrogen catalysed enzyme nitrogenase.
4. **(d)** Manganese toxicity causes deficiency of iron, magnesium and calcium.
5. **(d)** Chlorosis will occur if a plant is grown in Fe - free medium.
6. **(d)** Very dilute solution
7. **(b)** Leg-haemoglobin is the oxygen scavanger in root nodules of legumes.
8. **(b)** Insectivorous plants grow where there is nitrogen deficient soil.
9. **(a)** *Thiobacillus* is a group of bacteria helpful in carrying out denitrification.
10. **(a)** Rhodospirillum is anaerobic and free-living. In addition, a number of cyanobacteria such as Anabaena and Nostoc are also freeliving nitrogen-fixers.

Assertion & Reason Questions

1. **(a)** Chlorosis is the loss of chlorophyll leading to yellowing in leaves. This symptom is caused by the deficiency of elements N, K, Mg, S, Fe, Mn, Zn and Mo.
2. **(b)** The prominent symptom of manganese toxicity is the appearance of brown spots surrounded by chlorotic veins. Manganese competes with iron and magnesium for uptake and with magnesium for binding with enzymes. Manganese also inhibits calcium translocation in shoot apex.
3. **(c)** The nitrate formed by nitrification is absorbed by plants and is transported to the leaves. In leaves, it is reduced to form ammonia that finally forms the amine group of amino acids. Nitrate present in the soil is also reduced to nitrogen by the process of denitrification. Denitrification is carried by the bacteria *Pseudomonas* and *Thiobacillus*.
4. **(a)** Leguminous plants have nodulated roots in which *Rhizobium* is present. So, these are able to fix nitrogen.
5. **(b)** The enzyme nitrogenase is a Mo-Fe protein and catalyses the conversion of atmospheric nitrogen to ammonia, which is the first stable product of nitrogen fixation. The enzyme nitrogenase is highly sensitive to molecular oxygen; it requires anaerobic conditions. The nodules have adaptations that ensure that the enzyme is protected from oxygen.

Case/Passage Based Questions

1. **(c)** Nitrogen is absorbed as NO3–, NO2– or NH4–.
2. **(b)** Phosphorus is absorbed by the plants from soil in the form of phosphate ions.
3. Nitrogen is the essential nutrient element required by plants in the highest amount. Nitrogen is required by all parts of a plant, particularly the meristematic tissues and the metabolically active cells. Nitrogen is one of the major constituents of proteins, nucleic acids, vitamins and hormones.
4. Ions is an important constituent of proteins involved in the transfer of electrons like ferredoxin and cytochromes.
5. Potassium is absorbed as potassium ion (K^+) plays an important role in opening and closing of stomata and activation of enzymes and in the maintenance of the turgidity of cells.

Very Short Answer Questions

1. Nitrogenase.
2. Nitrogenase enzyme.
   Mineral elements are molybdenum and iron.
3. Some of bacteria affecting the root hair of leguminous plants enlarge to become rod shaped bacteroids.
4. Phosphorus is a constituent of cell membranes, certain proteins, all nucleic acids and nucleotides, and is required for all phosphorylation reactions.
5. Tomato, Lettuce

6. Importance of calcium in cell division :
   (i) It is used for the synthesis of middle lamella.
   (ii) It is used for the formation of mitotic spindle.
7. Critical concentration refers to the concentration of the essential element, below which the plant growth is retarded.
8. Nitrogen.
9. *Nitrosomonas, Nitrococcus.*
10. Leguminous plants.
11. It is plant growth in liquid culture medium.
12. Carbon, hydrogen and oxygen are called framework elements.
13. Anaerobic condition.
14. **Active absorption :** The uptake of mineral ions against concentration gradient is called active absorption.
15. Nitrogen and calcium are the two macronutrients that usually play the most important role in limiting plant growth.
16. It reduces nitrate ions to ammonia.
17. *Azotobacter, Beijernickia.*

Short Answer Questions

1. It is the conversion of ammonium ion to nitrite and then to nitrate. *Nitrosomonas* converts ammonium into nitrites, *Nitrobacter* converts nitrites into nitrates.
2. Leguminous plants possess root nodules in which the symbiotic bacteria *Rhizobium* fixes nitrogen. The fixed nitrogen make the soil rich in nitrogen fertilizer where the leguminous plant is ploughed back in the field.
3. The nitrifying bacteria of soil are *Nitrosomonas* and *Nitrobacter.* They are called chemoautotrophs because they obtain energy liberated during nitrification or chemical reaction.
4. Both leghaemoglobin and haemoglobin are iron containing molecules but leghaemoglobin is present in the root nodules in the plants belonging to family fabaceae while haemoglobin is human blood pigment.

5.

	Element	Importance	Main deficiency symptoms
1.	Iron	It is an important constituent of ferredoxin and cytochromes involved in E.T.C.	Chlorosis initiates in intravenal regions and then in complete leaf.
2.	Zinc	It in necessary for the synthesis of auxin.	Malformed leaves and intervenal chlorosis.
3.	Phosphorous	It is the constituent of cell membrane, nucleic acid, nucleotide and etc.	Purple or red spots on leaves.

6. **Macronutrients and their function :**
   1. **Carbon, hydrogen and oxygen** - They constitute the essential parts of carbohydrates and are found in fats and proteins also.

2. **Nitrogen**-Essential constituent of proteins, nucleic acids, vitamins and many other organic molecules as chlorophyll. Also present in some hormones, coenzymes and ATP, etc.
3. **Phosphorous**-Essential constituent of plasma membrane, nucleic acid, nucleotides, many coenzymes and organic molecules on ATP.

7.

	Elements		General functions
1.	Carbon, hydrogen, nitrogen, oxygen.	1.	Components of biomolecules and hence present as structural elements.
2.	Phosphorus, magnesium	2.	Components of energy related chemical compounds e.g., posphorus in ATP, magnesium in chlorophyll.
3.	Magnesium, zinc	3.	Activator or inhibitor of enzymes e.g., Magnesium activates RuBP Carboxylase. Zinc activates alcohol dehydrogenase.
4.	Sodium, pottasium and chlorine	4.	Anion-cation balancers and to maintain osmotic potential of cells e.g., sodium, potassium, chlorine.

8. Boron is absorbed as $B_4O_7^{2-}$ or BO_3^{3-}
   It is required for :
   (i) Translocation of carbohydrates.
   (ii) Pollen germination.
   (iii) Absorption and utilisation of calcium.
   (iv) Cell elongation and differentiation.
9. Difference between micronutrients and macronutrients are as following :

	Micronutrients		Macronutrients
1.	Micronutrients form minor portion of dry weight of a plant.	1.	Macronutrients form major portion of dry weight of a plant.
2.	They are required in minute quantities *i.e.,* less than one milligram per gram of dry matter or trace quantities by the plants.	2.	They are required in relatively large quantities *i.e.,* at least one milligram per gram of dry matter by the plants.
3.	Most of them act as activators for enzymes *e.g.,* Manganese, Zinc, Boron, etc.	3.	They enter into the structure of macromolecules of the cell *e.g.,* Carbon. Hydrogen and Nitrogen
4.	These are called trace elements.	4.	These are called major elements.

Long Answer Questions

1. **Nitrogen cycle :** Plants compete with microbes for the limited nitrogen that is available in soil. Thus, nitrogen is a limiting nutrient for both natural and agricultural eco-systems.

In nature, lightning and ultraviolet radiation provide enough energy to convert nitrogen to nitrogen oxides (NO, NO_2, N_2O). Industrial combustions, forest fires, automobile exhausts and power – generating stations are also sources of atmosphere nitrogen oxides.

Decomposition of organic nitrogen of dead plants and animals into ammonia is called ammonification. Some of this ammonia volatilises and re-enters the atmosphere but most of it is converted into nitrate by soil bacteria in the following steps :

$$2NH_3 + 3O_2 \longrightarrow 2NO_2^- + 2H^+ + 2H_2O$$

$$2NH_3 + 3O_2 \longrightarrow 2NO_2^-$$

$$2NH_2^- + O_2 \longrightarrow 2NO_3^-$$

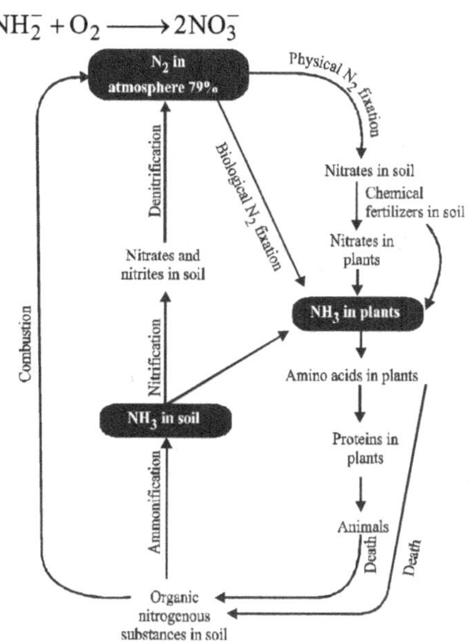

Fig. : Nitrogen cycle

2. Symbiotic biological nitrogen fixation is the fixing of atmospheric nitrogen into usable form by living organism *e.g. Nostoc, Anabaena, Rhizobium, Clostridium, Cyanobacteria,* etc. During this process atmosphere N_2 (dinitrogen) is reduced by the addition of hydrogen atom to ammonia.

$$N_2 + 8e^- + 8H^+ + 16ATP \rightarrow 2NH_3 + H_2 + 16ADP + 16\,Pi$$

The reaction is catalysed by the enzyme nitrogenase. The process requires energy in the form of ATP, which is provide by photosynthesis or respiration and strong reducing agent to transfer the hydrogen to nitrogen. Ammonium ions are absorbed by the plants and used for the synthesis of amino acid and proteins. Ammonia presents in the soil is converted to nitrite and then to nitrate which are then absorbed by plants.

3. (a) **Reduction amination -** In this process ammonia (formed by nitrogen assimilation) reacts with α ketoglutaric acid to form the amino acid - glutamic acid. Here α -ketoglutaric acid comes from Kreb's cycle and hydrogen is donated by co-enzyme NADH or NADPH.

$$\alpha\text{-Ketoglutaric acid} + NH_4^+ + NAD(P)H$$

$$\xrightarrow[\text{dehydrogenase}]{\text{Glutamate}} Glutamate + H_2O + NAD(P)$$

(b) **Transamination -** Once the glutamic acid is synthesized by reductive amination, other amino acids are synthesized by the transfer of amino group to other carbon skeletons. Glutamic acid is the starting material from which 17 other amino acid are formed by the transfer of amino group of an amino donor compound to the carboxyl position of an amino acceptor compound. Transaminase is the enzyme responsible for such reaction.

SECTION C — NCERT EXEMPLAR QUESTIONS 

MULTIPLE CHOICE QUESTIONS

1. Which one of the following roles is not characteristic of an essential element?
   (a) being a component of biomolecules
   (b) changing the chemistry of soil
   (c) being a structural component of energy related chemical
   (d) activation or inhibition of enzymes

2. Which one of the following statements can best explain the term critical concentration of an essential element?
   (a) essential element concentration below which plant growth is retarded
   (b) essential element concentration below which plant growth becomes enhanced
   (c) essential element concentration below which plant remains in the vegetative phase
   (d) None of the above

3. Deficiency symptoms of an element tend to appear first in young leaves. It indicates that the element is relatively immobile. Which one of the following elemental deficiency would show such symptoms?
   (a) Sulphur   (b) Magnesium
   (c) Nitrogen   (d) Potassium

4. Which one of the following symptoms is not due to manganese toxicity in plants?
    (a) Calcium translocation in shoot opex is inhibit
    (b) Deficiency in both iron and nitrogen induced
    (c) Appearance of brown spot surrounded by chlorotic veins
    (d) None of the above

5. Reaction carried out by N_2 fixing microbes include
    (a) $2NH_3 + 3O_2 \longrightarrow 2NO_2^- + 2H^+ + 2H_2O$ ...(i)
    (b) $2NO_2 + O_2 \longrightarrow 2NO_3$ ...(ii)
    Which of the following statements about these equations is not true?
    (a) Step (i) is carried out by *Nitrosomonas* or *Nitrococcus*
    (b) Step (ii) is carried out by *Nitrobacter*
    (c) Both steps (i) and (ii) can be called nitrification
    (d) Bacteria carrying out these steps are usually photoautotrophs

6. With regard to the biological nitrogen fixation by *Rhizobium* in association with soyabean, which one of the following statement/ statements does not hold true.
    (a) Nitrogenase may require oxygen for its functioning.
    (b) Nitrogenase is Mo-Fe protein
    (c) Leg-haemoglobin is a pink coloured pigment.
    (d) Nitrogenase helps to convert N_2 gas into two molecules of ammonia.

7. Plants can be grown in (Tick the incorrect option):
    (a) soil with essential nutrients.
    (b) water with essential nutrients.
    (c) either water or soil with essential nutrients.
    (d) water or soil without essential nutrient.

Very Short Answer Questions

1. Name a plant, which accumulate silicon.
2. Mycorrhiza is a mutualistic association. How do the organisms involved in this association gain from each other?
3. Nitrogen fixation is shown by prokaryotes and not eukaryotes. Comment.
4. A farmer adds *Azotobacter* culture to soil before sowing maize. Which mineral element is being replenished?
5. What type of conditions are created by leghaemoglobin in the root nodule of a legume?
6. Yellowish edges appear in leaves deficient in.
7. Name the macronutrient which is a component of all organic compounds but it not obtained from soil.
8. Name one non-symbiotic nitrogen fixing prokaryote.
9. Complete the equation for reductive amination ....

    $+ NH_4^+ + NADPH \xrightarrow{?} glutamate + H_2O + NADP$

10. Excess of Mn in soil leads to deficiency of Ca, Mg and Fe. Justify.

Short Answer Questions

1. How is sulphur important for plants? Name the amino acids in which it is present.

2. How are organisms like *Pseudomonas* and *Thiobacillus* of great significance in nitrogen cycle?

3. Carefully observe the following figure

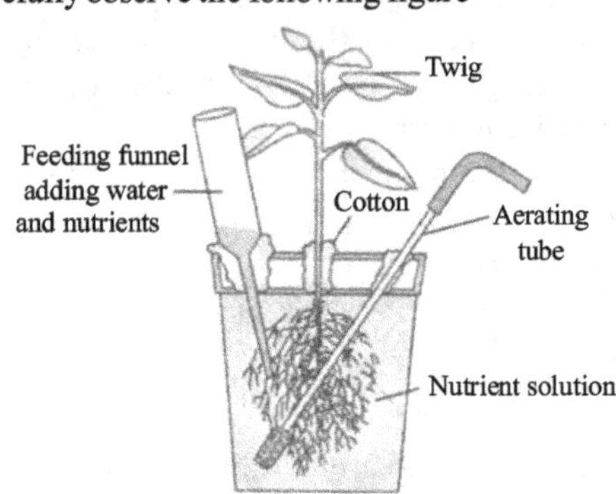

    (a) Name the technique shown in the figure and the scientist who demonstrated this technique for the first time.
    (b) Name atleast three plants for which this technique can be employed for their commercial production.
    (c) What is the significance of aerating tube and feeding funnel in this setup?

4. Name of most crucial enzyme found in root nodules for N_2-fixation? Does it require a special pink coloured pigment for its functioning? Elaborate.

5. Carnivorous plants exhibit nutritional adaption. Citing an example explain this fact.

6. A farmer adds/supplied Na, Ca, Mg and Fe regularly to his field and yet he observes that the plants show deficiency of Ca, Mg and Fe. Give a valid reason and suggest a way to help the farmer improve the growth of plants.

7. We find that *Rhizobium* forms nodules on the roots of leguminous plants. Also *Frankia* another microbe forms nitrogen fixing nodules on the roots of non-leguminous *plant Alnus.*
    (a) Can we artificially induce the property of nitrogen-fixation in a plant, leguminous or non leguminous?
    (b) What kind of relationship is observed between mycorrhiza and pine trees?
    (c) Is it necessary for a microbe to be in close association with a plant to provide mineral nutrition? Explain with the help of one example.

8. With the help of examples describe the classification of essential elements based on the function they perform.

9. Trace the events starting from the coming in contact of *Rhizobium* to a leguminous root till nodule formation. Add a note on importance of leghaemoglobin.

10. Give the biochemical events occurring in the root nodule of a pulse plant. What is the end product? What is its fate?

11. Hydroponics have been shown to be a successful technique for growing of plants. Yet most of the crops are still grown on land. Why?

SOLUTIONS

Multiple Choice Questions

1. **(b)** Changing the chemistry of soil is not a role of an essential element.

2. **(a)** The concentration of an essential element below which the plant growth is retarded is known as critical concentration. Plants start displaying deficiency symptoms if a particular element is present below the critical concentration.

3. **(a)** Plants show deficiency symptoms of an element when that particular nutrient is either not available to the plants or if is available, the plant is not able to use it.
   Sulphur is needed by young leaves, stem and root tips. Its deficiency symptoms which include
   (i) reduced growth
   (ii) extensive root growth
   (iii) hard and woody stem
   (iv) chlorosis of young leaves
   The immobile elements are transported in plant to the tip level, thus their deficiency appears first at the tips of growing apices of roots and shoots.

4. **(d)** Manganese is an essential micronutrient mainly required by the leaves and seeds of plants. Manganese becomes toxic when absorded by plants in higher amounts. Its toxicity causes reduced uptake of Fe^2, Mg^{2+} and N, inhibition of Ca^{2+} translocation in shoot apex, brown spots surrounded by chlorotic veins etc.

5. **(d)** The bacteria involved in the N_2 fixing process are not photoautotrophs but are chemoautotrophs. These bacteria oxidise inorganic substances like NH_3 and NO_2 and use the released energy. Hence they are called **chemoautotrophs**. They also help in the conversion of ammonia (NH_3) to absorbable form (NO_2^- and NO_3^-) of nitrogen.

6. **(a)** The enzyme nitrogenase is capable of nitrogen reduction. It is present exclusively in prokaryotes (e.g., *Rhizobium*). It is highly sensitive to O_2 and gets inactivated when exposed to it, thus does not require oxygen for its functioning.

7. **(d)** The plants can be grown in any medium, either water or soil if it is supported with all essential elements. Medium does not affect the plant growth but availability of all elements does affect the growth of the plants.

Very Short Answer Questions

1. *Oryza sativa* and *Triticum aestivum* are the plants that accumulates silicon. These plants absorbs silicon actively and accumulate them in their biomass.

2. Mycorrhiza is a mutualistic (symbiotic) association between fungus and roots of plants. The roots provide shelter and food to the fungus and the fungus helps plants in absorption of minerals, water uptake and protection against fungus.

3. Prokaryotes like *Rhizobium* and *Anabaena* are capable of nitrogen fixation as they contain enzyme nitrogenase but eukaryotes lack this enzyme.

4. *Azotobacter* provides nitrogen fixing bacteria which converts free nitrogen into nitrate and nitrites. It increases soil fertility.

5. Leghaemoglobin present in the root nodules of leguminous plants is responsible for creating anaerobic conditions and hence acts as an oxygen scavenger, protecting enzyme nitrogenase to come in contact with oxygen and help in the proper functioning of enzyme, *i.e.*, conversion of atmospheric nitrogen to ammonia (NH_3).

6. Yellowish edges or chlorosis appears in the leaves due to the deficiency of nitrogen. Its deficiency also causes delaying of flowering, interference in protein synthesis and dormancy of lateral buds.

7. Carbon is an essential macronutrient, which is a component of all organic compounds but is not obtained by soil. Plant take it from atmosphere in the form of CO_2. Its concentration in atmosphere is about 0.03%. Plants use CO_2 for photosynthesis (as a source of carbon) to synthesises glucose.

8. *Azotobacter* is a non-symbotic nitrogen fixing prokaryote. It flourishs in the rice fields.

9. a-ketoglutaric acid $+ NH_4^+ + NAD(P)H$

   $$\xrightarrow[\text{dehydrogenase}]{\text{Glutamate}} \text{Glutamate} + H_2O + NAD(P)$$

   Oxaloacetic acid $+ NH_4^+ + NAD(P)H$

   $$\xrightarrow[\text{dehydrogenase}]{\text{Aspartate}} \text{Asparatate} + H_2O + NAD(P)$$

10. When higher amounts of Mn^{2+} is absorbed by plants. The toxicity expressed in the form of brown sports surrounded by chlorotic vein.
    It is due to the following reasons
    (i) Reduction in uptake of Fe^{3+} and Mn^{2+}.
    (ii) Inhibition of binding of Mn^{2+} to specific enzymes.
    (iii) Inhibition of Ca^{2+} translocation in shoot apex.
    Thus, excess of Mn^{2+} causes deficiency of iron, magnesium and calcium.

Short Answer Questions

1. Sulphur is a macronutrient that is important for normal plant growth and development. It is also an integral part of some amino acids, proteins and helps in deciding the secondary structure of proteins as it forms disulphide bonds.

It is absorbed by the plants as SO_4^{2-} ion. It is present in vitamins (biotin, thiamine), proteins, coenzyme-A, amino acid (cystein and methionine) etc. It is also an essential component of plants like (onion, garlic) and mustard.

Its deficiency causes chlorosis in young leaves, extensive root growth, formation of hard and woody stem. It also causes the reduction in juice content of citrus fruit and tea yellow disease of tea.

2. In biological nitrogen fixation, the atmospheric N_2 gets reduced to NH_3 by the help of enzyme nitrogenase reductase present in some prokaryotes. NH_3 is then oxidised in to NO_2 and NO_3 by some other bacteria (*Nitrosomonas* and *Nitrobacter*) following are the various steps involved in nitrogen fixation.

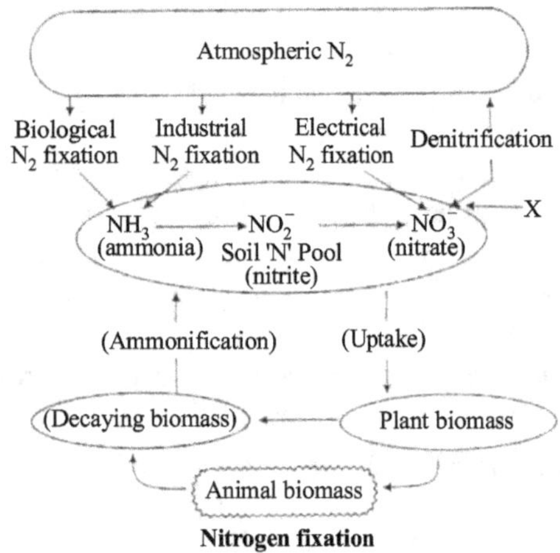

Nitrogen fixation

Pseudomonas and *Thiobacillus* are involved in the process of denitrification. They convert nitrate (NO_3^-) and nitrite (NO_2^-) into free nitrogen (N_2), that is released into the atmosphere.

3. (a) Hydroponics, Julius Von Sachs (1860)

(b) (i) *Solanum lycopersicum* (tomato)

(ii) *Hibiscus asculentus* (ladiesfinger)

(iii) *Solanum melongena* (brinjal)

(c) **Aerating tube** provides oxygen for the normal growth and development of the roots growing in the liquid solution. Feeding funnel is used to add water and nutrients in the hydroponic system when required.

4. The most crucial enzyme found in the root nodules for N_2-fixation is nitrogenase. It is a Mo – Fe protein that catalyses the conversion of atmospheric nitrogen to ammonia. Pink colour pigment present is root nodules of leguminous plants is called leghaemoglobin creates anaerobic conditions for the functioning of nitrogenase enzyme.

5. Carnivorous plants fulfill their nutritional requirements by feeding on small animals, like insects or protozoans. e.g. *Nepenthes*, Venus fly trap, *Utricularia* etc. Carnivorous plants grow in soil deficient in nitrogen. In pitcher plant leaves are modified into pitcher which stores the juice to lure an insect. When the insect come to suck this juice, chemicals present in nectar dissolve the skin of the prey and the plant obtains nutrients (mainly nitrogen) from its skin.

6. Plant can tolerate a specific amount of micronutrients. A lesser amount of micro- nutrient can cause deficiency symptoms and higher amount can cause toxicity. The concentration of mineral ion which reduces the dry weight of the tissues by 10% is called toxic concentration.

This concentration is different for different micronutrients as well as for different plants *e.g.*, Mn^{2+} is toxic beyond 600 mgg^{-1}; (for soyabean) and (for sunflower) and beyond 5300 μgg^{-1}. It has also been observed that the toxicity of one micronutrient causes the deficiency of other nutrients. To overcome such problems, farmers should use these nutrients in prescribed concentration so that the excess uptake of one element do not reduce the uptake of the element.

7. (a) Artificial induction in leguminous and non-leguminous plants have been tried by scientists. It's success rate is very low because expression of gene is highly specific phenomenon. When it desired gene is introduced that may not work because conditions for its expressions are very specific.

(b) Symbiotic mutualistic relationship (mutualism) is observed between the pine roots and mycorrhiza as both are benefitted mutually.

(c) Yes it is necessary for a microbe to be in close association with plant to provide mineral nutrition, to develop a physical relationship for example *Rhizobium* gets into the root and involve root tissues, then only helps in nitrogen-fixation.

8. Based on the diverse functions of essential elements, these are categorised into following categories given below:

(i) Constituent of biomolecules: These are the essential component of biomolecules. Hence, known as structural elements of cells, e.g., carbon, hydrogen, oxygen and nitrogen.

(ii) Energy related Chemical compound: Some elements also function in providing energy to the cell e.g. phosphorus is a component of ATP which function as energy currency of all the living system in which magnesium is a component of chlorophyll, which is involved in the conversion of light energy to chemical energy.

(iii) Enzyme showing catalytic effects: Many of the essential elements are required in the form of cofactors by enzymes. They function as the activator or inhibitor of enzymes, e.g., Mg^{2+} acts as an activator of several enzymes in both photosynthesis *e.g.*, Ribulose bisphosphate(RuBP), Carboxylase , Phosphoenol pyruvate carboxylase and respiration (e.g., hexokinase and phosphofructokinase). While Zn^{2+} acts as an activator of alcohol dehydrogenase while Mo of nitrogenase during the course of nitrogen fixation.

9. **Formation of Root Nodule** The coordinated activities of the *Rhizobium bacteria* regume depends on the chemical interaction between these symbiotic partners.

In the following diagram the principle stages in the nodule formation are summarised.

Diagram Refer to Q. 12.9 NCERT Exercise

1. Rhizobium bacteria growing in soil.
2. Roots of higher plant secrete chemical attractants like flavanoids, lectins and betaines.
3. The bacteria get colonise and get in contact with the roots of plant and release nod factor.
4. Curling of root hair around the bacteria and formation of infection thread.
5. Degradation of cell wall and penetration of infection thread inside cortex.
6. Infection thread grows along with the multiplication of bacteria and carries bacteria to the inner cortex, where it gets modified into rod shaped bacteroids and cause pericycle and cortical cell to divide.
7. Infected cortical and pericycle cell start dividing.
8. Intected cell enlarges and result in nodule formation.
9. It is complete with vascular tissues and is continuous with those of the roots. These tissues supplies nutrients to the nodule and carries the nitrogenous compound from the nodule to the rest of the plant.

Leghaemoglobin is an oxygen scavenger, that protects nitrogen enzyme from O_2 and also creates anaerobic conditions for the reduction of N_2 to NH_3 by *Rhizobium* bacteria.

10. Formation of root nodule in pulse plant is the result of infection of roots by *Rhizobium*. The following figure shows the process of nodule formation.

(a) *Rhizobium* divide near the root hair

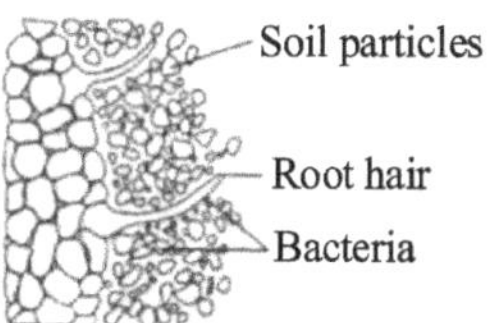

(b) Successful infection of the root hair causes it to curl

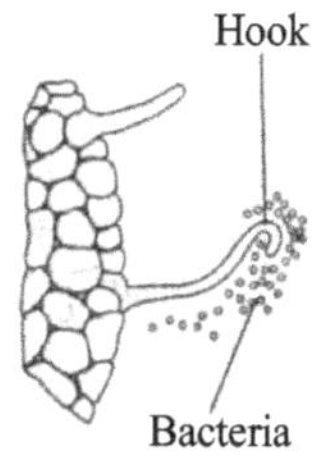

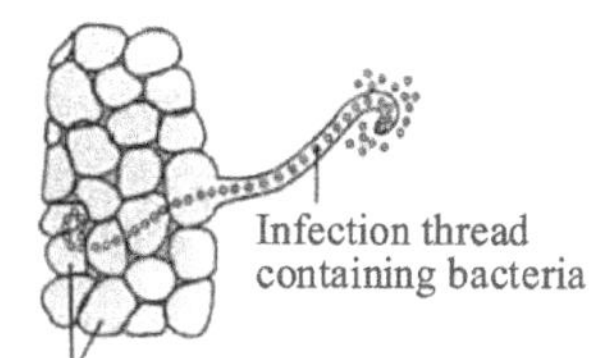

(c) Infected thread carries the bacteria to enter the cortex. Bacteria cause cortical and pericycle cells to divide, lead to nodule formation.

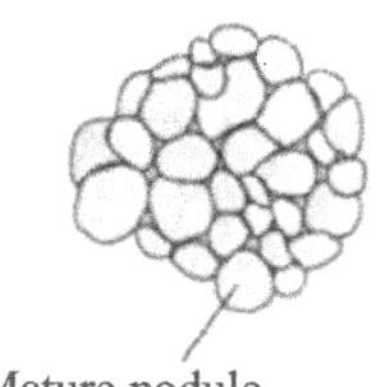

(d) Mature nodule with vascular tissues continuous with those of the roots.

The chemical reaction is as follows

$$N_2 + 8e^- + 8H^+ + 16\,ATP \rightarrow 2NH_3 + H_2 + 16\,ADP + P_1i$$

The reaction takes place in the presence of enzyme nitrogenase that acts in anaerobic conditions, which is created by leghaemoglobin.

Fate of Ammonia

There are two ways by which ammonia is further used.

(a) Reductive Animation

$$\alpha\text{-ketoglutaric acid} + NH_4^+ + NADPH$$

$$\xrightarrow[\text{Dehydrogenase}]{\text{Glutamate}} glutamate + H_2O + NADP$$

(b) Transmination

$$R_1 - \overset{\overset{\displaystyle H}{|}}{\underset{\underset{\displaystyle NH_3^+}{|}}{C}} - COO^- + R_2 - \overset{\overset{\displaystyle }{\|}}{\underset{\underset{\displaystyle O}{}}{C}} - COO^- \rightleftharpoons$$

$$R_1 - \overset{\overset{\displaystyle }{\|}}{\underset{\underset{\displaystyle O}{}}{C}} - COO^- + R_2 - \overset{\overset{\displaystyle H}{|}}{\underset{\underset{\displaystyle NH_3^+}{|}}{C}} - COO^-$$

This reaction and transfer of NH_2 group take place for amino acid to other amino acid catalysed by enzyme transaminase.

11. Hydroponics is a soil less culture and successful technique for plants, still many crops are grown on land because

(i) The major concern is its cost. The setting and handling of hydroponics requires much more investment than that of the soil based production.

(ii) Sanitization is extremely important, because especially with indoor hydroponic environments. Water borne disease can spread quickly through some methods of hydroponic production.

(iii) It is relatively a new technique and not used by the traditional farmers due to lack of knowledge.

(iv) Plants are less adaptable to the surrounding atmosphere. However weather and narrow oxygenation may minimise the production and quality of plant yield.

Photosynthesis in Higher Plants

13.1 By looking at a plant externally can you tell whether a plant is C_3 or C_4? Why and how?

Sol. C_4 plants are adopted to the xerophytic climatic conditions they can grow well in high temperature. It cannot be said conclusively that the plant is a C_3 or C_4 by looking at external appearance, some guess can be made by looking at fleshy leaf structure of C_4 plants.

13.2 By looking at which internal structure of a plant can you tell whether a plant is C_3 or C_4? Explain.

Sol. In C_4 plant internal structure of leaf possess special type of anatomy called 'Kranz' anatomy. 'Kranz' means '**wreath**' and is a reflection of arrangement of cells. The bundle sheath cells may form several layers around the vascular bundles; they are characterised by having large number of chloroplasts, thick walls impervious to gaseous exchange and no intercellular spaces. While in C_3 plants, there is no special type of leaf anatomy. There is only a single type of chloroplast in C_3 i.e. granal, while in C_4 chloroplasts are dimorphic, i.e, granal in the mesophyll cells and agranal in the bundle sheath cells.

13.3 Even though a very few cell in a C_4 plant carry out the biosynthetic-Calvin pathway, yet they are highly productive, can you discuss why?

Sol. (1) In C_4 plants, biosynthetic calvin cycle occurs only in bundle sheaths. Despite few number of cells performing calvin cycle in C_4 plants, they are highly productive due to minimum photorespiration losses.

(2) They are adopted to diverse climatic conditions as C_4 plants can synthesize at very low CO_2 concentration while for C_3 plants CO_2 concentration is the limiting factor.

(3) C_4 plants can synthesize at high temperature while C_3 plants cannot.

(4) Rapid withdrawl of photosynthates from the bundle sheath cells as they lie over the vascular bundles.

(5) Photosynthesis continues even when stomata are closed due to fixation of CO_2 released through respiration.

13.4 RuBisCO is an enzyme that acts both as carboxylase and oxygenase. Why do you think RuBisCO carries out more carboxylation in C_4 plants.

Sol. RuBisCO or Ribulose bisphosphate carboxylase - oxygenase enzyme can bind to both CO_2 and O_2. This binding is competitive. The relative concentration of CO_2 and O_2 determines which one of the two will bind to the enzyme. In C_4 plants photorespiration does not occur. This is because they have a mechanism that increases the concentration of CO_2 at the enzyme site. This takes place when oxaloacetic acid is broken down in the bundle sheath cells to release CO_2. It results in increasing intracellular concentration of CO_2. This ensures that the RuBisCO functions as carboxylase and minimising the oxygenase activity.

13.5 Suppose there were plants that had a high concentration of chlorophyll b, but lacked chlorophyll a, would it carry out photosynthesis? Then why do plants have chlorophyll b and other accessory pigments.

Sol. No, photosynthesis occurs in plants having high concentration of chlorophyll 'b' but lacks chlorophyll 'a' because chlorophyll 'a' molecule forms reaction center in both photosystem I and II which converts light energy into electrical energy and excites the electrons for photolysis of water.

Maximum photosynthesis occurs at the wavelengths which is absorbed by chlorophyll 'a' molecule i.e. blue and red regions.

Though chlorophyll a is the major pigment responsible for trapping light, other thylakoid pigments like chlorophyll b, xanthophylls and carotenoid, which are called accessory pigments, also absorb light and transfer the energy to chlorophyll a. Indeed they not only enable a wider range of wavelength of incoming light to be utilized for photosynthesis but also protect chlorophyll a from photo oxidation.

13.6 Why is the colour of a leaf kept in the dark frequently yellow, or pale green? Which pigment do you think is more stable?

Sol. Chlorophyll is unable to absorb energy in the absence of light and loses its stability, giving the leaf a yellowish colour. This shows that xanthophyll is more stable.

13.7 Look at leaves of the same plant on the shady side and compare it with the leaves on the sunny side. Or, compare the potted plants kept in the sunlight with those in the shade. Which of them has leaves that are darker green? Why?

Sol. In sunny plant colour of leaves is darker green because in sunny plant photosynthesis takes place while in shady plant rate of photosynthesis is low.

13.8 **Figure shows the effect of light on the rate of photosynthesis. Based on the graph, answer the following questions.**

(a) **At which point/s (A, B or C) in the curve is light a limiting factor?**

(b) **What could be the limiting factor/s in region A?**

(c) **What do C and D represent on the curve?**

Sol.

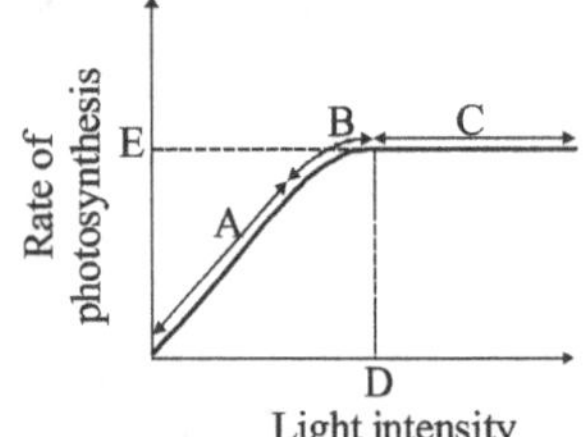

Fig.: Graph of light intensity on the rate of photosynthesis

(a) In the region 'A' and half of 'B' light is limiting factor because rate of photosynthesis is increasing with the intensity of light.

(b) All the other factors except light.

(c) C represents a region where factor other than light is limiting, e.g., CO_2. D represents the light intensity at which rate of photosynthesis is maximum under existing conditions (e.g., CO_2).

13.9 **Give comparison between the following :**

(a) **C_3 and C_4 pathways**

(b) **Cyclic and non-cyclic potophosphorylation**

(c) **Anatomy of leaf in C_3 and C_4.**

Sol. (a) Differences between C_3 and C_4 pathway

	Characters	C_3	C_4
1.	CO_2 acceptor	RuBP	PEP in mesophyll cells and RuBP in bundle sheath cells.
2.	First stable compound	PGA (3C compound)	Oxalo acetic acid (4C compound)
3.	Type of chloroplast involved	Only one type. Do not have kranz anatomy	Two types, bundle sheath chloroplast carry out C_3 cycle and Mesophyll cells carry out C_4 cycle
4.	CO_2	Work efficiently only if CO_2 concentration is high	Can work even in low concentration of CO_2
5.	Most active enzyme involved	RuBisCO	PEPcase
6.	Optimum temperature	$10 - 25°C$	$30 - 45°$
7.	Photorespiration	Present	Absent

(b) Differences between cyclic and non-cyclic photophosphorylation are

	Cyclic photophosphorylation	**Non-cyclic photophosphorylation**
1.	Only PSI involved	Both PSI and PSII involved
2.	No external source of electron is required	External source of electron is required.
3.	Photolysis of water not occurs	Photolysis occurs
4.	It occurs in stromal thylakoids	It occurs in grana thylakoids.
5.	It occurs when normal photosynthetic activity is inhibited.	It occurs under optimum light, aerobic condition and CO_2 concentration.
6.	No oxygen is released	Oxygen is released.
7.	No NADPH synthesized	NADPH synthesized
8.	Last electron acceptor is P_{700}	last electron acceptor is NADP.

(c) Diffferences between anatomy of leaf in C_3 plants and anatomy of leaf in C_4 plants are

	Anatomy of leaf in C_3 plants	**Anatomy of leaf in C_4 plants**
1.	The leaves do not posses Kranz anatomy.	The leaves have Kranz anatomy.
2.	Chloroplasts are of one type (mono-morphic)	There are two types of chloroplasts (dimorphic).
3.	Bundle sheath cells usually do not contain chloroplasts.	Bundle sheath cells possess prominent chloroplasts.
4.	In higher plants operating C_3 cycle, the chloroplasts are all granal.	There are two types of chloroplasts, granal in mesophyll cells and agranal in bundle shealth cells
5.	Mesophyll cells perform complete photosynthesis.	Mesophyll cells perform only initial fixation.

| SECTION B | **PRACTICE QUESTIONS** |

MULTIPLE CHOICE QUESTIONS

1. Photosynthesis is a/an:
   (a) physio-chemical process.
   (b) physical process.
   (c) chemical process.
   (d) energy wasting process.

2. The experiment material used by Van Neil, to prove that O_2 comes out from water was studied on
   (a) *Chlorella pyrenoidosa*
   (b) *Cladophora*
   (c) purple & green sulphur bacteria
   (d) blue green algae

3. Which one represents the correct empirical equation of photosynthesis?
   (a) $C_6H_{12}O_6 + 6O_2 \rightarrow 6CO_2 + 6H_2O + energy$
   (b) $C_6H_{12}O_6 + 6O_2 + 6H_2O \rightarrow$
   $$6CO_2 + 12H_2O + energy$$
   (c) $6CO_2 + 6H_2O \xrightarrow[\text{Chlorophyll}]{\text{Light}} 6O_2 + C_6H_{12}O_6$
   (d) $6CO_2 + 12H_2O \xrightarrow[\text{Chlorophyll}]{\text{Light}}$
   $$6O_2 + C_6H_{12}O_6 + 6H_2O$$

4. Which part of the plant do not perform photosynthesis?
   (a) Cactus stem
   (b) Guard cell of stomata
   (c) Mesophyll cells of leaf
   (d) Leaf epidermis

5. In a plant cell, which of the following pigments participates directly in the light reactions of photosynthesis?
   (a) Chlorophyll *a*   (b) Chlorophyll *b*
   (c) Chlorophyll *d*   (d) Carotenoids

6. Which one of the following statement correctly describes the cyclic photophosphorylation?
   (a) Cyclic photophosphorylation has both PS-I and PS-II.
   (b) Cyclic phosphorylation produces neither ATP nor $NADPH + H^+$.
   (c) Water is the ultimate source of e^- in cyclic phosphorylation.
   (d) Electrons are cycled in cyclic photophosphorylation.

7. In non-cyclic reactions of photosynthesis, electrons from chlorophyll molecules in photosystem-I are used in the formation of NADPH. What is the source of such electrons?
   (a) Light
   (b) NADPH
   (c) Photosystem-I
   (d) Photosystem-II, which splits water molecule

8. Site of photosynthesis in C_4 plant is:
   (a) mesophyll cells
   (b) bundle sheath cells
   (c) Both (a) and (b)
   (d) Cytosol

9. The primary CO_2 acceptor in C_4 plant is
   (a) RuBP
   (b) phosphoenol pyruvate
   (c) PEP carboxylase
   (d) PGA

10. According to Blackman's law of limiting factor, at any given time, photosynthesis can be limited by:
    (a) light only
    (b) CO_2 concentration only
    (c) both light and CO_2 concentration
    (d) either by light or by CO_2

ASSERTION & REASON QUESTIONS

DIRECTION (Qs. 1-5) : *These questions consists of two statements. Answer these questions selecting the appropriate option given below:*
(a) Both Assertion (A) and Reason (R) are true and Reason (R) is the correct explanation of Assertion (A).
(b) Both Assertion (A) and Reason (R) are true, but Reason (R) is not the correct explanation of Assertion (A).
(c) Assertion (A) is true, but Reason (R) is false.
(d) Assertion (A) is false, but Reason (R) is true.

1. **Assertion:** Six molecules of CO_2 six molecule of H_2O twelve molecules of $NADPH + H^+$ and 18 ATP are used to form one hexose molecule.
   Reason: Light reaction results in formation of ATP and $NADPH_2$.

2. **Assertion :** Under conditions of high light intensity and limited CO_2 supply, photorespiration has a useful role in protecting the plants from photo-oxidative damage.
   Reason : If enough CO_2 is not available to utilise light energy for carboxylation to proceed, the excess energy may not cause damage to plants.

3. **Assertion :** Rhoeo leaves contain anthocyanin pigments in epidermal cells.
   Reason : Anthocyanins are accessory photosynthetic pigments.

4. **Assertion :** Oxalo-acetic acid is first stable compound of C_4 plants.
   Reason : It takes place in mesophyll cell in the presence of RuBisCO.

5. **Assertion :** Dark reaction occurs only at night in the thylakoid of chloroplast.
   Reason : CO_2 fixation occurs during both C_3 and C_4 cycle..

CASE/PASSAGE BASED QUESTIONS

DIRECTIONS (Qs. 1-5) : *Read the following passage and answer the questions that follows.*

ATP synthesis is essential for the functioning of cells. Cells obtain energy through ATP molecules. In the given diagram ATP synthesis is show by Chemiosmosis.

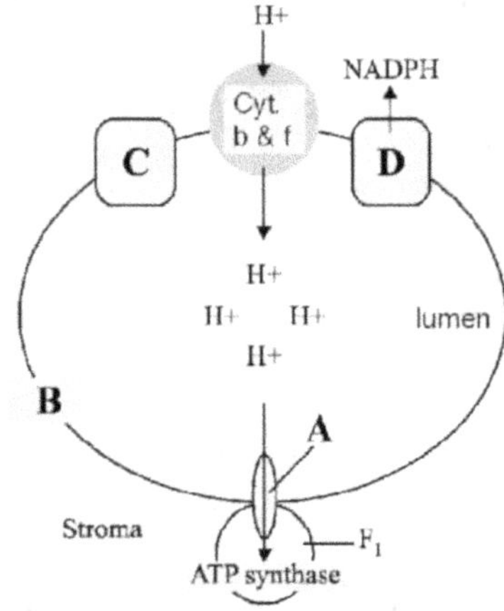

1. Which of the following labelling represents the thylakoid membrane?
   (a) D (b) B
   (c) A (d) C
2. Which of the following statement is true?
   (a) Reaction centre is made up of only chlorophyll b.
   (b) PSI reaction centre has absorption maxima of 700 nm.
   (c) Photosynthesis is a type of catabolic reaction.
   (d) All of them are true.
3. What is shown by labelling D?
   (a) Photosystem I (b) Photosystem II
   (c) ATP synthase (d) Thylakoid membrane
4. ATP synthesis takes place during chemiosmosis due to
   (a) Movement of ions across a semipermeable membrane along their electro chemical gradient.
   (b) Movement of ions across a semipermeable membrane down their electro chemical gradient.
   (c) Both option (a) & (b)
   (d) None of them
5. In eukaryotic organisms, chemiosmosis occurs in
   (a) Only in mitochondria
   (b) Only in chloroplast
   (c) Both mitochondria and chloroplast
   (d) Cytoplasm

VERY SHORT ANSWER QUESTIONS

1. Write one anatomical feature of C_4 plants.
2. Which of the following is not a useful function of the light reaction in photosynthesis?
   (a) splitting water
   (b) synthesis of NADPH
   (c) converting light energy into chemical energy
   (d) releasing oxygen for photorespiration

3. Which one is the most important limiting factor in photosynthesis?
4. Where is PS II located in a chloroplast?
5. Name the reaction centre of PS I and PS II.
6. Where are the photosynthetic pigments located in a chloroplast?
7. How many molecules of ATP and how many molecules of NADPH are spent to fix three molecules of CO_2 in Calvin cycle?
8. Why do the stomata of CAM plants open during night?
9. Mention one useful role of photorespiration in plants.
10. Cyanobacteria and some other photosynthetic bacteria don't have chloroplasts. How do they conduct photosynthesis?
11. What does the variegated leaf experiment of photosynthesis prove?
12. Name the organism Englemann used in his experiment.
13. Write the currently accepted equation of photosynthesis in plants.
14. What is a pigment?
15. Write the full form of NADP.
16. Expand RuBP.
17. Who discovered C_4 cycle?
18. Mention two conditions where light can become a limiting factor.
19. What are antenna molecules?
20. What is a quantasome? Where is it present?

SHORT ANSWER QUESTIONS

1. Specify how C_4 photosynthetic pathway increases carbondioxide concentration in bundle sheath cells of sugarcane?
2. Differentiate between absorption spectrum and action spectrum.
3. Why does chlorophyll appear red in reflected light and green in transmitted light? Explain the significance of these phenomena in terms of photosynthesis.
4. How does temperature influence the biosynthetic phase of photosynthesis ?
5. What is Blackman's law of limiting factors ?
6. In the condition of water stress why the rate of photosynthesis declines?
7. Why do scientist expect faster growth and more yield by C_3 plants, if the atmospheric CO_2 increases?
8. Why is photorespiration considered a wasteful process?
9. Give two reasons as to why photosynthesis is important for sustaining life on earth.
10. Why does the rate of photosynthesis decrease at higher light intensities? What plays a protective role in such situations?
11. Expand PEP. Where is it produced in C_4 plants? What is its role in the biosynthetic process?
12. What is kranz anatomy in plants?

LONG ANSWER QUESTIONS

1. How is photosystem I different from photosystem II?
2. Give the importance of C_4 plants.
3. Explain the process of biosynthetic phase of photosynthesis occurring in the chloroplasts.

SOLUTIONS

Multiple Choice Questions

1. **(a)** Photosynthesis is a physiochemical process by which green plants and some other organisms use sunlight to synthesize nutrients from carbon dioxide and water, and generates oxygen as a by-product.

2. **(c)** By studying purple sulphur bacteria and green sulphur bacteria, Cornelius Van Niel was the first scientist to demonstrate that photosynthesis is a light-dependent redox reaction in 1931, in which hydrogen from an oxidizable compound reduces carbon dioxide to cellular materials. This can be expressed as: $2 H_2A + CO_2 \rightarrow 2A + CH_2O + H_2O$, where A is the electron acceptor. His discovery predicted that H_2O is the hydrogen donor in green plant photosynthesis and is oxidized to O_2.

3. **(d)** Photosynthesis is the process by which plants use the energy from sunlight to produce sugar (fuel) used by all living things. The photosynthesis equation is a chemical representation of the process of photosynthesis which takes place in the chloroplasts. Plants take in carbon dioxide and water to produce glucose (carbohydrate) and oxygen. The following is the chemical equation, which explains this process:

$$6CO_2 + 12H_2O \xrightarrow[\text{chlorophyll}]{\text{sunlight}} C_6H_{12}O_6 + 6O_2 + 6H_2O$$

4. **(d)** Photosynthesis occurs particularly in specialized cell called mesophyll cells. These cells contain chloroplast, which is the actual sites for photosynthesis. The cactus stem and guard cell of stomata contain chloroplasts, so they can manufacture food by photosynthesis. The epidermal cells do not contain chloroplasts, so they do not perform photosynthesis.

5. **(a)** Chlorophyll *a* is the pigment that participates directly in the light reaction of photosynthesis. It absorbs the wavelengths of violet-blue and orange-red light and functions as a primary electron donor during the election transport chain in photosynthesis. It also functions in transporting energy to the reaction centre where P_{680} and P_{700} are located. The 'light-dependent reactions' is the first stage of photosynthesis, in which plants capture and store energy from sunlight. In this process, light energy is converted into chemical energy, in the form of the energy-carrying molecules ATP and NADPH.

6. **(b)** The function of water in photosynthesis is to supply electrons in the light dependent reaction. The light-dependent reactions take place in the membranous sections of the chloroplast - thylakoids (grana/lamellae) which offer a large surface area to absorb light energy. The main function of these reactions is to provide a source of ATP and reduced NADP, which are used to reduce CO_2 in the light independent reactions

7. **(d)** In non-cyclic reaction of photosynthesis, electrons from chlorophyll molecules in photosystem I are used in the formation of NADPH. The source of those electrons is photosystem II which splits water molecule.

8. **(c)** In C_4 plants, photosynthesis occurs in chloroplast of mesophyll and bundle sheath cells. While in C_3 plants photosynthesis occurs only in mesophyll cells.

9. **(b)** In C_4 plants, a 4 - C compound oxaloacetic acid (OAA) is the first stable product, and phosphoenol pyruvate (PEP) is the CO_2 acceptor. This reaction is catalyzed by the enzyme PEP carboxylase or PEP case in mesophyll cells of the leaf.

10. **(d)** According to Blackmans law of limiting factor, at any given time photosynthesis can be limited either by light or CO_2. Blackman proposed the law of limiting factors in 1905 to determine the rate of photosynthesis. According to this law, when a process depends on a number of factors, its rate is limited by the pace of the slowest factor.

Assertion & Reason Questions

1. **(b)** Light reaction or Hill reaction results in the formation of ATP and $NADPH_2$. $6CO_2$, $6H_2O$, $12NADPH_2$ and 18ATP are utilised to produce one molecule of glucose.

2. **(c)** Photorespiration is the uptake of O_2 and release of CO_2 in light and results from the biosynthesis of glycolate in chloroplasts and subsequent metabolism of glycolate acid in the same leaf cell. During photorespiration loss of carbon takes place in the form of CO_2.

3. **(c)** Anthocyanin pigments only give colouration since the epidermal cells mainly have potential colouring pigments. It is responsible of blue, red, pink and purple colours, observed in different parts of plants such as petals, stamens and fruits etc.

    Anthocyanin are also important for attracting insects for pollination and seed dispersal. Hence, anthocyanin pigments are not accessory photosynthetic pigments.

4. **(c)** In mesophyll cells, PEPcarboxylase fixes CO_2 with phosphoenol pyruvate (PEP) to form C_4 acid OAA, which then forms other 4-carbon compounds like malic acid or aspartic acid.

5. **(d)** Dark reaction is also known as light-independent phase. Unlike, light reaction, it does not require light as an essential factor. Thus, can take place both in the presence or absence of light. The term dark reaction does not mean that it takes place only in dark period or at night. CO_2 fixation occurs in both C_3 and C_4 cycle. In C_3 cycle, CO_2 is added by the enzyme, RuBisCO to a 5 carbon compound RuBP that is converted to 2 molecules of 3-carbon PGA. In C_4 cycle, the first product of CO_2 fixation (takes place in mesophyll) is a 4-carbon compound, oxaloacetic acid. It is seen in some tropical plants.

Case/Passage Based Questions

1. **(b)** Labelling B-represent the thylakoid membrane.

2. **(b)**

3. **(a)** Labelling D shows photosystem I.

4. **(b)** ATP synthesis takes place during chemiosmosis due to movement of ions across a semipermeable membrane down their electro chemical gradient.

5. **(c)** In eukaryotic organisms, chemiosmosis occurs in both mitochondria and chloroplast.

Very Short Answer Questions

1. Kranz anatomy in leaf.
2. (d) Releasing oxygen for photorespiration.
3. Carbon dioxide.
4. PS II is located in the appressed regions of grana thylakoid
5. P_{700} & P_{680}.
6. In the thylakoid membrane.
7. 9 ATP and 6 NADPH
8. As these plants grow in dry area , they keep stomata close during day to conserve water and open their stomata during night for the diffusion of gases.
9. It protects the plants from photooxidative damage.
10. Cyanobacteria have bluish pigment phycocyanin, which they use to capture light for photosynthesis. Some green bacteria (cyanobacteria) are red or pink due to pigment phycoerythrin. Whatever the colour of cyanobacteria, they are photosynthetic and so can manufacture food.
11. It proves that chlorophyll is necessary for photosynthesis.
12. *Cladophora.*
13. $6CO_2 + 12H_2O \xrightarrow{\text{Light}} C_6H_{12}O_6 + 6H_2O + 6O_2$
14. A pigment is a substance that absorbs light of certain wavelength(s).
15. NADP – Nicotinamide adenine dinucleotide Phosphate.
16. Ribulose 1, 5 bisphosphate.
17. Hatch and Slack.
18. Conditions in which light can become a limiting factor :
    (i) Plants in the shade.
    (ii) Plants growing under the canopy in a dense forest.
19. Antenna molecules are light harvesting pigment molecules that occur on the outer side of a photosynthetic unit.
20. Quantasome means photosynthetic units. It is equivalent is 230 chlorophyll molecules. These are present in the grana lamellae.

Short Answer Questions

1. In C_4 pathway of sugarcane, CO_2 from atmosphere enters through the stomata in the mesophyll cell and combines with phosphoenol pyruvate to form a 4-C compound oxaloacetic acid. The OAA is then transported to the bundle sheath where it is decarboxylated to release CO_2 in bundle sheath.
2. The main differences between absorption spectrum and action spectrum are as followings.

	Absorption spectrum		Action spectrum
1.	It shows the amount of light absorbed at different wave lengths.	1.	It shows the use of light energy of different wave lengths in photosynthesis.
2.	Absorption spectrum is the graphic representation of wavelengths absorbed by a pigment.	2.	It is the graphic representation of the rate of photosynthesis at different wavelengths of light.
3.	It requires a single exposure to light having itensity required for photosynthesis.	3.	It requires study of light utilization at various wavelengths.

3. In reflected light, the chlorophyll appears red because of fluorescence. The light absorbed by chlorophyll molecules loses its energy and emits light of wavelengths corresponds to red colour. In transmitted light, chlorophyll appears green because it absorbs only light of wavelengths correspond to green colour.
4. Influences of temperature on the biosynthetic phase of photosynthesis :
   (i) At higher temperature enzymes become inactive as it gets denatured.
   (ii) At low temperature also enzyme become inactive.
   (iii) Affinity of the enzymes for CO_2 decreases with increasing temperature.
5. F. F. Blackman (1905) extended a law to formulate the principle of limiting factors. "When a process is conditioned as to its rapidity by a number of separate factors, the rate of the process is limited by the pace of slowest factors."
6. Due to water stress stomata remain closed and so there is decrease in CO_2 concentration and the leaf water potential is also reduced, decline the rate of photosynthesis.
7. If the concentration of CO_2 in the atmosphere increases, the rate of photosynthesis by C_3 plants will increase for following two reasons.
   (a) High availability of substrate (CO_2) for carboxylation
   (b) Photorespiration is reduced due to more availability of CO_2 as enzyme will function only as carboxylase.
8. Photorespiration considered a wasteful process because
   (i) 25% of photosynthetically fixed carbon is lost in the form of CO_2.
   (ii) There is no energy rich useful compound produced during this process.
9. Photosynthesis is the most important process because :
   (i) it is the only natural process by which oxygen is liberated into the atmosphere.
   (ii) it is the process by which food is manufactured for all living organisms.
10. Rate of photosynthesis decreases for two reasons:
    (i) Other factors required for photosynthesis become limiting.
    (ii) Destruction of chlorophyll by photo oxidation.
    Carotenoids play a protective role by :
    (i) absorbing the excess light and
    (ii) acting as antioxidant to detoxify the effect of activated oxygen species.
11. PEP – phosphoenolpyruvate. It is produced in the mesophyll cells of leaves of C_4 plants. It is the primary acceptor of carbon dioxide and is converted into oxaloacetic acid (OAA). Thus it helps in carbon fixation in these plants. By this pathway the carbon dioxide concentration in the bundle sheath increases and photorespiration is prevented from occurring.
12. In **Kranz Anatomy** vascular bundles are surrounded by a layer of bundle sheath that contains large number of chloroplasts in mesophyl cells and it is present in C_4 plants e.g, Maize, Sugarcane, etc..

Long Answer Questions

1. The main differences between photosystem I and photosystem II are

	Photosystem I		Photosystem II
1.	The system is located in non-appressed part of grana thylakoid as well as stroma thylakoid.	1.	Photosystem II is present in the appressed part of grana thylakoid.
2.	The ratio of chlorophyll and carotenoid is high.	2.	The ratio of chlorophyll and carotenoid is low.
3.	Chlorophyll a content is more than twice that of chlorophyll b.	3.	Chlorophyll a and Chlorophyll b are approximately equal.
4.	Its photocentre is P_{700}.	4.	Its photocentre is P_{680}.
5.	It can perform cyclic photophosphorylation independently.	5.	It performs non cyclic photophosphorylation in conjunction with photosystem I.
6.	It is not connected with photolysis of water.	6.	It is connected with photolysis of water.
7.	Main function is ATP Synthesis.	7.	Main Function are ATP Synthesis and hydrolysis.

2. Importance of C_4 plants are :
   (1) C_4 plants have little photorespiration,.
   (2) C_4 plants are more efficient in picking up CO_2 even when it is found in low concentration because of high affinity of phosphoenolpyruvate (i.e. PEP).
   (3) Concentric arrangement of mesophyll cells produces a smaller area in relation to volume for better utilization of available water and reduce the intensity of solar radiation.
   (4) They are adapted to high temperature and intense radiation.
   (5) It prevents photorespiration

3. Biosynthetic phase of photosynthesis :
   - It occurs in the stroma of chloroplasts.
   - These reactions reduce the carbon dioxide into carbohydrates, making use of the ATP and $NADPH_2$ produced in the photochemical reactions.
   - The reactions are also called as Calvin cycle.
   - The three phases of Calvin cycle are as follows:
   (i) **Carboxylation**
   Six molecules of Ribulose 1, 5 bisphosphate react with six molecules of carbon dioxide to form six molecules of a short-lived 6C-compound.
   - The reaction is catalysed by RuBP carboxylase (RuBisCo).
   - The six molecules of the 6C-intermediate break into 12 molecules of 3-phosphoglyceric acid (3-PGA), a 3C-compound.
   - It is through this step that carbon dioxide is fixed in the plant.

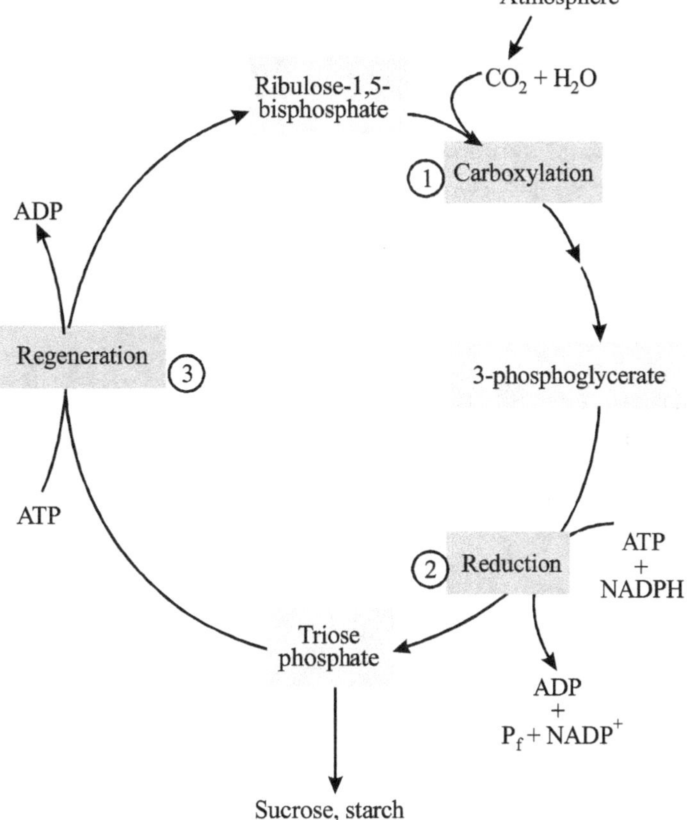

(ii) Reduction

12 molecules of 3-phosphoglyceric acid are converted into 12 molecules of 1, 3 diphospho-glyceric acid, utilising 12 molecules of ATP and then reduced to 3-phosphoglyceraldehyde making use of 12 molecules of NADPH. Two molecules of phosphoglyceraldhyde react to form one molecule of glucose. It is in this step that there is actual reduction of carbon dioxide leading to sugar formation.

(iii) Regeneration of RuBP

10 molecules of phosphoglyceraldehyde, by a series of c omplex enzyme-catalysed reactions, are converted into six molecules of ribulose 1, 5-bisphosphate; six molecules of ATP are needed for this step. This step of regeneration of RuBP is important for the cycle to continue.

SECTION C — NCERT EXEMPLAR QUESTIONS 

MULTIPLE CHOICE QUESTIONS

1. Which metal ion is a constituent of chlorophyll?
(a) Iron   (b) Copper
(c) Magnesium   (d) Zinc

2. Which pigment acts directly to convert light energy to chemical energy ?
(a) Chlorophyll-*a*   (b) Chlorophyll-*b*
(c) Xanthophyll   (d) Carotenoid

3. Which range of wavelength (in nm) is called Photosynthetically Active Radiation (PAR)?
(a) 100-390   (b) 390-430
(c) 400-700   (d) 760-100,00

4. Which light range is most effective in photosynthesis?
(a) Blue   (b) Green
(c) Red   (d) Violet

5. Chemosynthetic bacteria obtain energy from:
(a) sun   (b) infrared rays
(c) organic substances (d) inorganic chemicals

6. Energy required for ATP synthesis in PS II comes from
(a) proton gradient   (b) electron gradient
(c) reduction of glucose (d) oxidation of glucose

7. During light reaction in photosynthesis the following are formed:
(a) ATP and sugar
(b) hydrogen, O_2 and sugar
(c) ATP, hydrogen donor and O_2
(d) ATP, hydrogen and O_2 donor

8. Dark reaction in photosynthesis is called so because:
(a) it can occur in dark also
(b) it does not depend on light energy.
(c) it cannot occur during day light
(d) it occurs more rapidly at night

9. PEP is primary CO_2 acceptor in:
(a) C_4 plants   (b) C_3 plants
(c) C_2 plants   (d) both C_3 and C_4 plants

10. Splitting of water is associated with:
(a) photosystem I
(b) lumen of thylakoid
(c) both photosystem I and II
(d) inner surface of thylakoid membrane

11. The correct sequence of flow of electrons in the light reaction is:
(a) PS II, plastoquinone, cytochromes, PS I, ferredoxin
(b) PS I, plastoquinone, cytochromes, PS II, ferredoxin
(c) PS I, ferredoxin, PS II
(d) PS I, cytochromes, plastoquinone, PS II, ferredoxin

12. The enzyme that is not found in a C_3 plant is:
(a) RuBP carboxylase (b) PEP carboxylase
(c) NADP reductase   (d) ATP synthase

13. The reaction that is responsible for the primary fixation of CO_2 is catalysed by:
(a) RuBP carboxylase
(b) PEP carboxylase
(c) RuBP carboxylase and PEP carboxylase
(d) PGA synthase

14. When CO_2 is added to PEP, the first stable product synthesised is:
(a) pyruvate
(b) glyceraldehyde-3-phosphate
(c) phosphoglycerate
(d) oxaloacetate

VERY SHORT ANSWER QUESTIONS

1. Examine the figure.

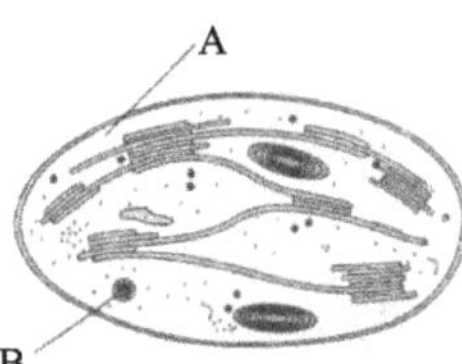

(a) Is this structure present in animal cell or plant cell?
(b) Can these be passed on to the progeny? How?
(c) Name the metabolic process taking place in the places marked (*A*) and (*B*).

2. $2H_2O \rightarrow 4H^+ + O_2 + 4e^-$

Based on the above equation, answer the following questions
(a) Where does this reaction take place in plants?
(b) What is the significance of this reaction?

3. Cyanobacteria and some other photosynthetic bacteria don't have chloroplasts. How do they conduct photosynthesis?
4. (a) NADP reductase enzyme is located on ....
   (b) Breakdown of proton gradient leads to release of ....
   (b) ATP molecules
5. Can girdling experiments be done in monocots? If yes, how? If no, why note?
6. $3CO_2 + 9ATP + 6NADPH + water \rightarrow$ Glyceraldehyde 3-phosphate $+9ADP+6NADP^+ +8Pi.$
   Analyse the above reaction and answer the following questions
   (a) How many molecules of ATP and NADPH are required to fix one molecule of CO_2?
   (b) Where in the chloroplast does this process occur?
7. Does moonlight support photosynthesis? Find out.
8. ATPase enzyme consists of two parts. What are those parts? How are they arranged in the thylakoid membrane? Conformational change occur in which part of the enzyme?

SHORT ANSWER QUESTIONS

1. Succulents are known to keep their stomata closed during the day to check transpiration. How do they meet their photosynthetic CO_2 requirements?
2. Chlorophyll-'*a*' is the primary pigment for the light reaction. What are accessory pigments? What is their role in photosynthesis?
3. Do reactions of photosynthesis called, as 'Dark Reaction' need light? Explain.
4. How are photosynthesis and respiration related to each other?
5. If a green plant is kept in dark with proper ventilation, can this plant carry out photosynthesis? Can anything be given as supplement to maintain its growth or survival?
6. Photosynthetic organisms occur at different depths in the ocean. Do they receive qualitatively and quantitatively the same light? How do they adapt to carry out photosynthesis under these conditions.
7. What conditions enable RuBisCO to function as an oxygenase? Explain the ensuing process.
8. Why does the rate of photosynthesis decrease at higher temperatures?
9. Explain how during light reaction of photosynthesis, ATP Synthesis is a chemiosmotic phenomenon.
10. In What kind of plants do you come across 'Kranz anatomy'? To which conditions are those plants better adapted? How are these plants better adapted than the plants, which lack this anatomy?
11. Tomatoes, carrots and chilies are red in colour due to the presence of one pigment. Name the pigment. Is it a photosynthetic pigment?

12. Observe the diagram and answer the following.

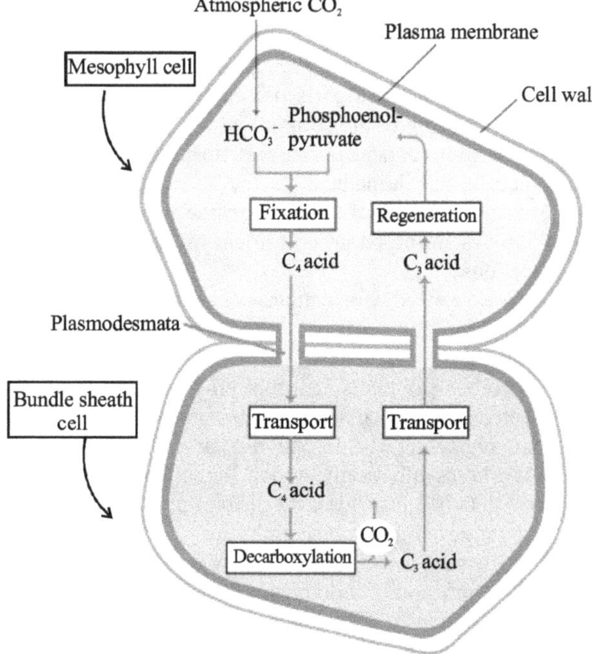

(a) Which group of plants exhibit these two types of cells?
(b) What is the first product of C_4 cycle?
(c) Which enzyme is there in bundle sheath cells and mesophyll cells?

LONG SHORT ANSWER QUESTIONS

1. In the figure given below, the back line (upper) indicates action spectrum for photosynthesis and the lighter line (lower) indicates the absorption spectrum of chlorophyll-*a*, answer the following

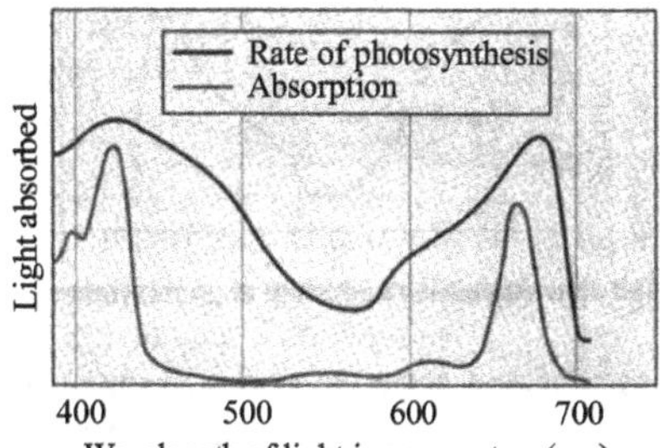

(a) What does the action spectrum indicate? How can we plot an action spectrum? Explain with an example.
(b) How can we derive an absorption spectrum for any substances?
(c) If chlorophyll-a is responsible for light reaction of photosynthesis, why do the action spectrum and absorption spectrum not overlap?
2. What are the important events and end products of the light reaction?
3. Why does not photorespiration take place in C_4 plants?

SOLUTIONS

Multiple Choice Questions

1. **(c)** Magnesium (Mg) is present in the centre of the porphyrin ring of the chlorophyll molecule. Other ions, such as iron, copper and zinc participate in other metabolic processes which include:
   Fe is an important part of **cytochrome** and **ferredoxin**.
   Cu plays an important role in enzyme catalysing redox reactions.
   Zn is associated with synthesis of auxin.

2. **(a)** Chlorophyll-*a* directly acts to convert light energy to chemical energy.
   The other pigments chlorophyll-*b*, xanthophyll and carotenoids are accessory pigments associated with the main pigment, i.e., chlorophyll-*a* harvest the light energy.

3. **(c)** Photosynthetically Active Radiation (PAR) ranges from 400-700 nm. This is the visible range of light energy.
   The range of other wavelengths are
   100-300 nm   :   Ultraviolet (UV) range
   390-430 nm   :   Infrared (NIR) range
   760-100,00 nm :   Mid Infrared (MIR) range

4. **(c)** The visible spectrum wavelength ranges from 400-700 nm of which red light has a wavelength of 700 nm.
   Red light is most effective in photosynthesis.
   In blue and violet hight photosynthesis takes place but the rate is slow. In green light the photosynthesis is least because plants do not absorb this range of light.

5. **(d)** Chemosynthetic bacteria were the first organism on earth to synthesise their own food by obtaining energy from chemicals like H_2S, NO_2, *etc.* Photosynthetic bacteria have originated from chemosynthetic bacteria.

6. **(a)** The synthesis of ATP is linked directly to the development of proton gradient across the thylakoid membranes of a chloroplast. It results when the water molecule splits inside the inner membrane and forms H^+ and OH^- ions.
   The energy for ATP synthesis comes from proton gradient which develops along the inner membrane, as in case of mitochondria in the electron transport chain and in chloroplast in the PS II.

7. **(c)** Light dependent reaction uses solar power to generate ATP and $NADPH_2$ which provides chemical and reducing power to sugar synthesising reaction of the Calvin cycle, while the O_2 is released as a by product of light dependent reaction.

8. **(b)** Dark reaction is called as such because it does not depend on light. It is also called as light independent reaction.

9. **(a)** C_4 plants have evolved PEP as the primary acceptor of CO_2 to avoid the sensitivity of RuBP carboxylase-oxygenase to high concentrations of oxygen. It prevents photorespiratory loss of CO_2 occuring in them.

10. **(d)** The thylakoid is a photosynthetic unit of the chloroplast. It is a membrane bound structure. The membrane consists of photosystems I and II embedded in it, in the form of chemicals and molecules. Splitting of water is associated with presence of Mn^{2+} and Cl^- ions on the inner surface of thylakoid membrane.

$$2H_2O \xrightarrow[Cl^-]{Mn^+} 4H^+ + O_2 + 4e^-$$

Photosystem I and II are associated with light reactions.

11. **(a)** Option (a) is the correct sequence for movement of electrons.

12. **(b)** PEP carboxylase enzyme is found in C_4 plants for initial fixation of CO_2.
   RuBP carboxylase operates in C_3 plants. NADP reductase is involved in electron transport chain. ATP synthase is used in ATP synthesis.

13. **(c)** In C_3 plants **RuBP carboxylase** fixes atmospheric CO_2 whereas while in C_4 plants **PEP carboxylase** is involved in primary CO_2 fixation.

14. **(d)** C_4 plants use PEP (phosphoenol pyruvate) to fix atmospheric CO_2. In a normal photosynthetic cycle RuBP carboxylase is used to trap CO_2 in C_3 plants.
   Oxaloacetate is a four carbon compound formed in C_4 cycle and is the first stable product, so such plants are called C_4 plants.

Very Short Answer Questions

1. (a) Figure shows the chloroplast, which is green in colour and performs photosynthesis in plants. The structure is present in plant cell.
   (b) *Yes*, chloroplast has the power of self replication because of presence of extra nuclear DNA. Hence, known as semi-autonomous organelle.
   (c) The metabolic processes that occurs in the marked places are as follows.
   A-It is the stroma of chloroplast, where dark reaction of photosynthesis takes place.
   B-It is the structure of extra nuclear DNA that is responsible for replication of chloroplast, when it is required in the photo synthesising cells.

2. (a) This reaction takes place in reaction centre PS II, that is located on the inner surface of thylakoid membrane. It is known as water splitting centre, where electrons are extracted from water and the reaction is catalysed by Mn^+ and Cl^- ions.
   (b) Splitting of water is an important event in photosynthesis are
   (i) It liberates molecular oxygen as byproduct of photosynthesis and is the significant source of oxygen in air, or is essential for all living beings on earth.
   (ii) Hydrogen ions produced takes part in reducing NADP to NADPH. It is a strong reducing agent.
   (iii) The electrons released are transferred from PS II to PS I through a series of electron carriers thus, creating a gradient for the ATP synthesis.

3. In Cyanobacteria complex lamellar system (thylakoids) are present instead of chloroplast. These thylakoids are functionally analogous to the plastids of eukaryotic cells. Pigment like chlorophyll-a, C-phycocyanin, C-phycoerythrin embedded in these lamellar system and they

trap solar energy and perform photosynthesis. They perform oxygenic photosynthesis. Photosynthetic bacteria possess related pigments called bacterichlorophyll which are of different types (a,b,c,d,e,f and g). Groups that contain chlorophyll, perform photosynthesis, but do not evolve oxygen. Bacteriochlorophyll, perform photosynthesis but do not evolve oxygen. Bacteriochlorophylls are photoreceptors similar to chlorophylls except for the reduction of an additional pyrrole ring and other minor differences that shift their absorption maxima to near infrared, to wavelength as long as 1000 nm. Thus, they utilize light wavelengths not used by green plants or cyanobacteria. Bacteriopheophytin is a variant of bacteriochlorophyll that has two protons are present instead of magnesium ion at its centre.

4. (a) NADP reductase enzyme is located on the outer side of thylakoid membrane.
   (b) ATP molecules

5. The girdling experiment cannot be done in monocots. The monocots vascular bundles are scattered all over the width of stem, so we cannot get the specific band of the phloem tissue which we get in dicot.

6. (a) 2 molecules of ATP for phosphorylation and two molecules of NADPH for reduction are required to fix one molecule of CO_2
   (b) The calvin cycle occurs in the stroma of the chloroplast.

7. Moonlight does not carry enough energy to excite chlorophyll molecules, i.e; reaction centre PSI and PSII, so light dependent reactions are not initiated. Thus, photosynthesis cannot occur in moonlight.

8. ATP synthase enzyme consists of two parts:
   (a) F_1- head piece is a peripheral membrane protein complex and contain the site for synthesis of ATP from ADP + pi (inorganic phosphate).
   (b) F_0-integral membrane protein complex that form the channel through which proton cross the inner membrane.

The arrangement of F_1 and F_0 in thylakoid membrane is as follows.

F_0- is a portion present within the thylakoid membrane.
F_1 is a portion of ATP synthase enzyme present in the stroma of chloroplast.
The conformational change occurs in F_1 portion of ATP synthase thus, it facilitates the ATP synthesis.

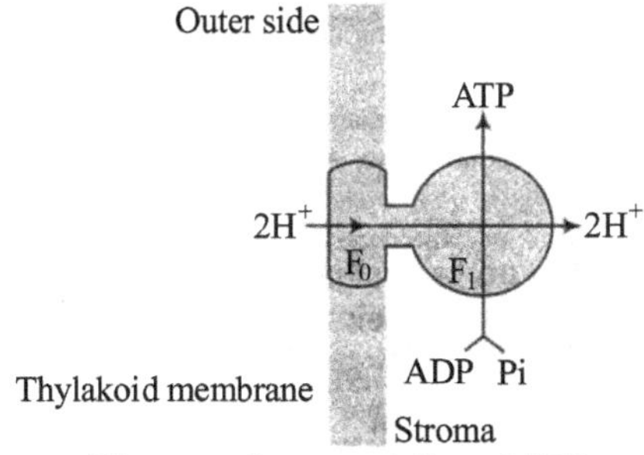

Diagramatic presentation of ATP synthesis in chloroplast

1. Succulent plants grow in dry and xeric conditions so, to prevent water loss through transpiration the stomata remains closed during day time. So that the gaseous exchange does not take place.
   Thus plants have developed the mechanism to fix CO_2 during night in the form of malic acid, which is a 4 carbon compound and are released during the day, inside the photosynthetic cells.

2. Accessory pigments are also photosynthetic pigments, like chlorophyll-*b*, xanthophyll and carotenoids which are not directly involved in emission of excited electron, but they help in harvesting solar radiation and pass it on to chlorophyll-*a*.
   This pigment itself absorbs maximum radiation at blue and red region. So the chief pigment of photosynthesis is chlorophyll and others (*i.e*, chlorophyll-*b* xanthophyll and carotenoid) are accessory pigments.

3. Dark reactions is a type of independent reactions. Through various biochemical reactions CO_2 is reduced to produce $C_6H_{12}O_6$ (glucose) which does not need light. But they depend on the products formed during light reactions, i.e., $NADPH_2$ and ATP.

4. Photosynthesis and respiration are related to each other as in both mechanisms, the plants gain energy.
   In photosynthesis, plants gain energy from solar radiations whereas, in respiration, they break down glucose molecule to get energy in the form of ATP molecules.
   The product of photosynthesis *i.e.*, glucose (food) is utilised in respiration to yield energy in the form of ATP. While doing so, it release many other simple molecules $(CO_2 + H_2O)$ that are utilised in photosynthesis to produce more sugar.

5. The plant in given conditions cannot carry out photosynthesis. Light is necessary for any green plant to make its own food. The plant should be watered properly for its survival.

6. Mostly algae are present at various depth in ocean. These show great variations in its photosynthetic pigment. These can absorb different wave lengths of light and could perform photosynthesis.
   Green algae–chlorophyll-*a*, (absorbs red) and b(absorbs blue violet).
   Brown algae-chlorophyll-*a*, *c* and fucoxanthin (absorbs yellow).
   Rhodophyceae–chlorophyll-*a*, *d* and phyocoerythrin.

7. This is an enzyme that has dual nature. When CO_2 concentration is good enough in atmosphere. It acts as carboxylase. But if concentration of O_2 increase, its nature changes and it binds with O_2 and acts as oxygenase enzyme that forces CO_2 to enter in C_2 cycle that leads to photorespiration and loss of CO_2.

8. Photosynthesis is an enzyme specific process. All enzymes works at an optimum temperature (*i.e.*, 25-35°C). As temperature increases, enzyme gets denatured thus leading to fall in the rate of photosynthesis.

9. In light reaction plants solar radiation is trapped by photosynthetic pigments, which converts light energy into chemical energy. Photophosphorylation is the main event of light reaction *i.e.*, formation of ATP from ADP + Pi by using energy of excited electron movement through electron transport chain, that is present in thylakoid membrane.

   The movement of ions across a selectively permeable membrane, down the electrochemical/proton gradient is known as chemiosmosis.

   Chemiosmosis hypothesis of ATP formation was first proposed by Mitchell (1961), according to ATP generated by enzyme ATP synthase *via* a membrane, proton pump and proton gradient. ATP synthase allows ions O_2 protons to pass through membrane and proton pump.

   Which creates a high concentration of protons (H^+) in the lumen and hence diffuses across the membrane to activate ATPase, releasing ATP molecules. One molecule of ATP is released for every two (H^+) ions passing through ATPase.

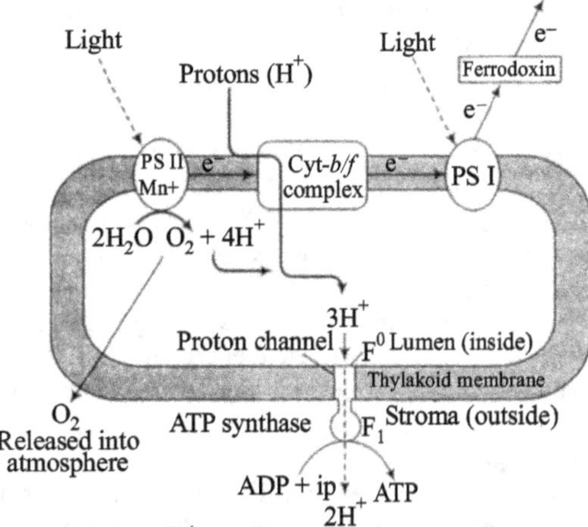

   Proton (H^+) gradient and ATP formation

10. Kranz anatomy how dimorphism in the chloroplast structure. It is found in C_4 plants. The cells of leaves consists two types of chloroplast in them.

    Granal Chloroplast is found in the mesophyll cells of leaves. Chloroplast have well developed grana in them. These chloroplast fixes CO_2 effectively even if it is present in lower concentrations. PEP carboxylase fixes CO_2 to form oxaloacetic acid (4 carbon compound).

    Agranal Chloroplast is found in bundle sheath cells of the leaves. C_3 cycle occurs in these cells in the presence of RuBisCo enzyme.

    The C_4 plants are well adapted to high O_2 concentrations and high temperature.

    C_4 plants can absorb CO_2 even when CO_2 concentration in much low thus C_4 plants can perform high rate of photosynthesis even the stomata are closed or there is the shortage of water thus, they can conserve water.

    Since, PEP-carboxylase is insensitive to O_2 thus excess O_2 has inhibitory effect in C_4 pathway and no photosynthesis occurs in C_4 plant.

    Thus, C_4 plants are better adapted to tropical and desert (hot acid habitats) areas than the plants, that lack kranz anatomy.

11. The pigments are chromoplasts, these are fat soluble carotinoid pigments like carotenes and xanthophylls. These are called accessory pigments, they absorb light and transfer energy to Chlorophyll *a*.

12. (a) Monocot plants that belongs to Graminae/Poaceae family, *e.g.*, sugarcane, maize etc., possess these two types of cells, *i.e.*, bundle sheath and mesophyll cell (in kranz anatomy).

    (b) First product of C_4 cycle is 4-carbon compound oxaloacetic acid.

    (c) Mesophyll cells consists PEP carboxylase enzyme to fix atmospheric CO_2 to form 4-carbon compound oxalo acetic acid, whereas bundle sheath cells consists RuBP carboxylase that fixes CO_2 to form 3-carbon compound 3 PGA (3 phosphoglyceric acid).

Long Answer Questions

1. (a) Action spectrum depicts the relative rates of photosynthesis at different wavelenghths of light. Action spectrum of photosynthesis can be plotted by measurement of oxygen evolution at different wavelength. Englemann (1882) by using a green algae plotted action spectrum.

   (b) Absorption spectrum of a substance can be derived by calculating amount of energy of different wavelength of light absorbed.

   (c) Chlorophyll a is responsible for light reaction of photosynthesis, but the action spectrum and absorption spectrum do not overlap because, though chlorophyll a is the main pigment responsible for the absorption of light, other thylakoids pigment like chlorophyll b, xanthophylls, carotenoids, which are accessory pigments also absorb and transfer the energy to chlorophyll a. Indeed they not only enable a wider range of wavelength of incoming light to be utilized for photosynthesis but also protect chlorophyll from photo-oxidation.

2. Following are important events of light reaction:
   (i) Excitation of chlorophyll molecule to release a pair of electrons and use their energy in the formation of ATP from ADP + Pi. This process is known as photophosphorylation.
   (ii) Splitting of water molecule
       (a) $2H_2O \rightarrow 4H^+ + 4e^- + O_2 \uparrow$
       (b) $NADP + 2H^+ \rightarrow NADPH_2$

   End products of light reaction are NADPH and ATP.

   Reducing power is produced in the light reaction *i.e.*, ATP and $NADPH_2$ molecules that are used up in dark reaction and O_2 is evolved as a by product by the splitting of water.

3. Photorespiration is associated with C_3 cycle, where plant lose CO_2 fixation due to the increase in concentrate ion of O_2 change in the nature of activity of RuBP carboxylase-oxygenase.

   While C_4 plants have evolved a mechanism to avoid loss of CO_2. There is not a direct involvement of RuBP carboxylase-oxygenase as C_3 cycle operates in bundle sheath cells, where both temperature and oxygen level low.

   CO_2 fixation occurs by another enzyme PEP carboxylase in mesophyll cells and oxaloacetate is formed, that is later converted into malic acid and transported to bundle sheath cells.

   There, it liberates CO_2, which is used in Calvin cycle, operating in bundle sheath cells of C_4 plants.

14 — Respiration in Plants

14.1 Differentiate between
- **(a)** Respiration and Combustion
- **(b)** Glycolysis and Krebs' cycle
- **(c)** Aerobic respiration and Fermentation

Sol. (a) Differences between respiration and combustion are as follows :

Respiration	Combustion
1. The breakdown of C-C bond of complex compounds inside the cells leading to release of considerable amount of energy is called respiration.	1. Conversion of total complex compounds into heat energy is called combustion.
2. Enzymes are used in different steps.	2. Enzymes are absent.
3. Energy stored in the form of ATP.	3. No energy is stored during combustion, so lot of energy is wasted.
4. It occurs in the cells of the living organisms.	4. It does not occur in the living organisms.

(b) Differences between glycolysis and krebs' cycle are as follows :

Glycolysis	Krebs cycle
1. It occurs inside the cytoplasm.	1. It occurs inside the matrix of mitochondria.
2. It is a linear pathway.	2. It is a cyclic pathway.
3. Glycolysis is the first step of respiration in which glucose is broken down to the level of pyruvate.	3. Krebs cycle is the second step in respiration where an active acetyl group is broken down completely.
4. The process is common to both aerobic and anaerobic modes of respiration.	4. It occurs only in aerobic respiration.
5. It degrades a molecule of glucose into two molecules of an organic substance, pyruvate.	5. It degrades pyruvate completely into inorganic substances $(CO_2 + H_2O)$.
6. Glycolysis consumes 2 ATP molecules for the initial phosphorylation of substrate molecule.	6. It does not consume ATP.
7. Net gain is two molecules of NADH and two molecules of ATP for every molecule of glucose broken down.	7. Krebs cycle produces six molecules of NADH, and 2 molecules of $FADH_2$ for every two molecules of acetyl CoA oxidised by it.

(c) Differences between aerobic respiration and fermentation are as follows :

Aerobic respiration	Fermentation
1. It involves exchange of gases between the organism and the environment.	1. An exchange of gases is absent.
2. It uses oxygen for breaking the respiratory materials into simple substances.	2. Oxygen is not used in the breakdown of respiratory substrates.
3. Respiratory material is completely oxidised.	3. Respiratory material is incompletely broken.
4. The end products are CO_2, water and energy.	4. The end products are organic acid, CO_2 and energy.
5. Every carbon atom of the food is oxidised and a large quantity of carbon dioxide is evolved.	5. Less quantity of carbon dioxide is evolved.

14.2 What are respiratory substrates ? Name the most common respiratory substrate.

Sol. The compounds that are oxidised during the process of respiration process are known as respiratory substrates. Usually carbohydrates are oxidised to release energy, but proteins, fats and even organic acids can be used as respiratory substrates in some plants, under certain conditions.

14.3 Give the schematic representation of glycolysis.

Sol.

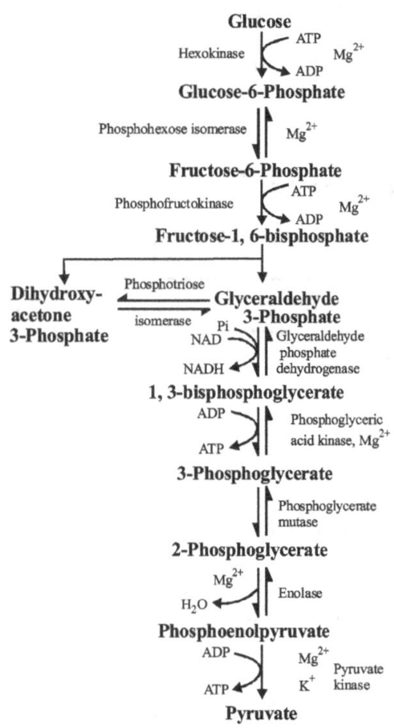

Schematic representation of glycolysis or EMP pathway

14.4 What are the main steps in aerobic respiration? Where does it take place ?

Sol. In aerobic respiration which takes place within the mitochondria, the final product of glycolysis, pyruvate is transported from the cytoplasm into the mitochondria. The crucial events in aerobic respiration are:

• The complete oxidation of pyruvate by the stepwise removal of all the hydrogen atoms, leaving three molecules of CO_2.

• The passing on of the electrons removed as part of the hydrogen atoms to molecular O_2 with simultaneous synthesis of ATP.

• The first process takes place in the matrix of the mitochondria while the second process is located on the inner membrane of the mitochondria.

• Pyruvate, which is formed by the glycolytic catabolism of carbohydrates in the cytosol, after it enters mitochondrial matrix undergoes oxidative decarboxylation by a complex set of reactions catalysed by pyruvic dehydrogenase. The reactions catalysed by pyruvic dehydrogenase require the participation of several coenzymes, including NAD^+ and Coenzyme A.

$$\text{Pyruvic acid} + \text{CoA} + NAD^+ \xrightarrow[\text{Pyruvate dehydrogenase}]{Mg^{2+}} \text{Acetyle CoA} + CO_2 + NADH + H^+$$

During this process, two molecules of NADH are produced from the metabolism of two molecules of pyruvic acid (produced from one glucose molecule during glycolysis). The acetyl CoA then enters a cyclic pathway, tricarboxylic acid cycle, more commonly called as Krebs' cycle.

14.5 Give the schematic representation of an overall view of Krebs' cycle.

Sol.

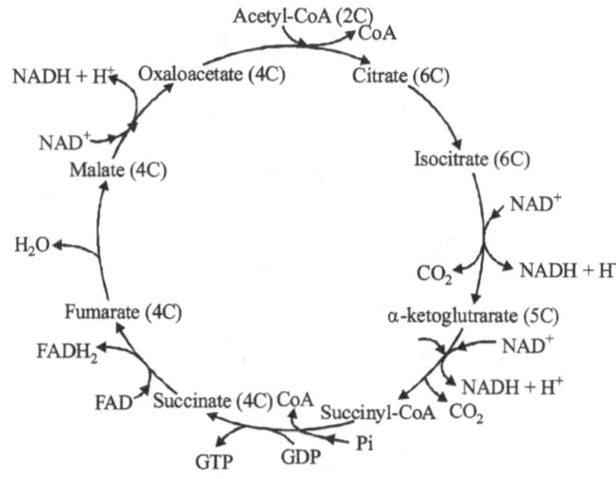

Fig.: Krebs' cycle

14.6 Explain ETS.

Sol. Electron Transport System (ETS)

- ETS occurs in the electron transport particles (ETP) on the inner surface of the inner membrane of mitochondria. It is a metabolic pathway through which electron passes from one carrier to another.
- Electrons from NADH produced in the mitochondrial matrix during citric acid cycle are oxidised by an NADH dehydrogenase (complex I), and electrons are then transferred to ubiquinone located within the inner membrane.
- Ubiquinone also receives reducing equivalents via $FADH_2$ generated during the oxidation of succinate by succinate dehydrogenase (complex II).
- The reduced ubiquinone, called ubiquinol, is then oxidised by transfer of electrons to cytochrome c, cytochrome bc_1 – complex (complex III).
- Cytochrome c acts as a mobile carrier between complex III and complex IV.
- Complex IV refers to cytochrome c oxidase complex containing cytochromes a and a_3 and two copper centres.
- When the electrons are pass from one carrier to another carrier via complex I to IV in the electron transport chain, they are coupled to ATP synthase (complex V) for the formation of ATP from ADP and iP.
- Oxygen functions as the terminal acceptor of electrons and is reduced to water along with the hydrogen atoms. It drives whole process by removing hydrogen from system.
- In respiration, energy of oxidation-reduction utilised for the production of proton gradient. So the process is called as oxidative phosphorylation.

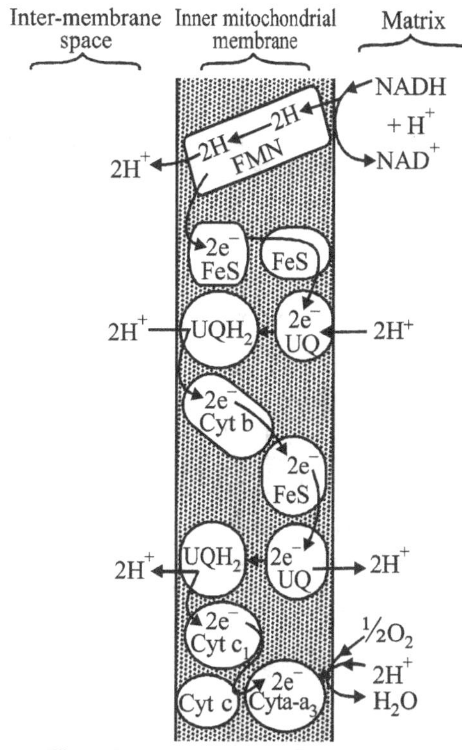

Fig.: Electron Transport System (ETS)

- Higher proton concentration in the outer chamber causes the protons to pass inwardly into matrix or inner chamber causes the protons to pass inwardly into matrix or inner chamber through the inner membrane.

- The energy of the proton gradient is used in attaching a phosphate radicle to ADP by high energy bond.
- Oxidation of one molecule of $NADH_2$ produces 3 ATP molecules while a similar oxidation of $FADH_2$ forms 2 ATP molecules.
- ATP synthase (complex V) helps in ATP synthesis. It consists two major components F_1 and F_0.
- F_1 (head piece) is a peripheral membrane protein complex and contains the site for ATP synthesis while F_0 is an integral membrane protein complex that forms channel through which protons cross the inner membrane.
- For each ATP produced, $2H^+$ passes through F_0 from the intermembrane space to the matrix down the electrochemical proton gradient.

14.7 Distinguish between the following :

   (a) Aerobic respiration and anaerobic respiration.
   (b) Glycolysis and fermentation.
   (c) Glycolysis and citric acid cycle.

Sol. Differences between aerobic respiration and anaerobic respiration are as follows :

	Aerobic respiration		Anaerobic respiration
1.	It is the type of respiration, that occurs in the presence of oxygen.	1.	It is the type of respiration, that occurs in the absence of oxygen.
2.	The respiratory substrate is completely oxidised.	2.	The respiratory substrate is only partially oxidised.
3.	Carbon dioxide, water and a large amount of energy are the end products.	3.	Ethyl alcohol or organic acids (acetic or lactic acid), CO_2 and energy are the end products.
4.	The reactions take place in the cytoplasm and mitochondria.	4.	The reactions take place only in the cytoplasm.

Differences between glycolysis and fermentation are as follows :

Glycolysis	Fermentation
1. It is the first step of respiration which occurs without requirement of oxygen and is common to both aerobic and anaerobic modes of respiration.	1. It is anaerobic respiration or respiration which does not require oxygen.
2. Glycolysis produces pyruvic acid.	2. Fermentation produces different products. The common ones are ethanol, CO_2 and lactic acid.
3. It produces two molecules of NADH per glucose molecule.	3. It generally, utilises NADH produced during glycolysis.
4. It produces 2 ATP molecules per glucose molecule.	4. It does not produce ATP.

Differences between glycolysis and citric acid cycle are as follows :

Glycolysis	Citric acid cycle
1. It is the first step of cellular respiration and its substrate is glucose.	1. It is the second step of cellular respiration and its substrate is acetyl CoA.
2. Glucose in broken down incompletely to form two molecules of pyruvate.	2. Activated acetate of acetyl CoA is completely broken down to inorganic state.
3. It occurs in cytoplasm.	3. It generally occurs inside the matrix of mitochondria (exception aerobic prokaryotes).
4. It is a linear or straight pathway.	4. It is a cyclic pathway.
5. It use two molecules of ATP.	5. It does not consume any ATP molecules.

14.8 What are the assumptions made during calculation of net gain of ATP ?

Sol. The calculations of net gain of ATP for every glucose molecule oxidised is made on certain assumptions that are as follows:

- There is a sequential, orderly pathway functioning, with one substrate forming the next and with glycolysis, TCA cycle and ETS pathway following one after another.
- The NADH synthesized in glycolysis is transferred into the mitochondria and undergoes oxidative phosphorylation.

14.9 Discuss "The respiratory pathway is an amphibolic pathway".

Sol. Glucose is the favoured substrate for respiration. All carbohydrates are usually first converted into glucose before they are used for respiration.

Respiration involves breakdown as well as synthesis of substrates, the respiratory process involves both catabolism and anabolism.

Glucose breakdown to release energy. This is called catabolism. Many compounds are also withdrawn from respiratory pathway for the synthesis new substrates (for example acetyl CoA is withdrawn from pathway to synthesis fatty acids when needed). This is called anabolism. Thus respiratory pathway involves in both anabolism and catabolism So it is called as an amphibolic pathway.

14.10 Define RQ. What is its value for fats ?

Sol. The ratio of the volume of CO_2 evolved to the volume of O_2 consumed is respiration is called respiratory quotient (RQ) or respiratory ratio.

$$RQ = \frac{\text{volume of } CO_2 \text{ evolved}}{\text{volume of } O_2 \text{ consumed}}$$

RQ is different for different substrates.

Fats : $2(C_{51}H_{98}O_6) + 145O_2 \longrightarrow$
Tripalmitin

$$102CO_2 + 98H_2O + \text{energy}$$

$$RQ = \frac{102CO_2}{145O_2} = 0.7$$

As RQ of fats is less than 1, so they (fats) require relatively greater amount of O_2 for oxidation.

14.11 What is oxidative phosphorylation ?

Sol. Oxidative phosphorylation is a metabolic pathway that uses energy released by the oxidation of nutrients to produce adenosine triphosphate (ATP).

During oxidative phosphorylation, electrons are transferred from electrons donors to electron acceptors such as oxygen, in redox reactions. These redox reactions release energy, which is used to form ATP. In eukaryotes, these redox reactions are carried out by a series of five protein complexes within mitochondria.

When the electrons pass from one carrier to another via complex I to IV in the electron transport chain, they are coupled to ATP synthase (complex V) for the production of ATP from ADP and inorganic phosphate. The number of ATP molecules synthesised depends on the nature of the electron donor. Oxidation of one molecule of NADH gives rise to 3 molecules of ATP, while that of one molecule of $FADH_2$ produces 2 molecules of ATP.

Oxygen acts as the final hydrogen acceptor. Unlike photophosphorylation where it is the light energy that is utilised for the production of proton gradient required for phosphorylation, in respiration it is the energy of oxidation-reduction utilised for the same process. It is for this reason that the process is called oxidative phosphorylation.

14.12 What is the significance of step-wise release of energy in respiration ?

Sol. During oxidation within a cell, all the energy contained in respiratory substrates is not released free into the cell, or in a single step. It is released in a series of slow step-wise reactions controlled by enzymes, and it is trapped as chemical energy in the form of ATP. Hence, it is important to understand that the energy released by oxidation in respiration is not used directly but is used to synthesise ATP, which is broken down whenever (and wherever) energy needs to be utilised. Hence, ATP acts as the energy currency of the cell. This energy trapped in ATP is utilised in various energy-requiring processes of the organisms, and the carbon skeleton produced during respiration is used as precursors for biosynthesis of other molecules in the cell.

SECTION B — PRACTICE QUESTIONS

MULTIPLE CHOICE QUESTIONS

1. Fermentation takes place
   (a) under anaerobic conditions in many prokaryotes and unicellular eukaryotes.
   (b) under aerobic conditions in many prokaryotes and unicellular eukaryotes.
   (c) under anaerobic conditions in all prokaryotes and unicellular eukaryotes.
   (d) under aerobic conditions in all prokaryotes and unicellular eukaryotes.

2. In alcoholic fermentation, NAD^+ is produced during the:
   (a) reduction of acetyldehyde to ethanol.
   (b) oxidation of glucose.
   (c) oxidation of pyruvate to acetyl CoA.
   (d) hydrolysis of ATP to ADP.

3. During glycolysis, glucose split into:
   (a) two pyruvic acid molecules.
   (b) two coenzyme A molecules.
   (c) two lactic acid molecules.
   (d) one lactic acid plus one ethanol molecule.

4. In glycolysis, there is one step where $NADH + H^+$ is formed from NAD^+, this is when 3-phosphoglyceraldehyde (PGAL) is converted to 1,3-bisphosphyglycerate (BPGA). This reaction shows
   (a) oxidative dehydrogenation
   (b) oxidative phosphorylation
   (c) oxidative dehydration
   (d) oxidation reduction

5. The enzymes, involved in the chemical reactions of glycolysis are located:
   (a) in the fluid matrix of cytoplasm.
   (b) in the mitochondrial matrix.
   (c) in the nuclear sap.
   (d) on the cristae of a mitochondria.

6. All of the following processes can release CO_2 except:
   (a) alcohol fermentation
   (b) oxidative decarboxylation and Krebs cycle
   (c) oxidative phosphorylation
   (d) Conversion of alpha-Ketoglutaric acid to succinic acid

7. By which of the following complex, proton is pumped to reach ATP synthase to participate in ATP synthesis?
   (a) Cytochrome b_6f (b) Cytochrome c oxidase
   (c) Cytochrome a - a_3 (d) Cytochrome bc

8. Cytochrome oxidase contain
   (a) Fe   (b) Mg
   (c) Zn   (d) Cu

9. Citrate synthase, an enzyme of TCA cycle is located in:
   (a) cytosol in prokaryotes.
   (b) mitochondrial matrix in eukaryotes.
   (c) both (a) and (b)
   (d) none of the above

10. Which of the metabolites is common to respiration mediated breakdown of fats, carbohydrates and proteins?
    (a) Fructose 1, 6 - bisphosphate
    (b) Pyruvic acid
    (c) Acetyl CoA
    (d) Glucose - 6 - phosphate

ASSERTION & REASON QUESTIONS

DIRECTION (Qs. 1-5) : *These questions consists of two statements. Answer these questions selecting the appropriate option given below:*
(a) Both Assertion (A) and Reason (R) are true and Reason (R) is the correct explanation of Assertion (A).
(b) Both Assertion (A) and Reason (R) are true, but Reason (R) is not the correct explanation of Assertion (A).
(c) Assertion (A) is true, but Reason (R) is false.
(d) Assertion (A) is false, but Reason (R) is true.

1. **Assertion :** Glycolysis is the first step of respiration in which glucose completely breaks into CO_2 and H_2O.
   Reason : In this process, there is net gain of eight molecules of ATP.

2. **Assertion :** Fermentation is incomplete oxidation of glucose.
   Reason : Pyruvic acid decarboxylase, Alcoholic dehydrogenase catalyse the reaction.

3. **Assertion :** Photorespiration is absent in C_4 plants.
   Reason : In C_4 plants, first CO_2 fixation product is formed in bundle sheath cells.

4. **Assertion :** Most of the enzymes of oxidative decarboxylation are present in mitochondrial matrix.
   Reason : ETS operates on inner membrane of mitochondria.

5. **Assertion :** Photorespiration decreases photosynthetic output.
   Reason : In photorespiratory pathway, neither ATP nor NADPH is produced.

CASE/PASSAGE BASED QUESTIONS

DIRECTIONS (Qs. 1-5) : *Read the following passage and answer the questions that follows.*

Glucose is a type of sugar and provides energy to the body. It is oxidised during respiration. The given figure shows the fate of glucose during aerobic and anaerobic respiration. Observe the diagram and answers the questions.

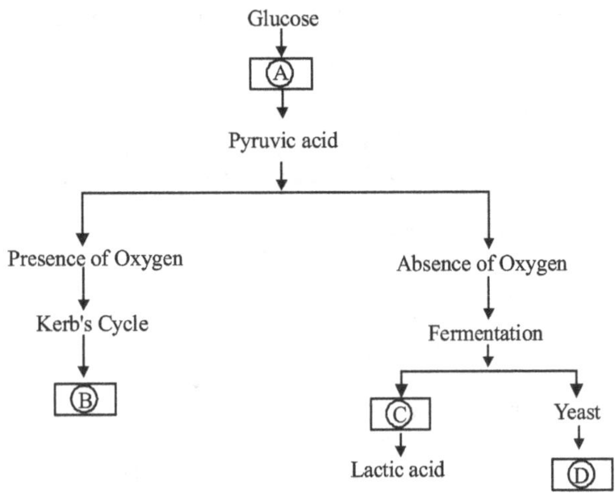

1. What is represented by labelling A?
   (a) Photosynthesis   (b) Glycolysis
   (c) TCA cycle   (d) None of them
2. Respiration is a type of-
   (a) Anabolic reaction   (b) Catabolic reaction
   (c) Both (a) and (b)   (d) None of them
3. Formation of ethyl alcohol and carbon dioxide is shown by labelling-
   (a) B   (b) A
   (c) D   (d) C
4. Kreb's cycle occurs in the presence or absence of O_2-
   (a) Presence of O_2 (b) Absence of O_2
   (c) In both (a) & (b)   (d) None of them
5. Which of the following statement is true about Lactic acid?
   (a) Lactic acid is formed during aerobic respiration.
   (b) It is formed in the muscle due to lack of O_2.
   (c) It is formed in the mitochondria.
   (d) All of them are correct.

VERY SHORT ANSWER QUESTIONS

1. Which organic compound acts as link between glycolysis and Kreb's cycle?
2. Name the final acceptor of electron in ETC.
3. Mention two functions of oxygen in aerobic respiration.
4. What term is given to the reduced ubiquinone?

5. Where does the electron transport system operate in the mitochondria?
6. Give the function of phosphofructokinase in glycolysis.
7. Name the enzyme that catalyses phosphorylation of glucose.
8. Where does the formation of acetyl CoA take place in a cell?
9. What is the first step of reaction in TCA cycle?
10. What happens to fatty acids before they form the respiratory substrates?
11. Name the oxidative pathway through which intermediate metabolites of glucose, fatty acids and amino acids are finally oxidised.
12. How many ATP molecules are obtained in the process of respiration?
13. What are the two molecules obtained by the action of aldolase from fructose -1, -6–biphosphate?
14. What occurs with proton gradient when protons move across F_oF_1 particle?

SHORT ANSWER QUESTIONS

1. How is proton gradient established?
2. Describe the steps in the formation of lactic acid from pyruvic acid.
3. How is ATP formed by the energy released during the electron transport system in mitochondria?
4. Give a detailed account on the net gain of ATP at different stage of respiration.
5. Enumerate the functions of ATP.
6. Where is cytochrome *c* located? What is its function?
7. Define respiratory quotient.
8. What is oxidative phosphorylation?
9. The energy yield in terms of ATP is higher in aerobic respiration than during anaerobic respiration. Why is there anaerobic respiration even in organisms that live in aerobic condition like human beings and angiosperms?
10. Comment on the statement- "Respiration is an energy producing process but ATP is used in some steps of the process".

LONG ANSWER QUESTIONS

1. Explain the major steps in Krebs' cycle. Why is this cycle also called citric acid cycle?
2. Name the end product of glycolysis. Where is it produced in the cell? Discuss oxidative decarboxylation.
3. Represent schematically the interrelationship among metabolic pathways in a plant, showing respiration mediated breakdown of different organic compounds.
4. How do plants manage exchange of gases? Give an overview of respiration in plants.

SOLUTIONS

Multiple Choice Questions

1. **(a)**
2. **(a)** Alcoholic fermentation is a process in which molecules such as glucose etc. are converted into cellular energy and thereby produce ethanol and carbon dioxide as metabolic waste products. During alcoholic fermentation, NAD^+ is produced when acetaldehyde is reduced to ethanol.
3. **(a)** Glycolysis is a partial breakdown of glucose molecule into two molecules of pyruvic acid. It occurs in cytoplasm and a common phase of aerobic and anaerobic respiration.
4. **(a)** In glycolysis, we find that there is one step where $NADH + H^+$ is formed from NAD^+; this is when 3-phosphoglyceraldehyde (PGAL) is converted to 1, 3-bisphosphoglycerate (BPGA). Two redox equivalents are removed (in the form of two hydrogen atoms) from PGAL and transferred to a molecule of NAD.
5. **(a)** Glycolysis occurs in the cytosol, where the glucose molecule is converted into two molecules of the 3C compound, pyruvate. The enzymes are located in the fluid matrix of cytoplasm.
6. **(c)**
7. **(a)** With the help of cytochrome b_6f, proton is pumped to reach ATP synthetase to participate in ATP synthesis.
8. **(a)**
9. **(c)** Enzymes of citric acid cycle are located in the cytosol in prokaryotes and mitochondrial matrix in eukaryotes.
10. **(c)** Acetyl CoA is common to respiration mediated breakdown of fats, carbohydrates and proteins. Fats are brokendown to fatty acid and glycerol and again fatty acid degraded to acetyl CoA. Protein first degraded by proteases to individual amino acids which deaminated to pyruvic acid and further decarboxylised to acetyl CoA.

Assertion & Reason Questions

1. **(d)** Glycolysis is the process of breakdown of glucose or similar hexose sugar into two molecules of pyruvic acid through a series of enzyme mediated reactions, releasing energy (ATP) and reducing power ($NADH_2$). It is the first step of respiration, which occurs inside the cytoplasm and is independent of O_2. In glycolysis, two molecules of ATP are consumed during double phosphorylation of glucose to form fructose 1, 6 diphosphate. Four molecules of ATP are produced in the conversion of 1, 3-diphosphoglycerate to 3-phospho-glycerate and phosphenol pyruvate to pyruvate whereas, two molecules of $NADH_2$ are formed during oxidation of glyceraldehyde 3-phosphate to 1,3-diphosphoglycerate. Since, each NADH is equivalent to 3 ATP, so net gain in glycolysis is 8 ATP.
2. **(a)** In fermentation, the incomplete oxidation of glucose is achieved under anaerobic conditions by sets of reactions where pyruvic acid is converted to CO_2 and ethanol. The enzymes, pyruvic acid decarboxylase and alcohol dehydrogenase catalyse these reactions.

3. **(c)** In C_4 plants photorespiration does not occur. This is because they have a mechanism that increases the concentration of CO_2 at the enzyme site. Primary acceptor of CO_2 in C_4 plants is PEP in the mesophyll cells to form C_4 acid.
4. **(b)**
5. **(a)** In photorespiration, RuBisCO acts as an oxygenase enzyme instead of carboxylase enzyme. Active site of this enzyme is same for both of these activities. In C_3 plants, some O_2 always bind to RuBisCO.

$$\underset{(5C)}{Ribulose - 1,5 - biphosphate} + O_2$$

$$\xrightarrow[\text{Oxygenase}]{\text{RuBp}} \underset{(3C)}{PGA} + \underset{(2C)}{Phosphoglycolate}$$

Photorespiration does not produce energy or reducing power. Rather, it consumes energy. Further, it undoes the work of photosynthesis. There is 25% loss of fixed CO_2.

Case/Passage Based Questions

1. **(b)**
2. **(b)** Respiration is a type of catabolic reaction.
3. **(c)** Formation of ethyl alcohol and carbon dioxide is shown by labelling D.
4. **(a)** Kreb's cycle occurs in the presence of O_2.
5. **(b)**

Very Short Answer Questions

1. Acetyl Co-A acts as link between glycolysis and Krebs cycle.
2. Oxygen is the electron acceptor of ETC.
3. Function of oxygen in aerobic respiration :
   (i) It acts as the final electron acceptor.
   (ii) It drives the whole process by removing hydrogen from the system.
4. Ubiquinol is a reduced form of ubiquinone.
5. Phosphofructokinase catalyses the formation of fructose 1, 6 bisphosphate from fructose 6-phosphate.
6. Hexokinase-helps in phosphorylation of glucose.
7. The formation of acetyl CoA takes place in the mitochondrial matrix.
8. The first step in Krebs cycle is the condensation of acetyl group (acetyl CoA) with oxaloacetic acid (OAA) to form citric acid and release the Coenzyme A.
9. Fatty acids may be converted to acetyl CoA before they from the respiratory substrates.
10. Krebs' cycle.
11. 36 ATP/38 ATP molecules are obtained in the process of respiration and it is related to the aerobic respiration type.
12. The two molecules obtained by the actions of aldolase from fructose –1, 6–biphosphete are :-
Glyceraldehyde 3–phosphete and Dihyroxy acetone–3–phosphate.
13. ATP is produced.

Short Answer Questions

1. Proton gradient is established by passing proton (H^+) from the matrix across the inner mitochondrial membrane into intermembrane space with the energy released during electron transfers in ETC.

2. Pyruvic acid is catalysed by the enzyme lactic dehydrogenase. NADH formed in glycolysis is used up for the reduction.

$$\text{Pyruvic Acid} + \text{NADH} \xrightarrow[\text{FMN, Zn}^{2+}]{\text{Lactic dehydrogenase}} \text{Lactic acid} + \text{NAD}^+$$

3. ATP formations require enzyme called ATP synthase. It has two component $F_0 - F_1$. ATP-synthase become active in ATP formation when concentration of H^+ on F_0 side is higher than F_1 side. Higher proton concentration in outer chamber cause the proton to pass inner chamber. F_1 particle induced by flow of proton through F_0 channel. The energy of proton gradient attaches the phosphate radicle to ADP. This produces ATP.

4.

Stages of respiration	Sources	No. of ATP Molecules produces
Glycolysis	Direct	2
	2 molecules of NADH	6
	(one molecule of NADH yeild 3 ATP)	
Pyruvic acid to acetyl CoA	2 molecules of NADH	6
Citric acid cycle	6 NADH	18
	2 FADH$_2$	4
	(one molecule of FADH$_2$ yeild 2 ATP)	
	Direct (GTP)	2
	Total yield of ATP moleculs	38

In most eukaryotic cells 2 molecules of ATP are required for transporting NADH produced in glycolysis to mitochondria for further oxidation . Hence net gain of ATP is 36 molecules.

5. Functions of ATP :-
   (i) ATP functions as universal energy carrier of living systems.
   (ii) ATP stores small packets of energy in its molecules.
   (iii) It is mobile in the cell. Therefore, it reaches all parts of cell away from the region of ATP synthesis.
   (iv) It activates a number of chemicals by functioning as phosphorylating agent.
   (v) ATP provides energy for muscle contraction.
   (vi) It is involved in transport of substances against concentration gradient.

6. Cytochrome *c* is located on the outer surface of the inner mitochondrial membrane. It acts as a mobile carrier for the transfer of electrons between complex III and complex IV of the electron transport system.

7. Respiratory quotient is defined as the ratio of the volume of carbondioxide evolved to the volume of oxygen consumed in respiration.

8. The whole process by which oxygen effectively allows the production of ATP by phosphorylation of ADP is called oxidative phosphorylation.

9. Aerobic organisms do face situations where oxygen availability is little. For example, overworked muscles do not receive enough oxygen during strenuous exercise. Similarly deep seated tissues of angiosperms do not receive enough oxygen through diffusion from outside. In such situations only anaerobic respiration can help in survival of the tissue.

10. ATP is required in all those reactions where phosphorylative activation of substrate is required. Therefore, despite producing energy (as ATP), respiration requires ATP in certain steps, e.g., glucose $\rightarrow$ glucose 6-phosphate, fructose 6-phosphate $\rightarrow$ fructose 1, 6-bisphosphate.

Long Answer Questions

1. **Krebs cycle :** This process occurs in the mitochondrial matrix.
   Major steps of krebs cycle are as follows :
   – Acetyl Co-A, formed by the oxidative decarboxylation of pyruvic acid enters the Krebs' cycle.
   – It combines with oxalo acetic acid (OAA), a 4C-compound, to form a 6C-compound, citric acid; the reaction is catalysed by citrate synthase.
   – Citrate is then isomerised into isocitrate.

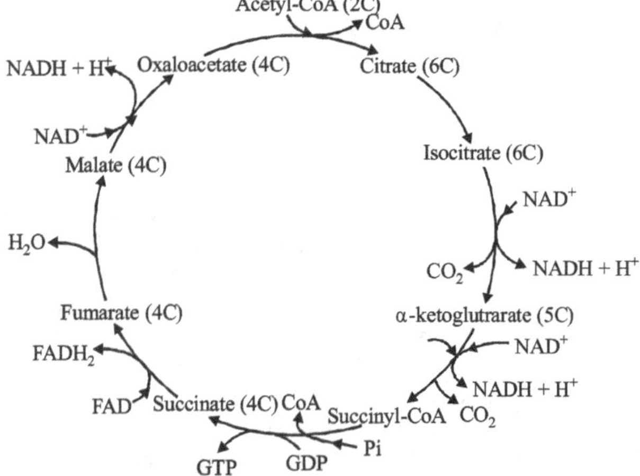

Fig. The Citric acid cycle

   – Isocitrate is converted into oxalosuccinic acid in the presence of NAD and isocitrate dehydrogenase.
   – Oxalosuccinic acid is then decarboxylated into α-ketoglutaric acid (KG), in the presence of a decarboxylase enzyme.

- α-ketoglutaric acid is converted into succinyl Co-A in the presence of NAD, Co-A and enzyme α-ketoglutarate dehydrogenase.
- When succinyl Co-A is converted into succinic acid, one molecule of GTP is formed and Co-A is released.
- In the remaining part of the cycle, succinic acid is converted into OAA, so that the citric acid cycle can continue to operate.
- During this cycle three molecules of NAD and one molecule of FAD are reduced to NADH and FADH respectively.
- This cycle is called as citric acid cycle because the first product is citric acid which is 3-C compound.

2. Glycolysis results in the formation of two molecules of pyruvic acid, NADH and ATP. It occurs in the cytosol of the cell.

Aerobic oxidation : One of the three carbons of pyruvic acid is oxidised to carbon dioxide in the reaction called oxidative decarboxylation. Pyruvic acid is first decarboxylated and then oxidised by the enzyme pyruvic dehydrogenase. The two-carbon units are readily accepted by coenzyme-A (Co-A) to form acetyl Co-A. The summary of the reaction is given in the following equation :

$$\text{Pyruvic acid} + \text{Co} - \text{A} + \text{NAD}^+$$

$$\xrightarrow[\text{Mg}^{2+}]{\text{Pyruvate dehydrogenase}}$$

$$\text{Acetyl Co} - \text{A} + \text{NADH} + \text{CO}_2$$

Thus, pyruvic acid enters Krebs cycle as acetyl Co-A. Krebs' cycle occurs in the mitochondrial matrix.

Acetyl Co-A, formed by the oxidative decarboxylation of pyruvic acid enters the Krebs' cycle.

3. Schematic representation among metabolic pathways showing respiration mediated breakdown of different organic molecules to CO_2 and H_2O :

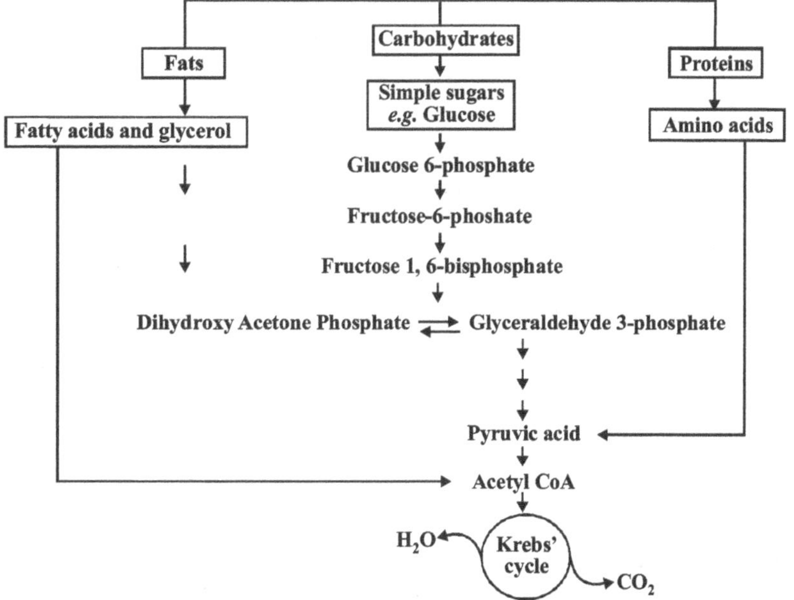

4. Plants, unlike animals, have no specialised organs for gaseous exchange but they have stomata and lenticles for this purpose. There are several reasons why plants can get along without respiratory organs.
- Each plant part takes care of its own gas-exchange needs. There is very little transport of gases from one plant part to another.
- Plants do not present great demands for gas exchange. Roots, stems and leaves respire at lower rate than animals do. Only during photosynthesis, large volumes of gases exchanged and, each leaf is well adapted to take care of its own needs during these periods. When cells perform photosynthesis, availability of O_2 is not a problem in these cells since O_2 is released within the cell.
- The distance that gases must diffuse even in large, bulky plants is not great. Each living cell in a plant is located quite close to the surface of the plant. Even in woody stems, the 'living' cells are organised in thin layers inside and beneath the bark. They also have openings called lenticels. The cells in the interior

are dead and provide only mechanical support. Thus, most cells of a plant have atlest a part of their surface in contact with air. This is also facilitated by the loose packing of parenchyma cells in leaves, stems and roots, which provide an interconnected network of air spaces.
- The complete combustion of glucose, which produces CO_2 and H_2O as end products, yields energy. Most of the energy is given out as heat.

$$C_6H_{12}O_6 + 6O_2 \longrightarrow 6CO_2 + 6H_2O + \text{Energy}$$

- If this energy is to be useful to the cell, it should be able to utilise it to synthesis other molecules that the cell requires. The strategy that the plant cell uses is to catabolise the glucose molecule in such a way that not all the liberated energy goes out as heat. The key is to oxidise glucose not in one step but in several small steps enabling some steps to be just large enough so that the energy released can be coupled to ATP synthesis.

SECTION C — NCERT EXEMPLAR QUESTIONS

MULTIPLE CHOICE QUESTIONS

1. The ultimate electron acceptor of respiration in an aerobic organism is:
   (a) cytochrome (b) oxygen
   (c) hydrogen (d) glucose

2. Phosphorylation of glucose during glycolysis is catalysed by:
   (a) phosphoglucomutase
   (b) phosphoglucoisomerase
   (c) hexokinase
   (d) phosphorylase

3. Pyruvic acid, the key product of glycolysis can have many metabolic fates. Under aerobic condition it forms
   (a) lactic acid (b) $CO_2 + H_2O$
   (c) acetyl Co - A + CO_2 (d) ethanol + CO_2

4. Electron Transport System (ETS) is located in mitochondrial
   (a) outer membrane (b) inter membrane space
   (c) inner membrane (d) matrix

5. Which of the following exhibits the highest rate of respiration?
   (a) Growing shoot apex (b) Germinating seed
   (c) Root tip (d) Leaf bud

6. Choose the correct statement:
   (a) Pyruvate is formed in the mitochondrial matrix.
   (b) During the conversion of succinyl Co A to succinic acid a molecule of ATP is synthesized.
   (c) Oxygen is vital in respiration for removal of hydrogen.
   (d) There is complete breakdown of glucose in fermentation.

7. Mitochondria are called powerhouses of the cell. Which of the following observations support this statement?
   (a) Mitochondria synthesise ATP
   (b) Mitochondria have a double membrane
   (c) The enzymes of the Krebs' cycle and the cytochromes are found in mitochondria
   (d) Mitochondria are found in almost all plants and animal cells.

8. The end product of oxidative phosphorylation is
   (a) NADH (b) oxygen
   (c) ADP (d) ATP + H_2O

VERY SHORT ANSWER QUESTIONS

1. Energy is released during the oxidation of compounds in respiration. How is this energy stored and released as and when it is needed?

2. Different substrates get oxidised during respiration. How does Respiratory Quotient (RQ) indicate which type of substrate, *i.e.*, carbohydrate, fat or protein is getting oxidised?

$$R.Q. = \frac{A}{B}$$

What do A and B stand for?
What type of substrates have R.Q. of 1, < 1 or > 1?

3. $F_0 - F_1$ particles participate in the synthesis of ....

4. When does anaerobic respiration occur in man and yeast?

5. Which of the following will release more energy on oxidation? Arrange them in ascending order.
   (a) 1 gm of fat
   (b) 1 gm of protein
   (c) 1 gm of glucose
   (d) 0.5 gm of protein + 0.5 gm glucose

SHORT ANSWER QUESTIONS

1. If a person is feeling dizzy, glucose or fruit juice is given immediately but not a cheese sandwich, which might have more energy. Explain.

2. Pyruvic acid is the end product of glycolysis. What are the three metabolic fats of pyruvic acid under aerobic and anaerobic conditions? Write in the space provided in the diagram.

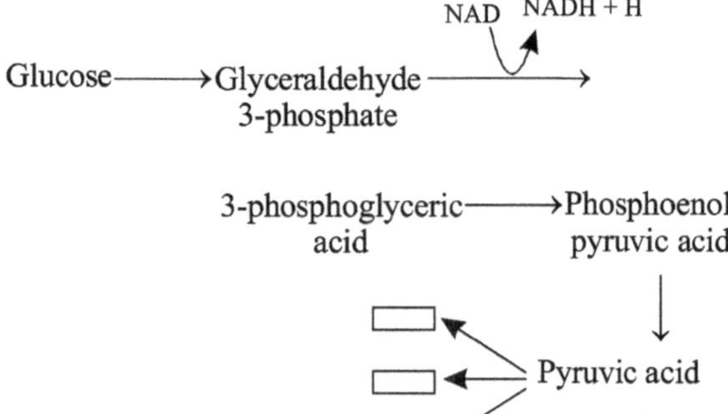

3. Oxygen is an essential requirement for aerobic respiration by it enters the respiratory process at the end? Discuss.

4. The figure given below shows the steps in glycolysis. Fill in the missing steps *A, B, C, D* and also indicate whether ATP is being used up or released at step *E*?

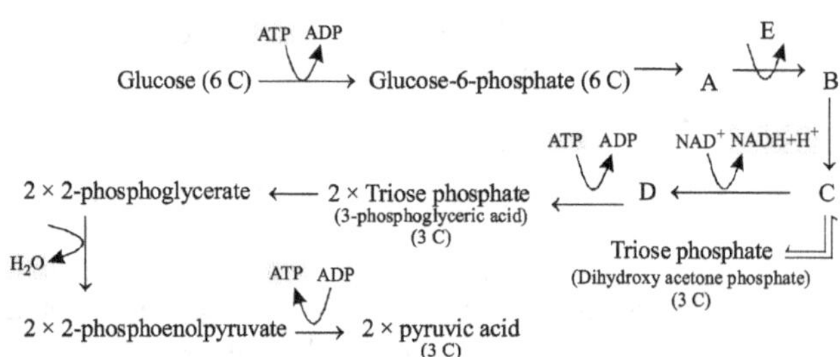

5. Do you know any step in the TCA cycle where there is substrate level phosphorylation.
   Which one?

6. In a way green plants and cyanobacteria have synthesised all the food on the earth. Comment.
7. When a substrate is being metabolised, why does not all the energy that is produced get released in one step. It is released in multiple steps. What is the advantage of step-wise release?
8. Respiration requires O_2. How did the first cells on the earth manage to survive in an atmosphere that lacked O_2?
9. It is known that red muscle fibres in animals can work for longer periods of time continuously. How is this possible?
10. RuBP carboxylase, PEPcase, pyruvate dehydrogenase, ATPase, cytochrome oxidase, hexokinase, lactate dehydrogenase, Select/choose enzymes from the list above which are involved in
   (a) Photosynthesis
   (b) Respiration
   (c) Both in photosynthesis and respiration

11. How does a tree trunk exchange gases with the environment although it lacks stomata?
12. Mention the important series of events of aerobic respiration that occur in the matrix of the mitochondrion as well as one that take place in inner membrane of the mitochondrion.

LONG ANSWER QUESTIONS

1. Oxygen is critical for aerobic respiration. Explain its role with respect to ETS.
2. Enumerate the assumptions that we undertake in making the respiratory balance sheet. Are these assumptions valid for a living system? Compare fermentation and aerobic respiration in this context.

SOLUTIONS

Multiple Choice Questions

1. **(b)** The ultimate hydrogen acceptor in aerobic respiration is oxygen because at the end of electron transport chain it accepts a pair of electron and combines with hydrogen atom to form a water molecule.
2. **(c) Hexokinase** catalyses the conversion of glucose into glucose-6-phosphate by the use of ATP molecule in the phosphorylation reaction.
   Phosphoglucomutase is an enzyme that transfers a phosphate group in D-glucose monomer from 1to 6 position of carbon in forward direction.
   Phosphoglucoisomerase catalyses conversion of glucose-6-phosphate to fructose-6-phosphate.
   Phosphorylase is an enzyme which catalyses the addition of phosphate PO_4^- group from inorganic phosphate to an acceptor.
3. **(c)** Pyruvate, the product obtained at the end of glycolysis, gets oxidised with carboxy group as CO_2, to give acetyl CoA, under aerobic conditions. This acetyl CoA is further oxidised completely to CO_2 and H_2O in the citric acid cycle.
   Lactic acid is formed in muscles under anaerobic conditions.
   Ethanol and CO_2 are products of anaerobic respiration in yeast cells. CO_2 and H_2O are final and complete reaction products released at the end of cellular respiration.
4. **(c)** Electron transport system is present in the inner mitochondrial membrane, which has several groups of proton (H^+) and electron (e^-) acceptors.
5. **(b) Germinating seeds** have the highest rate of respiration. As soon as the water is imbibed by seeds, hydrolytic enzymes come into action and mobilise the reserve food materials, so the seeds show high metabolic activity and germinate into a tiny plant.
   All these activities require energy, which is derived from increased rate of respiration.

6. **(c)** Oxygen is vital in respiration for removal of hydrogen.
7. **(a)** Mitochondria are a double membrane bound structures and are the site of ATP production the energy currency of the cell.
8. **(d)** Complete oxidation of glucose molecule produces 38 ATP molecules, water and carbon dioxide with the help of energy released during oxidation of reduced co-enzymes. This process is called oxidative phosphorylation.

Very Short Answer Questions

1. The energy currency of every living cell Adenosine Triphosphate (ATP).
   Complex organic food molecules such as sugars, fats and proteins are rich sources of energy for cell because much of the energy used to form these molecules is stored within the chemical bonds that hold them together. So, the cells release the stored energy through a series of oxidation reactions. During oxidation of food, the product of reaction has a lower energy content than the donor molecule. At the same time, electron acceptor molecules capture some of the energy lost during oxidation and store it for later use.
   Cells convert the energy from oxidation reactions to energy-rich molecules such as ATP that can be used through the cell for metabolism and construct new cellular components.
2. The ratio of CO_2 evolved and O_2 consumed in respiration is called the Respiratory Quotient (RQ) or respiratory ratio.

$$R.Q. = \frac{A}{B} = \frac{\text{Volume of } CO_2 \text{ evolved}}{\text{Volume of } CO_2 \text{ consumed}}$$

Example:
(i) During aerobic respiration carbohydrates have RQ = 1
(ii) During germination of seeds proteins and fats have RQ of < 1.
(iii) Under aerobic conditions substrates like organic acids have RQ of > 1

3. $F_0 - F_1$ particles present in the inner mitochondrial membrane are involved in the Adenosine Triphosphate synthesis. It is known as the energy currency of the cell.

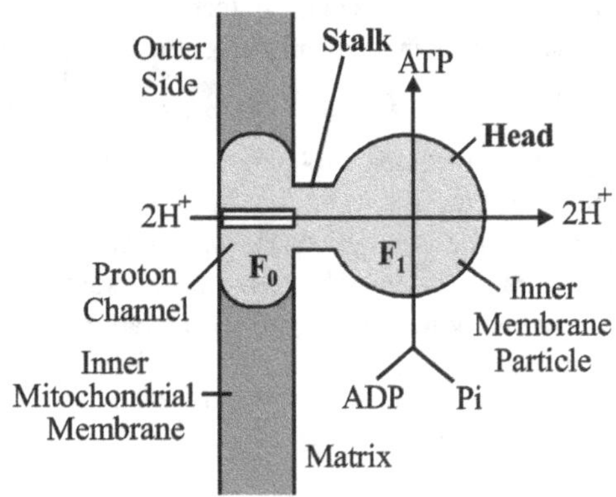

ATP synthesis by $F_0 - F_1$ particle

4. In animals anaerobic respiration occurs in the situation of oxygen deficiency during heavy exercise, when pyruvic acid is reduced to lactic acid by the enzyme lactate dehydrogenase.

   In yeast, the incomplete oxidation of glucose occurs in anaerobic conditions, during which pyruvic acid is converted to CO_2 and ethanol by the action of enzyme pyruvic acid decarboxylase and alcohol dehydrogenase.

5. The ascending order of substrate that will release more energy on oxidation will be as follows

   1 gm protein < 0.5 gm in protein < 1 gm glucose < 1 gm fat + 0.5 gm glucose

Short Answer Questions

1. The glucose is absorbed and reaches blood quickly and gives instant energy. Whereas, cheese sandwich require time for digestion, and absorption. Sick person needs immediate energy supply, so glucose or fruit juices containing glucose are given to them.

2. The three metabolic products formed under aerobic and anaerobic conditions are Lactic acid, Ethanol and Acetyl Co-A

   Lactic acid is formed under anaerobic condition in skeletal muscles by the oxidation of pyruvic acid.

   Ethanol is formed under anaerobic condition by the oxidation of pyruvic acid in yeast.

   Acetyl Co-A is formed by the oxidation of pyruvic acid that take place within the mitochondria under aerobic condition.

   $$\text{Pyruvic acid} + Co-A + NAD^+ \xrightarrow[\text{Pyruvate dehydrogenase}]{Mg^{2+}}$$

   $$\text{Acetyl } Co-A + CO_2 + NADH + H^+$$

3. Aerobic respiration needs oxygen in order to generate ATP. Oxygen acts as final acceptor in respiratory process.

   In pulse e^- (electrons) that energy from the electron transport chain ETC and take up protons from medium to form water.

It plays a vital role in respiration. O_2 enters in the respiratory process at the end. It drives the process of aerobic respiration by removing hydrogen from the system. Thus, acting as final hydrogen acceptor.

By the process of oxidative phosphorylation the energy is produced, utilising the energy of oxidation reduction reactions.

4. *Process of glycolysis is summarised as follow*

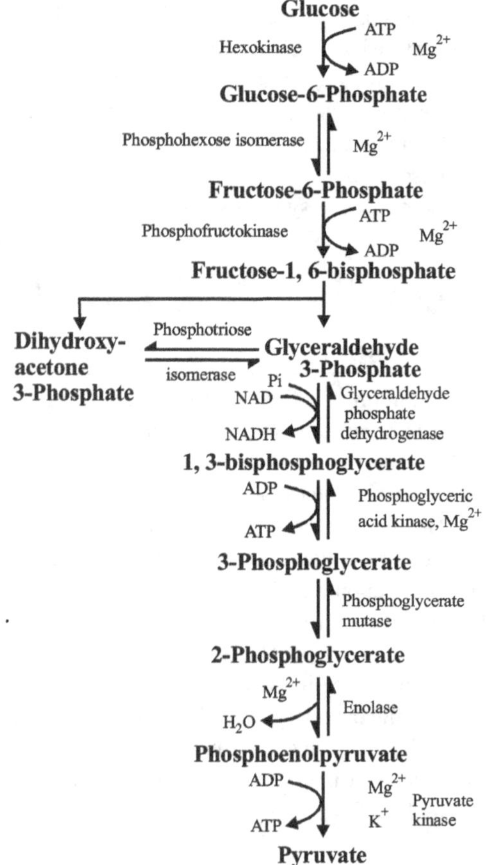

Schematic representation of glycolysis or EMP pathway

5. In an intermediate reaction TCA cycle, succinyl Co-A is converted succinic acid and one GTP molecule is synthesised through substrate level

   $$\underset{O}{\overset{CH_2-COO^-}{\underset{|}{\overset{|}{CH_2-S-Co-A}}}} \xrightarrow[GTP\ GDP\ Co-A-SH]{\text{Succinyl Co-A Synthetase}} \underset{COO^-}{\overset{CH_2-COO}{\underset{|}{\overset{|}{CH_2}}}}$$

   GTP formed in this reaction gives rise to ATP as follows
   $$GTP + ADP \rightarrow GDP + ATP$$

6. Cyanobacteria are unicellular prokaryotic organisms. Besides, some primitive cellular cell organelles, they have photosynthetic lamellae where photosynthetic pigments like chlorophyll-a c, phycocyanin and phycoerythrin, are present.

These coloured pigments confer typical blue green colour to the bacteria and enable them to manufacture food for themselves and aquatic animals. Green plants are multicellular are organisms, which is capable of making food by using CO_2, H_2O and light energy in specialized cell organelles called chloroplast. So bacteria and green plants make food for living organisms on earth.

7. The aerobic respiration process is divided into four phases- glycolysis, TCA cycle, ETS and oxidative phosphorylation. The process of respiration and ATP production in each phase takes place in a synchronized manner.

   The product of one pathway forms the substrate of the other pathway and these substrates enter or withdrawn from the path according to the necessity ATP gets utilised wherever needed and enzymatic rates are controlled generally. Thus, the step-wise released energy makes the system more efficient in extracting and storing energy.

8. Respiration always does not require O_2. There are some organisms which respire in anaerobic condition *i.e.* in the absence of O_2.

   The first cells of earth *i.g.*, chemosynthetic bacteria, which are the primitive organisms found earlier on earth. They obtain energy by breaking down inorganic molecules like H_2S, NO_2^-, etc.

   $$12H_2S + 6CO_2 \rightarrow C_6H_{12}O_6 + 6H_2O + 12S$$

9. There are basically two kinds of muscle fibres red muscles and white muscles

   Red muscles work continuously for a longer time because
   (i) These muscle fibres are dark red, due to the presence of red haemoprotein called myoglobin. It binds and stores oxygen as oxymyoglobin in the red fibres. Oxymyoglobin liberates oxygen for utilisation during muscle contraction.
   (ii) Mitochondria are more in numbers, hence they work for long periods of time.
   (iii) Red muscles possesses less sarcoplasmic reticulum.
   (iv) They carry out considerable aerobic oxidation without accumulating much lactic acid. Thus without fatigue red muscle fibres can contract for a longer period.
   (v) These muscle fibre have slow rate of contraction for long periods. *e.g.*, extensor muscles of the human back.

10. RuBP Carboxylase is an enzyme that takes part in dark reaction of photosynthesis. It catalyses the fixing of CO_2 in C_3 cycle. PEPcase an enzymes that takes part in photosynthesis of C_4 plants. It catalyses the reaction of fixing of CO_2 to form first stable product oxaloacetate. 4 carbon compound.

    Pyruvate dehydrogenase is an enzyme involved in aerobic respiration and catalyses the reaction of formation of acetyle Co-A from pyruvic acid. It requires the participation of NAD and Co-enzyme-A.

    Pyruvic acid + Co – A + NAD$^+$

    $$\xrightarrow[\text{Pyruvate dehydrogenase}]{Mg^{2+}} \text{Acetyl Co} - A + CO_2$$

    $$+ NADH + H^+$$

ATPase is a part of both respiration and photosynthesis. Both these processes uses etc, associated proton pump and ATP synthase. These all play a key part in the process is used by ETC pump hydrogen ions across a membrane. The protons flows back through ATP synthase, driving the production of ATP.

Cytochrome Oxidase is involved in both respiration and photosynthesis. It acts as electron carrier in the electron transport chain.

Hexokinase is an enzymes which is also involved in, respiration. In glycolysis, it catalyses the first reaction, *i.e.*, formation of glucose -6- phosphate from glucose molecule. It uses one ATP molecule which transfers PO_4 group to glucose molecules.

The first step of glycolysis $\longrightarrow$

$$\text{ATP} \underset{\text{Mg}^{2+}}{\overset{\boxed{\text{Glucose}}}{\diagdown}} \bigg| \text{Hexokinase}$$
$$\text{ADP} \diagup \qquad \downarrow$$
$$\boxed{\text{Glucose-6-phosphate}}$$

Lactate Dehydrogenase is an enzyme which is involved in anaerobic respiration in bacteria *Lactobacillus*.

Pyruvic acid formed at the end of glycolysis is converted to lactic acid by the help of homo-fermentative lactic acid bacteria. Hydrogen from NADH molecule is transferred to pyruvate is then transferred to pyruvate molecule lactic acid molecule leading to the formation of acid.

$$\underset{\text{Pyruvic acid}}{CH_3COCOOH} + NADH \xrightarrow[\text{Dehydrogenase}]{\text{Lactate}} \underset{\text{Lactic acid}}{C_3H_6O_3} + NAD$$

11. The old tree trunk is covered by dead woody tissue called cork. The epidermal layers of such tree get ruptured and outer cortical cells are loosely arranged. These structures are called as **lenticels**.

    These are the sites of gaseous exchange and transpiration.

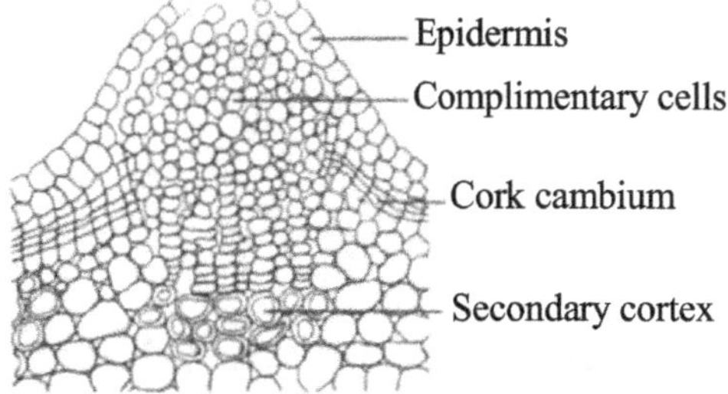

Structure of lenticel

12. Kreb's cycle occurs in the matrix of mitochondria. It is given in the following series of reactions

    Figure Refer to Practice Solution Long Answer 1.

    The inner mitochondrial membrane is specific about possessing proton (H^+) and electron (e^-) acceptors in a particular sequence called electron transport chain. It consists four enzyme complexes.

    The electrons either follow the pathway of complexes I, III and IV or II, III and IV that depends that upon the substrates from Kreb's cycle.

Following are the ways through which the transfer of electrons and hydrogen atoms takes place.

Complex I It consists of flavoproteins of NADH dehydrogenase (FP_N), of which FMN is the prosthetic group. It is combined with the flavoprotein is non-heme iron of NADH dehydrogenase. This complex spans inner mitochondrial membrane and is also able to translocate protons across it form matrix side to outer side.

Complex II It consists of flavoprotein of succinate dehydrogenase, of which FAD is the prosthetic group. It is combined with the flavoprotein is non-heme iron of succinate dehydrogenase.

Between complexes II and III the mobile carrier coenzyme-Q (Co-Q) or ubiquinone (UQ) is present

Complex III It consists of cytochrome-*b* and cytochrome-*c* that is associated with cytochrome-*b* is non-heme iron of complex III. Between complexes III and IV is the mobile carrier cytochrome-*c*.

Complex IV It consists of cytochrome-a and cytochrome-a_3, and bound copper that are required for this complex reaction to occur. This cytochrome also called **cytochrome oxidase**. It is the only electron carrier in which the heme iron has a free ligand that can react directly with molecular oxygen.

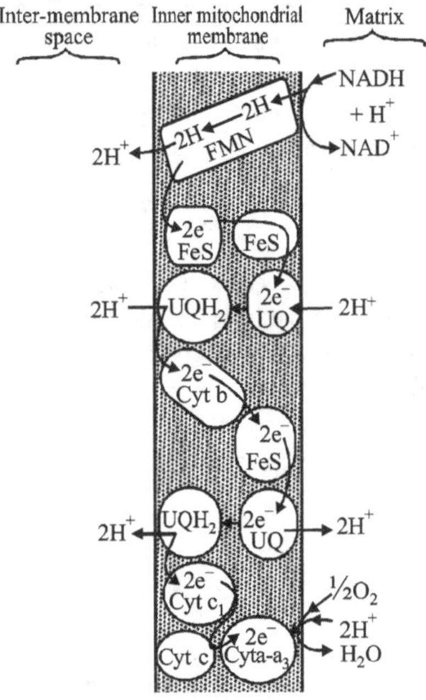

Electron Transport System (ETS)

Thus, hydride ions are transferred from the substance to be oxidised to NAD$^+$. From NAD$^+$ the hydrogen atoms are transferred to FMN of flavor protein 1 (Fp'N). After FMN the hydrogen atom splits into an electron and a proton.

In further stages transfer of e^-s occur but there is no longer a transfer of hydrogens. The electron passes to co-enzyme-Q, and from co-enzyme Q to cytochromes- *b*, *c$_1$*, *c*, *a* and *a$_3$*. The proton is released free.

As the hydrogen atom or electron passes down by F_0-F_1 particle at the same time oxidation of one coenzyme and reduction occurs at another steps. Oxygen is able to diffuse inside the mitochondria.

It is converted to anionic form O$^-_2$, combines with 2H$^+$ and forms metabolic water reduced co-enzyme NADH + H$_+$ that helps in pushing out three pairs of H$^+$ to outer chamber while FADH$_2$ sends two pairs of H$^+$ to outer chamber.

Oxidative phosphorylation is the synthesis of ATP molecules, with the help of energy liberated during oxidation of reduced co-enzyme (NADH$_2$, FADH$_2$) produced in respiration. The enzyme required for this synthesis is called ATP synthase present in inner mitochondria membrane.

Long Answer Questions

1. The oxidation of glucose starts with glycolysis in cytoplasm which followed by Krebs' cycle and finally Electron transport Chain (ETC) in inner mitochondrial membrane. The end of ETC O$_2$ is required.

   Where, it acts as final hydrogen acceptor. O$_2$ is responsible for removing electrons from the system. In the absence of oxygen, electrons could not be passed through the co-enzymes, inturn proton pump will not be established and ATP will not be produced *via* oxidative phosphorylation. Thus oxygen plays an important role in aerobic respiration in mitochondrial matrix.

2. The assumption that we undertake is making the respiratory balance sheet one as follows:
   (i) Respiratory substrate is glucose
   (ii) There is sequential pathway i.e., glycolysis in cytoplasm, TCA cycle in mitochondrial matrix and ETS in inner mitochondriol membrane.
   (iii) NADH synthesised in glycolysis enters into ETC for phosphorylation.
   (iv) None of the intermediates in the pathway are utilised to synthesise any other compound.

   These assumptions are not valid for a living system because of following reasons:
   (i) Glycolysis, TCA and ETC work simultaneously and do not take place one after the other.
   (ii) ATP is uutilised when needed.
   (iii) Rate of enzyme actions are controlled by multiple means.

   Comparison between fermentation and aerobic respiration in this context is as follows:
   (i) Fermentation is partial breakdown of glucose whereas aerobic respiration is complete breakdown of glucose.
   (ii) Net gain of only 2 ATP in fermentation whereas in aerobic respiration 38 ATP is produced.

15 Plant Growth and Development

15.1 Define growth, differentiation, development, dedifferentiation, redifferentiation, determinate growth, meristem and growth rate.

Sol.
(i) **Growth :** Growth is permanent and irreversible increase in size of living structure which is accompanied by an increase in dry weight and the amount of protoplasm.

(ii) **Differentiation :** The cells are derived from root apical and shoot apical meristems and cambium differentiate and mature to perform specific functions. This act leading to maturation is called as differentiation.

(iii) **Development :** Development includes all changes in an organism which occur during the life-cycle from seed germination to growth, maturation and senescence. Development is a qualitative change referring to the changes in nature of growth made by organism.

(iv) **Dedifferentiation :** The living differentiated cells loose their capacity of division. These cells may regain their capacity to divide under certain conditions. This phenomenon is called as dedifferentiation.

(v) **Redifferentiation :** The products of dedifferentiated cells which lose the capability to divide but mature to perform specific functions are called redifferentiated cells. This phenomenon is called as redifferentiation.

(vi) **Determinate growth :** When growth occurs only for some time it is called as determinate growth.

(vii) **Meristems :** Meristems are cells that divide continuously to produce new cells.

(viii) **Growth rate :** The expression of increased growth per unit time is called growth rate.

15.2 Why is not any one parameter good enough to demonstrate growth throughout the life of a flowering plant?

Sol. Growth, at a cellular level is a consequence of increase in the amount of protoplasm, which is difficult to measure directly. As a result, growth is manifested in different forms. It may be manifested as increase in weight or volume, length or cell number or a combination of these so no single parameter can be used.

15.3 Describe briefly :
(a) **Arithmetic growth**
(b) **Geometric growth**
(c) **Sigmoid growth curve**
(d) **Absolute and relative growth rates**

Sol.
(i) **Arithmetic growth :** In this type of growth after mitosis, only one daughter cell continues to divide while the others take part in differentiation and maturation *e.g.*, root elongating at constant rate. Here a linear curve is obtained.

(ii) **Geometric growth :** In most systems, the initial growth is slow (lag phase), and it increases rapidly thereafter - at an exponential rate (log or exponential phase). Here both the progeny cells following mitotic cell division divide continuously.

(iii) **Sigmoid growth curve :** Sigmoid or S-shaped growth curve consists of three phases *i.e.*, lag phase, log phase and stationary phase. During lag phase plant growth is slow (in phase of cell division), but increases at log or exponential phase (due to cell enlargement). During stationary phase the growth again slows down due to the limitation of nutrients.

(iv) **Absolute and relative growth rates :** Measurement and comparison of total growth per unit time is called the absolute growth rate. The growth of the given system per unit time expressed on a common basis *e.g.*, per unit initial parameter is called the relative growth rate.

15.4 List five main groups of natural plant growth regulators. Write a note on discovery, physiological functions and agricultural/horticultural applications of any one of them.

Sol. The five main groups of natural growth regulators are
(a) auxins (b) gibberellins
(c) cytokinins (d) ethylene
(e) abscisic acid

Gibberellins

Discovery : - They are another kind of promotory PGR. There are more than 100 gibberellins reported from different organisms such as fungi and higher plants. They are denoted as GA_1, GA_2, GA_3. E. Kurosawa reported the symptoms of the disease in infected rice seedings when they were treated with filtrates of the fungus. *Gibberalla fujikuroi* caused, 'bakane' (foolish seedling) a disease of rice seedlings. The active substances were later identified as gibberellic acid.

Physiological functions
(i) They cause an increase in length of axis is used to increase the length of grapes stalk.
(ii) Gibberellins cause fruit like apple to elongate and improve its shape.
(iii) They also delay senescence. Thus the fruits can be left on the tree longer so as to extend the market period.

Agricultural Applications

(i) Spraying sugarcane crop with gibberellins increases the length of stem. Thus increasing the yield as much as 20 tonnes per acre.

(ii) Spraying juvenile conifers with GAs hastens the maturity period, thus leading to early seed production.

(iii) Gibberellins also promotes bolting (internode elongation just prior to flowering) in beet, cabbages and many plants with rosette habit.

15.5 What do you understand by photoperiodism and vernalisation? Describe their significance.

Sol. Photoperiodism : Flowering in certain plants depends not only a combination of light and dark exposures but also their relative durations. This response of plants to periods of day/night is termed photoperiodism.

Some hormonal substances (e.g. florigen) migrates from leaves to shoot apices for inducing flowering only when the plants are exposed to the necessary inductive photoperiod.

Vernalization : It is the process of enabling low temperature to some temperate plants artifically so as to reduce the duration of vegetative phase and intiate onset of reproductive phase or flowering verialisation has been successfully used in many winter annuals biennial plants. e.g. winter wheat winter barley, winter lye, winter rat, cabbage, pea, but etc.

15.6 Why is abscisic acid also known as stress hormone?

Sol. Abscisic acid is known as stress hormone because it stimulates the closure of stomata in the epidermis and increases the tolerance of plants to various kind of stresses.

15.7 'Both growth and differentiation in higher plants are open' Comment.

Sol. In higher plants new cells are always being added to the plant body by the activity of the meristem. This ability of the plants is due to the presence of meristems at certain locations in their body. Meristems have the capacity to divide and self-perpetuate. The cells formed by these meristems later differentiate into different types of tissues and organs.

15.8 'Both a short day plant and a long day plant can flower simultaneously in a given place'. Explain.

Sol. There are two different plants one is Oat which is a long day plant and the other one is *Xanthium* which is a short day plant. Both have different photoperiods i.e. 9 hrs in Oat and 15.6 hrs in *Xanthium*. At 9.5 hrs both Oat and *Xanthium* will be flowering simultaneously.

15.9 Which one of the plant growth regulators would you use if you are asked to :

(a) **induce rooting in a twig**

(b) **quickly ripen a fruit**

(c) **delay leaf senescence**

(d) **induce growth in axillary buds**

(e) **'bolt a rosette plant'**

(f) **induce immediate stomatal closure in leaves.**

Sol. (a) Auxin   (b) Ethylene

(c) Cytokinin   (d) Cytokinin

(e) Gibberellin   (f) Abscisic acid

15.10 Would a defoliated plant respond to photoperiodic cycle? Why?

Sol. No, because the site of perception of light/dark durations are leaves which is absent in defoliated plant, hormone florigen will not migrate to shoot apices to induce flowering.

15.11 What would be expected to happen if:

(a) **GA_3 is applied to rice seedlings**

(b) **dividing cells stop differentiating**

(c) **a rotten fruit get mixed with unripe fruits**

(d) **you forget to add cytokinin to the culture medium.**

Sol. (a) It causes elongation of stems and leaf sheaths.

(b) A callus of undifferentiated cell will be produced.

(c) It stimulates ripening of unripe fruits.

(d) It inhibits the growth of callus.

SECTION B — PRACTICE QUESTIONS

MULTIPLE CHOICE QUESTIONS

1. Arithmetic growth is expressed as
   (a) $L_t = L_0 + rt$ (b) $L_0 = L_0 + rt$
   (c) $W_1 = W_0 e^{rt}$ (d) $W_0 = W_1 e^{rt}$

2. The exponential growth can be expressed as $W_1 = W_0 e^{rt}$. What is 'r' in the expression ?
   (a) Relative growth rate and depends on final size.
   (b) Absolute growth rate and depends on initial size.
   (c) Relative growth and also referred to as efficiency index.
   (d) None of the above

3. Arithmetic growth includes all the following except:
   (a) constant growth rate.
   (b) it is found in root and shoot cells.
   (c) its characteristic graph is sigmoid.
   (d) it is expressed as $L_t = L_0 + rt$.

4. Which of the following statement is not the characteristic of growth of an organism?
   (a) It is an irreversible permanent increase in size of an organ / its part / an individual cell.
   (b) It is accompanied by metabolic processes.
   (c) It is quantitative and intrinsic.
   (d) None of the above

5. Maximal size in terms of wall thickening and protoplasmic modification are achieved by:
   (a) cells of divisional phase.
   (b) cells of maturation phase.
   (c) cells of elongation phase.
   (d) cells of meristematic tissue.

6. Which of the following hormones causes fruits like apple to elongate and improve its shape?
   (a) GA   (b) ABA
   (c) NAA   (d) 2,4D

7. Removal of apical (terminal) bud of a flowering plant (or pruning of a flowering plant) leads to
   (a) formation of new apical buds.
   (b) formation of adventitious roots on the cut side.
   (c) early flowering (or stopping of floral growth).
   (d) promotion of lateral branches.

8. Auxin regulates cell growth by which of the following mechanisms?
  (a) Altering the elasticity of cell walls.
  (b) Altering the plasticity of cell walls.
  (c) Synthesizing new cell walls.
  (d) Breaking down cell walls in growing cells.

9. The fruits can be left on the tree longer so as to extend the market period. This is due to which function of GA?
  (a) Bolting   (b) Delay senescence
  (c) Internodal elongation (d) Parthenocarpy

10. The site of perception of light in plants during photoperiodism is:
  (a) Axillary bud   (b) Shoot apex
  (c) Leaf   (d) Stem

ASSERTION & REASON QUESTIONS

DIRECTION (Qs. 1-5) : *These questions consists of two statements. Answer these questions selecting the appropriate option given below:*
(a) Both Assertion (A) and Reason (R) are true and Reason (R) is the correct explanation of Assertion (A).
(b) Both Assertion (A) and Reason (R) are true, but Reason (R) is not the correct explanation of Assertion (A).
(c) Assertion (A) is true, but Reason (R) is false.
(d) Assertion (A) is false, but Reason (R) is true.

1. **Assertion:** The constantly dividing cells both at the root apex and the shoot apex. Show the meristematic phase of growth.
  Reason: The cells of this region are rich in protoplasm and are without nuclei.

2. **Assertion:** Development is a sum of growth and differentiation.
  Reason: Development in plants is under the control of extrinsic factors only.

3. **Assertion:** Auxin help to prevent fruits and leaves drop at early stages.
  Reason: Auxin promote the abscission of older mature leaves and fruits.

4. **Assertion:** Ethylene cause climacteric ripening of fruits.
  Reason: Climacteric fruits shows a rise in respiration at the time of ripening.

5. **Assertion:** Vernalisation is acceleration of subsequent flowering by low temperature treatment.
  Reason: Site of vernalisation is apical meristem.

CASE/PASSAGE BASED QUESTIONS

DIRECTIONS (Qs. 1-5) : *Read the following passage and answer the questions that follows.*

Plants like other organisms are made up of cells, plant growth involves an increase in cell numbers by cell division and an increase in cell size. Cell division itself is not growth, as each new cell is exactly half the size of the cell from which it is formed. Only when it grows to the same size as its progenitor has grown been realised. Nonetheless, as each cell has a maximum size, cell division is considered as providing the potential for growth.

1. The given figure indicates the stages of seed germination

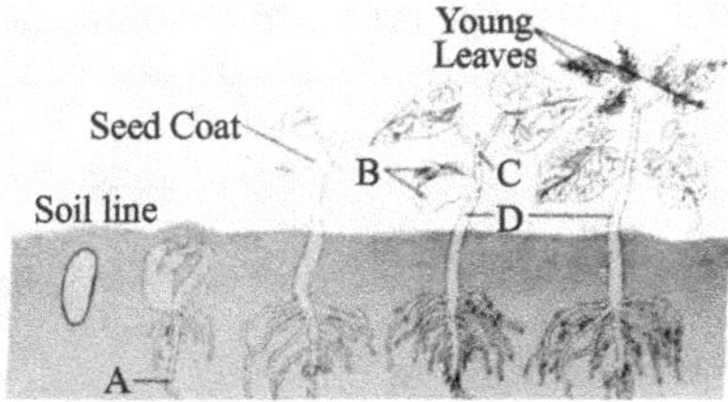

Identify A, B, C and D respectively.
  (a) Root hair, Catyledons, Epicotyl and Hypocotyl
  (b) Mesocotyl, Cotyledons, Epicotyl and Hypocotyl
  (c) Radicle, Cotyledons, Epicotyl and Hypocotyl
  (d) Plumule, Cotyledons, Epicotyl and Hypocotyl

2. See the figure and choose the correct option from table.

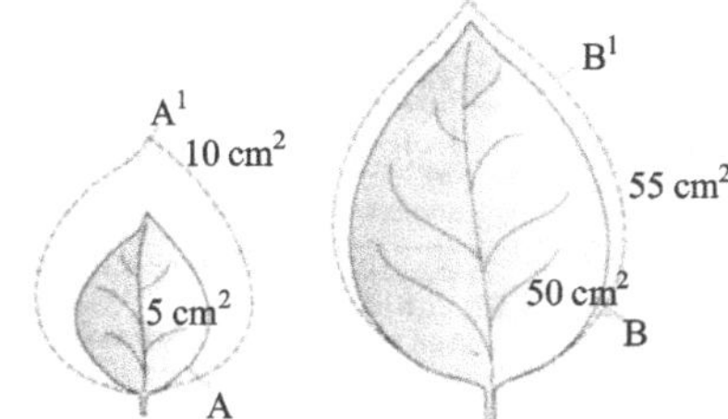

	A-leaf		B-leaf	
	AGR	RGR	AGR	RGR
(a)	0.5	100%	1.5	100%
(b)	5	100%	5	10%
(c)	100%	5	10%	5
(d)	1%	1	2%	2

3. Given below is a graph drown on the parameters of growth versus A, B, C respectively represent.

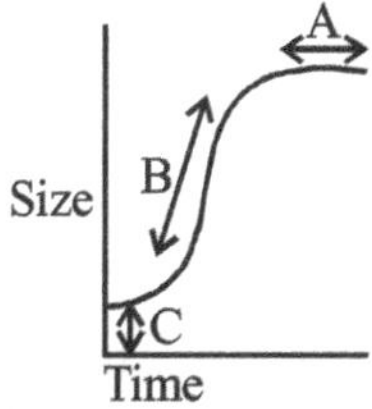

  (a) Exponential phase, log phase and steady phase.
  (b) Steady phase, log phase and lag phase.
  (c) Slow growing phase, lag phase and steady state phase.
  (d) lag phase, steady state phase and logarithmic phase.

4. Growth is maximum in the zone of
  (a) cell division   (b) cell maturation
  (c) cell elongation   (d) All of these

5. Which of the following instrument can be used to record plant growth by seconds i.e. in fraction of a minute.
  (a) Arc auxanometer   (b) Arc indicator
  (c) Space marker disc (d) Crescograph

VERY SHORT ANSWER QUESTIONS

1. What is the full form of IAA?
2. What is source of zeatin?
3. Name stress hormone in plants that functions during drought.
4. Name the hormone that makes the plant more tolerant to various stresses.
5. In a wheat field, some broad leaved weeds were seen by a farmer. Which plant hormone would you suggest to get rid of them?
6. A farmer grows cucumber plants in his field. He wants to increase the number of female flowers in them. Which plant growth regulator can be applied to achieve this?
7. Why is a beet root plant called a long day plant?
8. Define growth rate.
9. Who isolated auxin? Name the plant source.
10. Name the plant in which Darwin first observed phototropic curvature.

11. Name the causative agent of 'bakane' disease in rice seedlings.
12. Define climacteric.
13. What would happen when branch from short day plant after floral induction is grafted on a non-induced long day plant?
14. What is the most abundant natural cytokinin that was isolated from corn kernels and coconut milk?
15. Which plant hormone was first isolated from human urine?

SHORT ANSWER QUESTIONS

1. List some structural modifications which occur during cell differentiation.
2. How do you induce lateral branching in a plant which normally does not produce them? Give reasons in support of your answer.
3. Define growth regulators.
4. Why is the term 'long day plant' a misnomer?
5. Define plasticity.
6. What is growth? How will you measure the rate of growth?
7. Explain the different phases of growth with the help of a diagram.
8. Describe three different actions of ethylene in plants.

9. Where are auxins synthesised in plants? Mention any two of their functions.
10. Where are cytokinins synthesised in plants? Mention any two of their functions.
11. Explain apical dominance. Name the hormone that controls it.
12. How does abscisic acid act antagonistically to auxins and gibberellins?
13. What is ethephon? How does it function in plants? Give any two of its functions.
14. What is the sigmoid growth curve ? Write the names of the three phases in it.
15. Differentiate between phototropism and Geotropism.
16. What are Terpenoids?

LONG ANSWER QUESTIONS

1. What is meant by vernalization? Explain the significance of vernalization.
2. Discuss the role of gibberellins in plant growth and development.
3. What is meant by seed dormancy? Describe the methods to overcome the seed dormancy.
4. Describe the phenomenon of photoperiodism.

SOLUTIONS

Multiple Choice Questions

1. **(a)** Arithmetic growth is a type of growth in which the rate of growth is constant and increase in growth occurs in arithmetic progression *i.e.*, 2, 4, 6, 8 etc. Here after mitosis, only one daughter cell continues to divide, other takes part in differentiation and maturation. In this type of growth, a linear curve is obtained with positive value. Arithmetic growth is expressed as $L_t = L_0 + rt$. *Where*, L_t = Length after time t, L_0 = Length at the beginning, r = growth rate.

2. **(c)** In the expression $W_1 = W_0 e^{rt}$, r is the relative growth rate and is also the measure of the ability of the plant to produce new plant material, referred to as efficiency index.

3. **(c)** S-shaped or sigmoid shape curve is obtained in case of geometric growth. In arithmetic growth, on plotting length of the organ at different times, a linear curve is obtained.

4. **(d)** All the given statements are the characteristics of growth of an organism. Growth can be defined as an irreversible permanent increase in size of an organ or its parts or even of an individual cell.

5. **(b)** The period of growth is generally divided into three phases: meristematic (cells of apical meristem divide), elongation (proteins, protoplasm, cell wall material is synthesized) and maturation (secondary walls are laid down). Maximal size in term of wall thickening and protoplasmic modification are achieved by cells of maturation phase.

6. **(a)** Gibberellins (GAs) causes fruits like apple to elongate and improve in shapes. GA are plant hormones that regulate growth and influence various developmental processes, including stem elongation, germination, dormancy, flowering, sex expression, enzyme induction, and leaf and fruit senescence. GA is also responsible for bolting (internode elongation just prior to flowering).

7. **(d)** The phenomenon of apical dominance can be seen in most of the vascular plants in which, in the presence of apical bud, growth of lateral buds (formed just below the apex) is suppressed. At the removal of apical bud, the lateral buds grow vigorously. It shows that apical bud suppresses the growth of lateral bud (axillary bud) just below it. This is known as apical dominance. It is widely used in tea plantation and hedge making.

8. **(c)** Altering the plasticity allows for permanent changes in cell wall shape. The cell wall must increase in size in order for cell growth to occur.

9. **(a)** Removal of all yellow leaves and spraying the remaining of the leaves with 2, 4, 5 trichlorophenoxyacetic acid could be most beneficial to obtain maximum seed yield from the premature yellowing of leaves of a pulse crops with decreased yield.

10. **(b)** The site of perception of light in plants during photoperiodism is leaf.

Assertion & Reason Questions

1. **(c)** Growth, differentiation and development are closely related events in the life of a plant development is sum of growth and differentiation development in plant in under control of both intrinsic and extrinsic factors.

2. **(a)** Unlike animals, plants do not stop growing after reaching maturity. They continue to grow and bear new roots, leaves and branches etc. while roots, stems and their branches have indefinite growth, other organs like leaves, flowers and fruits show limited growth or definite growth. They appear and fall off periodically and sometimes repeatedly. In lower plants, growth is diffused as every cell can divide and enlarge. Higher plants possess specific areas which take part in the formation of new cells.

3. **(b)** Auxin delays abscission of young leaves and fruits. Its effect is through formation of abscission zone below a leaf or fruit. Abscission zone cuts off nutrients and water supply. However, auxin promotes the abscission of mature or older leaves and fruits.

4. **(b)** In fruits the rate of respiration will undergo a sharp rise and then fall near the end of ripening. kidd and west termed this phenomenon "climacteric rise". The climacteric

act as a trigger that sets in progress those changes that rapidly transform the fruit from an unripe to a ripe condition. Finally application of ethylene to unripe fruit will bring on a premature climacteric and accelerate ripening.

5. **(b)** The physiological mechanism of flowering in plant is controlled by two factors: light period and low temperature. The cold treatment of plant to induce flowering is called as vernalisation. As a result of vernalisation is apical meristem.

Case/Passage Based Questions

1. (c) 2. (c) 3. (b)
4. (c) Growth is maximum in the zone of cell elongation.
5. (d) Crescograph can be used to record plant growth by seconds i.e. in fraction of a minute.

Very Short Answer Questions

1. Indole acetic acid
2. Zeatin obtained from corn-kernels and coconut milk.
3. Abscisic acid
4. Abscisic acid
5. 2, 4-dichlorophenoxy acetic acid (2, 4-D)
6. Ethylene
7. Beet root plant is called a long day plant because it requires a light period longer than the critical photoperiod for flowering.
8. The increased growth per unit time is called as growth rate.
9. F.W. Went isolated auxin. He isolated it from tips of coleoptiles of oat seedlings.
10. Darwin firstly observed phototropic curvature in canary grass.
11. *Gibberella fujikuroi*
12. Climacteric refers to the increased rate of respiration during ripening of fruits.
13. The long day plant would start flowering because short day plant is capable to induce flowering in long day plant.
14. Zeatin is the most abundant natural Cytokinin that was isolated from corn Kernels and Coconut milk.
15. Auxin was first isolated from human urine.

Short Answer Questions

1. During differentiation, cells undergo few to major structural changes both in their cell walls and protoplasm. For example, to form a tracheary element, the cells would lose their protoplasm. They also develop a very strong, elastic, lignocellulosic secondary cell walls, to carry water to long distances even under extreme condition.

2. Apical bud checks the sprouting of lateral buds due to presence of auxins. When apical bud is removed, lateral branches are produced. Due to removal of apical bud effect of auxins is destroyed inducing the lateral buds to grow rapidly.

3. The plant growth regulators (PGRs) are small, simple molecules of diverse chemical composition. They could be indole compounds (indole-3-acetic acid, IAA); adenine derivatives (kinetin), derivatives of carotenoids (abscisic acid, ABA); terpenes (gibberellic acid, GA_3) or gases (ethylene, C_2H_4). Plant growth regulators are variously described as plant growth substances, plant hormones or phytohormones.

4. Flowering in long day plant is determined by the period of short night. Thus the appropriate term for these plants is - 'short night plants'.

5. Plants follow different pathways in response to environment or phases of life. It leads to formation of different structures. This ability is called plasticity.

6. Growth is defined as a permanent or irreversible increase in dry weight, size, mass or volume of a cell, organ or organism. Generally growth is accompanied by metabolic processes (both anabolic and catabolic). At the cellular level, growth is due to increase in amount of protoplasm. However, it is difficult to measure increase in protoplasm. Increase in protoplasm leads to increase in cell, cell number and cell size. This fact is used in calculating growth which, therefore, is a quantitive or measurable phenomenon. The parameters used for measuring growth are increase in fresh weight, dry weight, length, area, volume and cell number.

7. The period of growth is generally divided into three phases – meristematic, elongation and maturation.

   Meristematic phase : The constantly dividing cells, both at the root apex and the shoot apex, represent the meristematic phase of growth. The cells in this region are rich in protoplasm possess large conspicuous nuclei. Their cell walls are primary in nature, thin and cellulosic with abundant plasmodesmatal connections.

   Elongation phase : The cells proximal to the meristematic zone represent the phase of elongation. Increased vacuolation, cell enlargement and new cell wall deposition are the characteristics of the cells in this phase. Maturation phase : The cells of this zone, attain their maximal size in terms of wall thickening and protoplasmic modifications.

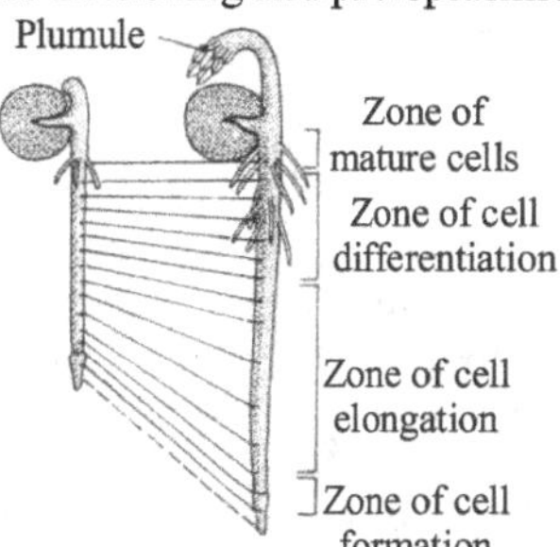

Fig.: Detection of zones of elongation by the parallel line technique. Zones A, B, C, D immediately behind the apex have elongated most

8. Influences of ethylene on plants include horizontal growth of seedlings, breaking seed and bud dormancy, initiates germination in peanut seeds, sprouting of potato tubers. Ethylene promotes rapid internode/petiole elongation in deep water rice plants. It is highly effective in inducing fruit ripening when it is produced in large amount. Ethylene increases the permeability of cell because of which the fruit is softened and entry of oxygen into fruit is accelerated.

9. Auxins are produced in the growing shoot apices and root apices.
   Functions of auxins are as follows :
   (i) Auxins control apical dominance, i.e., they suppress the growth of lateral buds into branches.
   (ii) They help to prevent fruit and leaf drop at early stages but promote the abscission of older mature leaves and fruits.

10. Cytokinins are synthesised in plant parts where rapid cell division occurs, like root apices, shoot buds, young fruits, etc.
    Functions of cytokinis are as follows :
    (i) Cytokinins influence cell division (cytokinesis), cell enlargement and differentiation.

11. Apical dominance is the phenomenon in which the apical bud suppresses the growth of lateral buds into branches. Auxin is the hormone that controls it.

12. ABA induces formation of abscission layer, while auxins prevent the formation of abscission layer.
    ABA induces seed dormancy and bud dormancy, while gibberellins break seed dormancy and bud dormancy.

13. Ethephon :
    – It is a compound used as a source of ethylene for plant growth.
    – It is an aqueous solution that is easily absorbed by the plants and transported within the plant.
    – It releases ethylene slowly.
    Functions of ethephon are as follows :
    (i) It accelerates abscission in flowers and thinning in cotton, walnut and cherry etc.
    (ii) It promotes the development of female flowers in cucumbers thereby increasing the yield.

14. S-growth curve : The rate of the growth whether measured as length area, volume or weight is not uniform. Under ideal conditions when the rate of growth is plotted against time, an S-shaped curve called the sigmoid curve.
    (i) Lag phase : Growth is slow in the initial stage.
    (ii) Exponential period of growth : It is second phase of maximum growth. Here, both the progeny cells follow mitotic cell division retain the ability to divide.
    (iii) Stationary phase : When the nutrients become limiting, growth slow down.

15.

Phototropism		Geotropism
(i)	It is response of plant with respect to light.	– It is response of plants with respect to gravity.
(ii)	The stem is positively phototrophic to light and the root us negatively phototropic.	– The stem is negatively geotropic but the root is positively geotrophic.
(iii)	It is due to unequal distribution of auxin under the influence of light of gravity.	– It is due to unequal distribution of auxin under the influence
(iv)	Leaves are diphototropic	– Secondry roots and stem branches are phagotropic.

16. Terpenoids are derivatives of terpenes, includes abscisic acid and gibberlin and the carotenoid and chlorophyll pigments.

Long Answer Questions

1. Vernalization may be defined as the method of inducing early flowering in plants by pretreatment of their seeds at low temperatures. It is the acquisition or acceleration of the ability to flower by chilling treatment. Some cereals such as wheat, barley, oat and rye have two kinds of varieties : winter and spring varieties.
    The 'spring' variety are normally planted in the spring and come to flower and produce grain before the end of the growing season. Winter varieties, however, if planted in spring would normally fail to flower or produce mature grain within a span of a flowering season. Hence, they are planted in autumn. They germinate, and during winter come out as small seedling, resume growth in the spring, and are harvested usually around mid-summer.
    Another example of vernalisation is seen in biennial plants. Biennials are monocarpic plants that normally flower and die in the second season. Sugarbeet, cabbages, carrots are some of the common biennials. Subjecting the growing of a biennial plant to a cold treatment stimulates a subsequent photoperiodic flowering response.

Significance of vernalization are as follows :
(i) It reduces vegetative period of plant.
(ii) It prepares the plants for flowering.
(iii) It increases yield, resistance to cold and diseases.
(iv) Vernalization is beneficial in reducing the period between germination and flowering. Thus, more than one crop can be obtained during a year.

2. The role of gibberellins in plant growth and development are as follows:
   (i) The gibberellins induce elongation of the internodes. The elongation of stem due to rapid cell division and cell elongation.
   (ii) In many plants leaves become broader and elongated when treated with gibberellic acid. This leads to increase in photosynthetic area which finally increases the height of the plant.
   (iii) They cause fruits like apple to elongate and improve its shape.
   (iv) They also delay senescence.
   (v) GA_3 is increase the yield of malt from barley grains.
   (vi) Spraying of sugarcane crop with gibberellins increases length of stem and yield of sugarcane to as much as 20 tonnes/ acre.
   (vii) They also promote bolting (internode elongation just prior to flowering) in beet, cabbages and many plants with rosette habit.

3. **Seed dormancy**
   There are certain seeds which fail to germinate even when external conditions are favourable. Such seeds are undergoing a period of dormancy which is controlled not by external environment but are under endogenous control or conditions within the seed itself.
   • Impermeable and hard seed coat; presence of chemical inhibitors such as abscissic acids, phenolic acids, para-ascorbic acid; and immature embryos are some of the reasons which causes seed dormancy. Seed dormancy however can be overcome through natural means and various other means e.g. the seed coat barrier in some seeds can be broken by mechanical abrasions using knives, sandpaper etc. or vigorous shaking. In nature, these abrasions are caused by microbial action, and passage through digestive tract of animals.
   • Effect of inhibitory substances can be removed by subjecting the seeds to chilling conditions or by application of certain chemicals like gibberellic acid and nitrates.
   • Changing the environmental conditions, such as light and temperature are other methods to overcome seed dormancy.

4. The effect of photoperiods or day duration of light hours (and dark periods) on the growth and development of plants, especially flowering, is called photoperiodism. On the basis of photoperiodic response to flowering, plants have been divided into the following categories :
   (a) Short day plants : They flower when the photoperiod or day length is below a critical period. Most of winter flowering plants belong to this category, *e.g., Xanthium, Chrysanthemum,* rice, sugarcane, etc.
   (b) Long day plants : These plants flower when they receive long photoperiods or light hours which are above a critical length, *e.g.,* wheat, oat, sugar beet, spinach, radish, barley etc.
   (c) Day neutral plants : There are many plants, however, where there is no such correlation between exposure to light duration and induction of flowering response; such plants are called day-neutral plants e.g. tomato, cucumber etc.

SECTION C	NCERT EXEMPLAR QUESTIONS 

MULTIPLE CHOICE QUESTIONS

1. The affect of apical dominance can be overcome by which of the following hormone?
   (a) IAA   (b) Ethylene
   (c) Cytokinin   (d) Gibberellin

2. Apples are generally wrapped in waxed paper to:
   (a) prevent sunlight for changing its colour
   (b) prevent aerobic respiration by checking the entry of O_2
   (c) prevent ethylene formation due to injury
   (d) make the apples look attractive

3. Growth can be measured in various ways. Which of these can be used as parameters to measure growth?
   (a) increase in cell number
   (b) increase in cell size
   (c) increase in length and weight
   (d) All of these

4. Plasticity in plant growth means that:
   (a) plant roots are extensible
   (b) plant development is dependent on the environment
   (c) stems can extend
   (d) None of the above

5. To increase sugar production in sugarcanes, they are sprayed with:
   (a) IAA   (b) cytokinin
   (c) gibberellin   (d) ethylene

VERY SHORT ANSWER QUESTIONS

1. Fill the places with appropriate word/words.
   (a) A phase of growth which is maximum and fastest is ....
   (b) Apical dominance as expressed in dicotyledonous plants is due to the presence of more ...... in the apical bud than in the lateral ones.
   (c) In addition to auxin, a .... must be supplied to culture medium obtain a good callus in plant tissue culture.
   (d) .... of a vegetative plants are the sites of photoperiodic perception.

2. Plant Growth Substances (PGS) have innumerable practical applications. Name the PGS you should use to
   (a) increase yield of sugarcane
   (b) promote lateral shoot growth
   (c) cause sprouting of potato tuber
   (d) inhibit seed germination

3. A primary root grows from 5 cm to 19 cm in a week. Calculate the growth rate and relative growth rate over the period.

4. Gibberellins were first discovered in Japan when rice plants were suffering from bakane (the foolish seedling disease) caused by a fungus *Gibberella fujikuroi*.
   (a) Give two functions of this phytohormone.
   (b) Which property of gibberellin caused foolish seedling disease in rice?

5. Classify the following plants into Long Day Plants (LDP), Short Day plants (SDP) and Day Neutral Plants (DNP) *Xanthium*, henbane (*Hyoscyamus niger*), spinach, rich, strawberry, *Bryophyllum*, sunflower, tomato, maize.

6. A farmer grows cucumber plants in his field. He wants to increase the number of female flowers in them. Which plant growth regulator can be applied to achieve this?

7. Where are the following hormones synthesised in plants?
   (a) IAA
   (b) Gibberellins
   (c) Cytokinins

8. Growth is one of the charactristic of all living organism? Do unicellular organism also grow? If so, what are the parameters?

9. In the figure of sigmoid growth curve given below, label segments 1, 2 and 3.

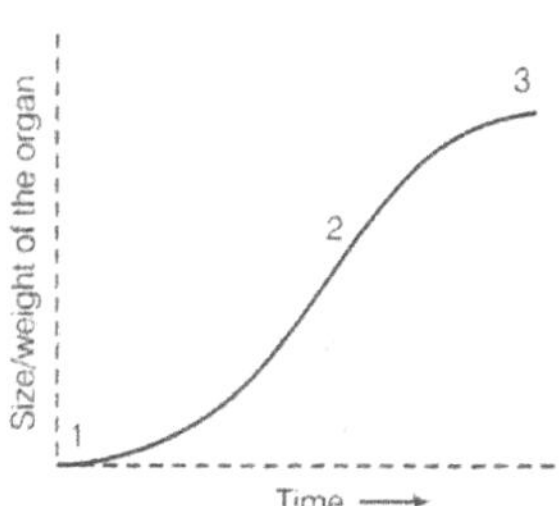

10. The rice seedlings infected with fungus *Gibberella fujikuroi* is called foolish seedlings? What was the reason behind it?

SHORT ANSWER QUESTIONS

1. *Nicotiana tobacum*, a short day plant, when exposed to more than critical period of light fails to flower. Explain.

2. Explain in 2-3 lines each of the following terms with the help of examples taken from different plant tissues.
   (a) Differentiation
   (b) De-differentiation
   (c) Re-differentiation

3. The role of ethylene and abscissic acid is both positive and negative. Justify the statement.

4. In animals, there are special glands secreting hormones, whereas there are no glands in plants. Where are plant hormones formed? How are the hormones translocated to the site of activity?

5. In a slide showing different types of cells can you identify which type of the cell may be meristematic and the one which is incapable of dividing and how?

6. A rubber band stretches and reverts back to its original position. Bubble gum stretches, but it would not return to its original position.
   Is there any difference between the two processes? Discuss it with respect to plant growth (hint elasticity (reversible) plasticity (irreversible).

7. Label the diagram.
   A. This is which part of a dicotyledonous plants?
   B. If we remove part 1 from the plant, what will happen?

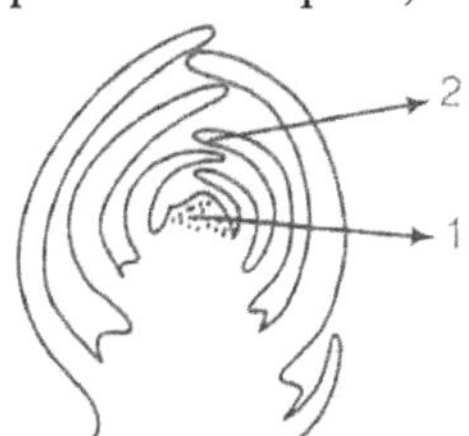

8. Both animals and plants grow. Why do we say that growth and differentiation in plants is open and not so in animals? Does this statement hold true for sponges also?

9. Define parthenocarpy. Name the plant hormone used to induce parthenocarpy.
10. While eating watermelons, all of us wish it was seedless. As a plant physiologist can you suggest any method by which this can be achieve.
11. On germination a seed first produces shots with leaves, flowers appear later,
    A. Why do you think this happens?
    B. How is this advantageous to the plant?
12. Fill in the blanks
    A. Maximum growth is observed in .... phase.
    B. Apical dominance is due to ....
    C. .... initiate rooting.
    D. Pigment involved in photo photoperception in flowering plants in ....

LONG SHORT ANSWER QUESTIONS

1. Some varieties of wheat are known as spring wheat while others are called winter wheat. Former variety is sown and planted in spring and is harvested by the end of the same season. However, winter varieties, if planted in spring, fail to flower or produce mature grains within a span of a flowering season. Explain, why?
2. Name a hormone which
    A. is gaseous in nature
    B. Is responsible for phototropism
    C. induces femaleness in flowers of cucumber
    D. is used for killing weeds (dicots)
    E. induces flowering in long day plants.

SOLUTIONS

Multiple Choice Questions

1. **(c)** Cytokinin is antagonistic to the action of auxin and thus help to overcome the phenomenon of apical dominance. IAA helps in apical dominance, ethylene in ripening of fruits and gibberellin in overcoming bud and seed dormancy.
2. **(b)** Apples respire as they have lenticels on their skin. They are wrapped in wax paper after harvesting so as to prevent the respiration and over ripening of the apples.
3. **(d)** All the given statements are true for growth in a living organism.
4. **(b)** Plants have a remarkable ability to adapt to the environment for their survival.
   They can change their phenotype according to the changes in environment. So, plant growth shows plasticity (ability to change/adapt according to environment).
5. **(c)** Gibberellin sprayed on sugarcane induces growth in the internodal area of the sugarcane plant. Larger is the area, larger will be the sugar content, as sucrose is the main constituent in the of sap of sugarcane stem.

Very Short Answer Questions

1. (a) A phase of growth which is maximum and latest is **exponential phase**.
   (b) Apical dominance as expressed in dicotyledonous plants is due to the presence or more **auxins** in the apical bud than in the lateral ones.
   (c) In addition to auxin, a **cytokinin** must be supplied to culture medium to obtain a good callus in plant tissue culture.
   (d) **Leaves** of vegetative plants are the sites of photoperiodic perception.
2. (a) Spraying gibberellins
   (b) Application of auxins
   (c) Ethylene
   (d) ABA
3. Growth depends upon three factors – initial size (W_0), rate of growth (r) and time interval ($+$) for which the rate of growth is retained.
   Where, $W_1 = W_0 e^{rt}$
   W_1 = final size,
   W_0 = initial size,
   r = growth rate,
   t = time

e = base of natural logarithim.

$$19 = 5 \times (2.7)^{r \times 7}$$

$$\frac{19}{5} = (2.7)^{r \times 7}$$

$$3.8 = (2.7)^{r \times 7}$$

$$\text{Log } 38 = r \times 7 \times \log(2.7)$$

$$0.5798 = r \times 7 \times 0.4314$$

$$\frac{0.5798}{7 \times 0.4314} = r = 0.1907$$

Relative growth rate =

$$\frac{\text{Growth in given time period}}{\text{Measurement at start of time period}}$$

$$= \frac{19}{5} = 38 \text{ cm}$$

Thus absolute growth rate is 0.1907 while relative growth rate is 3.8 cm.

4. Following are the two functions of gibberellin:
   (i) It produces the phenomenon of bolting *i.e.*, the growth of the internodal region of stem in rosette plants.
   (ii) It induces seed germination and break bud and seed domancy.
   (b) The rice seeding/plant show excessive growth in their internodal region when gets infected by fungus *Gibberella fujikuroi*. This fungus produces excessive amount of plant hormone GA that makes plants taller in comparison to the normal plant foolishly and many results into death of the plant.
5. **Long Day Plant** (LDP) The plants that requires the exposure light for a longer period exceeding a well defined critical duration of light are long day plants . Among the above given plant LDP are for henbane, *Bryophyllum* and spinach.
   Short Day Plants (SDP) The Plants that requires light for a period less than well defined critical duration of light, *e.g.*, *Xanthium*, rice, strawberry.
   Day Natural Plants (DNP) The exposure to light does not affect the flowering in certain plants, *e.g*, DNP, sunflower, tomato, maize.
6. Ethylene, is a plant growth regulator that has feminizing effect on sex expression. Ethylene promotes formation of female flowers in monoecious plants like cucumber.

7. (a) **IAA** *i.e.*, Indole acetic acid. It is synthesised at the growing apices of the plant, *e.g.*, shoot tip, leaf primordia and developing seeds.

(b) **Gibberellins** It is synthesised in the apical shoot buds, young leaves, root tips and developing seeds.

(c) **Cytokinins** are synthesised mainly in routs, but synthes also occurs in the endosperm of seeds, growing embryo etc.

8. 1. Lag phase- In this phase growth is slow.

2. Exponential phase- It shows rapid growth and maintains maximum growth for sometime.

3. Stationary phase- In this phase Growth diminishes and ultimately stops.

9. Growth is the main characteristic that distinguish living organisms from non-living. All living organism grow in number and then accumulate biomass and grow in size as well.

Increase in number of cells as well as increase in size and length of each cell, exhibits growth of all living organism. **In unicellular organism**, the growth is synchronized with reproduction. These organism when divide they produce offspring (reproduction) *i.g.*, each cell accumulate (synthesise) protoplasm and increase in size but at a certain a limit and divide to from two cells.

10. The rice seedling infected with fungus *Gibberella fujikuroi* are called foolish seedling because infected plants grow excessively taller than rest of the non infected rice plants in the field fall over and be unharvestable.

Short Answer Questions

1. Short day plants are those plants that flower only when the exposure to duration of light is below critical period. Tobacco, being a short day plant is unable to show flowering when it is exposed to light above than the critical period.

2. (a) Differentiation is permanent in composition structure size and function of cells, tissue or organs. For example the meristematic tissues in plants gives rise to new cells which then mature and get differentiated into tissue or an organ of the plant, *e.g.*, cells, distal to root apical meristem form root cap, cell of the periphery form epiblema, followed by cortex, *etc.*

(b) **De-differentiation** is the process of regain of differentiated cells so that they again become differentiated and able to divide. *e.g.*, in dicot stem, the cortical cells get de-differentiate and become meristematic to form cambium (interfascicular cambium, and fascicular cambiums).

(c) **Re-differentiation** The cambium cells thus formed, again re-differentiate to form secondary cortex cells, secondary xylem and phloem elements and phelloderm in case of secondary growth of woody dicot plants.

3.

Hormone	Positive Effects	Negative Effects
Ethylene	• It promotes horizontal/transverse growth. It makes stem positively geotropic.	• It inhibits longitudinal growth. It decreases sensitivity to gravity, *i.e.* root become apogeotropic
	• It promotes apical dominance.	• It enhances sense of leaves and flowers, fruits.
	• It breaks seed and bud dormancy.	• It prolongs dormancy of lateral buds.
	• It enhances fruits ripening and root initiation.	• It mediates formation of ABA under water stressed conditions.
Abscissic Acid	• It is used as anti transparent, by reducing water requirement and during irrigation (by partial closure of stomata).	• It promotes abscission of flower and fruits.
	• It also induces flowering and root initiation in some plants.	It stimulates sensescence of leaves by • stopping protein and RNA synthesis.
	• It is use in prolonging dormancy of buds and seeds.	It promotes bud and seed dormancy. Retards • cambial activity by stopping mitosis in vascular strands and cambium. It acts as antagonist to gibberellins and counteracts the effect of other growth
	• It increases resistance of plants, to cold and other types of stresses thus also known as stress hormone.	• hormones (IAA and cytokinin). It inhibits seed germination and growth of embryos in them.

4. The plant hormones are synthesised by the plant cells needed. Few hormones are specifically synthesised at a particular part of the plant like auxin synthesised in growing shoot apices and ethylene is secretes by ripened fruits. Cytokinin is found in dividing cells. Unlike plants animal being more advanced, and organised they have proper hormone secreting glands and organs. These are transported through the transport system of their body in both plant and animals. In plants, hormone are translocated via xylem and phloem to the site of activity.

5. On the basis of the following characteristics the meristemtic cells can be identified.
   (i) Cell consist thin cellulose wall and dense cytoplasm with large nucleus.
   (ii) Among meristematic cells, plasmodesmal connections are more numerous.
   (iii) Cell division, *i.e.*, mitosis and its various stages are distinctly visible.
   (iv) Chromosomes of cells replicate and divide into two homologous chromatids.

   All these features contribute to open ended growth where structure is in complete in meristematic regions.

   Whereas, cells incapable of dividing show features such as
   (i) Attains particular shape, size and thickening.
   (ii) Undergoes structural and physiological differentiation.
   (iii) Different types of cell are formed such as epidermis, cortex, vascular tissues.

6.

Elasticity	Plasticity
• It is stretchability of the plant cells or products, *e.g.*, rubber/latex etc. • The elastic substances can revert back to its original form in relaxed state. *e.g.*, stretching of rubber.	• Different pathways in response to environment or phases of life to form different kinds of structure is called plasticity. • The plastic substances and phenomenon of plasticity are not reversible, i.e., irreversible. e.g., difference in shapes of leaves produced in air and those produced in water in buttercup. This is also known as heterophylly.

7. Representation the labelling of the given diagram is as follows

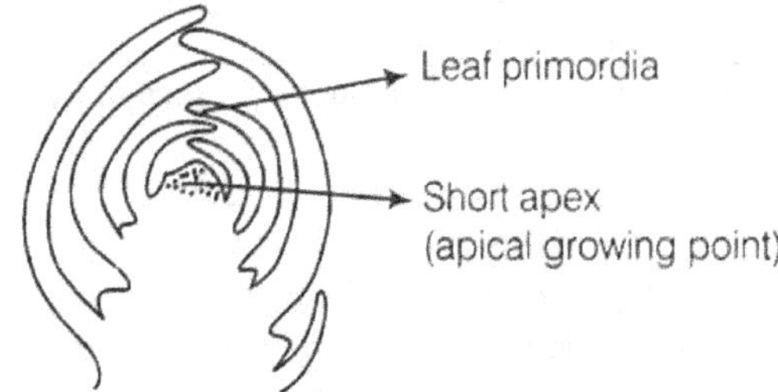

   A. The plant part in the given diagram is growing shoot apex.
   B. Removal of shoot apex will help to overcome the apical dominance. Thus, the lateral buds grow faster, giving rise to branches and give the plant a bushy appearance.

8. Growth in plant is totally different from the animal growth as growth in plant is unlimited and indefinite. Root and shoot in tips in the plants are open ended i.e. they always grow and form new organ to replace the older and senescent one due to presence of meristem cells, which are capable to grow and divide. Thus, the plant growth continues throughout the life. On the contrary, animal growth is limited as growth /stops as soon as they mature. Sponges are those animals which show cellular level of organisation. These animals posses totipotent cells which are capable of giving rise to all other cells in sponges. A small part detached from a sponge can regenerate into a whole new sponge. However growth in sponges cannot be called open or indefinite as they cannot grow beyond a certain size. Practically, they do not show open ended growth.

9. Parthenocarpy is the process where fruit develop without fertilisation and so, it lacks contain seed. Seedless fruits are developed in some plants. Certain phytohormone induce development of fruit without fertilisation. This can also be induced artificially by spraying auxin and gibberellins in certain plants like, grapes, papaya, etc.

10. The seedless, fruits can be produced by the process of parthenocarpy. In this fruits are developed without fertilisation, so, seeds are not formed in the fruit. Artifically parthenocarpy can be induced by spraying auxin and gibberellin to produce seedless watermelons.

11. **A.** With the germination of seeds the plant enters into vegetative growth period. This period takes light stimulus *i.e.*, photoperiod) and synthesise the florigen (a flowering hormone) that flowering.
    B. The vegetative growth period prepares the plant to bear reproductive structure like flower, fruits and seeds, and allows it to grow, mature and reproduce.

12. A. Exponential
    B. Auxin
    C. Cytokinin
    D. Phytochrome.

Long Answer Questions

1. Some annual plants such as wheat do not flower, unless they experience a low temperature during spring they remain vegetative but after receiving low temperature (in winter) they grow further to bear flowers and fruits.

   During winter the low temperature prevents precocious reproductive development in autumn, thus enabling the plant to reach vegetative maturity before reproductive phase. Thus, in spring when spring varieties are planted they flower and bear fruits prior to end of growing season. But, if the winter varieties are planted in spring, they fail to flower and produce mature grains before the end of growing season, as they could not perceive low temperature of winters.

2. A. Ethylene is a hormone which is gaseous in nature.
   B. Auxin (synthetic auxin 2-4D) is responsible for phototropism.
   C. Ethylene induces ferminising effect. External supply of very small quantity of ethylene can increase the number of female flowers and hence fruits as in cucumber.
   D. Synthetic auxin (2-4D) that kills broad leaved dicot weeds and is used as weedicides.
   E. Gibberellins induces flowering in long-day plants.

16 — Digestion and Absorption

16.1 Choose the correct answer among the following:

(a) Gastric juice contains
(i) pepsin, lipase and rennin
(ii) trypsin, lipase and rennin
(iii) trypsin, pepsin and lipase
(iv) trypsin, pepsin and rennin

(b) Succuss entericus is the name given to:
(i) a junction between ileum and large intestine
(ii) intestinal juice
(iii) swelling in the gut
(iv) appendix

Sol. (a) (i) Pepsin, lipase and rennin
(b) (ii) Intestinal juice

16.2 Match column I with column II

Column I		Column II
(a) Bilirubin and biliverdin	(i)	Parotid
(b) Hydrolysis of starch	(ii)	Bile
(c) Digestion of fat	(iii)	Lipases
(d) Salivary gland	(iv)	Amylases

Sol.

Column I		Column II
(a) Bilirubin and biliverdin	(ii)	Bile
(b) Hydrolysis of starch	(iv)	Amylases
(c) Digestion of fat	(iii)	Lipases
(d) Salivary gland	(i)	Parotid

16.3 Answer briefly :
(a) Why are villi present in the intestine and not in the stomach ?
(b) How does pepsinogen change into its active form ?
(c) What are the basic layers of the wall of alimentary canal?
(d) How does bile help in the digestion of fats ?

Sol. (a) Villi increases surface area for absorption and maximum absorption take place in intestine.
(b) Coming in contact with hydrochloric acid in stomach proenzyme pepsinogen convert to its active form pepsin, the proteolytic enzyme of stomach.
(c) There are four basic layers in the wall of alimentary canal *i.e.* serosa, muscularis, submucosa and mucosa.
(d) Bile helps in emulsification of fats *i.e.* breakdown the fats into very small micelles. Bile also activates lipases.

16.4 State the role of pancreatic juice in digestion of proteins.
Sol. The pancreatic juice contains inactive enzymes trypsinogen, chymotrypsinogen, procarboxy-peptidases, amylases, lipases and nucleases. Trypsinogen is activated by an enzyme enterokinase secreted by intestinal mucosa into active trypsin, which in turn activates the other enzymes in the pancreatic juice. These enzymes are concerned with protein, carbohydrate, fats and nucleic acid digestion.

16.5 Describe the process of digestion of protein in stomach.
Sol. The mucosa of stomach has gastric glands that secretes mucus, proenzyme pepsinogen, HCl and intrinsic factor. Intrinsic factor is essential for absorption of vitamin B_{12}. The food mix thoroughly with acidic gastric juice of stomach and called the chyme. The proenzyme pepsinogen on exposure to HCl gets converted to active enzyme pepsin. Pepsin converts proteins into proteases and peptones. Renin found in gastric juice of infants also helps in digestion of milk protein.

16.6 Give the dental formula of human beings.
Sol. Dental formula of human being is 2123/2123.

16.7 Bile juice contains no digestive enzymes, yet it is important for digestion. Why ?
Sol. Bile is a watery greenish fluid mixture containing bile pigments, bile salts, cholesterol and phospholipids. Bile helps in emulsification of fats i.e. breaking down of the fats into smaller micelles, it also activates lipases. Thus, it is important for digestion.

16.8 Describe the digestive role of chymotrypsin. Which two other digestive enzymes of the same category are secreted by its source gland ?
Sol. Chymotrypsin is a protein digestive enzyme that breaks down proteins, peptones and proteoses into dipeptides. Other two proteolytic enzymes are trypsin and carboxyl peptidase.

16.9 How are polysaccharides and disaccharides digested ?
Sol. (a) Digestion of carbohydrates starts in mouth cavity with the help of enzymes salivary amylase.

$$\text{Polysaccharides} \xrightarrow[\text{pH 6.8}]{\text{amylase}} \text{Disaccharides}$$

Intestinal juice contains **maltase, sucrase (invertase), lactase** and which act as follows :

$$\text{Maltose} \xrightarrow{\text{Maltase}} 2\ \text{Glucose}$$
$$\text{Sucrose} \xrightarrow{\text{Sucrase}} 1\ \text{Glucose} + 1\ \text{Fructose}$$
$$\text{Lactose} \xrightarrow{\text{Lactase}} 1\ \text{Glucose} + 1\ \text{Galactose}$$

16.10 What would happen if HCl were not secreted in the stomach?

Sol. Importance of HCl secreted by stomach:

HCl provides the acidic pH (pH 1.8) optimal for pepsins. It converts proenzyme pepsinogen into active enzyme pepsin, the proteolytic enzyme of the stomach.

HCl is also necessary to kill harmful bacteria which may be present in the food.

16.11 How does butter in your food get digested and absorbed in the body ?

Sol. Butter is a kind of fat. Fats are broken down by lipases with the help of bile into di- and monoglycerides:

$$\text{Fats} \xrightarrow{\text{Lipase}} \text{Diglycerides} \longrightarrow$$

$$\text{Monoglycerides} \longrightarrow \text{Fatty acid}$$

Fat is absorbed by villi in the small intestine.

16.12 Discuss the main steps in the digestion of proteins as the food passes through different parts of the alimentary canal.

Sol. (a) In stomach the proenzyme pepsinogen, on exposure to HCl converted into active pepsin that converts proteins into proteoses and peptones.

$$\text{Protein} \xrightarrow{\text{Pepsin}} \text{Protease, peptones, peptides}$$

(b) Proteins, proteoses and peptides in the chyme reaching the intestine are acted upon by proteolytic enzymes of pancreatic juice and converted to dipeptides.

$$\text{Large peptides} \xrightarrow{\text{Carboxypeptidase}}$$

$$\text{Dipeptide} + \text{Amino acids}$$

(c) The enzymes in succuss entericus act on the end product to form amino acids.

$$\text{Dipeptides} \xrightarrow{\text{Dipeptidase}} \text{Amino acids}$$

16.13 Explain the term thecodont and diphyodont.

Sol. Thecodont : In human beings, teeth are embedded in pits, the sockets of the jaw bones. Such teeth are called thecodont.

Diphyodont : The teeth that appear in two sets, i.e., milk-teeth which are later replaced by permanent teeth. This condition is called diphyodont.

16.14 Name different types of teeth and their number in an adult human.

Sol. Incisors – 8

Canines – 4

Premolars – 8

Molars – 12

16.15 What are the functions of liver ?

Sol. Functions of Liver :

1. The liver performs several roles in carbohydrate, lipid and protein metabolism.
2. The liver is responsible for the mainstay of protein metabolism, synthesis as well as degradation.
3. The liver produces and excretes bile (a greenish liquid) required for emulsifying fats.
4. The breakdown of insulin and other hormones
5. The liver breaks down haemoglobin, creating metabolites that are added to bile as pigment (bilirubin and biliverdin).
6. The liver converts ammonia to urea.

SECTION B	PRACTICE QUESTIONS 

MULTIPLE CHOICE QUESTIONS

1. The innermost layer of the digestive tract is the
   - (a) serosa membrane
   - (b) mucosa membrane
   - (c) submucosa membrane
   - (d) lumen

2. Crypts of lieberkuhn are present in
   - (a) intestine
   - (b) stomach
   - (c) oesophagus
   - (d) all of these

3. Where does bile go after it leaves the gall bladder?
   - (a) Duodenum   (b) Jejunum
   - (c) Ileum   (d) Caecum

4. The common bile duct in human is formed by the joining of
   - (a) pancreatic duct and bile duct.
   - (b) cystic duct and hepatic duct.
   - (c) cystic duct and pancreatic duct.
   - (d) hepatic duct and pancreatic duct.

5. The sphincter of Oddi is present between
   - (a) oesophagus and cardiac stomach.
   - (b) pyloric stomach and duodenum.
   - (c) hepatic duct and cystic duct.
   - (d) hepato-pancreatic duct and duodenum.

6. Succus entericus is a term used for
   - (a) the junction of ileum and colon
   - (b) inflammation of intestine
   - (c) vermiform appendix
   - (d) digestive juice of intestine

7. Oxyntic cells are located in
   - (a) Islets of langerhans.
   - (b) gastric epithelium and secrete pepsin.
   - (c) kidneys and secrete renin.
   - (d) gastric epithelium and secrete HCl.

8. Hydrochloric acid in the stomach is secreted by
   - (a) Chief cells
   - (b) Zymogen cells
   - (c) Parietal cells
   - (d) None of these

9. Rennin acts on milk protein and changes
   (a) caesinogen into caesin.
   (b) caesin into paracaesin.
   (c) caseinogen into paracaesin.
   (d) paracaesin into caesinogen.
10. Trypsin changes
    (a) fats into fatty acids.
    (b) proteins into peptones.
    (c) starch and glycogen into maltose.
    (d) maltose into its components.

Assertion & Reason Questions

DIRECTION (Qs. 1-5) : *These questions consists of two statements. Answer these questions selecting the appropriate option given below:*
(a) Both Assertion (A) and Reason (R) are true and Reason (R) is the correct explanation of Assertion (A).
(b) Both Assertion (A) and Reason (R) are true, but Reason (R) is not the correct explanation of Assertion (A).
(c) Assertion (A) is true, but Reason (R) is false.
(d) Assertion (A) is false, but Reason (R) is true.

1. **Assertion:** The amino acid glycine comes under the category of non-essential amino acids.
   Reason: This is due to the fact that it can not be synthesised in the body.
2. **Assertion:** Bile is not a true digestive juice.
   Reason: Bile lacks digestive enzymes.
3. **Assertion :** In human gut, small intestine is the smallest part of digestive system.
   Reason : Different type of food like proteins, fats and carbohydrates are digested completely in this smallest part of human alimentary canal.
4. **Assertion :** Presence of HCl in stomach is necessary for the process of digestion.
   Reason : HCl kills and inhibits the growth of bacteria in the stomach.
5. **Assertion :** Trypsin helps in digestion of blood of predator animals.
   Reason : Trypsin hydrolyses fibrinogen.

Case/Passage Based Questions

DIRECTIONS (Qs. 1-5) : *Read the following passage and answer the questions that follows.*

The inflammation of the intestinal tract is the most common ailment due to bacterial or viral infections. The infections are also caused by the parasites of the intestine like tapeworm, roundworm, threadworm, hookworm, pin worm, etc.

Jaundice – The liver is affected, skin and eyes turn yellow due to the deposit of bile pigments.

Vomitting – It is the ejection of stomach contents through the mouth. This reflex action is controlled by the vomit centre in the medulla. A feeling of nausea precedes vomiting.

Diarrhoea – The abnormal frequency of bowel movement and increased liquidity of the faecal discharge is known as diarrhoea. It reduces the absorption of food.

Constipation – in constipation, the faeces are retained within the colon as the bowel movements occur irregularly.

PEM – Protein-energy malnutrition (PEM) may affect large sections of the population during drought, famine and political turmoli. PEM affects infants and children to produce Marasmus and Kwashiorkar. Marasmus is produced by a simultaneous deficiency of proteins and calories. It is found in infants less than a year in age, if mother's milk is replaced too early by other foods which are poor in both proteins and caloric value. In Marasmus, protein deficiency impairs growth and replacement of tissue proteins; extreme emaciation of the body and thinning of limbs results, the skin becomes dry, thin and wrinkled. Kwashiorkar is produced by protein deficiency unaccompanied by calorie deficiency. It results from the replacement of mother's milk by a high calorie low protein diet in a child more than one year in age.

1. Identify the correct statements.
   (i) Jaundice cause skin and eyes turn yellow due to the deposit of bile.
   (ii) Diarrhoea reduces the absorption of food.
   (iii) In constipation bowel movements occur irregularly.
   (iv) Inadequate enzyme secretion, is one of the cause of indigestion.
   (a) (i) and (ii) are correct.   (b) (ii) and (iii) are correct.
   (c) (iii) and (iv) are correct. (d) All statement are correct.
2. The reflex actions of vomiting are controlled by the vomit centre present in the
   (a) Hypothalamus   (b) Hepatic lobules
   (c) Medulla   (d) Pancreas
3. Name any two protein energy malnutrition condition.
4. Define Marasmus disorder with suitable example.
5. Given an account of adverse effects of protein energy malnutrition.

Very Short Answer Questions

1. What type of medium as is required for activity of trypsin?
2. Which is the food constituent that bile helps to digest and absorb?
3. What is the function of enterokinase?
4. What are chylomicron?
5. Mention the role of bile salt in the digestion of fats.
6. What is the role of HCl in protein digestion?
7. Name the hardest substance in the body.
8. Where is caecum located in the alimentary canals?
9. Mention two functions of mucus.
10. Name the secretion of goblet cells in human stomach.
11. Where the taste buds located?
12. How is the tongue attached to the floor of the buccal cavity?
13. What is the function of epiglottis?
14. Which part of the stomach continues into the duodenum?

15. What name is given to the major lymph vessel present in the intestinal villi?
16. Where are crypts of Leiberkuhn located?
17. Name the structural and functional unit of liver.
18. What is sphincter of Oddi?
19. What is a bolus?
20. What is chyme?
21. What is the meaning of deglutition?
22. Name the enzyme involved in the breakdown of nucleotides into sugars and bases.

SHORT ANSWER QUESTIONS

1. If the pancreatic duct of a person is blocked, how would it affect the digestion of fat in the duodenum?
2. Name the organs which secretes carboxypeptidases and aminopeptidases respectively. Give the function performed by these enzymes.
3. Name the watery fluid secreted from Brunner's gland in the duodenum. Mention its any two characteristics. What role does it play inside duodenum?
4. What are microvilli? State their functions.
5. Differentiate between micelles and chylomicrons.
6. How is our gut lining protected from its own secretion of proteases?
7. What would happen if hydrochloric acid is not secreted in our stomach?
8. How does the nervous system control the activities of gastro-intestinal tract?
9. What are the basic layers of the wall of alimentary canal?
10. What is pancreas ? Mention the major secretions of pancreas that are helpful in digestion.

LONG ANSWER QUESTIONS

1. Draw a labelled human digestive system.
2. Describe the major disorders of the human digestive system.
3. How is the DNA content in our diet digested in the body?

SOLUTIONS

Multiple Choice Questions

1. **(b)** The membranes of the digestive tract are from the inside to the outside: *mucosa*, submucosa, circular longitudinal muscles and serosa.
2. **(a)** Crypts of Lieberkuhn are tubular invaginations of the epithelium around the villi, lined largely with younger epithelial cells which are involved primarily in secretion. They are present in the *intestine*. It consists of two secreting cells - *Paneth cells* (found in duodenum) and argentaffin cells.
3. **(a)** Bile is stored temporarily in gall bladder until it is needed by the small intestine to emulsify fats. After it leaves the gall blader, it enters into the *duodenum*.
4. **(b)** Bile is drained from the liver by a bile duct which is formed by the joining of a *cystic duct* from the gall bladder and a *common hepatic* duct from different liver lobes.
5. **(d)** The opening of hepato-pancreatic duct in the duodenum is guarded by *sphincter of Oddi*.
6. **(d)** *Succus entericus* refers to the digestive juice of intestine. It is the alkaline secretion produced by the intestinal glands in the wall of the duodenum. It consists of water, mucoproteins, and hydrogen carbonate ions. It helps to neutralize the highly acidic and proteolytic chyme which enters the small intestine from the stomach, and thus protects the duodenum from damage.
7. **(d)** Oxyntic cells are found on the *inner wall of gastric glands* and secrete HCl.
8. **(c)**
9. **(b)** *Rennin*, also known as chymosin, is a proteolytic enzyme and synthesized by *chief cells* in the stomach. Its role in digestion is to curdle or coagulate milk in the stomach. It acts on milk protein and changes casein into paracasein. If milk were not coagulated, it would rapidly flow through the stomach and miss the opportunity for initial digestion of its proteins.
10. **(b)** Trypsin, produced in the pancreas as the inactive protease trypsinogen, cleaves proteins into peptones. Trypsin cleaves peptide chains mainly at the carboxyl side of the amino acids lysine or arginine, except when either is followed by proline. It is used for numerous biotechnological processes.

Assertion & Reason

1. **(c)** Non essential amino acids are those amino acids which need not be supplied in the diet because they can be synthesised by the body, particularly from carbohydrate metabolites. Glycine is one such non essential amino acid. On the contrary, essential amino acids are those amino acids which can not be synthesised in the animal body and must be supplied with food in adequate amounts. Out of twenty amino acids, eight are considered essential in human diet.
2. **(a)** Bile contains bile pigments (billirubin and biliverdin), bile salts, cholesterol and phospholipids but no enzymes. Hence, it is not regarded as true digestive juice.
3. **(d)** Small intestine of the human gut is a narrow long tube. Because of its small diameter, it is called small intestine. Its length is according to the height of individual. It is the major site of digestion and absorption of different type of food. Digestion and absorption of various food is carried out in a particular part of small intestine, like absorption of iron takes place in proximal part of duodenum.

Food digestion starts from oral cavity in humans, which continues in stomach and is digested completely in small intestine. Undigested and unabsorbed food (faeces) is transferred to long intestine where the water and some vitamins are absorbed.

4. **(b)** Presence of hydrochloric acid in stomach is necessary for digestion because acidic medium activates the action of gastric juice. HCl maintains a strong acidic pH of about 1-2 in the stomach. At this acidic pH, inactive pepsinogen is spontaneously hydrolysed to active pepsin and inactive pro-rennin is converted to active rennin. Pepsin and rennin digest proteins to peptones and proteoses. In addition, HCl helps to kill and inhibit the growth of bacteria and other harmful organisms that may enter in the stomach along with the food.

5. **(a)** Trypsin is protein digesting enzyme present in the intestine of animals. Though it cannot digest casein (a milk protein), in predator animals drinking the blood of their prey, trypsin hydrolyses fibriongen of blood into fibrin, leading to blood coagulation thus, help in blood digestion. It also activates other pancreatic proteases.

Case/Passage Based Questions

1. **(d)** All the above statements are correct.

2. **(c)** The reflex actions of vomiting are controlled by the vomit centre present in the medulla.

3. Protein energy malnutrition leads to produce Marasmus and Kwashiorkar.

4. Marasmus is condition which is developed by a simultaneous deficiency of proteins and calories. It is found in infants less than a year in age, if mother's milk is replaced too early by other foods which are poor in both proteins and caloric value there is high possibility of developing Marasmus.

5. Adverse effects of PEM
- Marasmus protein deficiency impairs growth and replacement of tissue proteins; extreme emaciation of the body and thinning of limbs results, the skin becomes dry, thin and wrinkled. Growth rate and body weight decline considerably. Even growth and development of brain and mental faculties are impaired.
- Kwashiorkor shows wasting of muscles, thinning of limbs, failure of growth and brain development. Unlike marasmus, some fat is still left under the skin; moreover, extensive oedema and swelling of body parts are seen.

Very Short Answer Questions

1. Alkaline medium.

2. Fats.

3. Enterokinase of intestinal juice activates the inactive trypsinogen into trypsin which digest protein in duodenum.

4. The reconstructed triglycerides combine with phospholipids and cholesterol are released into the lymph in the form of protein coated water soluble fat globules or droplets. These are called chylomicron.

5. Bile salts emulsify fat particles and reduce surface tension of fat droplets for increase the action of enzyme lipase.

6. Role of HCl :
(i) It activates pepsinogen into active pepsin.
(ii) It provides a suitable acidic medium for the action of proteases in the stomach.

7. Enamel.

8. Caecum is located at the junction of small intestine and colon (large intestine).

9. Role of mucus :
(a) Acts as lubricant.
(b) Protects the epithelial surface of stomach from the corrosive effect of hydrochloric acid and digestion by pepsin.

10. Goblet cells secrete mucus.

11. Taste buds are located in the papillae on the upper surface of the tongue.

12. Tongue is attached to the floor of the buccal cavity by frenulum.

13. Epiglottis prevents the entry of food into the trachea, by closing its opening called glottis.

14. Pyloric region

15. Lacteal

16. Crypts of Lieberkuhn are located in between the bases of the villi in the intestine.

17. Hepatic lobules

18. Sphincter of Oddi is the muscular structure, that guards the opening of hepato-pancreatic duct into the duodenum.

19. When the thoroughly masticated food mixes with the saliva, the food particles become adhered together by the mucus known as bolus.

20. After partial digestion in the stomach, the form of food is called chyme.

21. The act of swallowing is called deglutition.

22. Nucleotidases : Nucleotide $\longrightarrow$ Nucleoside + Phosphate

Nucleosidases : Nucleoside $\longrightarrow$ Nitrogen base + Sugar

Short Answer Questions

1. If the pancreatic duct is blocked, the pancreatic juice cannot reach the duodenum. As a result the enzymes like trypsin, chymotrypsin, carboxypeptidase, aminopeptidase (help in the digestion of protein); amylase (help in carbohydrate digestion), lipase (help in fat digestion) could not reach the duodenum. Digestion of carbohydrates, proteins and fats will remain incomplete.

2. Carboxypeptidases are secreted by pancreas. Aminopeptidases are secreated by intestine. Both the enzymes act on the terminal peptide bonds and release the terminal/last amino acids of the peptide chain.

3. The watery fluid secreted by Brunner's gland is called mucoid fluid or mucus.

    Characteristics :

    (i)   It is viscous.   (ii) It is enzyme free

    (iii) It is alkaline in nature.

    Functions :

    It enable the duodenum to withstand the acidic chyme entering from the stomach.

4. Microvilli are bristle like extensions of the free surface of epithelial cells that line the surface of villi. They increase the surface area of epithelum for absorption of nutrients.

5. The differences between micelles and chylomicrons are

1.	The products of fat digestion are incorporated into small, spherical water soluble molecules called micelles with the help of bile salts and phospholipids.	1.	The products of fats digestion are used for synthesizing new fats which are released by the intestinal cells into the lymph, in the form of droplets called chylomicrons.
2.	This is the form in which digested fats are absorbed into intestinal cells.	2.	This is the form in which the synthesized fats are liberated from the intestinal cells.

6. (i)   Protease are secreted in inactive form and pose no threat to the gut lining.

    (ii) The mucus provides protection to the epithelial lining.

7. If hydrochloric acid is not secreted in the stomach, the following will happen :

    (i)   Pepsinogen will not be converted into pepsin.

    (ii) An acidic medium needed for the action of proteases will not be created.

    (iii) Salivary amylase may continue to function.

8. The sight, smell and presence of food in the oral cavity can stimulate the secretion of saliva. Gastric and intestinal secretions are also stimulated by similar neural signals. Muscular activities of alimentary canal is coordinated by both local and CNS neural mechanisms. Hormonal control of secretion of digestive enzymes is carried out by local hormones.

9. The wall of alimenatry canal consists of four main concentric layers. Beginning from outside, these layers are (i) visceral peritoneum (ii) muscular layer (iii) sub-mucosa and (iv) mucosa.

10. Pancreas is carrot-shaped soft greyish pink gland that lies transversely below stomach between duodenum and spleen, which secretes digestive enzymes from its exocrine parts and hormones from its endocrine parts.

    Pancreas secretes three enzymes in inactive proenzyme or zymogen state and three in active enzyme state.

    Proenzymes. Trypsinogen, chymotrypsinogen and procarboxypeptidases.

    Active Enzymes. Amylase, lipase and nucleases.

Long Answer Questions

1. 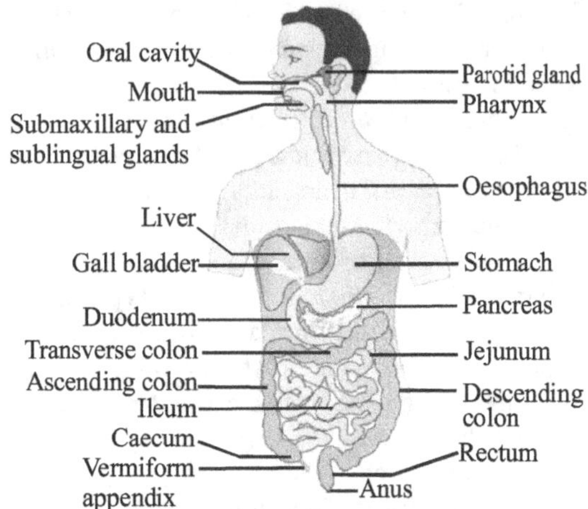

    The human digestive system

2. **Disorders of the digestive system :**

    (i) **Indigestion :**

    –   It is the condition in which the food is not properly digested leading to a feeling of fullness.

    –   It is caused by inadequate secretion of digestive enzymes, food poisoning, overeating or spicy food.

    (ii) **Constipation**

    –   It refers to the condition where the faeces are retained in the rectum for longer periods as the bowel movements occur irregularly.

    (iii) **Diarrhoea :**

    –   It refers to the abnormal frequency of bowel movement and increased liquidity of the faecal discharge; absorption of food is impaired.

    (iv) **Vomiting :**

    –   It is the ejection of stomach contents through the mouth; this reflex action is controlled by the vomit centre in the medulla.

    (v) **Jaundice :**

    –   It is due to viral infection, where liver is affected and digestion of fats is impaired.

    –   The eyes and skin turn yellow due to the deposit of bile pigments.

3. DNA content is digested in the intestinal part of our alimentary canal by the enzymes present in pancreatic juice and succus entericus.

$$DNA \xrightarrow[\text{enzyme}]{\text{Deoxyribonuclease}} Deoxyribonucleotides$$

$$Deoxyribonucleotides \xrightarrow[\text{enzyme}]{\text{Nucleosidase}} PO_4^+$$

Deoxyribonucleosides

$$Deoxyribonucleotides \xrightarrow[\text{Enzyme}]{\text{Nucleosidase}}$$

Deoxyribose + purine + pyrimidine

    DNAase is found in pancreatic juice while nucleotidase and nucleosidase occur in succus entericus and hydrolyse the DNA content in our diet.

MULTIPLE CHOICE QUESTIONS

1. Select what is not true of intestinal villi among following
   (a) they possess microvilli
   (b) they increase the surface area
   (c) they are supplied with capillaries and the lacteal vessels
   (d) they only participate in digestion of fats

2. Hepato-pancreatic duct opens into the duodenum and carries
   (a) bile
   (b) pancreatic juice
   (c) both bile and pancreatic juice
   (d) saliva

3. One of the following is not a common disorder associated with digestive system
   (a) Tetanus   (b) Diarrhoea
   (c) Jaundice   (d) Dysentery

4. A gland not associated with the alimentary canal is
   (a) pancreas   (b) adrenal
   (c) liver   (d) salivary glands

5. Match the enzyme with their respective substrate and choose the right one among options given.

	Column I		Column II
A.	Lipase	I.	Dipeptides
B.	Nuclease	II.	Fats
C.	Carboxypeptidase	III.	Nucleic acids
D.	Dipeptidases	IV.	Proteins, peptones and proteoses

   (a) A-II, B-III, C-I, D-IV
   (b) A-III, B-IV, C-II, D-I
   (c) A-III, B-I, C-IV, D-II
   (d) A-II, B-III, C-IV, D-I

6. Dental formula in human beings is

   (a) $\dfrac{3223}{3223}$ (b) $\dfrac{2123}{2123}$

   (c) $\dfrac{1232}{1232}$ (d) $\dfrac{2233}{2233}$

7. Liver is the largest gland and is associated with various functions, choose one which is not correct.
   (a) Metabolism of carbohydrate
   (b) Digestion of fat
   (c) Formation of bile
   (d) Secretion of hormone called gastrin

8. Mark the right statement among the following
   (a) Trypsinogen is an inactive enzyme
   (b) Trypsinogen is secreted by intestinal mucosa
   (c) Enterokinase is secreted by pancreas
   (d) Bile contains trypsin

VERY SHORT ANSWER QUESTIONS

1. The food mixes thoroughly with the acidic gastric juice of the stomach by the churning movements of its muscular wall. What do we call the food then?

2. Trypsinogen is an inactive enzyme of pancreatic juice. An enzyme, enterokinase, activates it. Which tissue/cells secrete this enzyme?/ How is it activated?

3. In which part of alimentary canal does absorption of water, simple sugars and alcohol takes place?

4. Name the enzyme involved in the breakdown of nucleotides into sugars and bases?

5. What do we call the type of teeth attachment to jaw bones in which each tooth is embedded in a socket of jaws bones?

6. Stomach is located in upper left portion of the abdominal cavity and has three major parts. Name these three parts.

7. Does gall bladder make bile?

8. Correct the following statements by deleting one of entries (given in bold).
   (a) Goblet cells are located in the intestinal mucosal epithelium and secrete chymot-rypsin/mucus.
   (b) Fats are broken down into di-and monog-lycerides with the help of amylase/lipases.
   (c) Gastric glands of stomach mucosa have oxyntic cell/chief which secrete HCl.
   (d) Saliva contains enzymes that digest starch/protein.

SHORT ANSWER QUESTIONS

1. What is pancreas? Mention the major secretions of pancreas that are helpful in digestion.

2. Name the part of the alimentary canal where major absorption of digested food takes place. What are the absorbed forms of different kinds of food materials?

3. List the organs of human alimentary canal and name the major digestive glands with their location.

4. What are three major types of cells found in the gastric glands? Name their secretions.

5. How is the intestinal mucosa protected from the acidic food entering from stomach?

LONG SHORT ANSWER QUESTIONS

1. A person had roti and dal for his lunch. Trace the changes in those during its passage through the alimentary canal.

   $$\alpha - \text{Dextrins} \xrightarrow{\alpha-\text{dextrinose}} \text{Glucose}$$

2. Discuss mechanisms of absorption.

SOLUTIONS

Multiple Choice Questions

1. **(d)** **Intestinal** villi do not participate in the digestion of fats but help in their **absorption** and absorption of various other food substances such as **water, mineral, salts, amino acids, vitamins,** etc.

2. **(c)** The **hepatic duct** from the liver and the duct of **gall bladder** form the **common bile duct**. The bile duct and the pancreatic duct together open into the duodenum as a common hepato-pancreatic duct which carries both **bile** and **pancreatic juice**.

3. **(a)** **Tetanus** is a medical condition characterised by a prolonged contraction of the skeletal muscle fibres. This disorder is not associated with digestive system.

4. **(b)** **Adrenal gland** is present at the anterior part of each kidney acting as an endocrine gland, involved in regulating body growth and developmental mechanisms. It is not associated with the alimentary canal.

5. **(d)** **Lipase** is an enzyme that digests fat.
   Nuclease digests nucleic acid.
   Carboxypeptidase are the enzymes involved in the digestion of proteins, peptones and proteases.
   Dipeptidases are the enzymes that break dipeptides into **amino acids**.

6. **(b)** An adult human possesses 32 permanent teeth which are of four different types, namely **Incisors** (I), **Canine** (C), **Premolar** (PM) and **Molar** (M). Arrangement of teeth in each half of the upper and lower jaw in the order I, C, PM, M is represented by a dental formula, which in humans is $\dfrac{2123}{2123}$.

7. **(d)** Liver is involved in the production of bile, which helps in the digestion of fats in the small intestine by the **emulsification process** (conversion of large fat droplets into small ones).
   Liver also plays a critical role in controlling rate metabolism by maintaining the glucose concentration in the normal range. Gastrin is secreted by G-cells in the pyrolic region of stomach. It stimulates gastric glands to secrete and release gastric juices.

8. **(a)** **Trypsinogen** is an inactive pancreatic enzyme that is activated by enterokinase, an enzyme secreted by intestinal mucosa. Active form of trypsinogen is called trypsin, which in turn activates other enzymes present in the pancreatic juice.

Very Short Answer Questions

1. For 4-5 hours, the food is stored in stomach and gets thoroughly mixed with the acidic gastric juice of stomach by the churning movements of its muscular wall. The food at this stage is called as chyme.

2. Trypsinogen is activated to trypsin in the presence of which enzyme enterkinase is secreted by the intestinal mucosa.

3. The absorption of water, simple sugars, alcohol and some lipid soluble drugs take place by the stomach wall.

4. The enzymes nucleotidases and nucleosidases are involved in the breakdown of nucleotides into sugars and bases.

$$\text{Nucleotides} \xrightarrow{\text{Nucleotidases}} \text{Nucleosides}$$

$$\xrightarrow{\text{Nucleosidases}} \text{Sugars + Bases}$$

5. The type of attachment where teeth are embedded in the socket of jaw bone is called thecodont.

6. The three major of stomach are cardio, fundus and pylorus.

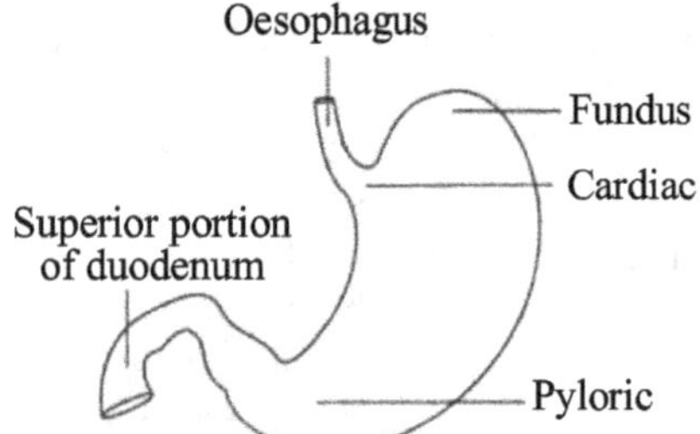

Outline structure of stomach

7. Gall bladder is involved in the storage of bile and not associated with the bile formation rather, bile is secreted and from the hepatic cells of the liver.

8. (a) Goblet cells are located in the intestinal mucosal epithelium and secrete mucus.

   (b) Fats are broken down into di and monoglycerides with the help of lipases.

   $$\text{Fats} \xrightarrow{\text{Lipases}} \text{Diglycerides} \longrightarrow \text{Monoglycerides.}$$

   (c) Gastric glands of stomach mucosa have oxyntic cells which secrete HCl

   (d) Saliva contains enzymes that digest starch

   $$\text{Starch} \xrightarrow[\text{pH 6.8}]{\text{Salivar yamylase}} \text{Maltose + Isomaltose} + \alpha - \text{dextrins}$$

Short Answer Questions

1. The pancreas is both exocrine and as well as gland endocrine situated between the limbs of 'U' shaped duodenum.

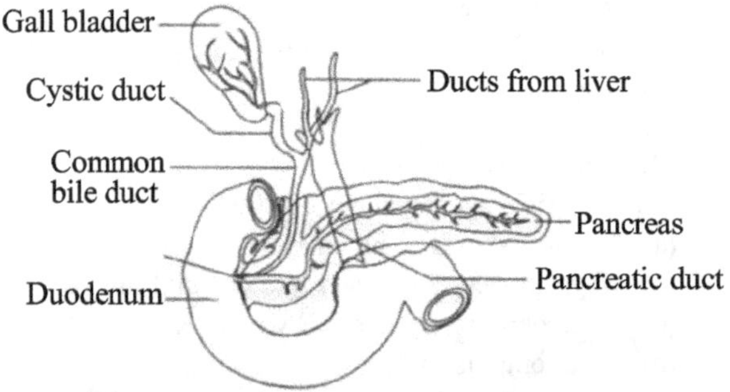

Diagrammatic representation of pancreas

Internal structure of pancreas consist of two parts, i.e., the exocrine and endocrine part.

(i) Exocrine part consists of rounded lobules called acini, that secretes alkaline pancreatic juice of pH 8.4 and is mainly involved in the digestion of starch, proteins, fats and nucleic acids.

(ii) Endocrine part secretes hormones like, insulin and glucagon that regulate glucose metabolism.

2. The principle organ for the absorption of nutrients small intestine is the proces's of digestion complete here and the final products of digestion are absorbed through the mucosa into the blood stream.

The absorbed form of different food materials are

Food Material	Absorbed Form
Carbohydrate	Glucose
Protein	Amino acid
Fat	Fatty acid

3. Human digestive system consists of two main parts: alimentary canal and digestive glands. The organ of human alimentary canal are mouth, pharynx oesophagus, stomach, small intestine, large intestine, rectum and anus. Major digestive glands with their locations are as follows :

Digestive glands	Location in body
Salivary Gland	It is located in buccopharyngeal cavity
Gastric Gland	Inner epithelial lining of the stomach wall
Liver	In the abdominal cavity below the diaphragm
Pancreas	Between the limbs of U shaped duodenum

4. Following are the three major types of cells found in gastric glands.

(i) Mucous cells (Goblet cells) are involved in the secretin of mucus and are present throughout the epithelium of gastrointestinal tract.

(ii) Peptic of Chief cells (Zymogenic cells) are Involved in the secretion of gastric enzymes such as proenzymes pepsinogen and prorenin and usually basal in location.

(iii) Parietal or oxyntic cells are large and most numerous present on the side walls of the gastric glands. They are involved in the secretion of HCl and Castlis intrinsci Factor (CIF).

5. The intestinal mucosal epithelium has goblet cell which secrete mucus. The mucus along with bicarbonate present in the gastric juice help in lubrication and protection of mucosal epithelium from the acidic food entering from the stomach.

Long Answer Questions

1. Digestion of Roti (Carbohydrates)

(a) Digestion of Carbohydrates in the Oral Cavity

In oral cavity, the roti get mixed with saliva that contains an enzyme salivary amylase (ptyalin), which converts starch of roti into maltose, isomaltose and small dextrins called α – dextrin. 30% of starch is hydrolysed in the oral cavity.

$$\text{Starch} \xrightarrow[\text{pH 6.8}]{\text{Salivary Amylase}} \text{Maltose} + \text{Isomaltose} + \alpha - \text{Dextrins}$$

(b) Digestion of Carbohydrates in the Small Intestine

The partially digested roti passes from oral cavity to oesophagus and then reaches to stomach by peristalsis. The stomach stores the food for 4-5 hours. The gastric juice does not contain carbohydrate digesting enzyme. The partially digested food is now called as chyme. In intestine, following action occurs.

(i) Action of Pancreatic Juice – Carbohydrates in the chyme are hydrolysed by pancreatic amylase into disaccharides.

$$\text{Polysaccharides(starch)} \xrightarrow{\text{Amylase}} \text{Disaccharides}$$

(ii) Action of Intestinal Juice – Intestinal Juice contain maltase, isomaltase, sucrase (invertase), lactase and α – dextrinase. In the presence of these enzymes food is converted into simpler compounds like glucose, fructose, galactose, etc.

$$\text{Maltose} \xrightarrow{\text{Maltase}} \text{Glucose} + \text{Glucose}$$

$$\text{Isomaltose} \xrightarrow{\text{Isomaltase}} \text{Glucose} + \text{Glucose}$$

$$\text{Sucrose} \xrightarrow{\text{Sucrase}} \text{Glucose} + \text{Fructose}$$

$$\text{Lactose} \xrightarrow{\text{Lactase}} \text{Glucose} + \text{Galactose}$$

$$\alpha - \text{Dextrins} \xrightarrow{\alpha-\text{dextrinose}} \text{Glucose}$$

Digestion of Protein

Proteins are made up of amino acids. So proteins are broken down to amino acid during the process of digestion.

Saliva lacks any protein digesting enzyme so, digestion starts further in stomach.

(a) Digestion of Protein in Stomach. The stomach normally stores food for 4-5 hours. The gastric glands of the stomach secrete gastric juice that contains HCl, proenzymes like-pepsinogen and prorennin. Various reactions in stomach are discussed bwlow.

$$\underset{\text{(proenzyme)}}{\text{Pepsinogen}} \xrightarrow{\text{HCl}} \text{Pepsin}$$

$$\text{Proteins} \xrightarrow{\text{Pepsin}} \text{Peptones and proteoses}$$

$$\underset{\text{(Proenzyme)}}{\text{Prorennin}} \xrightarrow{\text{HCl}} \text{Rennin}$$

(b) Digestion of Protein in Small Intestine

    (i) Action of Pancreatic Juice – The enzymes trypsinogen, chymotrypsinogen and procarboxypeptidase in pancreatic juice are all concerned with the protein digestion.

$$\text{Trypsinogen} \xrightarrow{\text{Enterokinase}} \text{Trypsin}$$

$$\text{Proteins} \xrightarrow{\text{Trypsin}} \text{Dipeptides}$$

$$\text{Chymotrypsinogen} \xrightarrow{\text{Trypsin}} \text{Chymotrypsin}$$

$$\text{Peptones} \xrightarrow{\text{Chymotrypsin}} \text{Dipeptides}$$

$$\text{Procarboxypeptidase} \xrightarrow{\text{Trypsin}} \text{Carboxypeptidases}$$

$$\text{Proteoses} \xrightarrow{\text{Carboxypeptidases}} \text{Dipeptides}$$

    (ii) Action of Intestinal Juice – Intestinal juice contain enzymes enterokinase, amino peptidase and dipeptidase.

$$\text{Peptides} \xrightarrow{\text{Amino peptidase}} \text{Amino acid}$$

$$\text{Dipeptides} \xrightarrow{\text{Dipeptidase}} \text{Amino acid}$$

The macromolecules are broken down into simpler components are the products of roti and dal (carbohydrates and proteins) which are further absorbed by the villi in small intestine and the rest undigested food is removed in the form of faeces by large intestine.

2. Absorption is a process by which the end product of digestion passes through the intestinal mucosa into the blood or lymph. It is carried out by passive, active or facilitated transport mechanism. Small amount of monosaccharide like glucose, amino acids and some electrolytes like chloride ions are absorbed by simple diffusion. Some of the substance like fructose and some amino acids are absorbed with the help of the carrier ions like Na^+ are absorbed by the active transport. Fatty acid and glycerol are insoluble, thus they cannot be absorbed by the blood. They are first incorporated into small droplets called micelles which move into the intestinal mucosa. They are reformed into very small protein coated fat globules called chylomicrons which are transported into the lacteals of the villi. The lacteals ultimately release the absorbed substance into the blood stream. The maximum absorption of food takes place in small intestine.

17.1 Define vital capacity. What is its significance?

Sol. The maximum volume of air a person can breathe in after a forced expiration. This includes ERV, TV and IRV or the maximum volume of air a person can breathe out after a forced inspiration.

It represent the maximum amount of air one can renew in the respiratory system in a single respiration. Thus, greater the vital capacity more is the energy available to the body for doing strenous work. Vital capacity is higher in athletes and mountain dwellers. Young persons would possess more vital capacity as compared to children or older persons.

17.2 State the volume of air remaining in the lungs after a normal breathing.

Sol. Volume of air remaining in lungs after a normal respiration is called functional residual capacity. It includes ERV + RV = Expiratory reserve volume + residual volume

17.3 Diffusion of gases occurs in the alveolar region only and not in the other parts of respiratory system. Why ?

Sol. Alveoli are the primary sites of exchange of gases. Alveolar region is having enough pressure gradient to facilitate diffusion of gases. Other regions of the respiratory sytsem don't have the required pressure gradient. Additionally the membrane of alveoli is thin enough to facilitate exchange of gases in a convenient manner.

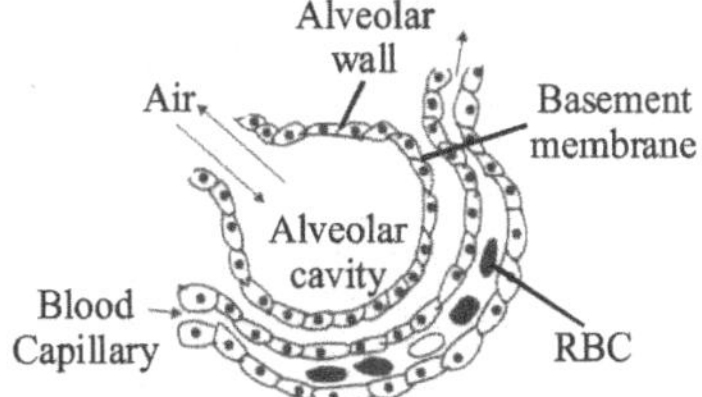

Exchange of gases in alveoli

17.4 What are the major transport mechanisms for CO_2 ? Explain.

Sol. Transport of carbon dioxide : About 4 ml of carbon dioxide is transported by every 100 ml of blood.

CO_2 is transported in three forms in the blood.

(i) In the dissolved form in plasma about 7% of CO_2 dissolves in plasma of blood, just as it gets dissolved in water.

(ii) As bicarbonates

- Erythrocytes have a high concentration of the enzyme, carbonic anhydrase which catalyses the following reactions;

$$CO_2 + H_2O \rightleftharpoons H_2CO_3$$
$$H_2CO_3 \rightleftharpoons H^+ + HCO_3^-$$

About 70% of CO_2 is transported as bicarbonates.

(iii) As carbaminohaemoglobin

- CO_2 combines with of the globin part of haemoglobin and forms carbamino haemoglobin. About 23% of CO_2 transported in this manner.

17.5 What will be the pO_2 and pCO_2 in the atmospheric air compared to those in the alveolar air ?

(i) pO_2 lesser, pCO_2 higher

(ii) pO_2 higher, pCO_2 lesser

(iii) pO_2 higher, pCO_2 higher

(iv) pO_2 lesser, pCO_2 lesser

Sol. (ii) pO_2 higher, pCO_2 lesser

pO_2 higher will create the pressure gradient to facilitate the movement of O_2 from atmosphere to alveoli and pCO_2 lesser will create the movement of CO_2 from alveoli to atmosphere.

17.6 Explain the process of inspiration under normal conditions.

Sol. Inspiration occurs when pressure within lungs is less than the atmospheric pressure, *i.e.*, there is a negative pressure in the lungs with respect to atmospheric pressure.

Inspiration is initiated by the contraction of diaphram which increases the volume of thoracic chamber in the antero-posterior axis. The contraction of external inter-costal muscles lifts up the ribs and the sternum causing an increase in the volume of a thoracic chamber in the dorso-ventral axis. The overall increase in thoracic volume causes a similar increase in pulmonary volume. An increase in pulmonary volume decreases the intra pulmonary pressure to less than atmospheric pressure which forces the air from outside to move into the lungs *i.e.*, inspiration.

17.7 How is respiration regulated ?

Sol. Respiratory rhythm centre, present in medulla region of brain is responsible for respiration regulation. Its function can be moderate by pneumotaxic centre, present in pons region of brain. A chemosensitive area present adjacent to rhythm centre, is highly sensitive to CO_2 and H^+. Chemosenstive centre due to increase in CO_2 and H^+ can signal the rhythm centre to make adjustment to eliminate these substances. Receptors associated with aortic arch and carotid artery also can recognise changes in CO_2 and H^+ concentration and send necessary signals to rhythm centre for remedial actions.

17.8 What is the effect of pCO$_2$ on oxygen transport?

Sol. At low pCO$_2$,blood can carry the maximum amount of oxygen as oxyhaemoglobin. At high pCO$_2$, the affinity for oxygen decreases and oxyhaemoglobin dissociates to free oxygen.

$$Hb_4O_8 \xrightarrow{H^+,CO_2} Hb_4 + 4O_2$$

So at high pCO$_2$, oxygen transport is inhibited.

17.9 What happens to the respiratory process in a man going up a hill ?

Sol. When a man is going uphill or doing some strenuous exercise then there is more consumption of oxygen. This decreases the partial pressure of oxygen in haemoglobin resulting in more demand of haemoglobin. As a result there is an increased breathing rate to fill the gap.

17.10 What is the site of gaseous exchange in an insect ?

Sol. Insect have a complex system of intercommunicating air tubes called tracheae to enable them to exchange gases between the environment and the body cells (tracheal respiration).

17.13 Distinguish between

    (a)   **IRV and ERV**

    (b)   **Inspiratory capacity and Expiratory capacity.**

    (c)   **Vital capacity and Total lung capacity.**

Sol.

17.11 Define oxygen dissociation curve. Can you suggest any reason for its sigmoidal pattern?

Sol. Oxygen dissociation curve: It is graphic respresentation of relationship between partial pressure of oxygen or pO$_2$ and percentage saturation of haemoglobin with oxygen. The graph is sigmoid as at low pO$_2$, there is reduced synthesis of oxyhaemoglobin. Percentage of oxyhaemoglobin rises with higher pO$_2$ till at about pO$_2$ is 100mm Hg, the haemoglobin becomes fully saturated with O$_2$. Further rise in pO$_2$ cannot increase the value of oxyhaem-oglobin as the blood is already saturated with it.

17.12 Have you heard about hypoxia ? Try to gather information about it, and discuss with your friends.

Sol. Hypoxia refers to shortage of oxygen supply to the body. It is of different types : 1. Anaemic hypoxia (deficiency of haemoglobin), 2. Cytotoxic hypoxia (impaired utilization as in cyanide poisoning) 3. Stagnant hypoxia. Due to heart failure or reduced pumping activity of heart. 4. Hypoxic hypoxia. Insufficient oxygen in air as at high altitude. 5. CO Poisoning. Carbon monoxide binds to haemoglobin irreversibly. Oxygen transport is correspondingly reduced.

IRV	ERV
1. It is extra volume of air, a person can inspire forcefully beyond normal tidal volume.	1. It is the extra volume of air that can be breathed out beyond the normal tidal volume.
2. It is about 2500-3000 mL.	2. It is about 1000-1100 mL.
Inspiratory capacity (ic)	**Expiratory capacity (ec)**
1. It is the total volume of air that can be inhaled forcefully after a normal expiration.	1. It is the total volume of air that can be exhaled forcefully after a normal inspiration.
2. It is the sum total of tidal volume and inspiratory reserve (TV + IRV) volume	2. It is the sum total of tidal volume and expiratory reserve volume (TV + ERV)
Vital capacity	**Total lung capacity**
1. It is the amount of air which can be maximum inspired and also maxium expired.	1. It is the total amount of air present in the lungs and the respiratory passage after a maximum inspiration.
2. It is the sum of tidal volume, inspiratory reserve volume and expiratory reserve volume.	2. It is the sum of the vital capacity and residual volume.
3. It varies from 3400 to 4800 mL.	3. It varies from 5000 to 6000 mL.

17.14 What is tidal volume ? Find out the tidal volume (approximate value) for a healthy human in an hour.

Sol. Volume of air inspired/breath during normal respiration. It is approximate 500mL.Number of breaths per minute 12 to 16.

    Tidal volume per minute = 500 × 12 to 16

                   = 6000 – 8000 mL or 6 –8 litres

    Tidal volume per hour = 6 to 8 × 60 = 360 – 480 litres.

| **SECTION B** | # PRACTICE QUESTIONS  |

MULTIPLE CHOICE QUESTIONS

1. The structure which does not contribute to the breathing movements in mammals is
(a) larynx (b) ribs
(c) diaphragm (d) intercostal muscles

2. Even when there is no air in it, human trachea does not collapse due to presence of
(a) bony rings (b) turgid pressure
(c) chitinous rings (d) cartilaginous rings

3. Which of the following are the stages of respiration in correct order?
I. Gaseous transport II. Cellular respiration
III. Tissue respiration IV. Breathing
(a) I – IV – III – II (b) IV – I – III – II
(c) IV – I – II – III (d) IV – III – II – I

4. When 1200 mL air is left in the lungs, it is called
(a) vital capacity
(b) tidal volume
(c) residual volume
(d) inspiratory reserve volume

5. Functional residual capacity can be represented as
(a) TV + ERV (b) ERV + RV
(c) RV + IRV (d) ERV + TV + IRV

6. O_2 dissociation curve is plotted between pO_2 and ....
(a) % Hb saturation (b) pCO_2
(c) Hb concentration (d) RBC/mm^3 of blood

7. CO_2 combines with Hb to form :
(a) Carbaminohaemoglobin (b) Carboxy haemoglobin
(c) Oxyhaemoglobin (d) Methaemoglobin

8. Dissociation of oxyhaemoglobin can be promoted by
(a) low pCO_2 (b) high pCO_2
(c) low body temperature (d) high blood pH

9. Dissociation curve shifts to the right when
(a) pH increases.
(b) CO_2 concentration increases.
(c) O_2 concentration decreases.
(d) 2,3 D-P-G decreases.

10. When, under certain conditions, the P_{50} value of haemoglobin rises, the affinity of the pigment of combining with O_2 will
(a) remain same (b) rise
(c) fall (d) first rise and then fall

ASSERTION & REASON QUESTIONS

DIRECTION (Qs. 1-5) : *These questions consists of two statements. Answer these questions selecting the appropriate option given below:*
(a) Both Assertion (A) and Reason (R) are true and Reason (R) is the correct explanation of Assertion (A).
(b) Both Assertion (A) and Reason (R) are true, but Reason (R) is not the correct explanation of Assertion (A).
(c) Assertion (A) is true, but Reason (R) is false.
(d) Assertion (A) is false, but Reason (R) is true.

1. **Assertion :** Expiration is the process by which the alveolar air is released out.
Reason : The relaxation of diaphragm and intercostal muscles leads to the process of expiration.

2. **Assertion :** Volume of air inspired a forcible inspiration is called tidal volume.
Reason : Additional volume of air a person can expire by a forcible expiration is called Expiratory Reserve Volume.

3. **Assertion :** Many visitors to the hills suffer from skin and respiratory allergical problems.
Reason : Conifer trees produce a large quantity of wind-borne pollen grains.

4. **Assertion :** The respiratory rhythm centre, present in the medulla is responsible for respiration regulation.
Reason : The function of respiratory rhythm centre is moderated by pneumotaxic centre.

5. **Assertion :** Oxyhaemoglobin dissociates near the organ tissue due to Bohr's effect and oxygen is released.
Reason : Increased CO_2 concentration reduces the affinity of haemoglobin for oxygen.

CASE/PASSAGE BASED QUESTIONS

DIRECTIONS (Qs. 1-5) : *Read the following passage and answer the questions that follows.*

Ravi is a chain smoker and all his friends know about his habit. One day he started experiencing problems such as short breadth. He decided to consult a doctor and open consultation he revealed that he was a chain smoker.

1. Which of the following disorders is he diagonesed with
(a) Asthma (b) Emphysema
(c) Tuberculosis (d) Asphysia

2. Which of following is damaged in emphysema patients.
(a) Trachea (b) Larynx
(c) Alveolar walls (d) Nasal passage

3. Why is damange of alveoliar walls presented with serious consequences such as emphysema?
(a) alveoli receives rich blood supply provided by a rich network of interconnected capillaries.
(b) act as site of diffusion of O_2 & CO_2.
(c) the alveolar wall is also known as diffusion membrane or respiratory membrane that enables the exchanges of gases.
(d) All the above

4. Choose the correct option:
(A) alveoli has high pO_2 and pCO_2
(B) diffusion of gases donot depend on the respiratory membrane
(C) diffusion depends only on the difference in partial pressure of O_2 and CO_2 in blood and tissues.
(D) the binding of O_2 to haemoglobin is inclusive of pCO_2, H^+ ion concentration andv temperature
(a) A & C (b) A, C & D
(c) A, B, C (d) Only A

5. With reference to the conditions in the alveoli choose the right options

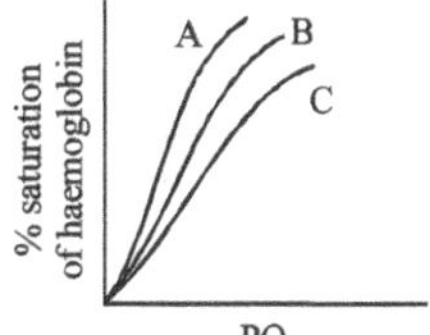

(a) A-low pCO_2, B-normal blood pCO_2, C-high blood pCO_2
(b) A-normal temperature, B-high temperature, C-low temperature
(c) A-A & B
(d) None of the above

VERY SHORT ANSWER QUESTIONS

1. Name the enzyme which catalyses the bicarbonate formation in RBC's.
2. What is carbamino haemoglobin ?
3. What is tidal volume?
4. What term is used for the volume of air left in the lungs even after the most powerful expiration?
5. Name the respiratory organ of
   (a) Butterfly and   (b) Frog larva.
6. What is the role of oxyhaemoglobin after releasing molecular oxygen in the tissue?
7. What are the two factors that contribute for the dissociation of oxyhaemoglobin in the atrial blood to release molecular oxygen in active tissue?
8. Name the double-walled sac which covers the lungs in mammals.
9. What prevents the collapsing of our trachea during breathing?
10. Define inspiratory reserve volume.
11. Which part(s) of the brain control(s) breathing movements?
12. What is oxyhaemoglobin?
13. How much of oxygen is transported by 100 ml of blood under normal physiological conditions?
14. Write the chemical reaction catalysed by enzyme carbonic anhydrase.
15. How does penumotaxic centre alter the respiratory rate?
16. What is the percentage of CO_2 transported as sodium bicarbonate?
17. What will happen if the human blood becomes acidic?

SHORT ANSWER QUESTIONS

1. Write four conditions necessary to facilitates efficient gaseous exchange between human respiratory surface and environment.
2. Differentiate between pharynx and larynx.
3. Why is haemoglobin called conjugated protein? What happen to the molecule at high and low partial pressure of oxygen?
4. Differentiate between inspiratory capacity and expiratory capacity.
5. Diffusion of gases occurs in the alveolar region only and not in the other parts of the respiratory system. Why ?
6. What percentage of oxygen is transported by erythrocytes in the blood? What happens to the remaining?
7. What is asthma? Explain.
8. What is the emphysema? What is its major cause?
9. Draw a labelled diagram of a section of an alveolus with a pulmonary capillary.
10. What will happen if the patient has been inhaling polluted air containing high content of CO?
11. What is pneumonia? What are its causes?

LONG ANSWER QUESTIONS

1. What do you mean by occupational lung disease? Enumerate the prevention measure that should be adopted by a person likely to be exposed to substances that cause occupational diseases ?
2. Explain the regulation of respiration by nervous system.
3. How does exchange of respiratory gases take place in the alveoli or lungs ?
4. How are inspiration and expiration take place in human ?

SOLUTIONS

Multiple Choice Questions

1. **(a)** Though larynx is a part of air passage connecting the pharynx with trachea it does not contribute to the breathing movements. A cartilaginous larynx (sound box or voice box) helps in sound production.
2. **(d)** Trachea is a membranous tube supported by "C" shaped cartilage ring. The cartilage ring protects the trachea from collapse and injury.
3. **(b)** The correct sequence of stages of respiration is: breathing-gaseous transport- tissue respiration- Cellular respiration.
4. **(c)** Residual volume (RV) is the volume of air remaining in lungs even after a forcible expiration. It is about 1100-1200 ml.
5. **(b)** Functional residual capacity is the volume of air remaining in the lungs after a normal expiration (ERV + RV). It is about 2100-2300 ml.
6. **(a)**   7.   **(a)**
8. **(b)** The higher concentration of pCO_2 stimulates dissociation of oxyhaemoglobin.
9. **(b)** When the relationship between the pO_2 and the percent saturation of haemoglobin is represented on a graph, then it is termed as oxygen - haemoglobin dissociation curve. A rise in pCO_2, H^+ ions (fall in pH), temperature and diphosphoglyceric acid raises the p50 value and shifts the oxygen - dissociation curve to right or vice versa.
10. **(c)** The affinity of the haemoglobin pigment of combining with O_2 will fall, when the p50 value of the haemoglobin rises.

Assertion & Reason Questions

1. **(a)** The relaxation of diaphragm and intercostal muscles returns the diaphragm and sternum to their normal positions and reduce the thoracic volume and thereby the pulmonary volume. This leads to an increase in intra-pulmonary pressure to slightly above the atmospheric pressure causing expiration.
2. **(d)** Tidal volume refers to the volume of air inspired or expired during a normal respiration. The additional volume of air a person can expire by a forcible expiration is called Expiratory Reserve Volume (ERV). Residual volume refers to the volume of air remaining in the lungs even after a forcible expiration.
3. **(b)** The skin problem could be due to pollen allergy and respiratory problem could be due to the decrease in oxygen content, since the atmosphere becomes thin as one goes up the hill.
4. **(a)** The pnemotaxic centre is present in the pons region of brain.
5. **(a)** Bohrs effect is the effect of CO_2 on oxyhaemoglobin. Body tissues obtain oxygen from oxyhaemoglobin because of its dissociation caused by low O_2 and high CO_2 concentration. The increased CO_2 concentration reduces the affinity of haemoglobin for oxygen.

Case/Passage Based Questions

1. **(b)** Emphysema is characterised by shortness of breadth and is due to chain smoking.
2. **(c)** The alveolar walls are damaged in emphysema patients.
3. **(d)** All the reasons listed are important and due to this a damage in alveolar wall lead to decrease in respiratory surface area.
4. **(b)** **(A, C, D)** The exchange of gases in alveoli depends on high pO_2 and low CO_2. The gases diffuse by simple diffusion which occurs on the alveolar membrane and is influenced by factors such as high pO_2, low pCO_2, H^+ ion concentration & temperature.
5. **(a)** The graph depicts effect of pCO_2 on oxygen affinity for haemoglobin, whose binding takes place in the alveolar wall.

Very Short Answer Questions

1. Enzyme carbonic anhydrase.
2. It is a complex formed by the combination of carbondioxide with the globin part of haemoglobin.
3. The volume of air inspired or expired with every normal breath during effortless respiration is called tidal volume.
4. Residual volume.
5. (i) Butterfly - trachea   (ii) Frog larva - gills.
6. Oxyhaemoglobin after releasing oxygen collects carbon dioxide from the tissue and form carbaminohaemoglobin.
7. The two factors are :
   (a) Low pO_2 (b) High pCO_2
8. Pleura.
9. C-shaped cartilages at regular intervals.
10. The extra volume of air that can be inspired beyond the normal tidal volume, is called inspiratory reserve volume.
11. Medulla and pons.
12. Oxyhaemoglobin is a complex formed when oxygen combies with the Fe^{2+} part of haemoglobin.
13. About 5 mL.
14. Carbonic anhydrase catalyses the following reaction :

$$CO_2 + H_2O \rightleftharpoons H_2CO_3 \rightleftharpoons H^+ + HCO_3^-$$

$$H_2CO_3 \rightleftharpoons H^+ + HCO_3^-$$

15. Pneumotaxic centre can reduce the duration of inspiration and alter the respiratory rate.
16. 70% of CO_2 is transported as sodium bicarbonate.
17. Oxygen carrying capacity of haemoglobin will decrease.

Short Answer Questions

1. Conditions for efficient gas exchange are as followings :
   (a) The membrane should be thin.
   (b) It should be highly vascularized.
   (c) It should be highly permeable to gases.
   (d) There should a partial pressure difference on both sides of lung.
2. The main differences between pharynx and larynx are as followings :

	Pharynx		Larynx
1.	It is lined by squamous epithelium.	1.	It is lined mainly by ciliated columnar epithelium.
2.	It lacks cartilage.	2.	It is made up of a hyoid bone and some cartilage.
3.	Oral cavity and nasal chamber open into it.	3.	Pharynx opens into it through glottis.
4.	It is crossing centre for food and air.	4.	It is a sound producing organ.

3. Haemoglobin : It is called conjugated protein because it consists of a basic protein globin and a non-protein heme. The haemoglobin when exposed to high partial pressure of oxygen combines with oxygen to form oxyhaemoglobin which carries 4 molecules of oxygen loosely bound to the four Fe^{2+} ions. When this oxyhaemoglobin reaches the tissues where there is low oxygen pressure oxyhaemoglobin dissociates into oxygen and deoxyhaemoglobin.
4. The differences between inspiratory and expiratory capacity are :

Oxyhaemoglobin	Carbaminohaemoglobin
It is formed by the combination of oxygen with the Fe^{2+} part of haemoglobin	It is formed by the combination of carbon dioxide with the amine radical of haemoglobin.
Its formation occurs on the alveolar surface.	Its formation occurs in the tissues.

5. The alveoli have very thin walls consisting of squamous epithelium. The alveolar wall is provided with as extensive network of blood capillaries; due to the intimate contact of the blood capillareis and alveolar wall, there is exchange of gases taking place easily. In the other part the membrane/wall is not so thin to allow for diffusion.
6. About 97% of the oxygen is transported by erthyrocytes. The remaining 3% is transported in dissolved form in the plasma.
7. Asthma : It is the hypersensitivity of bronchioles to any foreign substance, characterised by the spasm of the smooth muscles of the walls of the bronchioles.
8. Emphysema : Emphysema is a chronic disorder is which alveolar walls are damaged and hence the surface area for exchange of gases is reduced. It is caused mainly by cigarette smoking.
9.

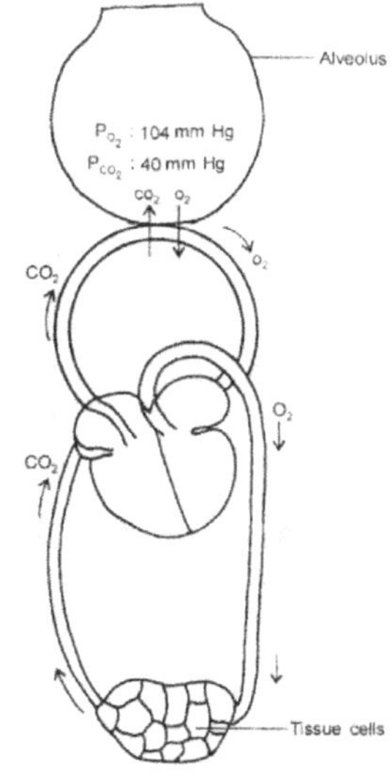

Fig. Exchange of gases

10. Haemoglobin has much more affinity about 250 times for CO than oxygen. It readily combines with CO to form most stable compound called carboxyhaemoglobin. It may be fatal for the patient.

11. Pneumonia is a respiratory disease in which oxygen has difficulty in diffusing through the in flammed alveoli and the blood O_2 may be drastically reduced and blood PCO_2 remains normal. It is caused by streptococcus penumoniae. Its symptoms are trembling, pain in chest, fever, cough, etc. It is mostly observed in children and old age.

Long Answer Questions

1. Occupational lung disease as the name suggests it is the disease of lung due to the occupation of the human.

   Cause : These are caused by the harmful substances, such as gas fumes or dusts, present in the environment where a person works. Silicosis and asbestoses are common examples, which occur due to chronic exposure of silica and asbestos dust in the mining industry.

   Symptoms : It is characterised by proliferation of fibrous connective tissue (**fibrosis**) of upper part of lung, causing inflammation.

   Prevention : The occupational disease expresses symptoms after chronic exposure (*i.e.,* 10-15 years or even more). Most of occupational diseases including silicosis and asbestosis is are incurable. Therefore, the person which is exposed to such irritants should adopt preventive measures. These protective measures are as follows:

   (i) Minimize the exposure of harmful dust at the work place.

   (ii) Workers should be informed about the harm of the exposure to such dusts.

   (iii) Workers must have the protective gears and clothing at the work place.

   (iv) Health of the workers should be regularly checked up.

2. **Regulation of respiratory rhythm**
   - The ability to maintain and moderate the respiratory rhythm according to the demand of the body tissues is due to the neural control.
   - Respiratory rhythm centre located in the medulla of the brain, is primarily responsible for this regulation. Pneumotaxic centre present in the brain functions as the 'switch off' point for regulation; by altering the duration of inspiration, it can alter the respiratory rate.
   - A chemosensitive area is situated adjacent to the rhythm centre; it is highly sensitive to carbon dioxide and hydrogen ions.
   - An increase in the concentration of these substances activates this centre which in turn sends signals to rhythm centre to make necessary adjustments in the 'respiratory process.
   - Receptors associated with aortic arch and carotid artery also are sensitive to carbon dioxide and H^+ ions; they too send signals to the respiratory rhythm centre.
   - Oxygen plays only an insignificant role in the regulation of respiratory rhythm.

3. Gaseous exchange in alveoli :
   - The alveolar wall is very thin and contains a rich network of inter connected capillaries.
   - Due to this the alveolar wall seems to be sheet of flowing blood, and is called the respiratory membrane.
   - It consists mainly of alveolar epithelium, epithelial basement membrane, a thin interstitial space, capillary basement membrane and capillary endothermal membrane. All these layer cumulatively form a membrane of 0.2 mm thickness.
   - The respiratory membrane has a limit of gases exchange between alveoli and pulmonary blood. It is called diffusing capacity. It is dependent on the solubility of respiratory gases.
   - The partial pressure of oxygen (pO_2) in the alveoli is higher (104 mm Hg) than that in the deoxygenated blood in the capillaries of the pulmonary arteries (40 mm Hg). As the gases diffuse from higher to a lower concentration, the movement of oxygen is from the alveoli to the blood. The reverse is the case in relation to carbon dioxide.
   - The partial pressure of carbon dioxide (pCO_2) is higher in deoxygenated blood (45 mm Hg), than in alveoli (40 mm Hg), therefore, CO_2 passes from blood to alveoli.

4. The inflow (inspiration) and outflow (expiration) of air occurs between atmosphere and lungs by the expansion and contraction of lungs.

   Inspiration : It is the process by which fresh air enters the lungs.
   - The external intercostal muscles present between the ribs contract and pull this ribs and sternum upward and outward increasing the volume to thoracic cavity.
   - Diaphragm becomes flats and gets lowered by the contraction of its muscles thereby increasing the volume of thoracic cavity.
   - The abdominal muscles relax and allow on the compression of abdominal organ by diaphragm.
   - As the volume of the thoracic cavity increases and as a result there is a decrease of air pressure in the lungs. The greater pressure outside the body causes air to flow rapidly into nostrils through the respiratory track to the lungs.

   Expiration : It is a process by which the foul air (CO_2) is expelled out from the lungs.
   - Internal intercostal muscles contract so that they pull in ribs downward and inward decreasing the size of thoracic cavity.
   - The muscle fibres of diaphragm relax making it convex, decreasing the volume of the thoracic cavity.
   - Contraction of abdominal muscles compresses this abdomen and pushes its towards the diaphragm.
   - The overall volume of the thoracic cavity decrease and foul air goes outside from the cavities of alveoli through the respiratory tract.

SECTION C — NCERT EXEMPLAR QUESTIONS

MULTIPLE CHOICE QUESTIONS

1. A person suffers punctures in his chest cavity in an accident, without any damage to the lungs its effect could be
   (a) reduced breathing rate
   (b) rapid increase in breathing rate
   (c) no change in respiration
   (d) cessation of breathing
2. It is known that exposure to carbon monoxide is harmful to animals because
   (a) it reduces CO_2 transport
   (b) it reduces O_2 transport
   (c) it increases CO_2 transport
   (d) it increases O_2 transport
3. Mark the true statement among the following with reference to normal breathing
   (a) inspiration is a passive process whereas expiration is active
   (b) inspiration is a active process whereas expiration is passive
   (c) inspiration and expiration are active processes
   (d) inspiration and expiration are passive processes
4. A person breathes in some volume of air by forced inspiration after having a forced expiration. This quantity of air taken in is
   (a) total lung capacity   (b) tidal volume
   (c) vital capacity   (d) inspiratory capacity
5. Mark the correct pair of muscles involved in the normal breathing in humans.
   (a) External and internal intercostal muscles
   (b) Diaphragm and abdominal muscles
   (c) Diaphragm and external intercostal muscles
   (d) Diaphragm and intercostal muscles

VERY SHORT ANSWER QUESTIONS

1. Define the following terms?
   (a) Tidal volume   (b) Residual volume
   (c) Asthma

2. A fluid filled double membranous layer surrounds the lungs. Name it and mention its important function.
3. Cigarette smoking causes emphysema. Give reason.
4. What is the amount of O_2 supplied to tissues through every 100 mL of oxygenated blood under normal physiological conditions?
5. A major percentage (97%) of O_2 is transported by RBCs in the blood. How does the remaining percentage (3%) of O_2 transported?
6. Complete the missing terms
   (a) Inspiratory Capacity (IC) = ... + IRV
   (b) .... = TV + ERV
   (c) Functional Residual Capacity (FRC) = ERV + ...
7. Name the organs of respiration in the following organisms.
   (a) **Flatworm** ....   (b) Birds. ....
   (c) Frog ....   (d) Cockroach ....

SHORT ANSWER QUESTIONS

1. State the different modes of CO_2 transport in blood.
2. For completion of respiration process, write the given steps in sequential manner.
   (a) Diffusion of gases (O_2 and CO_2) across alveolar membrane.
   (b) Transport of gases by blood.
   (c) Utilisation of O_2 by the cells for catabolic reactions and resultant release of CO_2.
   (d) Pulmonary ventilation by which atmospheric air is drawn in and CO_2 rich alveolar air is released out.
   (e) Diffusion of O_2 and CO_2 between blood and tissues.

LONG ANSWER QUESTIONS

1. Explain the mechanism of breathing with neat labelled sketches.

SOLUTIONS

Multiple Choice Questions

1. **(d)** The movement of air in and out of the lungs is performed by creating a pressure gradient between the lungs and the surrounding atmosphere. The pressure within the lungs is less than the atmospheric pressure so there is a negative pressure in the lungs with respect to atmospheric pressure. A puncture in the chest affects this pressure gradient maintained by the lungs and thus may cause cessation of breathing.

2. **(b)** Haemoglobin consists of a protein globin and pigment heme. The four portions of iron in heme combine with molecule of oxygen. It is an easy reversible reaction to form oxyhaemoglobin

$$Hb + O_2 \rightleftharpoons HbO_2$$

Whereas, the complex formed by the reaction of carbon monooxide and haemoglobin is incredibly strong

$$\underset{\text{(Haemoglobin)}}{Hb} + CO \rightleftharpoons \underset{\substack{\text{(Carboxy} \\ \text{haemoglobin)}}}{HbCO}$$

As a result of this strong bonding between the haemoglobin and carbon monooxide the haemoglobin loses its affinity to oxygen thus may lead to choking or even death.

3. **(b)** Inspiration is an active process while expiration is a passive process. Inspiration occurs when the muscles of diaphragm contract to increase the overall volume of the thoracic cavity. Thus the pressure within the lungs or intra-pulmonary pressure is less in comparison to the atmospheric pressure, *i.e.*, there is a negative pressure in the lungs with respect to the atmospheric pressure. Inspiration is thus called an active process. As the muscles use energy for contraction. During expiration diaphragm muscles relax without the use of energy. Intra-pulmonary pressure becomes higher than the atmospheric pressure and air gushes out. Thus, it is a passive process.

4. **(c)** Vital capacity is the maximum volume of air that a person can breathe in after force expiration or the maximum volume of air that a person can breathe out after force inspiration

$$\underset{\text{(Inspiratory reserve volume)}}{VC = IRV} + \underset{\text{(Expiratory reserve volume)}}{ERV} + \underset{\text{(Tidal volume)}}{TV}$$

The value of vital capacity ranges from 3400 mL to 4800 mL. Tidal volume is the air inspired or expired during normal breathing.

Total lung capacity is the volume of air present in lungs and respiratory passage after maximum inspiration. While, inspiratory capacity is the total volume of air that a person can inspire after normal inspiration.

5. (d) The diaphragm and a specialised set of muscles, called **external muscles** present between the ribs are involved in the normal breathing process in humans. They are involved in generating a pressure gradient of air between the lungs and the atmosphere, to facilitate the intake of air.

Very Short Answer Questions

1. (a) **Tidal Volume** (TV) is volume of air inspired or expired during a normal respiration. It is approx. 500 ml. *i.e.*, a healthy man can inspire or expire approximately 6000 to 8000 mL of air per minute.
   (b) **Residual Volume :** (RV) is volume of air remaining in the lungs even after a forcible expiration. This averages 1100 mL to 1200 mL.
   (c) **Asthma** is an allergic reaction that causes constriction of the bronchiole muscles, thereby reducing the air passage thus the amount of the air that can get to the alveoli.

2. Pleural membrane is a fluid filled double membranous layer surrounds the lung. It protects the lung and provides lubrication to it.

3. Emphysema is a chronic disorder of respiratory system, in which inflation or abnormal distension of alveolar wall occurs. Cigarette smoking and the inhalation of smoke or toxic substances over a time period causes the damaging of septa present between the alveoli, and its elastic tissue is replaced by the connective tissue in lungs.
   Hence, decreases the respiratory surface and causes emphysema. It causes shortness of breath, production of sputum, chronic bronchitis, etc.

4. Every 100 mL of oxygenated blood can deliver around 5 mL of O_2 to the tissue under normal physiological conditions.

5. About 97% of O_2 is transported by RBCs in the blood. The remaining 3% of O_2 is carried in a dissolved state through the plasma.

6. (a) Inspiratory Capacity (IC) = (TV) + (IRV) Tidal Volume. Inspiratory Reserve Volume
   (b) Expiratory Capacity (EC) = (TV + (ERV) Tidal Volume. Expiratory Reserve Volume.
   (c) Functional Residual Capacity (FRC) = (ERV) Expiratory + (RV) Reserve Volume. Residual Volume.

7. (a) **Flatworm** General body surface
   (b) **Birds** Lungs
   (c) **Frog** Lungs and moist skin
   (d) **Cockroach** Tracheal tubes.

Short Answer Questions

1. The blood carries carbon dioxide in three forms.
   (i) In dissolved State About 7% of CO_2 is carried by physical solution. Under normal temperature and pressure.
   (ii) As carbamino Compounds – Carbon dioxide binds directly with Hb to form an unstable compound carbamino compounds (CO_2Hb). About 23% CO_2 is transported in this form. When pCO_2 is high and pO_2 is low as in the tissues, more binding of CO_2 occurs whereas, when pCO_2 is low and pO_2 is high as in alveoli as tissue dissociation of CO_2 from carbamino-haemoglobin takes place.

$$HbO_2 + CO_2 \rightleftharpoons HbCO_2 + H^+ + O_2$$

(iii) As bicarbonate lons CO2 reacts with water in the presence of carbonic anhydrase to form carbonic acid (H_2CO_3) in RBC H_2CO_3 dissociates into hydrogen and bicarbonate ions (HCO_3^-).
The whole reaction proceeds as follows

$$CO_2 + H_2O \underset{\text{Anhydrase}}{\overset{\text{Carbonic}}{\rightleftharpoons}} \underset{\text{Carbonic acid}}{H_2CO_3}$$

$$\underset{\text{Carbonic acid}}{H_2CO_3} \rightleftharpoons \underset{\text{Hydrogen ion}}{H^+} + \underset{\text{Bicarbonate ion}}{HCO_3^-}$$

The carbonic anhydrase reaction mainly occur in RBC as it contain high concentration of enzyme carbonic anhydrase and minute quantity of it is present in plasma too.

2. Sequential steps of respiration process are:
   Pulmonary ventilation by which atmospheric air is drawn in and CO_2 rich alveolar air is released out.
   $\downarrow$
   Diffusion of gases (O_2 and CO_2) across alveolar membrane
   $\downarrow$
   Transport of gases by blood
   $\downarrow$
   Diffusion of O_2 and CO_2 between blood and tissues.
   $\downarrow$
   Utilization of O_2 by cells for catabolic reactions and resultant release

Long Answer Questions

1. Mechanism of breathing involves two stages:
   Inspiration is the process, during which atmospheric air is drawn in expiration is the process by which the alveolar air is released out.
   The movement of air into and out ofa the lungs is carried out by creating a pressure gradient between the lungs and the atmosphere, with the help of diaphragm and inter costal muscles.

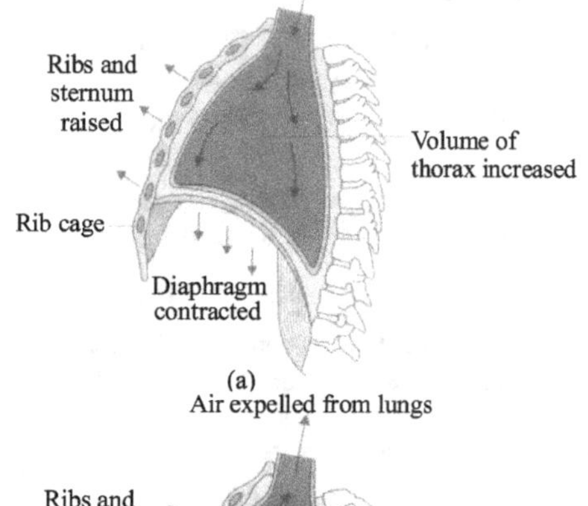

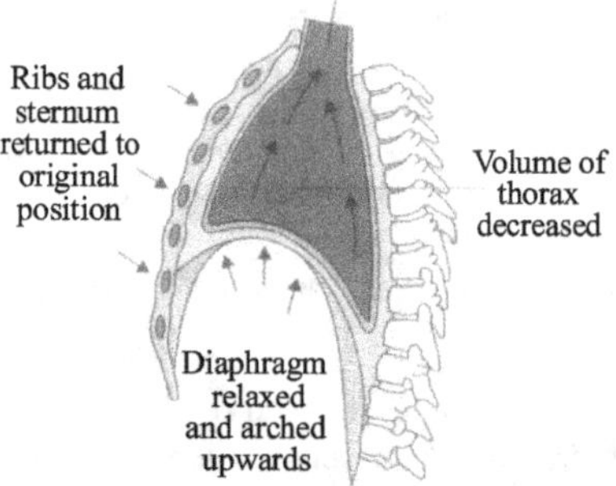

Fig. : Mechanism of breathing showing :
(a) inspiration (b) expiration

18   Body Fluids and Circulation

18.1   **Name the components of formed elements in the blood and mention one major function of each of them.**

Sol.   Blood is a mobile connective tissue composed of a fluid, the plasma and formed elements.
Formed elements includes erythrocytes, leucocytes and platelets.

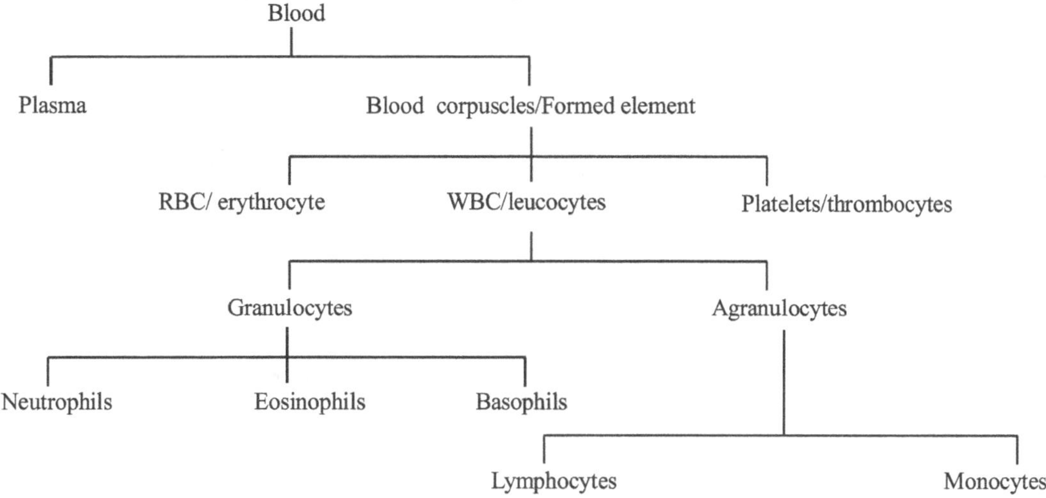

Blood corpuscles.

(a) Erythrocytes are most prevalent corpuscles (approx. 5 to 5.5 million /mm^3 of blood). They contain carbonic anhydrase enzyme which help in transportation of CO_2 and haemoglobin pigment which helps in transportation of O_2.

(b) Leucocytes lacks of any pigment and most active motile constituents of blood (approx. 6000-8000/mm^3 of blood). They may be of two types.

1. Granulocytes are the cells containing granules and a polymorphic nucleus.
    (i) Neutrophils : resposible for protection against infection.
    (ii) Eosinophils : play important role in allergic reaction.
    (iii) Basophils : significant in inflammatory reaction.

2. Agranulocytes are cells which lack granules
    (i) Lymphocytes play a key role in immunological reactions.

    (iii) Monocytes are phagocytic in nature.

(c) Platelets
    There are involved in the coagulation or clotting of blood

18.2   **What is the importance of plasma proteins ?**

Sol.   Fibrinogen, globulin and albumins are the proteins found in plasma. Fibrinogens are needed for clotting of blood. Globulins are involved in defence mechanisms of the body and albumins help in osmotic balance.

18.3   **Match Column I with Column II :**

Column I		Column II	
(a)	**Eosinophils**	(i)	**Coagulation**
(b)	**RBC**	(ii)	**Universal recipient**
(c)	**AB blood Group**	(iii)	**Resist infection**
(d)	**Platelets**	(iv)	**Contraction of heart**
(e)	**Systole**	(v)	**Gas transport**

Sol.

	Column I		Column II
(a)	Eosinophils	(iii)	Resist infections
(b)	RBC	(v)	Gas transport
(c)	AB blood Group	(ii)	Universal Recipient
(d)	Platelets	(i)	Coagulation
(e)	Systole	(iv)	Contraction of heart

18.4 Why do we consider blood as a connective tissue ?

Sol. Blood is considered a connective tissue for two basic reasons.

(i) Embryologically, it has the same origin as other connective tissue.

(ii) Blood connects the body systems together bringing the needed oxygen, nutrient, hormones and removing the wastes.

18.5 What is the difference between lymph and blood?

Sol. Differences between blood and lymph are as following :

	Blood		Lymph
1.	It consists of plasma, erythrocytes, leucocytes and platelets.	1.	It consists of plasma and leucocytes (lymphocytes most abundant).
2.	It is red in colour due to the presence of haemoglobin in erythrocytes.	2.	It is colourless as haemoglobin is absent.
3.	Its plasma has more proteins, calcium and phosphorus.	3.	Its plasma has fewer proteins and less calcium and phosphorus.
4.	Glucose concentration is less in blood.	4.	Glucose concentration is higher in lymph.
5.	Amount of CO_2 and other metabolic wastes is normal.	5.	Amount of CO_2 and other metabolic wastes is much more.
6.	It carries materials towards and away from the tissue, therefore, it acts as a "vehicle".	6.	It transfers materials from the blood to the body cells and vice-versa, therefore, it acts as "middle man".

18.6 What is meant by double circulation ? What is its significance ?

Sol. Double circulation : It is the passage of the same blood twice through the heart in order to complete one cycle. One component of the circulation is passage of deoxygenated blood to lungs for oxygenation. It is called pulmonary circulation. The oxygenated blood comes back to heart for being pumped into various parts of the body for providing oxygen. It is called systemic circulation. The deoxygenated blood comes back to heart for being pumped to lungs again.

Significance : (i) Double circulation checks the mixing of oxygenated blood and deoxygenated blood. (ii) Oxygenated blood carries more oxygen per unit volume. It is, therefore, able to provide more oxygen for metabolism. (iii) Deoxygenated blood can carry more CO_2 for removal.

18.7 Write the differences between

(a)	**Blood and Lymph**	**(b)**	**Open and closed system of circulation**
(c)	**Systole and Diastole**	**(d)**	**P-wave and T-wave**

Sol. (a) See answer 5.

(b) Differences between open and closed systems of circulation are as following :

	Open System of Circulation		Closed System of Circulation
1.	Blood does not remain confined in the blood vessels and comes to certain spaces.	1.	Blood remains confined to the blood vessels.
2.	Blood flows at low pressure.	2.	Blood flows at high pressure.
3.	Exchange of materials is direct between blood and body cells.	3.	Exchange of materials occurs through the tissue fluid.
4.	It is less efficient.	4.	It is more efficient.
5.	Found in leech, prawns, crabs, lobsters, insects, spiders, pila, etc.	5.	Found in earthworm, squid and all vertebrates.

(c) Differences between systole and diastole are as following :

	Systole		Diastole
1.	The contraction of cardiac (heart) chambers is called systole.	1.	The relaxation of the cardiac (heart) chambers is called diastole.
2.	Blood is pumped out of the cardiac chambers.	2.	Blood is received in the cardiac chambers.
3.	The valves are closed to prevent backflow of blood.	3.	The valves are opened to allow entry of blood.

(d) Differences between P-wave and T-wave are as following :

P-Wave		T-Wave	
1.	This wave represents depolarization of atria (atrial contraction).	1.	It represents ventricular repolarisation (ventricular relaxation).
2.	Blood is pumped into the ventricles.	2.	Blood is received by the atria.

18.8 Describe the evolutionary change in the pattern of heart among the vertebrates.

Sol.

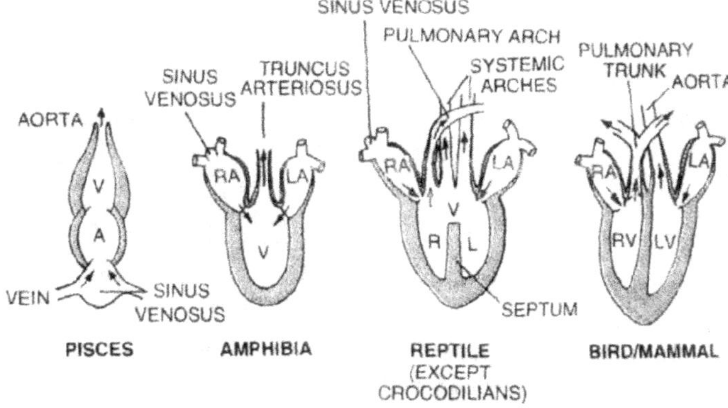

Hearts of different vertebrates. A = Auricle, V = Ventricle, R = Right, L = Left.

As it is clear from the following diagram the heart of fish has two chambers. This means there is no separate circulation for oxygenated and deoxygenated blood. There is separation of two chambers in the atrium of amphibians. This has further evolved to partial separation of ventricle in reptiles. Finally in birds there is complete separation of oxygenated and deoxygenated blood circulation with advent of four chambers in the heart. Mammal heart is the most developed having the most efficient double circulatory system.

18.9 Why do we call our heart myogenic ?

Sol. Normal activities of the heart are regulated intrinsically, i.e., auto regulated by specialised muscles (nodal tissue), hence the heart is called myogenic.

18.10 Sino-atrial node is called the pacemaker of our heart. Why ?

Sol. The SA node is located in the wall of right auricle slightly below the opening of the superior vena cava. It has a unique property of self excitation which enables it to act as the pacemaker of the heart. It spontaneously initiates a wave of contraction which spreads over both the auricles more or less simultaneously along the muscle fibres.

18.11 What is the significance of atrio-ventricular node and atrio-ventricular bundle in the functioning of heart ?

Sol. Atrio-ventricular node (AVN) is a mass of neuro-muscular tissues and is situated in the wall of right atrium. The AV node picks up the wave of contraction originated by SAN. Bundle of HIS is a mass of specialised fibres which originates from the AV node. The Bundle of HIS and Purkinje fibres which forms atrio-ventricular bundle convey impulses of contraction from the AV node to the muscles of the ventricle.

18.12 Define a cardiac cycle and the cardiac output.

Sol. **Cardiac cycle.** A regular sequence of three events : (i) auricular systole, (ii) ventricular systole, and (iii) joint diastole or complete cardiac diastole (relaxation of both auricles and ventricles) during the completion of one heart beat is known as heart cycle or cardiac cycle.

Cardiac output. The amount of blood pumped by heart per minute is called cardiac output or heart output. Heart beats 72 times per minute and pumps out about 70 ml of blood during each beat. Therefore, 72×70 or 5040 ml (roughly 5 liters) is the cardiac output.

18.13 Explain heart sounds.

Sol. The rhythmic closening and opening of the valves forms the sound of heart beat. The first sound lub (duration 0.16-0.90 sec) is created by closer of atrioventricular valves. The second sound dub (duration 0.10 sec) is created by the closure of semilunar valves.

18.14 Draw a standard ECG and explain the different segments in it.

Sol. The recording of electrical potential generated by the spread of cardiac impulse, is called electrocardiogram (ECG). ECG is the graphic record of electronic current produced by the excitation of cardiac muscles. A normal electrocardiogram is composed of P wave, QRS complex and T wave, P wave indicate the depolarisation of the atria. QRS complex expresses the ventricular depolarisation. T wave indicate an repolarisation of ventricles.

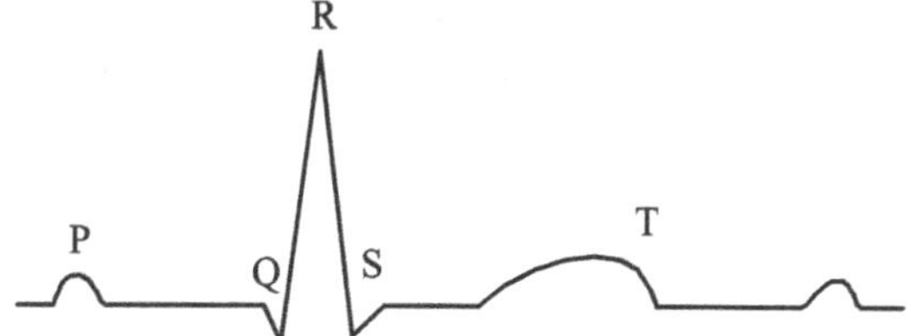

Fig. Diagrammatic presentation of a standard ECG

SECTION B — PRACTICE QUESTIONS

MULTIPLE CHOICE QUESTIONS

1. In blood
   (a) WBCs are more than RBCs
   (b) RBCs are more than WBCs
   (c) RBCs are less than platelets
   (d) Platelets are less than WBCs

2. Which one engulfs pathogens rapidly?
   (a) Acidophils
   (b) Monocytes
   (c) Basophils
   (d) Neutrophils

3. Which of the following is responsible for ABO grouping?
   (a) Presence or absence of clotting factors.
   (b) Compatibility of blood groups during blood transfusion.
   (c) Presence or absence of surface antigens (A and B) on WBCs.
   (d) Presence or absence of two surface antigens (A and B) on the RBCs.

4. Rh factor is named after
   (a) monkey   (b) *Drosophila*
   (c) rat   (d) man

5. Which of the following cations is required for the conversion of prothrombin into active thrombin by thromboplastin?
   (a) Cu^{2+} (b) Fe^{3+}
   (c) Fe^{2+} (d) Ca^{2+}

6. Contraction of the ventricle in the heart begins by the command from
   (a) Purkinje fibres   (b) AV node
   (c) chordae tendinae   (d) SA node

7. The pacemaker of the human heart is
   (a) SA node   (b) tricuspid valve
   (c) AV node   (d) SV node

8. In mammals the blood from the right ventricle goes to
   (a) systemic aorta   (b) precavals
   (c) truncus arteriosus   (d) pulmonary aorta

9. In a standard ECG, which one of the following alphabets is the correct representation of the respective activity of the human heart?
   (a) P-Depolarization of the atria
   (b) R-Repolarization of ventricles
   (c) S-Start of systole
   (d) T-End of diastole

10. 'Bundle of His' is a part of which one of the following organs in humans?
    (a) Brain   (b) Heart
    (c) Kidney   (d) Pancreas

ASSERTION & REASON QUESTIONS

DIRECTION (Qs. 1-5) : *These questions consists of two statements. Answer these questions selecting the appropriate option given below:*
(a) Both Assertion (A) and Reason (R) are true and Reason (R) is the correct explanation of Assertion (A).
(b) Both Assertion (A) and Reason (R) are true, but Reason (R) is not the correct explanation of Assertion (A).
(c) Assertion (A) is true, but Reason (R) is false.
(d) Assertion (A) is false, but Reason (R) is true.

1. **Assertion:** The spleen act as the graveyard of RBC.
   Reason: The RBCs are destroyed in spleen after 120 days.

2. **Assertion:** Blood coagulates in uninjured blood vessels.
   Reason: Blood release an anticoagulant heparin which prevent blood clotting.

3. **Assertion:** The cardiac cycle and cardiac output are same.
   Reason: The duration of cardiac cycle is 0.8 seconds.

4. **Assertion:** A special neural centre in the medulla oblongata can moderate the cardiac function through autonomic nervous system.
   Reason: Adrenal medullary hormones increase the cardiac output.

5. **Assertion :** Lub is a heart sound which is produced during each cardiac cycle.
   Reason : It is associated with the closure of the tricuspid and bicuspid valves.

CASE/PASSAGE BASED QUESTIONS

DIRECTIONS (Qs. 1-5) : *Read the following passage and answer the questions that follows.*

On a sunday afternoon, Ravi his wife and 2 kids were in the garden. The kids were playing and Ravi and his wife were having tea together. Suddenly he experienced severe pain in the chest and became unconcious. Ravi had cardiac arrest and was admitted to the hospital. Upon the cardiologist's recommendation he was connected to a machine with 3 electrical leads.

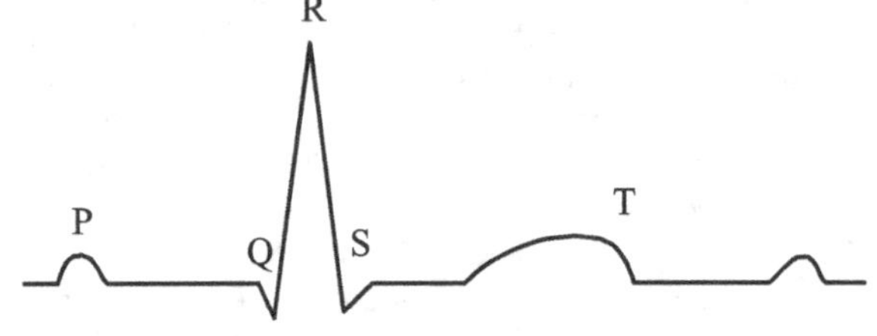

1. Based on the above diagram name the graph obtained and how were the leads pinned to the patient's body
   (a) Electrocardiogram, one to each wrist and the third lead was connected to left ankle.
   (b) Electrocardiogram, 2 leads were connected to each wrist and the 3rd one was connected to chest (left side)
   (c) Electroencephalogram, one to each wrist and the third lead was connected to right side of chest
   (d) Electrocardiogram, 2 leads were connected to wrist and the third lead was connected to right ankle.
2. Which of the following options refer to the end of systole in the above diagram?
   (a) QRS
   (b) initiation of the next P wave
   (c) End of T wave
   (d) Start of T wave
3. Which of the following refers to deflection from the normal heart beat.
   (a) Enlarged Q and R waves (b) Taller T wave
   (c) None of these   (d) Both A & B
4. Which of the following factors regulate the heart beat?
   (a) the length of QRS complexes
   (b) hormones of adrenal medulla
   (c) chemoreceptors sensitive for CO_2, O_2 and blood pressure
   (d) activity of pineal gland
5. In the options below, the rate of heart beat cycle can be referred to as:
   (a) Number of QRS complex in a given time period
   (b) starting from one QRS complex to the next
   (c) PQRST segment
   (d) PR segment

Very Short Answer Questions

1. What do you understand by joint diastole?
2. What is meant by open circulatory system?
3. What is the role of basophils in human body?
4. Write down the main function of neutrophils.
5. What are the functions of lymphocytes?
6. What is tunica externa?
7. Mention the function of pericardial fluid.
8. What does the QRS complex indicate?
9. Name the most common disorder of blood circulatory system.
10. What is atherosclerosis?
11. Name the type of granulocytes that play an important role in detoxification.
12. What transmits the cardiac impulse from the atria to the ventricles?

13. What is RBCs density in the blood of an adult human?
14. Name the reptile that has a four-chambered heart.
15. What are Purkinje fibres?
16. Name two vital organs affected by high blood pressure or hypertension.
17. What is the main symptom of heart failure?
18. Which vein carries oxygenated blood?
19. Name the layers of heart through which heart is covered?
20. Which human organ is known as "graveyard of RBCs"?

Short Answer Questions

1. What are thrombocytes? Where are they produced in human body?
2. What is serum?
3. Name the different types of granulocytes. Give the function of the one of which constitutes maximum percentage of total leucocytes.
4. Why closed circulatory system is more efficient than open circulatory system?
5. Name a portal system present in man. Write its one function.
6. Write down the functions of lymph.
7. What kind of circulatory system do the molluscs have? List the characteristics of such a system.
8. What is average number of thrombocytes in human blood? What is their function?
9. How many chambers are present in the heart of a fish? Name them.
10. What is meant by single circulation? Give an example.
11. Where and from which cells do platelets originate? What is their life span? How do they act when blood vessels get injured?
12. What do you mean by myogenic and neurogenic heart?
13. What is Arteriosclerosis? What are its causes?
14. Define Vagus escape.
15. What is erythroblastosis foetalis? How it occurs?
16. Why capillaries are known as exchange vessels?

Long Answer Questions

1. Describe step by step what happens during different phases of cardiac cycle in human being.
2. (a) Draw the L.S. of human heart showing the internal structure. Label the parts of the left side of the heart and the blood vessels that enter and leave the chambers of the same side.
   (b) What is the significance of the remnant of sinus venosus in the mammalian heart?
3. Describe briefly the steps involved in the coagulation of blood at the site of injury of a blood vessel.
4. Why is it necessary to check the Rh-factor of the blood of a pregnant woman?

SOLUTIONS

Multiple Choice Questions

1. **(b)**
2. **(d)** Neutrophils are a type of leucocyte (WBCs) that can take all types of stain (acid-basic-Neutral). It is most abundant (60–70% of total WBCs) and most active type of WBCs i.e., they are the most actively phagocytic in nature.
3. **(d)** ABO grouping is the classification of human blood based on the inherited properties of red blood cells (erythrocytes). It is determined by the presence or absence of the antigens A and B, which are carried on the surface of the red blood cells. Persons may thus have type A, type B, type O, or type AB blood. The A, B, and O blood groups were first identified by Austrian immunologist **Karl Landsteiner** in 1901.
4. **(a)** Rh factor is named after the Rhesus monkey. Experiments by Karl Landsteiner and Alexander S. Wiener, showed that rabbits, when immunised with rhesus monkey red cells, produce an antibody that also agglutinates the red blood cells of many humans.
5. **(d)** Thrombokinase hydrolyses prothrombin to thrombin in presence of Ca^{2+}. Thrombin converts soluble fibrinogen to insoluble fibrin.
6. **(d)** The SA node has the inherent power of generating a wave of contraction and controlling the heartbeat. Hence, it is known as the pacemaker.
7. **(a)** Sino-atrial node (SA node) initiates and maintains contraction of heart by generating action potentials (70-75/min). So it is called the pacemaker.
8. **(d)** In mammals the blood from the right ventricles goes to the pulmonary aorta.
9. **(a)** The P-wave indicates atrial depolarisation.
10. **(b)** 'Bundle of His' is a typical cardiac muscle fibres, connecting the atria with ventricle.

Assertion & Reason Questions

1. **(a)** The RBCs are formed in the bone marrow and destroyed in the spleen.
2. **(c)** When an injury is caused to a blood vessel, bleeding starts which is stopped by blood clotting. At the site of injury blood platelets release platelet factor - III and injured tissues release thromboplastin. The two combine to form prothrombinase enzyme which converts prothrombin to thrombin. The latter stimulates formation of fibrin thread or clot. Blood contains an anticoagutant heparin which prevents blood clotting in uninjured vessels.
3. **(d)** The cardiac cycle consist of one heart beat or one cycle of contraction and relaxation of the cardiac muscles. The duration of a cardiac cycle is 0.8 seconds. The amount of blood pumped by heart per minute is called cardiac output.

4. **(b)** The neural signals through the sympathetic nerves can increase the rate of heart beat, the strength of ventricular contraction and thereby the cardiac output. The para sympathetic neural signals can decrease the rate of heart beat, speed of conduction of action potential and thereby the cardiac output.
5. **(b)** Lubb and dub are two heart sounds, which occurs due to the closure of cuspid valves and semilunar valves respectively. Lubb is the first heart sound which is formed due to closure of atrioventricular valves at the beginning of ventricular systole. It is low pitched of long duration (0.15 sec).

Case/Passage Based Questions

1. **(a)**
2. **(c)** The end of T wave mark the end of systole.
3. **(d)** Any deviation from the normal heart beat suggest a difference in ECG. The ECG of the healthy individual is given above. The cardiace output of an athlete would be larger than a normal person, however, the ECG remains the same.
4. **(a)** The regulation of heart beat in controlled by factors such as: (a) chemosensitive receptors present in medulla oblongata (b) neural signal through the sympathetic nerves (c) adrenal medullary hormones etc.
5. **(a)** The heart beat refers to one cycle of contraction and relaxation of the cardiac muscle and the rate of heart beat is determined by the number of QRS complex formed in a given time.

Very Short Answer Questions

1. Joint diastole is a phase in the cardiac cycle during which both atria and ventricles are released simultaneously.
2. When the blood does not remain confined to the blood vessels and flows into open spaces called sinus. It is termed as the open circulatory system.
3. Basophils are significant in allergic reactions.
4. Neutrophils are mainly responsible for protection against infection.
5. Lymphocytes play an important role in cell-mediated immunity.
6. Tunica externa is the outermost layer of blood vessels (artery and vein) made up of fibrous connective tissue with collagen fibres.
7. Pericardial fluid keeps the surface of heart moist and prevents the friction between heart wall and surrounding tissues.
8. QRS complex represent the ventricular depolarizations.
9. Hypertension.
10. Atherosclerosis is the deposition of lipids (specially cholesterol) on the wall lining of large and medium sized arteries.
11. Eosinophils.

12. Atrio – ventricular bundle from the atrio – ventricular node transmits the cardiac impulse from the atria to ventricles.

13. About $5.0 - 5.5$ millions/mm^3 of blood.

14. Crocodile.

15. The minute branches of the right and left AV-bundles, that are found throughout the ventricular musculature of the respective sides, are called Purkinje fibres.

16. Brain, kidney.

17. Congestion of the lungs.

18. Pulmonary vein.

19. Endocardium, myocardium and pericardium.

20. Spleen.

Short Answer Questions

1. Thrombocytes or blood platelets are colourless formed elements of blood which appear round, or biconvex or irregular and helps in clotting of blood. They are produced from the megakaryocytes (special cells in the bone narrow).

2. Serum is straw coloured fluid left after the clotting of blood. It is also called blood serum.

3. Granulocytes are of three types neutrophils, eosinophils, basophils.
Neutrophils constitute the maximum percentage of the total leucocyte, mainly responsible for protection against infection. They engulf the foreign substances by phagocytosis.

4. Advantage of closed circulatory system : -
(i) Flow of blood is faster in closed circulatory system as compared to open circulatory system. Sufficiently high blood pressure can be maintained.
  – Blood does not come in contact with the tissues/ organs.
  – The volume of blood flowing to a particular tissue/organ can be regulated according to the need.
(ii) The blood flows under pressure so that all parts of the body receive blood with equal efficiency.
(iii) It transports materials efficiently.
(iv) There are checks for regulation of amount and speed of blood passing into an organ according to the requirement of that organs.

5. Hepatic portal system.
Significance : The blood which comes from the alimentary canal contains digested food like glucose and amino acids. The excess of glucose is converted into glycogen which is stored in the liver for later use.

6. Functions of lymph :
(i) Lymph acts as a 'middle man' which transports oxygen, food materials, hormones etc. to the body cells and brings carbon dioxide and other metabolic wastes from body cells to blood.
(ii) It keeps the body cell moist.
(iii) It maintains the volume of blood.
(iv) It absorbs and transports fat and fat soluble vitamins from the intestine.

7. Molluscs have open circulatory system.
  – In this type, the blood flows through open spaces (lacunae) and channels (sinuses) and not confined to closed blood vessels.
  – A sufficiently high blood pressure cannot be developed in lacunae and sinuses and so blood flows at a very slow velocity.
  – Blood directly comes in contact with the body tissues.
  – The volume of blood flowing to different tissues and organs cannot be regulated according to the need.

8. 1,50,000 to 3,50,000 platelets/mm^3 of blood
  – They release substances that are concerned with the clotting of blood.

9. There are two chambers one atrium and one ventricle.

10. Single circulation
  – Single circulation is the phenomenon in which the heart of an animal receives and pumps blood once for e.g. fish.
  – The heart of fish is two-chambered with an atrium and a ventricle.
  – The heart pumps only deoxygenated blood, to the gills for oxygenation.

11. Platelets originate from the megakaryocytes in the bone marrow.
  – They live for about seven days.
  – They release thromboplastins, which help convert prothrombin of the plasma into thrombin and thus they are involved in clotting of blood.

12. **(i)** Myogenic heart is the one which generates its own electrochemical impulse with the help of special muscles called myogenic muscles. e.g., molluscs, chordates.
(ii) Neurogen-ic heart is the one where electrochemical impulse for its contraction originates from a nerve ganglion or mass of nerve cells present nearby, e.g., most arthropods, annelids.

13. It is thickening, hardening and loss of elasticity of the wall of arteries. This process progressively restricts the blood flow to one's organs and tissues and can lead to severe health risks. It is caused by the build-up of fatty plaque, cholestrol and some other substances in and on the artery wall.

14. The stimulation of vagus nerve decreases the heart rate but its continuous stimulation shows no further decrease. This is known as vagus escape.

15. It is a type of haemolytic disease of new-borns due to ABO blood type A, B, or O is not compatible with blood group of foetus. It develops in a foetus, when IgG molecules produced by the mother passes through the placenta.

16. These have very thin walls which allows the passage of nutrients from blood into body tissues. It also allows the passage of waste product came from body tissues. So, capillaries are known as exchange vessels.

Long Answer Questions

1. Different phases of cardiac cycle in human being are as follow:
   (i) Atrial systole : As soon as atria contract due to contraction wave of SA node, the blood is forced into ventricle through open bicuspid and tricuspid valves.
   (ii) Beginning of ventricular systole : As soon the wave of contraction stimulates ventricle, bicuspid and tricuspid valves are closed immediately producing lub sound.
   (iii) Complete ventricular systole : With complete contraction of ventricle the blood flows into pulmonary trunk and aorta opening semilunar valves.
   (iv) Beginning of ventricular diastole: It is marked by closing of semilunar valves producing second heart sound. The ventricles start relaxation.
   (v) Complete ventricular diastole : As the ventricles are relaxed completely, the bicuspid, tricuspid valves open (due to fall in pressure of ventricles) and blood flows in it from atria.

2. (a)

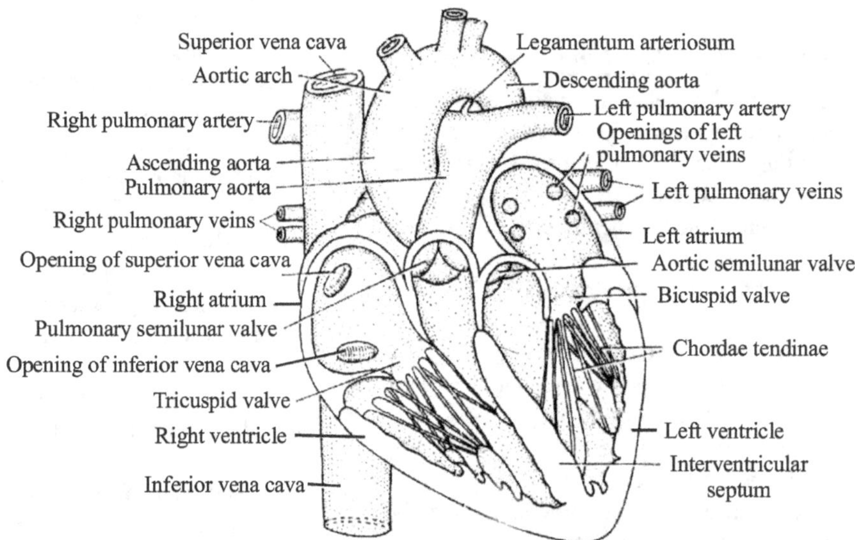

Fig. Internal structure of human heart

   (b) It is believed that the remnant of sinus venosus is modified into sino-atrial node (SA Node) in the mammalian heart which is nothing but a mass of neuromuscular tissue laying in the wall of right atrium near the openings of superior vena cava. It originates impulses for regulation of heart beat. Thus acts as pace maker of heart.

3. Blood exhibits coagulation or clotting in response to an injury or trauma. This is a mechanism to prevent excessive loss of blood from the body. We would have observed a dark reddish brown scum formed at the site of a cut or an injury over a period of time. It is a clot or coagulam formed mainly of a network of threads called fibrins in which dead and damaged formed elements of blood are trapped. Fibrins are formed by the conversion of inactive fibrinogens in the plasma by the enzyme thrombin. Thrombins, in turn are formed from another inactive substance present in the plasma called prothrombin. An enzyme complex, thrombokinase, is required for the above reaction. This complex is formed by a series of linked enzymic reactions (cascade process) involving a number of factors present in the plasma in an inactive state. An injury or a trauma stimulates the platelets in the blood to release certain factors which activate the mechanism of coagulation. Certain factors released by the tissues at the site of injury also can initiate coagulation. Calcium ions play a very important role in clotting.

4. Rh-Factor
   - Rh-antigen is present on the surface of erythrocytes in about 80-85% of the human beings.
   - The individuals who possess this antigen are called Rh-positive and those who do not have it are called Rh-negative.
   - An Rh-negative person, when exposed to Rh-positive blood, develops anti-Rh-antibodies.
   - If a pregnant women who is Rh-negative, bears an Rh-positive foetus, will develop anti-Rh-antibodies during the first delivery, when the foetal blood comes in contact with her blood.
   - These antibodies linger in the blood for sufficiently longer periods.
   - If she carries a second foetus, that is Rh-positive, the anti-Rh-antibodies in her blood enter the foetal circulation and cause damage to the foetal RBCs and could become fatal.
   - This condition is called *erythroblastosis foetalis*.

| SECTION C | **NCERT EXEMPLAR QUESTIONS**  |

Multiple Choice Questions

1. Which of the following cells do not exhibit phagocytotic activity?
   (a) Monocytes   (b) Neutrophil
   (c) Basophil   (d) Macrophage
2. One of the common symptoms observed in people infected with dengue fever is
   (a) significant decrease in RBCs count
   (b) significant decrease in WBC count
   (c) significant decrease in platelets count
   (d) significant increase in platelets count
3. Which among the following is correct during each cardiac cycle?
   (a) The volume of blood pumped out by the Rt and Lt ventricles is same
   (b) The volume of blood pumped out by the Rt and Lt ventricles is different
   (c) The volume of blood received by each atrium is different
   (d) The volume of blood received by the aorta and pulmonary artery is different
4. Cardiac activity could be moderated by the autonomous neural system. Tick the correct answer.
   (a) The parasympathetic system stimulates heart rate and stroke volume
   (b) The sympathetic system stimulates heart rate and stroke volume
   (c) The parasympathetic system decreases the heart rate but increase stroke volume
   (d) The sympathetic system decreases the heart rate but increase stroke volume
5. Mark the pair of substances among the following which is essential for coagulation of blood.
   (a) heparin and calcium ions
   (b) calcium ions and platelet factors
   (c) oxalates and nitrates
   (d) platelet factors and heparin

Very Short Answer Questions

1. Name the blood component which is viscous and straw coloured fluid.
2. Complete the missing word in the statement given below.
   (a) Plasma without _______ factors is called serum.
   (b) _______ and monocytes are phagocytic cells.
   (c) Eosinophils are associated with _______ reactions.
   (d) _______ ions play a significant role in clotting.
   (e) One can determine the heart beat rate by counting the number of _______ in an ECG.
3. Name the vascular connection that exists between the digestive tract and liver.
4. Given below are the abnormal conditions related to blood circulation. Name the disorders.
   (a) Acute chest pain due to failure of O_2 supply to heart muscles.
   (b) Increased systolic pressure.
5. Which coronary artery disease is caused due to narrowing of the lumen of arteries?
6. Define the following terms and give their location.
   (a) Purkinje fibre
   (b) Bundle of His
7. State the functions of the following in blood
   (a) fibrinogen
   (b) globulin
   (c) neutrophils
   (d) lymphocytes
8. How will you interpret an electocardiagram (ECG) in which time taken in QRS complex is higher?

Short Answer Questions

1. The walls of ventricles are much thicker than atria. Explain.
2. Differentiate between
   (a) blood and lymph
   (b) basophilsand eosinophils
   (c) tricuspid and bicuspid valve
3. Briefly describe the followings
   (a) anaemia   (b) angina pectoris
   (c) atherosclerosis   (d) hypertension
   (e) heart failure
   (f) erythroblastosis foetalis
4. Explain the functional significance of lymphatic system?

Long Answer Questions

1. Explain Rh-Incompatibility in humans.
2. Explain different types of blood groups and donor compatibility by making a table.
3. In the diagrammatic presentation of heart given below, mark and label. SAN, AVN, AV bundles, bundle of his and Purkinje fibres.

SOLUTIONS

Multiple Choice Questions

1. **(c) Basophils** are the least common granulocyte, only composed of 0.01% to 0.3% of the circulating white blood cells. These are involved in specific kinds of inflammatory reactions, especially those which cause allergic reactions and do not exhibit phagocytotic activity.
   Monocytes on the other hand, migrate from blood stream to tissue and differentiate into resident macrophage, like kupffer cells in liver and neutrophils target bacteria and fungi. Macrophages are also phagocytotic in nature.

2. **(c)** Low platelet count leads to life threatening conditions. It is one of the most common symptoms observed in people infected with dengue fever.

3. **(a) Cardiac Cycle** consists of one heart beat or one cycle of contraction and relaxation of the cardiac muscles. The contraction phase is called the systole and the relaxation phase is called the diastole.
   The purpose of the cardiac cycle is to pump the blood effectively. The right ventricle pumps the volume of deoxygenated blood to the lungs through pulmonary artery. After the oxygenation of blood the volume of blood carried through pulmonary vein is pumped through left ventricle into the aorta and transferred to the entire body.

4. **(b)** Neural signals through the sympathetic nerves can increase the rate of the heart beat, the strength of ventricular contraction and stimulate the cardiac output. Thus the sympathetic system is involved in stimulating heart rate and stroke volume.

5. **(b)** Certain factors released by the tissues at the site of injury can initiate coagulation processes.
   Calcium ions and platelet factor act first towards coagulation.

Very Short Answer Questions

1. Blood is a special connective tissue consisting of a fluid matrix, plasma and cells.

2. (a) Clotting
   (b) Neutrophils
   (c) allergic
   (d) Calcium
   (e) QRS complex

3. Hepatic portal system is the vascular connection that exists between the digestive tract and liver.

4. (a) Angina
   (b) High Blood Pressure

5. Atherosclerosis is the coronary artery disease caused due to the narrowing of the lumen of arteries due to deposition of calcium, fat, cholesterol and fibrous tissue the arteries become narrow, affecting vessels that supply blood to the heart muscles.

6. (a) Purkinje Fibres are the fibres that conduct impulse, and the contraction impulses from AV node into the walls of ventricles.
   (b) Bundle of His are mass of specialised fibres that originates from the AV node.

7. (a) Fibrinogens are the components of blood plasma that are inactive. In the presence of enzyme thrombin, they form a clot or coagulum of a network of threads called fibrin, in which dead and damaged elements of blood are trapped.
   (b) Globulins are primarily involved in immunity. i.e., defence mechanisms of the body.
   (c) Neutrophils are phagocytic cells, that destroy foreign organisms entering the body.
   (d) Lymphocytes are specialised cells which are responsible for the immune responses in the body. There are two major types of lymphocytes, that are involved in this process are B and T-lymphocytes.

8. **Electrocardiograph** (ECG) is a graphical representation of the electrical activity of the heart during a cardiac cycle. A patient is connected to the machine having three electrical leads (one to each wrist and one to the left ankle) that continuously monitor the activity of heart. Multiple leads are attached to the chest regions, for a detailed evaluation of the heart functions
   The **QRS complex** represent the depolarisation of the ventricles, that initiates the ventricular contraction. The contraction starts shortly after Q and marks the beginning of the systole. The time taken in QRS complex is 0.12 second in normal ECG
   The larger Q and R wave indicate a myocardial infarction (heart attack). The S-T segment is elevated in acute myocardial infarction and depressed when the heart muscle receives insufficient oxygen.

Short Answer Questions

1. The walls of ventricles are thicker than the atria. It is due to the greater pressure exerted by pumping out of blood through ventricles of heart in compare to atria. Ventricles need to pump blood further and with much force.

2. (a) Difference between blood and lymph are as follows

Blood	Lymph
Blood is a type connecting tissue that consists erythrocytes, leucocytes and platelets present in fluid called plasma.	Lymph is also a connective tissue which has large number of WBC (leucocytes) in plasma and devoid of RBC.
It flows in all blood vessels.	It flows only in lymphatic system and is also found extracellularly inside the tissue.

(b) Difference between basophils and eosinophils are as follows

Basophils	Eosinophils
These possess 3 lobed nucleus less number of coarse granules.	These possess bilobed nucleus and coarse granules in cytoplasm.
These take acidic	These take acidic stain
These are 0.1% Part of blood.	These are 1-6% part of blood.

(c) Difference between tricuspid valve and bicuspid valve are as follows

Tricuspid Valve	Bicuspid Value
It separates the right atria from right ventricle.	It separates the left atria from left ventricle.
It is made of 3 cusps or flaps.	It is made of 2 cusps or flaps.
This is also known as right atrio ventricular valve.	This is also called mitral valve or left atrio ventricular valve.

3. (a) **Anaemia** This is the most common disorder of the blood, which is caused due to decrease in the number of RBC than the normal amount and also due to less quantity of haemoglobin than the normal value in blood. This is the most common disorder of the blood.

(b) **Angina Pectoris** When there is blockage in coronary artery, thus insufficient supply of blood reaches to heart muscles. That results in chest pain, fear, anxiety, pale skin, profuse sweating and vomiting. The pain usually starts in the centre of the chest spreads down to the left arm which last for only few second.

(c) **Atherosclerosis** It refers the deposition of cholesterol or fatty substance in the inner lining of arteries called atherosclerotic plaque. Sometimes arteries get completely blocked, this may result in stroke of heart attack.

(d) **Hypertension** It is sometimes also known as arterial hypertension. The blood pressure in the arteries gets elevated. It could be primary or secondary hypertension which are caused by various conditions which affect kidneys, arteries heart or endocrine system.

(e) **Heart Failure** It is the state of heart, causes in when heart does not pump blood effectively enough to meet the requirement of the body.

(f) **Erythroblastosis foetalis** It is a haemolytic disease causes in new borns, which is an allo-immune condition that develops in foetus, when igG molecules produced by mother pass through placenta and attack RBC. It causes reticulocytosis and anaemia. It develops due to Rh incompatibility between the couples.

In a man with RH$^+$ blood and women with Rh$^-$ blood, the second pregnancy foetus may have this problem due to IgG accumulation in women during first child development and delivery.

4. Lymphatic system comprises blood vessels that carries a fluid called lymph. It contains white blood cells, which are responsible for fighting against any diseases. It removes and filter the interstitial fluid from tissues, later absorbs and transports fatty acids and fats as chyle from digestive system and also transport cells to immune system.

Long Answer Questions

1. In nearly 80% of human Rh antigen is observed on the surface of RBCs. Such individuals are called Rh positive (Rh$^+$) and those individuals where this antigen is not present are called Rh negative (Rh$^-$).

Both Rh$^+$ and Rh$^-$ individuals are phenotypically normal. The problem in them arises during blood **transfusion** and **pregnancy**.

(i) **Incompatibility During Blood Transfusion** The first blood transfusion of Rh+ blood to the person with Rh$^-$ blood causes no harm because the Rh$^-$ person develops **anti** Rh **factors** or **antibodies** in his/ her blood, but second transfusion of Rh$^+$ blood to the Rh$^-$ person because anti Rh factors are already formed it destroys the red blood corpuscles of the donor.

(ii) **Incompatibility During Pregnancy** If father's blood is Rh$^+$, mother blood is Rh$^-$ and the foetus blood is Rh$^+$. It will lead to a serious problem. Rh antigens of the foetus do not get exposed to the Rh$^-$ ve blood of the mother in the first pregnancy as the two bloods are well separated by the **placenta**.

But in the subsequent Rh$^+$ foetus, the anti Rh factors (antibodies) present in causes mother destroys the foetal RBC due to mixing of blood. This causes the **Haemolytic Disease of the New Born** (HDN), called as **erythroblastosis foetalis**. In some cases new born may survive but will be anaemic and may also suffer with jaundice.

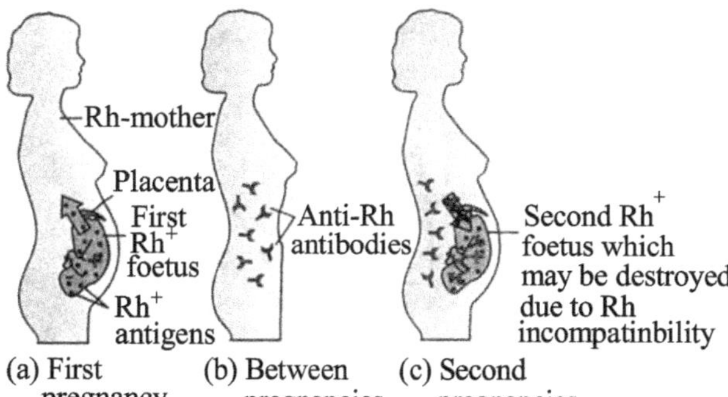

Diagram depicting Rh is incompatibility during pregnancy

This condition can be avoided by administering anti-Rh antibodies to the mother immediately after the delivery of the first child.

2. There are more than 30 surface antigens in blood cells which give rise to different blood groups.

   ABO Grouping on basis of the presence or absence of two surface antigens on the RBCs namely, A and B. The plasma of different individuals contain two natural antibodies. The distribution of antigen and antibody in divided four groups into. A, AB, B and O.

Human ABO Blood Groups and their Compatibility

Blood Group	Genotype	Antigens on Red Blood Corpuscles	Antibodies in Blood Plasma	Donor	Recipient
A	$I^A I^A$ or $I^A I^o$	A	b	A, AB	A, O
B	$I^B I^B$ or $I^B I^o$	B	a	B, AB	B, O
AB	$I^A I^B$	AB	None	AB	AB, A, B, O
O	$I^o I^o$	None	a, b	AB, A, B, O	O

Form the given table it is evident that group 'O' blood can donate to persons with any other blood group and hence 'O' group individuals are called **'Universal donors'**. Person with 'AB' blood can accept blood from persons with AB, as well as the other groups of blood. Hence, such persons are called **'Universal recipients'**.

3. The diagrammatic presentation of heart with labelled SAN, AVN, AV bundles bundle of His and purkinje fibres in heart is shown below.
   Refer Diagram from Practice Solution Q.1 of Long Answer Question

19 Excretory Products and their Elimination

19.1 Define Glomerular Filtration Rate (GFR).

Sol. Glomerular filtration rate refers to the quantity of the filtrate formed by the kidneys per minute.

It is 125 ml per minute *i.e.*, 180 litres per day.

19.2 Explain the autoregulatory mechanism of GFR.

Sol. – This mechanism in Kidney is present to regulate glomerular filtrate rate.

– Juxtaglomerular apparatus (JGA) is a specialised cellular region located where the distal convoluted tubule and afferent arteriole, come in contact with each other.

– A fall in GFR can activate the JG cells to release renin which acts through a complex series of reactions called renin-angiotensin aldosterone mechanism, can stimulate blood flow and thereby the GFR back to normal.

19.3 Indicate whether the following statements are true or false :

(i) Micturition is carried out by a reflex.

(ii) ADH helps in water elimination, making the urine hypotonic.

(iii) Protein-free fluid is filtered from blood plasma into the Bowman's capsule.

(iv) Henle's loop plays an important role in concentrating the urine.

(v) Glucose is actively reabsorbed in the proximal convoluted tubule.

Sol. (i) True (ii) False (iii) True (iv) True (v) True.

19.4 Give a brief account of the counter current mechanism.

Sol. The loop of Henle and *vasa recta* are responsible for concentrating the filtrate. The mechanism is called as counter current mechanism. The flow of filtrate in limbs of Henle's loop and vasa recta is opposite direction so, forms a counter-current system. The proximity as well as counter current in them maintains osmolarity increasing 300 $mOsmolL^{-1}$ in cortex and 1200 $mOsmolL^{-1}$ in inner medulla.

19.5 Describe the role of liver, lungs and skin in excretion.

Sol. Lungs is responsible for elimination of large amount (18 litres/day) of CO_2 and water vapour.

Liver secretes bile, degraded steroid hormones, drugs and certain vitamins.

Skin excretes certain substance through glands present in it *e.g.*, glands which excrete sweat produce cooling effect and sebaceous glands eliminate wastes through sebnum.

19.6 Explain micturition.

Sol. Micturition or urination is the process of explusion of urine from the urinary bladder through the urethra.

This is accomplished by the simultaneous contraction of the smooth muscles of urinary bladder wall and relaxation of the skeletal muscles of the sphincter around the opening of the bladder.

The expulsion of urine from the urinary bladder is called micturition. It is a reflex process, but in grown up children and adults, it can be controlled voluntarily to some extent.

19.7 Match the items of column I with those of column II.

	Column I		Column II
(a)	Ammonotelism	(i)	Birds
(b)	Bowman's capsule	(ii)	Water reabsorption
(c)	Micturition	(iii)	Bony fish
(d)	Uricotelism	(iv)	Urinary bladder
(e)	ADH	(v)	Renal tubule

Sol. (a) – (iii) ; (b) – (v) ; (c) – (iv), (d) –(i), (e) – (ii)

19.8 What is meant by the term osmoregulation ?

Sol. Osmoregulation. It is the maintenance of a fixed osmotic concentration inside the body cells and the extracellular fluids by controlling the amount of water and salts.

19.9 Terrestrial animals are generally either ureotelic or uricotelic, not ammonotelic, why?

Sol. Land animals have an integument that is impervious to gas exchange. Ammonia is highly toxic and it has to be eliminated as rapidly as it is formed. It requires a large volume of water for its elimination. They do not have access to such a large volume of water needed for elimination of ammonia. So, they are either ureotelic or uricotelic.

19.10 What is the significance of juxta glomerular apparatus (JGA) in kidney function ?

Sol. The JGA plays a complex regulatory role. A fall in glomerular blood flow/glomerular blood pressure/GFR can activate the JG cells to release renin which converts angiotensinogen in blood to angiotensin I and further to angiotensin II. Angiotensin II, being a powerful vasoconstrictor, increases the glomerular blood pressure and thereby GFR. Angiotensin II also activates the adrenal cortex to release aldosterone. Aldosterone causes reabsorption of Na^+ and water from the distal parts of the tubule. This also leads to an increase in blood pressure and GFR. This complex mechanism is generally known as the **Renin-Angiotensin** mechanism.

19.11 Name the following :
 (a) **A chordate animal having flame cells as excretory structures.**
 (b) **Cortical portions projecting between the medullary pyramids in the human kidney.**
 (c) **A loop of capillary running parallel to the Henle's loop.**

Sol. (a) *Amphioxus.*
 (b) Columns of Bertini.
 (c) *Vasa recta.*

19.12 Fill in the gaps :
 (a) **Ascending limb of Henle's loop is .... to water whereas the descending limb is .... to it.**
 (b) **Reabsorption of water from distal parts of the tubules is facilitated by hormone ....**
 (c) **Dialysis fluid contain all the constituents as in plasma except ....**
 (d) **A healthy adult human excretes (on an average) .... gm of urea/day.**

Sol. (a) impermeable, permeable
 (b) ADH (vasopressin)
 (c) nitrogenous wastes
 (d) 25 to 30 gm

SECTION B   PRACTICE QUESTIONS 

MULTIPLE CHOICE QUESTIONS

1. Uricotelic mode of passing out nitrogenous wastes is found in
   (a) reptiles and bird
   (b) birds and annelids
   (c) amphibians and reptiles
   (d) insects and amphibians

2. Excretion of nitrogenous waste product in semi-solid form occur in
   (a) amniotes   (b) desert animals
   (c) ureotelic animals   (d) uricotelic animals

3. The projections of renal pelvis are called
   (a) hiluses
   (b) calyces
   (c) medullary pyramids
   (d) renal columns

4. Glomerulus and Bowman's capsule constitute
   (a) nephrotome
   (b) renal corpuscle
   (c) renal capsule
   (d) malpighian tubule

5. Blood vessel leading to glomerulus is called
   (a) renal artery   (b) renal vein
   (c) efferent arteriole   (d) afferent arteriole

6. The part of the nephron impermeable to water is
   (a) proximal tubule
   (b) distal tubule
   (c) ascending limb of Henle's loop
   (d) collecting duct

7. The ascending loop of Henle is permeable for
   (a) ammonia   (b) glucose
   (c) sodium   (d) water

8. In nephron water absorption is maximum in
   (a) proximal convoluted tubule (PCT).
   (b) ascending limb of Henle.
   (c) descending limb of Henle.
   (d) distal convoluted tubule (DCT).

9. The cells named podocytes occur in
   (a) inner wall of Bowman's capsule
   (b) outer wall of Bowman's capsule
   (c) in the wall of glomerulus
   (d) in the wall of Henle's loop

10. The function of renin is
    (a) degradation of angiotensinogen
    (b) stimulation of corpus luteum
    (c) to reduce blood pressure
    (d) vasodilatation

ASSERTION & REASON QUESTIONS

DIRECTION (Qs. 1-5) : *These questions consists of two statements. Answer these questions selecting the appropriate option given below:*
(a) Both Assertion (A) and Reason (R) are true and Reason (R) is the correct explanation of Assertion (A).
(b) Both Assertion (A) and Reason (R) are true, but Reason (R) is not the correct explanation of Assertion (A).
(c) Assertion (A) is true, but Reason (R) is false.
(d) Assertion (A) is false, but Reason (R) is true.

1. **Assertion:** Flame cells are the excretory structures in cockroach.
    Reason: Nephridia are found in earthworm.
2. **Assertion:** Cortical nephrons have short loop of Henle.
    Reason: Juxtamedullary nephrons have longer loop of Henle.
3. **Assertion:** In vertebrates, the liver is also referred as an accessory excretory organ.
    Reason: Liver helps kidneys in the secretion of urine.
4. **Assertion:** A decrease in glomerular blood pressure results in the release of renin.
    Reason: Renin convets angiotensinogen in blood to angiotensin I and then to angiotensin II.
5. **Assertion:** Ultrafiltration takes place in presence of effective filtration pressure.
    Reason: In ultrafiltration process, blood is filtered in Bowman's capsule, filtered fluid contain protein & blood corpuscles also.

CASE/PASSAGE BASED QUESTIONS

DIRECTIONS (Qs. 1-5) : *Read the following passage and answer the questions that follows.*

The given diagram, a nephron of human excretory system is represented. Observe the diagram and answers the questions.

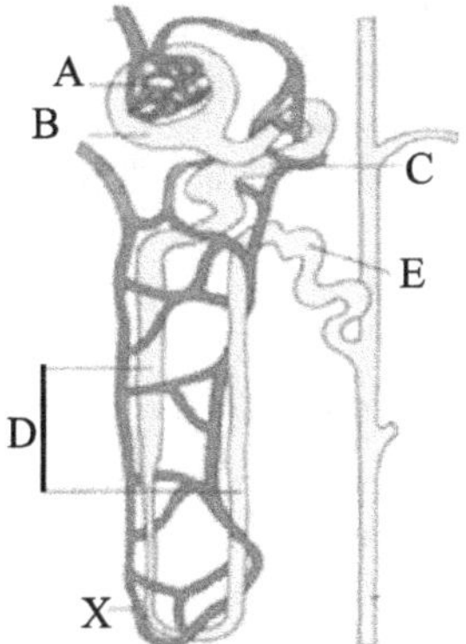

1. The label X represents ________ that function in ________.
    (a) Vasa recta- Reabsorption of water, minerals and digestive end products.
    (b) Henle's loop- Filtration of plasma leaving the blood.
    (c) Vasa recta- Filtration of plasma leaving the blood.
    (d) Henle's loop- Reabsorption of water, minerals and digestive end products.
2. Which blood component would not usually pass through the membranes from region A to region B?
    (a) Mineral salts (b) Red blood cells
    (c) Urea (d) Water
3. After the blood enters the kidney, it travels to the ________?
    (a) A (b) B
    (c) C (d) D
4. Which of the following statement is true?
    (a) Nephron is a functional unit of living organism.
    (b) Nephron is present in the liver cells.
    (c) Nephron is a functional unit of the kidney.
    (d) All of these
5. The main organ of excretory system is
    (a) Liver (b) Intestine
    (c) Kidney (d) All of them

VERY SHORT ANSWER QUESTIONS

1. Name the nitrogenous waste excreted by larval and adult stage of frog respectively.
2. In which organ ammonia is converted to urea ?
3. Define ammonotelism.
4. What is haemodialysis?
5. Define ketonuria.
6. What is columns of bertini?
7. In which part of the nephron does filtration take place?
8. What difference is observed in the ascending and descending limbs of Henle's loop with reference to permeability to water?
9. Name the body part through which ammonia is eliminated in a bony fish.
10. What is *vasa recta* ?
11. What is the driving force for glomerular filtration?
12. How are the filtration slits formed?
13. Why is glomerular filtration also called as ultrafiltration?
14. Name the mechanism that acts as a check for the Renin-angiotensin mechanism.
15. What is uremia?
16. What term is given to the inflammation of glomerulus in nephron?
17. Which limb of loop of Henle is impermeable to water?
18. What is afferent arteriole?
19. Which hormone promotes reabsorption of water from glomerular filtrate?

SHORT ANSWER QUESTIONS

1. How does the proximal convulated tubule of the nephron contribute in homeostasis ?
2. What are the functions of nephridia ? Name an animal having protonephridia.

3. Kidney do not play a major role in excretion in ammonotelic animals. Justify.

4. What are the functions of ADH?

5. What is the ultimate method of correcting acute renal failure ? Describe.

6. Mention the role of DCT in urine formation.

7. Why do persons suffering from very low blood pressure pass no urine?

8. Name the passage in sequence through which urine passes from kidneys to the outside in humans. How is urine prevented from flowing back into the ureters?

9. (a) The two human kidneys do not occur at the same level-explain.

   (b) Why are Kidneys called retro-peritoneal?

10. Differentiate between Cortical Nephron and Juxtamedullary Nephron.

11. What is the chemical composition of human urine.

12. What is Erythropoietin? What is its function?

LONG ANSWER QUESTIONS

1. Describe the structure of kidney.

2. Describe the role of organs other than kidney in the process of excretion in human being.

3. Describe the structure of nephron.

4. Describe the process of haemodialysis.

SOLUTIONS

Multiple Choice Questions

1. (a) An uricotelic organism produces uric acid as a result of de-amination. Examples of such organism are birds and insects.

2. (d) Excretion of nitrogenous waste product in semi-solid form is found in uricotelic animals.

3. (b) Hilus leads to funnel shaped cavity called renal pelvis with projections called calyces.

4. (b) Malpighian corpuscle (renal corpuscle) comprises glomerulus and Bowman's capsule. The malpighian corpuscle is named after Marcello Malpighi, an italian physician and biologist.

5. (d) Glomerulus is a tuft of capillaries formed by afferent arteriole (a fine branch of renal artery).

6. (c) The ascending limb of Henle's loop is impermeable to water but allows transport of electrolytes like sodium. So, the filtrate gets diluted.

7. (c) The ascending limb is impermeable to water but allows transport of electrolytes like sodium. So, the filtrate gets diluted.

8. (a) PCT increases the surface area for reabsorption. PCT reabsorbs most of the nutrients, and 70-80% of electrolytes and water.

9. (a) Podocytes are found in the inner wall of Bowman's capsule. Podocyles send foot processes over the length of the glomerulus.

10. (a) Renin converts angiotensinogen in blood to angiotensin I and further to angiotensin II (a vasoconstrictor).

Assertion & Reason Questions

1. (d) Flame cells are found in flatworms, rotifes etc. Malpighian tubules are the excretory structures in cockroaches. Nephridia are found in earthworm and prawns contain antennal glands or green glands for excretion.

2. (b) The cortical nephrons have short loop o Henle and Juxtamedullary nephrons have longer loop of Henle and vasa recta.

3. (c) In vertebrates, the lungs, liver & skin are referred as accessory excretory organs because besides the urinary system these organs also participate in the removal of waste products from the body. The liver is the principal organ for the excretion of cholesterol, bile pigments (bilirubin and biliverdin) and inactivated products of steroid hormones, some vitamins and many drugs. It secretes these substances in the bile and indirectly helps in formation of urea through amino acids in ornithine cycle. It has no role in secretion of urine

4. (a) Upon a fall in glomerular blood flow, JG cells are activated to release renin. The angiotensin II formed increases the glomerular blood pressure and thereby GFR.

5. (c) Ultrafiltration takes place in renal corpuscle of uriniferous tubule. It takes place in presence of effective filtration pressure. During the process, blood is filtered and contains only blood plasma – proteins. The filtered blood entering into Bowman's capsule is called glomerular filtrate.

   Glomerular filtrate = Blood – (Blood corpuscles + plasma proteins)

Case/Passage Based Questions

1. (a) The label X represents vasa recta that function in the reabsorption of water, minerals and digestive end products.

2. (b) In the given figure of nephron, red blood cells would not usually pass through the membranes from the region A (Glomerulus) to region B (Bowman's capsule). Capillaries of the glomerulus are lined by endothelial cells. These contain numerous pores (called fenestrae) 70-100 nm in diameter. These pores allow for the free filtration of fluid, plasma solutes and protein. However they are not large enough that red blood cells can be filtered.

3. **(a)** Label represents glomerulus. After the blood enters the kidney, it travels to the glomerulus.

4. **(c)** Nephron produces urine and removes the waste and excess materials from the blood so called as functional unit of the kidney.

5. **(c)** Kidney is an important organ that plays important role in the excretory system.

Very Short Answer Questions

1. Larval stage - ammonia, Adult stage - urea.
2. Liver.
3. Excretion of ammonia is called ammonotelism.
4. The process of removal of excess urea from the blood of a patient (normally suffering from uremia) using an artificial kidney is known as haemodialysis.
5. Presence of high ketone bodies in the urine is called as ketonuria.
6. These are the extension of the renal cortex between the medullary pyramids as renal columns.
7. Bowman's Capsule/Renal Corpuscle.
8. Ascending limb is impermeable to water and permeable to solutes.
   Descending limb is permeable to water and impermeable to solutes.
9. Gill membranes.
10. The U-shaped peritubular capillary that runs parallel to the Henle's loop is called *vasa recta*.
11. The driving force for filtration is the blood pressure in the glomerular capillaries.
12. The podocytes are arranged in an intricate manner so as to leave some minute spaces called filtration slits.
13. Blood is filtered so finely through these membranes, that almost all the constituents of the plasma except the proteins pass onto the lumen of the bowman's capsule. Therefore, it is considered as a process of ultra filtration.
14. Arterial Natriuretic Factor (ANF) Mechanism.
15. Uremia is a condition of excess accumulation of urea in the blood caused by the malfunctioning of kidneys.
16. Glomerulonephritis.
17. Bowman's capsule and glomerulus are collectively called malpighian body.
18. Blood vessels leading to glomerulus is called afferent arteriole.
19. Vasopressin promotes reabsorption of water from glomerular filtrate.

Short Answer Questions

1. All essential nutrients, and 70–80 per cent of electrolytes and water are reabsorbed by PCT segment. So it helps to maintain the pH and ionic balance of the body fluids by selective secretion of hydrogen ions, ammonia and potassium ions into the filtrate and by absorption of HCO_3^- from it.
2. Nephridia help to eliminate nitrogenous wastes and maintain a fluid and ionic balance. Protonephridia are present in *Amphioxus*, Rotifers, *Planaria*, etc.

3. Ammonia is readily soluble in water and diffuses across the body surface.
   In fish it is excreted as ammonium ions through gill surface. So kidneys do not have any significant role in elimination of ammonia.

4. (i) ADH facilites water absorption from distal tubule.
   (ii) It also affect the kidney function by its constrictory effects also on blood vessels.

5. Kidney transplantation is the ultimate method in the correction of acute renal failures (kidney failure). A functioning kidney is used in transplantation from a donor, preferably a close relative, to minimise its chances of rejection by the immune system of the host.

6. Distal convoluted tubule plays the following roles:
   - Conditional reabsorption of Na^+ & water takes place in this segment.
   - It also reabsorbs HCO_3^-
   - It helps in selective secretion of hydrogen and potassium ions to maintain the pH and sodium-potassium balance in blood.

7. The blood passes into the glomerulus under high pressure during glomerular filtration. If blood pressure is less then it result in the failure of ultrafiltration process in the glomerulus and hence, no urine formation occurs.

8. Kidneys $\rightarrow$ ureters $\rightarrow$ urinary bladder $\rightarrow$ urethra
   Urine is prevented from flowing back into the ureters because the terminal part of each ureter passes obliquely through the bladder wall.

9. (a) Left kidney is slightly longer, narrower, median and lies at a level 1.25 cm higher than the right kidney. Right kidney is lower in position due to presence of right lobe of liver over it.
   (b) **Retroperitoneal**. It is space that lies between peritoneum and vertebral column. Kidneys occur in this space so that they are lined by peritoneum only on the ventral side.

10.

Cortical Nephron	Juxtamedullary Nephron
1. It is found in cortex.	– It is found at the function of renal cortex and medulla.
2. These have relatively short loop of Henle.	– These have longer loop of Henle and Vasarecta.
3. Under normal water the control of blood volume.	– In deficient water condition, this supply, increased nephron deals with water retention occurs through this nephron.

11. Human urine is transparent, yellowish in colour and variable in chemical composition. It consists primarily of water (95%), with organic solutes including urea (2.6%), creatinine, uric acid, and trace amounts of enzymes, carbohydrates, hormones, fatty acids, pigments, and mucins, and inorganic ions such as Na^+, K^+, Cl^- Mg^{2+}, Ca^{2+}, and phosphates.

12. Erythropoietin is a glycoprotein hormone that controls erythropoieses, or the formation of red blood cells. It acts as a cytokine (proteinsignaling molecule) for RBC precursors in bone marrow. It is produced by enterstitial fibroblasts in the kidney in close association with peritubular capillary and tubular epithelial tubule.

Long Answer Questions

1. Kidneys are reddish brown, bean shaped structures situated between the levels of last thoracic and third lumbar vertebra close to the dorsal inner wall of the abdominal cavity. Each kidney of an adult human measures 10-12 cm in length, 5-7 cm in width, 2-3 cm in thickness with an average weight of 120-170 g. Towards the centre of the inner concave surface of the kidney is a notch called hilum through which ureter, blood vessels and nerves enter. Inner to the hilum is a broad funnel shaped space called the renal pelvis with projections called calyces. The outer layer of kidney is a tough capsule. Inside the kidney, there are two zones, an outer *cortex* and an inner *medulla*. The medulla is divided into a few conical masses (medullary pyramids) projecting into the calyces (sing.: calyx). The cortex extends in between the medullary pyramids as renal columns called **Columns of Bertini.**

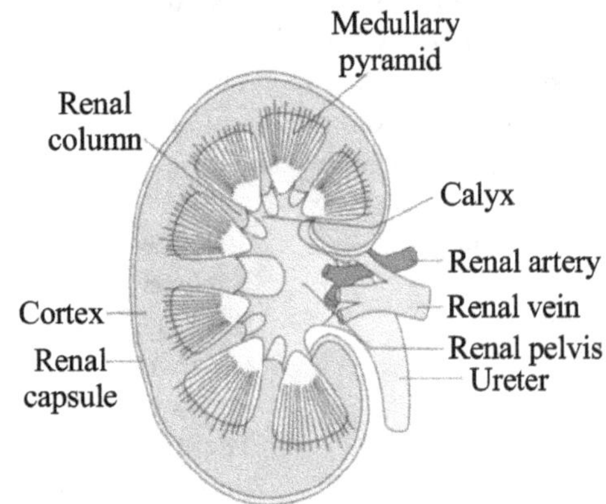

Diagram of Kidney

2. The organs other than kidney envolved in the process of excretion are (i) Lungs (ii) Skin (iii) Liver (iv) Intestine (v) Salivary glands.

   Our lungs remove large amounts of CO_2 (18 litres/day) and also significant quantities of water every day. Liver, the largest gland in our body, secretes bile-containing substances like bilirubin, biliverdin, cholesterol, degraded steroid hormones, vitamins and drugs. Most of these substances ultimately pass out alongwith digestive wastes.

The **sweat** and **sebaceous glands** in the skin can eliminate certain substances through their secretions. Sweat produced by the sweat glands is a watery fluid containing NaCl, small amounts of urea, lactic acid, etc. Though the primary function of sweat is to facilitate a cooling effect on the body surface, it also helps in the removal of some of the wastes mentioned above. Sebaceous glands eliminate certain substances like sterols, hydrocarbons and waxes through sebum. This secretion provides a protective oily covering for the skin.

3. **Structure of nephron**

   A nephron has two parts-the glomerulus and the renal tubule

   (i) **Glomerulus :** It is a tuft of capillaries formed by the afferent arteriole, which is a fine branch of the renal artery.

   (ii) **Renal tubule** has three part
   (a) proximal convoluted tubule
   (b) loop of Henle
   (c) distal convoluted tubule

   (a) **Proximal convoluted tubule** – The renal tubule is closed at the proximal end; it is expanded and curved inwardly to form a double walled cup-shaped structure called Bowman's capsule.

   The glomerulus is located in the hollow of the Bowman's capsule and together they constitute the renal corpuscle.

   The lumen of the capsule is continous with the narrow lumen of the entire tubule.

   The tubule continues to form a highly convoluted proximal convoluted tubule (PCT).

   (b) **Loop of Henle** – It arises from the end of the proximal convoluted tubule and ends at the starting of the distal tubule.

   It is a hairpin-like, with a descending limb (that extends into the medulla) and an ascending limb, that crosses back to the cortex.

   (c) **Distal convoluted tubule** – The ascending limb, on entering the cortex becomes the distal convoluted tubule.

   It then continues as a short straight collecting tubule, that joins the collecting duct.

   Each collecting duct receives the collecting tubule of a number of nephrons.

   Many collects converge, run through renal pyramids and open into the renal pelvis through the openings called renal papillae, at the tip of pyramids.

4. **Haemodialysis :** Blood from the artery of an uremia patient is taken, cooled to $0°C$ and mixed with an anti-coagulant like heparin. The unit contains a coiled cellophane tube surrounded by a fluid (dialysing fluid) having the same composition as that of plasma except the nitrogenous wastes. The porous cellophane membrane of the tube allows the passage of molecules based on concentration gradient. As nitrogenous wastes are absent in the dialysing fluid, these substances freely move out, thereby clearing the blood. The cleared blood is pumped back to the body through a vein after adding anti-heparin to it. This method is a boon for thousands of uremic patients all over the world.

SECTION C — NCERT EXEMPLAR QUESTIONS

MULTIPLE CHOICE QUESTIONS

1. Filtration of the blood takes place at
   (a) PCT
   (b) DCT
   (c) Collecting ducts
   (d) Malpighian body

2. Which of the following statement is incorrect?
   (a) ADH prevents conversion of angiotensinogen in blood to angiotensin
   (b) Aldosterone facilitates water reabsorption
   (c) ANF enhances sodium reabsorption
   (d) Renin causes vasodilation

3. A large quantity of one of the following is removed from our body by lungs.
   (a) CO_2 only
   (b) H_2O only
   (c) CO_2 and H_2O
   (d) ammonia

4. The pH of human urine is approximately
   (a) 6.5 (b) 7
   (c) 6 (d) 7.5

5. Which one of the following statement is incorrect?
   (a) The medullary zone of kidney is divided into a few conical masses called medullary pyramids projecting into the calyces
   (b) Inside the kidney the cortical region extends in between the medullary pyramids as renal pelvis
   (c) Glomerulus along with Bowman's capsule is called the renal corpuscle
   (d) Renal corpuscle, Proximal Convoluted Tubule (PCT) and Distal Convoluted Tubule (DCT) of the nephron are situated in the cortical region of kidney

VERY SHORT ANSWER QUESTIONS

1. Where does the selective reabsorption of glomerular filtrate take place?

2. What is the excretory product from kidneys of reptiles?

3. What is the composition of sweat produced by sweat glands?

4. Identify the glands that perform the excretory function in prawns.

5. What is the excretory structure in Amoeba?

6. The following abbreviations are used in the context of excretory functions, what do they stand for?
   (a) ANF (b) ADH
   (c) GFR (d) DCT

7. Differentiate glycosuria from ketonuria.

8. Mention any two metabolic disorders, which can be diagnosed by analysis of urine.

9. What are the main processes of urine formation?

10. Fill in the blanks appropriately

Organ	Excretory wastes
(a) Kidneys	____________
(b) Lungs	____________
(c) Liver	____________
(d) Skin	____________

SHORT ANSWER QUESTIONS

1. Show the structure of a renal corpuscle with the help of a diagram.

2. What is the role played by renin-angiotensin in the regulation of kidney fuctions?

3. The composition of glomerular filtrate and urine is not same. Comment.

4. What is the procedure advised for the correction of extreme renal failure? Give a brief account of it.

5. Explain, why a haemodialysing unit called artificial kidney?

LONG SHORT ANSWER QUESTIONS

1. Explain the mechanism of formation of concentrated urine in mammals.

2. Describe the structure of a human kidney with the help of a labelled diagram.

SOLUTIONS

Multiple Choice Questions

1. **(d)** Filtration of blood occurs at the **Malpighian body**. Malpighian body or corpuscle comprises of **glomerulus** and **Bowman's capsule.** Filtration of blood takes place in glomerulus through glomerular filtration in which blood enters in the glomerules through an afferent arteriole and leaves it through efferent arteriole.

2. **(a)** ADH (Antidiuretic Hormone) or vasopressin is secreted by the posterior pituitary gland. It facilitates water reabsorption from later parts of the tubule, and thus prevents diuresis.
   It regulates water excretion by increasing permeability of the collecting duct for water and salt by accelerating water and ion transfer determined by the osmotic gradient.

3. **(c)** Human lungs remove large amounts of CO_2 (18L / day) and also siginificant amount of water everyday. While respiration, CO_2 alone cannot be eliminated from the body and the same holds true for H_2O. Ammonia is highly toxic, and thus it is immediately converted to non-toxic form.

4. **(c)** The pH of human urine is approximately 6.0.

5. **(b)** Inside the kidney the cortical region extends between the medullary pyramids as renal pelvis and are called **column of Bertini**.

Very Short Answer Questions

1. The selective reabsorption of glomerular filtrate takes place in Proximal Convoluted Tubules (PCT) and Distal Convoluted Tubules (DCT).

2. The excretory product from the kidney of reptile is uric acid.

3. Sweat produced by sweat glands is a watery fluid that containing NaCl, small amounts of urea, lactic acid, etc. It's primary function is to facilitate a cooling effect on the body surface and also to helps in removal of water.

4. In prawns, the excretory organs are known as antennary glands or green glands. These glands are white pea sized structures and opaque enclosed in the coxa of each 2nd antenna. They mainly excrete ammonia.

5. Conractile vacuole performs the function of excretion as well as osmoregulation in amoeba.

6. (a) ANF Stands for Atrial Natriuretic Factor
    (b) ADH Stands for Antidiuretic Hormone
    (c) GFR Stands for Glomerular Filtration Rate
    (d) DCT Stands for Distal Convoluted Tubule

7. Difference between glycosuria and ketonuria is as follows

Glycosuria	Ketonuria
The presence of glucose in urine is known as glycosuria. It occurs in diabetes mallitus.	Presence of abnormally high ketone bodies in urine is termed as ketonuria. Increase ketones in urine usually occurs at the time of longtime

8. Metabolic disorders that can be diagnosed by analysis of urine are

(i) **Hematuria-** It is a disorder in which blood cells are present in the urine, which could be a sign of kidney stone or a tumor in urinary tract.

(ii) **Albuminuria-** It is a disorder in which albumin is present in urine and occurs in nephritis i.e., inflammaton of glomeruli. In this condition the size of filtering slits becomes enlarged.

9. Urine formation includes glomerular filtration (ultra filteration), selective reabsorption and tubular secretion that occurs in different parts of the nephron.
    Glomerular filteration is carried out by glomerulus and is involve the filteration of blood.
    Selective reabsorption is the absorption of filtrate through renal tubules either activity or passively.
    Tubular secretin involves secretion through tubular cells in urine in order to maintain ionic and acid-base balance of body fluids.

10. | Organ | Excretory wastes |
    |---|---|
    | (a) Kidneys | Urine |
    | (b) Lungs | CO_2 |
    | (c) Liver | Urea |
    | (d) Skin | Sweat |

Short Answer Questions

1. The structure of a renal corpuscle is shown below.

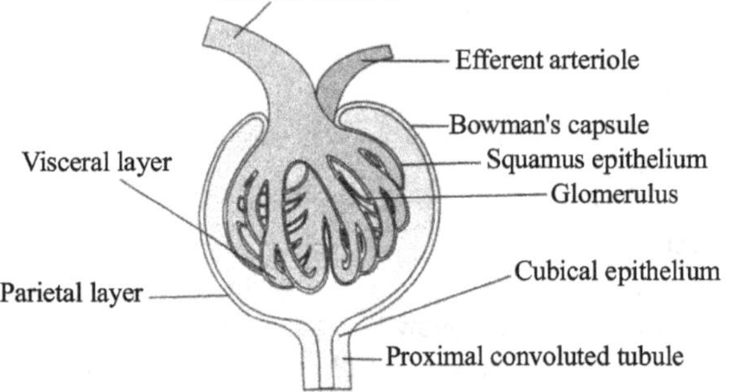

2. On activation by fall in the glomerular blood pressure/flow renin is released from the Juxta-Glomerular Apparatus (JGA). It converts angiotensinogen in blood to angiotensin I and further to angiotensin II. Angiotensin II, being a powerful vasoconstrictor, increases the glomerular blood pressure and thereby Glomerular Filteration Rate (GFR). Angiotensin II also activates the adrenal cortex to release aldosterone. This Aldosterone causes reabsorption of Na+ and water from the distal parts of the tubule. Which leads to an increase in blood pressure and GFR. This complex mechanism is generally known as Renin Angiotensin Aldosterone System of RAAS.

3. Glomerular filtrate contains all the content of the blood plasma except proteins. About 180 litres of glomerular filtrate like water, glucose, nutrients ions etc. occurs. As a result, now the composition of urine is quite different from that of the glomerular filtrate. Some ions are also added to this fluid by tubules *i.e.* tubular secretion to maintain ionic and acid base balance of body fluids. Thus the composition of glomerular filtrate andd urine is not same.

4. The ultimate method for the correction of acute/extreme renal failure (kidney failure) is, Kidney transplantation it is to minimise chances of rejection by the immune system of the host, functional kidney is used as a transplant from a donor, preferably close relative modern clinical procedures have increased the success rate of such a complicated technique.

5. Haemodialysis is a method that become a boon for thousands of uremic (accumulation of urea in blood) patients all over the world.

   Haemodialysing unit act as artificial kidney by removing urea from patients blood due to kidney failure. In this process blood is drained from artery and pumped into a dialysing unit after the addition of an anticoagulant named heparin.

   The unit contains a coiled cellophane tube which is surrounded by a dialysing fluid having the same composition as that of plasma except nitrogenous waste. The porous cellophane membrane of the tube allows the passage of molecules that is based on concentration gradient. Absence of nitrogenous water in dialysing fluid these substances freely move out thereby clearing the blood.

   In the end the cleared blood is pumped back to the body through a vein after the addition of anti-heparin to it thereby completing the process.

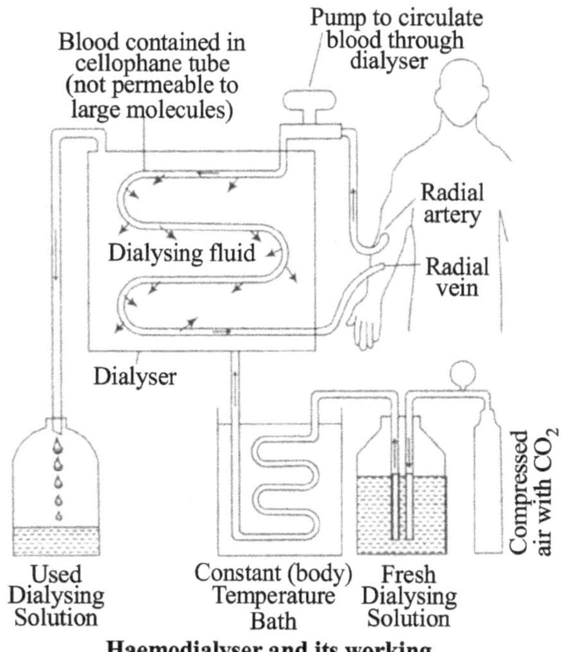

Haemodialyser and its working

Long Answer Questions

1. Mammals have the ability to produce concentrated urine. The loop of Henle and vasa recta play important role in it, which is discussed as follows:

   (i) The proximity between the Henle's loop and vasa recta, as well as the counter current that is formed due to the flow of filtrate in two limb's of Henle's loop in opposite direction and help in maintaining an increasing osmolality towards the inner medullary interstitium, i.e., from 300 mOsmoL^{-1} in the cortex to about 1200 mOsmol^{-1} in the inner medulla.

   (ii) This gradient is caused mainly due to NaCl and urea ascending limb of Henle's loop transports NaCl, that is exchanged with the descending limb of vasa recta.

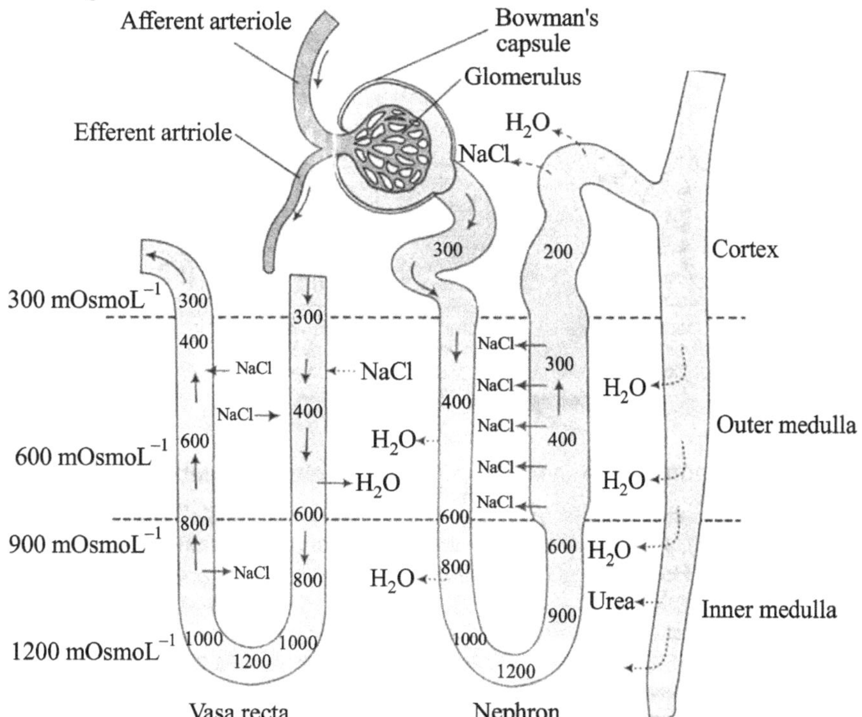

Diagrammatic representation of a nephron and vasa recta showing counter current mechanism

(iii) Through the ascending portion of vasa recta. NaCl is returned to the interstitium.

(iv) Similarly, a small amount of urea enters the thin segment of the ascending limb of Henle's loop, which is transported back to the intersitium by the collecting tubule.

(v) This special arrangement of Henle's loop, and vasa recta, is called the counter current mechanism.

(vi) The rate of dissipation is reduced by the counter current exchange. This in turn, reduces the rate at which the current must pump Na^+ to maintain any given gradient.

(vii) Presence of such interstitial garden helps in an easy passage of water from the collecting tubule thereby concentrating the filtrate (urine).

(viii) Human kidneys produces urine nearly four times concentrated than the initial filtrate formed.

2. Human kidney are reddish-brown, bean-shaped structures that is situated between the last thoracic and third lumbar vertebra, which is closer to the dorsal inner wall of the abdominal cavity. Each kidney of an adult human measures 10-12 cm in length, 5-7 cm in width, 2-3 cm in thickness with an average weight of 120-170 gm.

The kidney is covered by a fibrous connective tissue i.e., the renal capsula, that protects the kidney. Internally, it consists of outer dark cortex and an inner light medulla, both containing nephron, nephron is the structural and functional units of kidney.

The median concave border of a kidney contains a notch called hilum, that functions as route entry and exit of blood vessels, nerves and ureter.

The renal cortex is granular in appearance that contains convoluted tubules that malpighian corpuscles. The renal medulla contains loop of henle, collecting ducts and tubules and ducts of Bertini.

Medulla is divided into conical masses, the medullary pyramids that further form papillae. The papillae form calyces, which join to renal pelvis leading to ureter. Between the medullary pyramids, cortex extends into medulla and forms renal columns which are called as column of Bertini.

Figure Refer to Practice Solution Long Answer Q.1.

20. Locomotion and Movement

20.1 **Draw the diagram of a sarcomere of skeletal muscle showing different regions.**

Sol.

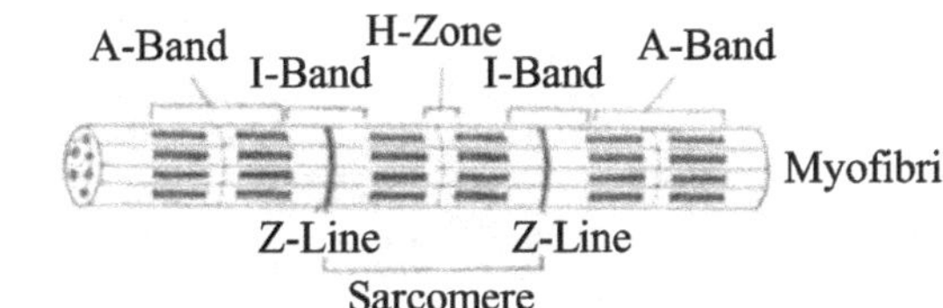

20.2 **Define sliding filament theory of muscle contraction.**

Sol. Sliding filament theory states that contraction of a muscle fibre takes place by the sliding of the thin filaments over thick filaments.

20.3 **Describe the important steps in muscle contraction.**

Sol. **Steps in muscle contraction :**

– A nerve impulse arriving at the neuromuscular junctions initiates the contractile response.

– A neurotransmitter released at the neuromuscular junction enters the sacromere through its membrane channel.

– The opening of the channel also results in the inflow of Na^+ ions inside the sacromere and generates an action potential that travels along the entire length of the muscle fibres.

– The sacromere reticulum releases Ca^{++} ions, which bind with the specific sites present on the troponin component of the thin filament.

– As a result of conformational changes in the troponin, the active sites on the F-actin are exposed.

– These are the active sites specific to myosin head, which exhibits myosin-dependent ATPase activity.

– The myosin heads acts as hooks and attach to F-actin to form cross bridges.

– When the muscle is stimulated to contract, the cross bridges move, pulling the two filaments past each other.

– When thousands of actin and myosin filaments interact this way the entire muscle cell shortens. This concept is **the sliding filament theory**.

20.4 **Write true or false. If false, change the statement so that it is true.**

(a) Actin is present in thin filament.

(b) H-zone of striated muscle fibre represents both thick and thin filaments..

(c) Human skeleton has 206 bones.

(d) There are 11 pairs of ribs in man.

(e) Sternum is present on the ventral side of the body.

Sol. (i) True

(ii) False : H-zone of striated muscle fibre represents only thick filaments.

(iii) True

(iv) False : There are 12 pairs of ribs in man.

(v) True

20.5 **Write the differences between.**

(a) **Actin and Myosin**

(b) **Red and White muscles**

(c) **Pectoral and Pelvic girdle**

Sol. (a) Differences between actin and myosin are as following :

	Actin		Myosin
1.	It is thin protein of sacromere or myofibril.	1.	It is thick protein of a sacromere or
2.	It is called as thin filament.	2.	It is called as thick filament.
3.	It is made of two 'F' actins helically wound to each other.	3.	Myosin is made of monomeric protein.
4.	It forms the light band or isotropic band.	4.	It forms the dark band or anistropic band

(b)   The main difference between red muscles and white muscles are as following :

Red muscles	White muscles
1. They have large quantity of myoglobin that gives the red colour.	1. They have very little amount of myoglobin hence are not red in colour.
2. They have a number of mitochondria and blood capillaries.	2. They have less number of mitochondria and blood capillaries.
3. Sacroplasmic reticulum is less.	3. Sacroplasmic reticulum is more.
4. They can work for longer periods, without getting fatigued.	4. They can work for shorter periods only.
5. These muscles fibres are thinner and smaller.	5. These muscle fibres are thicker and bigger.

(c)   The main difference between pectoral girdle and pelvic girdle are as following :

Pectoral girdle	Pelvic girdle
1. It occurs in the shoulder region, hence also called shoulder girdle.	1. It occurs in the hip region, hence also called hip girdle.
2. There are two separated pectoral girdles.	2. There is one pelvic girdle.
3. Each pectoral girdle has a glenoid cavity into which the head of humerus is articulated.	3. Each innominate bone has a deep depression called the acetabulum to which the head of the femur is articulated.
4. It has no articulation with vertebral column.	4. It has articulation with vertebral column.
5. Bones are light because it is not subject to much stress.	5. Bones are thick because it is subject to much stress.

20.6   Match Column I with Column II

	Column I		Column II
(a)	Smooth muscle	(i)	Myoglobin
(b)	Tropomyosin	(ii)	Thin filament
(c)	Red muscle	(iii)	Sutures
(d)	Skull	(iv)	Involuntary

Sol.   (a) - (iv); (b) - (ii), (c) - (i), (d) - (iii)

20.7   What are the different types of movements exhibited by the cells of human body ?

Sol.   Ciliary movements, amoeboid movement, muscular movement.

20.8   How do you distinguish between a skeletal muscle and a cardiac muscle ?

Sol.   The main difference between skeltal muscle and cardiac muscle are as following :

Skeletal muscle	Cardiac muscle
1. Closely associated with the skeletal components of the body.	1. Cardiac muscles are the muscles of heart.
2. Also called striated muscles because of striped appearance under microscope.	2. Striated but branched pattern.
3. Voluntary in nature.	3. Involuntary in nature.
4. Intercalated discs are absent.	4. Intercalated discs are present.

20.9   Name the type of joint between the following :
(a)   **Atlas/Axis**
(b)   **Carpal/metacarpal of thumb**
(c)   **Between phalanges**
(d)   **Femur/acetabulum**
(e)   **Between cranial bones**
(f)   **Between pubic bones in the pelvic girdle**

Sol.   (a)   Pivot joint
(b)   Saddle joint
(c)   Gliding joint
(d)   Ball and socket joint
(e)   Fibrous joint
(f)   Cartilagenous joint

20.10   Fill in the blank spaces :
(a)   **All mammals (except a few) have .... cervical vertebra.**
(b)   **The number of phalanges in each limb of human is ....**
(c)   **Thin filament of myofibril contains 2 'F' actins and two other proteins namely .... and ....**
(d)   **In a muscle fibre Ca^{++} is stored in ....**
(e)   **............... and .... pairs of ribs are called floating ribs.**
(f)   **The human cranium is made of .... bones.**

Sol.   (a)   Seven
(b)   Fourteen
(c)   Troponin, tropomyosin
(d)   Sarcoplasmic reticullum
(e) $11^{th}, 12^{th}$
(f)   Eight

SECTION B — PRACTICE QUESTIONS

MULTIPLE CHOICE QUESTIONS

1. The macrophages in human body exhibit
   (a) ciliary movement
   (b) amoeboid movement
   (c) no movement
   (d) movement with the blood flow only

2. Which set clearly identify striated muscles?
   (a) Cylindrical, Syncytial and Unbranched
   (b) Spindle, Unbranched and Uninucleated
   (c) Cylindrical, Striped and Nucleated
   (d) Cylindrical, Striped and Branched

3. Cardiac muscles are different from that of skeletal muscles as the former are
   (a) striated but involuntary.
   (b) non striated and involuntary.
   (c) smooth or unstriated.
   (d) voluntary in action.

4. Red muscle fibres are rich in
   (a) golgi bodies   (b) mitochondria
   (c) lysosomes   (d) ribosomes

5. According to the sliding filament theory of muscle contraction,
   (a) actin binds ATP and breaks it apart as actin pulls against myosin.
   (b) calcium ions are released from myosin as the filaments slide by.
   (c) the thick and thin filaments do not change length during this process.
   (d) all of the above

6. Part of the body having a single pair of bones is called
   (a) pelvic girdle   (b) external ear
   (c) wrist   (d) lower jaw

7. Identify the joint between sternum and the ribs in humans.
   (a) Fibrous joint
   (b) Gliding joint
   (c) Cartilaginous joint
   (d) Angular joint

8. Which of the following is a single U shaped bone, present at the base of the buccal cavity and it is also included in the skull?
   (a) Hyoid   (b) Malleus
   (c) Sacrum   (d) Scapula

9. An acromian process is characteristically found in the:
   (a) pelvic girdle of mammals
   (b) pectoral girdle of mammals
   (c) skull of frog
   (d) sperm of mammals

10. Total number of bones in the hind limb of man is
    (a) 14   (b) 30
    (c) 24   (d) 21

ASSERTION & REASON QUESTIONS

DIRECTION (Qs. 1-5) : *These questions consists of two statements. Answer these questions selecting the appropriate option given below:*
(a) Both Assertion (A) and Reason (R) are true and Reason (R) is the correct explanation of Assertion (A).
(b) Both Assertion (A) and Reason (R) are true, but Reason (R) is not the correct explanation of Assertion (A).
(c) Assertion (A) is true, but Reason (R) is false.
(d) Assertion (A) is false, but Reason (R) is true.

1. **Assertion:** The repeated activation of muscle causes fatigue.
   Reason: The muscle fatigue results in the accumulation of lactic acid in the muscle cells.

2. **Assertion:** The process of muscle contraction is signalled by acetyl choline.
   Reason: The neurotransmitter acetyl choline imparts the action potential to sareolemma causing the release of Ca^{2+} ions into the sarcoplasm.

3. **Assertion :** The phase of muscle contraction occurs when myosin binds and releases actin.
   Reason : Muscle contraction is initiated by a signal sent by the peripheral nervous system via motor neuron.

4. **Assertion:** Pectoral girdle consists of two coxal bones.
   Reason: Each coxal bone is formed by the fusion of 3 bones.

5. **Assertion:** The inflammation of joints is called arthritis.
   Reason: Muscular dystrophy is an age related disorder.

CASE/PASSAGE BASED QUESTIONS

DIRECTIONS (Qs. 1-5) : *Read the following passage and answer the questions that follows.*

Muscle contraction occurs due to the sliding of the thin filaments over the thick filaments. Observe the diagram and answer the questions.

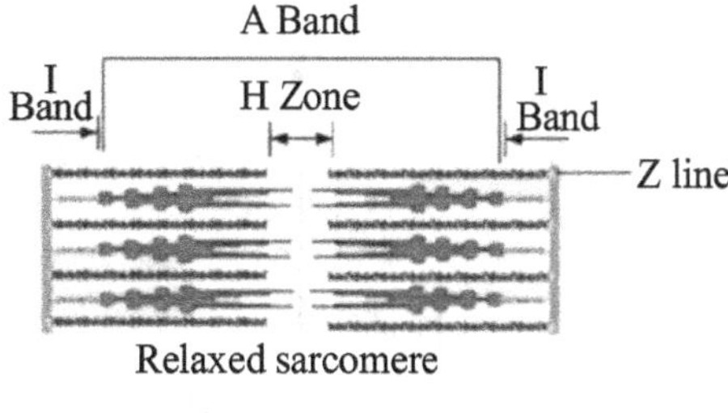

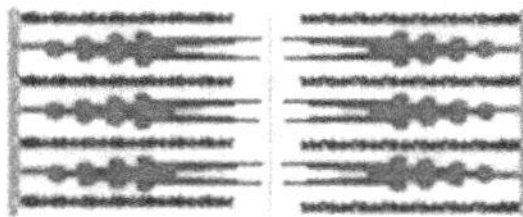

1. Which of the following has a centre for ATP hydrolysis during muscle contraction?
   (a) Actin (b) Myosin head
   (c) Both (a) & (b) (d) None of them
2. Choose the right option with respect to muscle contraction.
   (a) I band gets reduced, 'A' band remains same.
   (b) Both I and A bands remain same.
   (c) I and A bands get reduced.
   (d) 'A' band get reduced and 'I' bamd remain same.
3. The term sarcomere can be referred to as:
   (a) Between two Z lines (b) Between two I bands
   (c) Between two A lines (d) Between two H lines
4. What happens during relaxation of muscle fibres?
   (a) 'Z' line returns back to their original position.
   (b) 'Z' line pulled inwards.
   (c) 'Z' line pulled upwards.
   (d) None of these
5. Read the following statements (i to iv) and select the one option that contains both correct statements.
   (i) Z line is present in the centre of the light band.
   (ii) Thin filaments are firmly attached to the M line.
   (iii) The central part of thick filaments, not overlapped by thin filaments is called Z-band.
   (iv) Light bands contains only thin filaments.
   (a) (i), (iii) and (iv) (b) (ii), (i) and (iii)
   (c) (i), (ii) and (iii) (d) (ii), (i) and (iv)

Very Short Answer Questions

1. What causes gouty arthritis in human?
2. How many tarsals are there in the ankle?
3. What are the bones of the heel called?
4. How many types of movement shows by human body?
5. Name the lubricant which is responsible for the movable joint at the shoulder.
6. Give two disorders of skeleton and joints
7. Mention two sites on all body where striated muscles are present.

8. Name the two filaments which forms the cross-bridges during muscle contraction?
9. Name the monomers of myosin.
10. How many ribs are present in adult man?
11. Name the single U-shaped bone present at the base of buccal cavity.
12. Name the location where Z-line is present in sacromere.
13. What is the total number of bones present in the left pectoral girdle and the left arm respectively in a normal human ?
14. Name the kind of joint which permits movements in a single plane only.
15. What are neuromuscular junctions ?
16. Why are the ribs described as bicephalic ?
17. What is acromion ?
18. What is arthritis?
19. What is sarcomere?
20. Which muscle protein acts as ATPase?

Short Answer Questions

1. What causes osteoporosis?
2. Why a red muscle fibre can work for a prolonged period, while a white muscle fibre suffers from fatigue soon?
3. Name the major components of appendicular skeleton.
4. What is sarcoplasmic reticulum? What is its function?
5. Differentiate between A and I bands.
6. Draw the labelled diagram of pectoral girdle and upper arm.
7. Differentiate between bone and cartilage.
8. Describe the vertebro-chondral ribs.
9. How muscular contraction is triggered?

Long Answer Questions

1. Draw a well diagram of human skull.
2. Write short notes on :
   (a) Muscular dystrophy
   (b) Tetany
   (c) Myasthenia gravis
3. Give differences between movable and immovable joints ?

SOLUTIONS

Multiple Choice Questions

1. **(b)** Movement of leucocyte, macrophages and cytoskeletal elements in our body exhibits amoeboid movement. It is a type of movement which occur with the help of pseudopodia formed by cytoplasmic streaming (as in *Amoeba*).
2. **(a)** Striated muscles are cylindrical, syncytial and unbranched.
3. **(a)** Cardiac muscle fibres are striated but involuntary in action while skeletal muscle fibres are striated but voluntary in action.

4. **(b)** A red muscles fibre is a muscle in which small dark fibers predominate and myoglobin and mitochondria are abundant. Red muscle fibres contract and fatigue more slowly than white fibres and generate ATP by aerobic catabolism of glucose and fats, utilizing myoglobin-bound O_2.
5. **(c)** The thick and thin filaments do not change length during muscle contraction.
6. **(a)** Part of the body having a single pair of bones is pelvic girdle. Pelvic girdle, also called bony pelvis, is a ring-like structure, located in the lower part of the trunk. It connects the axial skeleton to the lower limbs. The bony pelvis consists of the two hip bones (also known as innominate or pelvic bones), sacrum and coccyx.

7. **(c)** Cartilaginous joints are connected entirely by cartilage (fibrocartilage or hyaline). These joints allow more movement between bones than a fibrous joint but less than the highly mobile synovial joint. Cartilaginous joint is found in between the sternum and the ribs in human. They also form the growth regions of immature long bones and the intervertebral discs of the spinal column.

8. **(a)** Hyoid is a horseshoe-shaped (or U shaped) bone situated in the anterior midline of the neck between the chin and the thyroid cartilage. At rest, it lies at the level of the base of the mandible in the front and the third cervical vertebra (C_3) behind. The hyoid bone provides attachment to the muscles of the floor of the mouth and the tongue above, the larynx below, and the epiglottis and pharynx behind. The hyoid bone helps in tongue movement and swallowing.

9. **(b)** Each half of pectoral girdle has two bones i.e. clavicle and scapula. A spine like, acromian process is attached to scapula for articulation with clavicle bone.

10. **(b)** Each hind limb contain 30 bones namely 1 femur in the thigh, 1 petala in the knee, 1 tibia and 1 fibula in the lower leg, 7 tarsals in the ankle, 5 metatarsals in the sole and 14 phalanges in toes.

Assertion & Reason Questions

1. **(a)** The lactic acid is produced as a result of anaerobic respiration.

2. **(a)** The increase in Ca^{2+} levels leads to the binding of calcium with a subunit of troponin on actin filaments and thereby remove the masking of active sites for myosin.

3. **(c)** The phase of muscle contraction occurs when myosin binds and releases actin. Muscle contraction is initiated by a signal sent by the central nervous system via a motor neuron. A motor neuron along with the muscle fibres connected to it constitutes a motor unit.

4. **(d)** The pelvic girdle consist of 2 coxal bones and pectoral girdle consist of clavicle and scapla. Each coxal bone is formed by the fusion of 3 bones-ilium, ischium and pubis.

5. **(c)** Muscular dystrophy is a genetic disorder marked by the progressive degeneration of skeletal muscle.

Case/Passage Based Questions

1. **(b)** The site of ATP hydrolysis is myosin head.

2. **(a)** During contraction of the muscle, the 'I' bands get reduced and 'A' band retain the length.

3. **(a)** The part between two 'Z' lines is referred to as sarcomere.

4. **(a)** Relaxation is marked by the return of 'Z' line back to their original position.

5. **(a)** Thin filaments are firmly attached to 'Z' line. 'Z' bond is a thin membrane in a myofibril and seen on longitudinal section as a dark line in the centre of the I band. The central part of thick filament, not overlapped by thin filament.

Very Short Answer Questions

1. Gouty arthritis (= *Gout*) is caused either due to excessive formation of uric acid or inability to excrete it.

2. Seven.

3. Metatarsals.

4. Three types of movements : amoeboid, ciliary and muscular movement.

5. Synovial fluid.

6. Arthritis and Osteoporosis.

7. Limbs and tongue.

8. Actin and myosin.

9. Meromyosins.

10. Twelve pairs.

11. Hyoid.

12. Centre of I band.

13. Left pectoral girdle   –   2
Left arm   –   30

14. Hinge joint.

15. The junction between a motor neuron and the sarcolemma of a muscle fibre, is known as neuromuscular junction.

16. Since each rib has two articulation surfaces on its dorsal end, it is described as bicephalic.

17. It is a flat expanded process projecting from the spine of the scapula; clavicle articulates with it.

18. Arthritis is painful stiffness and inflammation of joints.

19. A sarcomere is a structural unit within a microfibril bounded by Z lines that contain actin and myosin.

20. Myosin.

Short Answer Questions

1. Osteoporosis is a disease in which bone loses minerals and fibres from its matrix. There are more chances of fractures. Decreased level of estrogen is a common cause.

2. Red muscle fibres contain myoglobin that stores oxygen in the form of oxymyoglobin.
Since, there is a continuous supply of oxygen; for oxidation of food materials to release energy, the red muscles fibres retain energy and do not become fatigued and work for long periods whereas white muscle fibres lack myoglobin. At times they carry out the anaerobic respiration and become fatigued.

3. It is situated at the lateral sides which actually extend outwards from the principal axis. It consists of pectoral and pelvic girdles and bones of arms and legs.

4. Endoplasmic reticulum of muscle fibre is called sarcoplasmic reticulum which acts as a store house of calcium ions.

5. The main differences between A-band and I-band are as following :

	A – band		I – band
1.	It has wide H-zone.	1.	It has thin Z-line.
2.	It gives dark appearance and hence also called dark band.	2.	It gives light appearance hence also called light band.
3.	It contains myosin filaments and parts of actin filaments.	3.	It contains part of actin filaments.
4.	Its length remains unchanged during muscle contraction.	4.	It shortens during muscle contraction.

6.

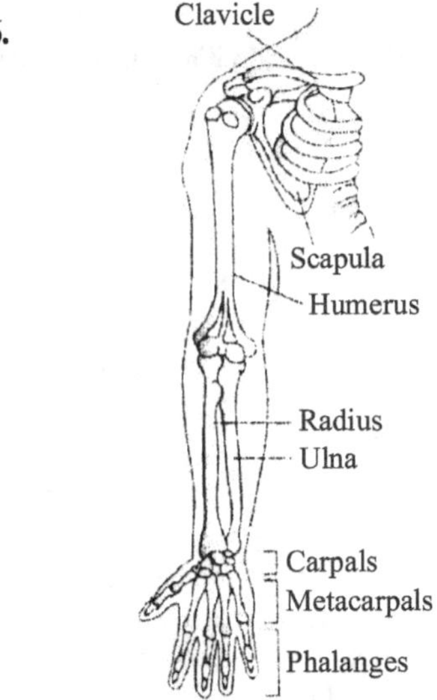

Fig. Right pectoral girdle and upper arm (Frontal view)

7. The main differences between bone and cartilage are as following :

	Bone		Cartilage
1.	It is a hard/rigid connective tissue.	1.	It is semi-rigid but hard connective tissue.
2.	The matrix is deposited with calcium salts.	2.	The matrix does not contain calcium salts.
3.	One osteocyte (bone cell) is found in a lacuna.	3.	2/3/4 chondrocytes (cartilage cells) are present in a lacuna.

8. Vertebro-chondral ribs
- 8th, 9th and 10th pairs of ribs are called vertebro-chondral (false) ribs.
- They remain attached dorsally to the respective thoracic vertebrae and vertrally to the sternum through the seventh rib by hyaline cartilage.

9. It is triggered by nerve releasing a neurotransmitter, which in turn triggeres the sarcoplasmic reticulum to release calcium ions into muscle interior. Where they bind to troponin, thus causing tropomyosin to shift from the face of the actin filament to which myosin heads need to produce contraction.

Long Answer Questions

1.

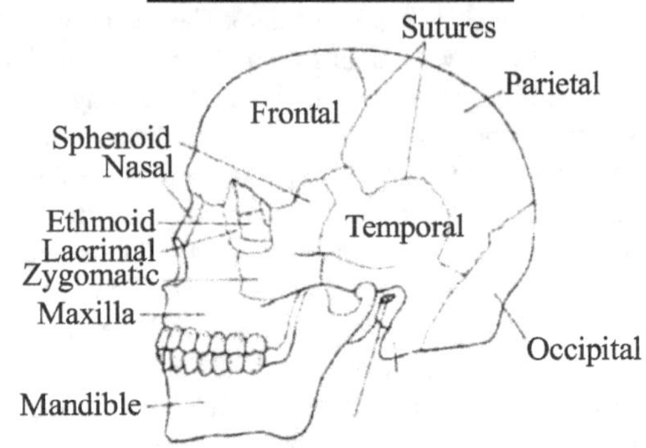

Fig. Human skull

2. Muscular dystrophy

The abnormality of muscles associated with dysfunction and ultimately deterioration is called muscular dystrophy. It is a genetic disorder caused by lack of dystrophin.

Myasthenia gravis : It is an auto-immune disorder that affecting neuro-muscular junction and leads to fatigue, weaking and paralysis of skeletal muscles.

Tetany : The rapid spasm and (wild contractions) is called tetany. In this case the muscles do not get a chance to relax at all. It is caused due to deficiency of parathyroid hormone and thus lowering Ca^{++} in blood fluid.

3. Differences between movable and immovable joint are tabulated below :

	Immovable joints		Movable joints
1.	It is also called fibrous joints.	1.	It is called either cartilagenous (slightly movable) or synovial (free movable) joints.
2.	There is white fibrous tissue between the ends of the two bones taking parts in the joints.	2.	There is either a pad of white fibro cartilage or synovial membrane between the ends of joints.
3.	The joints are marked by suture. There is no need of any specialized structure as the joint is fixed.	3.	Synovial membrane secretes synovial fluid that gets as cushion to prevent friction between bony surface. The joints are modified into various articular surface.

SECTION C — NCERT EXEMPLAR QUESTIONS

MULTIPLE CHOICE QUESTIONS

1. Ribs are attached to
   (a) scapula   (b) sternum
   (c) clavicle   (d) ilium

2. Which one of the following is showing the correct sequential order of vertebrae in the vertebral column of human beings?
   (a) Cervical - lumbar - thoracic - sacral - coccygeal
   (b) Cervical - thoracic - sacral - lumbar - coccygeal
   (c) Cervical - sacral - thoracic - lumbar - coccygeal
   (d) Cervical - thoracic - lumbar - sacral - coccygeal

3. Which one of the following pair is incorrect?
   (a) Hinge joint - between humerus and pectoral girdle
   (b) Pivot joint - between atlas, axis and occipital condyle
   (c) Gliding joint - between the carpals
   (d) Saddle joint - between carpel and metacarpals of thumb

4. Macrophages and leucocytes exhibit
   (a) ciliary movement   (b) flagellar movement
   (c) amoeboid movement   (d) gliding movement

5. Which one of the following is not a disorder of bone?
   (a) Arthritis   (b) Osteoporosis
   (c) Rickets   (d) Atherosclerosis

VERY SHORT ANSWER QUESTIONS

1. Name the cells/ tissues in human body which
   (a) exhibit amoeboid movement
   (b) exhibit ciliary movement

2. Locomotion requires a perfect coordinated activity of muscular .... systems.

3. Sarcolemma, sarcoplasm and sarcoplasmic reticulum refer to particular type of cell in our body. Which is this cell and to what parts of that cell do these names refer to?

4. Label the different components of actin filament in the diagram given below

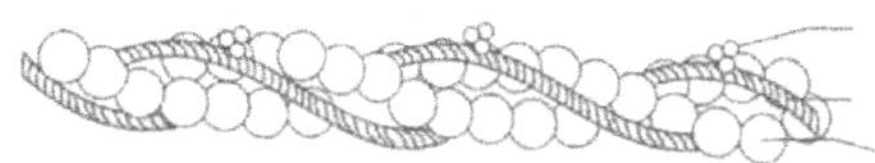

5. What is the difference between the matrix of bones and cartilage?

6. Which tissue is affected by mysthenia gravis? What is the underlying cause.

7. How do our bone joints function without grinding noise and pain?

8. Give the location of a ball and socket joint in a human body.

SHORT ANSWER QUESTIONS

1. With respect to rib cage, explain the following
   (a) bicephalic ribs   (b) true ribs
   (c) floating ribs

2. Exchange of calcium between bone and extracellular fluid takes place under the influence of certain hormones
   (a) What will happen if of Ca^{2+} is in extracellular fluid?
   (b) What will happen if very less amount of Ca^{2+} is in the extracellular fluid?

3. Rahul exercises regularly by visiting a gymnasium. Of late he is gaining weight. What could be the reasons? Choose the correct answer and elaborate.
   (a) Rahul has gained weight due to accumulation of fats in body
   (b) Rahul has gained weight due to increased muscle and less of fat
   (c) Rahul has gained weight because his muscle shape has improved
   (d) Rahul has gained weight because he is accumulating water in the body

4. Radha was running on a treadmill at a great speed for 15 minutes continuously. She stopped the treadmill and abruptly came out. For the next few minutes, she was breathing heavily/fast. Answer the following questions.
   (a) What happened to her muscles when she did strenuously exercised?
   (b) How did her breathing rate change?

5. Write a few lines about gout.

6. What are the points for articulation of pelvic and pectoral girdles?

LONG ANSWER QUESTIONS

1. How does a muscle shorten during its contracting and return to its original form during relaxation?

Multiple Choice Questions

1. **(b)** **Sternum :** is a flat bone present just beneath the skin in the middle of the chest. It is about 15 cm long. It consists of three parts, **manubrium** (the upper most part), **body** (the middle portion) and **xiphoid process** at the tip of the bone. The true ribs (7 pairs) are attached to the **sternum.** The, **scapula** and clavicle together combine to form pectoral girdle, and **Ilium** is a part of the **pelvic girdle.**

2. **(d)** The correct sequence showing the vertebral column of human being is as follows.
   Cervical—thoracic—lumbar — sacrals —coccygeal

3. **(a)** The joint present between the humerus and the pectoral girdle is ball and socket joint. Hinge joint is present between atlas and axis and not between humerus and pectoral girdle. The examples of hinge joints are the elbow, knee, ankle and interphalangeal joint.

4. **(c)** Certain specialised cells in blood like macrophages and leucocytes exhibit amoeboid movement. They have the ability to reach the interstitial fluid by squeezing through the thin walls of blood vessels, while ciliary movement, flagellar movement or gliding movement are not shown by macrophages and leucocytes.

5. **(d)** Atherosclerosis (**ateriosclerotic vascular disease**) is a condition where arteries wall get thickened as a result of invasion and accumulation of WBCs, containing both living active WBCs and remnants of dead WBC's along with **cholesterol** and **triglycerides** arthritis, osteoporosis and rickets are bone disorders.

Very Short Answer Questions

1. (a) Macrophages and leucocytes in blood exhibit amoeboid movement. Cytoskeletal elements like microfilaments are also involved in amoeboid movement.

   (b) Ciliary Movement occurs mostly in the internal organs, lined by the ciliated epithelium, e.g., cilia in trachea helps in removing dust particle and foreign substances inhaled along with atmospheric air.
   Passage of ova through the female reproductive tract is also facilitated by the ciliary movement. This is due to the presence of ciliated epithelium in the Fallopian tube.

2. Locomotion requires a prefect coordinated activity of muscular, skeletal and neural systems.

3. Muscle fibre is lined by the plasma membrane called sarcolemma. Muscle fibre is a syncitium because **sarcoplasm** (the cytoplasm) of muscle fibre contains number of nuclei and **sarcoplasmic reticulum** is the endoplasmic reticulum of the muscle fibre and is the store house of calcium ions.

4. Each actin filament is made of two 'F' (filamentous) actins helically wound to each other and each 'F' actin is a polymer of monomeric 'G' (globular) actins.
   The different components of action filament can be represented as

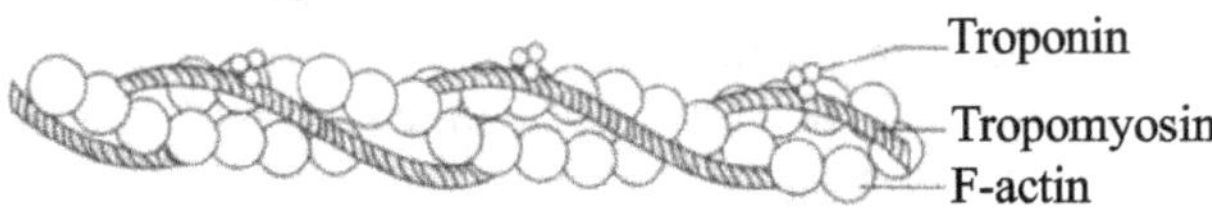

5. Difference between the matrix of ones and cartilage

Matrix of Cartilage	Matrix of Bones
Matrix of cartilage has a flexible material, the chondrin.	Matrix is bones has an inflexible material, the ossein.
Calcium salts may or may not be present in matrix.	Matrix of bones contains calcium salts.

6. Myasthenia gravis is autoimmune disorder of skeletal muscle, which affects neuromuscular junction, that leads to fatigue, weakening and paralysis of the skeletal muscle.

7. The presence of synovial fluid, between articulating surface of the two bones enclosed within synovial cavity of synovial joints to enables out joints to function without grinding noise and pain.

8. In human body Ball and socket joint are present between humerus and pectoral girdle. These joints allows free movement of bone in all direction. E.g., shoulder joints (humerus bone in socket of pectoral girdle) and hip joints femur bone in socket pelvic girdle.

Short Answer Questions

1. There are 12 pairs of ribs. Each rib consist of a thin flat bone dorsally connected to the vertebral column and ventrally to the sternum.
   (a) Bicephalic ribs each rib has two articulating surfaces on its dorsal end hence, are called as bicephatic ribs.
   (b) The first seven pairs of ribs are **true ribs.** These ribs are dorsally attached to the thoracic vertebrae and ventrally connected to the sternum with the help of hyaline cartilage.
   (c) The last two pair (11th and 12th) of ribs are not connected ventrally to the sternum therefore, called as floating ribs.

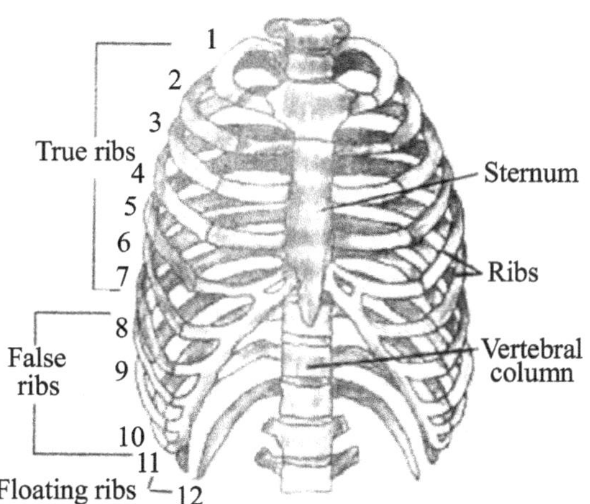

Diagram representing ribs and rib cage

2. Parathyroid and thyroid glands, function under the feed back control of blood calcium

   (a) More Ca^{2+} concentration in extracellular fluid is associated with hyperparathyroidism. It causes demineralisation, resulting in softening and bending of the bones. This condition leads to osteoprosis.

   (b) Very less amount of Ca^{2+} in extracellular fluid is associated with hypoparathyroidism. This increases the excitability or nerves and muscles, causing cramps, sustained contraction of the muscles of larynx, face, hands and feet. This disorder called parathyroid tetany or hypercalcemic tetany.

3. (b) Rahul has gained weight because the shape of his muscle has changed. Regular exercise increases the body muscle. There is an enlargement of muscles due to increase in the amount of sarcoplasm and mitochondria and the strength he to developed led him to gain the mass and size of body muscle and reduction in fat content.

4. (a) Her muscles got fatigues due to continuous exercise because of the accumulation of lactic acid within skeletal muscles. Pain is also often experienced in the fatigued muscles.

   (b) Her breathing rate changes from normal to high as during as her body muscles require thus oxygen for the ATP production, than the normal value, her breathing thus enhances, to take most oxygen from the atmosphere.

5. Gout is a disease caused due to improper purine metabolism. It causes accumulation of uric acid and its crystals in the joints. The level of uric acid and crystals of its salts get raised in blood causing their accumulation in the joint to which causes **gouty arthritis**. The excess of urates in blood can also lead to the formation stones in the kidneys.

6. Each half of the pectoral girdle consist of a clavicle and a scapula. The dorsal flat, triangular body of scapula has a slightly elevated ridge called the spine that, projects flat expanded process called the acromion and the clavicle articulating with it.

   There a depression below the acromion is called the glenoid cavity which articulates with the head of the humerous to form the **shoulder joint. Pelvic girdle** consist of two coxal bones, each formed by the fusioin of three bones, **ilium, ischium** and **pubis.** It articulates with femur through a cavity called **acetabulum** forming thigh joint.

Long Answer Questions

1. Muscles contract due to formation of cross-bridge between the actin and myosin filament

   (i) An ATP molecule joins the active site on the head of myosin myofilament. These heads contains an enzyme, **myosin ATPase** along with Ca^{2+} and Mg^{2+} ions that catalyses the break down of ATP.

$$ATP \xrightarrow[Ca^{2+}Mg^{2+}]{Myosin\ ATPase} ADP + P_i + Energy$$

(ii) The energy is transferred to myosin head which straightens to join an active site on actin myofilament, forming a across-bridge.

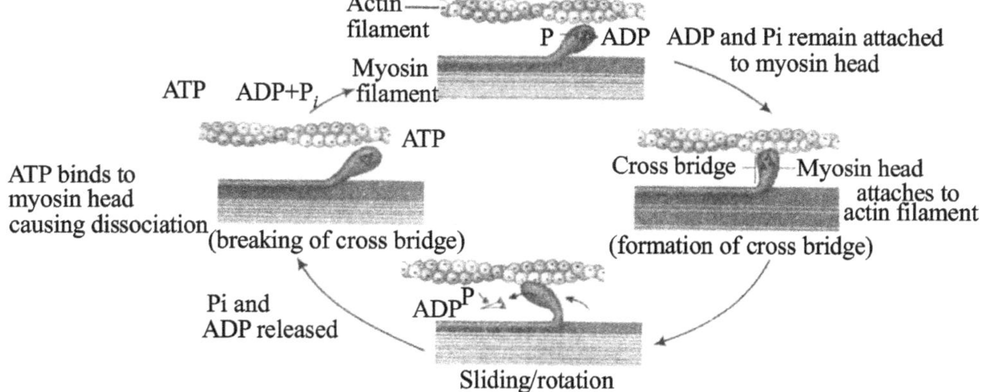

Stages in cross-bridge formation, rotation of head and breaking of cross-bridge

(iii) The energised cross-bridges move, causing the attached actin filaments to move towards the centre of A-band. The Z-line is also pulled inwards causing shortening of sarcomere, contraction. During contraction A-bands retain the length, while I-bands get reduced.

(iv) The myosin head releases ADP and Pi where relaxes to its low energy state. The head detaches from actin myofilaments when new ATP molecule joins it and cross-bridge are broken.

(v) In the next cycle, the free head cleaves the new ATP. The cycles of cross-bridge formation and breakage is repeated causing further sliding.

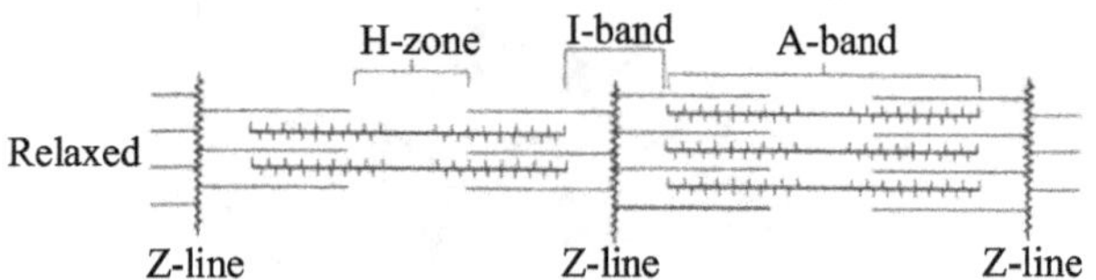

Movement of the thin filaments and the relative size of the I-band and H-zones

(vi) After contraction muscle relaxation occurs when the calcium ions are pumped back to the sarcoplasmic cisternae, thus, blocking the sites on actin myofilaments. The Z-line returns to original positions or relaxation.

Neural Control and Coordination

21

21.1 Briefly describe the structure of the following :
   (a) **Brain**   (b) **Eye**
   (c) **Ear**

Sol. **Structure of brain :**
The brain is the central information processing organ of the body,
- The human brain is well protected by the skull.
- Inside the skull, cranial meninges cover the brain. These are tough tissue layers.

- Meninges consist of 3 layers which are as follows :
  (i) The outermost - layer is **dura mater**
  (ii) The middle layer is **arachnoid**
  (iii) The inner layer is **piamater**.

The brain can be divided into three major parts which are given below :
(i) forebrain
(ii) midbrain
(iii) hindbrain

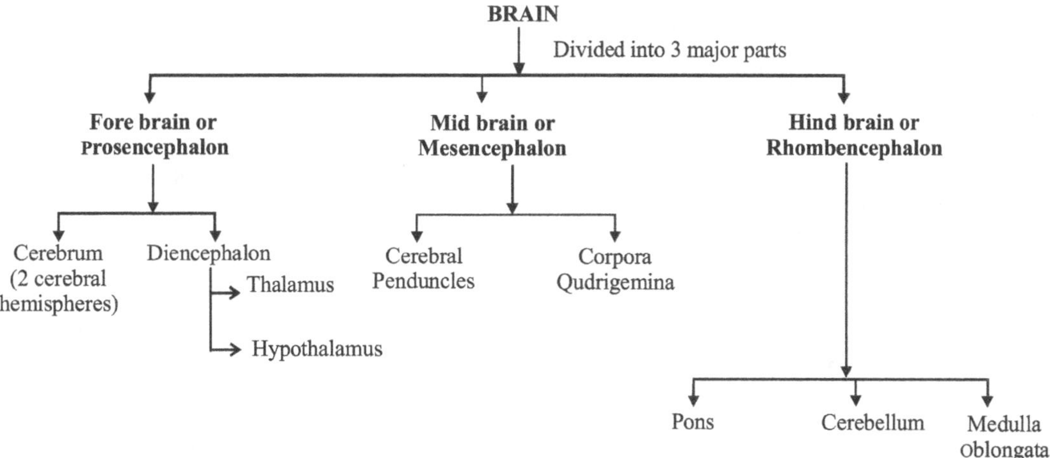

(i) Forebrain :
1. Cerebrum consists two cerebral hemisphere on the dorsal surface. It is connected by a tract of nerve fibres called corpus collasum. Cerebral hemispheres are covered by the layer of cells called cerebral cortex and are thrown into prominent folds referred as grey matter. Inner part of the cerebral hemisphere is white matter.
2. Diencephlon is the posterior part of fore-brain. It consists of thalamus and hypothalamus.
   - Thalamus is a major co-ordinating centre for sensory and motor signaling. It forms 80 % of diencephlon.
   - Hypothalamus contains a number of centres which control many functions Like – hunger, thirst, sleep, sweating, body temperature and emotions

(ii) Midbrain :
It is located between the thalamus/hypothalamus of the forebrain and pons of the hindbrain.
It forms the brain stem with the hindbrain. Anterior part of mid-brain contains two cerebral peduncles, which controls the muscle of limbs and Posterior part of mid-brain in four optic lobs called corpora quadri gemiana i.e. two upper and two lower.

(iii) Hindbrain :
Hindbrain consists of pons. Cerebellum and medulla of longata.
   - Pons is present below the midbrain and upper side of medulla oblangata. It posseses pneumotaxic area of respiratory centre.

- Cerebellum is the 2nd largest part of brain, which lies behind cerebrum and provides the additional space for many neuron and maintains equillibrium or posture of the body.
- Medulla oblongata lies below cerebellum and continues into spinal-cord. It contains respiratory centre for regulating breatheing, Cardiac centre for regulating heart beat and blood pressure and also has reflex centre for swallowing, coughing, sneezing, etc.

(b) Structure of eye :
- Our paired eyes are located in sockets of the skull called orbits.
- The adult human eye ball is nearly a spherical structure.
- The wall of eye ball is composed of three layers which are given below :
- The external layer is composed of a dense connective tissue and is called the **sclera**. The anterior portion of this layer is called the **cornea**.
- The middle layer is called **choroid** contains many blood vessels and looks bluish.
- The choroid layer is thin over the posterior two-thirds of the eye ball, but it becomes thick in the anterior part to form the **ciliary body**.
- The ciliary body itself continues forward to form a pigmented and opaque structure called the **iris** which is the visible coloured portion of the eye.
- The eye ball contains a transparent crystalline **lens** which is held in place by ligaments attached to the ciliary body.
- In front of the lens, the aperture surrounded by the iris is called the **pupil**. The diameter of the pupil is regulated by the muscle fibres of iris.
- The inner layer is the **retina** and contains three layers of cells- ganglion cells, bipolar cells and photoreceptor cells.

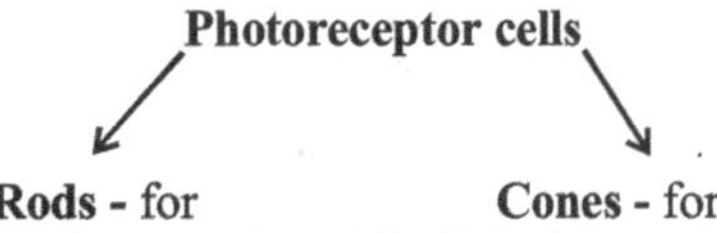

Rods - for twilight scotopic vision.   **Cones - for** Daylight (photopic) vision and colour vision.

In the human eye, there are three types of cones which possess their own characteristic photopigments that respond to red, green and blue lights.

The sensations of different colours are produced by various combinations of these cones and their photopigments. When these cones are stimulated equally, a sensation of white light is produced.

The **optic nerves** leave the eye and the retinal blood vessels enter it at a point medial to and slightly above the posterior pole of the eye ball.

Photoreceptor cells are not present in that region and hence it is called the **blind sport**. At the posterior pole of the eye lateral to the blind spot, there is a yellowish pigmented spot called macula lutea with a central pit called the **fovea.**

The fovea is a thinned-out portion of the retina where only the cones are densely packed. It is the point where the visual acuity (resolution) is the greatest.

(c) Structure of ear :
Anatomically, the ear can be divided into three major sections called the **outer ear**, the **middle ear** and the **inner ear**.

Outer ear. The outer ear consists of the **pinna** and **external auditory meatus** (canal). The pinna collects the vibrations in the air which produce sound.

The external auditory meatus leads inwards and extends up to the **tympanic membrane** (the **ear drum**).

There are very fine hairs and wax-secreting sebaceous glands in the skin of the pinna and the meatus.

The tympanic membrane is composed of connective tissues covered with skin outside and with mucus membrane inside.

Middle ear : The middle ear contains three ossicles called **malleus, incus** and **stapes** which are attached to one another in a chain-like fashion. These ossicles transmit sound waves further inside the ear.

An **Eustachian tube** connects the middle ear cavity with the pharynx. The Eustachian tube helps in equalizing the pressures on either sides of the ear drum.

Inner ear the fluid-filled inner ear called **labyrinth** consists of two parts, the bony and the membranous labyrinths. The bony labyrinth is a series of channels. Inside these channels lies the membranous labyrinth, which is surrounded by a fluid called perilymph. The membranous labyrinth is filled with a fluid called endolymph. The coiled portion of the labyrinth is called **cochlea**.

The membranes constituting cochlea, the reissner's membrane and basilar membrane, divide the surrounding perilymph filled bony labyrinth into an upper scala vestibuli and a lower scala tympani.

The **organ of corti** is a structure located on the basilar membrane which contains **hair cells** that act as auditory receptors. The hair cells are present in rows on the internal side of the organ of corti.

The inner ear also contains a complex system called **vestibular apparatus,** located above the cochlea. The vestibular apparatus is composed of three **semi-circular canals** and the **otolith organ** consisting of the saccule and utricle.

The base of canals is swollen and is called ampulla, which contains a projecting ridge called **crista ampullaris** which has hair cells. The saccule and utricle contain a projecting ridge called macula. The crista and macula are the specific receptors of the vestibular apparatus responsible for maintenance of balance of the body and posture.

21.2 Compare the following :
(i) **Central Neural System (CNS) and Peripheral neural system (PNS)**
(ii) **Resting potential and action potential**
(iii) **Choroid and retina**

Sol. Differences between central neural system and peripheral nervous system are as follows :

I	Central Neural System (CNS)		Peripheral Neural System (PNS)
1.	In vertebrates it consists of brain and spinal cord.	1.	In vertebrates it compries cranial nerves (connect the brain) and spinal nerves (connect the spinal cord).
2.	The group of neurons are called nuclei.	2.	The groups of neurons are called ganglia.
3.	Brain in vertebrates is protected by the cranium (brain box) which is present in the skull. Spinal cord is protected by vertebral column (back bone).	3.	Such protective structures are not found.
4.	Brain and spinal cord receive stimuli from the receptors (sense organs) and act through effectors.	4.	Cranial and spinal nerves carry stimuli from receptors to the brain and spinal cord and from brain and spinal cord to the effectors.

Differences between resting potential and action potential are as follows :

II.	Resting potential		Action potential
1.	The electrical potential difference across the resting plasma membrane is called as the resting potential.	1.	The electrical potential difference across the plasma membrane at the site of stimulus is called the action potential.
2.	Neuron is not involved in conduction of impulse.	2.	Neuron gets involved in conduction of impulse.
3.	Neuron membrane is permeable to K^+ ions and impermeable to Na^+.	3.	Neuron membrane becomes permeable to Na^+ ions.
4.	Membrane is impermeable to the negatively charged proteins of axoplasm and also Cl^- ions.	4.	Membrane gets deposited, and becomes permeable to negatively charged proteins of axoplasm.

Differences between choroid and retina are as follows :

III.	Choroid		Retina
1.	It is the middle layer of eye ball.	1.	It is the inner most layer of eye ball.
2.	It contains many blood vessels and looks bluish in colour.	2.	It contains three layers of cells which are ganglion cells, bipolar cells and photoreceptor cells.
3.	It does not contain photosensitive cells.	3.	It contains photosensitive cells which are rods and cones.
4.	No image is formed on choroids.	4.	Inverted image is formed on retina.

21.3 **Explain the following processes :**
  (a) **Polarization of the membrane of a nerve fibre**
  (b) **Depolarization of the membrane of a nerve fibre**
  (c) **Conduction of a nerve impulse along a nerve fibre**
  (d) **Transmission of a nerve impulse across a chemical synapse**

Sol. **(a)** **Polarization of the membrane of a nerve fibre :**
  – When a neuron is not conducting any impulse, i.e., at rest the axon membrane is more permeable to potassium ions (K^+).
  – It is impermeable to sodium ions (Na^+), negatively charged proteins and Cl^- ions.
  – Consequently, the axoplasm inside the axon contains high concentration of K^+ and negatively charged proteins and low concentration of Na^+.
  – In contrast, the fluid outside the axon contains a low concentration of K^+, a high concentration of Na^+ and thus form a concentration gradient. These ionic gradients across the resting membrane are maintained by the active transport of ions by the sodium – potassium pump which transports 3 Na^+ outwards for 2K^+ into the cell.
  – As a result, the outer surface of the axonal membrane possesses a positive charge while its inner surface becomes negatively charged and therefore is polarised.
  – The electrical potential difference across the resting plasma membrane is called **resting potential**.

  – The electrical potential that occurs across the membrane of an axon, when stimulated by threshold stimulus is called depolarisation.

(b) **Depolarisation of the membrane of a nerve fibre:**
  – When a stimulus is applied at a site on the polarised membrane, the membrane becomes more permeable to sodium ions (Na^+) than to potassium ions (K^+).
  – The potential difference in the stimulated/depolarised membrane is called action potential.
  – The action potential spreads like a wave along the membrane in the form of impulse or spike.

(c) **Conduction of nerve impulse along a nerve fibre:**
  – When a stimulus is applied at a site on the polarised membrane the membrane at the site A becomes freely permeable to Na^+.
  – As a result polarity gets reversed by a rapid inflow of Na^+.
  – After the reversal of polarity of the membrane, the membrane becomes depolarised.
  – The electrical potential difference across the plasma membrane at the site A is called the action potential; which is termed as **nerve impulse**.
  – The axon membrane (site B) has a positive charge on the outer surface and a negative charge on its inner surface. As a result, a current flows on the inner surface from site A to site B.

- On the outer surface current flows from site B to site A, to complete the circuit of current flow.
- Hence, the polarity at the site is reversed, and an action potential is generated at site B.
- Thus, the **impulse** generated at site A arrives at site B. The sequence is repeated along the length of the axon and consequently impulse is conducted.
- The rise in the stimulus-induced permeability to Na^+ is extremely short-lived.
- It is quickly followed by a rise in permeability to K^+. Within a fraction of a second, K^+ diffuses outside the membrane and restores the resting potential of the membrane at the site of excitation and the fibre becomes once more responsive to further stimulation.

(d) Transmission of a nerve impulse across chemical synapse:
- A nerve impulse is transmitted from one neuron to another through junction called **synapses**.
- Electrical current can flow directly from one neuron to the other across these synapses.
- The membrane of the pre-and post-synaptic neurons are separated by fluid-filled space called synaptic deft.
- Chemicals called neurotransmitters are involved in the transmission of impulses at these synapses.
- The axon terminals contain vesicles filled these neurotransmitters.
- When an impulse (action potential) arrives at the axon terminal, it stimulates the movement of the synaptic vesicles towards the membrane where they fuse with the plasma membrane and release their neurotransmitters in the synaptic cleft. The released neurotransmitters bind to their specific **receptors**, present on the post-synaptic membrane. This binding opens ion channels allowing the entry of ions which can generate a new potential in the post-synaptic neuron. The new potential developed may be either excitatory or inhibitory.

21.4 Draw labelled diagrams of the following :

  (a) **Neuron**   (b) **Brain**
  (c) **Eye**   (d) **Ear.**

  (a) **Neuron -**

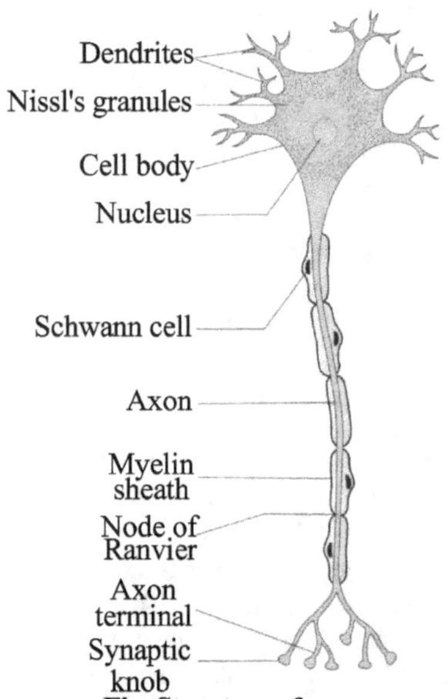

Fig. Structure of a neuron

  (b) **Brain -**

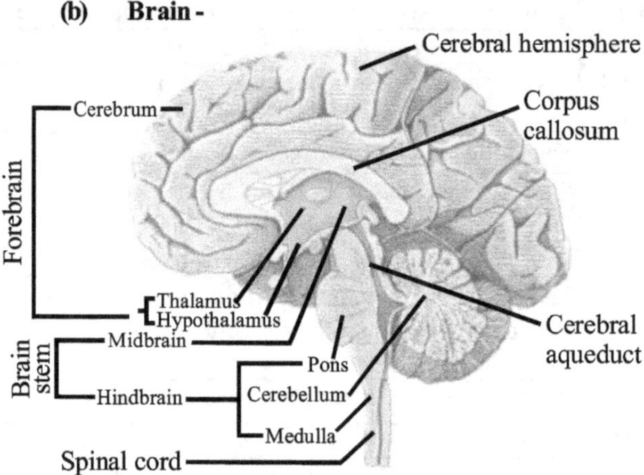

Fig. Diagram showing sagital section of the human brain

  (c) **Eye-**

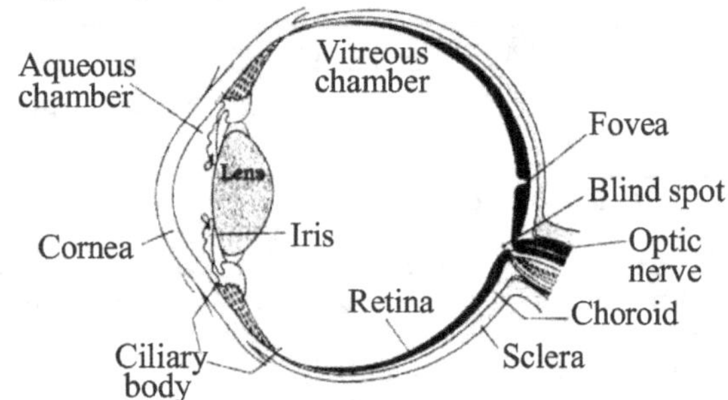

Fig. Structure of eye

  (d) **Ear -**

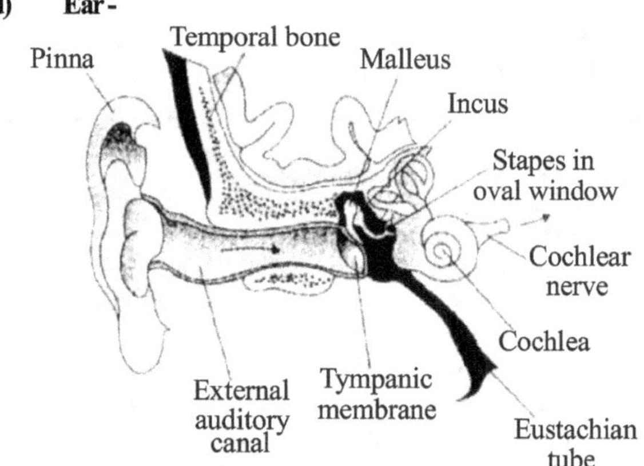

Fig. Diagrammatic view of ear

21.5 Write short notes on the following

  (a) **Neural coordination**   (b) **Forebrain**
  (c) **Midbrain**   (d) **Hindbrain**
  (e) **Retina**   (f) **Ear ossicles**
  (g) **Cochlea**   (h) **Organ of corti**
  (i) **Synapse**

Sol. (a) **Neural co-ordination :** The functions of the organs/ organ systems in our body must be coordinated to maintain homeostasis. **Coordination** is the process through which two or more organs interact and complement the functions of one another. For example, when we do physical exercises, the energy demand is increased for maintaining an increased muscular activity. The supply of oxygen is also increased. The increased supply of oxygen necessitates an increase in the rate of respiration, heart beat and increased blood flow via blood vessels. When physical exercise is stopped, the activities of nerves, lungs, heart and kidney gradually return to their normal conditions. Thus, the functions of muscles, lungs, heart, blood vessels, kidney and other organs are coordinated while performing physical exercises. In our body the neural system and the endocrine system jointly coordinate and integrate all the activities of the organs so that they function in a synchronised fashion.

(b) Forebrain : The forebrain consists of **cerebrum, thalamus** and **hypothalamus**. Cerebrum forms the major part of the human brain. A deep cleft divides the cerebrum longitudinally into two halves, which are termed as the left and right **cerebral hemispheres**. The hemispheres are connected by a tract of nerve fibres called **corpus callosum**.

The cerebral cortex contains motor areas, sensory areas and large regions that are neither clearly sensory nor motor in function. These regions called as the association areas are responsible for complex functions like intersensory associations, memory and communication.

The cerebrum wraps around a structure called thalamus, which is a major coordinating centre for sensory and motor signaling. Another very important part of the brain called hypothalamus lies at the base of the thalamus. The hypothalamus contains a number of centres which control body temperature, urge for eating and drinking. It also contains several groups of neurosecretory cells, which secrete hormones called hypothalamic hormones.

The inner parts of cerebral hemispheres and a group of associated deep structures like amygdala, hippocampus, etc., form a complex structure called the limbic lobe or limbic system. Along with the hypothalamus, it is involved in the regulation of sexual behaviour, expression of emotional reactions (e.g., excitement, pleasure, rage and fear), and motivation.

(c) Midbrain :
- It is located between the thalamus hypothalmus of the forebrain and pons of the hindbrain.
- The dorsal portion of the midbrain consists of four small lobes called as **corpora quadrigemina**.
- A canal called **the cerebral aqueduct** passes through the midbrain.

(d) Hindbrain :
- It consists of **pons, cerebellum** and **medulla-oblongata**.
- Cerebellum has very convoluted surface to provide the additional space for many more neurons.
- The medulla is the part that continues as a spinal cord.
- The medulla contains centres which control respiration, cardiovascular reflexes and gastric secretions.

(e) Retina : The **retina** contains three layers of cells - from inside to outside ganglion cells, bipolar cells and photoreceptor cells.

There are two types of photoreceptor cells, namely, **rods** and **cones**. These cells contain the light-sensitive proteins called the photopigments. The daylight (photopic) vision and colour vision are functions of cones and the twilight (scotopic) vision is the function of the rods. The rods contain a purplish-red protein called the rhodopsin or visual purple, which contains a derivative of vitamin A.

In the human eye, there are three types of cones which possess their own characteristic photopigments that respond to red, green and blue lights. The sensations of different colours are produced by various combinations of these cones and their photopigments. When these cones are stimulated equally, a sensation of white light is produced.

(f) Ear ossicles -
- The middle ear contains three ossicles called **malleus, incus** and **stapes** which are attached to one another in a chain-like fashion.
- Malleus is attached to the tympanic membrane and the stapes is attached to the oval window of the cochlea.
- The ear ossicles increase the efficiency of transmission of sound waves to the inner ear.

(g) Cochlea : The fluid-filled inner ear called **labyrinth** consists of two parts, the bony and the membranous labyrinths. The coiled portion of the labyrinth is called **cochlea**.

The membranes constituting cochlea, the reissner's and basilar, divide the surounding perilymph filled bony labyrinth into an upper scala vestibuli and a lower scala tympani. The space within cochlea called scala media is filled with endolymph. At the base of the cochlea, the scala vestibuli ends at the oval window, while the scala tympani terminates at the round window which opens to the middle ear.

(h) Organ of corti : The **organ of corti** is a structure located on the basilar membrane which contains hair cells that act as auditory receptors. The **hair cells** are present in rows on the internal side of the organ of corti. The basal end of the hair cell is in close contact with the afferent nerve fibres. A large number of processes called stereo cilia are projected from the apical part of each hair cell. Above the rows of the hair cells is a thin elastic membrane called **tectorial membrane**.

(i) Synapse : A nerve impulse is transmitted from one neuron to another through junctions called synapses. A **synapse** is formed by the membranes of a pre-synaptic neuron and a post-synaptic neuron, which may or may not be separated by a gap called **synaptic cleft**. There are two types of synapses, namely, electrical synapses and chemical synapses.

Electrical synapse : At electrical synapses, the membranes of pre-and post-synaptic neurons are in very close proximity. Electrical current can flow directly from one neuron into the other across these synapses. Transmission of an impulse across electrical synapses is very similar to impulse conduction along a single axon. Impulse transmission across an electrical synapse is always faster than that across a chemical synapse. Electrical synapses are rare in our system.

Chemical synapse : At a chemical synapse, the membranes of the pre- and post-synaptic neurons are separated by a fluid-filled space called synaptic cleft. Chemicals called neurotransmitters are involved in the transmission of impulses at these synapses. The axon terminals contain vesicles filled with these neurotransmitters. When an impulse (action potential) arrives at the axon terminal, it stimulates the movement of the synaptic vesicles towards the membrane where they fuse with the plasma membrane and release their neurotransmitters in the synaptic cleft. The released neurotransmitters bind to their specific **receptors**, present on the post-synaptic membrane. This binding opens ion channels allowing the entry of ions which can generate a new potential in the post-synaptic neuron. The new potential developed may be either excitatory or inhibitory.

21.6 Give a brief account of :

(a) **Mechanism of synaptic transmission**

(b) **Mechanism of vision**

(c) **Mechanism of hearing**

Sol. (a) **Synaptic transmission can be of two types :**

(i) Transmission of nerve impulse through electrical synapse.

(ii) Transmission of nerve impulse through chemical synapse.

Electrical synaptic transmission : At electrical synapses, the membranes of pre- and post- synaptic neurons are in very close proximity. Electrical current can flow directly from one neuron into the other across these synapses. Transmission of an impulse is very similar to impulse conduction along a single axon.

Chemical synaptic transmission : The membranes of the pre- and post-synaptic neurons are separated by a fluid-filled space called synaptic cleft. Neurotransmitters are involved in the transmission of impulses. When an impulse (action potential) arrives at the axon terminal, it stimulates the movement of the synaptic vesicles towards the membrane where they fuse with the plasma membrane and release their neurotransmitters in the synaptic cleft. The released neurotransmitters bind to their specific receptors, present on the post-synaptic membrane. This binding opens ion-channels allowing the entry of ions which can generate a new potential in the post-synaptic neuron.

(b) **Mechanism of vision**

The light rays in visible wavelength focussed on the retina through the cornea and lens generate potentials (impulses) in rods and cones.

The photosensitive compounds (photopigments) in the human eyes is composed of **opsin** (a protein) and **retinal** (an aldehyde of vitamin A). Light induces dissociation of the retinal from opsin resulting in changes in the structure of the opsin. This causes membrane permeability changes. As a result, potential differences are generated in the photoreceptor cells. This produces a signal that generates action potentials in the ganglion cells through the bipolar cells.

These action potentials (impulses) are transmitted by the optic nerves to the visual cortex area of the brain, where the neural impulses are analysed and the image formed on the retina is recognised based on earlier memory and experience.

(c) **Mechanism of hearing**

– The external ear receives sound waves and directs them to the ear drum. The ear drum vibrates in response to the sound waves and these vibrations are transmitted through the ear ossicles (malleus, incus and stapes) to the oval window.

– The vibrations are passed through the oval window on the fluid of the cochlea, where they generate waves in the lymphs.

– The waves in the lymphs induce a ripple in the basilar membrane.

– These movements of the basilar membrane bend the hair cells, pressing them against the tectorial membrane.

– As result, nerve impulses are generated in the associated afferent neurons. These impulses are transmitted by the afferent fibres via auditory nerves to the auditory cortex of the brain, where the impulses are analysed and the sound is recognised.

21.7 Answer briefly :

(a) **How do you perceive the colour of an object ?**

(b) **Which part of our body helps us in maintaining the body balance ?**

(c) **How does the eye regulate the amount of light that falls on the retina?**

Sol. (a) Cones are responsible for colour vision. They require brighter light than rods. There are three types of cones, maximally sensitive to longwavelength, medium-wavelength, and short-wavelength light (often referred to as red, green, and blue, respectively, though the sensitivity peaks are not actually at these colours). The colour seen is the combined effect of stimuli to, and responses from, these three types of cone cells. When these cones are stimulated equally, a sensation of white light is produced.

(b) The inner ear has three semi-circular canals forming cochlea. The inner ear also contains a complex system called vestibular apparatus, located above the cochlea. The vestibular apparatus is composed of three semi-circular canals and the otolith organ consisting of the saccule and utricle. The base of canals is swollen and is called ampulla, which contains a projecting ridge called crista ampullaris which has hair cells. The saccule and utricle contain a projecting ridge called macula. The crista and macula are the specific receptors of the vestibular apparatus responsible for maintenance of balance of the body and posture.

(c) The light rays in visible wavelength focussed on the retina through the cornea and lens generate potentials (impulses) in rods and cones. Light induces dissociation of the retinal from opsin resulting in changes in the structure of the opsin. This causes membrane permeability changes. As a result, potential differences are generated in the photoreceptor cells. These action potentials are transmitted by the optic nerves to the visual cortex area of the brain, where the neural impulses are analysed and the image formed on the retina is recognised based on earlier memory and experience.

21.8 Explain the following :
(a) **Role of Na$^+$ in the generation of action potential.**
(b) **Mechanism of generation of light-induced impulse in the retina.**
(c) **Mechanism through which a sound produces a nerve impulse in the inner ear.**

Sol. **(a)** **Role of Na$^+$ in action potential :**
- At the point of stimulation, the membrane becomes freely permeable to sodium ions (Na$^+$).
- As sodium ions enter the axoplasm, the interior becomes positively charged and the exterior is negatively charged.
- The positive ions travel from the depolarised region to the next polarised region through the axoplasm and create an action potential there.
- It results in forming wave of excitation along the nerve fibre which is called nerve impulse.

(b) **Mechanism of generation of light induced impulse in the retina :**
- Light induces the dissociaton of retinal (an aldehyde of vitamin A) and opsin (a protein), this results in change in the structure of opsin.
- The permeability of the membrane changes as a result of the above dissociation.
- The potential differences generated in the photoreceptor cells produce a signal that generates action potential in the bipolar neurons.
- These impulses/action potentials are transmitted by the optic nerve to the visual cortex.
- The neural impulses are analysed and image formed is recognised based on the earlier memory and experience.

(c) **Mechanism through which a sound produces a nerve impulse in the inner ear :**
- The sound waves vibrate the eardrum.
- The vibrations produced in response to these waves are transmitted through the ear ossicles to the oval window from where they reach the fluid of the cochlea.
- The waves produced in the perilymph and endolymph induce a ripple in the basilar membrane.
- The movements of the basilar membrane bend the hair cells which press them against the tectorial membrane.
- Nerve impulses are generated in the associated afferent neurons.
- The afferent fibres transmit the impulses via auditory nerves to the auditory cortex of the brain where the impulses are analysed and the sound is recognised.

21.9 Differentiate between :
(a) **Myelinated and non-myelinated axons**
(b) **Dendrites and axons**
(c) **Rods and cones**
(d) **Thalamus and Hypothalamus**
(e) **Cerebrum and Cerebellum**

Sol. Differences :

(a)	Myelinated axons		Non-myelinated axons
1.	The nerve fibres have a lipid rich myelin sheath around the axon.	1.	The nerve fibre does not form a myelin sheath around the axon.
2.	The conduction of nerve impulse is faster	2.	The conduction is comparatively slow.
3.	Action potential occurs only in the nodes of Ranvier.	3.	Action potential occurs all along nerve fibres.
4.	It is found in the spinal and cranial nerves.	4.	It is commonly found in autonomous and the somatic neural systems.
(b)	Dendrites		Axons
1.	Short fibres which branch repeatedly and project out of the cell body also contain Nissl's granules and are called dendrites.	1.	The axon is a long fibre like structure of neuron, whose distal end is branched.
2.	Dendrites conducts impulse towards the cell body.	2.	Axons conduct the impulse away from the cell body.
3.	The terminals of dendrites become as receptors.	3.	Axon ends in a group of branches called synaptic knob which possess synaptic vesicles containing chemical called neurotransmitters.
4.	A number of dendrites arise from the cyton	4.	Only single axon arises percyton.
(c)	Rods		Cones
1.	These are more sensitive to light and are meant for vision in dim light (scotopic vision).	1.	These are meant for vision in bright light (photopic vision)
2.	They do not have the ability to make coloured images.	2.	They have the ability to make coloured images.
3.	These contain the visual pigment rhodopsin formed from vitamin-A.	3.	These contain the pigment iodopsin.
(d)	Thalamus		Hypothalamus
1.	It lies below the cerebrum.	1.	It lies at the base of the thalamus.
2.	It is a major co-ordinating centre for sensory and motor signaling.	2.	It is a major centre for regulation of the body temperature, thirst, hunger, etc.
3.	It does not secrete any hormone.	3.	It secretes many hormones.
(e)	Cerebrum		Cerebellum
1.	It is a part of forebrain.	1.	It is a part of hind brain.
2.	It consists of two cerebral hemispheres.	2.	It consists of two cerebellar hemispheres and a vermis.

21.10 Answer the following :

    (a) **Which part of the ear determines the pitch of a sound ?**

    (b) **Which part of the human brain is the most developed ?**

    (c) **Which part of our central neural system acts as a master clock ?**

Sol. **(a)** Pitch represents the perceived fundamental frequency of a sound. Pitch is a subjective sensation in which a listener assigns perceived tones to relative positions on a musical scale based primarily on the frequency of vibration. As sound is finally perceived by the temporal lobe of the cerebral cortex so it can be said that cerebral cortex perceives the pitch of the sound.

    (b) Cerebral cortex   **(c)** Hindbrain

21.11 The region of the vertebrate eye, where the optic nerve passes out of the retina, is called the

    (a) **fovea**   **(b)** **iris**   **(c)** **blind spot**   **(d)** **optic chaisma**

Sol. Blind spot.

21.12 Distinguish between

    (a) **afferent neurons and efferent neurons**

    (b) **impulse conduction in a myelinated nerve fibre and unmyelinated nerve fibre**

    (c) **aqueous humor and vitreous humor**

    (d) **blind spot and yellow spot**

    (e) **cranial nerves and spinal nerves.**

Sol. Differences :

(a)	Afferent neurons		Efferent neurons
1.	They conduct impulses from the receptors/sense organs to CNS.	1.	They conduct impulse from CNS to the receptors/ sense organs.
2.	The terminals of dendrons/dendrites become modified to form receptors.	2.	The axon terminals become modified as motor end plate.
3.	They are sensory in nature.	3.	They are motor in nature.
(b)	Conduction of impulse in myelinated nerve fibre		Conduction of impulse in un-myelinated nerve fibre
1.	The depolarisation occurs only in the nodes of Ranvier, where myelin sheath is absent.	1.	Depolarisation occurs all along the length of the nerve fibre.
2.	Action potential jumps from one node of Ranvier to another.	2.	Action potential travels along the entire length of the fibre.
3.	Conduction is much faster and is also called saltatory conduction.	3.	Conduction is slower.
4.	Energy expenditure is less.	4.	Energy expenditure is high.
(c)	Aqueous humour		Vitreous humor
1.	The space between the cornea and the lens is called the aqueous chamber.	1.	The space between lens and the retina is called the vitreous chamber.
2.	Aqueous fluid present in the anterior chamber which is called aqueous humor.	2.	Jelly like substance present in the posterior chamber, which is called vitreous chamber.
3.	It provides nutrition to lens and cornea and supports lens.	3.	It supports the lens.
(d)	Blind spot		Yellow spot
1.	The optic nerves leave the eye and the retinal blood vessels enter it at a point medial to and slightly above the posterior pole of the eye ball. Photoreceptor cells are not present in that region and hence it is called blind spot.	1.	At the posterior pole of the eye lateral to the blind spot, here is a yellowish pigmented spot called macula lutea with a central concave point of yellow spot called Fovea centralis.
2.	There is no vision in the blind spot.	2.	Vision is the sharpest in yellow spot (fovea).
3.	No rods or cones are present.	3.	It contains mainly cones.
(e)	Cranial nerves		Spinal nerves
1.	Nerves which arise from different parts of the brain.	1.	Nerves arise from different segments of spinal cord.
2.	Cranial nerves are sensory, motor or mixed in nature.	2.	All spinal nerves are mixed nerves.
3.	There are twelve pairs of cranial nerves present in human being.	3.	There are thirty one pairs of spinal nerves present in human being.

SECTION B — PRACTICE QUESTIONS

MULTIPLE CHOICE QUESTIONS

1. An example of autonomous nervous system is
   (a) swallowing food
   (b) pupillary reflex
   (c) peristalsis of intestine
   (d) knee-jerk response

2. Which of the following statements are correct?
   (i) Somatic nervous system- Conducts impulses from CNS to skeletal muscles.
   (ii) Autonomic nervous system- Conduct impulses from CNS to internal organ muscles.
   (iii) Central nervous system- Consists of brain and spinal cord
   (iv) Peripheral nervous system- Consists of nerves carrying impulses to brain and spinal cord only
   (a) Only (ii) and (iii)
   (b) Only (iii) and (iv)
   (c) Only (i), (ii) and (iii)
   (d) All of these

3. The controlling centre of autonomic nervous system is
   (a) hypothalamus
   (b) spinal cord
   (c) cerebellum
   (d) pons

4. Centre for sense of smell is
   (a) cerebellum   (b) olfactory lobes
   (c) pons   (d) midbrain

5. Which of the following is a thin middle layer of cranial meninges?
   (a) Duramater   (b) Arachnoid
   (c) Piamater   (d) Optic nerve

6. The thinned-out portion of retina where only cones are densely packed is called
   (a) blind spot
   (b) corpus luteum
   (c) macula lutea
   (d) fovea

7. The amount of light that falls on retina is regulated by
   (a) lens   (b) cornea
   (c) iris   (d) ciliary muscles

8. The region of vertebrate's eye where the optic nerve passes out of the retina is called
   (a) yellow spot
   (b) optic chiasma
   (c) fovea
   (d) blind spot

9. Which of the following is devoid of blood supply?
   (a) Retina   (b) Choroid
   (c) Cornea   (d) Scleroid

10. Receptor cells for balance in human ear are located in
    (a) utricle, saccule and semicircular canal
    (b) malleus, incus and stapes
    (c) organ of corti
    (d) Eustachian tube

ASSERTION & REASON QUESTIONS

DIRECTION (Qs. 1-5) : *These questions consists of two statements. Answer these questions selecting the appropriate option given below:*

(a) Both Assertion (A) and Reason (R) are true and Reason (R) is the correct explanation of Assertion (A).
(b) Both Assertion (A) and Reason (R) are true, but Reason (R) is not the correct explanation of Assertion (A).
(c) Assertion (A) is true, but Reason (R) is false.
(d) Assertion (A) is false, but Reason (R) is true.

1. **Assertion:** The myelinated nerve fibres are found in spinal and cranial nerves.
   Reason: The gaps between 2 adjacent myelin sheaths are called nodes of Ranvier.

2. **Assertion:** A reflex action occurs involuntainly.
   Reason: The process of response to a peripheral nervous stimulation that requires the involvement of a part of the CNS is called a reflex action.

3. **Assertion:** The eustachian tube connects the middle ear cavity with the pharynx.
   Reason: The ear ossicles increase the efficiency of transmission of sound waves to the inner ear.

4. **Assertion:** The organ of corti contains hair cells that act as auditory receptors.
   Reason: The hair cells are present in rows on the internal side of the organ of corti.

5. **Assertion :** Tongue is a olfactory receptor.
   Reason : Receptors for gustatory sensations are located in taste buds.

CASE/PASSAGE BASED QUESTIONS

DIRECTIONS (Qs. 1-5) : *Read the following passage and answer the questions that follows.*

The change in potential due to stimulation of a nerve fibre is called action potential, which is otherwise termed as nerve impulse. This cause the adjacent inner part of the membrane to reverse its potential from −70mV to +3mV. The reversal repeats itself over and ever until the nerve impulse is conducted through the length of the neuron.

1. Refer the given figure which shows the axon terminal and synapse with their parts marked as 1 to 7. Identify the correct parts whose constitution forms the structure of synapse.

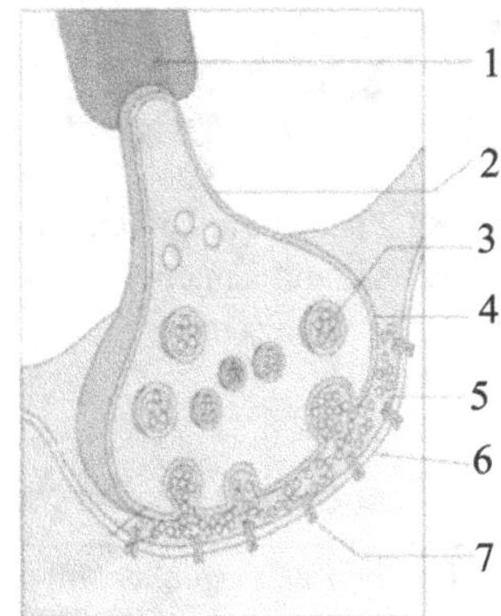

(a) 1, 2, 3   (b) 3, 4, 5
(c) 4, 5, 6   (d) 5, 6, 7

2. During the transmission of nerve impulse through a nerve fibre , the potential on the inner side of the plasma membrane has which type of electric charge?
  (a) First positive, then negative and again back to positive.
  (b) First negative, then positive and again back to negative.
  (c) First positive, then negative and continue to be negative.
  (d) First negative, then positive and continue to be positive.

3. In a nerve if sodium pump is blocked, which of the following is most likely to happen ?
  (a) Na^+ and K^+ will increases outside the cell.
  (b) Na^+ outside the nerve will increase.
  (c) Na^+ inside the nerve will increase.
  (d) K^+ inside the nerve will increase.

4. Which of the following helps in maintaining ionic gradients across the resting membrane potential?
  (a) Na– K potassium
  (b) reduced energy production by mitochondria
  (c) Ca^{2+} pumps
  (d) depletion of action potential

5. During the propagation of a nerve impulse, the action potential results from the movement of :
  (a) K+ ions from extracellular fluid to intracellular fluid
  (b) Na+ ions from intracellular fluid to extracellular fluid
  (c) K+ ions from intracellular fluid to extracellular fluid
  (d) Na+ ions from extracellular fluid to intracellular fluid

VERY SHORT ANSWER QUESTIONS

1. Name the band of nerves fibres that joins the cerebral hemispheres in mammals.
2. How many types of nerve fibres do PNS have ? Name them.
3. Name the functional unit of nervous system.
4. How many types of axons are present in CNS? Name them.
5. Name the functional junction between two neurons.
6. What does synaptic vesicles contain ?
7. Name the fluid in which membranous labyrinth of the inner ear floats.
8. Why is blind spot devoid of the ability of vision?
9. Name the canal which passes through midbrain.
10. Name the type of neuron which carries the signal from CNS to the effector organs.
11. Name the fluid which fills anterior chamber of eye.
12. Name the cells which are responsible for photopic (daylight) and colour vision.
13. Name the part through which middle ear communicates with the internal ear.
14. Name the specific receptors of the vestibular apparatus.
15. Give the technical names of the auditory ossicles in their natural sequence.
16. Name the membranes constituting the cochlea.
17. What is brain stem ?
18. What is optic chiasma?
19. Name the largest and longest cranial nerve?

SHORT ANSWER QUESTIONS

1. What are Nissl's granules.
2. Describe the location and the role of ciliary body in human eye.
3. Explain the structural and functional significance of fovea in human eye.
4. What is a reflex action?
5. Where are synaptic vesicles found? Name their chemical contents? What is the function of these contents?
6. Write short notes on hindbrain.
7. Enumerate the functions of hypothalamus.
8. Write a brief note on autonomic nervous system.
9. What are nodes of ranvier?

LONG ANSWER QUESTIONS

1. Explain briefly the structure and functions of middle ear.
2. What is a synapse? How is the nerve impulse transmitted across a synapse?

SOLUTIONS

Multiple Choice Questions

1. **(c)** Peristalsis of intestine is the example of autonomic nervous system. The autonomic nervous system (ANS) regulates the functions of internal organs (the viscera) such as the heart, stomach and intestines. It is part of the peripheral nervous system and controls some of the muscles within the body.

2. **(c)** The statements (i), (ii) and (iii) are correct while the statement (iv) is incorrect. The peripheral nervous system consists of nerves carrying impulses to and from brain and spinal cord.

3. **(a)** Hypothalamus is the controlling centre of autonomic nervous system. Hypothalamus lies at the base of the thalamus and contains a number of centres which control body temperature, urge for eating & drinking.

4. **(b)** Olfactory lobes receive the sensation of smell but relay the same to temporal lobe of cerebrum.

5. **(b)** The meninges are three layers of protective tissue called the dura mater, arachnoid mater, and pia mater that surround the brain and spinal cord. The meninges of the brain and spinal cord are continuous, being linked through the magnum foramen. The arachnoid or arachnoid mater is the middle layer of the meninges. In some areas, it projects into the sinuses formed by the dura mater and transfer cerebrospinal fluid from the ventricles back into the bloodstream.

6. **(d)** Fovea is a small depression in the centre of macula lutea. It has only cone cells. They are devoid of rod cells. Hence, fovea is the place of most distinct vision.

7. **(c)** The amount of light that falls on retina is regulated by iris. Iris is the anterior part and lies behind the cornea.

8. **(d)** The spot at the back of the eye, from where optic nerve fibres leave is free from rods & cones. This spot is devoid of the ability for vision and is called blind spot.

9. **(c)** Cornea is a transparent anterior portion of eye that lacks blood vessels and is nourished by lymph from the nearby area.

10. **(a)** The receptor cells for balance in human ear are located in utricle, saccule and semi-circular canal.

Assertion & Reason Questions

1. **(b)** The myelinated nerve fibres are enveloped with Schwann cells, which form a myelin sheath around the axon.

2. **(a)** The reflex pathway consist of atleast one afferent neuron and one efferent neuron. The afferent neuron received signal from a sensory organ and transmit the impulse via a dorsal nerve root into the CNS the efferent neuron then carries signals from CNS to the effector.

3. **(b)** An Eustachian tube connects the middle ear cavity with the pharynx. It helps in equalising the pressures on either sides of the ear drum.

4. **(a)** The basal end of the hair cell is in close contact with the afferent nerve fibres.

5. **(d)** Gustatoreceptors are chemoreceptors, enclosed within taste buds. These receptors are located on tongue.

Case/Passage Based Questions

1. **(c)** The parts labelled as 4, 5 and 6 are respectively pre-synaptic membrane, synaptic cleft and post-synaptic membrane. These parts constitute the structure of synapse. A synapse is a structure that permits a neuron (or nerve cell) to pass an electrical or chemical signal to another cell (neural or otherwise). Synapses are essential to neuronal function. At a synapse, the plasma membrane of the signal-passing neuron (the presynaptic neuron) comes into close apposition with the membrane of the target (postsynaptic) cell. Both the presynaptic and postsynaptic sites contain extensive arrays of molecular machinery that link the two membranes together and carry out the signaling process. In many synapses, the presynaptic part is located on an axon, but some postsynaptic sites are located on a dendrite or soma.

2. **(b)**

3. **(c)** The ionic concentration gradients across the resting membrane are maintained by active transport of ions by sodium-potassium pump which transports 3 Na^+ outwards for 2 K^+ into the cell. Hence, if sodium pump is blocked, sodium inside the nerve will increase.

4. **(a)** Sodium potassium pumps contributes to the ionic gradient across a resting neuron.

5. **(d)** Total sum of physio-electrochemical changes that takes place along the length of nerve fibre is known as nerve impulse. Change in potential due to stimulation of nerve fibre is called action potential. During propagation of nerve impulse, Na+ enters inside so (+ve) charge is formed inside the membrane. K+ ions come out.

Very Short Answer Questions

1. The hemispheres are connected by a tract of nerve fibres called corpus callosum.

2. The nerve fibres of the PNS are of two types :
   (a) afferent fibres
   (b) efferent fibres

3. The functional unit of nervous system is neuron.

4. There are two types of axons, namely, myelinated and non-myelinated.

5. A synapse is the functional junction between two neurons.

6. Synaptic vesicles contain chemicals called neurotransmitters.

7. The fluid in which membranous labyrinth of the inner ear floats is perilymph.

8. Blind spot have no photoreceptor cells (rods & cones) and hence it is devoid of vision.

9. Cerebral aqueduct is the canal which passes through midbrain.

10. Efferent neuron carries the signal from CNS to the effector/organs.

11. An aqueous fluid which fills anterior chamber of eye is aqueous humor.

12. Cones are responsible for photopic (day light) and colour vision.

13. Oval window helps the middle ear communicates with the internal ear.

14. The crista and macula are the specific receptors of the vestibular apparatus.

15. The technical names of the auditory ossicles are malleus, incus, staps.

16. Reissner's membrane and basilar membrane constitute the cochlea.

17. **Brain stem** is part of brain that lies in continuation of spinal cord, viz., medulla oblongata, pons and mid brain (with or without diencephalon of forebrain)

18. A cross like structure found on anterior surface of hypothalamus is called optic chiasma.

19. The largest cranial nerve is Trigeminal nerve and the longest cranial nerve is vagus nerve.

Short Answer Questions

1. The cell body contains cytoplasm with typical cell organelles and certain granular bodies called Nissl's granules.

2. Ciliary body is thick vascular, less pigmented ring shaped muscular structure occuring at the junction of choroid and iris. Ciliary body controls the size of pupil and in this way controls the amount of light entering the eye.

3. **Fovea**
   - The fovea is a thinned-out portion of the retina where only the cones are densely packed. It is the point where the visual acuity (resolution) is the greatest.
   - It is a slightly depressed, tiny circular area found in the retina, just above the blind spot.

4. A sudden withdrawal of a body part which comes in contact with objects that are extremely hot, cold pointed or animals that are scary or poisonous. The entire process of response to a peripheral nervous stimulation, that occurs involuntarily, i.e., without conscious effort or thought and requires the involvement of a part of the central nervous system is called a **reflex action**.

5. Synaptic vesicles are found in the bulbous expansion called synaptic knob, at the nerve terminal.
   - Each synaptic vesicle contains as many as 10,000 molecules of a neurotransmitter substance, that is responsible for transmission of nerve impulse across the synapse.
   - When a wave of depolarisation reaches the presynaptic membrane, the voltage-gated calcium channels concentrated at the synapse open and Ca^{++} ions diffuse into the terminal from the surrounding fluid.
   - The Ca^{++} ions stimulate the synaptic vesicles to move to the terminal membrane, fuse with it and then rupture by exocytosis into the cleft.
   - This neurotransmitter diffuses across the synapse and stimulates the membrane of the next neuron.

6. The hindbrain comprises **pons**, **cerebellum** and **medulla** (also called the medulla oblongata). Pons consists of fibre tracts that interconnect different regions of the brain. Cerebellum has very convoluted surface in order to provide the additional space for many more neurons. The medulla of the brain is connected to the spinal cord. The medulla contains centres which control respiration, cardiovascular reflexes and gastric secretions.

7. **Functions of hypothalamus are as follows :**
   (i) Hypothalamus maintains homeostasis *i.e.*, internal equilibrium of the body.
   (ii) It has centres for regulation of hunger, thirst, emotions.
   (iii) It organises behaviour like fighting, feeling etc., related to survival of species.
   (iv) It maintains a constant body temperature.
   (v) It secretes neurohormones, some of which control the functioning of pituitary glands called hypothalamic hormones.

8. Autonomic nervous is a part of peripheral nervous system. It controls activities occur in our body that are normally in voluntary such as heart beat, gut peristalsis, etc. Most of the actions of this system is controlled within the spinal cord or brain by reflexes known as visceral reflexes. It is maintanied by centre in medulla and hypothalamas. It maintains homeostasis. These are divided into two systems sympathetic and parasympathetic nervous system. The sympathetic nervous system mainly functions in quick responses and parasympathetic nervous system functions in actions which do not require immediate response.

9. These are the periodic gaps or breakes in the myelin sheath these breaks helps in the conduction of electricity in neurons the resistance to current flow between the axoplasm and fluid outside the cell is low these nodes set up the local circuits to flow current inside neurons as a result, the action potential jump from node to node and passes along the myelineted axon faster compared to the series of small local circuits in a non-myelinated axon.

Long Answer Questions

1. The middle ear is an air-filled chamber on the inner side of eardrum. Its cavity communicates with an air-filled tube called eustachian tube, which maintains a balanced air pressure on either side of the tympanum. The small bones called auditory ossicles are present in the middle ear. The malleus is attached to the ear-drum on one side and to the incus on the other side.

The incus inturn articulates with the stapes.

The stapes is attached to the membrane over an oval-window between the middle ear and the internal ear.

Functions :

– The auditory ossicles transmit the sound-induced vibrations of the ear-drum to the endolymph in the internal ear.

– The eustachian tube balances and maintains a constant pressure on either side of the ear-drum.

2. **Synapse :** The functional/intercommunicating, junction between two neurons, the axon of one neuron and the dendron/dendrite/soma of another neuron, through which impulse is conducted, is called a synapse.

Conduction of nerve impulse across a synapse :

– When a nerve impulse reaches the pre-synaptic membrane (membrane of synaptic button), the voltage-gated calcium channels, concentrated in the synapse, open.

– Calcium ions from the fluid in the synapse diffuse into the synaptic button and stimulate the synaptic vesicles to move to the terminal membrane, fuse with it and then rupture (exocytosis) to release the neurotransmitter.

– The neurotransmitter quickly diffuses across the synaptic cleft in the fluid and stimulates certain specific receptor molecules on the post-synaptic membrane (membrane of the next dendron/dendrite) and causes sparking and electrical current, passing the signal.

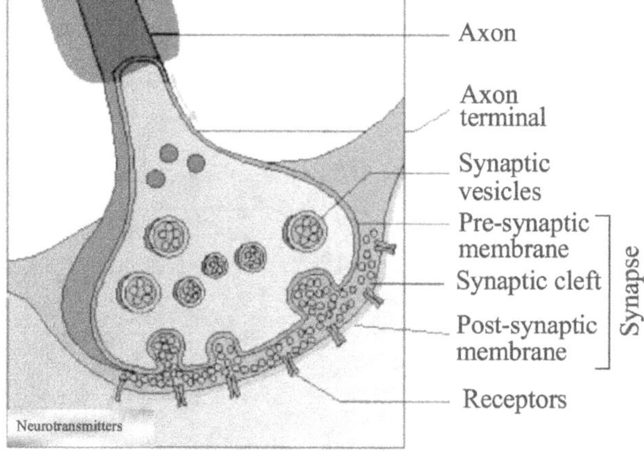

Fig. Diagram showing axon terminal and synapse

SECTION C — NCERT EXEMPLAR QUESTIONS

MULTIPLE CHOICE QUESTIONS

1. Chemicals which are released at the synaptic junction are called
   (a) hormones   (b) neurotransmitters
   (c) cerebrospinal fluid   (d) lymph

2. Potential difference across resting membrane is negatively charged. This is due to differential distribution of the following ions.
   (a) Na^+ and K^+ ions   (b) CO_3^{2-} and Cl^- ions
   (c) Ca^{2+} and Mg^{2+} ions   (d) Ca^{+4} and Cl^- ions

3. Resting membrane potential is maintained by
   (a) hormones   (b) neurotransmitters
   (c) ion pumps   (d) None of these

4. The function of our visceral organs is controlled by
   (a) sympathetic and somatic neural system
   (b) sympathetic and parasympathetic neural system
   (c) central and somatic nervous system
   (d) None of the above

5. Which of the following is not involved in knee-jerk reflex?
   (a) Muscle spindle   (b) Motor neuron
   (c) Brain   (d) Inter neurons

VERY SHORT ANSWER QUESTIONS

1. Rearrange the following in the correct order of involvement in electrical impulse movement.

2. Which cells of the retina enable us to see coloured objects around us?

3. Arrange the following in the order of reception and transmission of sound wave from the ear drum. Cochlear nerve, external auditory canal, ear drum, stapes, incus, malleus, cochlea.

4. During resting potential, the axonal membrane is polarized, indicate the movement of +ve and –ve ions leading to polarisation diagrammatically.

5. Our reaction like aggressive behaviour, use of abusive words, restlessness etc. are regulated by brain, name the parts involved.

6. What do grey and white matter in the brain represent?

7. Where is the hunger centre located in human brain?

8. Complete the statement by choosing appropriate match among the following.

	Column I		Column II
A.	Resting potential	1.	Chemicals involved in the transmission of impulses at synapses.
B.	Nerve impulse	2.	Gap between the pre synaptic and post synaptic neurons.
C.	Synaptic cleft	3.	Electrical potential difference across the resting neural membrane.
D.	Neurotransmitters	4.	An electrical wave like response of a neuron to a stimulation.

SHORT ANSWER QUESTIONS

1. The major parts of the human neural system is depicted below. Fill in the empty boxes with appropriate words.

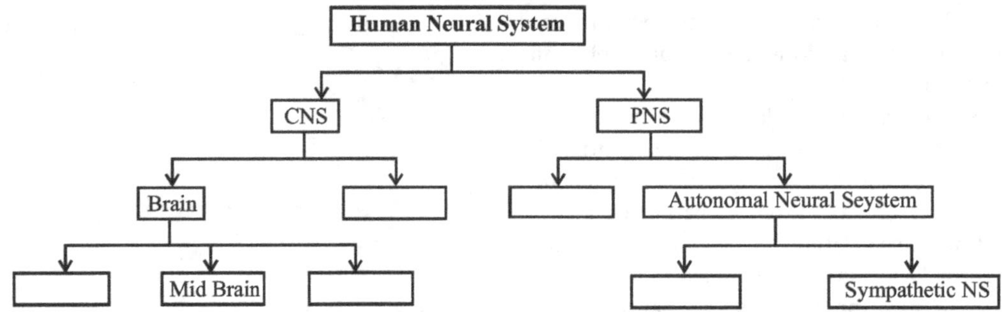

2. Neuron system and computers share certain common features. Comment in five lines.
3. What is the function described to Eustachian tube?

LONG SHORT ANSWER QUESTIONS

1. Explain the process of the transport and release of neurotransmitter with the help of a labelled diagram showing a complete neuron, axon terminal and synapse.
2. Explain the structure of middle and internal ear with the help of diagram.

SOLUTIONS

Multiple Choice Questions

1. **(b)** Neurotransmitters are involved in the transmission of impulses at the chemical synapses. They are present in the synaptic vesicles at the axon terminals.

   Hormones are non-nutrient chemicals which act as intercellular messengers produced in trace amounts.

   Cerebrospinal fluid is present in the subarachnoid space. It provideds shock resistance to brain.

   Lymph is a colourless fluid containing specialised lymphocytes which are responsible for the immune responses of the body. It is an important carrier of nutrients, hormones, *etc.* Fats are absorbed through lacteals (lymph vessels) present in microvilli of intestine.

2. **(a)** The ion gated channels on the neurolemma control the movement of Na^+ and K^+ ions on both inner and outer sides of a nerve cell.

   Ca^{2+}, CO_3^{2-}, Mg^{2+} and Ca^{2+} ions are not related with nerve excitation, rather are involved in other biological functions. Ca^{+2} ions are related to muscle metabolism where Mg^{2+} ions act as a cofactor in some reactions.

   Cl^- ion channels are important for cell's resting membrane potential, transepithelial salt transport and the acidification of internal and extracellular compartments.

3. **(c)** The ionic gradients across the resting membranes are maintained by the active transport of ions by the sodium- potassium pumps which transport 3 Na^+ outward for every 2K^+ into the cell.

4. **(b)** Sympathetic and parasympathetic neural system control all the visceral organs of the body. Somatic neural system is a part of peripheral nervous system and is not related to the regulation of visceral organs.

5. **(c)** Brain is not involved in any reflex action (e.g., knee-jerk reflex) while the muscle spindle, inter neuron and motor neutron are the part of reflex arc.

Very Short Answer Questions

1. The correct order of involvement in electrical impulse movement is as follows:
   (i) Dendrites   (ii) Cell body
   (iii) Axon   (iv) Axon terminal
   (vi) Synaptic knob

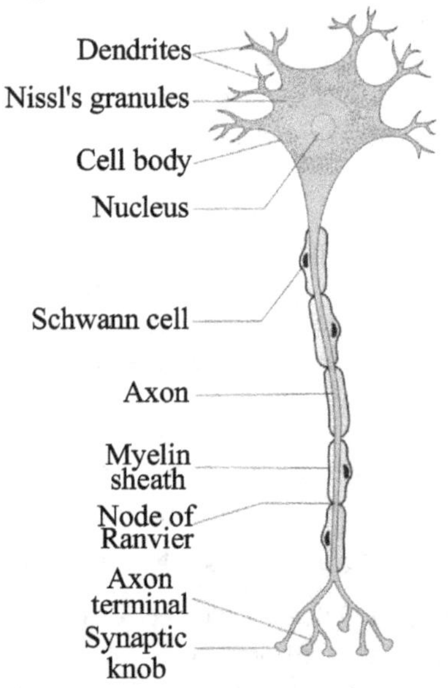

2. Cone cells present in unable us to see the colours. There are three types of cones which possess their own characteristic photopigments that respond to red, green and blue light.

3. The reception and transmission of sound waves occurs in following order – External Auditory canal → Eardrum → Malleus → Incus → Stapes → Cochlea → Cochlear nerve

4. 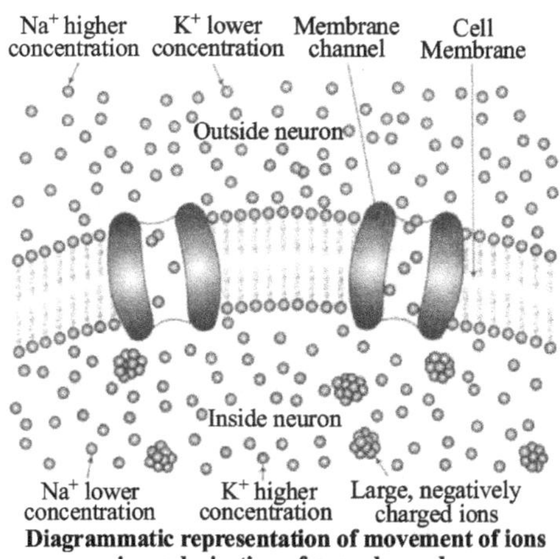

Diagrammatic representation of movement of ions causing polarisation of axonal membrane

5. Functions as aggressive behaviour, use or abusive words, restlessness, etc. The inner part of cerebral hemispheres and a group of associated deep structures called limbic lobe or limbic system along with hypothalamus are involved.

6. A major component of CNS is Grey matter consisting of neutronal cell bodies, dendrite, unmyelinated axons, glial cells and capillaries.
   White matter is also a component of CNS and consists mostly of gilal cell and myelinated axons.

7. Hypothalamus in human brain contains many centres which control urge for eating and drinking.

8. A. → (3), B. → (4), C. → (2), D. → (1)

Column I		Column II	
A.	Resting potential	1.	Electrical potential difference across the resting neural membrane.
B.	Nerve impulse	2.	An electrical wave like response of a neuron to a stimulation.
C.	Synaptic cleft	3.	Gap between the pre synaptic and post synaptic neurons.
D.	Neurotransmitters	4.	Chemicals involved in the transmission of impulses at synapses.

Short Answer Questions

1. The major parts of the human neural system is filled in the boxes with appropriate words

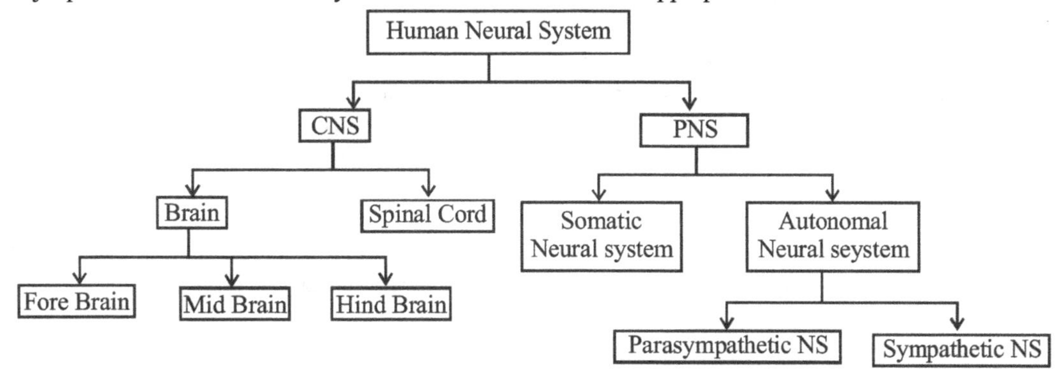

2. In various organs the sensory neurons is present to sense the environment and extend the message to the brain. So, it is equivalent to input device of computers.
   Brain acts as the CPU, or Central Processing Unit. The information gathered by sensory neurons is processed by brain and it gives command to the concerned organ to act accordingly. This message is taken or conveyed by motor neurons which act as output devices.

3. The eustachian tube forms connection between the middle ear cavity with the pharynx. It helps in equalising the pressure on either sides of the ear drum. At the pharyngeal opening of the eustachian tube there is a valve which normally remains closed.
   The valve opens during yawning, swallowing and during an abrupt change in altitude, when air enters or leaves the tympanic cavity to equalise the pressure of air on the two sides of the tympanic membrane.

Long Answer Questions

1. The three main parts of a neuron include the
   (i) Cell body
   (ii) Axon
   (iii) Dendrites
   Stimulus or nerve impulse of any kind passes from one neuron to another via axon. This nerve impulse is wave of bioelectric/electrochemical disturbance that passes along the neuron during conduction of an excitation.

Refer Figure from NCERT Exemplar Solution, Very Short Answer Q.1.

Within a synapse transport and release of a neuro transmiter occurs. At a chemical synapse, the membranes of the pre- and post-synaptic neurons are separated by a fluid-filled space called synaptic cleft. Chemicals called neurotransmitters are involved in the transmission of impulses at these synapses. The axon terminals contain vesicles filled with these neurotransmitters.

Upon arrival of an impulse (action potential) at the axon terminal, it stimulates the movement of the synaptic vesciles towards the membrane, where they fuse with the plasma membrane and release their neurotransmitters in the synaptic cleft.

The released neurotransmitters bind to their specific receptors, present on the post-synaptic membrane. This binding opens ion channels allowing the entry of ions, that can generate a new action potential in the post-synaptic neuron.

Refer Figure from Practice Solution, Long Answer Q.2.

2. Ears are a part of statoacoustic organ meant for balancing and hearing the external ear in most mammals is a heap of tissue also called pinna. It is a part of auditory system. The human ear consists of three main parts external ear, middle, ear and internal ear.

Structure of Middle Ear

The middle ear consists of three bones or ossicles-the **malleus** (hammer), **incus** (anvil and **stapes** (stir-up). These bones are attached to one another in a chain-like manner. The malleus is attached to the tympanic membrane and the stapes is attached to the oval window (a membrane beneath the stapes) of cochlea. These three ossicles increase the efficiency of transmission of sound waves to the inner ear. The middle ear also opens into the eustachian tube, which connects with the pharynx and maintains the pressure between the middle ear and the outside atmosphere.

Structure of Internal Ear

The inner ear consists of a labyrinth of chambers filled with fluid within temporal bone of the skull. The labyrinth consists of two parts the bony and membranous labyrinth. The bony labyrinth is a series of channels.

Membranous labyrinth lies inside these channels which is surrounded by a fluid called perilymph. The membranous labyrinth is filled with a fluid called endolymph. The coiled portion of the labyrinth is called cochlea.

The cochlea has two large canal separated by a small **cochlear duct** (scala media). An upper vestibular canal (scala vestibuli) and a lower tympanic canal (scala tympani). The vestibular and tympanic canals contain perilymph and the cochlear duct is filled with endolymph.

The wall of membranous labyrinth comes in contact with the fenestra ovalis at the base of scale vestibuli while the fenestra rotunda.

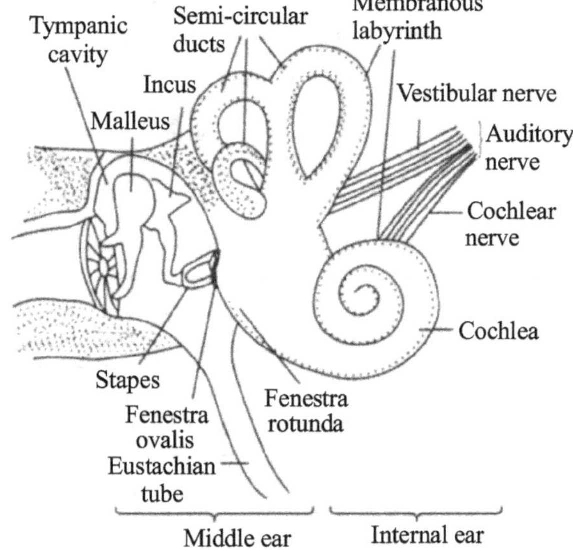

Diagram representing middle ear and internal ear

22 Chemical Coordination and Integration

22.1 Define the following :
- **(a) Exocrine glands**   **(b) Endocrine glands**
- **(c) Hormones**

Sol.
- (a) **Exocrine glands :** These glands have ducts. The secretions of these glands are carried by ducts to a particular organ to regulate some metabolic activities.
- (b) **Endocrine glands :** They lack ducts and their secretions (hormones) released directly into the blood for transport to the target tissues.
- (c) **Hormones :** Hormones are non-nutrient chemicals which act as intercellular messengers and are produced in trace amounts.

22.2 Diagrammatically indicate the location of the various endocrine glands in our body.

Sol.

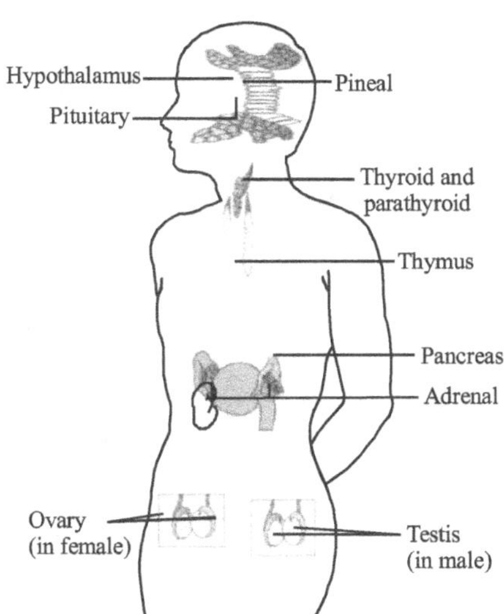

Fig. Location of endocrine glands

22.3 List the hormones secreted by the followings.
- **(a) Hypothalamus**   **(b) Pituitary**
- **(c) Thyroid**   **(d) Parathyroid**
- **(e) Adrenal**   **(f) Pancreas**
- **(g) Testis**   **(h) Ovary**
- **(i) Thymus**   **(j) Atrium**
- **(k) Kidney**   **(l) G-I Tract**

Sol.
- (a) **Hypothalamus :** Gonadotrophic releasing hormone (GnRH), somatostatin.
- (b) **Pituitary :** Growth hormone, prolactin, thyroid stimulating hormone, luteinizing hormone and follicle Stimulating hormone, oxytocin, vasopressin.
- (c) **Thyroid :** triiodothyronine (T_3) and tetraiodo thyronine (T_4).
- (d) **Parathyroid :** Parathyroid hormone.
- (e) **Adrenal :** Adrenaline or epinephrine and noradrenaline or norepinephrine.
- (f) **Pancreas :** Insulin and glucagon.
- (g) **Testis :** A group of androgens mainly testesterone.
- (h) **Ovary :** Estrogens and progesterone.
- (i) **Thymus :** Thymosins.
- (j) **Atrium :** Atrial Natriuretic factor (ANF)
- (k) **Kidney :** Erythropoietin.
- (l) **G-I tract :** Gastrin, secretin, cholecystokinin (CCK).

22.4 Fill in the blanks :

Hormones	Target gland
(a) Hypothalamic hormones	....
(b) Thyrotrophin (TSH)	....
(c) Corticotrophin (ACTH)	....
(d) Gonadotrophins (LH, FSH)	....
(e) Melanotrophin (MSH)	....

Sol.
- (a) Anterior pituitary and posterior pituitary.
- (b) Thyroid glands
- (c) Adrenal cortex
- (d) Gonads (testis and ovary)
- (e) Pituitary

22.5 Write short notes on the functions of the following hormones :
- **(a) Parthyroid hormone (PTH)**
- **(b) Thyroid hormones**
- **(c) Thymosins**
- **(d) Androgens**
- **(e) Estrogens**
- **(f) Insulin and Glucagon**

Sol.
- (a) **Parathyroid hormone (PTH)**
  - When the level of calcium ions in the plasma decreases, PTH is secreted.

- It increases the level of Ca^{2+} ions in the blood/plasma by
  - (i) bone reabsorption (demineralisation/dissolution of bones).
  - (ii) stimulating reabsorption of Ca^{2+} ions by the renal tubules.
  - (iii) stimulating the absorption of Ca^{2+} from the alimentary canal.
  - (iv) since it increases the level of Ca^{2+} ions in the blood, it is called hypercalcemic hormone.
- Along with TCT, PTH plays an important role in the calcium balance of the body.

(b) **Thyroid hormones :** Two types of thyroid hormones -
  - (i) Tetraiodothyronine (T_4)
  - (ii) Triiodothyronine (T_3)

  Thyroid hormones perform the following functions :
  - (i) They regulate the basal metabolic rate.
  - (ii) They control the metabolism of carbohydrates, fats and protein.
  - (iii) They influence the maintenance of water and electrolyte balance.
  - (iv) They support the process of red blood cells formation.

(c) **Thymosin :** Thymosin is secreted by thymus and plays a major role in the differentiation of T-lymphocytes, which provided cell mediated immunity. Thymosins also promote production of antibodies to provide humoral immunity.

(d) **Androgens :** Androgens are secreted from the leydig cells of testis.

  Functions :
  - (i) Androgens regulate the development, maturation and functioning of the male secondary sex organs.
  - (ii) They stimulate spermatogenesis.
  - (iii) They act on the CNS and the influence on male sexual behaviour.
  - (iv) They produce anabolic effects on proteins and carbohydrate metabolism.

(e) **Estrogens :** Ovarian hormone.

  Functions : Stimulates the growth and functioning of female sex organs.
  - It stimulates the development of female sex-characteristics.
  - It regulates the female sexual behaviour.

(f) **Insulin and Glucagon :** Secreted by pancreas.
  - Insulin is a peptide hormone which plays a major role in the regulation of glucose homeostasis. Insulin mainly acts on hepatocytes and adipocytes (cells of adipose tissue) and enhancing cellular glucose uptake and utilisation.
  - Glucagon is also a peptide hormone and plays an important role in maintaining the normal blood glucose levels.
  - Glucagon acts mainly on the liver cells (hepatocytes) and stimulates glycogenolysis resulting in an increased blood sugar (hyperglycemia).
  - This hormone also stimulates the process of gluconeogenesis which also contributes to hyperglycemia.
  - Glucagon reduces the cellular glucose uptake and utilisation. Thus glucagon is a hyperglycemic hormone.

22.6 **Give example(s) of :**
  - (a) **Hyperglycemic hormone and hypoglycemic hormone**
  - (b) **Hypercalcemic hormone**
  - (c) **Gonadotrophic hormones**
  - (d) **Progestational hormone**
  - (e) **Blood pressure lowering hormone**
  - (f) **Androgens and estrogens**

Sol.
  - (a) **Hyperglycemic hormone :** Glucagon.
    Hypoglycemic hormone : Insulin.
  - (b) **Hypercalcemic hormone :** Parathyroid hormone.
  - (c) **Gonadotrophic hormone :** Follicle stimulating hormone(FSH) or luteinizing hormone (LH).
  - (d) **Progestational hormone :** Progesterone.
  - (e) **Blood pressure lowering hormone :** Atrial Natriuretic factor (ANF)
  - (f) **Androgen :** Testosterone. **Estrogen :** Estrogens, estrone, estradiole.

22.7 **Which hormonal deficiency is responsible for the following :**
  - (a) **Diabetes mellitus**   (b) **Goitre**
  - (c) **Cretinism**

Sol. **Diabetes mellitus :** Insulin deficiency.

  Goitre : Deficiency of thyroid hormones due to deficiency of iodine.

  Cretinism : Deficiency of thyroid hormones during childhood.

22.8 **Briefly mention the mechanism of action of FSH.**

Sol. **Mechanism of FSH :**
  - FSH is a protein hormone.
  - It binds to membrane bound receptor and stimulates the production of second messenger, cyclic AMP or Ca^{++}.
  - The second messenger brings about biochemical responses, which results in the production of physiological response.

    e.g.- growth of the ovarian follicles and secretion of estrogens from the follicle cells.

22.9 **Match the following :**

	Column I		Column II
(a)	T_4	(i)	**Hypothalamus**
(b)	**PTH**	(ii)	**Thyroid**
(c)	**GnRH**	(iii)	**Pituitary**
(d)	**LH**	(iv)	**Parathyroid**

Sol. (a) $\rightarrow$ (ii); (b) $\rightarrow$ (iv); (c) $\rightarrow$ (i); (d) $\rightarrow$ (iii)

SECTION B — PRACTICE QUESTIONS

MULTIPLE CHOICE QUESTIONS

1. Anterior lobe of pituitary secretes
   (a) ACTH, TSH and oxytocin
   (b) STH, GH and ADH
   (c) TSH, ADH and prolactin
   (d) FSH, GH and LH

2. Which of the following hormone is known as 'milk let-down factor'?
   (a) Prolactin   (b) Mammotropin
   (c) Estrogen   (d) Oxytocin

3. Which of the followings is the more scientific definition of hormone?
   (a) They are extracellular messengers.
   (b) They always act at distantly located target organ.
   (c) They are the products of well organized endocrine glands.
   (d) They are non-nutrient chemicals that act as intercellular messengers.

4. Which of the following gland is often referred in connection with AIDS?
   (a) Thymus   (b) Thyroid
   (c) Adrenal   (d) Pancreas

5. Hypothyroidism in adults and hyperparathyroidism in children will respectively lead to
   (a) myxoedema and cretinism
   (b) Grave's disease and Hashimoto's disease
   (c) myxoedema and osteitis fibrosa cystica
   (d) Addison'a disease and cretinism

6. Blood glucose level in man is regulated by
   (a) insulin only
   (b) adrenaline
   (c) glucagon and insulin
   (d) all of the above

7. After four months of pregnancy if the ovaries are removed
   (a) It will cause abortion
   (b) The foetus will be mentally retarded
   (c) There will be no effect on foetus
   (d) The physical development of the foetus will be affected

8. In a normal pregnant woman, the amount of total gonadotropin activity was assessed. The result expected was
   (a) high levels of FSH and LH in uterus to stimulate endometrial thickening.
   (b) high level of circulating HCG to stimulate estrogen and progesterone synthesis.
   (c) high level of circulating FSH and LH in the uterus to stimulate implantation of the embryo.
   (d) high level of circulating HCG to stimulate endometrial thickening.

9. In hormone action, if receptor molecules are removed from target organ, the target organ will
   (a) continue to respond to hormone.
   (b) not respond to hormone.
   (c) continue to respond but requires higher concentration.
   (d) continue to respond but in the opposite way.

10. The hormone secretin is produced in
    (a) pancreas and influences conversion of glycogen into glucose.
    (b) small intestine and stimulates pancreas.
    (c) adrenal glands and accelerates heartbeat.
    (d) testes and produces male secondary sexual characters.

ASSERTION & REASON QUESTIONS

DIRECTION (Qs. 1-5) : *These questions consists of two statements. Answer these questions selecting the appropriate option given below:*
(a) Both Assertion (A) and Reason (R) are true and Reason (R) is the correct explanation of Assertion (A).
(b) Both Assertion (A) and Reason (R) are true, but Reason (R) is not the correct explanation of Assertion (A).
(c) Assertion (A) is true, but Reason (R) is false.
(d) Assertion (A) is false, but Reason (R) is true.

1. **Assertion :** Hormone calcitonin has antagonistic effect to that of parathormone.
   Reason : Calcitonin decreases blood calcium level while parathormone increases blood calcium level.

2. **Assertion:** Failure of secretion of hormone insulin causes diabetes mellitus in the patient.
   Reason: Vasopressin increases the volume of urine by increasing the reabsorption of water from the urine.

3. **Assertion :** The person with diabetes insipidis feels thirsty.
   Reason : A person with diabetes insipidus suffers from excess secretion of vasopressin.

4. **Assertion:** Erythropoietin hormone circulates to red bone marrow where it increases stem cell mitosis and speed up development of RBCs.
   Reason: The regulation of RBC production is accomplished by cortisol.

5. **Assertion:** Glucagon is a type of hypoglycemic hormone.
   Reason: Glucagon increase the level of glucose.

CASE/PASSAGE BASED QUESTIONS

DIRECTIONS (Qs. 1-5) : *Read the following passage and answer the questions that follows.*

Endocrine system is made of different types of endocrine glands that produces hormones. In the given diagram, the location of human endocrine glands are shown by labelling I, II, III, IV and V. Study the diagram and answer the questions.

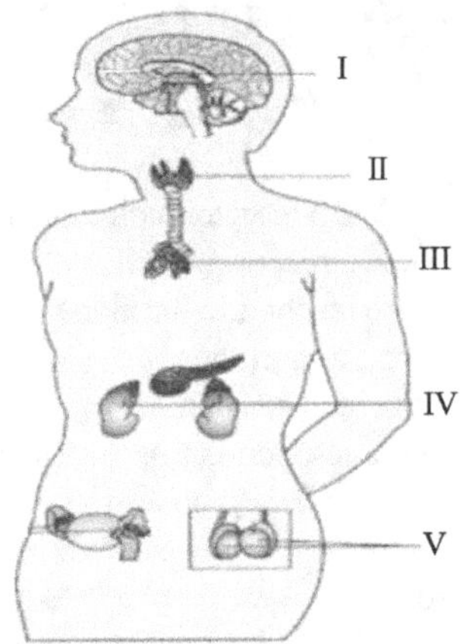

1. Which of the following labelling represents the secretion of melatonin ?
    (a) III   (b) I   (c) V   (d) II

2. Which of the following statement is true ?
    (a) Thymosine hormone is secreated by pituitary gland.
    (b) Testosteron is an androgenic hormone that is mainly secreted by the testes.
    (c) Adrenal gland is located on the liver.
    (d) All of them

3. Which of the following hormone is secreated by labelling IV ?
    (a) Thymosin   (b) Aldosterone
    (c) Insuline   (d) All of them

4. The gland with duct is known as :
    (a) Endocrine gland   (b) Exocrine gland
    (c) Both (a) and (b)   (d) None of them

5. Pancreas is a type of :
    (a) Only exocrine gland
    (b) Only endocrine gland
    (c) Exocrine as well as endocrine
    (d) It is not a gland

Very Short Answer Questions

1. Give two examples of endocrine glands.
2. Which gland secretes glucagon?
3. What is the location of pituitary gland?
4. Which hormone is secreted by pars intermedia?
5. Which hormone is secreted by pineal gland?
6. Name one disorder caused by hyper functioning of pituitary.
7. How many lobes does thyroid gland have?
8. Which gland produces the hormone called thyrocalcitonin (TCT) which regulates the blood calcium levels?

9. Name the organ which secretes progesterone.
10. Name two hormones of pancreas.
11. Which gland secretes somatostatin?
12. Which complex is formed during the binding of hormone to a receptor ?
13. Name one hormone secreted by gastro-intestinal tract.
14. Which hormone is secreted by testes and write the function of hormone also.
15. What are membrane bound receptors?
16. How many types of cells are present in Islets of Langerhans?
17. Why is oxytocin called as birth hormone ?
18. Why is vasopressin known as antidiuretic hormone?
19. What is cretinism ?
20. Which hormone interacts with membrane bound receptor and does not normally enter the target cell?
21. Which hormone opposes parathormone?
22. Which hormone is known as anti-aging hormone?

Short Answer Questions

1. Discuss the location and function of parathyroid hormone.
2. What is progesterone? Name two important functions of progesterone.
3. Name the principal mineralocorticoid secreted by adrenal cortex. Give its any two functions.
4. What are hormone receptors? What are the modes of their action ?
5. Name the gland that functions as a biological clock in our body. Where is this gland located ? Name its one secretion.
6. Where is thymus gland located in the human body ? Describe its role.
7. How does insulin act on high glucose content in the blood in a normal human body ?
8. What is corpus luteum ? Name its one secretion.

Long Answer Questions

1. Calcium plays a very important role in the formation of bones. Write the role of endocrine glands and hormones responsible for maintaining calcium homeostasis.
2. Draw a well labelled diagram showing the location of parathyroid gland. Discuss the function/(s) of parathormone and hyperparathyroidism.
3. What are the causes for following disorders?
    (a) Acromegaly
    (b) Cretinism
    (c) Gigantism
    (d) Myxoedema

SOLUTIONS

Multiple Choice Questions

1. **(d)** Anterior lobe of pituitary secretes follicle stimulating hormones, growth hormone and luteinizing hormone.
2. **(d)** Oxytocin stimulates the release of milk.
3. **(d)** Hormones are chemical messengers of the body that transfers information from one set of cells to another.

4. **(a)** Thymus is related to AIDS as it the first developing lymphoid organ whose main function is to develop immature T cells into immunocompetent T cells. AIDS (acquired immune deficiency syndrome) is a disease in which there is a severe loss of the body's cellular immunity, greatly lowering the resistance to infection and malignancy.

5. **(c)** Hypothyroidism in adults leads to myxoedema and hyper-parathyroidism in children lead to osteitis fibrosa cystica.

6. **(c)** Glucagon and insulin regulates the level of blood in man. Both the hormone is secreted from alpha and beta cell of pancreas respectively. Glucagon is secreted when the blood sugar level is low and it stimulates glycogen breakdown and glucose synthesis in the liver by increasing blood glucose concentration. Whereas rising level of blood glucose stimulates insulin secretion.

7. **(c)** There will be no effect on foetus because during second trimester of pregnancy the placenta is fully formed. So, removal of ovaries will not affect the foetus because sufficient amount of progesterone is secreted from placenta as this hormone is important for the maintainence of pregnancy.

8. **(b)** HCG (Human Chorionic Gonadotropin) is a placental hormone which maintains the corpus luteum for continuous secretion of progesterone and estrogen so as to maintain pregnancy.

9. **(b)** Hormones produce their effects by binding to the specific receptors located in the target tissues.

10. **(b)** Secretin is a hormone which is released into the bloodstream by the wall of the upper part of the small intestine (the duodenum) under the influence of stomach acid. It stimulates secretion of liver and pancreas.

Assertion & Reason Questions

1. **(a)** Calcitonin or thyrocalcitonin is secreted by parafollicular cells of thyroid stroma. It retards bone dissolution and stimulates excretion of calcium in urine. Thus, it lowers calcium level in extra cellular fluid (ECF). Parathormone is secreted by chief cells of parathyroid gland and is also known as Collip's hormone. It maintains blood calcium level by increasing its absorption from food in intestine and its reabsorption from nephrons in the kidney. Maintenance of proper calcium level is in fact, a combined function of parathormone and calcitonin. When calcium level falls below normal, parathormone maintains it by promoting its absorption, reabsorption and also by demineralisation of bones. When blood calcium level exceeds above normal then calcitonin hormone increases excretion of calcium in urine.

2. **(c)** Diabetes mellitus is caused due to the failure of insulin hormone secretion by the pancreatic islets. The osmotic effect of glucose in the urine considerably increases the volume of urine, due to which thirst is also enhanced. In extreme cases, the patient suffers from coma and may die.

3. **(c)** Vasopressin or antidiuretic hormone is secreted by posterior pituitary gland. The deficiency of vasopressin results in a disorder known as diabetes insipidus. The main symptoms of diabetes insipidus are increase in thirst and urination.

4. **(b)** The regulation of RBC production is accomplished by cortisol. Erythropoietin, a glycoprotein, is produced by the kidney when the oxygen level is low, then EPO stimulates the bone marrow to produce more red cells and thereby increase the oxygen-carrying capacity of the blood.

5. **(d)** Glucagon is a type of hormone that plays important role in maintaining the sugar level in the blood. Since it increases the glucose level in the blood so it is a hyperglycemic hormone.

Case/Passage Based Questions

1. **(b)** Labelling I represents the secretion of melatonin.
2. **(b)**
3. **(b)** Aldosterone hormone is secreated by labelling IV?
4. **(b)** The gland with duct is known as exocrine gland.
5. **(c)** Pancreas is a type of exocrine as well as endocrine.

Very Short Answer Questions

1. Examples of endocrine glands are
(i) pituitary gland
(ii) pineal gland.

2. Pancreas secretes glucagon.

3. The pituitary gland is located in a bony cavity called sella tursica and is attached to hypothalamus by a stalk.

4. Pars intermedia secretes melanocyte stimulating hormone (MSH).

5. Pineal gland secretes melatonin hormone.

6. Gigantism caused by hyper functioning of pituitary.

7. The thyroid gland is composed of two lobes which are located on either side of the trachea.

8. Thyroid gland secretes a protein hormone called thyrocalcitonin (TCT) which regulates the blood calcium levels.

9. Ovary secretes progesterone.

10. Glucagon and insulin are two hormones of pancreas.

11. Hypothalamus secretes somatostatin.

12. Hormone-receptor complex is formed during the binding of a hormone to a receptor.

13. Gastrin is secreted by gastro-intestinal tract.

14. Testosterone is secreted by testes. It controls growth and development of male secondary sexual characters.

15. Hormone receptors that are present on the cell membrane of the target cells are called membrane bound receptors.

16. There are two types of cells present in Islets of Langerhans which are α-cells and β-cells.

17. Oxytocin stimulates the contraction of smooth muscles of uterus and facilitates the child birth.

18. Vasopressin stimulates the reabsorption of water and electrolytes and reduces the loss of water through urine, known as diuresis. Hence it is called as anti-diuretic hormone.

19. Cretinism is reduction in body growth as well as underdevelopment of brain resulting in various structural and functional defects mainly due to deficiency of thyroxine (hypothyroidism) in infants and children.

20. Follicle stimulating hormone interacts with membrane bound receptor and does not normally enter the target cell.

21. Thyrocalcitonin opposes parathormone.

22. Melatonin, secreted by pineal gland is known as anti-ageing hormone.

Short Answer Questions

1. There are four parathyroid glands present on the back side of thyroid glands, two on each of the lobes of the thyroid gland.

The parathyroid glands secrete parathyroid hormone (PTH), a peptide hormone.

Parathyroid hormone (PTH) increases the Ca^{2+} levels in the blood. PTH acts on bones and stimulates the process of bone resorption (dissolution/ demineralization. PTH also stimulates reabsorption of Ca^{2+} by the renal tubules and increases Ca^{2+} absorption from the digested food.

2. Progesterone is a steroid hormone secreted by ovary. Functions of progesterone are as follows :
* It supports pregnancy.
* It acts on mammary glands and stimulates the formation of alveoli (sac-like structures which store milk) and milk secretion.

3. Aldosterone is main mineralocorticoid secreted by adrenal cortex.
Functions of aldosterone are :
* It stimulates reabsorption of Na^+ and water.
* It stimulates excretion of K^+ and phosphate ions.

4. Receptors are specific proteins present on the surface of target cell which bind with hormones and produce physiological changes in cell. Their are two types of hormone receptors which are discussed below :

	Locations of receptor	Classes of peptides	Principles of mechanism of action
1.	Cell surface receptors. (plasma membrane bound receptors)	Proteins and peptides	Generation of second messengers (cyclic AMP, IP₃, Ca^{++} etc.) which alter activity of other molecules usually enzymes. This happens due to the formation of hormone receptors complex which leads to conformation change in the target
2.	Intracellular receptors (Present inside the cell cytoplasm/molecules)	Steroids and thyroids	They regulate gene expression or chromosome function by interaction of hormone receptor complex with genome.

5. Pineal gland functions as a biological clock in our body.
– It is located on the dorsal side of the forebrain.
– It secretes melatonin.

6. The thymus gland is a lobular structure located on the dorsal side of the heart and the aorta.
– It secretes hormone thymosin, which has a stimulating effect on the immune system.
– Thymosin promotes proliferation and maturation of T-lymphocytes.

7. Insulin is a peptide hormone, which plays a major role in the regulation of glucose homeostasis.
* Insulin acts mainly on hepatocytes and adipocytes (cells of adipose tissue), and enhances cellular glucose uptake and utilisation. As a result, there is a rapid movement of glucose from blood to hepatocytes and adipocytes resulting in decreased blood glucose levels **(hypoglycemia)**
* Insulin also stimulates conversion of glucose to glycogen **(glycogenesis)** in the target cells.
* The glucose homeostatasis in blood is thus maintained jointly by the two enzyme insulin and glucagon.

8. Corpus luteum is the structure formed by the ruptured ovarian follicles after ovulation.
– It mainly secretes the hormone progesterone.

Long Answer Questions

1. **Calcitonin** (from thyroid) : Essential for maintaining bone strength as it does not allow calcium mobilisation from bones. It also lowers plasma level of calcium if the same is high.

Parathormone: Low level of parathormone secretion decreases blood plasma level of calcium, prevents reabsorption from bones and causes **tetany.** Higher levels of parathormone (PTH) increase plasma level of Ca^{2+} by withdrawal from bones resulting in (i) Inflammation and tenderness in bones due to dissolution of calcium from bones, formation of cavities which get plugged with fibrous nodes and cysts (osteitis fibrosa cystica) making bones soft deformed and prone to fracture. (ii) Excess plasma calcium gets deposited in various parts of body which often leads of obstruction and death.

2.

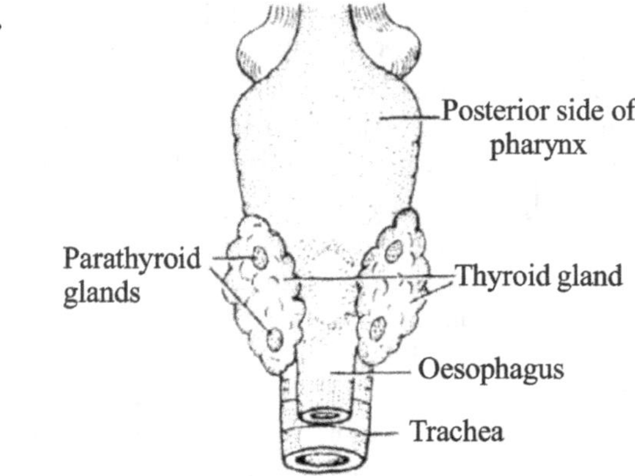

Fig. Parathyroid glands lie on the posterior surface of thyroid gland
Function : Parathormone (Collip's hormone) regulates the metabolism of calcium and phosphate between blood and other tissue.
(i) **Hyperparathyroidism :** It leads to demineralisation resulting in softing and bending of bones. An excess of parathormone cause osteoporosis and kidney stones.

3. **Disorders and their causes.**
(a) **Acromegaly** (*Acro-extremity, megaly – large*) – It is caused by excess secretion of growth hormone after adulthood is reached.
(b) **Cretinism :** It is caused by deficiency of thyroid hormone in infant.
(c) **Gigantism :** It is caused by excess of growth hormone from early age.
(d) **Myxoedema :** It is caused by deficiency of thyroid hormone in adults.

SECTION C	**NCERT EXEMPLAR QUESTIONS**

MULTIPLE CHOICE QUESTIONS

1. Which of the following hormones is not secreted by anterior pituitary?
   - (a) Growth hormone
   - (b) Follicle stimulating hormone
   - (c) Oxytocin
   - (d) Adrenocorticotrophic hormone
2. Mary is about to face an interview. But during the first five minutes before the interview she experiences sweating, increased rate of heart beat, respiration, etc. which hormone is responsible for her restlessness?
   - (a) Estrogen and progesterone
   - (b) Oxytocin and vasopressin
   - (c) Adrenaline and noradrenaline
   - (d) Insulin and glucagon
3. The steroid responsible for balance of water and electrolytes in our body is
   - (a) insulin
   - (b) melatonin
   - (c) testosterone
   - (d) aldosterone
4. Thymosin is responsible for
   - (a) raising the blood sugar level
   - (b) raising the blood calcium level
   - (c) differentiation of T-lymphocytes
   - (d) decrease in blood RBCs
5. In the mechanism of action of a protein hormone, one of the second messengers is
   - (a) Cyclic AMP
   - (b) Insulin
   - (c) T_3
   - (d) Gastrin
6. Leydig cells produce a group of hormones called
   - (a) androgens
   - (b) estrogens
   - (c) aldosterone
   - (d) gonadotropins
7. Corpus luteum secretes a hormone called
   - (a) prolactin
   - (b) progesterone
   - (c) aldosterone
   - (d) testosterone
8. Cortisol is secreted from
   - (a) pancreas
   - (b) thyroid
   - (c) adrenal
   - (d) thymus
9. A hormone responsible for normal sleep-wake cycle is
   - (a) epinephrine
   - (b) gastrin
   - (c) melatonin
   - (d) insulin
10. Hormones are called chemical signal that stimulate specific target tissues. Which is correct location of these receptors in protein hormones?
    - (a) Extra cellular matrix
    - (b) Blood
    - (c) Plasma membrane
    - (d) Nucleus
11. Blood calcium level is a resultant of how much dietary calcium is absorbed, how much calcium is lost in the urine, how much bone dissolves releasing calcium into blood and how much calcium from blood enters tissues. A number of factor play an important role in these processes. Mark the one which has no role.
    - (a) Vitamin-D
    - (b) Parathyroid hormone
    - (c) Thyrocalcitonin
    - (d) Thymosin
12. Which of the following conditions is not linked to deficiency of thyroid hormone?
    - (a) Cretinism
    - (b) Goitre
    - (c) Myxoedema
    - (d) Exophthalmia

VERY SHORT ANSWER QUESTIONS

1. Which of the two adrenocortial layers, zona glomerulosa and zona reticularis lies outside enveloping the other?
2. What is erythropoiesis? Which hormone stimulates it?
3. Name the only hormone secreted by pars intermedia of the pituitary gland.
4. Name the endocrine gland that produces calcitonin and mention the role played by this hormone.
5. Name the hormone that helps in cell-mediated immunity.
6. A patient complains of constant thirst, excessive passing of urine and low blood pressure. When the doctor checked the patients' blood glucose and blood insulin level, the level were normal or slightly low. The doctor diagnosed the condition a diabetes insipid us. But he decided to measure one more hormone in patients blood. Which hormones does the doctor intend to measure?
7. Correct the following statements by replacing the term underlined.
   - (a) Insulin is a steroid hormone.
   - (b) TSH is secreted from the corpus leteum.
   - (c) Tetraiodothyronine is an emergency hormone.
   - (d) the pineal gland is located on the anterior part of the kidney.
8. Match the following columns.

Column I	Column II
A. Oxytocin	1. Amino acid derivative
B. Epinephrine	2. Steroid
C. Progesterone	3. Protein
D. Growth hormone	4. Peptide

SHORT ANSWER QUESTIONS

1. What is the role-played by luteinising hormones in males and females respectively.
2. George comes on a vacation to India from US. The long journey disturbs his biological system and he suffers from jet lag. What is the cause of his discomfort?
3. Inflammatory responses can be controlled by a certain steroid. Name the steroid, its source and also its other important functions.
4. Old people have weak immune system. What could be the reasons?

LONG ANSWER QUESTIONS

1. Calcium plays a very important role in the formation of bones. Write on the role of endocrine glands and hormones responsible for maintaining calcium homeostasis.
2. Hypothalamus is a supper master endocrine gland. Elaborate.

SOLUTIONS

Multiple Choice Questions

1. **(c) Oxytocin** release from posterior pituitary gland. It acts on the smooth muscles of uterus and stimulates their contraction and also plays role in milk secretion.
   Follicle stimulating hormone stimulates growth of ovarian follicles in the female and spermatogenesis in the male.
   Growth Hormone stimulates body growth by promoting the synthesis and deposition of proteins in tissues and also in the growth of bones and muscles.
   Adrenocorticotrophic Hormone stimulates adrenal cortex of the adrenal gland to produce glucocorticoids and mineralocorticoids.

2. **(c)** Mary, during her first five minutes before interview experiences sweating, increased heart rate and respiration because of stress which leads to release of **emergency hormones** or **flight** and **fight,** hormones (adrenaline and noradrenaline.) These hormones stimulate the breakdown of glycogen resulting in increase concentration of glucose in blood.

3. **(d) Aldosterone** acts at the renal tubules stimulating the reabsorption of Na^+, water and excretion of K^+ and phosphate ions. Thus, it helps in maintenance of electrolytes, body fluid volume, osmotic pressure and blood pressure.
   Insulin is a peptide hormone, that plays an important role in maintaining the normal blood glucose levels.
   Testosterone is a male sex hormone that stimulates male features like muscular growth, facial and axial hair, aggressiveness, low pitch of voice, etc. and spermatogenesis.
   Melatonin Hormone has a very important role in regulating 24 hours (diurnal) rhythm of our body.

4. **(c) Thymosins** play a major role in the differentiation of T-lymphocytes, which provide cell mediated immunity. It also promotes antibody production to provide **humoral immunity**. It hastens the process attainment of sexual maturity.

5. **(a) Cyclic AMP** is one of the second messengers involve in the action of a protein hormone.

6. **(a)** The **Leydig cells** or **interstitial cells,** which are present in the interstitial spaces of testis produce a group of hormones called **androgens** mainly **testosterone.**
   Estrogen is secreted by the growing follicles in ovaries and stimulates growth and development of female secondary sex organs.
   Aldosterone is secreted by the adrenal gland helps in maintaining electrolytes in the body fluid, volume, osmotic pressure and blood pressure.
   Gonadotropins are secreted by anterior pituitary gland and stimulate the gonadal activity. These include LH and FSH.

7. **(b) Corpus luteum** secretes a hormone called as **progesterone** which supports pregnancy and stimulates the development of the **mammary gland** for the milk production in female.
   Prolactin also known as luteotropic hormone, it's a protein means hormone is involved in production of milk in females.

The source for secretion is anterior pituitary gland.
Testosterone stimulates muscular growth, growth of facial and axillary hair, aggressiveness, low pitch of voice, etc.
Aldosterone is secreted by adrenal cortex and plays a role in reabsorption of sodium ions, etc.

8. **(c)** The **zona fasciculata** region of adrenal cortex secretes **cortisol, corticosterone** and cortisone. These hormones are involved in maintaining glucose homeostasis.
   Pancreas is composite gland which secretes insulin glucagon and somatostatin.
   Thyroid gland secretes thyroxin or tetraiodothyronine (T_4) and triodothyronine (T_3) which regulate the metabolic rate of the body and maintain basal metabolic rate. It also secretes calcitonin.
   Thymus secretes thymosin, involved in providing cell mediated immunity to the body.

9. **(c) Melatonin** hormone plays a very important role in maintaining the normal rhythms of sleep-wake cycle.

10. **(c)** Hormone receptors are located in the target tissue and are present on the plasma membrane/cell membrane of the target cell.

11. **(d) Thymosin hormone** has no role in regulation of blood calcium homeostasis. It plays a major role in the differentiation of T-lymphocytes, which provides cell mediated immunity, vitamin-D, thyrocalcitonin and parathyroid hormone play a vital role in maintaining calcium homeostasis by regulating blood calcium levels.

12. **(d) Exophthalmia,** is a condition, caused due to over secretion of thyroid hormone. In this condition there is a bulging of the eye anteriorly out of the orbit.
    This is due to an increase in the amount of white blood cells (lymphocytes) in the eye and swelling due to excess accumulation of thyroid hormone, resulting the eyeballs being forced forward out of the eye sockets (orbits) whereas, cretinism, goitre and myxoedema are the diseases associated with thyroid deficiency.

Very Short Answer Questions

1. Zona glomerulosa envelops zona reticularis from the outside.

2. The process of formation of RBC is Erythropoiesis. Erythropoietin, a Peptide hormone secreted from the juxtaglomerular cells of kidney stimulates erythropoiesis.

3. The only hormone secreted by Pars intermedia of pituitary gland is Melanocyte Stimulating hormone (MSH). This hormone causes dispersal of pigment granules in the pigment cells, which darken the colour in certain animals like fishes and amphibians.

4. Calcitonin/thyrocalcitonin linear polypeptide hormone comprising of 32 amino acids that is produced in humans primarily by the parafollicular cells of the thyroid gland. It checks excess Ca^{2+} and phosphate in plasma by decreasing mobilization from bones.

5. The hormone thymosin plays a major role in the development and differentiation of T-lymphocytes, which provide cell-mediated immunity.

6. The doctor intends to measure the hyperglycaemia hormone, and its action is opposite to that of insulin Excess of glucose in blood suppresses the secretion of glucose, whereas fall in glucose level enhance glucose production.

7. (a) Insulin is a peptide hormone
   (b) TSH is secreted from the pars distalis region of pitutary.
   (c) Adrenaline is an emergency hormone.
   (d) The adrenal gland is located on the anterior part of the kidney.

8. The correct matching is

Column I	Column II
A. Oxytocin	– Peptide
B. Epinephrine	– Amino acid derivative
C. Progesterone	– Steroid
D. Growth hormone	– Protein

Short Long Answer Questions

1. LH and FSH stimulate activity of gonads and hence are called gonadotropins.

   Luteinising hormone (LH) in males stimulates the synthesis and secretion of hormones called androgens from testis. Androgens along with FSH (Follicle Stimulating Hormone) regulate spermatogenesis.

   LH induces ovulation of fully mature follicles in females and maintains the corpus luteum, formed from the remnants of the graafian follicles after ovulation. This secretes progesterone.

2. The melatonin hormone secreted by the pineal gland is also called as 'sleep hormone' as it promotes sleep-wake cycle.

   The disruption of the body clock as it is out of synchronisation because of the unfamiliar time zone of the destination causes Jet lag. The body experiences different patterns of light and dark conditions than it is normally used to, this disrupts the natural sleep-wake cycle. A hormone that plays a key role in body rhythms and causes jet lag is melatonin. Eyes perceive darkness after the sun sets and alert the hypothalamus to begin releasing melatonin, which promotes sleep. Conversely, when the eyes perceive sunlight, they induce the hypothalamus to with hold melatonin production.

   The hypothalamus however cannot readjust its schedule instantly and it may take several days, to overcome this problem.

3. Glucocorticoids cortisol in particular, produce anti-inflammatory reactions and suppress the immune response. The middle zone, in adrenal cortex which is the widest of three zones called zona fasciculata is the source for glucocorticoids.

   The glucocorticoids as the name suggests affect carbohydrate metabolism and metabolism of proteins and fats. They stimulate gluconeogenesis, lipolysis and proteolysis.

   They also inhibit utilization of amino acid and cellular uptake. Cortisol is also called stress hormone as it copes with stress.

4. A major role in the development of the immune system is played by thymus.

   The thymus gland is a lobular structure located on the dorsal side of the heart and the aorta. It is derived from the endoderm of the embryo. Thymus secretes a hormone named thymosin which stimulates the development of white blood cells (WBCs), involved in producing immunity. In old individuals, thymus is degenerated which results in decreased production of thymosin. The immune system as a result becomes weak, in old people.

Long Answer Questions

1. The hormones and endocrine glands that are responsible for maintaining calcium homeostasis, are thyroid and parathyroid glands and their associated hormones are **calcitonin** and **Parathyroid Hormone** (PTH).

   (i) **Parathyroid glands** – These glands developed from the endoderm of the embryo. The cells of parathyroid glands are of two types – chief cells and oxyphil cells. The chief cells of the parathyroid glands secrete parathyroid hormone (PTH).

   This hormone (PTH) is involved in regulation of calcium and phosphate balance between the blood and other tissue. It mobilises the release of calcium into the blood from bones. PTH increases reabsorption of calcium by the body organs like intestine and kidneys.

   (ii) **Thyroid gland** – It is the largest endocrine gland located anterior to the thyroid cartilage of the larynx in the neck. This gland plays a major role in maintaining calcium homeostasis. It releases thyrocalcitonin hormone produced by the parafollicular cells, also called, 'C' cells.

   This hormone is secreted when the calcium level in blood gets high. It is a 32 amino acid peptide hormone that lowers the calcium level by suppressing release of calcium ions from the bones. Calcitonin thus has an action opposite to that of the parathyroid hormone in calcium homeostasis.

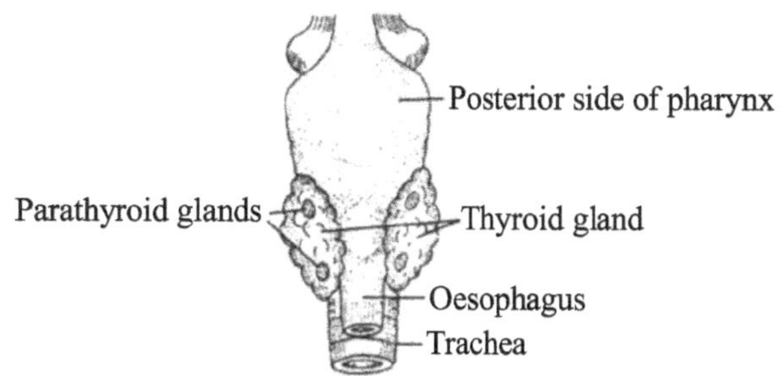

Parathyroid Glands and Thyroid Gland

2. Hypothalamus is a minor but extremely important part of the diencephalon that is involved in the mediation of endocrine, autonomic and behavioural function.

It consists of several groups of neuro secretory cells called nuclei which produce hormones. Hypothalamus provides anatomical connection between the nervous and endocrine system.

It controls the release of major hormones by hypophysis which include :

(i) **Growth Hormone Releasing Hormone** stimulates the anterior lobe of the pituitary gland to release growth hormone or somatostatin.

(ii) **MSH Releasing Hormone** stimulates the intermediate lobe of the pituitary gland to secrete Melanocyte Stimulating Hormone (MSH)

The hormones released from hypothalamus are involved in the processes like temperature regulation, control of water balance in body, sexual behaviour and reproduction, control of daily cycles in physiological state, behaviour and mediation of emotional response hypothalamus is thus called as super master endocrine gland of body.

(iii) **Prolactin Releasing Hormone (PRH)** stimulates the anterior lobe of the pituitary gland to secret prolactin.

(iv) **Gonadotropin Releasing Hormone** stimulates the anterior lobe of the pituitary gland to release gonadotropic hormones (FSH and IH).

(v) **Thyrotropin Releasing Hormone (TRH)** stimulates the anterior lobe of pituitary gland to release Thyroid Stimulating Hormone (TSH).

(vi) **Adrenocorticotrophic releasing Hormone** (ARH) stimulates the anterior lobe of pituitary gland to secrete Adrenocorticotropic Hormone (ACTH). ACTH stimulates the synthesis and secretion of steroid hormones called glucocorticoids by adrenal glands.

The hormones released from hypothalamus are involved in the processes like temperature regulation, control of water balance in body, sexual behaviour and reproduction, control of daily cycles in physiological state, behaviour and mediation of emotional responses. Hypothalamus is thus called as super master endocrine gland of body.

www.ingramcontent.com/pod-product-compliance
Lightning Source LLC
Chambersburg PA
CBHW081316150726
48001CB00021B/2980